DAVID STARKEY is Honorary Fellow of Fitzwilliam College, Cambridge, and the author of many books including *Elizabeth*, *Six Wives: The Queens of Henry VIII* and *Henry: Virtuous Prince*. He is a winner of the W. H. Smith Prize and the Norton Medlicott Medal for Services to History presented by Britain's Historical Association. He is a well-known TV and radio personality. He was made a CBE in 2007. He lives in London and Kent.

From the reviews of *Crown and Country*:

'Starkey is in a class of his own: the narrative rattles along like a lively lecture series, punctuated with interrogatives, mostly rhetorical, which are answered with authority'   *The Times*

'A masterpiece of accessible history, underscored with profound scholar-ship ... Above all, the author's passion for his subject, the royal tale of England, which is the backbone of this nation's story, explodes from every page'   *Guardian*

'A brilliant take on the relationship between ruler and subjects. An outstanding history of Britain from the Romans to the present day'
                                                    Sunday Express

'Excellent ... the really crucial events in the history of the British Monarchy since the Middle Ages are assessed with authority, wisdom and wit ... This is Starkey at his fluent and entertaining best'
                                                    Sunday Telegraph

'Vivid, lucid and engaging ... [Starkey's] judgements are often acute ... a very enjoyable book'   *Daily Telegraph*

ALSO BY DAVID STARKEY

Elizabeth: Apprenticeship
The Reign of Henry VIII: Personalities and Politics
Six Wives: The Queens of Henry VIII
The Monarchy of England: Volume I, The Beginnings
Monarchy: From the Middle Ages to Modernity
Henry: Virtuous Prince

Crown and Country

The Kings and Queens of England

DAVID STARKEY

Harper
Press

To all those who worked with me on the Channel 4
Monarchy *series for helping me understand history*
better and write it more clearly

Harper*Press*
An imprint of HarperCollins*Publishers*
77–85 Fulham Palace Road
Hammersmith
London W6 8JB

This Harper*Press* paperback edition published 2011

First published by Harper*Press* in 2010

Copyright © Jutland 2010

The Monarchy of England: Volume I, The Beginnings first published by
Chatto and Windus, a division of Random House, 2004

© Jutland 2004

Monarchy: From the Middle Ages to Modernity first published
by HarperPress 2006

© David Starkey 2006

5

David Starkey asserts the moral right to
be identified as the author of this work

A catalogue record for this book
is available from the British Library

ISBN 978-0-00-730772-2

Typeset in Bell MT by G&M Designs Limited, Raunds, Northamptonshire
Printed and bound in Great Britain by Clays Ltd, St Ives plc

MIX
Paper from
responsible sources
FSC
www.fsc.org **FSC® C007454**

FSC is a non-profit international organisation established to promote the
responsible management of the world's forests. Products carrying the FSC
label are independently certified to assure consumers that they come
from forests that are managed to meet the social, economic and
ecological needs of present and future generations.

Find out more about HarperCollins and the environment at
www.harpercollins.co.uk/green

LIST OF CONTENTS

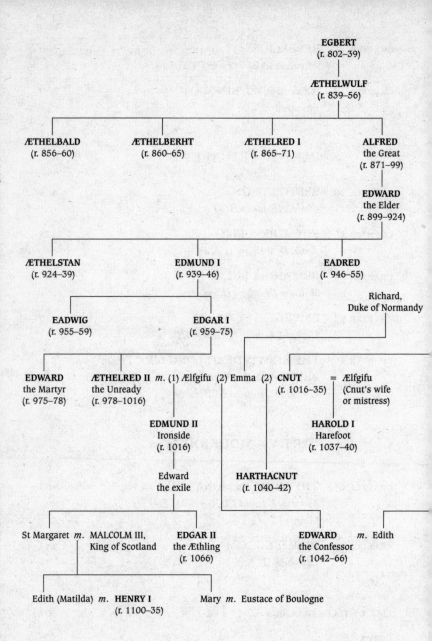

HOUSES OF GODWIN AND WESSEX

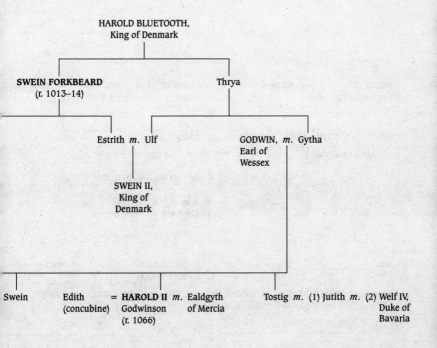

HAROLD BLUETOOTH,
King of Denmark

SWEIN FORKBEARD
(r. 1013–14)

Thrya

Estrith *m*. Ulf

GODWIN, *m*. Gytha
Earl of
Wessex

SWEIN II,
King of
Denmark

Swein

Edith
(concubine)

= **HAROLD II** *m*. Ealdgyth
Godwinson   of Mercia
(r. 1066)

Tostig *m*. (1) Jutith *m*. (2) Welf IV,
Duke of
Bavaria

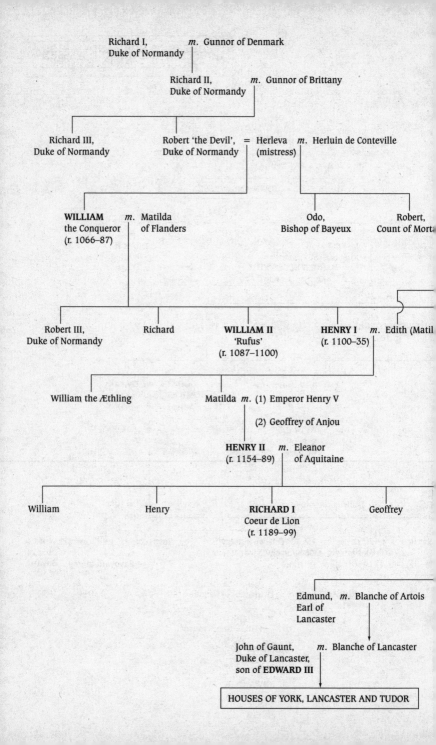

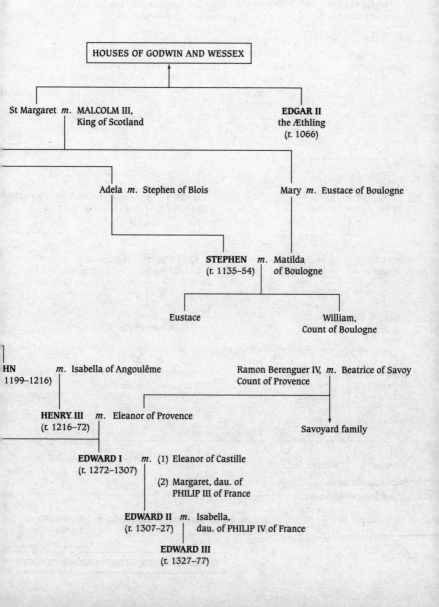

HOUSES OF NORMANDY, ANJOU
AND THE PLANTAGENETS

HOUSES OF GODWIN AND WESSEX

St Margaret *m*. MALCOLM III,
King of Scotland

EDGAR II
the Æthling
(r. 1066)

Adela *m*. Stephen of Blois

Mary *m*. Eustace of Boulogne

STEPHEN *m*. Matilda
(r. 1135–54) of Boulogne

Eustace

William,
Count of Boulogne

HN *m*. Isabella of Angoulême
1199–1216)

Ramon Berenguer IV, *m*. Beatrice of Savoy
Count of Provence

HENRY III *m*. Eleanor of Provence
(r. 1216–72)

Savoyard family

EDWARD I *m*. (1) Eleanor of Castille
(r. 1272–1307)

(2) Margaret, dau. of
PHILIP III of France

EDWARD II *m*. Isabella,
(r. 1307–27) dau. of PHILIP IV of France

EDWARD III
(r. 1327–77)

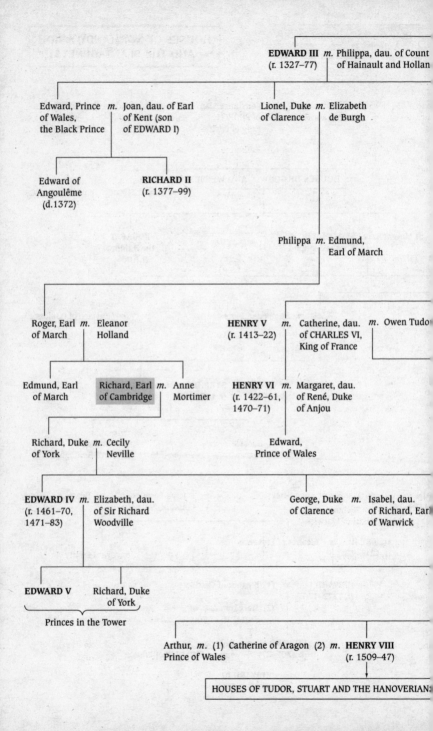

EDWARD III m. Philippa, dau. of Count
(r. 1327–77)   of Hainault and Hollan

Edward, Prince m. Joan, dau. of Earl
of Wales,   of Kent (son
the Black Prince   of EDWARD I)

Lionel, Duke m. Elizabeth
of Clarence   de Burgh

Edward of
Angoulême
(d.1372)

RICHARD II
(r. 1377–99)

Philippa m. Edmund,
              Earl of March

Roger, Earl m. Eleanor
of March   Holland

HENRY V m. Catherine, dau. m. Owen Tudo
(r. 1413–22)   of CHARLES VI,
                  King of France

Edmund, Earl
of March

Richard, Earl m. Anne
of Cambridge   Mortimer

HENRY VI m. Margaret, dau.
(r. 1422–61,   of René, Duke
1470–71)   of Anjou

Richard, Duke m. Cecily
of York   Neville

Edward,
Prince of Wales

EDWARD IV m. Elizabeth, dau.
(r. 1461–70,   of Sir Richard
1471–83)   Woodville

George, Duke m. Isabel, dau.
of Clarence   of Richard, Earl
                    of Warwick

EDWARD V   Richard, Duke
                of York

⎧ Princes in the Tower ⎭

Arthur, m. (1) Catherine of Aragon (2) m. **HENRY VIII**
Prince of Wales   (r. 1509–47)

HOUSES OF TUDOR, STUART AND THE HANOVERIAN:

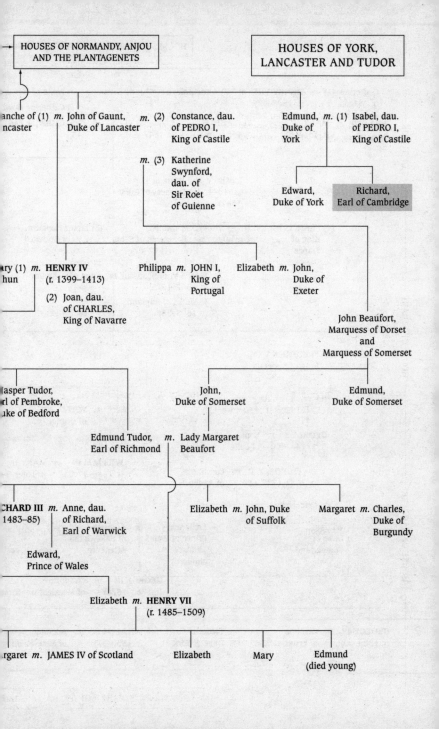

HOUSES OF NORMANDY, ANJOU AND THE PLANTAGENETS

HOUSES OF YORK, LANCASTER AND TUDOR

Blanche of (1) *m.* John of Gaunt, *m.* (2) Constance, dau. of PEDRO I, King of Castile
Lancaster   Duke of Lancaster

Edmund, *m.* (1) Isabel, dau. of PEDRO I, King of Castile
Duke of York

m. (3) Katherine Swynford, dau. of Sir Roët of Guienne

Edward, Duke of York

Richard, Earl of Cambridge

Mary (1) *m.* HENRY IV
Bohun   (r. 1399–1413)

(2) Joan, dau. of CHARLES, King of Navarre

Philippa *m.* JOHN I, King of Portugal

Elizabeth *m.* John, Duke of Exeter

John Beaufort, Marquess of Dorset and Marquess of Somerset

Jasper Tudor, Earl of Pembroke, Duke of Bedford

John, Duke of Somerset

Edmund, Duke of Somerset

Edmund Tudor, *m.* Lady Margaret Beaufort
Earl of Richmond

RICHARD III *m.* Anne, dau. of Richard, Earl of Warwick
(r. 1483–85)

Elizabeth *m.* John, Duke of Suffolk

Margaret *m.* Charles, Duke of Burgundy

Edward, Prince of Wales

Elizabeth *m.* HENRY VII
(r. 1485–1509)

Margaret *m.* JAMES IV of Scotland

Elizabeth

Mary

Edmund (died young)

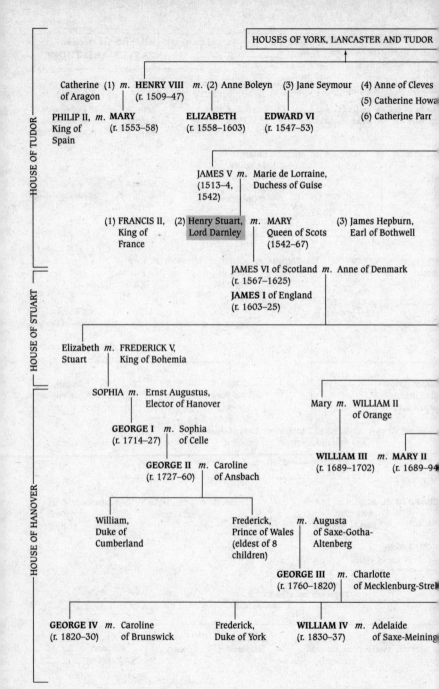

HOUSES OF YORK, LANCASTER AND TUDOR

HOUSE OF TUDOR

Catherine (1) *m.* **HENRY VIII** *m.* (2) Anne Boleyn (3) Jane Seymour (4) Anne of Cleves
of Aragon (r. 1509–47) (5) Catherine Howa
PHILIP II, *m.* **MARY** **ELIZABETH** **EDWARD VI** (6) Catherine Parr
King of (r. 1553–58) (r. 1558–1603) (r. 1547–53)
Spain

JAMES V *m.* Marie de Lorraine,
(1513–4, Duchess of Guise
1542)

(1) FRANCIS II, (2) Henry Stuart, *m.* MARY (3) James Hepburn,
King of Lord Darnley Queen of Scots Earl of Bothwell
France (1542–67)

JAMES VI of Scotland *m.* Anne of Denmark
(r. 1567–1625)
JAMES I of England
(r. 1603–25)

HOUSE OF STUART

Elizabeth *m.* FREDERICK V,
Stuart King of Bohemia

SOPHIA *m.* Ernst Augustus, Mary *m.* WILLIAM II
Elector of Hanover of Orange

GEORGE I *m.* Sophia
(r. 1714–27) of Celle

GEORGE II *m.* Caroline **WILLIAM III** *m.* **MARY II**
(r. 1727–60) of Ansbach (r. 1689–1702) (r. 1689–94

HOUSE OF HANOVER

William, Frederick, *m.* Augusta
Duke of Prince of Wales of Saxe-Gotha-
Cumberland (eldest of 8 Altenberg
children)

GEORGE III *m.* Charlotte
(r. 1760–1820) of Mecklenburg-Strel

GEORGE IV *m.* Caroline Frederick, **WILLIAM IV** *m.* Adelaide
(r. 1820–30) of Brunswick Duke of York (r. 1830–37) of Saxe-Meining

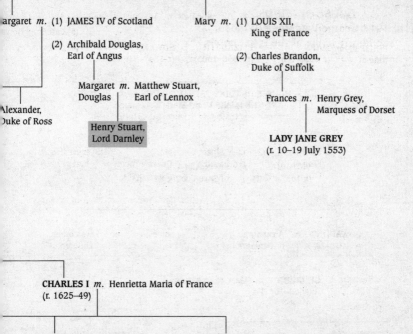

HOUSES OF TUDOR, STUART AND THE HANOVERIANS

Margaret *m.* (1) JAMES IV of Scotland

(2) Archibald Douglas,
Earl of Angus

Alexander,
Duke of Ross

Margaret *m.* Matthew Stuart,
Douglas   Earl of Lennox

Henry Stuart,
Lord Darnley

Mary *m.* (1) LOUIS XII,
King of France

(2) Charles Brandon,
Duke of Suffolk

Frances *m.* Henry Grey,
Marquess of Dorset

LADY JANE GREY
(r. 10–19 July 1553)

CHARLES I *m.* Henrietta Maria of France
(r. 1625–49)

CHARLES II *m.* Catherine
(r. 1660–85)   of Braganza

JAMES II   *m.* (1) Anne Hyde (2) Mary of Modena
(r. 1685–88)

ANNE   *m.* Prince George
(r. 1702–14)   of Denmark

James Francis Edward Stuart,
the Old Pretender

Charles Edward Stuart,
the Young Pretender

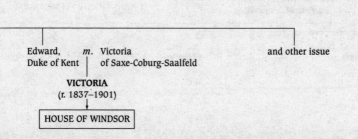

Edward,   *m.* Victoria   and other issue
Duke of Kent   of Saxe-Coburg-Saalfeld

VICTORIA
(r. 1837–1901)

HOUSE OF WINDSOR

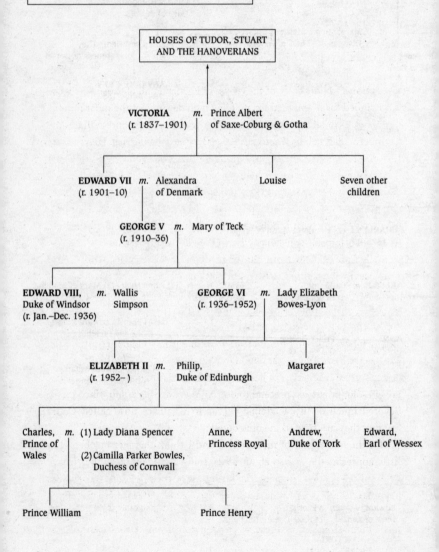

Simplified Family Tree

HOUSE OF WINDSOR
In 1917 George V adopted 'Windsor' as
the family name of the royal house

HOUSES OF TUDOR, STUART
AND THE HANOVERIANS

VICTORIA *m.* Prince Albert
(r. 1837–1901)   of Saxe-Coburg & Gotha

EDWARD VII *m.* Alexandra   Louise   Seven other
(r. 1901–10)   of Denmark   children

GEORGE V *m.* Mary of Teck
(r. 1910–36)

EDWARD VIII, *m.* Wallis   **GEORGE VI** *m.* Lady Elizabeth
Duke of Windsor   Simpson   (r. 1936–1952)   Bowes-Lyon
(r. Jan.–Dec. 1936)

ELIZABETH II *m.* Philip,   Margaret
(r. 1952–)   Duke of Edinburgh

Charles, *m.* (1) Lady Diana Spencer   Anne,   Andrew,   Edward,
Prince of   Princess Royal Duke of York   Earl of Wessex
Wales   (2) Camilla Parker Bowles,
               Duchess of Cornwall

Prince William   Prince Henry

FOREWORD

THIS BOOK IS THE STORY of the crown of England and of those who wore it, intrigued for it and died for it. They include some of the most notable figures of English and British history: Alfred the Great and William the Conqueror, who shaped and reshaped England; the great Henrys and Edwards of the Middle Ages, who made England the centre of a vast European empire; Henry VIII, whose mere presence could strike men dumb with fear; Elizabeth I, who remains as much a seductive enigma to us as she was to her contemporaries; and Charles I, who redeemed a disastrous reign with a noble, sacrificial death as he humbled himself, Christ-like and self-consciously so, to the executioner's axe.

Such figures leap from the page of mere history into myth and romance. I have painted these great royal characters – and the dozens of other monarchs, who, rightly or wrongly, have left less of a memory behind – with as much skill as I could.

But this is not a history of Kings and Queens. And its approach is not simply biographical either. Instead, it is the history of an institution: the Monarchy. Institutions – and monarchy most of all – are built of memory and inherited traditions, of heirlooms, historic buildings and rituals that are age-old (or at least pretend to be). All these are here, and, since I have devoted much of my academic career to what are now called Court Studies, they are treated in some detail.

But the institution of monarchy – and I think this fact has been too little appreciated – is also about ideas. Indeed, it is on ideas that I have primarily depended to shape the structure of the book and to drive its narrative. These are not the disembodied, abstract ideas of old-fashioned history. Instead, I present them through the lives of those who formu-lated them. Sometimes these were monarchs; more usually they were

advisers and publicists. Such men – at least as much as soldiers and sailors – were the shock-troops of monarchy. They shaped its reaction to
events; even, at times, enabled it to seize the initiative. When they were
talented and imaginative, monarchy flourished; when they were not, the
crown lost its sheen and the throne tottered.

So monarchy depends on its servants: its advisers and ideologues; its
painters, sculptors and architects, and – not least – its historians. And
these, too, are given voice, sometimes as chorus to the swelling scene,
occasionally as actors themselves.

The result is a task completed. It began in 2004 with the publication of
The Monarchy of England: The Beginnings. That book covered the period
from the fall of Roman Britain to the Norman Conquest and its aftermath,
and was intended to be the first of three volumes to accompany a Channel
4 series of the same name. A further volume, *Monarchy: From the Middle
Ages to Modernity*, appeared in 2006. But the Middle Ages themselves
remained untreated. This book brings together the two previously
published volumes. And it fills in the missing centuries in the same style
and with similar emphases.

I have also changed the book's title. *Monarchy* was chosen because of
the fashion at the time for portentous one-word titles for major television
series. And it did the job well enough. But *Crown and Country* does it
better. The crown is the oldest English institution and the most glittering. But its story, as I tell it, is finally the means to an end: the history of
England herself.

The Red House
Barham, Kent
July 2010

INTRODUCTION

RANK, ROMANCE AND THE ROYALS

IT SEEMS SUCH A STORY OF TODAY. William is the eventual heir to the oldest and most successful royal house in Europe and, on his marriage, will have a choice of titles that recall the gore and glory of the Middle Ages. Kate, on the other hand, descends from a line of Durham miners and has a mother who is a former air-hostess. The couple met, in the most ordinary way possible, while they were at university together. And, like most of their contemporaries, they have had a shot at being together (and indeed apart) before they decided to get married.

How very different in short from the love story of Charles and Diana – to say nothing of that of the queen and the duke of Edinburgh. No wonder the prime minister, David Cameron, has embraced their engagement as a sort of royal deluxe edition of his Big Society.

But, despite appearances and tabloid pontification, this royal romance is not a new beginning; it is scarcely even a new chapter. For nothing about it is quite what it seems or what we think.

Take their meeting at university. This may indeed be ordinary enough. But St Andrews is no ordinary academic institution. Instead, as the Chancellor boasted at Kate and William's graduation ceremony, it is 'the top match-making university in Britain'.

> You will have made lifelong friends; you may have met your husband or wife. Our title as the top match-making university … signifies so much that is good about St Andrews, so we rely on you to go forth and multiply.

Study, it would appear, is incidental. Instead this is university as a marriage-market. It is an updated version of the London Season of the first half of the twentieth century with its debuntantes and dowagers, and its student couples are as keen to pair off as their predecessors were in any royal court.

Nor are Kate's family as 'common' as some people think. Thanks to Party Pieces, the company in which Kate's mother appears to be the business brains, her parents have made money. Rather a lot of it indeed, since they have offered, with no sense of incongruity, to share the costs of the wedding with the queen and the prince of Wales. They live in a big, rambling, red-brick house, which is set in a garden large enough for William to use as a landing pad for his helicopter. The house is situated in a desirable village and surrounded by the rich, rolling countryside of Home Counties Berkshire. There is a hint of staff and the comfortable countrified life of the prosperous *nouveaux riches*, with their golf clubs and gymkhanas. And, most important of all perhaps, the Middletons have sent all three of their children to the elite public school of Marlborough College. Ever since the nineteenth century the public schools have been a principal gateway to gentility, mass producing little gentlemen and, latterly, little ladies. Kate, with her easy charm, confidence and style, is compelling evidence that the machine is still as purringly effective as ever.

But, it will be objected, this is a 'lifestyle' definition of gentility and class and, as such, essentially modern. What of lineage and ancestry? Are not they the proper and essential markers of class? Especially in earlier periods?

The answer is that they are not, at least in England. Nor have they been for several hundred years. 'As for gentlemen', wrote Sir Thomas Smith in his authoritative *De Republica Anglorum* (1565), 'they be made good cheap in England'.

> For whosoever studieth the laws of the realm, who studieth in the universities, who professeth liberal sciences, and to be short, who can live idly and without manual labour and will bear the port, charge and countenance of a gentleman, he shall be called *master*, for that is the title which men give to esquires and other gentlemen, and shall be taken for a gentleman.

For centuries, therefore, and whatever their remoter ancestry, girls like Kate, whose fathers have made money, lived genteely and could groom and educate them appropriately, have crossed the permeable and ever-fluctuating boundary of class and become ladies. They have even married royally. Even in the Middle Ages. Some indeed were also called Kate.

A royal wedding – whether the bride is Kate Middleton in the twenty-first century or her rather humbler predecessor Kate Swynford in the fourteenth – is a 'brilliant edition of a universal fact'. This means that it shares in the tension common to all marriages. Are the couple marrying for love? Or for property and power? And have they chosen each other? Or is the marriage arranged by their families for mutual advantage?

Nowadays, when even the rich have to earn their living, marriage is – or is supposed to be – about love. And the bride and groom expect to choose each other accordingly. In the Middle Ages, on the other hand, and for long afterwards, wealth was not so much earned as acquired by marriage or inheritance. This meant that marriage was too important to be left to the vagaries of emotion. Instead it was usually arranged and was primarily about property.

This was true, above all, of royal marriages, when it was not just property but the inheritance or acquisition of whole kingdoms that might be at stake. So royal children were married in their cradles and doddering old kings given blushing – and disgusted – young brides.

Feelings did not enter into it.

Except in England where, increasingly, they did.

This older, stranger story also begins, more or less, with another Kate. Katherine Roet was certainly no grander than Katherine Middleton, either by birth or family connections. Her father was a royal herald and her first husband, Sir Hugh Swynford, a royal servant. Yet Katherine finished up as a royal duchess and is the ancestress of all British monarchs from the Tudors to the Windsors.

Most striking of all, Katherine's own breakthrough came as a result of her employment – modest indeed – as a governess in a royal princely house-hold. John of Gaunt was the third son of King Edward III and, as duke of Lancaster, the richest and most powerful nobleman in England. He had vast lands, which are still the jewel of the Crown Estate, a string of noble castles, like Kenilworth, and a magnificent London palace at the Savoy.

In 1369 Gaunt's duchess, Blanche died after only nine years of marriage. She left three children and her widower turned to Katherine Swynford to look after them. Soon – as *au pairs* have had a habit of doing throughout the ages – Katherine began to look after Gaunt as well. In 1371, Gaunt remarried a royal princess, Constance of Castile. But his liaison with Katherine continued, and, after the death of her own husband, Sir Hugh, was publicly acknowledged.

The couple had four children, three boys and a girl, who were given the surname 'Beaufort', after one of Gaunt's French estates, and brought up as the duke's own. But the the ascent of Katherine and her family was not yet complete. Duchess Constance died, unlamented, in 1394 and Gaunt remarried Katherine in 1396. Their children were legitimated, first by the pope and then by the king and, within four generations, their descendants were sitting on the throne of England.

Katherine's rise, from mistress to wife and royal duchess, was unique for her own times. For us, of course, it bears a striking resemblance to the career of Camilla Parker Bowles. And the relationship was even more unpopular. Katherine was denounced as 'an enchantress and female devil'; Gaunt became the target of popular anger and disgust that nearly cost him his life in the Peasants' Revolt of 1381.

But then Gaunt – like Charles – had form with marriage. And the issue, as with Charles, was 'love, whatever that means'. Gaunt, as we have seen, was married three times. Only his second was a wholly conventional dynastic union. Gaunt, no more than second or third in line to the English throne, was in search of a kingdom and Constance, as daughter of the murdered Pedro I of Castile, had a claim to one. Love, even affection, did not enter into it and the couple were indifferent, if not actually hostile, to each other.

Gaunt's first marriage, to Blanche of Lancaster, had been a dynastic union too, since she was heiress to the greatest fortune in England. But it was more: the couple were young, high-born, glamorous and, it would seem, genuinely and passionately in *love*.

Or should that be in *lurve*? For Romantic Love – with its unrequited passions, its vows, its proposals on bended knee, its exchanges of rings and tokens, its protestations of eternal devotion and its living happily ever after – is an invention of the French Middle Ages. Its key text, all 21,000 lines of it, is the *Roman de la Rose*, from which the word *romantic* itself derives. The tradition was assimilated into English in John of Gaunt's own time. And the man who was primarily responsible was Gaunt's brother-in-law. For Geoffrey Chaucer was not only the greatest poet of the age but also husband to Philippa Roet, Katherine Swynford's sister and long-serving lady in waiting to successive duchesses of Lancaster. Chaucer may have translated the *Roman de la Rose*; certainly in countless other works he began to teach the English 'the craft of fyne lovynge'.

And one of his exemplars was Gaunt himself and *his* love for Blanche, which, in allegorical form, is the subject of Chaucer's early, exquisite poem, *The Book of the Duchess*. Gaunt's love, as Chaucer presents it, began when he was a mere stripling. He was overcome by Blanche's beauty: her fair face, her golden hair, and her neck, her throat and her hands all white. His passion became all consuming – she was:

> My suffisaunce, my lust, my lif,
> Myn hap, myn hele, and al my blisse,
> My worldes welfare and my lisse,
> And I hires hooly, everydel.

Twice she rejected him, without affectation but with a simple 'nay'. After a year, he tried again. This time she accepted; gave him a ring and the two became one:

> Therwith she was alway so trewe,
> Our Ioye was ever yliche newe;
> Our hertes wern so even a payre,
> That never nas that oon contrayre
> To that other, for no wo.

But their happiness was cut cruelly short and in 1369, during the last great visitation of the Black Death, Blanche succumbed. Silenced by grief and bereft of eloquence, all Gaunt can say is: 'She is deed'. And the only consolation Chaucer can offer is equally bleak and economical: 'It is routhe [pity]', he replies.

Of course, the knight in black and 'goode faire White' are not straight-forward portraits of Gaunt and Blanche. Chaucer is writing poetry after all, not prose reportage. Nevertheless, it seems clear that *The Book of the Duchess* embodies our first great royal love story. All the familiar elements are there: youthful infatuation, high romance and – what is the best box-office of all – a tragic ending. Such tales punctuate the succeeding centuries of our history. The staider sort of commentator tends to dismiss them as mere soap-opera or technicolour glitz. Actually, their impact has been as great as the most serious concerns of politics and principle.

This is due, above all, to the characteristically prosaic twist the English gave to the idea of Romantic Love. For the French, love was fairy matter and dwelt, like the unicorn, in a rarefied, otherworldly landscape of verdant and perpetual spring. Above all, it was distinguished from marriage. The delights of love were for the mistress; children, property and the plodding reality of everyday life were for the wife.

The English, however, tried to have their cake and eat it by combining love and marriage. In the English chivalric romances, the lovers marry – just as Gaunt had married Blanche. Similarly, many succeeding monarchs would try to marry for love, or even, like the aging Gaunt, endeavour to make their mistresses into wives.

The consequences were to be writ in blood, dynastic failure and religious revolution.

In 1399 Gaunt's eldest son by Blanche usurped the throne as Henry IV and founded the new Lancastrian dynasty. The second king of the dynasty, Henry V, Gaunt's grandson, carried England to the peak of power by his military genius and single-minded drive. He devoted all his energies to the conquest of France and swore that he would marry no one but Catherine, the daughter of the French king, Charles VI. He achieved both goals and by the time of his premature death in 1422 he had come within a whisker of establishing a dual monarchy of England and France. But his son, Henry VI inherited his grandfather Charles VI's madness and, under his feeble rule, the house of Lancaster lost first France and then England.

The beneficiary was the rival branch of the royal family, the house of York.

Edward, earl of March and son and heir of Richard, duke of York, was only nineteen when he seized the throne in 1461. He was hugely tall, strapping and handsome. He adored women and was irresistibly attractive to most of them. He also had an ugly streak of violence and had spent much of his short life fighting.

But he met his match.

Elizabeth Woodville was one of the two most controversial women to have been queen of England. She was the first commoner to marry a reigning sovereign. She was the daughter and grand-daughter of household servants – admittedly rather grand ones. She was a widow and already the mother of two sons. And her late husband had been on the losing side in the civil war.

How, with so many disadvantages, did she come to marry the victorious young Edward IV of York? The answer is love.

Or rather lust thwarted that *became* love. For their first meeting was more attempted rape than romantic courtship. Edward was taken with Elizabeth and decided to have her. So he held a dagger to her throat and demanded sex. Elizabeth responded with magnificent coolness. He could kill her, she said. But she would only sleep with him if he married her.

It was an audacious gamble. But it paid off. The king now yielded to the woman. Lust turned to love – and to marriage.

They were married secretly at her parents' house at Grafton Regis in Northamptonshire on 1 May 1464. The following year she was given a magnificent coronation when she was already pregnant with her first child, also christened Elizabeth, who was born on 11 February 1466.

The marriage was an appalling *mésalliance*. But it was made worse by Elizabeth's character. Her portraits show a supremely fashionable face: very pale, presumably whitened, a high forehead exaggerated by plucking back the hairline, and a striking geometric headdress. She was a beauty indeed, but a cold and arrogant one. A modern parallel, whose marriage also shocked both England and the royal family, would be Mrs Simpson. There is the same angularity, the same sense of an outsider.

It is also a question of style. Both women were incredibly stylish – too stylish indeed, like an over-polished stone. They were elegant, but frigidly so. And, most of all, they exuded pure, undiluted acquisitiveness. In the case of Mrs Simpson it was for jewel after jewel. In the case of Elizabeth Woodville it was for property after property; power base after power base; marriage after marriage.

Who could respect kings who seemed to be putty in the hands of such women?

Elizabeth's marriage had begun by outraging every convention. It continued by treading on every toe. Elizabeth was one of a large family. All were now married off into the high aristocracy, much to the disgust of other, more established families who found themselves shut out of the marriage market. Elizabeth also gave Edward a large family of his own of two boys and seven girls. Edward thought they would guarantee his immortality and secure the future of his dynasty. But Elizabeth packed the household of the prince of Wales with her family and friends as well. Thanks to her ruthless acquisitiveness, the Woodvilles were threatening to turn into the real ruling dynasty of England.

The thought was intolerable to many and after Edward's premature death the Yorkist establishment split into pro- and anti-Woodville factions and the regime tore itself apart.

Marriage motivated 'by blind affection and not by rule of reason' – in other words, marriage for love – had turned, as many conservative voices had predicted, into a dynastic disaster.

The end came swiftly. Only two months after Edward IV's death, his son was usurped by his uncle, Richard, duke of Gloucester, who played the anti-Woodville card to devastating effect. Only two years later still, however, the usurper, who reigned as Richard III, was himself defeated and killed in battle by Henry, earl of Richmond. Richmond, proclaimed king as Henry VII, was the Lancastrian claimant through his mother Margaret Beaufort. But the claim was remote in the extreme and, to cement his shaky hold on the throne, Henry VII married Elizabeth, eldest daughter of Edward IV.

The second, but only surviving, son of the marriage succeeded in 1509 as Henry VIII in the first peaceful accession for almost a century. The boy, for he was not yet eighteen, had a remarkable lineage. On his father's side he was descended from a lovechild of Gaunt's liaison with, and eventual marriage to, Katherine Swynford; on his mother's he was grandson of the even more flagrant love-match of Edward IV and Elizabeth Woodville.

Did he inherit the seeds of love from his ancestors? It would seem so for he was perhaps the most famous lover to have sat on the throne of

England. And certainly his love-affairs, and their tempestuous conclusions, had the greatest impact.

Henry's upbringing played its part as well. As a second son, he was not given the strict, male-dominated upbringing considered appropriate for the heir to the throne. His short-lived elder brother Arthur was sent off to Ludlow to rule Wales and fit himself to be king of England; Henry was kept at home. He was brought up by his mother and with his sisters in a largely female household till his early teens. It was a most unusual experience for a Tudor boy of the upper classes and it turned Henry into a man who needed women as no king had done before – or perhaps since. He could not live without them. But it had to be the right woman and he had to love and marry her. So intense was this quest for marital perfection – and such the frailty of womankind – that Henry, famously, married six times. And, as we know, there were casualties.

Henry's education was also important. He was taught French by a native-speaker and learned to read and write it fluently, perhaps almost as a native. This meant that, alongside his knowledge of the classics, which he acquired from a succession of distinguished Latin teachers, Henry was also soaked in the French literature of courtly love. He saw himself as a hero of romance, winning his lady with his lance. Every woman was a damsel in distress; every fortress a castle dangerous. And it was not only in the imagination: Henry was a superb jouster; a more-than-adequate poet who wrote (against weak competition, it is true) some of the best verse of his generation; and a talented musician, who excelled as both performer and composer. Indeed, his 'Pastime with Good Company', for which he wrote both the words and music, became the most popular lyric of the day. Henry in short was a crowned Don Quixote, except that his fantasies were real. Or at least his power made them appear so.

Something of this appeared even in his first marriage to Catherine of Aragon, where its dynastic and diplomatic foundations were overlaid by at least a veneer of high romance: 'I loved where I did marry', the king proclaimed in one of his early poems.

But it was in his second, protracted courtship of Anne Boleyn that his romantic yearnings found their mate. For Anne was brought up in the same Frenchified courtly tradition as Henry. Or rather, while he absorbed it at second-hand in England, she experienced the real thing, first in the

French-speaking household of the Archduchess Margaret, Regent of the Netherlands; then in the dazzling court of Francis I of France. And even in France she shone and was paid the highest compliment a Frenchman can pay: 'you would never have thought her English', an observer wrote, 'but taken her for a fine French lady'.

Anne was thus a swan among geese when she returned to the English court: the greatest poet of the age made passionate love to her but was spurned; the heir to the richest earldom became her suitor and betrothed her; and the king threw himself at her feet.

Literally. Henry's early love-letters to Anne are written in French in the high courtly style. He is prostrate; he proffers his services; he is her secretary; he languishes and only a word from her can save him. She is his *Mistress*.

But that was the one role that Anne was determined not to play. Like Elizabeth Woodville before her, she would be wife and queen or nothing. And Henry, like *his* grandfather Edward IV before him – whom he so much resembled in build, appearance and character – took the bait. They would marry, he swore. 'Either there [marriage], or nowhere'.

Henry's letters now change character. He is no longer the court lover but the passionate husband-to-be. Even the signature changes. Henry signs himself with the royal monogram, 'HR' (*Henricus Rex*) enclosing a heart inscribed with Anne's monogram, 'AB'. Sometimes he elaborates. He is 'immovable [in his determination]'. He 'seeks no other [than Anne]'. He enters into complex word play on her name and *an* (year) in French and *anno* (year) in Latin. And Anne no doubt replied in kind.

Here in short are two lovers in love with being in love. They play the game of love. They speak their own private language and they inhabit their own private world.

So long as they remained in that private world, all was well. But once they entered on the public stage of matrimony disaster befell. Anne, so masterful in the art of love, was temperamentally unsuited to being that shrunken thing, a wife. Above all, she failed to give Henry a son. The result was that Henry fell out of love with her almost as quickly as he had once thrown himself at her feet. Love turned to hate and marriage to divorce – and death.

The strange cycle of Henry's love then turned again. And again.

* * *

Elizabeth I, Henry VIII's daughter by Anne Boleyn, succeeded to the throne in 1558. She was the child of a love-match, admittedly one that went horribly wrong. And love, or rather the incompatibility in her case of love and marriage, is a dominant theme of her life and reign. For she was not, emphatically, a natural virgin. She loved men and children; she loved being in love or playing at being in love. She had been in love in earnest with her then step-father, Thomas, Lord Seymour of Sudeley, when she was still in her teens. And she fell passionately in love with Robert Dudley, her master of the Horse, soon after she became queen. Dudley was handsome and masterful. But he was widely distrusted and his reputation was blasted by the fact that both his father and grandfather had been executed as traitors.

It would, in short, have been madness to marry him and Elizabeth had the sense, unlike her cousin Mary Queen of Scots, to pull back from the brink. Dudley was transmuted from consort-to-be into favourite and Elizabeth retired, hurt, from the mating game. She never fully re-entered it. The dilemma on which she was impaled was neatly summarized by a contemporary politician: anybody that Elizabeth *could* marry, she would not, because she did not find them attractive; and anybody that she *would* marry, she could not because they were not of the right status.

Elizabeth never resolved the issue. Instead in time she turned her virgin state into a matter of policy and propaganda. It worked. But it meant that when she died in 1603, the direct line of the English royal house died with her.

After Elizabeth's death, James VI of Scotland, who descended from Margaret, elder sister of Henry VIII, succeeded as James I of England, or Great Britain as the new joint kingdom became known.

There followed three centuries of rule by foreign dynasties: Franco-Scottish, Dutch and German. And their marriage customs were foreign too. Out went love and low origins; in came strict rules about rank and suitability. But as rules about the choice of wife and queen became more restrictive, love – and lust – found their outlet elsewhere.

The age of license and the mistress had begun.

The Stuarts were a recent and insecure dynasty. Their title was weak and Scotland itself peripheral. The acquisition of England helped. But still they sought marriage with the great royal houses of Europe, the French and the Spanish, to reinforce their status and dignity. But, even with this prudential and calculating approach to matrimony, romance and chivalry cast their spell.

Marriage negotiations were opened for James's heir, Charles to marry the Spanish *infanta*. The negotiations stalled, and Charles and his friend and his father's favourite, the duke of Buckingham, resolved to journey to Spain to woo and win the lady in person. They departed like two knights in romance on a chivalric quest. But the land of Don Quixote proved unresponsive. The Spanish demands for Catholic toleration were too high and the *infanta* herself was loath to marry a heretic. So Charles and Buckingham were repulsed in their knightly quest and returned to England hurt and breathing vengeance. They would fight Spain and Charles would marry in France.

And so it came to pass. His bride was the fifteen-year-old Henrietta Maria, daughter of Henry IV of France. The marriage began disastrously, with tears and tantrums on the part of the youthful bride. But things settled down and, as sometimes happens in arranged marriages, the couple fell deeply and devotedly in love *after* matrimony. The contrast with James I's rackety court was notable and their family life became a model of decency and decorum.

This cut little ice with most of Charles I's subjects. For England – as a result primarily of Henry VIII's matrimonial adventures – was Protestant while Henrietta Maria was proudly, flagrantly Catholic. The result was to taint the monarchy with an alien creed. The perception played an important part in the outbreak of the Civil War which led to the downfall of the monarchy and the execution of the king in 1649. And it became even more pronounced after the Restoration in 1660 and Henrietta Maria's return to England as queen mother. Charles II, her eldest son, was received into the church of Rome on his deathbed while her younger son, who succeeded as James II in 1685, had converted long before. This was tolerable since his two children by his late first wife had been brought up as staunch Protestants. But in 1688 James's second Catholic wife, Mary of Modena, gave birth to a son who would certainly be brought up as a Catholic.

The prospect of a Catholic succession was the last straw and James was overthrown in the Glorious Revolution. The revolutionary settlement also introduced the first, formal limitation on the marriage of an

English sovereign. No future monarch, it declared, could be Catholic or could marry one.

And, over three hundred years later, the rule still holds. Happily, Kate Middleton's religion, in so far as it is discernible, appears to be of the right sort.

In 1701 the anti-Catholicism of the monarchy was further entrenched by the Act of Settlement. This transferred the succession to the only available Protestant heirs, the German family of Guelph, who were the rulers of the north German state of Hanover.

The result in 1714 was the accession of the Elector Georg of Hanover to the British throne as King George I.

The Hanoverians brought with them the full rigour of German dynastic customs, particularly with regard to marriage. These stood at the opposite extreme to the free and easy English practice. In the German tradition, social rank was legally defined and the choice of marriage partner had to follow suit: nobleman had to marry noblewoman; prince had to wed princess. Failure to do so led to *dérogeance*: the issue from the marriage took the mother's inferior rank and became ineligible to inherit their father's status and public position. Positively applied, these rules also led to to the idea of 'morganatic marriage'.

This was a private marriage for a public figure. The marriage was valid and the children were legitimate. But the wife did not assume her husband's status, nor were the the children able to inherit his royal or princely titles.

These German dynastic rules were never incorporated directly into English law. But they came in by the back door with the Royal Marriages Act of 1772. This declared that no royal marriage was valid without the consent of the king – and the king saw himself as guardian of the full rigour of dynastic tradition. The effect was to give the sanction of English law to the deeply un-English marriage customs of the royal house.

A clash between English and German values was now inevitable. For though the royal house was German, its children were brought up in England and acquired English values – especially in the matter of emotional satisfaction. George III (1760–1820) and Queen Charlotte had some seven sons. Only the duke of York made an officially approved marriage with a German princess. But the couple had no children and, in what is also rather English behaviour, lavished their affection on their dogs. The remaining sons entered into liaisons with English women. The resulting relationships were often long-lasting, affectionate and fertile, with the duke of Clarence and the actress Mrs Jordan, for example, having some ten children. Similarly George, prince of Wales, found the love of his life with Mrs Fitzherbert, who was 'fat, fair and forty'. Unfortunately, however, she was not only English but Catholic, which meant that their marriage, though probably canonically valid, was not recognized.

But in 1794, George, overwhelmed by debt thanks to his luxurious lifestyle and even more lavish building projects, succumbed. He offered a deal: in exchange for having his debts paid, he would throw over Mrs Fitzherbert and marry the required German princess. The chosen bride was Caroline of Brunswick. It was loathing at first sight. The prince's reluctance was so obvious that the archbishop of Canterbury, who was conducting the wedding service, paused meaningfully after reciting the words 'no lawful impediment'. And matters only got got worse on the marriage night. The bride was ugly and stank; the groom drank himself to oblivion with cognac and was found the following morning with his head in the hearth. They never spent another night together. Nevertheless, successful intercourse had taken place and a daughter, named Charlotte after her grandmother the queen, was born. Princess Charlotte was intelligent, gay and tomboyish. But she died in childbirth in 1817 after only eighteen months of marriage.

Charlotte's death triggered a dynastic crisis. King George III and Queen Charlotte had had twelve children who reached maturity. But, with the princess's death, there survived not one single legitimate grandchild.

The remaining royal dukes were now required to do their duty and a rush to the altar followed. Cambridge, Kent and Clarence all disposed of their English mistresses and married German princesses. The victor in the procreation stakes was Kent, to whom a daughter was born in 1819.

She was called Victoria, after her mother.

In 1837, Victoria succeeded at the age of only eighteen. She was lively, wilful – and unmarried. Her remote cousin Albert of Saxe-Coburg-Gotha, had already been suggested as a possible husband. But, as queen regnant, Victoria could not simply be ordered to marry; she also disapproved of arranged marriages and had a powerful appreciation of male beauty.

In 1839 Albert visited England again and something clicked. He is *'beautiful'*, Victoria confided to her diary. She, as queen, proposed and they were married the following February in the Chapel Royal, St James's.

The bride's orange-blossom trimmed headdress trembled throughout the ceremony and she developed a blinding headache. But then all dissolved in passion and bliss.

Victoria and Albert's happy marriage rescued the moral reputation of the monarchy from the degradation into which it had sunk under her 'wicked' Regency uncles.

But there was a price: it became more German than ever. Sitting at their adjacent desks at Osborne, Victoria and Albert spoke German to each other. Their artistic tastes were German; their music was German; the style of their family life – complete with the Germanic importation of Christmas trees – was German. Most importantly, of their nine children, six married German princes or princesses, two members of the Danish and Russian royal houses and only one at home, to a Scottish nobleman.

The result was that at the beginning of the twentieth century the dynasty was almost as German as it had been when the Hanoverians first arrived in Britain two hundred years before. Identities were fused, how far and how deeply we have almost forgotten: the German Kaiser Wilhelm II was Victoria's eldest and favourite grandson; the commander of the British navy was a German princeling.

None of this mattered in the cosy world of cross-Channel monarchy. But in 1914 this world was shattered for ever when Britain declared war on Germany and the First World War broke out. The British royal family, and every member of it, had to make the choice, however painful.

Were you English? Or German? For you could no longer be both.

The year was 1917. The First World War was at its height. At home, the fleet had mutinied at Spithead; abroad the Russian Empire was about to collapse and everywhere revolution was in the air. George V, king-emperor of Great Britain and William's great-great-grandfather, was the least likely of revolutionaries. He was a stiff-backed ex-sailor; punctilious in his dress and formal in his manners, whose only recreations were his stamp albums, his weather-gauge and his coverts of game-birds, of which he slaughtered prodigious numbers. And yet he had shrewd political instincts and even shrewder advisers. Together they decided to fight revolution with revolution.

Their enterprise was no less than to reinvent the British Monarchy. The first step was to make it British. Ever since the accession of the House of Hanover two hundred years previously in 1714, the royal family had been German – in blood, in its first language and, above all, in its name: Guelph or, latterly, Wettin or Saxe-Coburg-Gotha.

With Germany as the enemy, this was impossible and George resolved to change it. After a bit of discreet market-testing, he came up with the quintessentially English name of Windsor. With its echoes of Shakespeare and soft-soap it was the perfect choice. It also led to the only recorded joke by Kaiser Wilhelm II, George's cousin and opponent in the war, who declared that he was looking forward to the next performance of Shakespeare's 'Merry Wives of Saxe-Coburg-Gotha'!

But the change of name was only the first step.

What had kept the royal family German for two hundred years were its marriage customs. So George changed those as well. Hitherto, the royal family had followed the German practice. This required members of ruling houses only to marry people of equivalent rank – in other words princes and princesses of other German dynasties. Instead George declared by order in council that henceforth his children would be able to marry Englishmen and Englishwomen. 'It was an historic day', he confided to his diary.

It was. It sounds so simple. And yet the seed of everything that has followed, right up to the marriage of William and Kate, is there. Royal weddings – even to unknown and usually unattractive German princesses – have always aroused a lot of popular interest. But it was difficult to present such arranged dynastic marriages as romantic love stories. Once the brides were English and pretty, however, the floodgates of schmalz opened.

They did most conspicuously in the case of Prince William's great-grandparents, the future George VI and Queen Elizabeth (later the queen mother), who were married in 1923. The relationship was even on-off as well, since Elizabeth refused George's first two proposals. After she had accepted his third, the media storm broke. The newly-illustrated popular press and women's magazines featured endless photographs of the bride, her family and homes. Her trousseau and clothes were scrutinized and the interiors of the couple's new home at 145 Piccadilly pored over. Elizabeth even gave a press interview, though the appalled reaction of her father-in-law, George V, made sure that it was her last.

If Kate really wants to know what lies ahead, she could do worse than flick through the files of those yellowing cuttings.

There was even the same interest in the choice of venue for the wedding. In the Hanoverian centuries, and under the Stuart dynasty before that, royal weddings were semi-private affairs. They were held, almost invariably, in the Chapel Royal at St James's Palace. The chapel would be magnificently decorated. But nothing could disguise its mean interior and poky proportions.

The royal revolution of 1917 changed this too. A royal wedding was now a national wedding. Everybody was interested and everybody – metaphorically at least – was invited. Only one building was big enough or symbolic enough: Westminster Abbey.

In 1923 the wedding address in the Abbey was given by Cosmo Gordon Lang, Archbishop of York. It was solemn, even intimidating. 'You cannot', he told the bride and groom, 'resolve that [your marriage] will be happy. But you can and will resolve that it shall be noble'. Lang, good priest that he was, recognized the vagaries of human nature. But, in the case of the young royal couple before him, he required that those vagaries be hidden by a public facade: whatever the reality of their marriage, George and Elizabeth were required to keep up appearances.

Above all they must never, ever contemplate divorce. Ever since the Reformation, the law of England on marriage had corresponded more or less to the Church of England's teaching on the indissolubility of Christian marriage. This meant that divorce was difficult, expensive and subject to profound social stigma. Pressure to reform these impossibly restrictive laws grew on either side of the First World War. Lang set himself to oppose the movement for liberalization and did so with remarkable success. But his masterstroke was his wedding address of 1923 which enlisted the monarchy to his cause.

The result was a paradox. Once the demand for love had been an escape from the shackles of royal convention. Now a royal couple were required to have a happy, loving marriage – or least to keep up the appearance of one. One set of rules, it turned out, had only been replaced by another. The old German dynastic rules governing royal marriages had been discarded. But the price was the imposition of the new rule of compulsory marital happiness. And the new rule had the potential to make the old seem like freedom itself.

Especially for the man who would be king.

For George, duke of York, was only the second son of George V. The heir was Edward, prince of Wales, who was the antithesis of his shy, stuttering, conventional brother. The prince was handsome and dashing. He adored trousers with turn-ups, cocktails, flying, America, fast cars, Art Deco and every other fad and fashion of modernity. He also set the fashion himself, with his boyish figure and excellent dress sense. Above all, he was a confident and insatiable womanizer.

The only problem was that he preferred married women and showed no inclination to marry himself – until he met his match in Wallis Simpson. Wallis was Edward's alter ego. He loved America; she *was* American. And she was as smart, fashionable and ever-so-up-to-the-minute as he was. She was also much the stronger character and he yielded adoringly to her influence.

They would marry, he decided and nothing should stop them – not even the fact that Mrs Simpson was a married woman with one divorce already behind her. For so extreme a *mésalliance* it is necessary to go back to Edward IV and Elizabeth Woodville. Or Henry VIII and Anne Boleyn. Wallis and Edward even had a similar private language. And it too centred on a monogram: 'WE'. 'WE' stood, of course, for Wallis and Edward. But it took on a life of its own: 'WE' together. 'WE' different. 'WE' non-conformist. 'WE' doing what 'WE' want, not what 'WE' are told to do.

'WE', in short, against the world.

But the world proved unforgiving. In the midst of their affair, George V died. The next evening, the prime minister was to broadcast to the nation from Downing Street. Lang's friend, John Reith, the director general of the BBC, was invited to dinner and asked to comment on the script. He made crucial alterations 'bringing in the moral authority, honour and dignity of the throne'. But Edward would not be warned. His private secretary, Clive Wigram, then sought to invoke the law and consulted the Lord Chancellor 'about the marriage laws of a sovereign'. He expected to be told that marriage with a divorced woman, like Mrs Simpson, was explicitly excluded. He must have been surprised to be informed instead that the laws spoke only of marriage with a Roman Catholic and were silent on the subject of a union with a divorcée.

But if the law could not stop Edward, public and political opinion, astutely manipulated by the prime minister, Stanley Baldwin, could. Baldwin backed Edward into a corner and Edward, already riddled with doubts about the 'kinging business', failed to put up much of a fight. He abdicated on 11 December 1936 after reigning less than a year. That evening he was at last allowed to broadcast to the nation:

> You must believe me [he said] when I tell you I have found it impossible to carry the heavy burden of responsibility and to discharge my duties as king as I would wish without the help and support of the woman I love.

The new Windsor rules of loving – but holy – matrimony had claimed their first victim. He would not be the last.

His removal had also been easy because he had no direct heirs while his younger brother George already had two daughters, Princesses Elizabeth and Mary Rose. It was thus straightforward, as well as sound dynastic policy, to shunt Edward VIII aside and replace him with George VI. This is why the Abdication Crisis was over almost as quickly as it had begun. For the royal family it was a terrible trauma; for the nation at large, it was a nine-day wonder.

Soon it was as though the brief reign of Edward VIII had never been. Reith and Lang could breathe again, confident that in the new king they had a monarch who would play his appointed part. He was ably supported by his wife and, in time, by his eldest daughter Elizabeth, on whom the demands of royalty sat as lightly as they had been burdensome to her uncle.

And she was especially fortunate in the matter of love. She was swept off her feet by her handsome, sea-faring cousin, Prince Philip of Greece, and the two were married at Westminster Abbey in 1947. The ceremony, the archbishop of Canterbury declared was exactly the same as it would be for any cottager who might be married this afternoon in some small country church in a remote village in the Dales: the same prayers are offered; the same blessings given.

It was indeed the same, apart from the twelve wedding cakes at the reception and the 2,666 wedding presents, including a solid gold coffee set and a 54 carat pink diamond. But the imputed ordinariness made the ostentatious wealth somehow all right – like a welcome shaft of sunlight amid the grey austerity of postwar Britain.

Indeed, the ordinariness was a sort of pathetic fallacy. The pathetic fallacy proper is a literary device which attributes human feelings to the impersonal forces of nature. The pathetic fallacy of the Windsor monarchy – or rather of its subjects – was to attribute the democratic unction of ordinariness to the most extraordinary family of all. The result was that, while other thrones tottered and fell, the British monarchy seemed impregnable. 'Soon', one of the growing band of former monarchs, ex-King Farouk of Egypt, prophesied, 'there will only be five Kings left: the King of England, the King of Spades, the King of Clubs, the King of Hearts, and the King of Diamonds'.

Princess Elizabeth succeeded in 1952 after the early death of her father at the age of only 56. At her Accession Council she announced her intention 'always [to] work as my father did'. She has kept her promise.

Her children have found it far less easy and divorce has dogged all but one of them. Especially Prince Charles. At first, his marriage to Lady Diana Spencer seemed the embodiment of the Windsor dream. Are you 'in love', the couple was asked? 'Of course', Diana replied. 'Whatever "in love" means', answered the prince.

Not even the Abbey was big enough for the expectations aroused by their wedding and St Paul's Cathedral was chosen instead. 'This is the stuff of which fairy tales are made', said the archbishop in his address. Only one previous prince of Wales had been married there: Arthur, eldest son of Henry VII, who was dead within six months of the wedding.

It was not a happy precedent.

* * *

The fairy-tale wedding, notoriously, turned to nightmare and the prospect of divorce loomed. It was back to 1936 and the Abdication Crisis. But the balance of forces was different. This time, the Establishment spoke with forked tongues. Separation and even divorce would present no constitutional barrier to Prince Charles's eventual accession, the prime minister stated – certainly correctly. Even the archbishop of Canterbury temporized. Nevertheless, there was widespread unease. There was a feeling that the 'rules' (even if they were only unwritten conventions) had been broken and that Prince Charles had somehow 'broken his compact with the Nation', as the *Sun* put it.

Public opinion also decided, as public opinion tends to, that an older, rather unattractive man was in the wrong and a young and pretty woman was in the right. Finally, the Wars of the Wales, in which Charles and Diana slugged it out in public and traded scandal for scandal, brought the House of Windsor, for the first time in its history, into widespread contempt.

But times and values have changed – not least thanks to Diana herself. William, as his re-use of his mother's engagement ring shows, is profoundly attached to Diana's memory. And he seems to have found a kindred spirit in Kate. The result is that their relationship, in this regard at least, appears different from any previous Windsor couple. There is not a trace of high romance or grand, Mills & Boon-style passion. Instead, it is pragmatic, remarkably equal, and based (so they have told us) on a shared sense of humour. It also has already lasted some eight years.

Despite this good, level-headed beginning, they will be under enormous pressure to turn into figures from a romance and become Prince Charming and Cinderella in Jimmy Choos. The press wants it; the people want it; the world wants it. We all want our fairy tale.

It will be very difficult for them to resist. But it will be greatly to their advantage if they do. It will also be to ours since it will help us to admit that family values have indeed changed and that high romance and the workaday reality of marriage – even princely marriage – have very little to do with each other.

They will be under another pressure too: to put on a good show. For another of the paradoxes of the Windsor monarchy is that it has carried royal spectacle to heights of splendour and perfection rarely equalled even in the glory days of kingly power under the Plantagenets and Tudors. This is because a People's Monarchy is part of popular entertainment, which has high standards when it comes to spectacle.

On the other hand, siren voices have been raised to tell them to cut back. Remember the recession, says one Gradgrind; away with flummery, demands another kill-joy. This is very strange. The most ordinary couples try to make a bit of a splash with their weddings. How much more is expected of a royal union?

For this is the real point. As Walter Bagehot pointed out long ago in his masterly analysis of the Victorian monarchy, royalty is interesting while republics are boring. This is why that great republic, America, despite having got rid of George III, cannot get enough of the British monarchy. 'Kate and William are HUGE news here. Is anything else going on in the world?' an American friend has just emailed me.

Kate and William are now the latest stars of that great international circus. There are terrible dangers, as William knows only too well from his mother. But, helped by Kate, he shows signs of having learned that he must do things a bit differently and pour the wine of new, more modest values into the old bottle of the Windsor Family Monarchy.

Let's hope that it turns out to be champagne and doesn't go flat too quickly!

David Starkey
Barham, Kent
March 2011

PART I

BEGINNINGS

1

THE SHADOW
OF ROME

SOMETIMES, EVEN WHEN you are a case-hardened professional, you see history differently. I had one such moment when I first visited the Great Hall of the National Archives in Washington. I was faintly shocked by the way in which the Constitution and the Bill of Rights were displayed, like Arks of the Covenant, on a dimly lit altar and between American flags and impossibly upright American marines.

But what really struck me was the presence of a copy of Magna Carta. It was, as it were, in a side chapel. Nevertheless, here it was, this archetypically English document, in the American archival Holy of Holies.

It was placed there out of the conviction that it was the ancestor, however remote, of the Constitution and the Bill of Rights. And its presence set me thinking. Was this assumption correct? Does it help explain current concerns – like Britain's, or England's, reluctance to be absorbed in the European Union? Does it mean that there is an Anglo-Saxon way and a European way, as the French undoubtedly think? Does the difference derive from the contrast between Roman Law and English Common Law? Is it, finally, England *versus* Rome?

The first part of this book attempts to answer some of these questions. It uses the medium of narrative, which I think is the only proper means of historical explanation. And it goes back to the beginning, which is the only right place to start.

Indeed, if I may be excused Irish, it goes back *before* the beginning. The idea of the English does not appear until the eighth century, and the reality of England not till two hundred years later still. But I start a millennium earlier with the Roman invasions and occupation of Britain. I do so for two reasons. The first is that the great Anglo-Saxon historian Bede, who, more than anyone else, invented the idea of England, thought that this was the right place to start his *Ecclesiastical History of the English People*. The second is that Rome is indeed 'our common mother' and is the fount from which all modern western European countries spring.

But, in the case of England, Rome is at best a stepmother. There is, uniquely in the Western Empire, an absolute rupture between the Roman province of *Britannia* and the eventual successor-state of Anglo-Saxon England. Elsewhere, in France, Italy or Spain, there are continuities: of language, laws, government and religion. In Britain there are none. Instead the Anglo-Saxon invaders of the fifth century found, or perhaps made, a *tabula rasa*.

This is normally regretted. Civilization was destroyed, the common story goes, and the Dark Ages began. I am not so sure. For Rome was not as civilized as we think and the Dark Ages – at least in Anglo-Saxon England – were by no means so gloomy. The roots of the misunderstanding, I think, lie in the importance we attach to material culture. We too live in a comfortable age, so we are impressed – too impressed – with the apparatus of Roman comfort: the baths, the sanitation, the running water, the central heating and the roads.

All these are, indeed, very sophisticated. But the politics that underpinned them was surprisingly crude. Not only was the Empire a mere military despotism, it was also peculiarly mistrustful of any form of self-help, much less self-government, on the part of its subjects. This is shown by a famous exchange of letters between the Emperor Trajan and the senatorial aristocrat and man of letters Pliny the Younger, who was then governor of the province of Bithynia in Asia Minor. The important provincial city of Nicomedia, Pliny informed the emperor, had suffered a devastating fire. Might he encourage the citizens to set up a guild of firemen to fight future conflagrations? On no account, replied the emperor, since such bodies, whatever their ostensible purpose, become fronts for faction and political dissent.

It was this enforced passivity on the part of its civilian populations that helped make the Empire such easy meat for the barbarian invaders. It is also its sharpest point of contrast with the kingdom of Wessex, round which England coalesced in the ninth and tenth centuries. Wessex was not a democracy, or even a peasant commonwealth, as some of its more enthusiastic Victorian historians assumed. But it was a participatory society, which balanced a powerful and effective monarchy at the centre with institutions of local government which required – and got – the active involvement of most free men. It was this combination, which was unique in Europe at the time and long after, as well as good luck and inspired royal leadership, which enabled Wessex to survive, and finally to thrive, in the face of the Viking invasions that destroyed all the other Anglo-Saxon kingdoms.

The result was England. It was an early, perhaps indeed the earliest, nation-state, with a remarkable unity of language, culture and politics. The vernacular, Anglo-Saxon or Old English, not Latin as elsewhere, was the language of politics and administration. It was also the language of *The Anglo-Saxon Chronicle*. This was no episodic monastic annal; it was a book of national record that charted, self-consciously and deliberately, the birth and development of a nation. All this gave Anglo-Saxon England a powerful sense of national solidarity: it could negotiate collectively with its kings even when they were conquerors; it could also strive to settle political disputes without the bloodshed of civil war.

It was, in short, *different*.

I

Two thousand years ago there was only one power that counted in the Western world: Rome. It was perhaps the purest, the most absolute monarchy the world has ever seen. The emperor incorporated in his own person all the powers of the state: military, executive, judicial and (in practice if not at first in theory) legislative. As *imperator*, he was commander of the army; as holder of the 'tribunican powers', he represented the sovereign majesty of the people and was protected by the terrible penalties of *laesa maiestatis* or treason; as *pontifex maximus*, he was chief priest. He was even regarded as a god himself, who was worshipped by many of his subjects in life and by more in death. His person, his palace and his very treasury were 'sacred'.

And Britain, the province of *Britannia*, was just a tiny part of this monarchy, which, at its maximum extent, stretched from the Bay of Biscay in the west to the River Euphrates in the east and from the moors of Scotland in the north to the sands of the Sahara in the south.

The myriad peoples inhabiting the Empire spoke many different languages and honoured many different gods. But there were also powerful, supervening forces of unity as well. First, there was the army. It was the Roman army which had conquered most of the known world for Rome and it was the army which kept it Roman. So everywhere in the Empire the imperial army performed the same drills; built similar forts and wore the same uniforms. Close behind the soldier marched the tax collector and the lawyer. So everywhere too the imperial bureaucracy, which was mind-numbing in its size, hierarchical complexity and expense, collected the same taxes; enforced the same Roman law on all free men and used the same Roman weights and measures.

In these and all other forms of governmental administration, one official language was employed: Latin – though in the Eastern Provinces Greek also enjoyed a high status as a second, as yet unofficial, language. Everywhere, therefore, anybody who aspired to be anybody had to speak, read and write one or preferably both of these languages, which also carried a common Classical literature and culture with them. The same went for the visual arts where, yet again, there was a single official style – the Roman version of Classicism – which was used for buildings, artefacts and decoration throughout the Empire.

How would Britain, which the Romans disparaged as the 'ends of the earth', fit in with all this?

The first Roman expeditions to Britain were led by the proto-emperor Julius Caesar, in 55 and 54 BC. Born in c.102 BC into a noble if impoverished family, Caesar soon proved himself as ambitious as he was multi-talented. And, in achieving his ends, he set in train the events which transformed Rome from a Republic – a commonwealth of free men, if bitterly divided by class and interest group – into the absolute monarchy of the Empire.

Caesar's expeditions to Britain were an interlude in his conquest of Gaul. This established his reputation both as the power-broker of the Roman world and, thanks to his account of the conquest in his *De Bello Gallico* (*The Gallic War*), as a great, if self-serving, military historian. The first British expedition was little more than an armed reconnaissance raid. But in the second Caesar brought a substantial force of five legions with their auxiliaries, amounting to about 27,000 men. He defeated Cassivellaunus, and penetrated north of the Thames. Caesar never makes clear Cassivellaunus's precise status. But the best guess is that he was tribal king of the Catuvellauni. There was some attempt among the warring British tribes to sink their differences with the appointment of Cassivellaunus as overall commander, and some success with guerrilla tactics. But, finally, what turned the day for Caesar was not the force of the Roman army but the weakness and divisions of the British coalition. Nevertheless, Cassivellaunus had held out long enough to stop Caesar capitalizing on his gains. Instead, after signing treaties, Caesar withdrew to deal with more pressing problems in Gaul. The Roman legions would not return to Britain for nearly a hundred years.

In 44 BC, ten years after he had left Britain, Caesar was made life-dictator, though he ostentatiously refused the crown itself. Months later he was dead of multiple stab-wounds from the daggers of former friends and foes alike. The assassination was intended to save the Republic. In fact, it administered the death blow. For the man who emerged victorious from the years of civil war that followed Caesar's assassination was Caesar's great-nephew by marriage and adoptive son and heir Octavius, later surnamed Augustus.

Unlike Caesar, Augustus was as subtle as he was ruthless. So, instead of treating republican institutions with contempt, he cherished them. Indeed, he loved them to death. The Republic was 'restored', with much fanfare, in 27 BC. But, one by one, Augustus took over all the powers which had been carefully separated under the republican constitution.

But what to call this monarchy that dared not speak its name? Augustus himself liked to be addressed as *princeps* – that is, 'first (among equals)'. But he also used the style *imperator* or general. Since the command of the army was now the real key to power, his successors soon started to use *imperator* or emperor as their principal title. The title was deliberately *not* royal to avoid alienating residual republican feeling. But it betokened, as it still does, power that was greater, in both extent and intensity, than that of any mere king.

In AD 43, Claudius, one of the most historically minded emperors, determined to complete the task that Caesar had started. Claudius was eager to establish his warlike credentials, but could not afford to take any personal risks. The result was that this second Roman invasion of Britain became as much a piece of theatre as a military expedition, with its two initial leaders effectively acting the corresponding roles of impresario and general. They were Aulus Plautius, whom the Roman historian Tacitus called a 'famous soldier', and Narcissus, Claudius's all-powerful secretary and an imperial freedman, who accompanied Plautius as a kind of political commissar. But the oddly matched soldier and the manumitted ex-slave proved an effective double act. Plautius, with his Gaulish auxiliaries, fought his way to the Thames, at which point Narcissus informed the emperor that it was time for him to set out. Claudius eventually arrived, complete with ceremonial elephants and a vast cavalcade – and stayed only sixteen days. But it was long enough for him to take part in a set-piece campaign masterminded by Narcissus. He crossed the Thames 'at the side of his troops'; 'caused the barbarians to come to hand in battle' and entered Colchester, capital of the Catuvellauni, in triumph. He was repeatedly acclaimed *imperator* by the troops and received the submission of no less than eleven British kings.

And all this in barely more than a fortnight! The sense of theatrical artificiality was only heightened by the fact that, when he had returned to Rome, Claudius immediately ordered a repeat performance. He took part in an even grander triumph and laid on a re-enactment of the high-lights of his campaign in the Campus Martius. The scenes included 'the assault and sacking of a town' and 'the surrender of the British kings'. We don't know who played the British kings. But Claudius, 'presiding in his general's cloak', appears to have played himself.

Meanwhile, back in the real world of *Britannia*, the political situation was more complex. For in AD 43 the Romans, whatever the textbooks might say, did *not* conquer Britain. Instead, in the smallest of small colonial wars, they defeated a single dominant tribe, the Catuvellauni, and took over their territories in the south-east. Outside this area, other tribal kings continued to exercise their sway under Roman protection. Indeed, the Romans added to their number by setting up the renegade British prince Cogidubnus as king of a new, artificially created tribe called, signif-icantly, the *Regnenses* ('The King's Folk').

The reason for this apparent generosity was straightforward. British kings, who had started to issue Roman-style coins and to give themselves the Latin title of *rex*, had been the most effective agents of Romanization *before* Claudius's invasion and, led by that accomplished quisling Cogidubnus, they continued to play the same role afterwards.

But not for long. For rebellions, like that of Boudicca, queen of the Iceni, in AD 60, and deliberately fostered quarrels in the British royal families took their toll. The result was that, within thirty years, direct Roman rule covered most of southern Britain and was being aggressively extended far into modern Scotland.

There were to be no more kings in Britain till the Romans had gone.

With the coming of direct Roman rule, Romanization became a matter of public policy. It was pursued especially effectively by Agricola, who was governor for the unusually long period of six years from AD 78 to 84. Within a year of his arrival he had embarked on a major building programme, giving 'private encouragement and public aid to the building of temples, courts of justice and private dwelling houses'. He also provided a sophisticated Classical education for the sons of the British elite.

His campaign seems to have enjoyed quick success. As early as AD 79 or 81, an inscription was set up at *Verulamium* (St Albans) to commemorate Agricola's role in the creation of a splendid new *Forum* or marketplace. And the British elite at least eagerly embraced Latin, the *toga*, hot and cold baths and banqueting while reclining on couches. 'They called [it] civilization', Tacitus sardonically observes, 'when it was but a part of their servitude.'

Perhaps. But the prosperity brought to Britain by the *pax Romana* – 'the Roman peace' – was real enough: some six thousand miles of well-engineered, solidly metalled roads were built; towns grew and flourished; farmsteads expanded into substantial, luxurious villas; the spa-complex at *Aquae Sulis* (Bath) reached its greatest extent in the third and fourth centuries and the population of Britain rose to about four million, a figure that would not be reached again for a millennium.

But there was a price to be paid for this prosperity as Britain, like the rest of the Empire, became a target for raids by less civilized peoples beyond the frontiers. The Romans, borrowing a piece of racial snobbery from the Greeks, called such peoples 'barbarians'. The word meant 'non-Roman' or 'non-Greek'. But it quickly acquired overtones: of contempt, because the barbarians were uncivilized; and of fear because they were a threat to civilization. For the German tribes, in particular, had never accepted rule from Rome and not even Rome had been able to force them to bend the knee.

There were internal problems as well. All power, in theory and usually in practice, was in the hands of the emperor. He, as we have seen, was a god on earth, whose task it was to rule and defend the Empire. The duty of his subjects was to obey and pay their taxes. The idea that there might be any limit on what the emperor could do, or that his subjects should have a say in what got done, was simply inconceivable.

With no constitutional means of opposition, force was the only – and the frequent – resort. The result was that the later Empire was plagued with rebellions, military revolts and palace coups. Britain, with the strong garrison required by its exposure to barbarian raids, supplied more than its fair share of military usurpers who aspired to the purple. It was also, like other remote outposts of empire, used as a place of internal political exile. The exiles conspired with each other; suborned the troops and generally subverted the province from within.

All these problems came together in the single great crisis of AD 367, known as the *barbarica conspiratio*, 'the Conspiracy of the Barbarians'. *Britannia* was attacked from three sides: by the Picts from the north and the Scots (who then inhabited Ireland) from the west, while the Saxons rampaged on the Channel coast of Gaul and perhaps of Britain too. The Roman generals were killed or overwhelmed; internal conspiracy was given free rein and the fall of the Roman regime seemed certain. But the arrival of an expeditionary force commanded by a general-cum-politician of genius, Theodosius the Elder, saved the day. The barbarians were seen off; military discipline restored and the leading traitors executed.

So Roman Britain lived to fight another day. But just how Roman was it? For some time now it has been gospel among historians that *Britannia* was a province like any other, as loyal to Rome and as fully integrated into Roman ways. But there are some important pieces of evidence which refuse to fit the theory. For instance, the only Romano–British author whose works survive, Gildas, always distinguishes the 'Romans' from the 'British' and is almost uniformly hostile to the former: the Romans, he writes, had seized Britain by guile rather than honest victory in the field and they had imposed a rule that was both alien – 'so that [the country] was no longer thought to be Britain but a Roman island' – and oppressive, with 'taskmasters' and 'cruel governors'. Historians have explained away Gildas's hostility by arguing that, though he wrote fluent Latin, he reflected the views of those outside the Romanized elite.

Maybe. But there also have to be doubts about the political, as opposed to the social, Romanization of the elite itself. For even they failed to participate in the imperial administrative machine. Provincials, of course, were not allowed to hold office in their native province. But they could – and, in the case of the Gauls, frequently did – hold office elsewhere. Not so the British. Why? Perhaps, then as now, the *Oceanus Britannicus* (the English Channel) was seen as a real barrier. Perhaps, bearing in mind the booming prosperity of Britain in the third and fourth centuries, they were simply doing too well at home to want to risk their luck abroad.

We shall, finally, never know.

Whatever the reason, however, the British then remained semi-detached from the Empire, just as the British now are semi-detached from the European Union. And it is as different, semi-detached and even semi-barbarous, that they appear in our final glimpse of Roman Britain. It comes from the poem *De Reditu Suo* ('On his Return') by the Gallo-Roman poet Rutilius Claudius Namatianus, who was returning home after serving as a high official in Rome. He travelled by sea from port to port and in one of these he met his friend Victorinus, the former *vicarius* (governor) of Britain. Namatianus then gives a pen portrait of Victorinus, which turns into a back-handed picture of late Roman Britain. Victorinus, the poet writes, had been a just and upright administrator, who had worked to win the affection of the British people *despite the fact that they were so remote and primitive*.

Why such language after four centuries of Roman rule? There is only one explanation. Victorinus and Rutilius, Gauls though they were by birth, saw themselves as Romans and heirs to the culture and Empire of Rome. The Britons, on the other hand, were different. They might be within the Roman Empire. But they were outside the charmed circle of Romanness. They were subjects and natives. They were not Romans.

Such, probably, is the background to the strange death of Roman Britain. For the Romans did not abandon Britain in AD 409 of their own volition. Rather, it seems, they were expelled by their discontented British subjects, who thought that they could defend themselves better than the decadent power of Rome. Such provincial risings had occurred before and Rome had always fought back. Moreover, the leaders of the British 'cities', as the old tribes had been renamed, soon had second thoughts and appealed to Rome for help. But this time the Emperor Honorius had more important concerns on his mind as in AD 410 Rome itself had been captured by Alaric the Goth. The city, inviolate for a thousand years, was sacked and the emperor's own sister was among the booty carried off. In the circumstances, it is hardly surprising that Honorius rejected the British appeal and ordered the cities to look to their own defences.

Britannia was now on its own. How would it fare?

II

With the break between Britain and Rome, all legitimate political authority – which had been vested in the emperor – came to an end. Who filled the vacuum we do not know. Perhaps the representative British Council of the cities, which had existed in the early third century with largely ceremonial functions, was revived as a working government, like the Congress of the Revolutionary American Colonies.

And, like the Revolutionary Congress, the Council's first task was defence. For Britain's barbarian enemies took advantage of the departure of Roman officialdom and the field army to redouble their attack. At first the British, long unused to defending themselves and with inexperienced and divided leadership, did badly. But they soon learned to use the formidable defensive works which the Romans had left behind. Each was targeted against a different enemy. Hadrian's Wall defended the northern frontier against the Picts; a chain of forts along the west coast, from the Solway Firth to Cardiff, held off the Scottish raiders from their Irish homeland; while the massive fortifications of the Saxon Shore, which stretched from *Branodunum* (Brancaster) in the north to *Portus Ardaoni* (Porchester, near Portsmouth) in the west, were built to protect the East Anglian, Kentish and Channel coasts from the Saxon pirates from across the North Sea. Even today, the remains of the Saxon Shore forts are impressive. The walls of *Gariannonum* (Burgh Castle) in Norfolk are ten feet thick and still stand some twenty feet high; similarly, the vast circuit of the walls of Porchester seem framed to enclose a substantial town rather than a mere fortress.

How could barbarian raiders overcome such obstacles? The answer, probably, is that they did not. Instead, like the Greeks before the walls of Troy, they were inadvertently let in.

As it happens, we have, albeit imperfectly, both sides of the story. The British perspective is given by Gildas's *The Ruin of Britain*; the invaders' by Bede's *Ecclesiastical History of the English People*.

Bede was a Northumbrian, born in 673 on the lands of the monastery of St Peter at Wearmouth. At the age of seven, his parents sent him to St Peter's to begin his education. And there he remained, first as student and then as master, either at Wearmouth or at the twin monastery of St Paul at Jarrow on the River Tyne, till his death in 735 at the then ripe age of sixty-two.

It would be hard to think of a career that was more circumscribed or less eventful. But that is to see it simply in physical terms. Instead, Bede was an adventurer of the mind and his *terra incognita* was the great library accumulated by his own patron and teacher, Bishop Benedict Biscop, at Jarrow. Bede explored this library thoroughly and meticulously. But he was no dry-as-dust scholar. Rather, as with those who go into the unknown, there was a touch of boldness about him, and a willingness to think afresh.

The result was that this provincial monk, who never stirred more than a few dozen miles from his place of birth, became responsible for a remarkable series of scholarly innovations which changed the intellectual life of Europe.

He was particularly interested in chronology – that is, the ordering of events in time. This is the basic tool of the historian, and to help himself and others to date events accurately he wrote two handbooks. They listed world events from ancient times to his own day and – in place of the chaos of different eras used then and for long after – they popularized what has become our standard means of dating by the year BC or AD. He was also, since he was unusually scrupulous both about naming his sources and quoting from them accurately, one of the pioneers of the footnote and the bibliography. He had a clear understanding of causation, and wrote in a plain style which was refreshingly different from – say – Gildas's excitable rhetoric. Finally, Bede invented the idea of England, or at least the idea of the English as a single people. And he applied all of this to his late masterpiece, *The Ecclesiastical History of the English People*, which he finished only four years before his death. If the writing of history is one of the glories of England as a country and of English as a language (as I think it to be) then Bede, though he wrote in Latin, deserves an honoured place as the founder of a national tradition.

The British Gildas, like the Anglo-Saxon Bede, was a monk and he too wrote in Latin. But that is all the two men have in common. Otherwise, they and their works were as different as chalk and cheese. Gildas's is a diatribe; Bede's a sober history. The former is written in the heat and terror of events; the latter retrospectively, when the dust had begun to settle a little. But it is no emotion recollected in tranquillity; instead, Bede's contempt for the vanquished British is as fresh as when the two peoples first met and took an instant and lasting dislike to each other.

And the British were by no means the only ones to detest the Saxons. The Saxons were part of the great diaspora of Germanic peoples, who first threatened the Roman Empire and then, in the fifth century, overran it. Their homeland lay in the north German plains between the River Elbe to the east and the River Ems to the west in a region still known today as *Niedersachsen* (Lower Saxony). Here, the North Sea coast is flat and low-lying and even the hinterland rises only to a hundred-odd feet above sea-level. The result is that the frontier between land and water is uncertain: there are marshlands and fenlands; great rivers which are tidal for scores of miles and huge storms which sweep in across the coastal flats. And, above all, there is the sea.

Even now, the sea is dominant. Then, it was omnipresent, both as a threat and an opportunity: it forcibly inducted the Saxons into the arts of seamanship; it also drove them out, to search for plunder and for territories in softer lands to the west and south. Here they struck terror, along the coasts of Britain and Gaul, from the Wash to the Bay of Biscay. 'The Saxon', wrote the Gallo-Roman nobleman Sidonius Apollinaris, 'is the most ferocious of all foes.' Their ships were long, clinker-built and with high, curving prows, each carved with the image of a sea-serpent. The men on board were strange in appearance too to those accustomed to Mediterranean build and coloration. They were tall, fair-skinned, blue-eyed and with their blond hair shaved at the front, 'till the head looks smaller and the visage longer'. Neither the sea nor shipwreck, Sidonius continued, held any terrors for them; nor did the common rules of humanity. Instead, at the end of each summer's raiding party, they would drown one in ten of their captives as a sacrifice to their savage gods.

The Saxons first appeared in British waters in about AD 285, when the admiral sent against them, Carausius, rebelled against Rome and set up the first seaborne British Empire. His regime issued a remarkable series of propagandistic coins, and it was probably he who had the strategic imagination to conceive of the defensive scheme of the Saxon Shore forts.

Subsequently, after Constantius Chlorus had re-established Roman power in Britain, the forts became one of the great frontier commands of the Empire, under a high military official known as the Count of the Saxon Shore. The Saxons, and their fellow Germanic tribesmen to the west, the Franks, also played a part in the penultimate act of Roman Britain, the *barbarica conspiratio* of AD 367.

There was another reason for the almost superstitious dread which the Saxons aroused: their unrepentant, aggressive and, it would appear, bloodthirsty paganism. For Rome and Empire had become Christian. This story too began in Britain, when on 25 June 306, in the great legionary fortress of *Eboracum* (York), the troops of Constantius Chlorus, who had just died, acclaimed his son Constantine as emperor. Constantine, known to history as The Great, completed the evolution of the Empire into an oriental despotism; his 'conversion' in 312 also began the transformation of Christianity from a savagely persecuted sect into the official religion of the Empire – including the province of *Britannia*. Basilica-like churches were built in the major British cities and British bishops took part in the Councils of the Church.

But, despite the Saxons' ferocious credentials as heathens as well as barbarians, in the early fifth century it was the Picts and Scots who seemed the greater threat to post-Roman Britain. The result was one of the great miscalculations of history. Under the pressure of constant warfare against the Celtic invaders, the representative regime of the British cities had been quickly supplemented by the rule of military strongmen, who dignified themselves with the revived name of *rex* or king. And, in the middle years of the century, a certain Vortigern, whose name means 'Mighty King', may have established an overlordship over all *Britannia*.

Quite how the two forms of government, the royal and the representative, related to each other is uncertain. But, faced with renewed incursions from the Picts and Scots, both groups, according to Gildas, came together in the fateful decision. 'Then all the councillors, together with that proud tyrant, … the British King, were so blinded', Gildas reports, 'that, as a protection to their country, they sealed its doom by inviting among them (like wolves into the sheep fold) the fierce and impious Saxons, a race hateful both to God and men, to repel the invasions of the northern nations.' The Saxons, Gildas continues, who arrived in 'three ships of war', 'landed on the eastern side of the islands, by the invitation of the unlucky King' and there made their first settlement. The terms of Vortigern's invitation gave the Saxons 'an allowance of provisions', handed over each month, in return for their military support.

This sounds like the kind of arrangement which the Romans themselves had frequently made with their barbarian neighbours. For relations between Rome and the barbarians were not simply of hostility. They were more complex – and ambiguous – than that. Indeed, they bear a striking resemblance to our own, equally ambiguous, attitudes to immigrants and asylum seekers. On the one hand, we fear them and the threat they pose to our way of life and security; on the other, we recognize the vital contribution they make to our economies by doing the jobs our own people won't. The barbarians came to play a comparable role for Rome. For the people of the Empire soon began to disdain the hardships of the soldier's life. Instead, the best soldiers were drawn first from the hardy mountain tribesmen of the Balkans and later from Germany itself. Whole tribes were settled on the border territories of the Empire in return for military service. And individual Germans rose far and fast in the imperial armies until they started to dominate the senior ranks.

And it was in some such role as hired mercenaries that the Saxons first settled in post-Roman Britain. The arrangement was always risky. But in Britain it encountered the additional difficulty that the Roman structures of administration and taxation, which alone could guarantee a regular handover of supplies, had been dismantled – either deliberately by the Romano-Britons themselves, or consequentially following the drying-up of coin supplies from the Empire. The results were predictably disastrous as quarrels broke out over the sufficiency and regularity of the supplies. Gildas claims that the Saxons deliberately played up the quarrels. But they could equally have interpreted the irregularities as a sign of bad faith on the part of their hosts. At any event, the Saxons first threatened and then carried out reprisal raids. Soon, these escalated into an all-out war of conquest.

In the war, the initial Saxon settlement, as Gildas saw with the blinding clarity of hindsight, had handed all the advantage to the invaders. It acted as a Trojan Horse, getting the Saxons past the coastal fortifications which served as the first and chief British line of defence. It was also a beachhead, enabling the Saxons to bring over reinforcements as and when they pleased from their homeland. The Britons could not fight against these odds and their towns were sacked and their populations massacred from east to west of the island.

Gildas may have witnessed a late example of such a sack:

> All the columns [he writes] were levelled with the ground by the frequent strokes of the battering-ram, all the husbandmen routed, together with their bishops, priests, and people, whilst the sword gleamed and the flames crackled round them on every side. Lamentable to behold, in the midst of the streets lay the tops of lofty towers, tumbled to the ground, stones of high walls, holy altars, fragments of human bodies, covered with livid spots of coagulated blood, looking as if they had been squeezed together in a press.

Judging the writing of another age and in another language is always difficult. But this passage, though it may borrow from Classical models, is, to my ear at least, no mere rhetorical exercise but a piece of vivid war reporting. And it still chills.

As also does Gildas's description of the consequences. The survivors, who had managed to flee, soon faced either starvation or death from the elements. In this extremity, some surrendered to the invaders, to be killed or enslaved at their pleasure. Others fled abroad. While others took refuge among the mountains, forests and cliffs of the west of the island.

Gildas's account is, for once, history written by the losers. But the story did not change much when Bede came to rewrite it two and a half centuries later from the perspective of the victors. Bede supplies a date – 'in the year of Our Lord 449, Martian being made Emperor with Valentinian' – for Vortigern's invitation to the Saxons. And he gives the names of the Saxon leaders: 'Hengist' and 'Horsa'. But the date is clearly the result of intelligent guesswork while, with his usual scrupulousness, he qualifies the statement about Hengist and Horsa with the warning: these 'are said to have been' their names.

Where Bede is useful instead is in his account of the ethnography of the invasions. For he is clear that the Saxons were only one of several distinct German peoples to invade Britain, each of whom settled in a different part of the old Roman province.

Those who came over were of the three most powerful nations of Germany – Saxons, Angles, and Jutes. From the Jutes are descended the people of Kent, and of the Isle of Wight, and those also in the province of the West Saxons [Wessex] who are to this day called Jutes, seated opposite to the Isle of Wight. From the Saxons, that is, the country which is now called Old Saxony, came the East Saxons, the South Saxons, and the West Saxons [that is, the peoples of Essex, Sussex and Wessex]. From the Angles, that is, the country which is called Anglia, and which is said, from that time, to remain desert [i.e. unpeopled] to this day, between the provinces of the Jutes and the Saxons, are descended the East Angles, the Midland Angles, Mercians, all the race of the Northumbrians, that is, of those nations that dwell on the north side of the River Humber, and the other nations of the English.

Bede's account was a product of the best antiquarian scholarship of his own day. And it has been confirmed, in astonishing detail, by modern archaeology. Cremation urns of the same type, and probably indeed by the same potter, have been found in Wehden, Lower Saxony, and Markshall, Norfolk. Grave-goods discovered in both places, especially bracteates (decorated discs of gold), likewise confirm that there was a close connection between Kent and Jutland on the west coast of Denmark. The author is even right about the depopulation of Angeln, the homeland of the Angles. There rising sea-levels made long-established villages uninhabitable and their populations joined, almost certainly, in the emigration to Britain.

But, beyond these broad outlines, it is remarkably difficult to go. True, the much later compilation known as *The Anglo-Saxon Chronicle* does appear to give a detailed account of the conquest with dates and battles. But it is easy to show that the *Chronicle* narrative is riddled with repetitions, inconsistencies and glaring omissions. It is also shot through with formulaic foundation legends (the landing parties almost always sail in three ships) and mythical genealogies (almost all the royal houses spring from the Anglo-Saxon god Woden). In view of this, the best that can be said is that the invaders first settled on the coast and then penetrated inland along navigable rivers and Roman roads. The broad movement was from east to west and south to north. But it was patchy, often

slow and faced occasional serious reverses, like the battle of Mount
Badon, in which the British, led by Ambrosius Aurelianus, whom Gildas
calls the sole survivor of 'the Roman nation' in Britain, inflicted a heavy
defeat on the Anglo-Saxons, probably in the AD 490s. The area around
Luton and Aylesbury in the modern Buckinghamshire and Bedfordshire
did not fall till AD 571 and Bath not till six years later, after the battle
of Dyrham. And there were pockets of resistance even in the east – such
as *Verulamium*, the site of the death of the proto-martyr, St Alban, and
the principal cultic centre of British Christianity, or the little British
kingdom of Elmet in the modern Yorkshire – which held out longer
still.

By the end of the sixth century, however, the future political geogra-
phy of Britain was becoming clear. The Britons had held on to the territories to the north of Hadrian's Wall, to Cumbria and to the west of the
Severn and Wye valleys, while the Anglo-Saxons had conquered everything to the east and to the south.

Give or take a little, these are the approximate frontiers of modern
England.

III

We tend to think of the Norman Conquest as *the* turning point in the
history of England. But the Saxon Conquest was even more important,
since it created both the reality and the idea of England itself. Indeed, it
is scarcely possible to exaggerate the scale of the Saxon incursions.
Perhaps 200,000 people flooded into a native population which by then
had been reduced by raids, famine and disease to less than two million.
Proportionately, it was the largest immigration that Britain has ever
known. Moreover, as most of the incomers were men, it quickly turned
from immigration into conquest. In the areas of densest Anglo-Saxon
settlement, in the east and the Midlands, DNA evidence shows that up to
ninety per cent of the native male population was displaced – they were
driven west or killed – and their women, their villages and their farms
taken over by the incomers. This was ethnic cleansing at its most savagely
effective.

And it was not only blood that changed. The Anglo-Saxon immigrants
imposed their own language: Old English. Most former places of

habitation – towns, villages and villas – were abandoned and new ones established, to which new, English names were given. They also gave new names to natural features, such as mountains and rivers and woods. And they remade as well as renamed the landscape. In the fullness of time, they even gave the country they had conquered a new name: *Britannia* became the land of the Angles or *Ængla Land.*

This immigration at the point of the sword led to an outcome that was unique in the former territories of the Empire. For the sack of Rome in AD 410 had been followed sixty years later by the fall of the Empire itself in the west in AD 476. Nevertheless, in most places – in Italy and what were to become France and Spain – things continued pretty much as before. The cities with their bishops survived; 'senatorial' aristocrats continued to entertain each other in their opulent villas; the trade routes to the East remained open. The difference was that in place of the emperor, barbarian German leaders took over the imperial role. They divided it and localized it. But they kept all of the wealth, pomp and authority they could. For it was that which had made Rome such a magnet in the first place.

Even the Visigoths, who had sacked Rome, got in on the act. 'At first', Athaulf, the Visigothic king is reported as saying, 'I ardently desired that the Roman name should be obliterated.' But then he realized his mistake. 'I have therefore chosen the safer course of aspiring to the glory of restoring and increasing the Roman name by Gothic vigour.' Athaulf's lineage did not survive. But his aspirations did. The result was that, throughout the continental provinces of the Empire, a hybrid sub-Roman society continued to propagate Roman and Christian ideas of politics under the rule of Germanic kings; Roman buildings, such as churches and palaces, were still put up to enrich their capitals; their new Germanic nobility retained the names of the senior Roman military ranks – *comes* or count and *dux* or duke – as aristocratic titles; and, above all, Latin – if increasingly debased and diluted – continued to be the spoken and written language, used by the invaders and the native populations alike.

But in *Britannia* it was a different story. Here the fall of Rome really marked the end of Romanness. Despite their height and strength, the walls of *Rutupiae* (Richborough) and the other forts of the Saxon Shore were overwhelmed and abandoned. So were the walled towns. And their ruin marks the ruin of Britain. Or at least it marks the annihilation of everything that was Roman about Britain: the law, the language, the literature, the religion and the politics all vanished.

Quite why the Anglo-Saxons should have behaved so differently from their fellow Germanic tribesmen across the Channel it is hard to say. Perhaps the Britons, who, unlike the demoralized and by this time largely barbarian Roman field-army, were defending their own homes and families, simply fought too hard. Perhaps, in the fifty years since cutting off the imperial ties in AD 409, Romanized Britain had ceased to be a going concern, where, unlike the Continent again, there was nothing much for the barbarian invaders to buy into. Perhaps the Anglo-Saxons (and some of the Britons too) simply wanted to be different.

But the important thing is that in *Britannia*, uniquely in western Europe, there was a fresh start. For along with their new language, the Anglo-Saxons brought a new society, new gods and a new, very different set of political values. And from these, in time, they would create a nation and an empire which would rival Rome. A version of their tongue would replace Latin as the *lingua franca*; English Common Law would challenge Roman Law as the dominant legal system; and they would devise, in free-market economics, a new form of business that would transform human wealth and welfare. Most importantly, perhaps, they would invent a new politics which depended on participation and consent, rather than on the top-down autocracy of Rome.

It is a story to be proud of and, at its heart, lies a single institution: the monarchy.

2

CHRISTIAN KINGSHIP

Redwald, Æthelfrith, Æthelbert,
Penda, Offa, Egbert

THE ANGLO-SAXONS HAD BROUGHT MANY THINGS from Germany. But the idea of kingship was not among them. As late as Bede's own day, the Anglo-Saxons' ancestral people in the German homeland were kingless; likewise, the leaders of the first expeditions to Britain – Cerdic, Cynric and the rest – were called chiefs and never kings. Only in subsequent generations did their children and grandchildren begin to style themselves kings and invent impressive genealogies for themselves.

English kingship, that is to say, was a plant of English growth, developing in England out of the conditions which followed the Anglo-Saxon conquest.

I

The background was the peculiarly egalitarian nature of Germanic social structure and political values which the Anglo-Saxons brought with them to Britain. Since the Anglo-Saxons themselves, like other Germanic peoples, were illiterate, we have to depend for our knowledge of these on the account of a civilized Roman outsider, Tacitus. His *Germania* (*Germany*) has a double aspect. It was political propaganda, addressed to the Romans of his own day. But it was also a piece of serious ethnography.

Tacitus was a grand senatorial aristocrat, historian and biographer and son-in-law of Agricola, the conquering governor of Britain. He was born around AD 55 in the reign of the Emperor Nero and died *c.* AD 120 under Hadrian. Like many of his class, Tacitus was nostalgic for the Republic. So in *Germania* he turned its inhabitants into Noble Savages. They were physically handsome. They were morally virtuous. They remained uncorrupted by civilization and its delights. And, above all, they had preserved their manhood and their freedom.

Tacitus's essay, as well as being a serious piece of ethnography, is also remarkably accurate as prophecy. For, three centuries before the barbarian invasions which overran the Western Empire, Tacitus proclaimed that the Germans were Rome's most dangerous foe. Not even the great Middle Eastern empire of Parthia (in effect, the later Persia) presented such a challenge.

The Germans, Tacitus writes, have no cities and dislike close neighbours. Instead they live in separate dwellings in widely scattered hamlets. Their buildings are of wood and their dress is of the simplest, with both men and women, apart from the richest, wearing a one-piece garment held in place with a clasp. This clasp, elaborated into a brooch, was the most characteristic form of female adornment; for a man, however, it was the spear. Indeed, the spear *was* manhood and presentation with it was the *rite de passage* from a boy to a man: 'up to this time he is regarded as a member of the household, afterwards as a member of the commonwealth'.

Happy chance has preserved the remains of a series of such communities in the Lark valley in Suffolk. They belong to the earliest days of the Anglo-Saxon settlement in Britain and their archaeology confirms Tacitus's picture in striking detail. The hamlets were widely separated and the houses built of wood. They clustered in three groups, which probably formed the accommodation of three extended families. The larger building in the centre of each group was the hall where the family met, ate and caroused, and where, too, probably the young unmarried men slept. The immigrants depended on simple mixed farming, while their grave-goods suggest a remarkably homogeneous and egalitarian society. Each female grave contained a brooch and only a handful of males were buried with a sword rather than the ubiquitous spear.

For the right to bear arms was as important to the Anglo-Saxons as it was to the framers of the Second Amendment to the American Constitution. And for much the same reason: only a community that could defend itself was free and only someone who could share in that defence had the right to call himself a free man. 'They transact', Tacitus noted, 'no public or private business without being armed.' The result was a sort of armed democracy. 'When the whole multitude think proper, they sit down armed ... the most complimentary form of assent is to express approbation with their spears.' This was participatory politics and the polar opposite of the imperial command model of Rome.

Nevertheless, such communities still needed leaders, especially in times of war. But how did they arise? Our earliest sources on the German people, Tacitus and Bede, offer the same answer: they chose or 'elected' their kings. And, as the kings were made by the people, they had, as Tacitus again emphasizes, neither 'unlimited [n]or arbitrary power' over them. This, then, is the idea of government by consent, in which the leader is chosen by the people, or at least is answerable to them. It was an idea taken by the Anglo-Saxons from their homeland in Germany and transplanted to their new home in England, where it flourished and remains an essential element in the monarchy to the present day.

The contrast with the Rome of Tacitus's own day – where the emperor ruled and a fawning court adored; where the rich had sold their liberty for luxury and the poor for bread and circuses; where freedom was a memory and liberty an illusion – was all the stronger for being unspoken.

Meanwhile, England, in the immediate aftermath of the Anglo-Saxon conquest, offered special circumstances which encouraged the development of kingship beyond anything the Germans were familiar with back home. Most important was the long, hard-fought nature of the conquest itself. For the Anglo-Saxons' more-or-less permanent state of war to the death with the British required equally permanent leaders. Moreover, war in a prosperous country like Britain produced booty, which made the war leaders rich. From their new wealth they could reward their followers. This attracted fresh followers and consolidated the loyalty of the old, which made the leaders more powerful still. And so on. Finally, the power and the permanence coalesced into kingship.

The clearest evidence of the change from the relatively egalitarian communities of the early conquest period to a more complex society with greater extremes of rich and poor, of haves and have-nots, comes from the graves known to archaeologists as *Fürstengräber* ('princely graves'). They appear by the middle of the sixth century and have a distinctive style. A large mound or barrow was raised over the grave and a rich array and variety of goods placed within it, such as the silver-gilt-hilted sword, silver-studded shield, spear and knife, Kentish glass claw-beaker, Frankish bronze bowl and Frankish silver-gilt-and-garnet-encrusted belt buckle found under the largest barrow of the 'burial field' at Finglesham in East Kent.

We shall never know the exact names or ranks of the people buried at Finglesham. But the name Finglesham is itself a clue. Its earliest form, contemporary with the cemetery, is *Pengels-ham*: 'the Prince's manor'; while a couple of miles to the north-west is Eastry, a royal vil of the eventual kingdom of Kent. Almost certainly, therefore, the burials at Finglesham were those of Kentish princes. Were they cadets of an existing royal house? Or were they princes on their way to becoming kings? And what was the source of their wealth? From trade? Or war? Or both?

This halfway world to monarchy is also reflected in the great Anglo-Saxon epic poem *Beowulf*, which is written much later but appears to preserve folk memories of these earlier times. The poem's hero, Beowulf, was a local war leader chosen by the people of his district on the mainland. Thanks to his prowess, he eventually became a king, reigned gloriously for fifty winters and was given a magnificent funeral.

> The Geat People built a pyre for Beowulf,
> stacked and decked it until it stood foursquare,
> hung with helmets, heavy war-shields
> On a height they kindled the hugest of all
> funeral fires; flames wrought havoc in the hot bone-house
> burning it to the core … Heaven swallowed the smoke.

Then, after the body and weapons were consumed in the flames,

> … the Geat people began to construct
> a mound on a headland …
> It was their hero's memorial; what remained from the fire
> they housed inside it …
> And they buried torques in the barrow, and jewels
> and a trove [of golden treasure] …

But *Beowulf*, impressive though it is, is only literature and scholars were inclined to dismiss its tale of lavish buried treasure as mere embroidery. Then, in 1939, archaeologists began to excavate a mound at Sutton Hoo near Woodbridge in Suffolk. It revealed a burial of epic magnificence. The largest Dark Age ship yet known – ninety feet in length and fourteen feet across at its widest – had been dragged from the River Deben to the top of the hundred-foot-high ridge and laid in an enormous, pre-excavated trench. Then a gabled hut was built amidships and the body, dressed in the deceased's richest clothes, and surrounded with his weapons, insignia and treasures, was placed within. Finally the trench was filled in and a high mound raised over the ship and its precious cargo.

The mound stood out boldly on the skyline, like an English earth pyramid. Within, the deceased, who had been buried rather than cremated, was sent off on his voyage to the Other World with as rich an array of grave-goods as any pharaoh. The splendour of the contents paralleled or even exceeded the tomb-goods described in the epic. There is gold and garnet jewellery that is unequalled in Europe; weapons for the chase and battlefield; a bronze cauldron for cooking; silver-plate from Byzantium decorated with lavish Classical ornament for feasts; and a harp to accompany the festivities.

But who is buried here? Is he a prince, as at Finglesham? Or was he a king? The fact that the Anglo-Saxons were still illiterate means that the answers to these questions can never be known for certain. Nevertheless, there are several powerful indications, all of which point to Redwald, king of East Anglia and *bretwalda* or overlord of England. The Merovingian coins in his purse have been redated to *c.* 625, which corresponds closely to the date (627) given by Bede for Redwald's death; the location of the burial is a known centre of East Anglian royal power, while the wealth of the grave-goods echoes Bede's description of Redwald's great military and political success.

Moreover, the grave-goods seem to be more than just those of a very rich man or even of a prince. Instead, they point to the 'ceremony', which Shakespeare's Henry V identifies as the peculiar attribute of kings. For instance, there is a pattern-welded sword of the finest steel, of the kind we find named and celebrated in the epic poetry of the time; a silvered and gilt helmet based on the design of a late Roman general's helmet; a decorated whetstone polished from the hardest rock. These surely are regalia

– the symbols of a ritualized monarchy – and they include many objects which feature, later in English history, in formal coronation rituals: the sword; the sceptre (for it seems that the whetstone is a sceptre) and the crown (for in later times the Saxon word for crown was *cynehelm* or helmet of the people).

So it is clear that Redwald, if it be he, was much more than an elected war leader. He was a true king. Indeed, he was a king like Henry VIII. He was rich, like Henry, and his purse was filled with gold coins struck in Merovingian France. Like Henry, he was fond of music and he is buried with a lyre. Like Henry, he was a discerning patron of the arts, and he had court craftsmen who were able to make the finest jewellery in Europe. And like Henry, he delighted in the weaponry and accoutrements of the warrior world.

But Redwald's grave-goods show something else: he had contacts beyond the world of the North Sea. He reached out into France and, beyond that, into the surviving Roman Empire in Byzantium. Both of these were Christian. And there are traces of this too in two of the smaller items of the Sutton Hoo treasure: a pair of silver spoons of Mediterranean manufacture. One is clearly inscribed in Greek letters 'Paulos', and the other, more clumsily and debatably, 'Saulos'. They are the only things to be touched by literacy. And they are the only ones that may be Christian.

For Redwald was an English king on the cusp of a new world, the world of Christian monarchy.

II

The Anglo-Saxon world of the sixth century was rich, strange and bloody. It was peopled with monsters and dragons, miracle-working swords and kings who all claimed descent from Woden, chief of the Anglo-Saxon pagan gods.

As these genealogies suggest, both the kings and their peoples remained pagan. This meant that religion in post-Roman Britain continued to be divided along racial lines: Britons were Christian, after their fashion, and Anglo-Saxons pagan, after theirs. And traces of the Anglo-Saxons' beliefs survive in our language to the present: in the names of days of the week (Tuesday, Thursday and Friday are named, respectively, after the Anglo-Saxon deities for order and law, thunder and fertility and

Wednesday after Woden himself); in place-names (Wednesbury in Staffordshire means 'Woden's burgh' [fortified town]) and in the names of festivals ('Yule' is the modern form of the Anglo-Saxon *Giuli*, while Easter, the greatest feast of the Christian Church, derives its name from the pagan goddess *Eostre*, whose festival was also celebrated in the spring.

Later, Bede condemned the Britons in stinging terms for having made no attempt to convert the Anglo-Saxons to Christianity. 'Among other most wicked actions [of the Britons]', he observed, 'which their own historian Gildas mournfully takes notice of, they added this: that they never preached the faith to the Saxons, or English, who dwelt amongst them.' Nor did any of the Anglo-Saxons' other Christian neighbours, whether from Ireland or Gaul, make any moves towards their conversion either, and there is no reason to suppose they would have found them receptive if they had.

Then, in the last decade of the sixth century, there were signs of movement on the Christian and pagan sides alike. The first steps were probably taken by Æthelbert, king of Kent. Periodically, by guile or military prowess, one of the petty Anglo-Saxon kings would make himself first among equals, or even overlord (*bretwalda*) of most of England. Æthelbert was one of the most successful. His prestige seems to have derived from his access to the material and cultural riches across the Channel. There, in contrast to the former *Britannia*, where everything that was Roman had been wiped out, Roman institutions had survived the political collapse of the Empire. They did so because of the very different behaviour of the barbarian conquerors of Gaul, the Franks.

The Franks, another Germanic people, were the Saxons' neighbours to the west, with their lands lying along the lower Rhine. They spoke a similar language to the Saxons, and, to begin with, were equally feared as pirates. But their history was transformed by their king Clovis, or Chlodwig (*Louis* in modern French). Born in *c.* 466, he married a Christian princess, Clotilda, and was himself baptized into Roman Christianity at Reims in 496. Thereafter, the Gallo-Romans, led by their bishops, hastened to submit themselves to him, and by the age of forty he was master of all Gaul. The Franks long retained their own laws, language and identity, and even gave a new name, *Francia* (France), 'the land of the Franks', to Gaul. But equally, under their rule, most aspects of sub-Roman society – the architecture, language, literature, manners and, above all,

Roman Christianity – continued to flourish in the most successful regime since the fall of the Western Empire.

A connection with *Francia* was thus a glittering prospect for an ambitious Anglo-Saxon king like Æthelbert. So, probably in the 580s, he married Clovis's great-granddaughter, Bertha. In the marriage, two contrasting worlds – Anglo-Saxon paganism and Roman Christianity – were to meet and, in so doing, to transform the face of English kingship.

As was usual with royal inter-faith marriages, arrangements were made for Bertha to retain the practice of her own religion. She brought clergy, including a Frankish bishop, Luidhard; while her husband, a conscientious, believing pagan, gave her the little Romano-British church of St Martin's outside the walls of his 'metropolis' or capital at Canterbury to worship in. Perhaps Bertha's family had made it a condition, spoken or unspoken, of the marriage that Æthelbert would convert. Perhaps Æthelbert, for his part, saw himself as another Clovis who would complete his domination of Britain through his own baptism. At any rate, after a few years, word reached Pope Gregory in Rome that the people of England wished to be converted to the Christian faith.

Gregory was a great man in a great office. For the popes were already claiming to be heirs, not only of St Peter, but of the Roman emperors as well. Gregory's power was different, of course. It consisted not of legions of soldiers but of regiments of priests and monks. But they were organized with all the old Roman respect for discipline, hierarchy, efficiency and law. According to the famous story in Bede, Pope Gregory the Great first encountered the English when a party of merchants offered a group of boys for sale as slaves in the Forum: 'their bodies [were] white, their countenances beautiful and their hair very fine'. He was told they came from Britain, were pagans and were known as Angles. 'Not Angles but angels', he is supposed to have replied.

The tale has the air of being a little too well polished in the telling. Nevertheless, there is no reason to doubt its essential truth. This is shown by Gregory's own letters which make plain his interest in young Anglo-Saxon slave-boys. 'Procure with the money thou mayest receive,' he instructed the papal agent in Gaul, 'English boys of about seventeen or eighteen years of age, who may profit by being given to God in monasteries.'

Now Bertha's marriage to Æthelbert presented Gregory with the opportunity to go further and launch a new Roman conquest of England for Christianity. His chosen general in the campaign was an Italian monk of good family, named Augustine.

Augustine and his party of monks and priests set out from Rome in 595. They planned to travel by the usual route – by sea to Provence and thereafter across Gaul by land – and they carried letters of introduction to Gallo-Roman and Frankish notables, including the heads of Bertha's own family. But, hearing tales of the Anglo-Saxons' savagery, Augustine soon returned to Rome to beg for their recall. Instead, Gregory sternly ordered him to proceed, redoubling, at the same time, his own diplomatic efforts. The mixture of stick and carrot worked, and Augustine and his followers, complete now with Frankish interpreters, arrived in Kent in 597. They landed at Richborough, like those previous invaders Hengist and Horsa in 449 or the Emperor Claudius in AD 43.

Æthelbert, as soon as he was informed of Augustine's arrival, ordered him to remain in quarantine on the Isle of Thanet, which was then cut off from the mainland by the Wantsum Channel. After a few days, the king decided on a meeting. So he crossed into Thanet and held his court there in the open air. This was to protect him from Augustine's magical powers, which, the king and his advisers feared, might prove irresistible indoors. But, when he was summoned to the presence, Augustine employed instead the weapons of liturgical ceremony, which the Church had already polished to a fine art. Augustine entered the assembly robed and in procession, accompanied by his monks 'bearing a silver cross for their banner, and an icon of Jesus ("the image of Our Lord painted on a board") and singing the litany [in Latin]'.

Bede describes this entry as embodying 'divine, not magical, virtue'. But the strangeness of it all – the dress, the symbols, the language and the music – must have been as potent as any spell to the Anglo-Saxons. It was a new way of doing things. And, as we shall see, it was to prove profoundly attractive.

Augustine then preached 'the Word of Life' to the king and his courtiers and his 'interpreters of the nation of the Franks' translated. Æthelbert heard them out courteously before making his reply. 'Your words and promises are very fair', the king said to his visitors, 'but, as they are new to us, and of uncertain import, I cannot approve of them so far as to forsake that which I have so long followed with the whole English nation.' But, he continued, he would welcome the missionaries. He would also allow them to 'preach and gain as many as you can to your religion'.

Æthelbert was playing a subtle political game. He was well aware of the advantages which had accrued to the Franks after their conversion to Roman Christianity. But he needed to be convinced that it would work for him, for the political risks of conversion were enormous. So, in effect, he was inviting Augustine to market-test Christianity: there would be no Constantinian heroics of conversion; instead, Æthelbert would convert only when the people had shown it safe to do so.

Augustine got to work right away. The mission, with its formal preaching, teaching and services, was based in Bertha's little church of St Martin's, Canterbury. But equally effective in attracting converts, according to Bede, was the missionaries' exemplary monastic life. The result was a mass baptism of 10,000 Kentish people at Christmas 597. Some historians take this to mean that Æthelbert himself must have converted already. But Gregory makes no mention of this fact in his report of the incident. Instead, it seems clear that Æthelbert held out for some years more. Finally in 600–1, Gregory vented his feelings at the continuing delay in a letter to Queen Bertha. She had done much, he had heard. But she could – and should – have done more: 'you ought before now, as being truly a Christian, to have inclined the heart of our glorious son, your husband, by the good influence of your prudence, to follow, for the weal of his kingdom and of his own soul, the faith which you profess'.

Gregory's is the earliest surviving letter to an English queen consort and the first picture of her role. It is a remarkably familiar one. She is pious and literate and her husband is expected – rather optimistically in Æthelbert's case – to be putty in her hands. Gregory's letter also gives a sense of Bertha's place in the world, and, by extension, of England's too. Naturally, the 'world', as Gregory saw it, was – despite all the vicissitudes of the city – resolutely Roman. 'Your good deeds', he assured Bertha, 'are known, not only among the Romans ... but also through divers places, and have even come to the ears of the most serene prince [the emperor] at Constantinople.'

Within a few months of Gregory's letter to Bertha, Æthelbert was baptized, almost certainly at the hands of Augustine himself.

What had carried the day? True, the psychology of Augustine and Gregory in dealing with Æthelbert had been subtle. They had presented the Christian God as a great king, who would reward Æthelbert's service in this world and the next, just as he, the *bretwalda* of England, rewarded his own faithful servants. But, finally, the key was probably political. For Christianity would enhance Æthelbert's kingship with two things that were very attractive to a Dark Age ruler: Roman ideas about power and Roman ways of doing things. Like Rome, the Church used Latin. It had an elaborate system of law and administration, and it built in stone. Above all, the Roman Church was ruled by a monarch, the pope, who, like the emperors, claimed absolute and divinely ordained authority. The pope even used one of the imperial titles: supreme pontiff.

All this the Church made available to Æthelbert, now that he had converted to Christianity. The advantages for the king were obvious. One of the first things Æthelbert did after his conversion was to issue a Law Code, like Justinian and other Christian Roman emperors. But, though the *form* is Roman, the *content* of the Code is wholly Anglo-Saxon and merely sets down in writing the existing law of the folk in their own language, with the necessary adaptations to their new Christian status. Indeed, the Code may be the first document written in English and the story goes that Augustine himself had to devise additional new letters of the alphabet in order to write Anglo-Saxon down. And it is revered: at the top of the document, written in red, it reads: 'These are the dooms [judgements] that King Æthelbert fixed in Augustine's days.'

But could the Anglo-Saxon ideal of elective kingship survive these new trappings of divine and imperial authority and the power that went with them?

Over the next few years, the structure of the English Church was worked out in an exchange of letters between Gregory and Augustine. The English Church was to be self-governing under the pope. There were to be two provinces, each under a metropolitan or (as he was later known) archbishop: the northern based at York and the southern at London. Augustine himself was to be the first archbishop of the southern province with final authority over the whole English Church and (which became a point of bitter contention) over the surviving British bishops as well. The scheme was based partly on memories of the administration of later

Roman Britain and partly on the current reality of the geopolitics of the Anglo-Saxons, who divided themselves into South- and Northumbrians (those living south and north of the River Humber). In the event, Augustine and his successors continued to be based at Canterbury. Otherwise, the lineaments of the scheme have survived and continue to the present.

Augustine died in *c*. 605 and Æthelbert a decade later in about 616. Both were buried in the splendid abbey, later known as St Augustine's, which Augustine had founded after his mission outgrew St Martin's. Augustine's fellow missionaries and successors as archbishops were buried on one side of the church, and Æthelbert and Bertha and their successors as kings and queens of Kent on the other.

It was a symbolism of death to equal and outdo Sutton Hoo itself. It also spoke eloquently of the alliance of Church and king that, for a thousand years, would be one of the principal driving forces of English political life and practice.

III

The reigns of Æthelbert and Redwald marked the end of the domination of the south-east. Thereafter, the Anglo-Saxon balance of power swung away from the area of earlier settlement towards the north and west. Here, larger, newer kingdoms were being forged at the margins of Anglo-Saxon power: Northumbria in the north; Mercia in the Midlands and Wessex in the south-west. Each in turn was to dominate until finally, partly by accident and partly by design, a unified kingdom of *Ængla Land* (England) was created.

The outstanding contemporary of Redwald was Æthelfrith, king of Northumbria. Æthelfrith was a great warrior, and, thanks to his victories over the Scots under Aedan in 603 and the Britons of Powys in 613, he was the real founder of Northumbrian power. He was also a pagan. But this did not stop Bede from seeing him as the instrument of God's vengeance against the Celts, who were not only (Bede thought) of the wrong race but had also espoused the wrong sort of Christianity. Æthelfrith was another Benjamin, Bede enthused, and, like the Old Testament hero, '[he] shall ravin as a wolf; in the morning he shall devour the prey, and at night he shall divide the spoil'.

It was a verse that might have been the motto of any successful Anglo-Saxon king.

But in this dog-eats-dog world, even Æthelfrith got his comeuppance. It was administered by Redwald, who had given refuge to Edwin, a rival claimant to the Northumbrian throne. Æthelfrith demanded Edwin's surrender. But Redwald, deciding that attack was the best form of defence, launched a surprise campaign and defeated and killed Æthelfrith in battle in 616. Edwin succeeded to Northumbria while Redwald became unchallenged *bretwalda*. A decade later, Redwald died in *c.* 627 and Edwin emerged as *bretwalda* in turn. One of Edwin's first steps was to seek the hand of Æthelbert's daughter, Æthelberg, who arrived in Northumbria with Augustine's disciple, Paulinus, as her spiritual adviser. After the marriage, Edwin converted and Paulinus became archbishop of York. But when Edwin went the same way as most early Anglo-Saxon kings and was overcome in battle and killed in 633, Paulinus fled south, to become successively bishop of Rochester and archbishop of Canterbury.

The new king of Northumbria, Oswald, was also a Christian. But he drew his inspiration from the very different tradition of the Celtic Christianity of the Scotto-Irish world, where he had spent many years of exile. This is seen in the case of the Lindisfarne Gospels. Lindisfarne monastery on Holy Island, off the Northumbrian coast, had been founded by St Aidan, an Irish monk from Iona, as a base for his missionary activity under Oswald. The splendid decoration of the Gospels, produced in the late seventh century, testifies to the rich mixture of Celtic, Anglo-Saxon and Roman elements in Northumbrian Christianity.

Under Oswald's younger brother and successor, Oswy, the tensions between the two strands of Christianity, the Celtic and the Roman, became acute: it even divided the king and the queen, who took different sides on the matter. To settle the dispute, Oswy summoned a Council at Whitby in 664. Both sides argued their case with passion, particularly over the vexed issue of the dating of Easter. But the king declared that the Catholics had been victorious. He did so on simple grounds of authority. If he had to decide, the king said, between St Columba, the apostle of the Scots, and St Peter, the disciple to whom Jesus had given the Key of Heaven, he would choose St Peter.

In the wake of his decision, the Celtic leaders of the Northumbrian church withdrew and returned to Scotland. But much of their influence lingered on to contribute its share to the astonishing efflorescence of Northumbrian culture in the century and a half from *c.* 650 to *c.* 800. Monasteries were richly endowed with lands and books and relics and became outposts of sophisticated Mediterranean civilization in the north. They copied and illuminated magnificent manuscripts; sent out missionaries to convert their former homeland in Germany, and in Bede produced the greatest European polymath of the day. The intellectual centre of the world, it seemed, had moved from the banks of the Tiber to the Tyne.

But it was not to last.

Very different was the rival kingdom of Mercia. Here King Penda (*c.* 626–55) held out as an unrepentant pagan. Moreover, in an alliance of convenience with the Britons, he enjoyed a series of crushing victories over the Christian Northumbrians, defeating and killing King Edwin in 633 and King Oswald in 642. The struggle was crucial to the future of England, and the largest, richest and most important Anglo-Saxon archaeological discovery of the last fifty years may be a product of it.

The Staffordshire Hoard was discovered in 2009 in a field near Lichfield, then in the heart of Mercia. It consists of over 1,500 objects made of gold and silver and decorated with precious stones. The silver weighs about 1.3 kilograms and the gold an astonishing 5 kilograms. Only the Sutton Hoo treasure can compare with it. But the two are very different. The Sutton Hoo burial is a careful ritual deposit; the Staffordshire Hoard seems to have been quickly thrown together and hastily buried. Moreover, it consists of fragments: 86 pommel caps from swords; 135 hilt plates from swords and the decorative pieces of at least one Sutton Hoo-style helmet. All are items of male adornment; there is no female jewellery. There are also the crumpled remains of four or five Christian crosses, including one inscribed with the warlike verses from Psalm 68: *Surge domine*, 'Rise up, O Lord, and may Thy enemies be dispersed and those who hate Thee be driven from Thy face'.

Was this a processional cross, carried by the losing side in one of Penda's victories over the Christians of 633 or 642? And were the fragments of male adornment – the warrior bling of the day – torn from the bodies and weapons of the fallen Northumbrian warriors?

It seems very possible. But, alas, we are most unlikely ever to know for certain.

But, finally, Penda succumbed in turn, being defeated and killed by the Christian Oswy of Northumbria in 655. The previous year, in a temporary lull in the hostilities, Penda's son had married Oswy's daughter, who, as usual, arrived with Christian missionaries. This gave Christianity a toehold in Mercia even before Penda's death and it made rapid strides afterwards. One of the old pagan's sons even retired to an English monastery, while a grandson abdicated to become a monk in Rome. Soon after, Penda's direct line died out and the succession passed to his great-great-nephew, Æthelbald, who at last proved equal to his formidable ancestor.

The kingdom Æthelbald acquired was already extensive. Its base lay in the Tame valley north of Birmingham, with Tamworth and Lichfield as its main centres. Thence, the power of the kings of Mercia reached out in every direction along the two great Roman roads, Watling Street and the Fosse Way, which intersected in its heartland: north-east towards Lincoln; north-west into the borders of Wales, south-west to Bath and, above all, south-east to London, which, then as now, was the commercial heart of Britain.

Accurately, but prosaically, the Mercian kings have been called Lords of the A5.

Æthelbald was a man shrewd enough, and ruthless enough, to exploit this inheritance to the utmost. He also enjoyed, as all successful politicians must, good luck in the shape of the relative weakness of his most obvious rivals, the kings of Northumbria and Wessex. The result was that he quickly became dominant in the whole of southern Britain. Moreover, he maintained his sway throughout an unprecedentedly long reign of forty years (716–57).

But did that make him a true king of England, rather than a mere overlord? Many, then and now, have thought so. Indeed, a charter of 736 heaps titles on him: he is 'king not only of the Mercians, but also of all the *provinciae* which are called by the general name "South English"'; *rex Suutanglorum* ('king of the South English') or even *rex Britanniae* ('king of Britain'). But this was courtly hyperbole. Long-established kingdoms, such as Wessex and East Anglia, kept their separate identities and at least some freedom of action. Moreover, Æthelbald's dominance came at a price. His private life was denounced as wicked by St Boniface; he was also reviled as a 'tyrant' once he was safely dead.

Indeed, it is the manner of his death which reveals the real fragility of his kingship. For, after reigning forty-one years, he was murdered at the height of his power and in the heart of his kingdom by his own men. The deed was done at Seckington, near Tamworth, where Æthelbald was 'treacherously killed by his bodyguard at night ... in shocking fashion'. The king's remains were brought to Repton Church and buried in the mausoleum of the Mercian kings in its crypt. The crypt survives, though its alcoves and shelves are long stripped of the jewels and reliquaries they once contained. But then it would have been the setting for another spectacular royal funeral like those at Sutton Hoo and St Augustine's, Canterbury.

Perhaps, however, there's a wicked twist to the story. Was Æthelbald's murder really the work of nobodies with a grudge? Or was the man who seems to have been responsible for Æthelbald's splendid funeral also the man behind his murder? Certainly he was the one who profited from it, since, after a brief power struggle in which his rival too was murdered, he succeeded Æthelbald as king. He is one of the forgotten heroes of English history; a man who operated on a European scale and dominated the England of his day. His name was Offa, king of Mercia.

IV

Despite the sensational circumstances of his accession, Offa's reign (757–96) seems in many ways a rerun of his predecessor's: he even reigned for a similarly long period. In fact, there were important differences of scale and method.

Like Æthelbald, Offa had generally good relations with the two large rival kingdoms of Northumbria and Wessex, which were cemented in the usual way by marriage alliances. But elsewhere, in the south and east, he increasingly imposed direct rule. And by often brutal means. He took control of Kent in the 760s; lost it for nine years after his rare defeat at the battle of Otford in 776, and then moved decisively to recover it. Sussex, whose fortunes were closely linked with Kent's, followed a similar pattern, as a result of which Offa demoted its ancient kings to *ealdormen* or nobles. But most sensational was the case of Redwald's former realm of East Anglia, where, in 794, Offa ordered King Æthelbert to be beheaded. It was an assertion of pure, untrammelled power.

Offa was equally assertive with the Church. The archbishop of Canterbury was head of the English Church. But he was also a great Kentish magnate and, as such, appears to have played a part in local resistance to Offa's encroaching power. Offa's response was stunning: he would have an archbishop of his own. The scheme was negotiated with two papal legates at a Council of the English Church in 787. The Council was close fought. But, as usual, Offa got his way and Lichfield, in the Mercian heartland, was elevated into an archbishopric, with its incumbent safely in Offa's pocket.

The creation of the archbishopric of Lichfield opened the way to another project that was even closer to Offa's heart: to ensure the succession of his son, Ecgfrith. He proclaimed him king of Mercia in his own lifetime; he also decided that he should be anointed. The ceremony also took place in 787. We do not know where or who performed it. Perhaps it was the new archbishop of Lichfield. Or perhaps the papal legates. Or perhaps, since Offa never did things by halves, it was both together.

At any rate, Ecgfrith's is the first recorded consecration in English history, and it deployed the whole panoply of the Church to declare that the boy was inviolably royal and his father's unchallengeable successor. The ceremony was a Christian adaptation of the inauguration rites of Old Testament kings. But, as so often in Anglo-Saxon England, it was a hybrid, since it combined Judaeo-Christian anointing with older Anglo-Saxon traditions that went back to Sutton Hoo and beyond. For the boy was invested, not with a crown, but with a *cynehelm*, a royal helmet.

Offa's handling of the coinage was almost as novel. He issued a new-style coinage, in which the coins were bigger and thinner, had a better bullion content, were stamped with his image and prominently displayed his name and title of *Rex M[erciorum]* ('king of the Mercians') in bold capital letters. Offa was not quite the first English king to mint such a coinage. But his is incomparably the most important, in terms of both quality and quantity. Millions of coins seem to have been struck and they show an exuberant variety of 'portrait' types: some use Roman models; others appear to be based on the representations of the kings of Israel in Anglo-Saxon manuscripts. Obviously, Offa cared about the image-making power of the coinage. But it was its economic and fiscal functions that mattered more. The numbers struck reflected Offa's takeover of the wealth of the south-east; they helped that wealth to grow, especially by trade with *Francia*, and, in turn, they allowed Offa to tap the burgeoning economy for his own purposes.

A similar balance between image-making and practicality is to be found in the greatest achievement of his reign and the work for which he is still popularly remembered: Offa's Dyke. It originally stretched from sea to sea along the Welsh frontier. This is a distance of 135 miles or double the length of Hadrian's Wall. It consists of a ditch, originally six feet deep, backed by an earth rampart that was about twenty-five feet high. The rampart was probably reinforced with timber, and its siting displays great tactical ingenuity, commanding, as it does, long views into Wales.

But what was it for? Did it mark an agreed frontier, as an act of peace? Or was it a warlike gesture: to defend Mercia against Welsh attacks and to provide Offa with a forward base from which to launch his own campaigns against the Welsh? The latter now seems much more likely. In which case the Dyke was 'a work of almost studied contempt for the Welsh'. For, by a strange reversal of roles, its building would suggest that it is the former Anglo-Saxon invaders who now see themselves as rich and civilized while the Welsh have become wild, untrustworthy raiders. In short, it is the Welsh, the Dyke says, who are the barbarians now.

But does that mean that Offa had gone the whole hog and imagined himself in turn as an imperial Roman? There is some evidence to support this view. And certainly, it is what happened to the Anglo-Saxons' Frankish cousins across the Channel. For these are the years of the Carolingian revolution. It took place in two stages: the first royal, the second imperial. In 751, Pepin the Short, who had usurped the Frankish throne, was made king by the new royal inauguration ceremony of anointing. Forty-nine years later, his son Charlemagne, who had succeeded his father in 768 and had expanded the frontiers of *Francia* to run from the banks of the River Ebro to those of the Elbe, was crowned emperor in Rome by the pope on Christmas morning 800. The renewed empire was intended to be both Roman and Christian and Charlemagne took himself seriously in both capacities: he was soldier of the Faith and reformer of the Church, on the one hand, *and*, on the other, restorer of the Roman Empire, whose inheritance of law, language, literature, architecture and forms of government he was determined to revive.

Pepin and Charlemagne were thus Offa's contemporaries and the latter at least was well known to him. They had diplomatic relations; unsuccessfully negotiated a marriage alliance and corresponded. The only surviving letter from a European ruler to an Anglo-Saxon king is from Charlemagne to Offa in 796. In it he recognized Offa 'to be not only a most strong protector of your earthly country, but also a most devout defender of the holy faith'. He also addressed Offa as 'brother' and acknowledged him as an equal. Offa, for his part, was influenced by Charlemagne's revival of the apparatus of Roman power. But there is no sign that Offa understood or imitated its cultural dimension.

On the other hand, Englishmen played an important role in the Carolingian achievement and one, Alcuin, who was born in Northumbria and educated at York, was a central figure in the regime as a sort of minister for culture and education. Finally, Offa's takeover of the southeast of England brought him into close and direct commercial contact with *Francia*. This is why he modelled his changes in the currency on Pepin's monetary reforms. Pepin also provided the ultimate model for Ecgfrith's anointing. But there was a more immediate input since Alcuin, acting as envoy from Charlemagne, had accompanied the papal legates on their mission to England in 786. He played a major part in the ensuing Church Council; probably attended Ecgfrith's coronation and returned to England on another diplomatic errand a few years later. Alcuin's correspondence thus provides a sort of commentary on the apogee of Offa's power and on the nemesis which followed soon after.

At first, all seemed well. Offa was, Alcuin wrote in one letter, 'the glory of Britain'; in another, he saw him as having 'the kingdom … of all the English' within his grasp. And in Ecgfrith he had provided a worthy heir. Alcuin called the boy 'my son'; enjoined him to learn 'authority' from his father and 'compassion' from his mother and saw him as 'the hope of many'. It is not hard to see why. For, irrespective of Ecgfrith's personal qualities, Alcuin interpreted his anointing, which he may have helped to devise, as the promise of a new, better monarchy: more ordered, more Christian and better attuned to its responsibilities to the people of God. In short, Alcuin seems to have hoped that the ceremony of 787 would lead to a renewed kingdom of the English, just as the Carolingian revolution had restored the kingdom of the Franks and would, in the fullness of time, revive the Roman Empire itself.

But it was not to be. Offa died on 29 July 796. Ecgfrith duly succeeded. But he died less than six months later, on 17 December. The hopes had been cheated and 'the divinity that doth hedge a king' had failed at its first English test. Alcuin was forced to ask why. His answer was that the sins of the father had been visited on the son. 'For you know very well', he wrote to a leading Mercian noble, 'how much blood his father shed to secure the kingdom on his son.'

There were sins of omission on Offa's part as well. Though Alcuin had expressed his delight that Offa was 'so intent on education', there is no evidence that it came to very much. Certainly, there is nothing to compare with the Carolingian or the Northumbrian achievement: there is no Mercian renaissance or chronicle, no *Life of Offa*, no writings by the king himself. In short, if Offa were attracted to ideas of empire, it was to *imperium* in its simplest, crudest sense as the mere absoluteness of power. His conquest of the south-east, his construction of Offa's Dyke, his bloodlettings and regicides can all be read as embodying that. But it was not enough. Indeed, in the Anglo-Saxon political tradition, it may have been worse than useless. Or, in Alcuin's own words: 'this was not a strengthening of the kingdom but its ruin'.

But we must not anticipate. The man who emerged victorious from the power struggle which followed the royal deaths of 796 was Cenwulf. He, at best, was only a distant member of the royal kindred. But his style was pure Offa, as his treatment of Kent shows. The Kentishmen took advantage of the succession crisis and the consequent temporary eclipse of Mercian power to rebel and erect a certain Eadbert as their own king once more. But Cenwulf exacted a terrible revenge. The revolt was suppressed and Eadbert taken to Mercia. There he was ritually mutilated to disable him from kingship: his eyes were put out and his hands cut off. Not surprisingly, Kent subsequently remained quiet, though Cenwulf in turn made some concession to local pride by setting up his brother Cuthred as puppet-king of Kent.

Cenwulf himself died in 821. His death was followed by another, even more drawn-out struggle for the succession, which once more gave Mercia's enemies, internal and external alike, their opportunity. And this time the whole edifice of Mercian imperial power was brought crashing down. Fittingly, the man who struck the decisive blow was another victim of Offa's, Egbert.

Egbert was a scion of the royal house of Wessex. Somehow he had fallen foul of Offa, and, like many others, had fled 'in fear of death' to take refuge in *Francia* at the court of Charlemagne. But in 802, after the death of Offa's son-in-law King Beorhtric, Egbert the exile returned to succeed effortlessly to the throne of Wessex. Now, twenty years later, Cenwulf's death offered him the opportunity to avenge the slights he had suffered at Mercian hands. The year 825 was his *annus mirabilis*: Egbert himself defeated the new Mercian king Beornwulf at *Ellendun*; the East Anglians then rose against Mercian domination and killed Beornwulf as he tried to suppress the revolt; meanwhile, Egbert's son, Æthelwulf, occupied the remaining provinces of the former Mercian empire in Sussex, Kent and Essex, and, by some at least, was greeted as liberator. Four years later, Egbert scaled fresh heights: he conquered Mercia and marched against the Northumbrians, defeating them in battle and receiving submission and tribute.

A new great power had arisen in England: Wessex. But it would have to confront a new and even greater threat: the Vikings.

3

WESSEX

Æthelwulf, Æthelbald, Æthelberht, Æthelred, Alfred the Great

ONCE, IN THE FOURTH AND FIFTH CENTURIES, the Saxons had been Europe's most feared pirates, plundering the coasts of Britain and Gaul at will. Then they grew bolder and became settlers and conquerors.

Now the process was about to repeat itself with another Germanic people on the move: the Vikings. They came from further north, from Denmark and even Norway. They were intrepid seafarers, as the Anglo-Saxons had once been; they were also pagan and they were (despite the whitewash of some recent historians) even more savage. The Viking raids on England began in the late eighth century, when Offa still held sway. An isolated raiding party landed at Portland and killed the king's reeve, the leading royal official, at Dorchester. Then, in 793, they struck at the other end of the country and destroyed the monastic church on Lindisfarne.

Little more is heard of them for forty years. But from 835 the raids became regular. For Anglo-Saxon England was now rich – as rich, probably, as late Roman Britain and as vulnerable. Particularly attractive to the raiders were the forms of portable wealth which have appealed to thieves and robbers throughout the ages: the golden crosses and altar plate, the jewels surrounding the relics and studding the bindings of lavishly illuminated Bibles, the vast quantities of silver coin struck by Offa and his successors, the silver-mounted drinking horns and gold rings and brooches of the rich. Much of this portable wealth was concentrated in the minster-churches and monasteries, which thus became favourite Viking targets. Probably all that mattered was that these churches were rich. But the fact that they were centres of a rival faith *may* have made their destruction a duty to the pagan Vikings as well as a pleasure. Towns, which were also rich and lightly defended, were other victims of choice. As were captives, who could be ransomed, sold or enslaved.

All this was bad enough. But in the 860s there came a change in the raids that was both qualitative and quantitative: in 865 a 'great army' invaded England, and it was reinforced in 871 by 'a great summer army'. Thousands of men were involved; they had royal leadership and their aim was conquest. Within a decade, everything north and east of Watling Street had fallen: Northumbria in 867, East Anglia in 869 and most of Mercia in 874–7. The kingdoms of Northumbria and East Anglia were obliterated, never to revive, and their kings were offered as sacrifices to Odin (the Nordic Woden), perhaps in the gruesome ritual of the 'blood-eagle', in which the victim's ribcage was cut open and his lungs torn out and draped round his shoulders like an eagle's folded wings. The succession to five bishoprics was disrupted for long periods and three of them were never re-formed. Everywhere, libraries and archives were destroyed; learning itself perished and the whole achievement of Anglo-Saxon England seemed on the point of obliteration.

I

In the rout, only one Anglo-Saxon kingdom survived, Wessex, and even that hung by a thread. It had certain advantages, however, which might give it hope. These included a secure succession, an unusually effective structure of government and, above all, it was to prove, the personal qualities of its king, Alfred. Like all Anglo-Saxon kings, Alfred was a man of action and a warrior. But he was also, uniquely for his own age and for long after, a true philosopher-king. Moreover, unlike many philosophers and almost all kings, he wrote and published widely. The result is that his very words have come down to us and, for the first time in our history, we can hear the genuine voice of an English king.

It is a very attractive voice too: reasonable, practical and persuasive. So much so, indeed, that it is easy to forget that it is also the voice of a master politician, who had an agenda and wants us to see things from his point of view. Actually, it is very difficult not to, since almost everything that survives from the period is written by Alfred or influenced by him. To a remarkable extent therefore our image of Alfred as 'The Great' is – still, and after over a thousand years – a product of Alfred's own self-invention. It goes without saying that such a view is not impartial. But it has survived only because Alfred's achievements matched the grandiosity of his vision.

Alfred was a grandson of the great King Egbert. His own father, Æthelwulf, succeeded in 839 after having acted for many years as sub-king or viceroy in the eastern provinces of Wessex, which he had conquered in 825. His marriage, to his first wife Osburh, was unusually fruitful, with five sons who reached maturity. This could be a mixed blessing, as the results of Edward III's numerous progeny would show. But Æthelwulf was able to get his sons to agree to a sort of succession in survivorship, in which each brother would succeed his elder, saving all the time certain property rights to the children of the deceased. Rather surprisingly, the agreement held. Even more surprisingly, all four sons who survived Æthelwulf succeeded in turn to the throne.

Alfred, born in about 849, was the youngest of this band of brothers, being junior by at least twenty-five years to Æthelstan, the eldest. As the youngest of the family, he seems to have been a favourite child, indulged and even a little spoiled. He was also bright, curious, with an excellent memory and, like many younger sons, an unusually adventurous intelligence. But events were just as important in forming the man. His mother died when he was very young. Even more importantly, his father, taking advantage perhaps of his wife's death, decided that thirty years as viceroy and king was enough. Instead, in 855, when Alfred was about six, he embarked on a pilgrimage to Rome. Æthelbald, his eldest surviving son, was left as king in his place, but Alfred, as the youngest, seems to have accompanied his father. They travelled in style and stayed in the city for about a year. It was far fallen from its ancient splendour. But more than enough remained to fire the imagination of a sensitive and impressionable child like Alfred. Probably his interest in history dates from this experience. As does his ambition, his lust for fame and his determination, as it were, to build a new Rome in England's green and pleasant land.

But there was more to come. On the way back from Rome, Æthelwulf visited the Frankish court, and, on 1 October 856 at Verberie-sur-Oise near Paris, was married to Princess Judith, daughter of Charles the Bald, king of West *Francia*, and great-granddaughter of Charlemagne. At the same time, Judith was anointed and crowned queen by Archbishop Hincmar of Reims, the master-liturgist and inventor of tradition, in an *ordo* or form of service which he had devised. It was the first recorded coronation of an English queen and perhaps the first time as well that a crown had been used, rather than the royal helmet (which was, in any case, unsuitable for a woman). 'May the Lord crown you with glory and honour,' Hincmar intoned as he placed the crown on the queen's head, 'that ... the brightness of the gold and the... gleam of the gems may always shine forth in your conduct and your acts.'

Was Alfred present? If so, we can only guess at the impact of the words. But their import would not have been unfamiliar. For, according to the official narrative of the House of Wessex, Alfred himself had already undergone some form of consecration, whether as king or consul, at the hands of Pope Leo IV himself in Rome.

Æthelwulf did not long survive his return home and was succeeded by Æthelbald. Æthelbald also stepped into his father's bed and married his stepmother Judith. But Judith, who, after Æthelbald's own premature death, would elope with Count Baldwin of Flanders, was cultivated as well as brazen. She also seems to have taken a shine to Alfred. So far, according to Alfred's biographer, Asser, Alfred's education had been oral and had consisted of learning by heart long passages of Anglo-Saxon verse. But Judith, literate herself, stimulated Alfred to learn to read by playing on his competitive instincts. She showed him a book with a richly illuminated initial and promised to give it to whichever of the two brothers, Alfred and Æthelred, who was only a couple of years older, would first memorize its contents. Alfred won.

But a harsher contest was imminent. In 865 the third brother, Æthelberht, died after another brief reign. Æthelred, the loser in the book competition, now became king and Alfred stepped up to take his place as royal deputy and heir presumptive. Æthelred had need of all the help Alfred could give for his accession coincided with the arrival in England of the Viking great army.

Alfred's life task had begun.

At first, Wessex got off lightly, as the brunt of the Viking attack fell on, successively, East Anglia, Northumbria and Mercia. But in the early winter of 870–71 'the great army' turned south-west from East Anglia and occupied a fortified camp to the east of Reading as its new forward base. The choice was perfect strategically. The camp, situated at the confluence of the Rivers Thames and Kennet, could be reinforced up the then still navigable Thames; it lay on the disputed frontier between Mercia and Wessex; while to the south and west, and within easy ride, lay the rich lands of Wessex.

The *witan*, the advisory council or 'parliament' of the leading men, lay and ecclesiastical, of Wessex, met in emergency session at *Swinbeorg* (almost certainly Swanborough Tump, a prehistoric burial mound in the Vale of Pewsey, in Wiltshire). First, King Æthelred and his younger brother Alfred, facing the imminent prospect of death in battle, solemnly confirmed their father's arrangements for the succession; then they rode off, up the chalk road on to the Marlborough Downs and across the River Kennet to Reading, to try to dislodge the enemy. The results were mixed. A direct assault on the camp failed. But the West Saxons were victorious in a battle fought in the open field on the chalk ridge known as Ashdown. Alfred distinguished himself in the battle. But it failed to swing the campaign and two more Saxon defeats followed.

At this point disaster struck twice. The Vikings were reinforced by the arrival of 'the great summer army'. And in mid-April 871 King Æthelred, still only in his twenties, died. The body was taken to Wimborne Minster in Dorset for burial and the great men of the *witan*, gathered for the funeral, met once more and confirmed Alfred as king. He was just twenty-two or -three. There is no suggestion of a coronation. Perhaps in view of the crisis there was neither the time nor the inclination.

The crisis soon got worse. Only a month after his accession Alfred, seemingly caught off guard and with only a small force, was defeated at Wilton. The victorious Vikings were within twenty miles of Wimborne and Alfred had to sue for peace.

It was not a good start to a reign.

But, once more, events elsewhere in England gave Wessex respite. Faced with more pressing concerns, 'the great army' withdrew from Reading, first for London and then for the north, to deal with the Northumbrian revolt against their Viking overlords. Its suppression, and the ensuing partition of Mercia, occupied 'the great army' till 874–5. Then it split into three divisions. The leader of one was 'King'

Guthrum. And he had decided to carve out a real kingdom for himself – in Wessex.

First Guthrum struck south, cutting right across Wessex to Wareham on the south coast, which he held in 875–6. Then he turned west to Exeter, which he occupied for the following year. For three years, that is, Guthrum marched the length and breadth of Wessex, pillaging, burning and living off the land as he went. Alfred, for his part, was able to bottle Guthrum up in both Wareham and Exeter. But he was not strong enough to take them and, in both cases, had to agree terms. These the Vikings negotiated with almost flamboyant bad faith. That Alfred seems to have taken their worthless promises at face value means either that he was naive – or, more likely, that he had no choice.

After slinking out of Exeter under cover of night and with the solemn promise to Alfred, sworn 'on [his] holy armlet', that 'they would speedily depart from his kingdom', Guthrum took up winter quarters at Gloucester. Alfred shadowed him up to the northern border of Wessex, where he spent Christmas at his royal hall at Chippenham in Wiltshire. But on 6 January 878, the last day of the Christmas festivities known as Twelfth Night, Guthrum appeared before Chippenham. He had marched fast and in the depths of winter. Alfred was taken by surprise and had no choice but to flee. Guthrum now occupied the heartland of the defenceless kingdom and Wessex seemed about to go the way of the rest of Anglo-Saxon England.

II

In his flight, Alfred was accompanied only 'by a little band' and he deliberately avoided centres of population, seeking instead the cover of the forests and uplands of Wiltshire ('the woods and fastness of the moors'). Gradually, he moved south and west towards the Somerset fens and Athelney. Here at last he began to feel safe.

Athelney means 'royal island', and Alfred chose it as his fastness because the area at the confluence of the Rivers Parret and Tone was then an island. It was well screened in the middle of the marshes, and the water which flooded the fenlands in winter made it even more difficult to attack. His time here was the nadir of Alfred's fortunes. Later, in one of his writings, he seems to recall the self-examination it provoked:

> In the midst of prosperity the mind is elated, and in prosperity a man forgets himself; in hardship he is forced to reflect on himself, even though he be unwilling.

By this or other means, Alfred regained confidence in his own capacity. But the power of a king is not simply personal. It is also political or collective. Alfred understood this too. 'A man cannot work without tools,' he wrote in another of his works. And, he continued:

> In the case of a king, the resources and tools with which to rule are that he have his land fully manned. He must have praying men, fighting men and working men … without these tools no king may make his ability known … nor can he accomplish any of the things he was commanded to do.

In the adjacent kingdom of Mercia, these collective 'tools' seem to have consisted of little more than the king's war-band, which is why Mercian power was so vulnerable to challenge whenever the strong hand of an effective king, like Offa or Cenwulf, was removed. But in Wessex, luckily for Alfred, power was both more diffuse and more 'popular'. This meant, paradoxically, that it was more durable and could survive even such a debacle of royal power as Twelfth Night 878.

Which is where, perhaps, the story of Alfred and the cakes fits in. The king, the story goes, had taken refuge, incognito, in the hovel of a swineherd, where he found himself upbraided by the man's wife for letting her bread-cakes burn as he dreamed in front of the fire of regaining power. The story is, of course, a legend. But it is a very old one since it dates from Alfred's own lifetime or shortly thereafter. It also points, once again, to the closeness of monarch and people which would be the salvation of Wessex.

Alfred, as soon as he was able, moved to invoke these powers. At Easter, which fell very early that year on 23 March, he further strengthened Athelney's natural defences by building a fort. He was helped to do this by the *ealdorman* or governor of Somerset, while the men of 'that part of Somersetshire which was nighest to it' also joined in the raids against the Viking occupiers which the king now launched from his island fortress. But these raids were a mere morale-boosting exercise to prepare the way for the full-scale counter-attack which Alfred began to organize.

And the key to the counter-attack was, once again, the shires. Historic Wessex (that is, the kingdom before its expansion under Alfred's grandfather, Egbert) was divided into five 'shires' or, as we would now say using Norman-French rather than Anglo-Saxon, 'counties': Somerset itself, Devon, Wiltshire, Dorset and Hampshire. The shires were further subdivided into 'hundreds', so called because, in theory though rarely in practice, they contained a hundred 'hides' or parcels of land each sufficient to maintain a family. We do not know when the shires and hundreds began. The former are first mentioned in the seventh century and the latter in the eleventh. But they are clearly much older. Perhaps indeed they are immemorial and go back to the folk-moots of the first Saxon settlers in western *Britannia*. This would explain why their meetings took place in the open air, at traditional assembly points that were often marked by a prehistoric monument, like a tumulus or barrow. One such is Swanborough Tump in Wiltshire. Here, as we have seen, Æthelred and Alfred had met with the *witan* to settle their affairs on the eve of the Viking attack. And here, on a much humbler scale, the free men of the Hundred of Swanborough met once a month to settle their affairs.

These meetings, and the less frequent but more important shire assemblies, which took place twice a year, were later called 'courts'. They did indeed try legal cases, both criminal and civil. But they did much more. They kept the peace; levied taxes and raised troops. Finally, their sworn testimony, later systematized as the jury, supplied the basic information about property rights and inheritance without which royal government could not function: even William the Conqueror, in all his power, would depend on such juries to produce the myriad facts on which the Domesday Book was based.

For the hundred and shire were also, whatever their folk origins may have been, the agencies of royal government. It was one royal official, the reeve or bailiff, who presided over the Hundred Court, and another, much greater one, the *ealdorman*, who chaired the Shire Court. The *ealdorman* was the leading man in his shire and one of the greatest in Wessex. He commanded the shire levies, acted as intermediary between the court and the county, and used his authority to settle most local disputes.

Indeed, the *ealdorman* was so powerful that it was easy for him to forget that he was the king's servant and to aspire instead to become a territorial magnate in his own right. Alfred was well aware of the temptation and, in a well-judged interpolation in one of his translations, he denounced the *ealdorman* who turned his delegated authority (*ealdordome*) to lordship (*hlaforddome*) and caused 'the reverence of himself and his power to become the regular custom of the shire he rules'.

Alfred fought this tendency. So did his successors. So too, perhaps, did the people. The result was that the paths of government in Wessex and *Francia* started to diverge. In *Francia*, the nobility, like Alfred's ambitious *ealdorman*, soon took over the king's former powers in the localities and privatized justice, taxation and the raising of troops. In so doing, they interposed themselves between king and people: the people of a district were now their lord's, not the king's. In Wessex, this never quite happened. Here, instead, the partnership between king and people, into which rough and ready egalitarianism of the early Saxon settlers had developed, held. This partnership, with its sense of all being in it together, would make it easier for Alfred to impose heavy demands on his people as the crisis drew out over years and decades. It also provided, in 'the self-government at the king's command' of the shires and hundreds, and the collective self-consciousness which they fostered, the means for Alfred to begin his fight-back against Guthrum.

III

The planning of the campaign, once again, started at Easter. Over the following weeks Alfred sent out messengers from Athelney in all directions. They went to lords in their halls and to meetings of the common folk at their outdoor Hundred Courts. Seven weeks after Easter (11 May) all was ready and the signal was given. Alfred himself set out from Athelney and marched east towards the rendezvous at Egbert's Stone. There he was met 'by all the people of Somersetshire, and Wiltshire and that part of Hampshire which is on this side of the sea [that is, excluding the Isle of Wight]'. These were the forces of three out of the five shires of Wessex. It is unclear why the other two, Devon and Dorset, failed to send troops. Dorset may have been incapacitated by taking the brunt of the Viking occupation. But the Devonians were probably assigned to coastal defence. Earlier that year, Viking reinforcements had tried to land in Devon. The *ealdorman* Odda had driven them off with heavy losses and captured their sacred raven banner. But other landings must have been anticipated.

Alfred had chosen the rallying point carefully. Egbert's Stone has been recently identified as yet another prehistoric tumulus, high on the hills above the River Deverill on the edge of Salisbury Plain in western Wiltshire. It is close to the spot at which Somerset, Wiltshire and Dorset all meet, and it was here that Alfred's grandfather, Egbert, had marched his soldiers after a decisive and final victory over the British people of Cornwall. But Alfred was not just evoking Wessex's past glories. His campaign was also a kind of crusade: he was a Christian king and his enemies were pagans. Hence the launch of the campaign around Easter. This suited military realities. But it coincided as well with the most important feast of the Christian year, the feast of resurrection. The coincidence was not lost on his troops:

> when they saw the King, receiving him not surprisingly as if one
> restored to life after suffering such great tribulations, they were
> filled with immense joy.

The day after the rendezvous, Alfred struck camp at dawn. The army followed the course of the river north-east beyond its confluence with the Wylye to Iley Oak, the traditional site of another Wessex Hundred Court. It lies in a bend in the river and offers ample room for a force of about three thousand to bivouac. In the morning they would go out to meet Guthrum and his Vikings, marching up over Battlesbury Hill on to the high ground of Salisbury Plain.

For Guthrum had moved his forces to another royal estate at Edington (*Ethandun*). And it was there, probably on the hill above the village, that the two armies met. We cannot be sure, because there has been no systematic excavation of the site. But chance finds have turned up a number of bodies of the right date, some of them badly mutilated. That is not surprising. For the battle was to be both savage and bloody. There was too much at stake on both sides for it to be anything else. Guthrum knew that, for his takeover of the kingdom of Wessex to succeed, he had to kill Alfred outright. As for Alfred and the men of Wessex, they knew that this was probably their last chance of independence: if Guthrum won, Viking domination of Wessex and England would be complete. So both sides were hoping for a decisive result. They were not to be disappointed:

> Fighting fiercely with a compact shield wall against the entire Viking army, [Alfred] persevered resolutely for a long time. At length he gained the victory through God's will [and] destroyed the Vikings with great slaughter.

Alfred's victory at Edington was complete, and decisive. The broken remains of Guthrum's army fled back to their fortified base at Chippenham. Alfred pursued them, cutting down the stragglers on the way. Then he laid siege to the fort. After two weeks, the Viking leader surrendered. But this time Guthrum was in no position to equivocate. He promised to withdraw from Wessex and he confirmed his promise by agreeing to be baptized. The baptism occurred three weeks later. Alfred stood as Guthrum's godfather, which made the Viking his moral and political dependant. And the ceremony took place at Aller in Somerset, only three miles east of Athelney, which avenged Alfred's darkest hour.

The battle of Edington was the turning point in Alfred's life and one of the great turning points of English history. Alfred, fighting at the head of the shires, had established himself as a great war leader. And Wessex was saved, for the moment at least. But the future of the rest of England still hung in the balance.

Alfred's victory at Edington bought him almost a decade and a half of peace. But Alfred did not sleep on his laurels. Instead he embarked on a considered and ambitious programme of military and moral rearmament. As a result, Wessex was able, not only to survive a third Viking challenge, but also to expand until, within half a century of Alfred's death, it ruled, directly or indirectly, all *Britannia*.

The foundation of all this was Alfred's transformation of his kingdom into a society on a full-time war footing. He built a navy, with bigger ships constructed to his own design. There were early technical problems. But they seem to have been overcome and the sixty-oared vessel he pioneered became the standard unit of the Anglo-Saxon navy. He also reorganized the *fyrd* or army, 'so that always half its men were at home, [and] half on service'. This enabled him to put troops into the field at almost any time. Most effective of all, however, was his scheme of fortification. In the first Viking attacks in the 870s, Guthrum and his men had been able to range great distances throughout Wessex at will and virtually unopposed. Alfred's fortifications were designed to prevent any repetition.

The result was an undertaking on a massive scale. Thirty *burhs* or fortified settlements were built, strategically sited so that nowhere in Wessex was more than twenty miles (or a day's march) away from one, and 27,000 men were assigned to defend them. The figure was based on the assumption that four men were needed to man each pole (five and a half yards) of rampart. The circuit of each *burh* was measured (very accurately) and the number of its garrison calculated accordingly. Finally, each *burh* was assigned an endowment of land to maintain its garrison, on the basis of one hide for each man.

The document in which all this was set out, known as the Burghal Hidage, survives in a slightly later form, which probably dates from the early tenth century. The Burghal Hidage demonstrates the tremendous bureaucratic achievement of which Anglo-Saxon government was capable. But it also shows that its bureaucratic competence was firmly harnessed, as Alfred's high Christian concept of kingship required, to the common good. For these *burhs* were not private castles, owned by some lord or bishop and manned by his retainers. Instead, they were fortified communities, founded by the king, defended by his people, and defending and protecting them in turn.

Moreover, the significance of the *burhs* went beyond their defensive capacity, since many, though not all, developed into real towns. Once again, this seems to have been Alfred's intention from the beginning. For *burhs* like Winchester, which Alfred was to make into the capital of Wessex, were laid out as proper planned new towns, with a set, regular street pattern. Such places quickly became market centres and, most importantly of all, mint towns, where the king's coin was struck according to centralized patterns and fixed weights and fineness. The result of this rapid urbanization was a virtuous economic cycle in which everybody benefited. Trade boomed and with it taxes; the king got rich and his people grew prosperous, while the word 'borough', as we pronounce it today, started to assume its modern meaning of a self-governing urban community under royal patronage. In short, probably more by design than by accident, Alfred had turned the *burhs* into the urban equivalent of the hundreds, or, in the case of the largest of them, of shires in their own right.

And the *burh* of *burhs* was London. It was already the largest town and the commercial powerhouse of England. As such, it had been the jewel in King Offa's crown and the fiscal key to Mercian power. But it suffered the common fate of eastern Mercia and passed under Viking domination. This lasted, almost certainly, for fifteen years, from 871, when the 'great summer army' took up winter quarters there, to 886, when Alfred felt strong enough to take it. The result was a turning point in the history of the City – and of England.

The original Anglo-Saxon settlement, known as *Lundenwic*, was not based in the abandoned Roman city but further west at Aldwych, from which it sprawled out along the line of the modern Strand. Alfred moved most of the population back within the Roman walls, which he rebuilt and refortified. He also constructed another *burh* at Southwark, which is still known as 'Borough' today.

All this entitles Alfred to be regarded as the second founder of the City. But in what capacity did Alfred, king of Wessex, thus act in former Mercian territory? Alfred answered the question by giving charge of the refounded City to the *ealdorman* Æthelred. Æthelred, however, was not *ealdorman* of any of the historic shires of Wessex; instead, his charge was Mercia, or rather the rump of the kingdom to the south and west of Watling Street which had escaped the Viking conquest. How and when Æthelbert and Lesser Mercia passed into Alfred's sphere of influence is unclear. But Alfred moved to cement the relationship personally, by marrying Æthelbert to his masterful eldest child, Æthelflaed, who proved to be every inch her father's daughter. He also did so juridically, by starting to style himself in his charters 'king of the Angles and of the Saxons' or 'king of the Anglo-Saxons'. Could a claim to be King of All the English be far behind?

For that, de facto, was Alfred's position with the Viking destruction of all the other Anglo-Saxon kingdoms. And the position, it seems, was recognized *de jure* in the aftermath of his capture of London, when 'all the English people that were not under subjection to the Danes submitted to him'. Was there a formal ceremony? Did it involve oath-taking? We cannot know. But at this point the idea of a common 'English' identity, first (mis)understood by St Gregory and powerfully expounded by Bede, started to assume concrete political form.

Its first expression, appropriately enough – since Guthrum's defeat had been the making of Alfred – was in a treaty with King Guthrum which was agreed between 886 and Guthrum's death in 890. After his defeat and baptism in 878, Guthrum and his host had retreated east. Here Guthrum had found the kingdom he craved by becoming monarch of the Danes of southern England. He was called king of East Anglia. But the actual boundaries of his kingdom were much wider, embracing all England east of Watling Street and the Ouse and (probably) south of the Humber. Guthrum and Alfred thus negotiated as equals in power. But the preamble to the treaty defines their kingship differently. Guthrum's is the territorial kingship of (greater) East Anglia; Alfred's, in contrast, is national: he is the king 'of all the English nation' (*ealles Angelcynnes*) and his *witan* is Council of the English Nation too.

'Of all the English nation'. These few words contain the germ of a national political idea. But, in the circumstances of 886, in which the Vikings held half England and still threatened to take the whole, it was *only* an idea. Nor is it clear how many shared it, or thought that its realization was inevitable or even desirable. But, whatever their number, Alfred determined to increase it by a sustained programme of writing and publication. An earlier generation called the result scholarship. It was, of course. But it was also propaganda – for Alfred and for England. And the king was his own Minister for Information, and, as in everything else he did, a highly effective one.

But first Alfred had to address his own inadequacies. For most of his adult life, the king was literate only in Anglo-Saxon. That was enough for most practical purposes. But, for the task which he now had in hand, Alfred required access to the surviving riches of Classical culture which only a knowledge of Latin could give. His first, interim, solution was to get some of his more learned clergy to read Latin texts with him, translating and expounding as they went. This could have been the lazy man's way out. Alfred instead treated the experience as one-to-one language teaching and benefited accordingly. His pious biographer, Asser, presents the result as a miracle, in which, on 11 November 887, Alfred learned to read Latin at a stroke. We can discount the miracle, but accept the idea that by this stage the king felt confident enough to tease the good bishop by doing the translation himself. We should also take the date – a year after the occupation of London – seriously too. Alfred was now ready to launch his propaganda campaign.

It was announced in the Preface to his translation of St Gregory's *Pastoral Care*. Why, Alfred asked himself, had not the scholars of the pre-Viking golden age of Anglo-Saxon England translated the key works of Christianity into 'their own language'? Then knowledge of them would have survived into his own, post-Viking, iron age, when (he recollected of the time he came to the throne) there were very few 'who could ... even translate a single letter from Latin into English' and not 'a single one south of the Thames'. Moreover, by translating, they would only have been following a long line of distinguished precedents:

> Then I recalled how the Law was first composed in the Hebrew language, and thereafter, when the Greeks learned it, they translated it all into their own language, and all other books as well. And so too the Romans, after they had mastered them, translated all through learned interpreters into their own language ... Therefore it seems better to me ... that we too should turn into the language that we can all understand certain books which are the most necessary for all men to know.

His present translation would, Alfred hoped, set the ball rolling.

Finally, with characteristic attention to practical detail, Alfred set out how his text should be distributed: each bishop would be sent a copy, together with a pointer or *aestel*, worth the vast sum of fifty *mancuses* or the equivalent of six and a quarter pounds of silver. The book and its *aestel* must never, Alfred further stipulated, be separated and must be set up in church together. This, I think, makes clear how Alfred intended each copy of his book to be used: it was to be set up openly in church so that it could be used for public readings and instruction – for which, of course, the *aestel* would come into its own. Interestingly, a remarkably similar procedure (though without the precious *aestel*) was to be used by that later practical visionary, Thomas Cromwell, to disseminate the English translation of the Bible in Reformation England.

Alfred's practicality also extended to his approach to the art of translation itself. For his books were intended to be, not academic exercises, but things that were useful and were used. This meant in turn that Alfred had to prevent his readers from seeing the late Roman world of Gregory or Boethius, whose *Consolation of Philosophy* Alfred (like Queen Elizabeth I) also translated, as foreign to their own experience and therefore irrelevant to it. Instead, he cut his Roman cloth, very thoroughly, into English dress. The 'senate' becomes the 'Roman *witan*' and 'magistrates', '*ealdormen*'. Most ingenious is his rendering of Boethius's reference to the fleetingness of the fame of even the conqueror Fabricius. Alfred guessed that the name of the Roman hero would have meant nothing to his target English audience. Instead, he went to the root of the name in *faber* ('smith') and, for the unknown Roman, substituted a reference to Weland the Smith, the Germanic smith-god whose smithy the men of Wessex believed to have been a neolithic barrow on the Berkshire Downs. 'Where now', Alfred's inspired translation read, 'are the bones of the famous and wise goldsmith, Weland?'

It was also Alfred, or a member of his intimate court circle, who commissioned the national book of record known as *The Anglo-Saxon Chronicle*. Its chronicle form is deceptively simple (and has deceived many historians). In fact, it is a highly sophisticated piece of historical special pleading, to be put on a par (in approach if not in method) with Bede's *Ecclesiastical History*. Like Bede, the *Chronicle* is a providential history of the Anglo-Saxon people: of their conquest of Britain, of their conversion to (Roman) Christianity, and of their quest for political union. The novelty of the *Chronicle* lies in the role it assigns to Wessex. In Bede, we see the torch of the *bretwalda*-ship (or overlordship) passing from the southern kingdoms of Kent and East Anglia to the strong hands of his native Northumbria. The *Chronicle* picks up the story in the ninth century. In so doing, the intervening, century-long Mercian supremacy of Æthelbald, Offa and Cenwulf is ignored; instead, following his victories of 829, the *Chronicle* hails Egbert of Wessex, Alfred's grandfather, as the eighth *bretwalda*. Finally, the marriage of Æthelwulf, Alfred's father, into the sacred house of Charlemagne, Æthelwulf's pilgrimage to Rome and Alfred's own mysterious anointing there, confer divine sanction on the House of Egbert and mark out Alfred as the eventual heir to its glories.

'Who controls the past controls the future; who controls the present controls the past,' wrote another great Englishman, George Orwell. Alfred was determined that the future should be England as a greater

Wessex, with his own issue on the throne. But the language of the *Chronicle* is just as important as its subject matter. For, as we would expect from Alfred's general approach, the *Chronicle* is not written in Latin, like the chronicles produced elsewhere in Europe, but in the Anglo-Saxon vernacular. And that changed everything. The *Chronicle* was not written by churchmen for churchmen. Instead, it is a king talking to his people in the language that they understand and his people talking to themselves. The *Chronicle* is, in short, the greatest cultural achievement of Alfred's reign and a symbol of national independence and identity that was so powerful that not even the Norman Conquest could extinguish it outright.

Alfred's *kulturkampf* (cultural struggle) began in the years of uneasy peace. But it continued during the Third Viking War of 892–6. The war was as hard-fought as previously. But it was fought differently. For this time the Vikings, after an initial foray, were never able to cross large sections of Wessexian territory. The *burhs*, it seems, had done their work well.

So, too, had Alfred. Three years after the end of the war, Alfred died on 26 October 899, aged only fifty. He still ruled over only part of England. But, as he so clearly intended, his legacy was the permanent unification of the country. The actual work was the task of his sons and grandsons. But it was Alfred, who, in the crucible of the Viking invasions, had forged an idea of England that was more than simply cultural and linguistic, it was political as well. Or rather, uniquely in Europe at the time, it was a combination of all three.

In other words, *Ængla Land* was to be a nation-state, Dark Age style.

4

TRIUMPH AND DISASTER

Edward the Elder, Æthelstan, Edmund I,
Eadred, Eadwig, Edgar I, St Edward,
Æthelred II, Swein Forkbeard,
Edmund Ironside, Cnut, Harold Harefoot,
Harthacnut

AFTER ALFRED'S DEATH, HIS SON, King Edward the Elder, and his grandsons, Æthelstan, Edmund I and Eadred, continued Alfred's policy of uncompromising resistance to the Vikings. Soon they were able to turn the tables and go on the offensive. One by one the Viking kingdoms and lordships were defeated or forced to submit until in 920, at Bakewell in Derbyshire, Edward was acknowledged as overlord by all the surviving powers in northern Britain: Scots, Vikings and Angles alike. With this final piece of the jigsaw in place, Edward, who had already assumed direct rule in Mercia and received the submission of the British princes of Wales, now appeared, not only as king of *Ængla Land*, but as a veritable emperor of Britain.

There was resistance, of course, to this vast growth of West Saxon power, and not only from the Vikings. The Northumbrians had the proud and separate history recorded in Bede and were as reluctant as many of their descendants today to take orders from the south. And the same applied, even more strongly, to the Scots. The result was that the death of each West Saxon monarch was followed by a rebellion and a reassertion of northern independence. But each in turn was put down and the victories – Æthelstan's at *Brunanburgh* in 937 and Edmund's in the east Midlands in 942 – were celebrated by *The Anglo-Saxon Chronicle* in sanguinary verse. Edmund was hailed, in language taken from the old sagas, as 'lord of the English, guardian of kinsmen, loved doer of deeds', while his elder brother Æthelstan was 'lord of warriors and ring-giver to men'. But there was a political message too. The army at *Brunanburgh* was a joint force of Mercians and West Saxons; the achievement of each was celebrated, and the battle seen as the greatest victory since both peoples' ancestors had conquered Britain:

> Never was there more slaughter
> on this island, never yet as many
> people killed before this
> with sword's edge ...
> since from the east Angles and Saxons came up
> over the broad sea. Britain they sought,
> Proud war-smith who overcame the Welsh,
> glorious warriors they took hold of the land.

The message was clear: united we stand in a new, consolidated *Ængla Land.*

Administrative unity, too, was soon imposed on all England south of the Humber. Like Alfred's resistance, the reconquest from the Vikings had depended on the building of *burhs* – such as Hertford, Leicester, Nottingham and Huntingdon – to push the disputed frontier forward and to hold land taken. These *burhs* quickly followed the path of the southern *burhs* and became prosperous centres of population and trade. But they were made the administrative centres of new shires as well. These were modelled on the shires of Wessex and were likewise divided into hundreds. The difference was that they were largely artificial creations, imposed by a powerful and centralized administration and paying little or no regard to former regional and tribal boundaries which had existed before the Viking invasions.

I

This story of more or less unbroken success received a rude shock after the death of Eadred in 955. He was succeeded by his nephew, Eadwig, the elder son of Edmund I, who was crowned at Kingston a few months later.

But, aged only about fifteen, Eadwig had his mind fixed on something other than ceremony and, at the feast which followed the day after the coronation service, the king suddenly withdrew. St Dunstan, the outspoken and reforming abbot of Glastonbury, who had had the ear of both Edmund and Eadred, was deputed to bring him back. Dunstan marched into the royal bedchamber, where he found the king in a threesome with his future wife and mother-in-law, while 'the royal crown, which was bound with wondrous metal, gold and silver gems, and shone with many-coloured lustre, [lay] carelessly thrown on the floor'.

It was an inauspicious beginning. Within two years, Mercia and Northumbria had transferred their allegiance to Eadwig's younger brother, Edgar, and Eadwig's power was reduced to England south of the Thames. Two years later still, Eadwig died on 1 October 959 and was succeeded as king of all England by Edgar.

Edgar had won support by presenting himself as being as serious as his brother was irresponsible. And, once he had succeeded to his whole inheritance, he continued to win golden opinions. One of his first acts was to appoint Dunstan as archbishop of Canterbury. Edgar and Dunstan, who was a frequent attender at court, then went into partnership to enforce the programme of monastic reform which Dunstan had begun as abbot of Glastonbury. Each had his particular concern. Dunstan wanted to impose the order and discipline made possible by the rule of St Benedict. Edgar also saw the political possibilities of the reformed monasticism.

Most important, symbolically, was his purge of the two great adjacent minsters in his capital at Winchester, the Old, where Alfred was buried, and the New, founded by Edward the Elder. In 964, *The Anglo-Saxon Chronicle* notes with some surprise, Edgar 'drove' the existing clergy out of the two minsters, and 'replaced them with monks'. Two years later, in 966, he refounded the New Minster and his munificent gift was recorded in an unusually long and magnificent charter, written in book form. The frontispiece shows Edgar wearing the crown with four fleurons, which Eadwig had cast aside, and presenting the book-charter to Christ in Majesty.

By gifts such as these, Edgar was serving another god: he was promoting the idea of a united *Ængla Land*. Monasteries like Winchester were national institutions; they held land all over the country; they were centres of a self-consciously English culture and, above all, they were royal. Endowed by the king and reformed under his patronage, they were so many counterbalances to the overweening local power of *ealdormen* and other aristocrats. Naturally, some of the *ealdormen* were resentful. But, faced by the united front of king and archbishop, they had no choice but to submit to the reform programme, which carried all before it. At the beginning of his reign there was only one properly constituted Benedictine monastery, Dunstan's at Glastonbury; by the end there were twenty-two.

Another illustration of the ordered, reforming power of Edgar's government is the currency. Since Offa, as we have seen, the quality of the Anglo-Saxon coinage had tended to be high. But the Viking invasions had brought chaos here as everywhere else. In about 973 Edgar felt strong enough to issue a reforming ordinance. Thenceforward, every six years all the silver pennies in circulation were called in and melted down, and reminted with new designs. The reminting was done in local *burh*-mints. But the designs and dies were centrally supplied to the moneyers by the king. This arrangement not only ensured uniformity and maintained standards, it also allowed for a sophisticated management of exchange rates by increasing or decreasing the silver content. No other government in Europe would have been able to conceive or carry out such a programme, which continued to the end of Anglo-Saxon England and beyond. It gave England a currency that was unmatched in quality in Europe, and it laid the foundations for an enviable national prosperity.

But just as striking is the inscription on Edgar's coins. It read: *EADGAR REX ANGLO(RUM)*, 'Edgar, king of the English'. And where there are English, there is an England, or *Ængla Land*, as the Anglo-Saxons called it. The unification of England, as we have seen, was the work of Edgar's immediate predecessors, starting with his great-grandfather, Alfred the Great. Now, seventy years after Alfred's death, his great-grandson Edgar came to Bath to be crowned on Whit Sunday 973. Almost certainly, he had already been crowned long before, perhaps as king of the Mercians. But now, in a vastly grander ceremony, he was to be anointed king of the English; honoured as emperor of Britain, and revered as a second Christ.

Hence the choice of Bath for the ceremony. For here there was a unique combination of a Christian abbey next to the largest, most impressive ruins of Roman Britain. It was an incomparable setting and the ceremony matched the occasion's significance. St Dunstan himself, as archbishop of Canterbury, acted as ecclesiastical master of ceremonies and Edgar performed his part devoutly and decorously. First, he swore a threefold oath, administered by Dunstan: to keep the Church of God and the Christian people in true peace; to forbid rapacity and iniquity in all ranks; to do justice equitably and mercifully. Then he was acclaimed by the people as their king and anointed, as the choir sang the anthem 'Zadok the Priest and Nathan the Prophet anointed Solomon King'. Next he was invested with the insignia of kingship: the ring, the sword, the crown, the sceptre and the rod. Finally, there came the coronation banquet, at which no one, we are told, drank more than he could hold. The king presided, wearing an imperial diadem of laurel interwoven with roses, while the queen had her own separate table.

Immediately after the coronation, Edgar sailed with his fleet to Chester, where, in an acknowledgement of his imperial overlordship, he was rowed on the Dee by six or eight British, Scottish and Irish kinglets. To symbolize his kingship of England and overlordship of Wales, Scotland and the Western Isles his fleet would, every year, sail round the whole island of Britain. Finally, even the strange delay in this second coronation was turned to advantage since, *The Anglo-Saxon Chronicle* reported, the king was in his twenty-ninth year – the same as Christ when He, 'the lofty king/guardian of light', had begun His public ministry. Edgar's reign thus represents the apogee of the Anglo-Saxon monarchy with its idiosyncratic fusion of Germanic, Roman and Christian traditions.

Edgar's coronation ceremony impressed contemporaries – as was intended – and it is the first English coronation of which a full account survives. It also impressed foreigners as well since its text, almost unaltered, was used for coronation ceremonies as far afield as Normandy, Hungary, Milan and perhaps Poland. Even the French coronation, which had at first so influenced the West Saxon, now adopted the magnificent structures, rhythms and rhetoric of Edgar's service. What is most remarkable of all, however, is that the substance of Edgar's service has endured in England to the present, so that the same rituals were enacted and often the same words (in English rather than in Latin) rang out in Westminster Abbey on 2 June 1953 when Elizabeth II was crowned queen, aged twenty-seven and a week after Whitsuntide.

II

Only two years after the ceremony in Bath, Edgar died, still only in his early thirties. Immediately there was trouble, since, for all the political sophistication of England, there were no fixed rules of succession. Edgar left two surviving sons: the elder, Edward, by his first wife, and the younger, Æthelred, by his third, Ælfthryth. Edward was crowned king at Kingston. But Ælfthryth, who had shared in the triumph of Edgar's second coronation at Bath, felt that her son should have taken precedence. The opponents and advocates of monastic reform, the political hot potato of the day, also took sides: the former supported Æthelred and the latter Edward. The result was one of the darkest deeds in Anglo-Saxon history. On 18 March 978, only three years after his accession, Edward was attacked and killed at Corfe in Dorset by his half-brother's retainers, probably on the orders of his stepmother. Edward seems to have been a violent and unattractive young man, but the manner of his death meant that he quickly joined St Edmund as one of England's two most popular royal saints. *The Anglo-Saxon Chronicle* commemorated the transformation from sinful king to royal martyr in verse:

> Men him murdered,
> But God him glorified.
> He was in life an earthly king;
> He is now after death a heavenly saint.

Despite the horror at the assassination, the murder succeeded in its purpose and Æthelred became king.

Æthelred II had one of the longest reigns in English history and is still remembered today as one of our most disastrous kings. This is largely because of his nickname: 'Æthelred the Unready'. The proper Anglo-Saxon form of his nickname, however, was *Unraed*, that is, 'badly advised or counselled'. It is a pun on his name Æthelred, which means 'noble counsel', and it is a product of hindsight first appearing almost a century after his death.

It is also unfair, at least for the earlier decades of the reign. True, his brother's murder tainted his accession and Æthelred himself sowed wild oats in his youth. But, by the 990s, England was enjoying something of a golden age of church-building, and legal and administrative reform. It had also developed a politics of astonishing maturity. There was a rich and powerful aristocracy, whose ranks included scholars and eccentrics as well as soldiers and statesmen. At its apex stood the royal court. This too was peopled with familiar figures: there was a scheming queen mother, an ambitious, foreign queen consort and an unpopular and, as it turned out, treacherous royal favourite. The *witan*, which looked more and more like a proto-parliament, solemnly debated the issues of the day but rarely came up with a solution. Taxes rose to unheard-of levels. There were scandals, faction-fighting and palace coups. Give or take the odd murder or mutilation, it is a picture that could come from any time in the next thousand years of English history, till the death of aristocratic politics in the second half of the twentieth century.

Nevertheless, the essential charge against Æthelred II remains. In his reign, England faced a renewed Viking attack. His ancestor Alfred had made his name and his dynasty's reputation by the courage and resourcefulness with which he had seen off the first. Æthelred, in contrast, failed either to muster an adequate response himself or to inspire others to do so. The result was more than a personal failure. For, without adequate royal leadership, the English achievement of the tenth century turned against itself and the country became a rich, tempting and finally defenceless prey.

The Vikings had always been a dangerous enemy. But, when they returned to England in the 990s, they were stronger and better organized than ever. This was because, in Denmark as in England, the previous century had seen a rapid growth in royal power. Probably under the leadership of their first Christian king, Harold Bluetooth, the Danes had created a formidable military machine. It centred on purpose-built, circular fortresses, such as Trelleborg on the west coast of the island of Zealand. They are laid out with geometrical precision and embody engineering and organizational skills of a high order.

Trelleborg's initial purpose was to enable the Danish king to impose order on Denmark itself. But the Danish warrior-elite did not take kindly to order and there were many rebels. These rebels, dispossessed at home, probably formed the first wave of the renewed Viking attack on England. But they did so well that the Danish kings decided to take over the campaign themselves. The full force of the formidable military machine of Trelleborg was now to be turned on England. It was blitzkreig, even shock and awe, as the English troops assembled on the East Anglian coast were about to find out.

In 991, the Viking fleet sacked Ipswich and then made landfall on an island in the Blackwater estuary near Maldon in Essex. The whole of eastern England was threatened. The Danes' first move was to send a messenger to the English, demanding money to buy them off. The English commander, the *ealdorman* Byrhtnoth, retorted that they should come across the causeway, which linked the island to the mainland at low water, and fight it out like men.

The battle began badly for the English, as Byrhtnoth, who was easily picked out by his height and grey hair, was killed in the first engagement. But his men, outnumbered and outgeneralled though they were, fought on till they were overwhelmed. It was a defeat, but, in its way, a glorious one. The result was that, like the victory of *Brunanburgh*, the defeat at the Blackwater became the subject of another notable Anglo-Saxon war poem: *The Battle of Maldon*. The poem captures perfectly the Dunkirk spirit of the doomed army. But it also tells us in remarkable detail about the men who composed it: these are no faceless, helmeted figures, but real, named individuals. There is an aristocrat from the Midlands, called Ælfwine, a local man, the Essex *ceorl* (yeoman) called Dunnere, and, from far-off Northumbria, a warrior called Æscferth.

So every region of England was represented in this roll-call of the army and each rank of society from the top almost to the bottom. The result was to emphasize the unity of England as a country in which a common sense of nationhood overrode distinctions of locality and class. The poem is propaganda, of course; but it is unusual propaganda at a time when, in most of Europe, horizons were much narrower and loyalty to a local warlord came first and last.

The Battle of Maldon may succeed as literature. But it failed to stimulate another, Alfredian, campaign of resistance. Instead, in the immediate aftermath of the defeat, the English decided, on the advice of the archbishop of Canterbury, to pay a tribute or Danegeld to the Vikings. The intention was to persuade them to leave; the result, of course, was to encourage them to come back for more. And with each raid the violence, and the payments, rose: £10,000 was paid in 991, £16,000 in 994, £24,000 in 1002 and £30,000 in 1007.

The Viking campaign of 1006–7 marked a turning point. Thoroughly contemptuous now of the lack of effective English resistance, the raiders behaved with a flamboyant insolence. They made camp at Cuckhamsley Hill, the meeting place of the Shire Court of Berkshire. And they marched with their spoil past the gates of Winchester itself. They had struck into the heart of Wessex, and neither the shires nor the *burhs*, it seemed, availed anything. The reason, of course, was that these were royal instruments but the king, Æthelred, refused to wield them. Instead, as the people of his ancestral lands were despoiled, the king spent the winter of 1006–7 in safety in Shropshire, far from the raiders' range.

III

Only in foreign policy did Æthelred show any initiative with his decision to take Emma, daughter of Duke Richard I of Normandy, as his second queen. The core of Normandy, named after the *Normanni* ('Northmen'), had been granted by the French king to the leader of a party of Vikings in 911. The Normans had quickly assimilated to French language and culture. But they preserved an ancestral sympathy for their Viking cousins, who were allowed to overwinter in Normandy in 1000 before making the short Channel crossing to the Solent and attacking England in the spring. Æthelred's marriage put a stop to such help. Otherwise, he might have got more than he bargained for.

Emma is the first English queen to emerge fully into the light of history. She was handsome, astute and fertile. And she knew how to use a woman's power, which consisted largely in marriage and childbearing. The result was that, from the moment she married Æthelred and took up residence at Winchester, she became the axis around which English politics turned. For Emma was determined that – let who will be king – it should be her children who would sit on the throne of England.

Emma also had a profound effect on the politics of Æthelred's reign. His mother, to whom he was devoted, died in about 1000. This meant that Emma was not overshadowed by her, as Æthelred's first wife had been. Instead, she soon emerged as a political player in her own right. She may have had a role in the palace coup of 1006, in which several leading *ealdormen* were expropriated, executed or blinded. And she was almost certainly an ally of the man who rode to power on the back of the coup: Eadric

Streona ('the grasper'). Eadric was made *ealdorman* of Mercia the following year and became the king's favourite and minister. His rise, as usually
happens when a favourite monopolizes power, triggered deep resentment.
This further weakened English resistance and led directly to the self-
destruction of the great fleet which the English assembled to use against
the Vikings in 1009.

By this time it was clear to Swein Forkbeard, Bluetooth's son and
successor as king of Denmark, that England was his for the taking. He
invaded in force in 1013, and the north and east quickly submitted to him.
Then followed Winchester, until only London, where Æthelred had taken
refuge, held out. But finally the Londoners, 'because they dreaded what
[Swein] would do to them', surrendered as well. Æthelred sent Emma
and his two sons by her to safety in Normandy, while he first retreated to
the Isle of Wight before joining his family in exile.

But Swein was only a winter-king of England and died on 3 February
1014. What English arms had been unable to do, English weather,
perhaps, accomplished. His death was followed by a succession crisis. The
Danish occupying force chose Swein's younger son, Cnut, as king. But the
English had other ideas and sent to Æthelred to invite him to return – *but*
on certain conditions. As a pledge of good faith he sent his young son,
Edward, as a hostage, to begin negotiations. The complaints against
Æthelred included high taxation, extortion and the enslavement of free
men. By the end of the talks, Æthelred was forced to agree to govern
within the rules established by his predecessors. And the terms of the
agreement still exist today, for they were copied at the time into the
national book of record, *The Anglo-Saxon Chronicle.* It reports Æthelred's
undertaking as follows:

> that [Æthelred] would be their faithful lord, would better each of
> those things that they disliked, and that each of the things would be
> forgiven which had been done or said against him. Then was full
> friendship established in word and in deed and in compact on either
> side.

Embedded here in the prose of *The Anglo-Saxon Chronicle* is the text,
probably even the actual words, of a formal written agreement between
the king and his people. It is the Anglo-Saxon Magna Carta. The

circumstances in 1014, moreover, were very similar to those 200 years later. A political crisis and a foreign pretender brought the king, more or less naked, to the negotiating table. The throne would be his, but on conditions. The king agrees, since he has no choice. The terms and his consent to them are made public and the whole enshrined in a written document. The result is the first constitutional settlement in English history, and it began a tradition which descends through Magna Carta, the Petition of Right and the Reform Acts, down to the present.

And, even at the time, it seemed to open up a new chapter. Wulfstan, archbishop of York, soon afterwards preached a highly political sermon, almost certainly in the presence of the king and the *witan*, on the present discontents and their remedies:

> the rights of free men are taken away and the rights of slaves are restricted and charitable obligations are curtailed. Free men may not keep their independence, nor go where they wish, nor deal with their property just as they desire ...
>
> Nothing has prospered now for a long time either at home or abroad, but there has been military devastation and hunger, burning and bloodshed in nearly every district time and again ... And excessive taxes have afflicted us ...

But the real indication of change was that Æthelred moved decisively and unexpectedly against the Danes, who found their position untenable and retreated back home.

Æthelred's new resolution stemmed, almost certainly, from the new prominence of Edmund, his eldest son by his first wife. Father and son were opposites in character: the former took a firm stand on nothing but his kingly dignity; the latter, as his nickname 'Ironside' indicates, was a man of action in the best traditions of his house. But Edmund's rise meant Streona's decline, and the favourite resisted with all the black arts at his command.

The result drove Edmund to take over the former Viking dominions in the north and east, the so-called Danelaw, in an act of virtual rebellion against his father. At this point, the Danes reinvaded and father and son were reunited. Streona, slighted, betrayed Mercia and Wessex to the Danes, and on St George's Day, 23 April 1016, Æthelred died. Rival meetings of the *witan* took place: that in Southampton elected the Danish claimant; that in London chose Edmund.

Edmund now proceeded to show what Æthelred II, with all the time and resources at his command, could have accomplished if he had tried. In a whirlwind campaign, he fought the Danes to a standstill until finally a partition of England along the line of the Thames was agreed: Edmund took the south and the Danes the north, including London. But a month later, on 30 November 1016, Edmund died, aged about twenty-three. His Danish opponent, Cnut, who was even younger, was now acknowledged as *Rex totius Angliae* ('king of all England').

Would the constitutional ideas of 1014 survive and flourish? Would England? In the circumstances of 1016 it seemed rather unlikely.

IV

Cnut, who became 'king of all England' in 1016, was the most successful Viking ever. His ancestors had raided England; he conquered it. They had exacted tribute; but he, as king of England, controlled English taxes, the English mints and the English Treasury, and he poured out their wealth on his Danish followers. And he did all this while barely in his twenties. No wonder his *skalds*, or court poets, hailed him as the true heir of Ivar the Boneless, the master of the longships and the greatest Dane of them all.

Even before he became king, Cnut had given the English a foretaste of his ancestral Viking ruthlessness. When he had been forced to leave England after his father Swein's death, his last act had been to put in at Sandwich with his fleet. 'There', *The Anglo-Saxon Chronicle* reports, 'he landed the hostages that were given to his father and cut off their hands and ears and noses.' In 1017 it was heads that rolled. Those executed included the sons of three *ealdormen* and Eadric Streona himself, who Cnut seems to have felt had changed sides once too often. The purge extended to surviving members of the dethroned royal family: Eadwig, Ironside's brother, was first exiled and then lured back to England to his death, while Ironside's sons, Edgar the Æthling and Edmund, found refuge at the court of Hungary.

But, by the summer, there were already signs that Cnut wished to balance ruthlessness with reconciliation. 'Before the calends of August

[16 July]', *The Anglo-Saxon Chronicle* states, 'the king gave an order to fetch him the widow of the other king, Æthelred, the daughter of Richard [of Normandy], to wife.'

This statement leaves everything open. Was Cnut marrying Emma to reconcile the English? Or to buy off the Normans? Was she in Normandy? Or in England, perhaps under some form of restraint? And on what terms did the marriage take place? Emma already had two sons by Æthelred; while Cnut himself had an English wife or (as Emma preferred to call her) concubine, Ælfgifu, by whom he also had two sons, Swain and Harold Harefoot. According to Emma's side of the story her marriage agreement with Cnut cut the Gordian knot, since Cnut promised that 'if God should grant her a son by him, he would never appoint the son of any other wife as his successor'. Such a son, Harthacnut, was soon born, and the children of the couple's two previous relationships were disinherited, at least as far as England was concerned.

Emma, crowned queen of England a second time alongside Cnut in 1017 and mother of his heir, now emerged to play a leading part in a series of carefully calculated religious ceremonies which sought to lay the ghost of the recent bloody past. In 1020 Cnut went on progress in Essex, accompanied by Archbishop Wulfstan and other leading magnates. His destination was Ashingdon, where his final, decisive battle with Ironside had taken place. It had been a disastrous day for the English. 'There', lamented the Anglo-Saxon chronicler, 'had Cnut the victory, though all England fought against him ... And all the nobility of the English nation was undone.' On this progress, Cnut 'ordered to be built there a minster of stone and lime for the souls of the men who were there slain' – English as well as Danish. Emma's presence is not mentioned but the priest Cnut appointed to Ashingdon Minster was Emma's client, Stigand.

Emma's role three years later in the translation of the relics of St Ælfheah is much better documented. Ælfheah was the archbishop of Canterbury who had been martyred by the Danish army in England on 19 April 1012 in an orgy of drunken violence. He was half pelted to death with meat-bones and finally felled with an axe-blow to the head. Now Emma, queen of England, with Cnut's 'royal son, Harthacnut', came to Rochester 'and they all with much majesty, and bliss, and songs of praise carried [the body] into Canterbury'.

Long before this, however, Cnut, probably advised by Archbishop Wulfstan, had entered into a formal agreement with his English subjects. It was reached in a meeting of the *witan* held at Oxford in 1018. 'The Danes and English', as *The Anglo-Saxon Chronicle* summarizes, 'were united ... under King Edgar's Laws', which Cnut soon reissued with his own extensive modifications. Cnut then moved quickly to normalize his rule in England. Most of the Danish army and fleet were paid off with a Danegeld of £72,000 besides a separate payment by London. The sum was vast. But, for the first and last time, the Danegeld actually achieved its purpose and all but forty ships returned home. It was not quite business as usual, however, as Cnut continued the deeply unpopular tax known as the *heregeld* or army tax. This had first been imposed as an emergency measure by Æthelred in 1012 but Cnut kept it going to pay a standing army of *housecarls* or retainers. Some would have remained in England as a garrison, but many accompanied Cnut on his wanderings.

For Cnut's interests extended far beyond England: to Denmark, which he inherited in 1019, and Norway, which he occupied in 1028, and even to part of Sweden. The acquisition and retention of this vast empire kept Cnut abroad for most of the 1020s. But he was always careful to keep his English subjects informed. In 1019–20 he sent them an open letter from Denmark, and in 1027 another from Rome, whither he had gone to play an honoured part in the coronation of the Holy Roman Emperor, Conrad II. These letters, 'unparalleled in any other country', complement the spirit of the constitutional settlements of 1014 and 1018. Cnut, as chief executive of England, reports to his subjects as shareholders in a common enterprise. And the analogy of an Annual General Meeting is exact. For the letters – which are addressed, respectively, to 'all [the king's] people ... in England' and to 'the whole race of the English, whether nobles or *ceorls*' – were evidently intended to be read out aloud at Shire and Hundred Courts and *burh* moots. In view of this audience, part of their message is straightforwardly populist:

> I went myself with the men who accompanied me to Denmark [Cnut
> reported in 1019–20], from where the greatest injury has come to
> you, and with God's help I have taken measures so that never hence-
> forth shall hostility reach you from there as long as you support me
> rightly and my life lasts.

Like Alfred, in other words, Cnut is claiming to have settled the Danish question; and, like Alfred, he is a king who takes his people into his confidence.

V

The upshot of all this is that, within a few years of his accession, Cnut the Viking had become more English than the English – at least when he was in England. Nothing better illustrates this transformation than the famous story about Cnut and the incoming tide. Cnut's courtiers proclaimed that his power was so great that he really ruled the waves. To expose their folly, Cnut ordered his throne be carried to the seashore and placed at the water's edge. Cnut forbade the sea to advance. But the waves ignored him and soaked his feet. 'Let all the world know', Cnut told his now shamefaced courtiers, 'that the power of kings is empty and worthless' compared with the majesty of God.

The incident, if true, was a consummate piece of political theatre. But what really matters is that the story is only to be found in the twelfth-century English source of Henry of Huntingdon. For this is Cnut as the English wanted to remember him: the king they had severed from his harsher Nordic roots and remade in their own image as a Christian and a gentleman.

But, of course, a king who was absent from England for almost half his reign had to delegate power. Cnut had been quick to realize this and, as early as 1017, had taken 'the whole government of England ... and divided it into four parts': Wessex, East Anglia, Mercia and Northumbria. Wessex, for the time being, Cnut kept for himself; the other three he gave to so many trusted adherents. The result was to hasten the transformation of the Anglo-Saxon *ealdorman* into the Scandinavian loan-word *eorl* ('earl'). The *ealdorman* was a figure deeply rooted in his shire; the earl, who was responsible for several shires, was a royal appointee who ruled a vast area arbitrarily assigned by the king.

Several of these earls, naturally enough, were Danes. But two of the most successful were English: Leofric, who was made earl of Mercia, and Godwin, whom Cnut created earl of Wessex. Leofric, husband of the famous Lady Godgifu (Godiva), came from an established *ealdorman* family. But Godwin's origins are obscure and disputed. Most likely, he was the son of Wulfnoth, the *thegn* (knight) who had led the mutiny of the English fleet in 1009 against the henchmen of the hated Streona, and, beyond that, the great-grandson of the aristocratic chronicler, the *ealdorman* Æthelweard, who was himself of royal blood.

What mattered, however, was not Godwin's family origins, but the fact that Cnut trusted him – and trusted him enough to advance him to giddy heights. He became a member of the extended royal family through his marriage to Cnut's sister-in-law (some say sister), Gytha, by whom he had a fine brood of sons, who grew up to be proud, quarrelsome and able, and daughters who made good marriages. He built up a huge landed estate, which centred on his private port of Bosham on the Sussex coast. And, by the latter part of Cnut's reign, he operated as virtual viceroy of England: 'what he decreed should be written, was written; what he decreed should be erased, was erased'.

Then, on 12 November 1035, Cnut died at Shaftesbury and was buried in Winchester in the mausoleum of the English kings of the House of Wessex, with whom he had so carefully identified himself in life. Cnut's death in his early forties was evidently unexpected and left all the pieces on the political chessboard in the wrong places – at least from the point of view of the queen dowager, Emma. Her son by Cnut, Harthacnut, was in Denmark, where he had been titular king since 1028. On the other hand, Harold Harefoot, Cnut's son by Emma's rival Ælfgifu, *was* in England, together with his formidable mother, whose appetite for power had been whetted by five very unsuccessful years as regent of Norway.

Which queen would place her son as king? And what moves should Earl Godwin and his fellow power-brokers make? The *witan* met at Oxford soon after Cnut's death to decide the succession. But it split down the middle – or rather, along the Thames. Earl Leofric, 'almost all the *thegns* north of the Thames' and the commanders of the fleet in London threw their weight behind Harold Harefoot, while Godwin and the men of Wessex argued for Harthacnut. Godwin held out for as long as possible. But the weight of opinion against him was too great.

In most other countries, and in almost all subsequent centuries in England, from the twelfth to the seventeenth, such a situation would have led to civil war. But the extraordinarily consensual politics of late Anglo-Saxon England – with their precocious sense of a national interest – instead drove the parties to the unheard-of compromise of a regency.

Harefoot was 'to be governor [regent] of all England for himself and his brother Harthacnut'. The latter's interest was put in the capable hands of his mother, Emma, who, the *witan* also decreed, 'should remain at Winchester with the household of the king her son'. The queen dowager's residence in the capital, with the royal household, Cnut's treasures and Godwin himself as her right-hand man, meant in turn that she was effectively regent in Wessex.

The situation was awkward in any case. But it looks as though it was Emma's ambition that destabilized it. She launched a propaganda war by spreading scurrilous stories about Harefoot's birth. Harefoot struck back by stripping her of 'all the best [of Cnut's] treasure'. But, despite the slight, Emma held out in Winchester 'as long as she could'.

At this moment Emma's two sons by Æthelred, Edward and Alfred, decided to leave the safety of their exile in Normandy and fish in the troubled waters of an England which they had fled more than twenty years previously. Each claimed, innocently, to 'wish to visit his mother'. But no one was deceived. Had Emma encouraged their gamble? Or had Harefoot, as Emma was later to claim, tricked these possible rivals into putting themselves into his power?

Probably as reinsurance, the two travelled separately. Edward made for Southampton but was beaten off and returned to Normandy. Alfred, on the other hand, evaded the English fleet and successfully landed at Dover. But he was soon picked up by Godwin's troops and taken to Guildford. The upshot was another royal murder, which ranked as a *cause célèbre* with Edward the Martyr's death at Corfe. Alfred's men were killed or variously mutilated, while the *æthling* (prince) himself was taken to Ely, where he too was blinded, and 'so carelessly ... that he soon died'.

The deed was done 'by the king's [Harefoot's] men'. But what was Godwin's role? *The Anglo-Saxon Chronicle* said that he handed over Alfred 'because such conduct was very agreeable to Harold [Harefoot]'. Godwin himself later claimed on oath that he was only acting on Harefoot's orders. The issue is important morally: if the first were true, Godwin was an accessory before the fact in Alfred's murder; if the latter, he was innocent. But the political realities were the same. As early as 1036, Godwin had decided that, with Harthacnut still unable to leave Denmark, his cause and Emma's was hopeless, and it was time to conciliate Harefoot.

As usual, Godwin read the runes correctly, and in 1037, following Harthacnut's continued absence, Harefoot was universally accepted as king. Emma, irreconcilable, was driven out 'against the raging winter'. She found refuge in Flanders, where, under the protection of Count Baldwin V, she settled into a comfortable exile in Bruges. Meanwhile, Ælfgifu, who had been both indefatigable and imaginative in winning over support to Harefoot, was triumphant and probably acted as virtual regent for her colourless son.

But Emma in Bruges was not idle either. She had discussions with Edward. She poured out her troubles to her daughter by Cnut, Godgifu, who was married to Henry, son and heir of the Holy Roman Emperor, Conrad II. But everything depended on her beloved Harthacnut. Only he had the power. Finally, in 1039, an agreement with the now independent kingdom of Norway freed his hands in Scandinavia and he set sail with a great fleet of sixty-two ships to join Emma in Bruges. He overwintered there. But, before he could launch an invasion of England, Harefoot died at Oxford on 17 March 1040.

Once more, this time more by good luck than anything else, England had avoided civil war. Instead, the *witan* 'sent after Harthacnut to Bruges, supposing they did well'. But Emma and Harthacnut, who were taking no chances this time, brought the great fleet with them anyway. Raising the vast sums required to pay off the ships would bedevil the politics of the reign: England had got out of the habit of paying the Danegeld and saw no reason to recommence. Harthacnut's other concern was to take his revenge on the regime that had kept him, as he saw it, from his inheritance for five years. Harefoot's body, which had been buried at Westminster, was 'dragged up and thrown in a ditch', and moves, which came to nothing, were made against Godwin for his complicity in Alfred's murder.

Emma was now in her element. As *mater regis* ('queen mother'), she recovered all the wealth and more that she had lost in 1037. But how to guarantee the future? Her son Harthacnut was only in his early twenties. But he was unmarried and the males of Cnut's line were, it was now clear, not long-lived. In the circumstances, Emma turned to her other surviving son, Edward, as the spare, if not the heir that she had always considered Harthacnut to be. In 1041 Edward was recalled from Normandy and, according to *The Anglo-Saxon Chronicle*, 'sworn as king and abode in his brother's court'. It was during this strange period of double kingship that

Emma commissioned the *Encomium Emmae Reginae*, with its frontispiece showing her, Harthacnut and Edward, all three wearing crowns.

But the diarchy did not last long. Emma's fears about Harthacnut's longevity proved correct and he had a seizure during a drinking bout at a marriage at Lambeth. He survived the stroke itself but never recovered speech and died on 8 June 1042. He was unregretted: 'then were alienated from him', *The Anglo-Saxon Chronicle* reports, 'all that before desired him, for he framed nothing royal during his whole reign'. It is a damning verdict and shows that the years of uncertainty which had followed Cnut's death, and the heavy taxation of Harthacnut's reign, had dissipated any remaining English affection for Cnut's house. Its direct male line, in any case, was extinguished. Perhaps it was time to return to the House of Wessex.

5

CONFESSOR AND CONQUEST

Edward the Confessor, Harold Godwinson

EDWARD WAS NOMINATED AS KING almost before the life was out of his predecessor. 'Before [Harthacnut] was buried', *The Anglo-Saxon Chronicle* reports, 'all the people chose Edward for king at London.' Some historians have understood this to mean that Edward II was carried to the throne on a wave of patriotic sentiment for the House of Wessex. It is possible. On the other hand, the verdict of *The Anglo-Saxon Chronicle* suggests, at best, modified rapture: 'they received him as their king as was natural'.

I

By this time, Edward was already nearing forty. He had spent well over half his life as an exile in Normandy and was probably more French than English. Certainly, he seems to have been happier in Norman or French company. Both his coins, whose portrait type is the most realistic yet, and the Bayeux Tapestry show him with a long, rather lugubrious face, and moustache and beard. The beard began as a rather straggly imperial but became more luxuriant with age. In character, he seems to have had something of that other long-term exile, Charles II, about him. He was ordinarily rather lazy about affairs of state, but, when backed into a corner, he could be both cunning and decisive. And he, too, was determined never to go on his travels again.

The difference, of course, lay in their sexual appetites. Later, the fact that Edward was childless was misunderstood by his monkish admirers to mean that, though married for over two decades, he was voluntarily celibate. On this basis he was named 'the Confessor' and honoured as a saint.

But the real Edward was a man and a king of his time. And he did all the things an eleventh-century king had to do. He led his troops and his fleet. He loved hunting, and, when he relaxed of an evening, he liked to listen to the recital of bloodthirsty Norse sagas. Of course, like most English kings, he was pious and showy in his devotions – especially towards the end. But his childlessness, it seems clear, was the result, not of piety, but of mere bad luck – and perhaps of an impossible wife.

Edward's coronation was delayed for the unusually long period of nine months. This allowed for careful preparation; it also enabled the coronation to be timed to coincide with Easter, the principal feast of the Church. 'Early' on Easter Day Edward was crowned at Winchester 'with much pomp'. Archbishop Eadsige of Canterbury performed the ceremony and 'before all the people well admonished [the king]'. The Church, clearly, wanted another Edgar: it remained to be seen whether they had got him.

Eight months later, Edward took what he probably saw as his first steps towards becoming his own man. Accompanied by Earls Godwin and Leofric, he rode from Gloucester to Winchester, 'took his mother unawares' and stripped her, once more, of her lands and treasures. The reason, the Anglo-Saxon chronicler heard, was that Edward resented the fact that Emma's behaviour towards him had been lukewarm at best. 'She was formerly very hard upon the king her son, and did less for him than he wished before he was king, and also since.' Edward soon relented and made a partial restitution. But for Emma, the glory days were over. She was reduced from the regal state of *mater regis* to a mere royal widow. And, instead of dabbling in high politics, she seems to have retired to live out the last years of her life at her house in Winchester, where she died in 1052 and was buried next to Cnut.

But Edward soon exchanged one form of female domination for another. For, on 23 January 1045, he married Edith, Godwin's cultivated, forceful daughter. Her two older brothers had already been made earls: Swein of a new earldom carved out from Wessex and Mercia along the Welsh border, and Harold of East Anglia. United, it seemed, the Godwin family could carry all before it. But there now occurred the first of a series of disastrous quarrels. It was provoked by Swein, who, although the eldest, was the black sheep of the family and seems to have seen himself more as a Danish freebooter than an English aristocrat. He first seduced an abbess and then murdered his cousin, Earl Beorn. Harold was outraged, but Edward, perhaps slyly, eventually pardoned Swein.

Was Edward already tiring of Godwin and his over-mighty family? If so, this would explain why Edward was also building up his own, French, party. His nephew, Ralph of Mantes, son of his sister Godgifu's first marriage, was made earl of Hereford, which had formed part of Swein's much larger earldom. And Robert, the former abbot of the great Norman abbey of Jumièges, was made bishop of London. Then, in October 1050, Eadsige of Canterbury, who had been incapacitated for much of the previous decade, died. There followed a disputed appointment. The monks at Canterbury elected a kinsman of Godwin's. But Edward decided that Robert of Jumièges should have the archbishopric; overturned the election and sent Robert off to Rome to get his pallium (a narrow stole of white wool that marked the papal confirmation of the appointment of an archbishop) from the pope.

Edward can only have intended this as a deliberate challenge to Godwin. Not only was his kinsman slighted, but Canterbury lay at the heart of Godwin's sphere of influence. Worse was to come. In the course of the summer, another of Edward's extended French family, Count Eustace of Boulogne, came to visit the king. Eustace had married Edward's sister, Godgifu, as her second husband, and had had children by her. Was the purpose of his visit, perhaps, to discuss the succession which the childlessness of Queen Edith left vacant? Eustace planned to return via Dover. The unpopularity of the French, already endemic in England, led him to expect trouble, and perhaps even to provoke it. He and his men donned armour and then tried forcibly to quarter themselves in the town. One householder resisted and a Frenchman was killed. A general melee resulted, leaving twenty English dead, and nineteen French, beside the wounded. Eustace complained personally to Edward, giving a slanted version of the story. Edward, happy probably to humiliate Godwin, took Eustace's side and ordered Godwin, as earl of Wessex, to punish the town. But Godwin refused, 'because he was loath to destroy his own people'.

Faced with Godwin's direct challenge to royal authority, Edward convened the *witan* to meet at Gloucester on 8 September. Meanwhile, Godwin, who 'took it much to heart that in his earldom such a thing should happen', summoned his forces. So did Swein (back in the family fold when there was trouble). And so did Harold. The three met at their manor of Beverstone, fifteen miles south of Gloucester. Edward, taken by surprise at the size of Godwin's army, hastily called on the forces of the rival earls, headed by Leofric.

Once again, civil war seemed inevitable. But, once again, it was avoided. Cooler heads pointed out the obvious:

> It was very unwise that they should come together, for in the two armies was there almost all that was noblest in England. They therefore prevented this, that they might not leave the land at the mercy of our foes, whilst engaged in destructive conflict betwixt ourselves.

Matters were therefore postponed to give time for tempers to cool. Hostages were exchanged and the *witan* directed to reconvene in a fortnight in London. In the interim, the balance of forces shifted. The army of the royalist earls was constantly swollen with the arrival of recruits from the distant north. On the other hand, Godwin's 'army continually diminished'. By the time Godwin and his sons had taken up their positions in their London residence in Southwark on the south bank of the Thames, it was clear that the game was up. Stigand, Emma's former confidant, who was now bishop of Winchester, was sent to deliver Edward's ultimatum. Godwin, certain now that he would be condemned, refused to appear before the *witan*, and was immediately outlawed, together with his whole family. This then divided: Godwin, his wife and three of his sons fled to the family harbour at Bosham and thence to exile in Flanders. While Harold, with another brother, rode to Bristol, where a ship was ready prepared to take them to Ireland. Only their sister, Queen Edith, remained at the mercy of her family's enemies, who were now headed by her own husband. In a grim echo of his treatment of his mother, Edward stripped his wife too of her lands and treasures, and packed her off to a nunnery.

When everything was over, *The Anglo-Saxon Chronicle* reflected on the mutability of fortune:

Wonderful would it have been thought by every man that was then in England, if any person had said before that it would end thus! For [Godwin] before was raised to such a height, that he ruled the king and all England; his sons were earls, and the king's darlings; and his daughter wedded and united to the king.

Now all was lost.

It had not happened without planning, of course. Indeed, Edward, despite the apparently fortuitous course of events, seems to have prepared the ground for the coup with care. He even involved those outside the political elite by abolishing the hated *heregeld*, which won him instant popularity.

But the completeness of his success tempted Edward to overreach himself. The most obvious symptom was to invite his nephew William, duke of Normandy, to England. William arrived with 'a great force of Frenchmen' all of whom were entertained at court. We do not know what passed between uncle and nephew. But the suspicion must be that this was the moment when Edward formalized his nomination of William as his heir. According to Norman sources, Robert of Jumièges, on his way to Rome earlier in 1051, had paused in Normandy to convey the initial offer to William. Now, in Edward's moment of triumph, the deed was done. William paid homage and Edward received him as heir. The royalist earls pledged their support, and a son and grandson of Godwin's, who were already in Edward's hands as hostages, were handed over to William to make sure that the exiled Godwins acquiesced.

What was Edward doing? In retrospect, it looks as though he was taking a decision of enormous strategic importance and deciding – no less – that the future of England should be Norman, not Anglo-Saxon.

But, at the time, it may have appeared very different. For the offer to William was not irrevocable. Edward might yet have children of his own, especially if he changed wives, as Archbishop Robert was encouraging him to do. And, even if he did not, he could always change his mind about his nominated heir. Edward, in other words, was using the great expectations of the succession to manage the politics of the reign. Godwin and his family were down but not out. William might prove a useful ally if it came to a showdown. Or he might indeed be the best long-term bet as an acceptable king of England.

II

But such subtleties passed most Englishmen by. To them, it simply looked as if Edward were handing over England to the French. The result was that the balance of opinion, especially in the south-east, now started to shift to the Godwins. Realizing this, the Godwins decided to try their luck in England once more. Harold and his father effected a rendezvous at Portland on the Dorset coast and then made for the Thames estuary. Hitherto, they had behaved like any other marauding army. But now they set themselves to win hearts and minds – and, above all, men. Thanks in large part to Godwin's earlier protection of Dover, they succeeded. They were especially keen to recruit sailors and soon assembled a formidable fleet, which pledged its loyalty to Godwin's cause: 'then said they all that they would with him live or die'.

Godwin now felt strong enough to try the issue with Edward again. The king had taken his stand in London, with the royalist earls and the fleet. As the Godwins' armada approached from the east, Godwin sent to Edward formally to demand restitution, on behalf of himself and his family: 'that they might be each possessed of those things that which had unjustly taken from them'. Edward dismissed the appeal and Godwin's forces clamoured for a fight. But Godwin instead decided to tighten the noose. On Monday, 14 September, his ships successfully shot London Bridge, taking advantage of the flood tide and hugging the south bank at Southwark, where Godwin's own London *burh* was situated. Once past the bridge, Godwin's ships joined up with his land forces, who were drawn up along the Strand. The Godwin fleet and army thus formed 'an angle', as *The Anglo-Saxon Chronicle* puts it, and threatened to trap the king's fleet against the bridge.

It was a situation that would recur in English history. In 1399, for example, Henry Bolingbroke, who had been disinherited of the dukedom of Lancaster by Richard II, returned in force to England. At first Henry announced, like Godwin, that he required only the restitution of what was rightfully his. But, as royalist resistance crumbled, Henry overthrew Richard II and usurped his throne – as had probably been his real intention all along.

A similar outcome seemed on the cards in 1052. But, once again, the instinctive quest for balance in the Anglo-Saxon polity came into play:

They were most of them loath to fight with their own kinsmen – for there was little else of any great importance but Englishmen on either side; and they were also unwilling that this land should be more exposed to outlandish people, because they destroyed each other.

These were the same arguments as in 1051. But they had the opposite effect this time and it was the royalist forces that backed off. Negotiations began, with Bishop Stigand acting once more as intermediary. Meanwhile, Archbishop Robert, who had done so much to provoke the crisis, realized that the game was up and, with his fellow French bishop, Ulf of Dorchester, cut his way out of the City and fled for France 'on board a crazy ship'.

On the 15th the final scene was played out before the *witan*, which met in the king's palace at Westminster. Godwin protested his innocence of all the charges laid against him and exculpated himself before 'his lord King Edward and before all the nation'. Edward, though unwillingly, professed to believe him and gave him the kiss of peace. Godwin and his sons were then restored to their earldoms while his daughter, Edith, resumed her place as queen. It was now the turn of Edward's fallen French followers to be outlawed. The charges were that they had 'chiefly made the discord between Earl Godwin and the king', and, more generally, that they had 'instituted bad laws, and judged unrighteous judgements, and brought bad counsels into this land'. An exception, however, was made in favour of household servants, whom the king was permitted to keep on the proviso that they were 'true to him and all his people'.

Again, these self-same words and phrases echo through the succeeding centuries. In the thirteenth century Henry III was required to divest himself of his French favourites in 1234 and of his Poitevin relations in 1258; while in the seventeenth century the Civil War was ushered in with the charge against Charles I's minister, the earl of Strafford, that he had put discord between king and people. Even in the language of opposition, it would seem, the foundations of English politics were laid in Anglo-Saxon England.

Once the great crisis of 1051–2 was over, Edward II's reign takes on a very different character. The interesting times, apparently, were finished. *The Anglo-Saxon Chronicle*, which had given a breathless, blow-by-blow account of each political drama and its resolution, turns into a bare narrative of events. And there seem to have been rather few of those.

What had happened? And what was Edward's own role in the change? Some historians see him as a broken man. Forced against his better judgement into a reconciliation with a man and a family he detested, he went into a sort of internal exile. He abandoned the affairs of the ungrateful kingdom of England for the kingdom of Heaven and devoted himself, more and more, to his great new monastic foundation of Westminster Abbey.

Edward's Westminster Palace and the adjacent Abbey are represented in the Bayeux Tapestry – and archaeological evidence and contemporary descriptions confirm the broad accuracy of its representation. The Abbey, with a ground plan in the form of a Latin cross, was modelled on the great Norman foundations. One outstanding example is the abbey of Jumièges, which had been founded a decade before in a self-consciously Roman style of grandeur by its then abbot, Robert, Edward's notorious archbishop of Canterbury.

Westminster, however, would outdo all its Norman rivals. Despite the French inspiration, two of the master masons were English, while a third was probably German. Under their direction, work started probably in the late 1050s and proceeded rapidly. It began at the east end, which was the nearest point to the riverside palace which Edward had built a little earlier. The choir was made up of two double bays. Each bay consisted of a pair of semicircular arches resting on plain, round columns, while the bays were divided from each other by massive piers. The crossings, where the choir met the transepts and nave, was surmounted by a lantern, in which four corner staircase turrets clustered around the massive central square tower. The nave, also made up of double bays, was half as long again as Jumièges and probably even higher. At the west end, which the Tapestry shows as work in progress, were two more square towers.

The result was by far the largest and most magnificent church in England and one of the noblest in northern Europe. But why, in the first place, should Edward have bothered to rebuild the poverty-stricken Abbey and nominate it as his burial place? The site, on Thorney Island, was surrounded by barely drained marshland, and all Edward's dynastic connections pointed to Winchester. Contemporaries explained the king's choice by his devotion to St Peter, the Abbey's patron saint. This is no doubt true as far as it goes. But it was the Abbey's proximity to London which counted for most. London had always been the commercial capital. But the events of the eleventh century show it usurping the role of the political capital as well: it had been the last place to hold out against Cnut and it was the scene of the decisive encounters between Edward and the Godwins in 1051–2.

Edward's decision to site his abbey on Thorney Island both reflects this historical development and hastened it. And it means that, to all Edward's other achievements, we should add this: he is the founder of Westminster as the royal and political capital of England.

Edward's enthusiasm for Westminster is real enough. But it does not quite explain his apparent withdrawal and reconciliation with Godwin. Rather, Edward, the great survivor, decided that, if he could not get rid of the Godwins, then he would have to live with them. And, as he was no ascetic, he resolved to live with them as comfortably as possible.

Things were helped by the swift removal of Godwin himself from the political scene. For the tensions of 1051–2 seem to have been too much for the earl's constitution. Within a few days of his triumphant vindication at the Westminster *witan*, he was taken unwell and went back home. Six months later Godwin, with his sons Harold and Tostig, was celebrating Easter with the king at Winchester. On Easter Monday, 12 April 1053, as he was sitting with Edward at table, he had a stroke: 'he suddenly sank beneath [the table] against the foot-rail, deprived of speech and of all his strength'. He was carried into the king's bedchamber and was expected to recover. Instead, he remained speechless and helpless, and, after lingering for three days, died on the 15th. He was buried in the Old Minster, close to his first patron, Cnut.

Godwin's death drew the worst of the venom from Edward's feud with his family. For the king's inveterate dislike of the earl for his part in his brother Alfred's death in 1036 was personal; it did not extend to his sons. On the contrary, Edward's relations with them were correct and, in the fullness of time, even became warm.

This was especially true of Harold, who, following his brother Swein's death on the pilgrimage to Jerusalem, which he had undertaken to atone for his sins, was now the head of the family. He succeeded to his father's earldom of Wessex and soon to his role as *nutricius* or protector of the realm as the king's right-hand man. His other brothers did not have to wait long for their share: Tostig became earl of Northumbria in 1055, Gyrth of East Anglia in 1057 and Leofwin of a newly created earldom of the south-eastern counties bordering the Thames estuary in the same year.

This left the one non-Godwin earldom of Mercia surrounded. Earl Leofric himself, old and perhaps schooled to patience by his wife Godgifu (Godiva), remained impassive. But his son and heir, Ælfgar, kicked against the pricks. He was twice outlawed. And twice he responded by allying himself with the aggressive and successful Welsh king Gruffudd ap Llwelyn and attacking England. Yet twice, too, Ælfgar was pardoned. He was allowed to succeed to Mercia; died in his bed and was in turn succeeded by his young son.

It was almost as though Edward – and Harold – were secure enough once the crisis of 1051–2 was over to allow the luxury of dissent. We can see this strength in the silver penny issued shortly after. The image of the king on the coin is a sharply characterized, realistic portrait – the first such on an English coin. It is also remarkable for its weight of royal symbolism: not only is the king shown with a sceptre but his crown is doubly imperial. The upper portion of the crown is crossed with two arches, like the closed crown of the German Holy Roman Emperor; the lower jewelled circlet, however, is modelled on the diadem of the *basileus*, the Byzantine emperor, and features the same *cataseistae*, or pendants. The St Stephen Crown of Hungary, where Edward the Exile took refuge from Cnut, is of similar appearance and it may perhaps be conjectured that Edward introduced his Hungarian hosts both to the form of the crown and to the formulary of the English coronation, which was also adopted in Hungary.

Should the king be properly known as Edward the Emperor rather than Edward the Confessor?

For the second half of Edward's reign was a period of remarkable prosperity and stability. The continuing struggle for control of Cnut's Scandinavian empire between the rulers of Denmark and Norway meant that they were too busy fighting each other to think seriously of invading England. This meant in turn that the *geld*, or land tax, which continued to be levied despite Edward's ostentatious abolition of the *heregeld* itself, flowed directly into the king's coffers.

A rudimentary treasury was set up at Winchester to administer the funds. It began as a chest under the royal bed in the charge of one or more of the king's bedchamber servants or 'chamberlains'. The chest figures in one of the legends that gathered around Edward as a proto-saint. A thief entered the royal bedchamber; made sure, as he thought, that the king was sound asleep and stole from the chest. He did the same a second night. But, as he came back a third time, he was startled when Edward, who had silently observed his earlier depredations, warned him to be gone as Hugolin the chamberlain was about to enter.

This Hugolin was a real person and, as senior *bur-thegn* or chamberlain, had charge not only of the royal treasures but of important documents as well. But was the under-the-bed chest also real? Modern historians have been sceptical. They have calculated the size of the chest needed to hold the annual yield of the *geld*, and then observed, dismissively, 'some box, some bed'! But they may be being too clever by half. For hands-on royal management of the finances remained a feature of English government to the end of the Middle Ages and beyond. Henry VII counted and chested his own money with his treasurer of the chamber; while under Henry VIII the wealth of the monasteries was decanted into a cash hoard that was kept behind the royal bedchamber in Whitehall and administered by Sir Anthony Denny as chief gentleman of the Privy Chamber. Denny's other duties included the custody of valuables and documents, the control of access and the wiping of the royal bottom.

Where modern historians are right, of course, is that this 'primitive' system of cash hoarding, whether in the eleventh or in the sixteenth century, was underpinned by an elaborate and formalized system of revenue raising. Receipts, in the form of notched sticks or tallies, were issued, and written records, including tax assessments, were kept. And, in sharp contrast with later practice, they were kept in English.

At the same time, the royal writing office developed rapidly too. It was run by the king's priest Regenbald, who probably came from Lotharingia (Lorraine). He used the title of either *regis sigillarius* ('keeper of the king's seal') or *regis cancellarius* ('king's chancellor'). The seal, of which he was keeper, was a metal matrix, or mould, which was used to make a wax impression. The image of the seal, which showed the king enthroned in majesty, with crown, sword and sceptre, was modelled on the seal of the Holy Roman Emperors. But, uniquely, the English seal was double-sided and hung from the document on a tag rather than being impressed on its surface. This meant that even when the document was folded and tied up, the seal could still be left hanging outside, proud and visible.

The visibility of the king's image was important because the document, to which the seal was most frequently attached, was a peremptory royal letter of instruction. Known as a writ, it ordered a royal official that something should be done forthwith: that a case be heard in his court; that a tax be remitted; that a *burh* be punished for its misdemeanours. All this implied a highly sophisticated form of government: the person addressed was a royal official, not a feudal magnate; and the courts which would hear the case, in the shire and hundred, were royal also. But, though they were royal, they were not bureaucratic. Instead, they relied for their operations on the cooperation of the local community of free men. And a surprisingly high proportion was involved: on one Herefordshire estate, for example, it has been calculated that one free man in twenty was engaged in administration at one level or another.

Another mark of the stability of these years was the deliberate reconstitution of the royal family. As we have seen, after Cnut's triumph the children of his supplanted Anglo-Saxon rival, Edmund Ironside, had been packed off to Germany and thence to Hungary. Cnut's intention was that they should be murdered (at a safe distance from English eyes). Instead, they were received as honoured guests. The younger, Edmund, died in Hungary. But the elder, Edward the Exile, married the Princess Agatha and had 'a fair offspring'. In 1054, the princely Bishop Ealdred of Worcester, who was an intrepid traveller, went 'on the king's errand' to the imperial court. His mission was to persuade Edward and his family to return with him to England. The then state of relations between the Empire and Hungary frustrated Ealdred's mission. But the message got through and Edward, Agatha and their children arrived in England in 1057. Edward himself died almost immediately, to the grief of the Anglo-Saxon chronicler. But his wife and children remained in England and his young son, Edgar the Ætheling, was brought up by Edward as his own.

The most striking change, however, and the surest sign of recovery, was that England regained her tenth-century hegemony within Britain. In 1054, Earl Siward of Northumbria defeated Macbeth, the usurping king of Scots; killed many of the Scots nobility and seized immense booty. These events, imaginatively dramatized by Shakespeare, paved the way for the restoration of Malcolm III, son of Macbeth's predecessor, Duncan, in 1057. Two years later, in 1059, Malcolm visited the English court, escorted by Earl Tostig. It was the first such visit by a Scottish king since Kenneth I had come to Edgar's court eighty years previously, also to swear a form of fealty.

Likewise reminiscent of Edgar's reign was the fate of Wales. Harold tried to bring Gruffudd ap Llwelyn to heel in 1056 by negotiation from a position of strength. Gruffudd, recognizing that he was temporarily outmatched, 'swore oaths that he would be a firm and faithful viceroy to King Edward'. But, as soon as he dared, he was back to his old tricks. Finally, in 1063, Harold and his brother Tostig launched a two-pronged attack on Gruffudd: Harold by sea and Tostig by land. Their success provoked an internal rising against Gruffudd, who 'was … slain on 5 August by his own men'. His severed head was surrendered to Harold, who sent it as a trophy to Edward, together with the gilded figurehead and prow of Gruffudd's ship.

It is a remarkable achievement. Edward's coronation seems to have been intended to usher in a new 'age of Edgar'. An observer of Britain in 1063 would probably think that it had succeeded.

But he would have judged too soon.

III

The Anglo-Saxon Chronicle contains no entry at all for 1064. But this is the year, almost certainly, of Harold's ill-fated visit to William of Normandy. There are contemporary descriptions of the visit only in the Norman sources and even they disagree about details. But the broad outlines, as they are presented in the Bayeux Tapestry, seem reasonably clear. Harold took leave of Edward and rode to Bosham, hunting and hawking along the way. He prayed at Bosham Church and ate and drank in the hall before embarking in a single ship with his hawk still on his wrist and his hound under his arm. Was he on a royal mission to renew Edward's offer of the crown to William, as the Norman sources claim? Or was it a pleasure trip that went wrong, as some later English sources argue? At all events he was driven ashore in the hostile territories of Count Guy of Ponthieu. Thence he was rescued by William; accompanied the duke on a campaign against the refractory Bretons, in which he performed wonders of strength and bravery, and finally swore a great oath to support William's claim to the throne at Bayeux (or Rouen or Bonville-sur-Touques or Bur-le-Roi, depending on which version is to be believed). He then returned to England to an apparently grim reception from Edward, who pointed an admonitory finger at him.

What to make of all this? That the visit to Normandy took place and that Harold swore an oath we can accept. But it is impossible to believe that Harold acted voluntarily. However he got to Normandy, he was in the duke's power. As was his younger brother, Wulfnoth. Harold therefore swore under duress and would have discounted his oath accordingly.

Moreover, he soon had more pressing things to worry about.

For, at the beginning of October 1065, Northumbria rose in revolt against Earl Tostig, Harold's brother. Partly, it was a question of style. Tostig was a stranger to the area; he had tried to impose southern customs and he maintained, the northern men felt, unnaturally friendly relations with King Malcolm III of Scotland. But there were also more serious and specific charges: that he had perverted the law to kill his enemies; had robbed churches and had taxed disproportionately. The revolt was no hole-in-the-corner affair. Instead, the Northumbrian *thegns* (nobles) acted collectively and decisively. They killed Tostig's retainers, seized his arsenal at York and confiscated his treasury. Having thus emasculated Tostig's local power, they then chose as their earl Morkere, the younger brother of Earl Edwin of Mercia. Under the nominal command of their new earl, the rebels marched south, gathering the strength of three more counties of Nottinghamshire, Derbyshire and Lincolnshire on the way, till they came to Northampton. There Earl Edwin joined them with the Mercian levies.

All seemed set for another civil war: between north and south and between Godwins and the rest. But, once again, a way out was found, with Harold performing the crucial role of peacemaker. He had gone to Northampton as the king's representative at the meeting of the *witan* convened there, and had returned thence to put the rebels' demands to Edward. No doubt on Harold's advice, Edward accepted them at a second meeting of the *witan* on 28 October at Oxford; replaced Tostig with Morkere as earl of Northumbria and confirmed the Laws of Cnut, which embodied the separate legal status of the Danelaw.

Harold had played the statesman. He had put his country before his family and saved England from civil war. But there was a price: the Godwins were now irretrievably split and Harold's dispossessed brother Tostig had become his deadliest enemy. After the Oxford meeting, Tostig fled with his family to Flanders, where he spent the winter contacting allies and plotting his revenge.

Edward by this time was about sixty. It was old for the time but his health was excellent. When, for instance, he received the news of the Northumbrian revolt he was hunting with Tostig in Wiltshire. But the political storm of the autumn, which came from a blue sky, affected him badly. He celebrated Christmas Day with the usual pomp. But on the 26th he took to his bed and was too ill even to attend the consecration of his new abbey at Westminster on the 28th.

Over the next few days, his condition worsened and he alternated between fitful sleep and delirium. As he shook with a particularly violent seizure his terrified attendants roused him and all his old lucidity seemed to return. He had had a prophetic dream, he explained. God's curse was on England for her sins, and her troubles would cease only when the trunk of a green tree, which had been cut in half, reunited of itself and bore leaf again.

Was he really prophesying the fate of England and the House of Wessex? Or was it only, as the ever secularly minded Archbishop Stigand whispered to Harold, that he 'was broken with age and disease and knew not what he said'?

As well as the archbishop and Earl Harold, the group gathered in the royal bedchamber included Robert fitzWimarch, the king's kinsman and *staller* or master of the horse, and Queen Edith herself, 'who was sitting on the floor warming his feet in her lap'. Edward, now fully himself, first spoke to Edith, beseeching God to be gracious to her: 'for certainly she has served me devotedly, and has always stood close by my side like a beloved daughter'. Then he turned to Harold and said, 'I commend this woman and all the kingdom to your protection'. The words do not quite amount to a bequest of the crown, but they were the next best thing. That Edward had nominated Harold as his heir was also stated as sober fact by *The Anglo-Saxon Chronicle*; it was even admitted by the Norman sources – though, in view of the earlier undertakings of both Edward and Harold, they denied the validity of the bequest.

Edward's final request was that his death should not be concealed, so that all his subjects could pray for his soul. He had his wish. He died on 5 January and was buried in his new abbey on the 6th.

On that same day, the Feast of the Epiphany, and in the same place, Harold was crowned king of the English. It was a peaceful, unchallenged succession and, as the ceremony took place so quickly, it must have been both anticipated and prepared for. Harold's other moves display a similar confidence and good sense. He married Ealdgyth, sister of Earls Morkere and Edwin, as his queen. And he went on a progress to the north. He was back in London from York by Easter, which fell on 16 April.

But, a week later, on 24 April, Halley's comet appeared in the skies and remained there till 8 June. It was universally taken as a portent of disaster. In the Bayeux Tapestry a group of men marvel at the flaming comet in the sky; it is labelled ISTI MIRANT STELLA, 'these men marvel at the star'. A messenger is shown bringing the news to Harold, whose evident anxieties are reflected in the ghostly fleet of empty ships which appear beneath him, in the margin.

IV

But the disaster seemed long in coming. Tostig made the first moves, raiding from the Isle of Wight to Sandwich and thence to Lincolnshire. He fled from Sandwich with the approach of Harold, who had assembled 'so large a force, naval and military, as no king collected before in this land'. And he was driven out of Lincolnshire by the brother earls, Edwin and Morkere. He then took refuge with his bosom friend, Malcolm III, in Scotland.

With Tostig out of the way, Harold was able to put his forces to the use for which he had raised them and guard the south coast against William: 'for it was credibly reported that Duke William from Normandy, King Edward's cousin, would come hither'. Harold stationed himself on the Isle of Wight, which enabled him to shadow perfectly the fleet that William was building, directly opposite, at the mouth of the River Dives. But then, about 8 September, shortage of provisions forced Harold to stand his forces down. It was a blow. But not, apparently, a bad one as the usual campaigning season was almost over.

But, just when he seemed safe, events started to run hard against Harold. For the stand-off in Scandinavia, which had given England three decades' respite from the Vikings, now started to resolve itself. In 1062, King Harold Hardrada of Norway defeated King Swein of Denmark at the battle of Nissa, and two years later they made peace. Either was now free to take advantage of Edward's death and attack England as the self-proclaimed heir of Cnut.

Harold Hardrada took the initiative. Though just over fifty, he was a formidable warrior of the old Viking type. He was bloodthirsty, and, in his own saga, gloried in his deeds:

> Now I have caused the deaths
> Of thirteen of my enemies.
> I kill without compunction
> And remember all my killings.

Harold, he determined, should be his fourteenth victim. He set sail for England with a huge armada of 300 ships; landed at the Tyne and linked up with Tostig, who swore fealty to him. Then they sailed up the Ouse towards the old Viking city of York. En route, they were intercepted by Earls Edwin and Morkere. Both sides suffered heavy losses when they met on 20 September. But Hardrada and Tostig were left in possession of the field and entered York.

Harold, who meantime had force-marched his troops from London, arrived at Tadcaster on the 24th. There he heard that Hardrada and Tostig had already moved a few miles north-east of York to Stamford Bridge, to receive hostages and the submission of the countryside. Instead, Harold took them unawares in a headlong assault in which Hardrada and Tostig were both killed. As the invaders turned to flee, a lone Norseman held the bridge and prevented the English pursuit. But an Englishman somehow got under the bridge and 'pierced him terribly inward under the coat of mail'. The pursuit now became a massacre, which was halted only by Harold himself. Barely 25 of the 300 ships which Hardrada had brought were left to sail home.

It was the most total, complete victory that the English had ever won over the Vikings. But there was no time for celebration as, immediately after Stamford Bridge, the wind turned and William was able to set sail.

He landed unopposed at Pevensey on 28 September and occupied the old Roman fort of *Anderida*. Then he moved a few miles north-east to the more strategically important site of Hastings, where he erected a wood-stockade castle.

What would Harold do? To fight two major battles within days of each other was unheard of. But that was what Harold resolved on. After returning from the north, he spent about a week in London, gathering more men and resting such crack troops as he had brought down from the north. Then, before his preparations were fully complete, he force-marched south towards Hastings. His intention seems to have been to repeat the success of Stamford Bridge and take William unawares. Instead, William got news of his approach on 13 October and the two sides took up battle stations the following day: Harold on top of the hill where Battle Abbey now stands; William on Telham Hill. The English fought on foot, forming a shield wall as at Maldon, which they defended with battleaxes and throwing spears. The Normans attacked with mounted and armoured knights and foot archers. As they clashed the Normans cried *Dieux aide* ('God help us!'), while the English chanted *Ut, ut!* ('Out, out!')

The two sides were evenly matched and the balance, insofar as the different, contradictory accounts can be disentangled, swung this way and that. Harold's brothers, Earls Leofwin and Gyrth, were cut off and killed. But then a large detachment of Normans were worsted and threatened to flee. They were rallied by William's half-brother, Bishop Odo of Bayeux, waving his baton (*baculus*). More confusion was caused by a rumour that William was down, and he raised his helmet to identify himself. This seems to have been the turning point. Perhaps the English had broken ranks to pursue the apparently fleeing French. Perhaps the steady rain of arrows was beginning to tell. At any rate, first Harold's bodyguard was slaughtered; then the king himself was killed, disabled apparently by an arrow in the eye and then cut down with a sword-blow to the thigh. With the death of the king, the English fled and William was master of the field – and, as it turned out, of England.

The result was the death of one world and the birth of a new. Anglo-Saxon England had been a nation-state, in which rulers and ruled spoke the same language. This now ceased and, for the next four centuries, England was administered in Latin and governed in French.

Anglo-Saxon, instead, became the patois of the poor and dispossessed. On the site of his victory William founded Battle Abbey. It was built on the hill where the English formed their shield-wall phalanx and the high altar is said to mark the spot where Harold fell. The size of the abbey also tells its own story: like the Normans themselves, it dominates the landscape and crushes the nearby settlement. Even its name is foreign and French: *Bataille*.

But what of the ideas and institutions of the Anglo-Saxon state, with its notions of consensual politics, of participatory government and a monarchy that, as 1014 had shown, was in some sense responsible to the people? How would these fare under new rulers with a new language and new values? Would they vanish? Or would they transmute and survive?

PART II

THE MEDIEVAL
MONARCHY

6

SUBJUGATION

William I

THE FIRST PART OF THIS BOOK traced the history of Anglo-Saxon England from its beginnings to the crisis of the Norman Conquest, when, as one contemporary put it, 'God ordered that the English should cease to be a people'.

But the institutions of the Old English state proved more resilient and, within forty years of Hastings, the English could celebrate the English conquest of Normandy and the rebirth of an English nation. It was polyglot and multicultural and found itself retelling the Anglo-Saxon past in Latin or Norman French. But it was, finally, the values and practices of Anglo-Saxon politics which survived and came to dominate the history of medieval England.

I

William the Conqueror is perhaps the greatest man to have sat on the throne of England; he is certainly one of the most unpleasant. He was covetous, cruel, puritanical, invincibly convinced of his own righteousness and always ready to use terror as a weapon of first, rather than last, resort. He was also deeply pious and sure that God was on his side.

And the extraordinary course of his career gave him every reason for this belief.

William was born around the turn of the year 1027–8 in Falaise, Normandy. His father, Robert, was younger brother of Duke Richard III of Normandy and his mother, Herleva, was the daughter of a furrier or skinner. Six months later, Richard was dead, some said of poison, and

Robert succeeded him as duke. Robert was not an effective ruler. During his reign the great Norman landed families seized the leading offices in the ducal household and made them hereditary. They likewise took over the local position of *vicomte* or sheriff. This last was especially important. Since the *vicomte* controlled the local administration of finance and justice, it meant that the duke was losing control of his dukedom – just as his own independence vis-à-vis the king of France was a symptom of the fragmentation of the kingdom into a series of largely independent territorial principalities.

Robert's personal life was more successful. He and Herleva never married but their relationship was close, perhaps even loving, and Robert always treated William as his son. Shortly before he left on pilgrimage to Jerusalem in 1035, he had the Norman magnates swear fealty to William as his heir and had the bequest confirmed by his overlord, Henry I, king of France. Robert never returned from his pilgrimage, and later in 1035, William succeeded as duke. He was still only in his eighth year.

Predictably, his minority was troubled. Two of his guardians were killed; his steward, Osbern, was murdered in the duke's bedchamber as William slept, and in 1047 he was saved from deposition only by the personal intervention of King Henry I, who joined with William to defeat the rebels in battle at Val-ès-Dunes.

William was twenty and his victory marked his coming of age. He was now his own man and he quickly made his mark. In about 1050 he married Matilda, daughter of Count Baldwin V of Flanders; in 1051 he was apparently offered the throne of England by Edward the Confessor, and in the following year he was strong enough to go on the offensive against his enemies. These were headed by Count Geoffrey Martel of Anjou, who in 1051 conquered the county of Maine. This made him William's immediate neighbour with, thanks to the revolt of the lord of the castles of Alençon and Domfront, a back door into Normandy itself. William resolved to close it. Geoffrey backed off from battle and William was able to pick the disputed castles off, beginning with the lightly defended Alençon. The defenders beat pelts on the walls in mocking reference to William's birth. Once he had captured the place, William retaliated by cutting off their hands and feet. Domfront then surrendered without a struggle.

William had got what he wanted. But, in so doing, he had aroused a fear and loathing that he was never able to shake off. The immediate result was a *renversement d'alliances* in northern France, as Count Geoffrey and King Henry, hitherto inveterate enemies, went into alliance against the upstart. Two invasions of Normandy took place which William had difficulty in fighting off. But in 1060 both Geoffrey and Henry died and were succeeded, respectively, by a weakling and a minor. William never looked back from this extraordinary stroke of luck, which gave him a free hand in France and, it turned out, in England. He seized the county of Maine in 1062, claiming, as he was to do in England, that the late count had nominated him as his heir if he died childless. Then in 1064 he launched a successful attack on Brittany, in which, as we have seen, Earl Harold of Wessex had distinguished himself. Finally, in 1066, he won the battle of Hastings.

But winning the battle was not the same as winning England. To do that would take seven more years of almost continuous, often bloody fighting, and would involve an almost complete reversal of political strategy.

In the immediate aftermath of Hastings, it was far from clear that all was lost for the English: William had only a toehold on the south coast and only a tiny proportion of the available manpower had been thrown against him. The problem, essentially, was one of leadership. The Godwins had monopolized political power. But, between them, the two battles of Stamford Bridge and Hastings had wiped them out. The Mercian earls, Edwin and Morkere, survived, as did Earl Waltheof, the son of Siward of Northumbria. But the two former had been bloodied by Harold Hardrada and Tostig and were, in any case, more used to an oppositionist role against the Godwin hegemony than to leadership in their own right.

Archbishop Ealdred of York stepped into the breach. He had played a leading part in bringing back the family of Edward the Exile to England and now, together with the leading citizens of London, he sought to have Edward's surviving son, the fifteen-year-old Edgar the Æthling, nominated king, 'as he was quite natural to them'. Following this lead, Earls 'Edwin and Morkere promised that they would fight with them'. It was a moment for decisive action. Instead, as *The Anglo-Saxon Chronicle* bitterly observed, 'the more prompt the business should ever be, so was it from day to day the later and worse'.

And they faced an opponent, of course, who was both ruthless and a master of timing. After the battle, William had returned to his fortified camp at Hastings to wait and see whether the English would submit. When they did not, he first marched to the old Godwin manor of Southwark at the southern end of London Bridge. But the City held out and he decided that his forces, which probably numbered only about seven thousand men, were not strong enough for a frontal assault on London. Instead, he resorted to his favourite weapon of terror. Riding in a swift arc round London, from the south to the north-west, he 'ravaged all the country that he overran'. After a few days of this, the demoralized English leadership had had enough and made their formal submission to William twenty-eight miles north-west of London at Berkhamsted in Hertfordshire:

> where Archbishop Ealdred came to meet [William], with child Edgar, and Earls Edwin and Morkere, and all the best men from London: who submitted them for need, when the most harm was done.

It was a grim parody of the usual recognition ceremony by the *witan*.

Why had English morale collapsed so quickly and so completely? The explanation seems to be that the shattering defeat at Hastings was taken as God's judgement on the nation's sins. The possibility, after all, had always been latent in Bede's providential history of the Anglo-Saxon people. The Britons had forfeited their territory to the invaders, he explained, because of their sins. Now, clearly, it was the turn of the English to be deprived by the Normans for *their* wrongdoing. Hence the surprisingly unrancorous verdict of *The Anglo-Saxon Chronicle* that 'the Frenchmen gained the field of battle [at Hastings], as God granted them for the sins of the nation'.

How long this mood of resigned submissiveness would last was, of course, another matter.

Nevertheless, the Anglo-Saxon tradition of consensual monarchy still had some life left in it. Once again, it was Archbishop Ealdred who tried to rescue something from the wreck in William's coronation as king of England. This took place on Christmas Day 1066 in the Confessor's abbey at Westminster with Ealdred himself as the principal celebrant:

Archbishop Ealdred hallowed him king … and gave him possession with the books of Christ, and also swore him, ere he would set the crown on his head, that he would so well govern this nation as any before him best did, if they would be faithful to him.

Seen in this light, William's coronation becomes another contract between king and people, as had been agreed by the last foreign conqueror, Cnut, at the Oxford *witan* of 1018.

Maybe William, who was always vehement in his assertion that he was the true heir of his 'kinsman', Edward the Confessor, sincerely shared in these hopes. But the confusion which surrounded the remaining ceremonies of the coronation highlighted the difficulties in the way. After William had sworn the oath, Ealdred in English and Bishop Geoffrey of Coutances in French asked the people whether they would have William for their king. The loud acclamations that followed alarmed the troops guarding the Abbey and, as a precaution, they fired the surrounding houses. Much of the congregation, panicking in turn, rushed out of the church, leaving the clergy and the king, who is described as trembling from head to foot, to conclude the ceremony.

These events were sufficient to remind William of the dangers of remaining in London, exposed to the 'fickleness of the vast and fierce populace'. Soon after the coronation, he withdrew to Barking, at a safe distance to the east of the City. And thence, in March 1067, he returned to Normandy to spend the remainder of the year celebrating his victory. Along with vast spoils, William took with him (nominally as guests but in reality as hostages) most of the surviving English political elite, including Archbishop Stigand, Edgar the Æthling and Earls Edwin, Morkere and Waltheof. In their place, William left a wholly Norman government, headed by two of his closest associates: Bishop Odo of Bayeux, who was his half-brother by Herleva's subsequent marriage to Herluin de Conteville, and William fitzOsbern, one of the leading Norman magnates. And Odo and fitzOsbern lost no time in giving England the firm slap of Norman-style government: they 'wrought castles widely through this country', *The Anglo-Saxon Chronicle* reported, 'and harassed the miserable people'.

II

One of William's first acts in England had been to build a castle to secure his camp at Hastings. The scene is vividly represented in the Bayeux Tapestry. William sits in council with his two half-brothers, Bishop Odo and Robert, count of Mortain. The latter issues the order to build the castle. Workmen, with picks and shovels, throw up the pudding-shaped *motte* or mound, which is crowned with a wooded stockade. The motte was one essential feature of the castle. The other was the *bailey* or stock-aded enclosure at the foot of the motte.

These motte-and-bailey castles, like the mounted knights and archers who had won Hastings, were another mark of the Normans' military superiority. They were standardized, quick and easy to build using forced labour and the plentiful supplies of local timber; and, above all, they were effective.

On his march to London after the battle of Hastings, William strength-ened the fortifications of Dover and, from his residence at Barking, he used the first weeks of 1067 to supervise the construction of another castle at London, to the south-east of the City on the site of the present Tower. William's first two English castles, at Hastings and Dover, were designed to secure his communications with Normandy; his third, at London, was intended to overawe the capital city. Now Odo from his base at Dover, and Robert from his at Norwich, were building more.

Anglo-Saxon England had seen nothing like them. The *burhs*, or forti-fied towns, were designed to protect the people. The motte-and-bailey castles were there to intimidate them. And they did. With their raw earth and wood, set in a tree-denuded landscape, each was the symbol of a profoundly alien military occupation.

But, despite the castles and the heavy-handedness of William's two regents, the prospects for Anglo-Norman cooperation still seemed reasonably good when William returned to England on 6 December 1067, in time to celebrate the feast of Christmas in his new kingdom. Early in the new year, there was a little local difficulty at Exeter, where Harold's mother, Gytha, had taken refuge with her household. The town held out against the king for two weeks, despite William's typical tactic of having a hostage blinded within sight of the walls, and the defenders inflicted heavy casualties on William's troops. Nevertheless, they were granted easy terms: yet another castle was built; otherwise, William wanted to show that life could return to normal under his rule.

Indeed, by April William felt secure enough to bring his wife Matilda to England. And, on Whit Sunday, 11 May 1068, 'Archbishop Ealdred hallowed her for queen at Westminster'. William's reunion with Matilda was evidently a happy one and their youngest son, the future Henry I, was born within the year. The political climate equally seemed set fair. The court that gathered for the coronation was unusually full and it was evenly balanced between Norman and English magnates.

But, within a few months, this fair weather turned to foul and any hopes for an Anglo-Norman state were dead. In the course of the summer, some of the most distinguished English elite chose exile: Harold's mother, Gytha, 'and the wives of many good men with her', went to St Omer in Flanders; while Edgar the Æthling with his mother Agatha and sisters Margaret and Christina took refuge in Scotland at the court of Malcolm III. But others turned to rebellion: Earls Edwin and Morkere rose in the Midlands and Gospatric in Northumbria, where William had made him earl. Both their motives and strategy are obscure. And William, as usual, moved too fast for whatever plans they may have had to mature. First he advanced to Nottingham. This cut Edwin and Morkere off from their northern allies and they had no choice but to surrender. Then William marched to York, at which point Gospatric and 'the best men' fled to join Edgar in Scotland. Finally the king returned south via Lincoln. And everywhere he went he built a castle, as *The Anglo-Saxon Chronicle* reports:

> He went to Nottingham, and wrought there a castle; and so advanced
> to York, and there wrought two castles; and the same at Lincoln and
> everywhere in that quarter.

Most ambitiously of all, he set up a Norman, Robert de Commines, as earl of Northumbria, with another new castle at Durham.

With the north apparently settled, William and Matilda returned to Normandy in late 1068. But it proved to be a lull before a far greater storm. Early in 1069, the Northumbrians rose against Earl Robert; took Durham Castle; murdered the earl and slaughtered the garrison. Most ominously, having been joined by the exiles in Scotland, Edgar the Ætheling and Earl Gospatric, they took York, where, with the agreement of the citizens, Edgar was proclaimed king. At the same time, aid was solicited from King Swein of Denmark, who still persisted with his own claim to the English throne.

This was even worse than the Northumbrian revolt of 1065. Then, the Northumbrians had chosen their own earl; now they had elected their own king. Once more, William made a lightning march to York and took the rebels unawares. He captured and sacked the city, not sparing the Minster, and then, after refortifying and regarrisoning it, returned south.

But the leaders had escaped and were still at large when the Danish fleet landed in the Humber in September 1069. The Danes and the English rebels, who now included Earl Waltheof, joined forces and on 20 September captured York, where they demolished William's castles and slaughtered the French garrison. It was the third time that the city had changed hands within the year. And William had to set out on his third northern expedition to recover it. He was determined that it should be his last.

First, he came to terms with the Danes. Lacking the ships to attack their fleet, William bought them off with a Danegeld, in return for which they promised to leave before Easter. This distraction out of the way, he turned to settle accounts with his own subjects. Once again, his weapon was terror. But this time the scale was infinitely larger. On his march north through Yorkshire, he systematically ravaged the countryside: destroying crops, killing livestock and burning villages. He reached York in time for Christmas. The city was a ruin, but William kept the feast with his accustomed splendour and wore the crown and regalia which had been brought up specially from the treasury at Winchester. The north, he was determined, should know who was king, even if he were king of a wasteland.

After the celebrations, the destruction was carried still further north, far into Durham. Eighteen years later, the countryside still bore the scars and the Domesday Book describes dozens of villages between York and Durham as *wasta* ('waste'). 'Waste' is a technical term. It does not necessarily mean that the land had been devastated; rather, that it was uninhabited, uncultivated and hence untaxable. This technical distinction is important. But it was William's actions that had made so much of the north *wasta* in whatever sense of the term. And, in so doing, he had killed tens of thousands by the sword, starvation and disease.

The Harrying of the North, as it became known, shocked an unshockable age. Even the twelfth-century chronicler Orderic Vitalis, an Anglo-Norman and a self-consciously balanced writer, is unreserved in his condemnation:

> Never did William such cruelty; to his lasting disgrace, he yielded
> to his worst impulse, and set no bounds to his fury, condemning the
> innocent and the guilty to a common fate.

'I assert', Orderic concluded, 'that such barbarous homicide could not pass unpunished' – by God, if not by man.

But, whatever its morality, the terror achieved its purpose. The north would not trouble William again.

III

The centre of resistance now shifted south to the Fenlands of East Anglia. Its many monasteries, such as Peterborough and Ely, saw themselves as guardians of Anglo-Saxon faith and culture; while the landscape of marshes and islets, criss-crossed by a watery maze of rivers, streams and meres, provided ideal territory for guerrilla warfare. The leader of the Fenland revolt was a local *thegn*, Hereward, who was joined by a large and shifting coalition. His first allies in 1070 were the Danes, who had broken their promise to return home. Hereward joined forces with them to sack Peterborough and to strip it of its treasures to prevent them from falling into the hands of the Frenchman Thorold, whom William had appointed abbot. This sacrilegious attack, by an Englishman on a great English monastery, opened up a gulf between last-ditchers, like Hereward, and more cautious compromisers, like the Anglo-Saxon chronicler, himself a monk of Peterborough, who denounced 'Hereward and his gang'.

All members of the Anglo-Saxon elite faced a similar choice. Their eventual decision must have depended on personal circumstance, family connection and even chance. But, by and large, administrators, like the Anglo-Saxon chronicler himself, who 'lived sometime in [William's] court', chose compromise, as did the financiers and moneyers, while the political aristocracy joined Hereward in the last ditch. In the course of 1071 both the Mercian brothers Earls Edwin and Morkere renounced their allegiance and went underground, 'roam[ing] at random in woods and in fields'. Edwin was 'treacherously slain by his own men' on his way to Scotland, but Morkere made it 'by ship' to Hereward's last redoubt in the heavily fortified monastery of Ely. There he was joined by the rump of Northumbrian resistance, led by Bishop Æthelwine of Durham, who came 'with many hundred men'. William now launched an all-out amphibious assault. Ely was blockaded to the north by ships, while, to the west, the land attack took place along a specially built, two-mile-long causeway. Trapped, most of the rebels surrendered. Morkere was imprisoned for life; Æthelwine was deprived of his bishopric and sent to the monastery of Abingdon, where he soon died, while the lesser rebels were imprisoned, blinded or had limbs amputated 'as [William] thought proper'. Only Hereward and the diehards refused to bow the knee; instead Hereward 'led [them] out triumphantly' – to escape no one knows where and to live in legend for ever.

With the fall of Ely and the extinguishing of the last spark of English resistance, William was free to turn against Scotland. Malcolm III owed his very throne to Edward the Confessor. Moreover, in 1069 he had married Margaret, sister of Edgar the Ætheling. She was a powerful character, who became a force in Scottish politics in her own right. For all these reasons, Malcolm had been happy to offer protection and occasional assistance to English refugees from William. William now determined to close this back door into his kingdom. In 1072, he led a joint naval and military expedition to Scotland. At first, Malcolm retreated before William. But, beyond the Forth, the two kings met on the borders of Perthshire and Fife and agreed the Peace of Abernethy. Malcolm became William's vassal; surrendered hostages and, almost certainly, agreed to stop supporting his brother-in-law, Edgar the Ætheling.

But the process of disengagement was handled slowly and with due regard to decorum. Edgar returned to Scotland in 1074 from his then place of exile in Flanders. He was given a warm reception by the king and queen but was encouraged to seek a reconciliation with William. Edgar did as he was advised and William graciously accepted his overtures. Loaded with gifts, Edgar was then dispatched to William in Normandy.

'William received him with much pomp, and he was there afterwards in his court, enjoying such rights as he confirmed to him by law.'

At least Edgar's cage was golden.

It remained only for William to take over the English Church and Normanize it as completely as the English state. This, of course, was a battle which had to be fought with spiritual weapons. But William proved as adept at deploying these as fire and sword. Back in 1066, he had begun by a determined campaign to win papal support for his claim to the English throne. William's arguments were given a mixed reception in Rome, as Hildebrand, then an archdeacon and a leading figure of the papal court, reminded the king in a subsequent letter:

> I believe it is known to you, most excellent son, how great was the love I have always borne you ... and how active I have shown myself in your affairs; above all, how diligently I laboured for your advancement to royal rank. In consequence I suffered dire calumny through certain brethren insinuating that by such partisanship I gave sanction for the perpetration of great slaughter.

The premonitions of the 'certain brethren' were of course right. Nevertheless, the then pope, Alexander II (1061–73), was persuaded to give William's expedition his blessing and to equip it with a papal banner.

And the pope proved equally accommodating after William's victory by sending two cardinal-legates to oversee the reform of the English Church. The legates arrived in England in the spring of 1070 and were met by William, fresh from the Harrying of the North, at Winchester. There they celebrated Easter and the king and legates presided jointly over a council of the English Church. It began with William receiving – like the Carolingians but uniquely for an English king – a second, papal, coronation at the hands of the legates. Then the business of reform began. King and pope saw this differently. For the papacy, it was a question of removing unworthy bishops and abbots, who were incompetent, sexually incontinent or owed their appointment to anti-popes. For William, it was simpler: he wanted to get rid of politically unreliable Englishmen from high ecclesiastical office. Fortunately, the two different objectives coincided in practice, and when the council was over only two Englishmen retained bishoprics: one, Wulfstan of Worcester, would become a saint; the other, Siward of Rochester, was senile.

A second council, held at Whitsuntide, started to fill the resulting vacancies. William's favourite churchman, Lanfranc of Bec, was made archbishop of Canterbury in place of the deprived, disgraced and now imprisoned Stigand; while York, left vacant by Archbishop Ealdred's death in 1069, was given to Thomas, a canon of Bayeux, who was doubly qualified as both a former pupil of Lanfranc and a protégé of Bishop Odo.

There is no doubt that Lanfranc and the rest were infinitely superior as churchmen to those they replaced. But it is also the case that they were outsiders, with an outsider's indifference or even hostility to native customs and traditions. Buildings that the Anglo-Saxons thought venerable they saw merely as old-fashioned; locations that were sanctified by memory and the experience of countless English generations were merely inconvenient. The result was a wholesale relocation and rebuilding that transformed both the physical and the organizational fabric of the English Church. The seats of one third of English bishops were moved, from the countryside into thrusting towns. And everywhere, with the Norman fondness for glossy and grandiloquent structures, new buildings replaced old. The fate of Ely is typical. Within ten years of Hereward's final defeat and disappearance into legend, there was a Norman abbot at Ely and work had started on the building of the present vast church, whose massive walls and piers seem to crush out even the memory of revolt and transform the last centre of Anglo-Saxon resistance to William into an eloquent symbol of the Conquest and the permanence of Norman power. Work at Lincoln, whither the see of Dorchester had been transferred, started a decade earlier in the 1070s, while the foundations of Durham were ceremonially laid on 11 August 1093, after the Anglo-Saxon church had been entirely demolished the previous year.

We think of cathedrals as noble monuments to God and the Christian faith. Norman cathedrals, however, were ecclesiastical versions of Norman castles: at once centres of Norman administration, advertisements for a new, Norman, way of life, and monuments to the permanence of Norman power. Above all, they were visible proof that God was on King William's side.

IV

The 1070s were the nadir of England and the English. It was, wrote Henry of Huntingdon, who was himself half-English, an insult to be called English; William, despairing of his new subjects, abandoned his attempts to learn their language; while God Himself, it seemed, had 'ordered that they should no longer be a people' (*iam populum non esse iusserit*).

But, at the same time, there were signs of movement in the opposite direction. These eddying currents find their clearest expression in the so-called Bride's Ale revolt of 1075. The revolt took its name from the fact that it was planned at the marriage of Earl Ralph of East Anglia to the sister of Earl Roger of Hereford. It was a marriage at the highest level of the Anglo-Norman elite: Roger was the son of William's closest aristocratic ally, William fitzOsbern; Ralph, the son and heir of one of Edward the Confessor's Breton favourites, Ralph 'the Staller', while it was William himself who had arranged the match. Nevertheless, at the marriage feast at Norwich talk quickly turned to treason: there was 'Earl Roger and Earl Waltheof and bishops and abbots; who there resolved that they would drive the king out of England'. Earls Roger and Ralph were the prime movers and both tried to raise their earldoms against the king. But neither enjoyed much success and Ralph, in particular, confronted a remarkably hostile coalition: 'the castlemen that were in England and also the people of the land came against him, and prevented him from doing anything'. In other words Normans ('castlemen') and Englishmen ('the people of the land') had joined together in the king's name against an Anglo-Norman earl. The revolt now collapsed. Ralph succeeded in fleeing abroad while Roger was captured and imprisoned for life. But William's full vengeance was saved for the Englishman, Earl Waltheof.

Waltheof's career was a switchback. Youngest son of Earl Siward of Northumbria, he had been an enthusiastic participant in the northern revolt, and, at the battle of York, had personally slaughtered many of the Norman garrison, 'cutting off their heads one by one as they entered the gate'. Nevertheless, he was pardoned by William, who then went to great lengths to keep his loyalty. He gave him his father's earldom of Northumbria, as well as the earldom of Huntingdon, which he had been granted by the Confessor; he even gave him his niece, Judith, as his wife. In the face of such generosity, Waltheof's participation in the Bride's Ale revolt, hesitant and quickly regretted though it seems to have been, was unforgivable. He was beheaded at Winchester on 31 May 1076 and reburied at Crowland Abbey, where, as with the victims of earlier Anglo-Saxon political deaths, a popular cult quickly developed at his tomb.

The drama of Waltheof's execution, the pathos of his position as the last surviving English earl and his posthumous reputation for sanctity have conspired to obscure the real significance of the Bride's Ale revolt. It was *not* the last stand of the English. On the contrary. The English, or at least some lesser East Anglian landowners, had been actively loyal to William. Instead, the threat to the king was Norman. It came from within the Norman establishment; and its motives seemed to have been characteristically Norman as well.

For what had apparently outraged Earl Roger was that the king's sheriffs had been holding pleas in his lands. The office of sheriff had first appeared in the early eleventh century. The sheriff acted as immediate deputy to the earl; he was also the king's direct representative in the shire, presiding in the Shire Court and supervising the collection of the *geld* and the dues from the royal estates. The office had become necessary with the creation of the great earldoms of Cnut's reign, which embraced many counties and turned their holders into figures of central, even more than local, politics. In Normandy, as we have seen, the aristocracy had got control of the equivalent office of *vicomte* in the reign of William's father, Duke Robert. But in England, the king kept it firmly in his grasp – and no king more firmly than William.

All this makes it important to understand what changed in the socio-political structure of England, and what did not, with the Norman Conquest. There was, indisputably, a revolution in the aristocracy, by which a native Anglo-Saxon elite was replaced, almost entirely, by a foreign, Norman-French ruling class. These newcomers brought with them a new language, new values and new attitudes. But did these importations include what historians call 'feudalism'? For the great Victorian scholars, such as Stubbs and Freeman, it was axiomatic that they did: English feudalism was a Norman invention. More recent scholars reject this idea. They point out that Anglo-Saxon England, as King Alfred's works alone make clear, was fully familiar with the idea of 'lordship'. The earls acknowledged the king as their lord, probably in a formal ceremony of homage; the *thegns*, in turn, were the 'men' or vassals of the earls, and so on down the social scale. And each relationship of lord and vassal involved the granting of land by the lord in return for the supply of troops by the vassal.

In this sense of the word 'feudalism', little of substance changed at the Conquest. Noble estates, it is true, probably became larger. In part, this was a matter of necessity, since the Norman military innovations of the castle and the mounted knight were more expensive than their Anglo-Saxon equivalents. But it was also a question of opportunity, since, with the mass expropriation of the Anglo-Saxon elite, there was so much land to distribute among such a comparatively small group of people. This exceptionally rapid and wholesale turnover of land, and the fact that it took place in a foreign and often hostile environment, also meant that practices which had developed piecemeal and over time in Normandy became more explicit and schematic in England.

All of this, however, is far from the 'Feudal Revolution' imagined by the Victorians. Nevertheless, they were right, I think, to insist that some-thing *had* changed. For feudalism has another sense. It is not simply the hierarchical ordering of society as a chain of lords and vassals; it is also the displacement of 'state' structures by 'feudal' ones – so that, for exam-ple, lords take over royal powers of justice and taxation. This tendency was present, too, in Anglo-Saxon England, as, once again, King Alfred's writings bear witness. But in England, unlike France, the tendency was resisted, and resisted effectively, by the king.

But the Conquest made this resistance much harder. For it introduced, and lavishly endowed, a French ruling class who had a very high opinion of French practices in government, as in everything else, and a very low one of English. Hence Earl Roger's rebellion against William. And hence the increasing difficulties William had with the new Norman elites and with his own family most of all. The English found themselves caught in the middle. But for most the choice was easy. They would support the king, even a Norman king, against a feudal noble, especially a Norman one. And it was this occasional, mutually self-interested, alliance between king and people against a foreign aristocracy that marks the beginning of the English recovery from the shame of defeat and dispossession.

7

SONS OF CONQUEST

William II

WILLIAM HAD THREE SONS who survived to maturity: Robert 'Curthose', born in about 1053; William, born in 1060–5, and Henry, born in 1068. Robert, the most personally attractive of the siblings, had been acknowledged as heir of Normandy while still a boy. But his father was reluctant to allow him any real power. Robert was also jealous of the favour William showed to his second son and namesake, William 'Rufus'. Finally, there was a clash of personalities between father and eldest son: between the driven, ruthless king, and the brave, charming, dissolute prince. These are not qualities calculated to impress historians. But they did make Robert a hero for many of the younger members of the Anglo-Norman aristocracy. They also ensured that his career exemplified the dangerous, egotistical factiousness which the Normans brought with them to England.

I

The quarrel between father and son became open in 1078, and early the following year they met in battle at the castle of Gerberoi on the south-eastern frontier of Normandy. The two fought in personal combat and Robert wounded William in the hand. William's horse was also killed under him. But an English *thegn*, Toki, the son of Wigot of Wallingford, brought him another. Toki had, almost certainly, saved William's life – but at the cost of his own, as he was killed on the spot.

William and Robert soon patched up an agreement. But the dispute flared up again and in 1084 William banished his son from his domains.

Meanwhile, other members of the family were drawn into the quarrel. Queen Matilda tried to protect Robert and mediate between him and his father. She got little thanks from William, who threatened to blind one of her servants who had acted as intermediary with Robert. She died in 1083, and William made a great show of grief, which may have been sincere. Matilda had been one of his principal coadjutors in government; the other was his brilliant, ebullient half-brother Odo. But Odo, too, leaned to Robert, and in 1083 William had Odo arrested. At his trial, Odo protested that as bishop of Bayeux he was exempt from William's jurisdiction. William retorted that he respected his sanctity as bishop but was trying him as earl of Kent. The earl-bishop was condemned and imprisoned.

These family quarrels offered a field day to William's many enemies: France, Anjou and Scotland. Even the Danes joined in, and in 1085 Cnut, son of King Swein, threatened an invasion of England in alliance with the count of Flanders. William was in Normandy when the news arrived and his response was characteristically vigorous:

> He went into England with so large an army of horse and foot, from France and Brittany, as never before sought this land; so that men wondered how this land could feed all that force. But the king left the army to shift for themselves through all this land among his subjects, who fed them, each according to his quota of land.

In the event, after dissension in his own ranks prevented Cnut from launching the attack, William stood part of his mercenary army down, but kept the rest on stand-by over winter.

This security scare and the resulting difficulties in billeting troops formed the background to the most extraordinary administrative achievement of the reign: the great survey known as the Domesday Book. The decision to launch the survey was taken at a great council (as the *witan* was now known), which met at Gloucester immediately after Christmas:

> The king [had] a large meeting, and very deep consultation with his council about this land; how it was occupied and by what sort of men.

Once the scope of the survey was agreed, groups of commissioners were dispatched to cover all England south of the Rivers Ribble and Tees. They proceeded county by county, finding out who held what land, now and in 1066; what the estate was worth, again in 1066 and 1086; its assessment for the *geld*; the number of peasants who worked it and with how many ploughs; its stock of animals and its other amenities such as mills. Each individual landowner or his representative was interrogated and the information they supplied checked with the juries of the Shire and Hundred Courts. But it did not end there since, in some areas at least, second groups of commissioners were sent out to control the work of the first. These were deliberately chosen from men with no local connections who could be expected to operate without fear or favour.

Finally, the information was collated and written up fair for presentation to the king: 'Little Domesday', which deals with the East Anglian counties of Essex, Suffolk and Norfolk, and 'Great Domesday', which covers the rest and is beautifully written and elaborately rubricated (highlighted in red) for ease of reference.

And all this was done in a mere seven months.

The result astonished contemporaries. 'There was not one single hide,' the Anglo-Saxon chronicler writes, 'nor yard of land, nay, moreover (it is shameful to tell, though [William] thought it no shame to do it), nor even an ox, nor a cow, nor a swine was there left, that was not set down.' And it still astonishes. It is a tribute to the Anglo-Saxon systems of local administration and national taxation, on the one hand, and to Norman energy, ambition and efficiency, on the other. Above all, it represents the closing chapter of the Conquest. The chaotic turnover of land ownership of the last twenty years was now over, it signalled; instead, an entry in the Domesday Book would represent secure title, both then and for ever.

All this is no doubt true. But it is the Anglo-Saxon chronicler who goes further and grasps the essential. For he sees Domesday as a product of William's covetousness. The king had devoted the best years of his life to the acquisition of England, while the means he had used to get and keep it had risked his immortal soul. Now, at last, it was his and Domesday enabled him to hold it, literally, in his hands.

The survey was presented to the king on Lammas Day, 1 August 1086, at the great court held at Old Sarum in Wiltshire. The court was attended, not only by the council and the magnates, but also by 'all the landsmen [landowners] that were of any account over all England'. And there they all, each and every one, performed homage to the king. It was an extraordinary scene, and the Anglo-Saxon chronicler describes it with the precision of an eyewitness:

> They all bowed themselves before him, and became his men, and
> swore him oaths of allegiance that they would against all other men
> be faithful to him.

At first sight, this mass act of feudal homage looks like the ultimate Normanization of English politics. But the appearance is deceptive. For at Salisbury William received the oaths, not only of his own immediate vassals, or tenants-in-chief as they would later be called, but also of their tenants and sub-tenants as well. This looked forward to the idea of liege homage but it also looked back to the practice – which was as old as Alfred's time at least – of every free man swearing an oath to the king in the Hundred Courts. The result was to give English feudalism a decidedly English twist.

William left for Normandy immediately after the Oath of Salisbury. It was to be his last visit to England, and he left in typical fashion, having first exacted a heavy *geld*. The money was needed to finance William's struggle with the king of France, Philip I, who had taken advantage of the quarrels within William's family to try to cut his over-mighty vassal down to size. William's campaign went well, and in August 1087 he captured Mantes. The lightly defended town was sacked and fired, and many of the inhabitants, including two especially venerated hermits, perished in the flames.

This calculated use of terror was, as we have often seen, business as usual for William. But this time something went wrong. William's horse bolted in the chaos of the burning town and he was struck hard in his now-protuberant stomach by the pommel of his saddle. He was carried to Rouen, where he lay for three weeks. He remained lucid throughout and was expected to recover. But in early September his condition deteriorated and on the 9th he died.

The Anglo-Saxon chronicler honoured the dead king with a magnificent obituary. It is based on personal knowledge – 'we who often looked upon him' – and it is nuanced and balanced. The chronicler praised his wisdom and wealth, which were very great; his piety, which built and endowed so many monasteries; his dignity, which manifested itself in the crown-wearings which took place three times a year when he was in England; his force of will, which brooked no opposition, and struck down bishops, abbots and earls and even his own brother Odo. But, above all, he admired his harsh yet equitable justice, which brought peace and tranquillity to a distracted kingdom. To set against all these qualities, however, were William's vices: his insatiable covetousness, his inordinate pride and his addiction to hunting, which, for his mere pleasure, inflicted so much suffering on his subjects.

The chronicler extenuates none of these faults. But, finally and justly, he acknowledges William's stature as England's greatest king: 'he truly reigned over England', he concluded, and was 'more splendid and powerful than any of his predecessors'.

From an Englishman, this was high praise indeed.

But great king of England though he was, William remained a Norman at heart. As he requested, his body was taken for burial to the Norman abbey of St Etienne at Caen; all the bishops and abbots of Normandy were present at the ceremony, and the sermon was preached by the Norman bishop of Evreux. But a final hitch occurred. As the manner of his death makes clear, William had grown very fat in his later years. But his sarcophagus, probably made long before, took no account of the fact and some force was needed to fit the body in. The result was described by the Anglo-Norman monk Orderic Vitalis: 'the swollen bowels burst, and an intolerable stench assailed the nostrils of the bystanders and the whole crowd'. Not even the clouds of incense could mask it and the service was rushed to a conclusion.

It was a humiliating end for a man who had been so conscious of his dignity in life.

II

The three weeks William lingered on his sickbed at Rouen left him plenty of time to arrange his affairs and divide his estate among his sons: despite their quarrel, Robert, he decided, should have Normandy; William, England; while Henry was 'bequeathed immense treasure'. It was a decision that was guaranteed to perpetuate the divisions in the royal house long after his own death.

William II's accession was smooth. His father dispatched him to England before the life was out of his body and gave him sealed instructions for Archbishop Lanfranc. These were executed to the letter. Lanfranc anointed and crowned William at Westminster on 26 September and all the magnates did him homage. William then rode to Winchester; opened and viewed the Treasury; distributed the lavish bequests to monasteries, churches and the poor of each county which his father had made for the good of his soul, and released all political prisoners. He then returned to London for the winter.

It was a conventional beginning to a highly unconventional reign. For, in contrast to the older William with his piety and uxoriousness, the younger set himself to flout all contemporary norms of behaviour. Not only did he plunder the Church, he was actively irreligious. He never married or fathered children; instead, he had male 'favourites' and was almost certainly homosexual. Still worse, he made no bones about the fact.

This flamboyantly un-Christian mode of life led churchmen both to loathe him and to underestimate him. We should not make the same mistake. For, despite the great differences in their moral character, William also inherited many of his father's most impressive qualities. Like the Conqueror, Rufus was a skilled soldier and a natural leader of men. He was similarly strong-willed and determined to enforce his authority. And he went about it more imaginatively: he showed an occasional flair for public relations, while his building works transformed the physical setting of the monarchy.

All this made William II a powerful and effective king. But that very fact meant that much of the Norman baronage looked with envy across the Channel at the laxer rule of Duke Robert. They correctly saw Robert as one of themselves and longed to have him for their lord in England. The lead was taken by Bishop Odo, whom William had been persuaded, against his better judgement, to include in his deathbed amnesty for political prisoners. Odo was duly released and returned to his earldom of Kent, whence he plotted with his fellow malcontents. During Lent 1088, a formidable coalition was assembled and at Easter, 16 April, a coordinated series of provincial revolts broke out: in East Anglia, Durham, the

Midlands, the Welsh Borders, the West Country and, above all, in Odo's territories of Kent.

The rebellion polarized opinion – and the races – in England. The rebels, *The Anglo-Saxon Chronicle* noted, were 'all French', or rather they were the *crème de la crème*: 'the richest French men that were in this land'. And the chronicler castigates their behaviour severely: their purpose was to 'betray their lord the king'; they were guilty of 'great treachery'. But his harshest words are reserved for Odo: he was a veritable 'Judas', who planned 'to do by [William] as … Iscariot did by Our Lord'.

In contrast, English sentiment seems to have been solidly royalist. Bishop Wulfstan stood firm in Worcester and, with a comparatively small force, put the rebels to flight there. But the situation in Kent, where Odo had retreated with his spoil to his near-impregnable castle of Rochester, demanded sterner measures. The result was an appeal by William to his English subjects:

> He then sent after Englishmen, described to them his need, earnestly requested their support, and promised them the best laws that ever were in this land; each unright *geld* he forbade and restored to the men their woods and chases [that is, their hunting rights].

The promised abolition of the Forest Laws (of which more later) was, like the Laws themselves, an innovation. Otherwise, both the form and the content of William's appeal are remarkably similar to the compact hammered out between king and people as a condition of Æthelred II's restoration to the throne in 1014.

And it was equally effective. Thanks to the forces raised, William was able to bottle Odo up in Rochester. Finally, after inordinate wriggling on Odo's part, an agreement was reached: Odo would surrender all his offices and possessions in England, in return for which William would allow him to return unharmed to Normandy. The English troops, however, thought this more than Odo deserved and, as he emerged from the castle, cried out:

> Halters, bring halters, and hang this traitor bishop and his accomplices from the gallows!

A similar punishment awaited William of St Calais, who as bishop of Durham had begun the building of the mighty cathedral and castle. He had joined Odo and 'did all the harm that he could all over the north'. William Rufus besieged him and the bishop was forced to come to terms: he 'gave up the castle, and relinquished his bishopric, and went to Normandy'. This, as the Anglo-Saxon chronicler notes with satisfaction, was the common fate of most of the leaders of the revolt: 'many Frenchmen also abandoned their lands and went overseas; and the king gave many of their lands to the men that were faithful to him'.

The crisis over, William's promises to the English were forgotten. When he was taxed with this by Archbishop Lanfranc, the king smoothly retorted: 'who can be expected to keep all his promises?'

Despite his broken word, William was able to deploy the men and money of England to re-create and even to extend the Conqueror's empire. He first forced an effective division of Normandy, by taking the east of the duchy and leaving Robert with only the west. Finally, in 1096, Robert mortgaged him the whole of Normandy to finance his participation in the First Crusade. The price was 10,000 marks of silver. And it was raised, needless to say, by an English *geld* at the rate of four shillings per hide.

Even more remarkable was the fate of Scotland. As we have seen, Malcolm III had married Margaret, sister of Edgar the Æthling. The hope must have been to exploit Margaret's Anglo-Saxon royal blood to make England Scottish. The result instead was to make Scotland English or, at any rate, Anglo-Norman. In part, this was the work of Margaret herself. She was passionately Anglo-Norman, in both culture and churchmanship, and imposed these values when and where she could in Scotland. This inevitably led to a native Gaelic backlash and King Malcolm found himself caught in the middle. A complicating factor was Edgar the Æthling's reconciliation with William the Conqueror, which led, in effect, to his becoming an honorary member of the Norman dynasty.

With both his wife and his brother-in-law as Anglo-Norman agents, the pressure on Malcolm was intense. And it was not made any easier by William II's high-handed approach to his northern neighbour.

In the event, however, it was Malcolm who threw the first stone by taking advantage of William's absence in Normandy in 1091 to launch an invasion of England, which, after making considerable headway, was repulsed by William's regents. But then, as Malcolm's ill-luck would have it, William and Robert sank their differences and decided to celebrate their new-found friendship by joining in a punitive expedition to Scotland. The English fleet was destroyed in September. But the army swept into south-eastern Scotland and it was clear that Malcolm would have to submit. Duke Robert and Edgar the Æthling acted as intermediaries and it was agreed to renew the Peace of Abernethy, in return for which Malcolm performed homage to William on the same terms that he had done to his father.

But William, probably sensing Scottish weakness, had no intention of keeping his side of the bargain. Next year he came north with a large army; captured Carlisle and built and garrisoned the castle. He also rebuilt the town and planted an English colony around it: sending 'a vast number of rustic people with wives and with cattle ... thither, to dwell there in order to till the land'.

The establishment of Carlisle as a fortified outpost of England altered the whole balance of power along the vague and unstable Anglo-Scottish border. Malcolm had to respond. But, having learned the lesson of Anglo-Norman power, he tried negotiation and came under safe-conduct to the crown-wearing at Gloucester. There, however, William chose to inflict deliberate humiliation on him. 'But when he came to the king, he could not', *The Anglo-Saxon Chronicle* reported, 'be considered worthy either of our king's speech, or of the conditions that were formerly promised him.'

Malcolm returned to Scotland and, intent on revenge, launched a destructive raid on England. But the raid ended disastrously. Malcolm was entrapped near Alnwick and killed by Morel of Bamborough, the steward and kinsman of the earl of Northumberland and Malcolm's own intimate friend. Malcolm's son and nominated heir, Edward, was killed at the same time. The death of both her husband and son was too much for Margaret, who, almost maddened with grief, died a few days later. There followed a powerful Gaelic reaction in which Donald III Bane (White- or Fair-haired), Malcolm's backwoodsman brother, was made king and 'drove out all the English'. A counter-blow was struck when Duncan II, Malcolm's son by his first wife, briefly regained the throne as an English client. But he was soon forced to dismiss his foreign entourage and was then murdered and replaced once more by Donald III.

William, meanwhile, put his own house in order by bringing Robert de Mowbray, the rebel earl of Northumberland, to heel. But the earl's castle of Bamborough proved impregnable. Instead, William built a counter-castle, which he called *Malvoisin*, 'Evil Neighbour'. Earl Robert unwisely ventured outside his stronghold with a raiding party and was captured. William then forced the countess, who was mounting an intrepid defence of Bamborough, to surrender by resorting to one of his father's favourite tricks and threatening to blind the earl in front of the castle walls. With the surrender of the great fortress, William enjoyed greater direct power in the north than any previous king.

It remained to deal with Scotland. William's chosen instrument was Edgar the Æthling. He was dispatched north in 1097 with a large army; defeated and captured Donald III Bane, who was later blinded, and installed his namesake and nephew as King Edgar I.

Scotland was now, effectively, an English protectorate. A vassal-king, who was half-English in blood and wholly English in culture, had been put on the throne by an English prince at the head of an Anglo-Norman army. And under Edgar's ten-year rule, the English language, English colonizers and English ways of doing things spread far into the Lowlands. The result, paradoxically, made Scotland, as a mirror-image of England, all the more able to resist England when the time came.

Wales also suffered the relentless expansion of Anglo-Norman England. But here the consequences were different. In Scotland, the aftermath of the death of Malcolm III led to the eventual creation of a strengthened kingdom that was, in essential respects, another England. In Wales, in contrast, the death of the dominant native prince of south Wales, Rhys ap Tewdwr, also at the hands of a Norman and also in 1093, marked an end: 'and then fell the kingdom of the Britons', the Welsh chronicler lamented; or, as an English writer put it, 'from that day kings ceased to bear rule in Wales'.

The result was that 'English' Wales became the most purely Norman area in Britain. Here were feudal lordships, each based on a castle, that feuded ceaselessly with each other and with the king. And they did so more or less without restraint since the structures of royal government, which held firm over most of England, had never been imposed there.

III

Probably more important than these events on the periphery, both to the king and his subjects, was his redevelopment of London. It was, as we have seen, Edward the Confessor with his building of the Abbey who had taken the first crucial step in the establishment of London/Westminster as the political capital. But William II's building programme comes close behind. The programme included the construction of the first curtain-wall of the Tower; the rebuilding of London Bridge, in a piece of advanced engineering; and, most importantly of all, the erection of a new Great Hall at Westminster.

The Hall, at 240 feet long by 67 feet wide, was one of the largest secular buildings north of the Alps, and, reroofed and reskinned in the fourteenth century, it still stands as the most impressive surviving monument of the Anglo-Norman monarchy. One curious feature, however, is the lack of alignment between the fenestration on the two long walls, so that the windows on the west wall are four feet further north than their equivalents on the east. This has never been satisfactorily explained. It cannot, for example, be a question of the Hall's size defeating the technical ability of eleventh-century masons, since, big though it is, many English cathedrals are even bigger. One possibility, however, is that the problem was caused by building the new Hall round Edward the Confessor's hall, which was left standing and operational. Certainly we know that Westminster Hall was built in a rush, taking little more than the year 1098–9. This required plentiful use of forced labour, and, according to *The Anglo-Saxon Chronicle*, cost numerous lives: 'many men perished thereby'.

The Great Hall was finished in the first half of 1099. When he first saw it, one of the king's attendants is supposed to have said that, though it was impressive, he felt it was rather too big. William crushed him with his retort. It was, the king said, 'too big for a chamber but not big enough for a hall'. The remark was worthy of a Nero; indeed, the crown-wearings, for which the Hall was principally intended, were imperial in both their origins and their pretensions. The king sat in the middle of the dais, crowned, robed and enthroned, while the Latin text known as the *Laudes* ('Praises') was sung in his honour in an adjacent chapel. The text hailed him like a Roman emperor and wished him *Vita et Victoria*: 'long life and victory'.

It was at Whitsuntide, 29 May 1099, that William 'held his court the first time in his new building at Westminster'. Apart from ceremony, the principal item of business was the conferment of the great bishopric of Durham on Ranulf Flambard. The appointment was probably Ranulf's reward for having steered the king's massive building programme to a successful conclusion. But, like Flambard himself, it was deeply unpopular.

Flambard was William's chief minister, 'who had long directed and governed his counsels over all England'. As such, he was widely blamed for William's exactions and oppressive government. He was also, though a churchman himself, directly responsible for the king's sustained plundering of the Church. He kept bishoprics and abbacies vacant for long periods; seized the revenues to the king's use, and farmed the lands to his own profit. At Ely Ranulf did not even wait for the incumbent to die; instead, he took advantage of the last days of the aged Abbot Simeon to pension off the monks and take the surplus for the king (and himself).

But the most outrageous case was at Canterbury itself. Archbishop Lanfranc had died only two years after crowning William. Thereafter the see, with its vast revenues, had been kept vacant for four years. And it was only filled in 1093 thanks to the king's dangerous illness at Gloucester, when he 'was so sick, that he was by all reported dead'. Frightened by this brush with death, William decided to make amends by appointing Anselm as archbishop.

Anselm, a distinguished philosopher who had been Lanfranc's pupil and successor as abbot of Bec, was regarded as the natural choice. But the appointment turned out to be deeply unsatisfactory for both king and archbishop. Anselm had all the academic's unworldliness and refusal to compromise; while William, once he had recovered from his fright, was aggressive and unyielding in turn. Even the conditions of Anselm's appointment were subject to dispute and, within two years, William was intriguing at Rome to have Anselm deprived. The attempt failed; indeed, William, for once, was outsmarted and was manoeuvred into recognizing Urban II as pope without the quid pro quo of getting rid of his troublesome archbishop. But it was only a matter of time and in 1097 Anselm, finding his position impossible, went into exile. There he remained for the rest of the reign while the revenues from Canterbury fell once more into William's hands.

IV

William, like almost all kings in the Middle Ages and for long after, was a passionate huntsman. There was nothing new in this; Edward the Confessor, as we have seen, had been similarly addicted. First, Edward would attend divine service; then he would devote himself, equally assiduously, to the chase:

> He took much pleasure in hawks and birds of that kind which were brought before him and was really delighted by the baying and scrambling of the hounds.

To provide for such sport, Edward and his Anglo-Saxon predecessors had created special royal game reserves, such as Kingswood in the Kentish Weald, or Woodstock Chase in Oxfordshire.

But for the Normans these relatively modest provisions were nothing like enough and they introduced two major changes, both of which are associated with the imported Norman-French word *forêt* ('forest'). First, they enormously extended the area of the game reserves. The most notorious example is the New Forest in Hampshire. William I, it seems, found some 75,000 acres of almost deserted upland and rough country; added a further 15–20,000 acres of inhabited and cultivated land, and expelled some five hundred families as a precaution against poaching. And the New Forest was only one of many. At their maximum extent in the twelfth century, the Royal Forests covered almost a third of England; they stretched in a broad band from Lincolnshire to Oxfordshire, and included the whole of the county of Essex.

The second change was to subject this hugely extended area to a separate jurisdiction known as Forest Law. This had been the practice in Carolingian France and it had been adapted by the dukes for their own purposes in Normandy. But it seems to have been entirely unknown in Anglo-Saxon England and its importation, *The Anglo-Saxon Chronicle* makes clear, was one of the most deplorable aspects of the Conqueror's rule:

> He made many deer-parks; and he established laws therewith; so that
> whosoever slew a hart, or a hind, should be deprived of his eyesight.
> As he forbade men to kill the harts, so also the boars; and he loved
> the tall deer as if he were their father.

The results were unpopular among all classes; 'his rich men bemoaned it, and the poor men shuddered at it'. For everyone was affected. The rich found their own sport curtailed; the poor lost a useful source of food and saw their crops damaged; while churchmen disapproved both of the savagery of the laws and of the excessive commitment to sport which they represented. But there was a broader issue too. For the Laws were hated, above all, because they were perceived to be arbitrary. They were a product merely of the king's will and they served only his pleasure. In other words, they were 'un-English'. They were also the most vivid reminder that England was a conquered country, whose land, people and resources were the spoils of the victor to use or abuse as he wished.

Naturally, when William II made his bid for English support in 1088, an undertaking to abolish or moderate the Forest Laws was given a prominent place. But, equally naturally, the promise was forgotten when William's hour of need passed. Instead, he proved as ruthless a Nimrod as his father.

But in 1100 the hunter became the hunted. Late in the afternoon on 2 August the king was hunting in the New Forest near Brockenhurst with a small party that included his younger brother, Henry. One of the huntsmen, Walter Tirel, lord of Poix in Ponthieu, appeared to aim at a stag but instead hit the king with his arrow. William died instantly. There followed immediate panic – real or staged – and the party rode off, abandoning the body. It was left to a passing peasant to bundle it in a cart and bring it to Winchester, where it was hastily buried beneath the tower. Meanwhile, Tirel had fled abroad while Henry had ridden to Winchester, seized the Treasury and, on 3 August, had himself chosen king.

Was the death accident or design? There have been suggestions of a conspiracy by the great family of Clare, with Tirel, whose wife was a Clare, as the hit-man. Two members of the family were in the hunting party on the fatal day and, subsequently, they were treated with marked favour by Henry. But there are no more substantial clues. What matters instead is the old rule of *cui bono?* – 'who gains?' And the man who gained most from the death, clearly, was Henry. If he did not plan it, he exploited it with the cool skill which was to be a marked feature of his rule.

By this time, Henry was thirty-two. He was the Conqueror's youngest son; he was also the most 'English', being conceived, born and knighted in England. His status as a prince, or king's son, from birth also seems to have affected his upbringing. There is little sign, for example, that either his father or his brothers received any but the most elementary instruction: they were swordsmen first and penmen scarcely at all. Henry, on the other hand, was given the sophisticated education (at least for a layman) that led to his later nickname of 'Beauclerk':

> He was [writes his contemporary, William of Malmesbury] early
> instructed in the liberal arts and so thoroughly imbibed the sweets
> of learning that no warlike disturbance and no pressure of business
> could erase them from his noble mind.

'His learning,' William concluded, 'though obtained by snatches, assisted him much in the science of government.'

The evidence of this more reflective, calculating approach to kingship was quickly apparent. For Henry had seized the throne by means of a *coup d'état*, perhaps even by fratricide. His actions were palliated, no doubt, by William's widespread unpopularity. Even so, he badly needed legitimacy.

His first step was to bring forward his coronation. Normally, coronations took place on a great feast of the Church. Henry, however, could not wait. Instead, immediately after his election as king by an impromptu *witan* at Winchester – 'the statesmen that were then nigh on hand' – on Friday, 3 August, he rode post-haste to London and was crowned in the Abbey on the Sunday by Maurice, bishop of London. From the death of one king to the crowning of another had taken a mere four days.

Nevertheless, it was time enough for Henry to introduce an important modification to the coronation service. As we have seen, since at least the time of Edgar, English kings had sworn an oath at their coronation. The oath took a fixed form and was regarded by both king and people as defining the essence of good royal government. Twenty years after his own coronation, for instance, Edward the Confessor quoted his oath, more or less verbatim, in a charter. Henry, however, decided to go beyond the traditional form. He would not only promise to govern well; he would also renounce the bad government of his father and brother. This turned, and was clearly intended to turn, the oath from a promise into a manifesto.

The Anglo-Saxon Chronicle, alert as always to the 'constitutional' implications of events, notes the change with precision:

> On the Sunday ... before the altar at Westminster, he promised God
> and all the people to annul all the unrighteous acts that took place
> in his brother's time, and to maintain the best laws that were valid
> in any king's day before him.

Only once these promises were made was Henry crowned and given a general homage, in which 'all this land submitted to him, and swore oaths, and became his men'.

The oath, of course, was oral – though the king and the bishop must each have read from a written text. Henry's other innovation was to issue a version of this text as a Coronation Charter. There was something in it for everyone. The Church traditionally came first and the first clause of the Charter duly promised to end Rufus's policy of ecclesiastical plunder. It began sonorously, with the king's solemn, general undertaking to 'make free the Church of God'. Then each of Rufus's specific methods of extortion was renounced.

In fact, Henry, even in the short time available to him, had already begun to translate his words into action. Of the three bishoprics that were in the king's hands, he filled one on the very day of his election by giving the diocese of Winchester, vacant since 1098, to the chancellor, William Gifford. At Canterbury, likewise, the vacancy was quickly ended when the king, with the advice of his council, wrote letters of recall to Archbishop Anselm. And it was the same with the vacant abbeys, which included five out of the six richest. Nor was the scandal ever repeated.

Then the concerns of Henry's lay subjects were addressed. The aristocracy was promised security of inheritance; while everyone would benefit from Henry's renunciation of the *monetagium*, or levy on the coining of silver pennies. But it was Henry's promise to moderate the *murdrum* ('murder') fine which most struck a chord with the ordinary people.

The *murdrum* fine had been introduced by the Conqueror to try to protect his Norman followers from assassination by the disaffected English. It assumed that every murdered body was that of a Norman, unless it could be proved otherwise. If the proof were not forthcoming, a heavy fine was levied on the whole community where the body had been found. The principle of collective reprisals – the resort of occupying forces throughout the ages – was odious and the *murdrum* fine was linked with the Forest Laws as a badge of English oppression.

Henry's promise to tackle the issue was therefore a popular one. In the event, the grievance was mitigated rather than abolished. Nevertheless, a welcome signal of a return to normalcy had been given.

And it was this, really, that was the underlying purpose of the Charter. 'I abolish', the king swore, 'all the evil practices with which the realm was unjustly oppressed.' In their place, he undertook to 'restore to you the law of King Edward'. Strictly speaking, Edward the Confessor, unlike many of his predecessors, including, most recently, Cnut, had issued no law code. Instead 'the law of King Edward' was taken to mean the totality of all Anglo-Saxon law in force in 1066. This corpus was now researched by Henry's legal scholars and, with judicious modifications, was used to provide the basis of the Common Law that, henceforth, would be the law of England. And, though it was formulated by an Anglo-Norman legal establishment, this was, self-consciously, a native, English law.

But the Charter did not only look back to the legal status quo ante of 1066 or to the settlement of 1014. It was also rich in implications for the future. It was reissued by all subsequent twelfth-century kings and it was incorporated, almost word for word, into Magna Carta. But there was one grievance which Henry, as keen a huntsman as any of his house, could not bring himself to address. 'I have retained', Clause 10 declared baldly, 'the Forests in my own hands as my father did before me.' Even here, however, the naked arbitrariness of the Conqueror's legislation is cloaked with the claim that the retention of the Forests had been agreed 'by the common council of my barons'.

Just as important were the personal changes of 1100. William's hated minister, Ranulf Flambard, was thrown in the Tower. And Henry decided to get married; indeed, he may even have fallen in love. The woman in question was Edith, daughter of Malcolm III of Scotland and St Margaret and niece of Edgar the Æthling. She had been brought up at Romsey

Abbey, an aristocratic establishment, where her aunt Christina was a nun. There she had had many suitors and, though not professed, had worn the veil to keep them off.

But Henry was different. It was clearly Edith's pleasure to marry him; it was also her duty since, by the marriage, the House of Wessex would be restored to the throne of England. Henry, who revered his wife's fourteen generations of royal blood, saw the union in a similar light. As did all other observers, led by the Anglo-Saxon chronicler, who rejoiced that she was 'of the right royal race of England'. On 11 November they were married 'with much pomp at Westminster' by Anselm himself and Matilda, as she was known after her marriage, was anointed and crowned queen in the same ceremony. Three years later a son was born. He was christened William, after his Norman grandfather, the Conqueror; but surnamed Æthling, after his Anglo-Saxon royal blood. The cloven tree trunk of the Confessor's dream had, it seemed, knitted up and borne green leaf again.

There was soon an even stranger reversal of fortune. Flambard quickly escaped from the Tower and fled to Normandy. There he plotted with Duke Robert, who had returned from crusade, to dethrone Henry. The conspiracy failed. But it led to years of fratricidal war. The war ended with Robert's crushing defeat at Tinchebrai on 28 September 1106. Henry annexed Normandy and imprisoned his brother for life.

It was, to the day, the fortieth anniversary of the battle of Hastings. William of Malmesbury noted the coincidence with glee: the English had conquered Normandy; defeat was avenged and revenge was sweet.

8

THE TRIUMPHANT KING

Henry I

IN 1106, AT THE TIME OF HIS GREAT VICTORY at Tinchebrai over his eldest brother Robert, duke of Normandy, King Henry I was thirty-eight years old. Only six years previously, he had been a near-landless younger son, unmarried and with uncertain prospects. Then, in quick succession, he had seized the throne of England; married a queen of unimpeachably royal blood and fathered a son who was the heir of the Anglo-Saxon as well as the Norman kings. Now, with the conquest of the duchy of Normandy which followed the battle, he had reconstituted his father, William the Conqueror's, empire by his own hands.

I

Henry was also fortunate in his historian and younger contemporary, William of Malmesbury. William was the greatest English historian since Bede and in Henry he found a subject worthy of his talents. The king was, he writes:

> of middle stature; … his hair was black, set back on the forehead; his eyes mildly bright; his chest brawny; his body fleshy. He was facetious in proper season, nor did multiplicity of business cause him to be less pleasant when he mixed in society … He preferred contending by counsel rather than by the sword: if he could, he conquered without bloodshed; if it was unavoidable, with as little as possible …

He was plain in his diet ... He never drank but to allay thirst ... His
sleep was heavy and interrupted by frequent snoring. His eloquence
was rather unpremeditated than laboured; not rapid but deliberate.

The impression is of a man of powerful appetites, which were held in
control by an equally powerful will and intelligence. And, commanding
himself, he was able to command others as well. The result was that
contemporaries were convinced of his greatness as a ruler. He was,
William of Malmesbury concluded, 'inferior in wisdom to no king of
modern times and ... clearly surpassing all his predecessors in England'.

But Henry's standing has proved less easy to communicate to subsequent ages. Especially in England. Here Henry reigned thirty-five years.
Nevertheless, thanks to his iron grip, nothing much happened. In
Normandy, however, it was a different story. Partly this was due to the
primitiveness of the duchy's structure of politics and government and to
its faction-ridden and unruly nobility. But there was also the destabilizing
influence of the powerful and hostile rulers based just beyond the Norman
frontiers: to the east, the count of Flanders; to the south-west, the count
of Anjou; and to the south, the king of France, who was not only a neighbour but, in theory at least, the king-duke's feudal overlord. All were
jealous of Henry's power and took every opportunity of stirring the
seething pot of Norman politics.

Most dangerous of all, however, was the fact that Henry's brother
Robert left an infant son, William, who was aged five at the time of his
father's defeat and capture. Henry, once Duke Robert was safely in his
hands, showed no compunction in condemning him to a perpetual imprisonment that was ended only by his death twenty-eight years later in 1134
at the age of over eighty. The son, however, was another matter. Sensitive
as usual to public opinion, Henry felt obliged to leave him at liberty 'for
fear that it might be held against him if the boy came to any harm while
in his hands'. It was a bad blunder, of which Henry soon repented. But by
then it was too late. The boy was spirited out of his clutches and, flaunt-
ing the provocative surname of 'the Clito' or 'royal-born', grew up to
become a thorn in his uncle's flesh and, as pretender to Normandy and
perhaps to England, the focus of every plot and alliance against him.

The result of all this was that Normandy was to occupy a disproportionate amount of Henry's time: he spent the greater part of his reign in

the duchy. England, in contrast, was left to fend for itself. Which it did – as well as supplying the wealth that enabled Henry repeatedly to take on and defeat the apparently overwhelming coalitions lined up against him.

The extraordinarily divergent courses of Henry's reign in England and in Normandy gave rise to some of the most interesting analytical passages in contemporary historians. Shrewdest and most succinct, as usual, was William of Malmesbury:

> Normandy, indeed, though not very wide in extent, is a convenient and patient fosterer of the abandoned. Wherefore, for a long time, she well endures intestine broils; and on the restoration of peace becomes more flourishing than before; at her pleasure ejecting her disturbers, who feel themselves no longer safe in the province, by the open passes into France. Whereas England does not long endure the turbulent; but when once received into her bosom, either surrenders, or puts them to death; neither, when laid waste by tumult, does she again soon recover herself.

Henry's own *coup d'état* at the beginning of his reign perfectly illustrates the truth of this dictum: England had surrendered to his firm grasp in a matter of days and did not stray from its allegiance thereafter.

Moreover, the phenomenon was specifically *English* – that is, Anglo-Saxon. And Henry had likewise allied himself to this English sentiment by his marriage to Edith, even though as queen, Henry's English bride took the Norman name Matilda. The English naturally rejoiced and welcomed the couple, however optimistically, as one of them. But, despite the change of name, the Norman grandees sneered at the *mésalliance*: all but a handful, according to William of Malmesbury, who was half-English himself, 'openly branded their lord with sarcasms, calling him *Godric* and his consort, *Godgifu*'.

The satire was many-layered. *Godric* and *Godgifu* were the commonplace names of humble, God-fearing folk. So their employment mocked the new queen's rather ostentatious piety, which it was assumed Henry would share. Another target was the dullness of their court, which contrasted with the rackety brilliance of Rufus's establishment. Finally, and above all, the names were *Anglo-Saxon*, which, in the mouths of the

Anglo-Norman smart set, turned them into racial insults: Henry, the aristocracy was saying, had married a native and gone native himself.

And Henry's own behaviour gave substance to the charges. Above and beyond his marriage, he openly played the Anglo-Saxon national card and raised the *fyrd* (the old Anglo-Saxon land-army) against his brother Robert. The problem with the *fyrd*, however, as the battle of Hastings had shown all too clearly, was that its infantry tactics were no match for the Norman cavalry. Henry set himself to remedy this as well:

> He frequently went through the ranks [William of Malmesbury explained] instructing them how to elude the ferocity of the cavalry by opposing their shields, and how to return their strokes: by this he made them perfectly fearless of the Normans, and ask to be led out to battle.

Thus, by a strange reversal, a Norman king was teaching the Anglo-Saxons how to fight their Norman masters.

The Anglo-Norman elite drew its own conclusions. Henry, they decided, was about to become too powerful and they must close ranks. Another historian, Orderic Vitalis, who also straddled the cultures as the product of a mixed marriage of a Norman father with an English mother, takes up the story.

> The earls and magnates of the kingdom [he reports] met together and discussed fully how to reconcile the rebel [Robert of Bellême, earl of Shrewsbury] with his lord. For, as they said, 'If the king defeats a mighty earl by force and carries his enmity to the point of disinheriting him, as he is now striving to do, he will from that moment trample on us like helpless slave girls.'

'Let us', they therefore concluded, 'make every effort to reconcile them, so securing the advantage of our lord and our peer alike within the law, and, at the same time, by quelling the disturbance, we will put both parties in our debt.'

Henry met the peers in open-air conference near Robert of Bellême's castle of Bridgnorth and they did their best to win the king round to a compromise. But Henry's resolution was stiffened by the presence of a force of three thousand *pagenses milites* ('country knights or troops'). 'Henry, lord king,' they cried out, 'why do you listen to men who urge you to spare a traitor and let a conspiracy against your life go unpunished? … Storm the fortress … and make no peace with [the traitor] until you have him in your hands, dead or alive.'

'These words', according to Orderic, 'put heart into the king.' He rejected the proffered mediation; took a hard line and had all the success his nobles feared. First, he browbeat the garrison of Bridgnorth into surrender; then, having cleared a new road to bring up his vast army, he laid siege to Robert himself in Shrewsbury. Faced with overwhelming odds, Robert submitted. The king left him with his life. But he and his followers were stripped of all their English lands and sent into exile in Normandy.

II

Henry's absolute victory over his rebellious vassal marked a turning point. 'After Robert was exiled', Orderic writes, 'the realm of Albion [England] remained in peace and King Henry reigned prosperously for thirty-three years, during which time no one again dared to rebel against him in England or hold any castle against him.' And, on this side of the Channel at least, the king's triumph was widely welcomed. 'Rejoice,' the English told Henry, 'give thanks to the Lord God, for you have begun to rule freely now that you have conquered Robert of Bellême and driven him out of your kingdom.' Orderic couches these words in a kind of irregularly rhymed Latin verse: are they his translation of an early English political song?

But, while England rejoiced, Normandy suffered. Orderic, who witnessed events close at hand, resorted to the language of the Apocalypse to highlight the contrast. 'Like the dragon of whom John the Apostle writes … who was cast out of heaven and vented his bestial fury by warring on the dwellers on earth, [Robert of Bellême], driven from Britain, fell in wrath upon the Normans.' Moreover, what was most striking of all, Henry's own attitude also became different when he crossed the water and exchanged the role of king for that of duke.

The difference showed most clearly in Henry's conduct in war with France. Louis VI of France allied with Henry's deadly rival, William the Clito. In 1119, the French king determined to meet Henry in battle. The result was the disastrous skirmish at Brémule in which the French knights were defeated and their king himself fled from the field of battle, 'trembling' from fear of being betrayed or captured. This, despite its petty scale, was a victory to compare with his triumphs at Bridgnorth and Shrewsbury. But Henry exploited it differently. Indeed, save symbolically, he refused to exploit it at all.

He was of course sensitive to the fame he had won and eager to memorialize it by securing an appropriate trophy: 'King Henry', Orderic writes, 'purchased the standard of King Louis for twenty marks of silver from the knight who had captured it, and kept it as a memorial of the victory which God had given him.' Otherwise, his first concern was the comfort and dignity of his temporarily despoiled opponents. 'He sent back', Orderic continues, 'the king [of France]'s horse to him next day, with the saddle and bridle and all the trappings that become a king.' And he made sure that William the Clito's horse, which had also been captured in the melee, should be returned to him in the name of his own son and heir, William the Æthling, together with other necessaries for the exile.

Nor was there any chorus of vengeful 'country knights', as at Bridgnorth, clamouring for blood. Instead, both sides behaved with equal restraint:

> I have been told [Orderic reports] that in the battle of the two kings, in which about nine hundred knights were engaged, only three were killed. They were all clad in mail and spared each other on both sides, out of fear of God and fellowship in arms; they were more concerned to capture than to kill the fugitives. As Christian soldiers they did not thirst for the blood of their brothers, but rejoiced in a just victory given by God, for the good of holy Church and the peace of the faithful.

This clearly is not war as we understand it. Instead, it was a blood sport in which surprisingly little blood was spilled; a game, played according to strict rules, which minimized casualties both on the field of battle and after it; and a trial by battle, in which God was thought to be on the side, not of the big battalions, but of right and justice.

The name given to this complex of values is 'chivalry'. The name comes from the French *chevalier*: that is, horse-mounted soldier or knight.

Orderic, as we have seen, is careful to emphasize that the combatants at Brémule all belonged to this group. They were 'knights', he says; 'they were all clad in mail', while the fate of the horses in the battle figures almost as prominently in his account as that of their riders. Such heavily armed, mounted troops were another Norman innovation. As was the chivalric ethos which they personified. For not only had the Anglo-Saxons fought on foot, they had also taken a much more 'total' attitude to war. For them, all was fair in conflict: they usually killed defeated enemies, whatever their rank, and regularly employed unsporting devices like entrapment and assassination to eliminate their foes. Worst of all was the fate of captured royal rivals or pretenders. Instead of the 'courtesy' which Henry extended to the Clito, a defeated Anglo-Saxon claimant faced either death or, at best, savage mutilation by blinding and amputation.

Now clearly the Norman chivalric code was more 'civilized'. Indeed, in time, it would become a central element in a new hybrid Anglo-Norman identity. This saw England as a self-consciously 'civilized' nation in contrast to the barbarous peoples of the Celtic fringe, who still embraced the brutal pre-chivalric code and slaughtered each other (and, when they got the chance, the English) without mercy. That is the credit side of chivalry. But there was an equally strong downside which threatened to undo the remarkable political achievement of Anglo-Saxon England.

The issue was royal power. In theory, the king remained as much of a king as he had ever been, consecrated by holy Church and honoured by all. But with the Norman Conquest the reality of his position had undergone a fundamental shift. For the king was now a knight as well as a sovereign: he shared the chivalric ethos and was bound by its code. As were all his greater subjects. And the greatest of them all thought of themselves as his 'peers' or equals. They expected to be treated accordingly with consideration and kid gloves, while the king, for his part, had a severely limited range of sanctions which he could apply to bring them into line. Execution, in particular, was unacceptable; instead confiscation, exile and, as a last resort, life imprisonment, were the most extreme measures he could use. The effect was to license a high level of political dissent and disorder, as the case of Normandy shows.

But all this, as William of Malmesbury points out, was foreign to the Anglo-Saxon tradition. This is why post-Conquest England experienced the apparent paradox of rebellions which were led by Norman nobles while the English natives clamoured for the king to hang the rebels in the approved English fashion!

Henry I had benefited from this sentiment when he resolved on a final settlement of accounts with Robert of Bellême. And it helped guarantee him a trouble-free English reign thereafter.

III

In time the chivalric virus would spread to England. But, even before it did, the country needed proper government during the king's lengthy absences in Normandy. At first, Henry turned to his queen, Edith-Matilda. She gave birth to her daughter Matilda in 1102 and her son William the following year. Then, after a mere three years of marriage and having barely fulfilled her dynastic duty, she separated herself from her husband's bed and lived apart, in great splendour, at Westminster. Henry did not complain and she appears not to have complained either when he reverted to the habits of his unmarried youth and sought the solace of many other women.

There were also political advantages to the arrangement as it left Matilda free to act as regent of England. She presided over councils and conducted diplomatic business. She also gave government a human face as she was pious, charitable and cultured. She loved music and musicians and was lavish in her patronage of foreign scholars, since, as William of Malmesbury noted slyly, they would trumpet her fame abroad.

But Matilda died in 1118. Thereafter Henry turned to a man of sterner stuff: Roger of Salisbury.

Roger was a priest of humble birth. Like that other priest-minister Cardinal Wolsey, who was one of the last of the breed just as Roger was one of the first, stories abound of Roger's swift dispatch of business in his earlier days. Roger is supposed to have first attracted Henry I's attention by the speed at which he said mass. This may or may not be true. What it certainly shows, however, is that Roger, like Wolsey later, impressed contemporaries as a man who got things done, and, when it was necessary, got them done fast.

There were other resemblances, too. Like Wolsey, Roger flagrantly broke his vow of celibacy and openly lived with his mistress. Roger was also a great builder, particularly at Shaftesbury and Malmesbury.

> For there he erected extensive edifices at vast cost and with surpass-
> ing beauty; the courses of stone being so correctly laid, that the line
> of juncture escapes the eye, and leads one to imagine that the whole
> wall is composed of a single block. He built anew the church of Salis-
> bury and beautified it in such a manner that it yields to none in
> England.

'He was', William of Malmesbury concluded, 'a prelate of great mind, and spared no expense towards completing his designs.'

And it was, above all, this *magnanimity* or greatness of mind that was the key to his magnificently confident handling of power. Wolsey was supposed to be in the habit of saying *Ego et rex meus* ('I and my king'). But Roger actually saw fit to add his own authority to the king's by issuing a writ which contained the phrase: 'I order you, on the part of the king and myself".

Even the great Cardinal might have hesitated before committing such an expression to writing.

Finally, both men's careers ended in failure when they were humiliated and repudiated by the kings they had served so well. Nothing survived from the wreck of Wolsey's fortunes. But Roger fared better and estab-lished an enduring administrative dynasty that ruled England, in three successive generations, for almost the whole of the twelfth century: from Roger's own advent in about 1100 to 1196, when Richard fitzNigel, Roger's great-nephew, died, still in harness after nearly forty years as treasurer. Not even the Cecils would cling to power so long or so tenaciously.

Henry had appointed Roger head of his household while he was still a landless younger son. Then, as soon as he became king, he gave him swift promotion up the official ladder: Roger was made chancellor in 1101, bishop of Salisbury in 1102 and finally, at an unknown date, 'justiciar'. Or maybe it would be truer to say that it was Roger who made the post of justiciar. There were two distinct aspects to the position: the justiciar was head of the ordinary administration of finance and justice, or, as we might say, chief minister; he was also vice-regent during the king's absences abroad. Under the earlier Norman kings the two functions seem to have been discharged by different men. Roger, however, combined them in his own person and did so, moreover, for the unprecedentedly long period of two decades or more under two kings.

Most important, perhaps, was Roger's dominance of the machinery of finance. Here again he appears as an innovator, since he was, almost certainly, not simply England's first minister of finance but also the creator of the financial ministry itself. This was known then and for the following seven hundred years as the 'Exchequer'.

The Exchequer's origins are much disputed. All that can be said for certain is that in 1110 Henry issued a writ addressed to 'the barons of the Exchequer'. It dealt with the payment of an 'aid' (tax) for the marriage of the king's daughter to the Holy Roman Emperor, Henry V, and it was witnessed by Bishop Roger. This writ appears to be the earliest piece of evidence for the Exchequer; it points to Roger's role as its managing executive (if not its creator) and it suggests that the imposition and collection of the 'aid' may well have been the first large-scale undertaking of the new agency. Roger's formative role also features heavily in the *Dialogus de Scaccario* ('Treatise on the Exchequer'), written by Roger's great-nephew, treasurer Richard fitzNigel, in about 1178.

Like many medieval administrative agencies, the Exchequer was named after a thing. What made it unique, however, was the nature of the object. It was not a piece of furniture (like the King's Bench) or a room (like the Chamber). Instead, it was a calculating device. The Exchequer was a board, 5 feet wide and 10 feet long, set up on trestles like a table. The board was covered with a black cloth, replaced each Easter, and divided by a grid of vertical and horizontal wood laths into squares.

The resulting resemblance to the board for a game of chess, known as *scacci* in Latin and *eschecs* in Old French, gave the Exchequer its name. It also enabled the board to function as a form of abacus or calculator. The seven columns, running from right to left along the length of the board, were denominated according to monetary value: at the extreme right were pennies, then shillings, pounds, scores of pounds, hundreds, thousands, and finally tens of thousands of pounds. Counters representing a debt to the king were placed in an upper row (so many for each penny, shilling, pound and so forth) and counters representing monies paid on account put likewise in a lower row. The amount outstanding could then be determined by subtracting the lower row of counters from the higher.

The device was necessary because the clumsy form of Roman numbers and their lack of a zero made arithmetic on paper more or less impossible. It also represented cutting-edge technology. The abacus had first been described in the West in the tenth century, and treatises on it continued to multiply over the next two centuries. One of the most important was written by the great English scholar Adelard of Bath, while he was a teacher at Laon in the early 1100s. Laon was then the most flourishing and influential school in the West. And, it has been conjectured, it was from Laon (conveniently nearby in Picardy in northern France) that someone, almost certainly Roger of Salisbury himself, borrowed the idea of the abacus and adapted it to the demands of English royal finance.

But the key to the Exchequer's effectiveness lay not only in its technology but also in its personnel and procedures – in *who* sat round the board, *what* they did, and *when* they did it. Here, once again, we almost certainly see the hand of Bishop Roger, who sat as its first president and modelled it in his own image of brusque, businesslike efficiency.

The board was placed long-side-on at the end of the room furthest from the door, like a high table in a college hall, and was surrounded on all four sides with benches. At the head of the table sat the justiciar, with the chancellor on his left and another senior councillor on his right. On the long bench against the wall were placed the treasurer and beneath him the clerks who wrote out the rolls of the Exchequer in which the written records of its business were kept. On the opposite long bench, with their backs to the room, were those who performed the mechanical tasks on which the smooth operation of the whole system depended: the calculator, who placed and manipulated the counters, and the tally-cutter, who made the notched sticks which served as a tangible record of monies paid and received.

Finally, at the foot of the table, sat the man who was the object of this whole elaborate apparatus: the sheriff. With the assistance of his clerk, he was the accounting officer for the king's revenues in the county or counties which he administered and he appeared before the Exchequer as a kind of defendant. The prosecuting counsel, on the other hand, was the treasurer, whose job it was to press the revenue's case for the sheriff to pay over as much money as possible. While the other senior officers, known as the 'barons' of the Exchequer, acted as judges between them.

This meant that the metaphor of a chessboard took on another, grimmer significance. For the sheriff was like one player in a game of chess; his opponent was the treasurer, 'so ... it is chiefly between [these] two', the *Dialogus* notes, 'that the conflict takes place and the war is waged':

each counter in the upper row meant that the king received more; each in the lower, that the sheriff paid less. It was the difference between ruin and security for the sheriff and riches and pecuniousness (which in turn meant power or weakness) for the king.

By and large, it will come as no surprise to the modern taxpayer, the treasurer won on the king's behalf, while the sheriff, summoned to appear 'as you love yourself and all that you have', paid up.

Not all of this was new, of course. Tallies went back to the reign of Edward the Confessor at least. Similarly, later Anglo-Saxon England had a centralized treasury at Winchester, where were kept not only cash but written records and assessments. The innovations, on the other hand, were just as important: the siting of the Exchequer in Westminster; the use of Latin for the records; and, above all, the fixed rhythm of biannual audit: the first at Michaelmas (29 September), when the sheriff paid monies on account, and the second at Easter, when a final reckoning was agreed and any balance due handed over.

And it was this inexorable regularity, as well as the 'scientific' precision of the calculator and his counters, that gave the Exchequer its special edge. What was agreed at Easter and entered in the rolls was final: it could be changed only by the king himself and it would be pursued to the last penny and fraction of a penny, thanks to the attendance of the marshal and his officers on the board, who would imprison the defaulting or recalcitrant until they paid up or were discharged.

What the Exchequer did *not* do, however, was to handle cash. This, instead, was the role of the exchequer of receipt. And it was much less straightforward than merely counting coins. Not that there wasn't a lot of counting to do, since only one coin was then current in England: the silver penny.

But, beyond counting, there was the question of value. For the value of such coins rested, as would continue to be the case for almost the next millennium, not on their face value but on the actual quantity of precious metal they contained. Thus, for all the bureaucratic elaboration and sophistication of the Exchequer machine, the wealth of the king, like the wealth of England, rested on the quality and stability of the English coinage. This was yet another Anglo-Saxon creation. It had survived the reigns of the first two Norman kings largely unscathed. But, by Henry I's own time, there was significant deterioration and the face value of the coins was no longer supported by the quantities of silver in them. There are several possible explanations for this. The 'moneyers', or coiners, were paid neither a salary nor commission. This made the temptation to reduce the weight of the coins, or their fineness by adding base metals, very great. Above all, there was the scale of the king's own demands – the 'manifold impositions' of which the Anglo-Saxon chronicler repeatedly complains – which subjected the whole monetary system to intolerable strain.

The result was a cycle: debasement and inflation were followed in turn by measures of reform. But these, though dramatic, were never long lasting. The first attempts at reform took place early in the reign in 1108 when, on the advice of Anselm, archbishop of Canterbury, Henry issued legislation which threatened the coiners of substandard money with terrible punishment: they were to be castrated and their right hands amputated. Unsurprisingly perhaps, the consequence was an immediate improvement in both the appearance and fineness of the coinage. But the improvement was short lived and was followed by an even more precipitate decline.

By 1124 crisis had been reached. According to *The Anglo-Saxon Chronicle*, debasement and the consequent inflation hit record levels: 'the penny was so adulterated that a man who had a pound at a market could not exchange it for twelve-pence worth of goods'. The situation was exacerbated by crop failure and, as the price of staples soared beyond reach, public order threatened to break down. It was decided to make an example – or rather, several. In early December, at a court held in Leicestershire and attended by many of the king's knights, Ralph Basset, the king's justice, 'hanged more thieves than were ever known before'. 'A full heavy year was this,' the chronicler lamented, 'the man who had any property was deprived of it by severe taxes and severe courts; the man who had none died of hunger.'

All this was bad enough. But much more directly threatening to Henry was the reaction of his soldiers in Normandy, who complained vigorously about his attempt to pay them in English pennies that were little better than tin. This time something had to be done. As usual, Henry delegated the task to Roger of Salisbury. At Christmas 1125, all the moneyers in England were summoned to Winchester, where 'they were taken one by one and each deprived of the right hand and the testicles below'. The legislation of 1109 had at last been put into operation. In contrast to his sympathy for the thieves executed the previous year, the Anglo-Saxon chronicler had none for the moneyers:

> All was done with great justice, because they had ruined the whole country with their great counterfeitings. They all paid for it.

Here at last there was something that united all Henry's subjects: when it came to protecting the deservedly high reputation of the English currency, everyone, from the Norman king to the lowliest Anglo-Saxon peasant, was in agreement and was prepared to use the most savage means.

IV

In 1120, Henry's power reached an apogee. Long unchallenged in England, the king found that the victory over France at Brémule and the renewed exile of William the Clito gave him an equally free hand in Normandy. For the first time in almost four years, he would be able to return to England to spend Christmas with all the pomp of a conqueror.

But, on the way back, disaster struck the royal family, who, then as now, travelled separately. Just before twilight on 25 November, Henry and his court set sail from Barfleur in Normandy and, with a favourable wind, made a quick and safe passage. But his son and heir William the Æthling, who was aged seventeen and 'possessed everything but the name of king', decided to stay behind for a final evening of revelry. He and his suite of three hundred (which included the cream of the young Anglo-Norman nobility, who, as usual, were attracted to the rising sun) got thoroughly drunk. As did the crew. Nevertheless, towards midnight, they decided to embark in the *White Ship*. It was a crack vessel of the latest construction and the young sparks boasted that they would soon catch up with the king and his greybeards, even though they had left hours before.

But, less than half a mile out, the drunken pilot steered the ship on to a well-known hazard: a large rock that lurked just beneath the surface at high tide. A hole was ripped in the ship's side and the vessel started to fill with water. Despite the confusion, the ship's boat was launched and William was rowed off towards safety. But, hearing the cry of his illegitimate half-sister, the countess of Perche, William ordered the boat to return to rescue her. Desperate men, however, flung themselves into it; the tiny craft was overwhelmed and William was drowned. As was almost everyone else on board the *White Ship*, including William's half-sister and half-brother, his tutor and the earl of Chester and his countess, who was also of the blood royal. Only a single man survived.

It was, as they say, a moment that changed history: 'no ship', William of Malmesbury wrote, 'was ever productive of so much misery to England; none so widely celebrated throughout the world'.

News quickly reached England. But at first a terrified court withheld it from the king. When, over a day later, he was finally told, Henry collapsed and was helped to a private room, where he wept bitter tears. 'This mourning', Orderic noted, 'lasted for many days.'

'Many *days*'? In the context, 'days' seems almost bathetic. But Henry could not afford to indulge his grief for long. For he was a king and he had work to do. His only legitimate son's death had left him without an heir and his whole achievement in England and Normandy threatened to die with him. This could not be. Instead, on 6 January 1121, the last day of a miserable Christmas, the council, meeting in London, resolved that the king, widowed since the death of Edith-Matilda in 1118, should marry a new wife. The chosen bride was Adeliza, daughter of Godfrey VII, count of Louvain.

Henry had a single purpose in his second marriage: 'he was anxious for future heirs by [his] new consort'. And there was every reason to suppose that his wish would be fulfilled. Adeliza was 'a beautiful girl', who seems to have been chosen on grounds of her looks as well as her family connections; while Henry himself was a man of tremendous sexual appetites – and achievements. His nearest rival among English kings, Charles II, fathered eight sons and six daughters out of wedlock. Henry easily beat this: besides his two legitimate children, he had some nine sons and eleven daughters by at least six mothers of four different races: Anglo-Saxon, Norman, Welsh and Anglo-Danish.

But, like Charles's marriage to Catherine of Braganza, Henry's second union was to be barren. At the time it was the young bride who was blamed for a fruitless union. Adeliza, however, would mother seven children with her second husband, Henry's butler. Her blushes, in Henry's lifetime, spared the king's pride.

But as Henry's virility waned, some other means of settling the succession would have to be found.

Things were probably brought to a head by another death in the family. In 1114, Henry's daughter Matilda had been married to the Emperor Henry V. But, in May 1125, the emperor died. Matilda was now a widow of twenty-four and Henry's only surviving legitimate child. She travelled from Germany to join her father in Normandy and in September 1126 father and daughter returned to England together.

Much of the remainder of the year seems to have been spent in debating the succession question. One possibility lay in the children of Henry's sister, Adela. Adela had married in 1080 Count Stephen of Blois, by whom she had a brood of fine sons. The eldest, Theobald, had his future assured as heir to his father's county of Blois, sited strategically on the frontier of Normandy and the kingdom of France. But the two younger sons, Stephen and Henry, were attracted into the orbit of their uncle Henry I and made their fortunes in England.

Henry of Blois, like many younger sons, was destined for the Church and was educated at the abbey of Cluny in Burgundy. The abbey was notable for three things: its strict observance of the rule of St Benedict, which regulated monastic life throughout the West; the splendour of its liturgy; and, finally, its empire-building, as it spawned daughter-houses across Europe. The young Henry picked up on the splendour and the empire-building. But the strictness rather passed him by. Instead, in 1126 King Henry appointed his nephew abbot of Glastonbury and, three years later, bishop of Winchester. Since Glastonbury was one of the richest abbeys and Winchester was the richest see, the fact that Bishop Henry contrived to hold both of them together for the next forty years made him a veritable prince-bishop and the wealthiest prelate in the English Church, with an authority eventually outweighing that of Roger of Salisbury himself. Roger exercised power under the king and on his behalf; Henry, however, came to fancy himself as a kingmaker.

But the man who would be king was the middle brother, Stephen. Born in about 1096, he grew up to be a paragon of chivalry. He was handsome, brave and a fine warrior. These personal qualities made him an attractive candidate for the throne. In addition, his uncle King Henry showered him with lands and in 1125 engineered his marriage to Matilda of Boulogne. Matilda, herself a woman in the heroic mould, was a great heiress in

England as well as France. Even more importantly perhaps, she too was a descendant through her mother of the Anglo-Saxon royal house. This meant that Stephen's children, too, would carry the mystic bloodline of the House of Wessex.

Finally, there was Henry's only surviving legitimate child, the Empress Matilda, who was now, following her husband's death, back in the Anglo-Norman realm at her father's side. The fact that she was a woman, of course, was enough to rule her out in most eyes. And father and daughter had not seen each other since the girl was eight. Nevertheless, there was, Henry discovered, much to recommend her. She was beautiful, intelligent and capable and, still in her twenties, had not suffered that coarsening of character which would later make her so controversial and divisive. Her position as dowager empress augmented her status. And above all, she was her father's daughter and her mother's too. This double royal descent, all commentators agree, was decisive for Henry.

It remained only to enforce his decision.

V

At Christmas 1126 Henry summoned a great council in London. According to William of Malmesbury, he presented the case for Matilda forcibly. He reminded those present of her descent from the Norman kings on his side and from the Anglo-Saxon on her mother's. And he seems to have laid special emphasis on the latter.

Such an appeal to Anglo-Saxon history must have warmed the hearts of men like William of Malmesbury, who may have been research assistant for the speech. But William was under no illusion about the general attractiveness of the argument to Henry's audience of hard-bitten Anglo-Norman magnates. For what carried the day, he makes clear, was not Henry's words but his will: Henry 'compelled', William states baldly, 'all the nobility of England ... to make oath that ... they would ... accept his daughter Matilda as their sovereign'.

The clergy, headed by the archbishop of Canterbury, swore first; then it was the turn of the lay nobles. The first to take the oath was King David I of Scotland, who was Matilda's maternal uncle. His oath was followed by a good-natured dispute between Henry's oldest bastard, Robert, earl of Gloucester, and Stephen of Blois as to who should have the honour of swearing next: 'one alleging the privilege of a son, the other the dignity of a nephew'. In the event, Stephen won and swore second, while Robert had to be content with third place. Both men, of course, were possible contenders for the throne themselves. And, it would become clear, they took the oath with very different degrees of sincerity.

Many others present had reservations too. But, as usual, Henry got his way. For the time being at least.

Only a few months passed before Henry put the uneasy acquiescence of his nobility to a severe and arguably fatal test. The king, with his remarkable strategic sense, had long seen that Anjou held the key to the uneasy balance of power in northern France and he pursued an Angevin alliance with his usual undeviating determination. But there were obstacles on both sides. On the one hand, Count Fulk V of Anjou was a flighty opportunist; on the other, the Norman nobility nursed an inveterate dislike of the Angevins as the hereditary enemies of the duchy. Henry had sought to overcome their hostility by marrying his heir, William the Æthling, to the daughter of Count Fulk. But this hope, like so many others, foundered with the *White Ship*. Now that Matilda was securely nominated as his heir, Henry's first thought was to return to the Angevin alliance. But he recognized that he had to proceed by stealth.

In late spring 1127, Henry sent Matilda to Normandy, where, on Whitsunday, 22 May, she was betrothed to Geoffrey, son and heir of Count Fulk. Henry soon followed in person to celebrate the marriage. Throughout the affair, Henry took into his confidence only a handful of his family and intimates.

And for good reason. The marriage was deeply unpopular. 'All the French [Normans] and English', the Anglo-Saxon chronicler wrote, 'disapproved of this.' Simple xenophobia played its part. But there was a more substantial point. Geoffrey, as Matilda's husband, might be expected to play an important part in the government of England. In other words, the Anglo-Norman elite were complaining about having a monarch thrust on them by the back door and without their consent. Swallowing Matilda had been hard enough; to submit to her husband as well was a step too far.

The marriage and the underhand way in which it had been brought about fatally undermined Matilda's position. 'I have frequently heard',

William of Malmesbury reports, 'Roger, bishop of Salisbury say that he was freed from the oath which he had taken to the empress; for that he had sworn conditionally, that the king should not marry his daughter to anyone out of the kingdom, without his consent and that of the rest of the nobility.' But, no doubt, while Henry lived Roger kept his thoughts to himself.

Moreover, it was even doubtful whether the marriage would last. After the wedding, Fulk had set out again on crusade to the Holy Land, leaving his newly married son Geoffrey, barely aged fourteen, as the ruler of Anjou. Geoffrey and his wife, who shared the same imperious temperament, now proceeded to quarrel. Within a year, they separated and Geoffrey sent Matilda, bag and baggage, back to her father in Rouen. The separation, which lasted for two years, was brought to an end in 1131. On 8 September, the nobility renewed their solemn oath to Matilda and also advised that she should return to her husband. In the course of the next few years, three sons were born in quick succession: Henry on 5 March 1133, Geoffrey (from whose birth Matilda nearly died) in 1134 and William in 1136.

The birth of the young Henry seemed to settle the problem of the succession. It also offered the prospect of the union of Normandy and Anjou, which had been the lifetime goal of King Henry's diplomacy. Overjoyed, Henry, hastening to be at his grandson's side, left England for Normandy in August 1133.

He never returned.

It was not for want of trying. Three times he made arrangements to leave. But each time the journey had to be put off. The reason was a new family quarrel between the king and his son-in-law, Count Geoffrey. Geoffrey was eager to step into the old man's shoes; Henry was having none of it. In revenge Geoffrey stirred up rebellion in Normandy and it almost came to open war between them.

But not even rebellion and family quarrels were allowed to interfere with Henry's passion for the chase. On Monday, 25 November 1135, he arrived at the *château* of Lyons-la-Forêt and made arrangement to go hunting the following day. But in the night he was suddenly taken ill. He lingered for almost a week. In that time he confirmed his disposition of the crown: 'he awarded', William of Malmesbury writes, 'all his territories, on either side of the sea, to his daughter in legitimate and perpetual

This mosaic from Cogidubnus's palace at Fishbourne near Chichester suggests the sophisticated lifestyle of the Romanized British elite.

The 'Venerable Bede', who chronicled the Anglo-Saxon invasions and immigration of the fifth and sixth centuries, which destroyed what was left of Romano-British civilization. Bede also invented the idea of England, or at least the idea of the English as a single people.

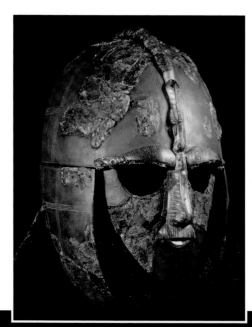

Anglo-Saxon England was a warrior culture, with a taste for splendid male jewellery. It also had metal-working skills of the highest order. LEFT: The royal helmet, perhaps of King Redwald of East Anglia, from the Sutton Hoo ship burial, is modelled on a Roman centurion's helmet and made of iron overlaid with plaques of silvered and gilt bronze. BELOW: Gold and garnet-inlaid fragments from the recently discovered Staffordshire Hoard, including the twisted remains of a cross (RIGHT). This suggests that the hoard may be the result of a victory by the pagan King Penda of Mercia over his Christian rivals.

Anglo-Saxon England quickly developed a sophisticated culture of its own. RIGHT: After his conversion to Christianity, Æthelbert of Kent issued a Law Code, like the Christian Roman emperors. But the content of the Code is wholly Anglo-Saxon – indeed, it may be first document written in English. BELOW: Offa of Mercia's silver penny, stamped with his name and image, and his gold coin, with his name and title inside an Arabic inscription copied from a dinar issued by the caliph Al-Mansur.

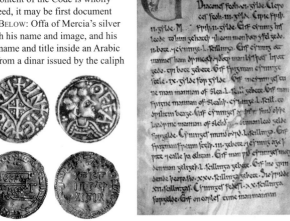

A dragon-headed Viking ship, as depicted in a late tenth-century Anglo-Saxon chronicle. The mobility of the Vikings, on both sea and land, was the greatest threat to Anglo-Saxon England.

The gold ring of Alfred the Great's father, King Æthelwulf of Wessex, whose name and title appear round the base. The shape of the ring might refer to a mitre, or perhaps to the *cynehelm*, in which case it is our only representation of this earliest form of Anglo-Saxon crown.

The 'Alfred Jewel' was discovered in 1693, not far from Athelney where Alfred hid in the marshes during his campaign against the Danes. The inscription reads AELFRED MEC HEHT GEWYRAN ('Alfred had me made').

Edgar, crowned and flanked by St Peter and the Virgin Mary, offering to Christ his charter of the New Minster at Winchester, which he refounded as a reformed Benedictine monastery. Edgar's reign represents the apogee of the Anglo-Saxon monarchy with its idiosyncratic fusion of Germanic, Roman and Christian traditions.

Cnut and his queen, Emma, presenting a giant gold cross to the New Minster at Winchester. The illustration, modelled on the similar image in Edgar's refoundation charter of the New Minster, is yet another sign that Cnut, the Viking invader, presented himself as the legitimate successor of Edgar, the Anglo-Saxon king whose rule came to be seen as a golden age. But there are differences. In accordance with his high view of kingship, Cnut's crown is placed on his head by an angel. Likewise, the near-equal status accorded to Emma is a break with English tradition.

The silver penny which Edward issued in 1051 after his triumph over the Godwins. The image of the king is a sharply characterized, realistic portrait – the first such on an English coin. The upper portion of the crown is crossed with two arches, like the crown of the Holy Roman Emperor; the lower jewelled circlet is modelled on the diadem of the Byzantine emperor.

The end of Anglo-Saxon England: the final stages of the Battle of Hastings, as shown in the Bayeux Tapestry. The first scene, which is captioned *HIC HAROLD REX INTERFECTUS EST* ('Here King Harold was killed'), shows on the left Harold trying to remove an arrow from his eye, and on the right the king being struck down with a sword blow to the thigh. The second scene, the caption of which begins with *ET FUGA* ('And in flight'), shows the English shield wall crumbling and the soldiers beginning to flee.

The presentation copy of the Domesday Book, given to William the Conqueror at Salisbury on 1 August 1086. Its elaborate survey of the landed wealth of England enabled William, as it were, to hold the Conquest in his hand.

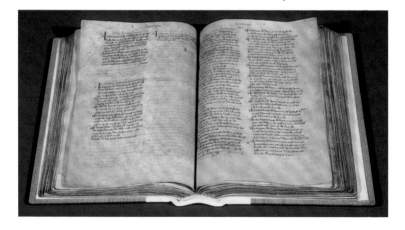

ET FVGA: VE...

The coronation of William II
'Rufus' at Westminster on
26 September 1087 by
Archbishop Lanfranc.

The Great Hall of Westminster
looking towards the dais. The
hammer-beam roof is fourteenth
century; otherwise the vast
dimensions of the hall are as William
II left them. The Hall remains the
most impressive monument of the
Anglo-Norman monarchy.

William the Conqueror on horseback as commander from the Bayeux Tapestry. Chivalry (from the French *chevalier,* knight or mounted warrior), with its code of values and anarchic politics, was one of the most important and unsettling Norman imports into England.

Henry I, youngest son of William the Conqueror, who seized the throne after the death of William Rufus in a hunting accident, proved a highly effective ruler. Here, in John of Worcester's *Chronicle*, written in about 1140, we see Henry dreaming of the problems of kingship: above are protesting peasants, submitting a written list of their complaints to the king and, below, violent barons who threaten him with their swords and spears.

Henry I laid the foundations of the main administrative and legal institutions of medieval England. This early fifteenth-century miniature shows the Court of King's Bench in session in Westminster Hall: the red-robed judges sit above; the clerks write the rolls of the proceedings at the green baize table; an usher swears in the jury on the left; the accused in leg-irons is in the middle, with counsel wearing the white coif (headdress) pleading on either side; and other prisoners are chained at the bar at below.

Henry II (BELOW) and Eleanor of Aquitaine in their tomb effigies at Fontevrault, the mausoleum of the counts of Anjou. Henry I's death without a male heir led to almost two decades of civil war between his daughter Matilda and his nephew Stephen and it was not until 1154 that Matilda's son became unchallenged king as Henry II. Henry, inheriting Anjou from his father as well as England and Normandy from his mother and ruling Aquitaine in right of his wife, was Europe's most powerful ruler and one of England's ablest kings. His weakness was his fraught relationship with his wife and three warring sons.

Henry II was a passionate believer in royal justice. But his attempt to punish criminal clergy led to a clash with Thomas Becket, archbishop of Canterbury and his sometime favourite and chancellor. Words uttered during one of Henry's volcanic fits of rage led four knights to murder Becket in his own cathedral in 1170, as shown on the front of this enameled casket. Henry was only able to head off the consequences of this act by doing penance at Becket's tomb, in which the martyr is shown being laid on the casket lid.

These tiles show Richard 'Coeur de Lion' (LEFT) defeating Saladin during the crusade to recover the Holy Lands in the late twelfth century. In fact, Saladin did not die at Richard's hands: this scene represents a dramatic invention intended to act as a tribute to Richard's bravery in battle. The subject had a natural appeal for English kings and was a particular favourite of Henry III, who had it painted on the walls of the Antioch Chamber at Clarendon Palace.

The tomb effigy of John at Worcester Cathedral. John, Henry II's spoilt youngest son, succeeded his heroic crusader brother Richard I in 1199 and quickly proved a disaster. He was grasping, treacherous and an unsuccessful general. He quarrelled with the pope, lost Normandy and, by the time of his death, was within a whisker of losing England too.

After the loss of Normandy, the nobility took advantage of John's weakness to force him to concede *Magna Carta*, shown here in the third version issued by John's successor, Henry III. The Charter addressed the grievances of the church and the barons but it also contained the famous general clauses promising not to punish without trial or deny or sell justice. However, the proviso that authorized the barons to use force to compel the king to adhere to the charter led to its being annulled by Pope Innocent III, to whom John had reconciled himself and done homage.

Henry III, from his tomb effigy at Westminster Abbey. Henry, who succeeded at the age of nine, was crowned immediately but real power was exercised by a series of regents. He inherited high ideas of kingship, but grew up to be easygoing, luxurious, unwarlike and in thrall to stronger personalities, especially from his wife's extended family, who quarrelled among themselves and were hated as foreigners.

A self-portrait of the chronicler Matthew Paris kneeling at the feet of the Virgin. Paris's gossipy, lavishly illustrated chronicles give a richly detailed picture of the politics of Henry III's reign – albeit one bitterly hostile to the king, with whom he nevertheless enjoyed good personal relations.

The Battle of Evesham, fought on 4 August 1265 between Simon de Montfort and Henry III's eldest son Edward. De Montfort, Henry's brother-in-law, had capitalized on widespread discontent with Henry's government to impose a 'constitutionalist' regime that turned the king into the cypher of a baronial council. After his defeat at Evesham his body – as shown here – was dismembered as that of a traitor.

The gatehouse tower of Edward I's Caernarfon Castle in north Wales, crowned with eagles and with walls banded in lighter coloured stone like those of Constantinople, symbolizes Edward's imperial ambitions. Warlike and legalistic, Edward restored royal authority in England and was determined to extend it to Wales and Scotland. But, to pay for his wars, he had to accept the legacy of Magna Carta and to work with Parliament.

Edward II, in a copy of his tomb effigy at Gloucester Cathedral. Edward, who succeeded in 1307, was tall and strong like Edward I. But he inherited his grandfather's weak and indulgent character and his reign saw a violent replay of the constitutional and political struggles of the thirteenth century.

Sir Hugh Despenser, favourite of Edward II, is emasculated and disembowelled as a traitor in 1326. Feeling against the king and his favourites was exacerbated by rumours of Edward's homosexuality. Piers Gaveston, Despenser's predecessor, had been brutally murdered in 1312 and Edward himself was done to death at Berkeley Castle after his deposition in 1327.

Edward III (LEFT) in the blue mantle of the Order of the Garter, from the Garter Book of 1435. The Garter, founded in 1348, symbolized Edward's chivalric view of kingship. He enjoyed excellent relations with his nobility, like his cousin, Thomas, duke of Lancaster (RIGHT), and led them to a series of great victories in France, of which he claimed to be king in 1340.

Richard II, assisted by his patron saints, praying to the Virgin and Child in the Wilton Diptych. As this exquisite painting suggests, Richard was intelligent, sensitive and artistic – and quite unsuited to managing the warrior monarchy perfected by his grandfather, Edward III.

succession'. Finally, on Sunday, 1 December, towards midnight, Henry died.

The Anglo-Saxon chronicler had found plenty to criticize in Henry's rule while he was still alive, in particular 'the manifold impositions' of taxation which had borne so heavily on the common folk. But, when he was dead, he delivered a very different verdict on the king:

> A good man he was; and there was great dread of him. No man durst do wrong with another in his time. Peace he made for man and beast. Whoso bare his burthen of gold and silver, durst no man say ought to him but good.

The difference in the judgements arose, no doubt, from the fact that the chronicler was writing his obituary with the benefit of hindsight.

For Henry had changed the monarchy – and England. At his deathbed one of his attendants said, 'God grant him peace, for peace he loved.' This and more he had achieved by force of will, by ruthlessness and patient calculation. He had imposed royal justice on his people and centralized power in permanent departments of state. He had restored his father's empire and extended it into Wales. He had dominated Scotland and held Normandy together. All these were remarkable achievements. But, for the English, there was one that stood out at the time. It was the imposition of the king's peace – intimidating, irresistible and complete. And it would be in short supply now that he was gone.

Henry's body was taken in solemn procession to Rouen. There it was disembowelled and embalmed in preparation for its eventual journey to England. This was delayed by adverse winds and bad weather and it was not until 4 January 1136 that it was buried in the abbey at Reading which Henry had built and in the England which he had made his own.

His successor was present at the funeral. But, despite all Henry's efforts, it was not his daughter Matilda.

9

CIVIL WAR

Stephen and Matilda

BACK IN 1126, STEPHEN OF BLOIS had competed to be second to swear the oath to his cousin Matilda. Now he was the first to break it. As soon as he heard the news of his uncle Henry's death, he took ship for Dover. There the townsfolk refused to admit him. As they did at Canterbury. But in London it was a different story. The citizens welcomed him with open arms, and, claiming to act as a proxy for all the English, elected him king by acclamation. It was the first direct participation by the English in the choice of a monarch since the Norman Conquest.

Then Stephen, following in Henry I's own footsteps, made straight for Winchester, where he seized the royal treasury and was acclaimed by the people of the second capital. That done, he returned to London for his coronation on Sunday, 22 December. It was a scratch affair. According to William of Malmesbury, three bishops were present: 'but there were no abbots and scarcely any of the nobility'. Thinly attended though it was, it was enough to put the indelible mark of kingship on Stephen.

A mere twenty-two days separated the death of Henry I and Stephen's coronation. It was done 'without delay, without struggle, as though in the twinkling of an eye'.

I

That much is clear. But *how* the *coup d'état* was effected is more debatable. One school of thought sees it merely as the result of Matilda's ill-luck and ill-judgement. If her relations with her father had remained good and she had been present at his deathbed then, it is argued, she would have been recognized as queen by the large number of nobles and bishops 'whom the report of [Henry's] sickness ... quickly gathered around him', and that would have been that. I wonder, however, whether it were quite so simple. Had Stephen really not thought of the possibility of claiming the throne? Had he really taken no soundings? Was the well-oiled machine of the seizure of power really extemporized? It seems hard to believe.

The other view would see longer-term causes at work: simmering resentment at Matilda's nomination and marriage on the one hand, and careful preparation by Stephen on the other. The latter is plainly hinted at by William of Malmesbury: 'yet, not to conceal the truth from posterity,' he writes, 'all [Stephen's] efforts would have been in vain, had not his brother, Henry, bishop of Winchester, granted him his entire support'. For Henry's firm commitment and smooth tongue brought over other crucial figures: the archbishop of Canterbury, Roger of Salisbury and William de Pont de l'Arche, the treasurer. Between them, these men gave Stephen the key to three of the four power centres of the Anglo-Norman state: the Church, the administration and the royal treasures. Only the fourth, the nobility, remained uncommitted.

But not for long. Here, once again, Stephen's remarkable and universal popularity came into play. 'Stephen,' William of Malmesbury concedes, 'before he came to the throne, from his complacency of manners, and readiness to joke, to sit and make good cheer, even with low people, had gained so much on their affections as is hardly to be conceived.' Soon, the same easy talent had the nobility eating out of his hand as well and they 'all ... willingly acknowledged him'. And where his own popularity couldn't reach, his uncle's treasures, estimated at £100,000 in cash besides plate and jewels, and now at his entire disposal, did.

Stephen's swift and complete seizure of power presented Matilda and her leading supporters with a fait accompli, and even her half-brother Robert, earl of Gloucester, rendered conditional homage at the specially summoned great council. The other principal business of the council was the issuing of a major charter of liberties. There was something in it for everyone, but most for the Church. 'I, Stephen ... do grant the Holy Church to be free,' the charter began and went on to confirm the most generous and far-reaching interpretation of the rights, privileges, property and autonomy of both Church and churchmen. Stephen also surrendered all the new forests which had been added by Henry I; 'entirely

[did] away all exactions ... and injustices, whether illegally introduced by the sheriffs or anyone else', and finally swore to 'observe the good and ancient laws and just customs in murders, pleas and other causes'.

The charter, witnessed by the impressively large number of fourteen bishops and twenty-nine lay magnates, marked the definitive acceptance of Stephen by the realm. But, even at this high tide of his support, there were disturbing signs of weakness. Immediately on hearing of the death of Henry, David I of Scotland had invaded England and captured several important towns, including Carlisle and Newcastle, which were the key to the west and east borders respectively.

Was David being merely opportunistic? Or was he also registering his disapproval of Stephen's overriding of Matilda's claim, of which (the Anglo-Saxon chronicler implies) the Scottish king had been a prime mover? At any event, Stephen moved north with an intimidatingly large army. But, instead of crushing David, he came to terms. David kept Carlisle.

Similarly, Earl Robert of Gloucester, in return for rendering a reluctant homage, 'received everything that he wanted' from the king. But most notorious was the case of Baldwin de Revières, who held Exeter Castle against Stephen. Stephen took personal charge of the siege, which dragged on through three swelteringly hot summer months. Like the siege of Bridgnorth, thirty years previously at the beginning of Henry I's reign, it was a high-profile military action, conducted 'before the eyes of all the barons'. Also as at Bridgnorth and no doubt for the same reasons, the barons were reluctant for the king to press things to a conclusion and counselled leniency. But there the parallel ends. For Stephen, unlike Henry, listened to the siren voices and allowed the garrison and Baldwin de Revières himself to go free on their surrender.

Stephen, men were learning fast, might be a good soldier. But he was a poor negotiator, with the knack of snatching defeat from the jaws of victory.

The lesson was driven home, on the largest and most damaging scale, by Stephen's expedition in 1137 to Normandy to take possession of his other, ducal realm. The Norman barons had been no keener on the succession of Matilda than the English and their first thought after Henry's death was to offer the duchy to Stephen's elder brother, Theobald, count of Blois. Theobald accepted, and it was only with a bad grace that he was subsequently persuaded to renounce his claim in favour of Stephen. Stephen, for his part and with his now customary generosity, sweetened the pill with a pension of 2000 marks (£1333 6s 8d) a year for his brother.

A much more severe challenge to Stephen's possession of Normandy came from Geoffrey of Anjou. Geoffrey, acting in right of his wife Matilda, was able to exploit the ever-fractious Norman baronage and invaded in June. Stephen determined to meet him head-on. But once again the barons demurred. Faced with this division in his own ranks, Stephen had no choice but to come to terms, and Geoffrey too was bought off with an annual pension of 2000 marks. Stephen even paid the first year's instalment on the spot.

Stephen never returned to Normandy, which was left – increasingly unhappily – to fend for itself.

The outcome of this disastrous Norman expedition was a turning point. It made clear that Stephen was squandering his political capital almost as quickly as his uncle's cash mountain. It emboldened his enemies everywhere. The Scots invaded in the new year and, after Easter, there were risings against Stephen throughout the West Country.

In response, Stephen laid about him in all directions: rushing, in the space of a few months, from Scotland to Bristol to Castle Cary and finally to Shrewsbury. Here, for the first time, he showed his teeth by having 'five men of rank ... hanged' after the surrender of the garrison. And a much greater victory was won in Stephen's absence in the north. There, on 22 August, the northerners, led by Archbishop Thurstan of York and fighting under the banners of the northern Anglo-Saxon saints, defeated King David of Scots. The victory entered into legend as the Battle of the Standard. But, despite the scale of the Scottish military defeat, it was David who triumphed in the peace negotiations by gaining Newcastle and the earldom of Northumbria. With these gains, the Scots now ruled the northern counties from coast to coast.

The effective dismemberment of England had begun.

II

The key defector from Stephen was Earl Robert of Gloucester. Robert's motives have been much debated by modern historians. Had he been covertly committed to Matilda all along? Or was he a Johnny-come-lately to her cause and motivated more by pique at Stephen than by loyalty to his half-sister? In fact, there seems little reason to doubt the explanation of Robert's behaviour offered by his contemporary and apologist, William of Malmesbury. For it is based, above all, on Robert's caution. This was a quality which Robert displayed – often to excess – throughout his career. Robert, William of Malmesbury explains, found himself on the horns of a dilemma: 'if he became subject to Stephen, it seemed contrary to the oath he had sworn to his sister; if he opposed him, he saw that such conduct [in view of Stephen's apparently impregnable position] could nothing benefit her or his nephews, but would certainly most grievously injure himself'.

The upshot was that Robert played a waiting game. But the moment the cracks in Stephen's position made it safe and sensible to do so, he had renounced the homage he had reluctantly given.

That was in May 1138. But it took almost another eighteen months before Robert felt it safe to land in England. Meanwhile, Stephen's position had undergone a further, abrupt deterioration. And this time it touched, not the fringes, but the heart – or rather, the soul – of his power. From the beginnings of English kingship, the relationship of Church and state had been of the most intimate. But Stephen, more even than most kings, had begun his reign as a creature of the Church. As we have seen, the support of his brother Henry, bishop of Winchester, had been crucial in his seizure of the crown. And thereafter the Church had continued to be exceptionally supportive.

But now Stephen risked throwing all this away by engineering a confrontation with Bishop Roger of Salisbury and his clan at the summer court of 1139. The court was convoked to meet at Oxford on 24 June and Bishop Roger was summoned with the rest. But he went reluctantly and with foreboding. 'I shall be of much the same service at court as a foal in battle.'

Roger's premonitions were fulfilled when a fracas took place between his servants and those of Stephen's favourite, Alan, count of Brittany. The king leapt at the opportunity. He had disgraced the king's court and broken his peace, Roger was told. To make amends, he was required to reaffirm his allegiance and surrender his castles of Salisbury, Malmesbury, Sherborne and Devizes. Roger's nephew Alexander, bishop of Lincoln, was likewise required to surrender his castles of Newark and Sleaford.

The shock of his fall proved too much for Bishop Roger, who, Wolsey-like to the last, died before the end of the year.

Stephen's professed motive was to deprive Earl Robert and Matilda, who were expected to arrive at any moment in England, of allies and strongholds. But his actions had more or less the opposite effect. Bishop Henry, appointed papal legate earlier in 1139, donned the mantle of affronted ecclesiastical power and summoned a council of the Church to condemn Stephen's actions.

A month later, on 30 September, Earl Robert and the Empress Matilda landed in England, accompanied by only 140 knights. This was more of an escort than an army and would have been quite inadequate to force a landing at any of the main ports. Instead, they had done a deal with the queen dowager, Adeliza, who resided in her castle at the river port of Arundel in Sussex. The party was allowed to land there and Matilda was received into her stepmother's protection. Robert slipped away almost immediately and, with only a dozen knights, made his way through hostile country to his stronghold of Bristol. Halfway there he was joined by Brian Fitzcount, also one of the original supporters of Matilda's marriage, and henceforward her unshakeable partisan.

Meanwhile, Stephen moved in force against Arundel and forced Adeliza to withdraw her protection. Matilda was saved by two things: by chivalry, which made it unthinkable that Stephen would use violence against a woman, and by Bishop Henry's advice to his brother that, to contain the Angevin threat in one place, Matilda should be allowed safe-conduct to Bristol as well. Was Henry being too clever by half? Or down-right treacherous? And why did Stephen, who had had one confrontation with him already over the fate of Bishop Roger, accept his brother's advice? Contemporaries were equally puzzled: Matilda's escape was 'quite incredible', one well-informed chronicler thought.

Robert met his half-sister at what was already called 'the frontier' and escorted her to Bristol. Soon, Gloucester submitted as well, followed in the course of the year by most of the Welsh marches, as 'partly by force and partly by favour, [the whole region] espoused the side of the empress'. Matilda even managed to make her half-brother Reginald earl of Cornwall.

Stephen had already lost the north; now he had lost the West Country as well and his writ would never run there again. The result was the effective partition of England: the north and west belonged to the empress, while the south and east remained loyal to Stephen. And neither side was able to make much headway into the territory of the other.

In 1140, there were attempts at resolving the stalemate by negotiation. A peace conference was held at Bath, at which the empress was represented by Earl Robert, and Stephen by Bishop Henry, Archbishop Theobald of Canterbury and by Stephen's wife, Queen Matilda.

The queen, indeed, was emerging as her husband's most effective and dogged advocate – so much so that at times the civil war appears as a women's war of the two Matildas: empress against queen. Moreover, though Queen Matilda yielded nothing to her cousin the empress in courage or strength or determination, she was able to express these qualities in a way which did not overtly challenge the conventions of the period. This enabled her to play both gender roles and plead as a woman and command as a man. In the Empress Matilda, on the other hand, the female was too often swallowed up in the male. 'She was', her panegyrist wrote, 'a woman who had nothing of the woman in her.' That was intended as praise. But it meant that her behaviour tended to grate and that she had only to see toes to tread on them.

The Bath peace conference came to nothing. Instead, in the new year, both sides tried to settle the issue by a single, bold throw of the dice. For Stephen, with his manic warrior energy, which repeatedly took him from one end of the country to the other, this was thoroughly in character. But for Earl Robert, whose motto, according to William of Malmesbury, was 'to do what he could, when he could not do what he would', it was a novel departure. Nevertheless, at first it seemed to pay off handsomely.

III

The background, once again, lay in the effective partition of England. One of the principal beneficiaries was Earl Ranulf of Chester, who was the dominant magnate in the north Midlands. This was now a debatable land between the rival spheres of influence of Stephen and Matilda, and both sides were eager to win the earl's support. In late 1140 Stephen seemed to have outbid the opposition by conceding Earl Ranulf's claims (through his mother) to Lincoln and giving him as well a great swathe of territories across the Midlands.

These joined together Ranulf's original centre of influence in Chester and his new one in Lincoln. But they also trespassed on the power bases of many of Stephen's other loyal supporters, who made their feelings plain at the Christmas court, which was also held at Lincoln. The result was a characteristic volte-face by Stephen: having come to terms with Ranulf before Christmas, in the new year he turned against him.

This was the moment that Robert, with all his caution, had been waiting for. With an ally as powerful (and as powerfully motivated) as Earl Ranulf, he could strike a decisive blow against Stephen. Calling up his full strength, he marched his army through the Midlands; joined forces with Ranulf at Derby and arrived before Lincoln on 2 February with a formidable force.

Stephen, too, was spoiling for a fight. That day, 2 February, is the Feast of the Purification of the Blessed Virgin Mary or Candlemas and, early in the morning, the king had carried the customary candle in procession to mass in the cathedral. But, as it was being lit, the candle broke in two. Stephen, however, brushed the ill-omen aside. He also ignored the advice of his council of war that, since the army of the earls was bigger and stronger, he should stage a tactical retreat. Instead, as Orderic observes, 'the wilful prince turned a deaf ear to the advice of prudent men' and ordered his men to prepare for battle.

The armies met on the water meadows which lie between the River Witham (which the earls had to cross) and the city on its steep hill, which, then as now, is crowned by the cathedral and castle. The odds were heavily stacked against the royalists. In accordance with the latest tactics, both Earl Ranulf and King Stephen dismounted to lead the resistance to the cavalry charges of the enemy. But the royalist charge broke almost immediately on the earls' lines. At this point, much of Stephen's army, including the flower of the English nobility, decided that their cause was hopeless and fled the field.

Stephen, in contrast, stood his ground, and though quickly surrounded on three sides, fought bravely on. First he laid about him with his sword; then, when that was broken, with an old-fashioned two-headed battleaxe handed to him by one of the Lincoln militia. But finally, when the battleaxe too was broken, he was overcome and knocked out with a blow to his helmet from a heavy stone. 'Here everybody! Here! I've got the king!' cried his captor, who was one of Earl Robert's household knights.

Robert, according to William of Malmesbury, treated his royal captive with every respect. He was first taken to Gloucester, where he was presented to the Empress Matilda, and then sent to Bristol Castle, where he was imprisoned. At first his captivity was honourable. But then, after trying to escape or bribe his gaolers, he was kept in chains.

The last vestige of his royal dignity was gone. And it had gone, contemporaries felt, 'by the just judgement of God'.

It now remained, it seemed, only to give effect to the judgement of battle by conferring the sovereignty on Matilda. Matilda sent notice of her intention to Bishop Henry, who, as usual, accommodated himself to an outcome which he may also have wished for. They met on Sunday, 2 March, in the open air to the west of Winchester. Matilda, for her part, promised to be guided by Henry in all matters relating to the Church and to ecclesiastical appointments; while Henry, for his, swore his allegiance to her as queen.

The next day she was conducted in procession to the cathedral, where she was received as queen by the bishops and abbots of 'her' part of England. A few days later, Archbishop Theobald of Canterbury arrived. But he refused to join his fellow bishops in swearing allegiance to Matilda until Stephen in person had released him from his oath to him. Stephen, bowing to the inevitable, gave the necessary release.

A month later, Henry, as papal legate, convened a Church Council at Winchester to effect the transfer of sovereignty. William of Malmesbury was present and gave a unique account of the event, in which he tells us as much about what happened backstage as in the glare of the spotlights. And the former, at least to begin with, was vastly more important than the latter. For Bishop Henry was determined his council should be as smoothly stage-managed as any modern British party conference or American presidential convention. In a clear case of divide and persuade, he spent the first day in a series of separate, private meetings with each rank of the senior clergy: the bishops, the abbots and the archdeacons. All were sworn to secrecy and nothing emerged publicly. Informally, it was a different matter, and a swirl of gossip and speculation filled the cloisters of power as 'what was to be done engrossed the minds and conversation of all'.

With opposition bought off or at least silenced, Bishop Henry was ready to go public and anoint (though not yet literally) Matilda as the chosen candidate. This was the business of the second day and it went like clockwork. Henry summarized recent events: the peace and good order England had enjoyed under Henry I; the oath to Matilda; her absence from the country on her father's death which led to Stephen's nomination as king; Stephen's breach of his oath to protect the Church and the mounting disorder of his rule and finally the judgement which God had passed on Stephen, 'by permitting him, without my knowledge [Henry added, surely unnecessarily], to fall into the hands of the powerful'. Therefore, Henry concluded, he had summoned this council 'of the English clergy, to whose right it principally pertains to elect a sovereign, and also to crown him'.

The result of the 'election', of course, had been fixed the day before. All that was left was for Henry to announce it, which he did in suitably ringing terms:

> We elect [he proclaimed] the daughter of that powerful, that glorious, that rich, that good, that in our times incomparable king, as sovereign of England and Normandy, and promise her fidelity and support.

His audience knew what was expected and 'all present', William of Malmesbury reports, 'either becomingly applauded his sentiments, or by their silence assented thereto'. Following her election, Matilda was known as 'lady of the English', which was the appropriate variation on the title of 'lord of the English' given to a king before he had been crowned.

It only remained for the people to rubber-stamp the decision of the clergy, and Henry concluded the day's proceedings by reporting that a delegation of Londoners, 'who, from the importance of their city in England, are nobles, as it were', had been summoned and were expected to arrive the next day – as they duly did.

It is clear that Henry expected no more problems with the Londoners than with his malleable fellow clergy. But he was quickly undeceived. Far from meekly acquiescing, the Londoners dared to request that Stephen, as 'their lord the king', might be released from captivity. Henry tried to face them down. Instead, the whole smooth machine of the council derailed, as a clerk belonging to Stephen's queen, Matilda, followed up the Londoners' plea by presenting a letter on her behalf to Henry. Clearly flustered, Henry, 'exalt[ing] his voice to the highest pitch', sought to shout him down. But the man was not to be silenced and, 'with notable confidence', read out the queen's letter. This restated the Londoners' request in still bolder and more personal terms. She required the council, 'and especially the bishop of Winchester, the brother of her lord', to restore Stephen, 'whom abandoned persons, and even such as were under homage to him, had cast into chains'.

The council now broke up in disorder, but not before Henry, in a final show of authority, had excommunicated several leading royalists.

The debacle of the Winchester Council put Matilda's candidacy on the back foot and it never recovered the smooth momentum which would have carried her effortlessly to the throne. Instead, it inched forward. Almost three months (from the beginning of April to the end of June) were spent in persuading the Londoners to agree, reluctantly, to allow Matilda to enter Westminster for her coronation. The time was not wholly wasted and Earl Robert, who was an effective consensus politician, had notable successes in winning over more of the aristocracy to his sister's claim. He used every device: 'kindly addressing the nobility, making many promises, and intimidating the adverse party'.

But Matilda's entry into Westminster, which should have crowned both her and the whole enterprise, instead turned into a disaster. For she displayed none of her half-brother Robert's emollient skills. Instead her imperious instincts came to the fore. She tried to command the Londoners when she should have wooed them. She refused to renew the privileges with which a grateful Stephen had rewarded their support. She even tried to tax them.

The result was that the Londoners, always lukewarm to her cause, became violently hostile and rose in force to drive her out of Westminster. Faced with overwhelming numbers, Matilda and her escort, which included her two chief supporters, her uncle David I of Scotland and her half-brother Robert of Gloucester, as well as Bishop Henry, fled.

As they made good their escape, the citizens plundered the palace, while Queen Matilda of Boulogne, who had been encamped on the South Bank, retook the City for her husband Stephen, to whom it henceforward remained steadfastly loyal.

Matilda and her friends regrouped at Oxford, where she lavishly rewarded the loyalty of her followers. This looked like wisdom. But it had the effect of further deepening partisan divisions. It also led to another crucial rift in the coalition which had so nearly swept her to the crown. For she now quarrelled with Bishop Henry. Despite having abandoned his brother, Henry was determined that his nephew Eustace, Stephen's elder son, should succeed to his maternal inheritance of the county of Boulogne. Matilda was equally adamant that he should not. Was it vengeance? Or the fact that, as part of her distribution of largesse, she had already promised it to others? In any case, it led to a fatal breach with Henry, who refused her summons to attend her court at Oxford.

In the space of a few days, the empress had contrived to lose both her capital and, in effect, the Church.

Events now started to run strongly against her. Bishop Henry met Queen Matilda of Boulogne at Guildford and reached agreement with her by which he renewed his allegiance to Stephen and repudiated Matilda. In riposte, Matilda marched to Winchester, entered the city and laid siege to the bishop in his adjacent palace at Wolvesey. Henry retaliated by firing much of the city, including the suburban monastery of Hyde, where stood the great golden cross, given long ago by Cnut. Meanwhile, Queen Matilda of Boulogne and the Londoners joined in the fray and besieged the besiegers. As the trap started to close round them, Matilda and her forces decided to retreat and left the city on 14 September, the Feast of the Exaltation of the Holy Cross. But 'the retreat became a flight, the flight a rout'. Matilda herself escaped, riding astride her horse like a man, and reached the safety of Gloucester. Robert of Gloucester was cut off and captured at Stockbridge.

The symmetry powerfully struck contemporaries: within nine months of each other, the leaders of the two sides, King Stephen and Earl Robert, had each been defeated and captured in battle, and both events had taken place on a great feast day of the Church. The result was the status quo ante, as the battle of Lincoln was cancelled out by the rout of Winchester. Two months later, the two captives were exchanged for each other.

Faced with stalemate once more, Matilda, who had resumed residence at Oxford, decided to appeal to her husband for support. But Geoffrey, who had been quick to exploit the battle of Lincoln by launching his soon-to-be-successful conquest of Normandy, preferred to remain on his own side of the Channel and bought time by stating that he would agree the terms of his support for his wife only in personal negotiations with Earl Robert. Robert duly set sail for Normandy, leaving Matilda in safety, as he thought, at Oxford. He even extended his stay to help Geoffrey conquer further territory in the duchy.

His absence presented Stephen with an opportunity and, with characteristic speed, the king raised an army and laid siege to Matilda in Oxford. Robert was unable to return in time and by December 1142 Oxford was on the brink of surrender. Determined to avoid the capture that had been the fate of her rival Stephen, Matilda decided on a daring plan of escape. Clad in white cloaks as camouflage, she and a little escort of only three or four knights slipped out of Oxford by a postern gate, crossed the frozen Thames and trudged through the winter landscape to Abingdon. Thence she rode to Wallingford, Brian Fitzcount's border fortress, before retreating still further west, to Devizes, where, in the almost impregnable castle built by Bishop Roger, she set up her new headquarters.

IV

Matilda was to remain at Devizes for six years, during which time she was never able to break out of her western heartland, which corresponded roughly to the ancient kingdom of Wessex. But neither was Stephen, equally secure in the east, ever able to make serious inroads against her. Instead, the effective partition of England, which had been apparent from the earliest days of the civil war, perpetuated itself and showed dangerous signs of consolidation, even permanence.

The symptoms were many and various. In view of their pretensions to sovereignty, it was only natural that Matilda in the west, Stephen in the east, and King David I of Scots in the north should each issue separate coinages from the mints under their control. But so did other great lords with no claim to royalty. These included the earls of Leicester, Salisbury and Northumbria, together with mere barons in the remoter fringes of the country, such as the lords of Alnwick and Gower. Even Earl Robert of Gloucester challenged his half-sister's jealously guarded regality by issuing coins bearing his own name from the mint he had taken over at Bristol. From all directions, therefore, the royal monopoly on coinage, which had alone guaranteed its uniformity and quality and had been one of the great legacies of Anglo-Saxon England, came under severe and sustained challenge.

Nor was the coinage the only royal right usurped by the greater earls. Equipped with the whole panoply of royal power, they even presumed to negotiate with each other like more or less autonomous powers. Most dramatic was the *conventio* ('agreement') between Ranulf, earl of Chester, and Waleran's twin brother, Robert, earl of Leicester. The former's relentless expansionism brought him into contact with the latter's sphere of influence and the agreement tried to limit the resulting friction. A formal defiance was to give fifteen days' warning of any attack by the one on the other; a demilitarized zone was created round Leicester as a no man's land in which neither might build castles; and, in the event of a breach, pledges deposited for safe-keeping with two local bishops were to be surrendered by the offending party. The detail is impressive; so is the fact that the king is almost ignored. But not quite: if the king attacks either party the other may assist him according to his allegiance. But he must do so with only twenty knights (a fraction of the forces available to him) and any plunder must be returned.

Divided, therefore, the English monarchy was falling into the state of the French. The monarch, whoever he or she might be, was more or less respected as a distant, somewhat ineffectual, feudal overlord. But his or her interventions on the ground were neither expected nor much welcomed, nor greatly to be feared.

And it was Stephen's inability to instil fear or 'dread' that the Anglo-Saxon chronicler saw as the key to the disasters of his reign:

> When the [rebellious lords] saw that he was a mild man, and soft, and good, and did not exact the full penalties of the law, they perpe-trated every enormity.

'For every rich man built his castles', the chronicler continued, 'and when the castles were made, they filled them with devils and evil men', who plundered and burned and taxed and tortured without mercy. At particular risk were those of the common people who were thought to be prosperous and to have hoarded wealth:

They put them in prison and tortured them with indescribable torture to extort gold and silver ... They were hung by the thumbs or by the head, and [heavy] chains were hung on their feet. Knotted ropes were put round their heads and twisted till they penetrated to the brains. They put them in prisons where there were adders and snakes and toads, and killed them like that. Some they put in an instrument of torture, that is in a chest which was short and narrow and not deep, and they put sharp stones in it and pressed the man so that he had all his limbs broken.

'To till the ground', the writer concluded, in one of the finest and last pieces of prose to be written in the old tongue, 'was to plough the sea; the earth bare no corn, for the lands was all laid waste by such deeds; and [men] said openly that Christ slept and his saints.'

The Anglo-Saxon chronicler was writing at Peterborough in East Anglia. Similar pictures were painted by William of Malmesbury, writing in Wiltshire; Ailred of Rievaulx, writing in Yorkshire; and Henry of Huntingdon, also writing in East Anglia. There is no reason to doubt that these writers reported accurately what they had seen and heard. But each had the misfortune to live in a hotly contested area. The Anglo-Saxon chronicler was especially unfortunate in being a neighbour of Geoffrey de Mandeville.

De Mandeville's father had been constable of the Tower when Ranulf Flambard effected his daring escape and was stripped of a third of his lands by Henry I as a punishment for his carelessness. His son devoted his career to winning back what his father had lost: first by conspicuous loyalty to Henry I, later by *dis*loyalty to everybody in the civil war. He changed sides at least three times, and each time increased his fame and fortune. Finally he became too powerful for his own good and Stephen, resorting to his favourite trick of arresting him at court, forced him to disgorge his castles. De Mandeville, faced once more with the ruin of his family, reacted with a furious nihilism. He flung himself from the royal court 'like a vicious and riderless horse, kicking and biting'. Then he embarked on a regional reign of terror in East Anglia and the Fenland in revenge. He sacked Cambridge; pillaged the Isle of Ely; seized Ramsey Abbey and made it his headquarters. But his warlordism came to an abrupt end in 1144, when he died of the wounds he had received while attacking the royal stronghold at Burwell. Since he died excommunicate, his body remained unburied for twenty years.

Almost certainly, the sadistic excesses described by the Anglo-Saxon chronicler were the work of de Mandeville and his henchmen, William de Say and Hugh Bigod, earl of Norfolk. But, at the other end of the scale, Brian Fitzcount, Matilda's partisan and one of the best educated and most civilized of the nobility, was also driven to survive by pillage and forced taxation around his border stronghold of Wallingford. And he mounted a powerful defence of his actions to Bishop Henry of Winchester, who had written him a curt letter of reproof. The civil war, he told him, had led to the loss of most of the lands he had received from King Henry. 'As a result', he continued, 'I am in the greatest distress and am not harvesting one acre of corn from the land which he gave me.' And this necessity was the sole reason for his depredations: 'neither I nor my men are doing this for money or fief or land'.

But both de Mandeville and Brian Fitzcount were, in their very different ways, exceptional. Each was a product of a frontier; elsewhere, in the solid blocks of territory held by each of the three main parties to the war, Stephen, Matilda and David I of Scotland, there was what one chronicler calls *umbra quaedam pacis* ('the shadow or simulacrum of peace'): a certain level of public order was maintained, taxes and dues were collected, charters were issued and even justice was done – if with a backward glance at happier, more stable times.

> I am, as you see [a witness began his testimony at a meeting of the Shire Court in Norwich], a very old man, and I remember many things which happened in King Henry's time and even before that, when right and justice, peace and loyalty flourished in England. But because in the stress of war, justice has fled and laws are silenced, the liberties of churches, like other good thing, have in many places perished.

This testimony was given shortly after 1148, and it suggests that there was already a profound and pervasive war-weariness. This extended even to one of the principals. That same year, Matilda left for Normandy. There she spent the last nineteen years of her life in a dignified and pious retirement. She never returned to England and she never used the title of 'lady of the English' again.

But if Matilda had given up the struggle for herself, she had only passed on the torch to her son, Henry. Henry, then aged nine, had first been brought to England by his uncle, Earl Robert, in the aftermath of Matilda's flight from Oxford in 1142. For the next seven years, he divided his time between England, where he stayed with either his mother or his uncle, and Normandy, where his father Geoffrey, having completed the conquest of the duchy, was formally invested as duke in 1144. The intention, clearly, was to present Henry as the rightful heir to both halves of the Anglo-Norman realm.

To begin with, however, Henry had no better luck in enforcing his claim in England than his mother. In 1147, he ran out of money to pay his mercenaries and had to be rescued by – of all people – Stephen, who, with characteristic chivalry, paid off his rival's debt. The generosity was not repaid. Henry returned two years later in 1149, was knighted by his uncle David I of Scots at Carlisle and joined in a pincer attack on Yorkshire. But this too was thwarted by Stephen; while Stephen's son and heir, Eustace, shadowed Henry on his march south through the Welsh marches. Having failed, yet again, to alter the balance of power in England, Henry returned to Normandy in 1150.

On Stephen's side, too, the focus was shifting to the next generation, as Stephen, following French custom, sought to secure Eustace's position by having him crowned king in his own lifetime. But here the alteration in the king's relations with the Church counted heavily against him. While his brother Bishop Henry remained papal legate, the two had run the Church as a family concern: three family members were made abbots and one a bishop. But when the new pope, Eugenius III, deprived Bishop Henry of his legation, relations rapidly cooled and Stephen's nepotistic candidates for York and Lincoln were turned down by the pope 'indignantly and with harsh language'. In the circumstances, Eustace's coronation became a bargaining counter and the English hierarchy played for time by claiming that it would be against precedent.

V

The crippling stalemate in England was broken, as it turned out, by events far away in France. In 1150, Henry, having returned from his second, less-than-successful expedition to England, was invested as duke of Normandy by his father Geoffrey. Shortly after Geoffrey died, leaving Henry as count of Anjou as well as duke of Normandy.

Henry's dizzying rise to international power was aided by another twist of fate. Louis VII of France had married Eleanor of Aquitaine in 1137, but they were divorced in 1152. Eleanor immediately gave her hand and her duchy to Henry. They married the following 18 May, thus adding her vast inheritance to his own. In two years Henry had gone from almost nothing to lord of the better half of France.

With his hand thus strengthened, Henry sailed to England in January 1153, determined to add it too to his empire. He won no great military victories. But he had no need to: the tide of events was now running strongly in his favour. There was a palpable longing for peace. Most of the great lords, with one eye on their lands across the Channel, were eager to come to terms. And Stephen had given up the attempt to keep the throne in his family. For the last few years had been as fatal to him as they were beneficial to Henry. His queen, Matilda of Boulogne, died in 1152 and his son and heir Eustace in 1153.

But despite these losses and his relatively advanced age of fifty-seven, Stephen was not ready to give up without a struggle and he tried to bring Henry to battle at Malmesbury. But he found his support drifting away – and drifting towards Henry. Following this, the Midlands – always a hotly contested zone – surrendered to Henry, and Stephen, in desperation, sought to make a last stand at Wallingford. Instead, both sides were brought to agree to negotiate a comprehensive peace settlement.

Its broad outlines had been sketched several times before, in the abortive negotiations which had punctuated the conflict. Stephen should remain as king for his lifetime, for he was the crowned and anointed sovereign. But Henry should succeed him, since he was generally viewed as 'the lawful heir'.

Both sides came together in a great court at Winchester on 6 November. Stephen and Henry, now acknowledged as Stephen's adoptive son and heir, made a joint progress to Westminster to celebrate Christmas together. Huge, cheering crowds lined the way; there were solemn processions and assemblies and a dawning realization that peace had come at last. There was gratitude for the negotiators, such as the archbishop of Canterbury, who was congratulated on having 'restored order to our distracted country', and almost millenarian hopes for Henry: he was, the prior of Westminster told him, 'the new light ... a leader given to us by God ... [who] shall found a new Jerusalem'.

For five months following the treaty, England was ruled by an effective diarchy of king and duke. Stephen, by virtue of his rank, was the senior partner. But it was Henry who impressed the Anglo-Saxon chronicler as the real power behind the throne: 'all the people loved him', he reports, 'for he did good justice, and made peace'. As was only to be expected after two decades of civil war, there were eddies of mistrust and even rumours of rupture between the two former opponents. These the chroniclers (who thrived on stories of conflict in high places as much as any modern journalist) assiduously played up. But Henry was more relaxed. Indeed, he was so confident about the durability of the arrangements for the succession that he left England at Easter to return to Normandy along with his two leading adherents: Earl Reginald of Cornwall and Earl Robert of Leicester.

He did not have to wait for long. After a brief Indian summer as unchallenged king, Stephen died in October. His body was taken to Faversham in north-east Kent and buried alongside his wife Matilda and son Eustace in the abbey which he had founded there. Few seemed to mourn his passing.

Instead all eyes turned to 'the new light'. Contrary winds kept Henry in Normandy till 7 December. But despite this six-week absence, 'no man', the Anglo-Saxon chronicler noted approvingly, 'durst do other than good for the great fear of him'.

Finally, the weather turned. Henry set sail from Barfleur and landed the following day on the coast of Hampshire. Like Henry I, he made straight for Winchester to secure the treasury. That done he went to London and was crowned at Westminster on 19 December 'before an immense concourse of people'.

So far so good. But whether he would 'found a new Jerusalem' remained to be seen.

10

'TOUCH NOT MINE ANOINTED'

Henry II

HENRY WAS TWENTY-ONE when he became king. But, having first intervened in English affairs seven years before, at the age of only fourteen, he was already a political old hand and fully able to recognize the weight of expectation vested in him. He had also had time to develop his own model of kingship and deploy his own extraordinary talents.

Henry was gifted with genuine charisma: he had piercing grey eyes and his physical presence was mesmerizing: 'his face was one upon which a man might gaze a thousand times and still feel drawn to gaze on again'. And he had a single, overriding goal: after years of anarchy and the degradation of the monarchy he was determined to restore the crown to the power it held under Henry I. For this Henry was his grandsire's grandson: in abilities, temperament, political skill and even, to a large extent, in appearance. Like Henry I, he was shortish, barrel-chested and with a tendency to run to fat. He had also inherited his grandfather's inexhaustible energy, his restlessness, his addiction to hunting, his gross sexual appetites, his personal simplicity, his attention to detail, his acute intelligence and his memory.

But his Angevin ancestors left their mark as well. He had that family's red hair, which he kept close cropped, and a redhead's temper to boot. Napoleon jumped on his hat in his rages; both Kissinger's feet left the ground simultaneously in his; while Hitler, allegedly, chewed carpets during his paroxysms. Henry went further, and, on one documented occasion, ate his bedding. He 'fell out of bed screaming, tore up his coverlet, and threshed around the floor, cramming his mouth with the stuffing of his mattress'.

And all because someone had uttered a misplaced word of praise for the king of Scots!

These ungovernable rages could easily have undone all his good qualities. But Henry knew himself well enough rarely to take important decisions in them. And his councillors and attendants likewise knew him well enough to disregard what he uttered when the rage was on him.

Only once, and with immeasurable consequences, do they seem to have taken him at his angry word.

I

Henry's first task was to assemble the personnel of his government. Here again, he was building on the foundations his grandfather had laid. The great administrative offices of state had originally appeared in the first Henry's reign; so had the pools of administrative talent. And Henry drew directly on these in his reappointment of Bishop Nigel, the surviving representative of Roger of Salisbury's administrative clan, as treasurer. But service to Stephen was no drawback either in Henry's eyes, and he appointed men of talent regardless of previous loyalties and betrayals.

Henry's final appointment was to the chancellorship. Here he was guided in his choice by Archbishop Theobald, who recommended his favourite clerk, Thomas Becket, archdeacon of Canterbury. Becket, son of a middling City merchant of Norman stock, was the consummate man of business. Indeed, he was to the chancellorship what Roger of Salisbury had been to the justiciarship: he made the office rather than the office making him. Hitherto it had been a second-rank position, whose holder remained in charge of the king's chapel as well as supervising the staff of royal writing clerks who made up the Chancery proper. Becket elevated the chancellorship from this clerical-bureaucratic backwater into a kind of ministry of all departments, with himself as minister of all the talents: secretary, soldier, diplomat and judge. He excelled at every role he took; won the king's absolute confidence and friendship; became very rich and spent his wealth with a delighted ostentation which made the sharpest contrast with the frugality of the king.

In 1158, for example, he performed a formal entrée into Paris to begin negotiations for a marriage between Louis VII's daughter and Henry's eldest surviving son. Chancellor Becket rode in procession through the streets, surrounded by a swarm of flunkies and squires and followed by wagons loaded with barrels of beer and chests of gold and richly caparisoned packhorses mounted with monkeys. When Henry himself arrived, he was less impressively equipped than Becket's servants.

But it was all done, as Becket's successor in the chancellorship and namesake, Thomas Wolsey, would have said, for the king's honour.

Henry's administrative appointments were all very well. But the real weakness of royal government in Stephen's reign lay, not so much at the centre, as in the localities. It was this that Henry now proceeded to remedy. He would show himself to his kingdom: seeing and being seen. And, above all, he would impose his will – even on his greatest subjects. One of the most contentious clauses of the Treaty of Winchester, which had ended the civil war, was the requirement that the barons should demolish unlicensed or (in the contemporary jargon) 'adulterine' castles. At the Christmas court, held at Bermondsey immediately after his coronation, Henry reiterated this order.

And woe betide any great lord who defied the young king's command. Henry confronted a series of over-mighty lords who had taken advantage of royal weakness and established quasi-regal power in their domains. One by one the defiant grimaces were wiped off their faces and they surrendered their castles to the overwhelming royal force that appeared in their locales.

Hugh de Mortimer was not to be faced down, however. 'Estimating the king to be a mere boy and indignant at his activity', he tried to fortify his castles of Cleobury, Wigmore and Bridgnorth against the king. Henry marched against him in person, put all three castles under siege, and surrounded Bridgnorth with a wall and ditch so that Hugh could not escape.

Hugh's submission to the king was turned into a piece of high political theatre. It was witnessed by a specially convened and impressively well-attended great council of bishops, earls and barons.

Bridgnorth had also been the scene of an earlier royal victory. Over fifty years previously, in 1102, Henry I had defeated *his* over-mighty subject, Robert of Bellême, in a similar set-piece siege, and, by his victory, had secured an unchallenged hold on England. In view both of his identification with his grandfather and the fact that he had 'at his finger tips a ready knowledge of nearly the whole of history', it seems inconceivable that the younger Henry was unaware that he was treading so precisely in the older Henry's footsteps.

Another person who took a serious interest in history was Bishop Henry of Winchester. For twenty years this princely bishop, secure in his royal blood, his vast wealth and his talents as a political intriguer, had helped make and unmake the rulers of England. No more. Faced after Bridgnorth with the need to bow the knee to Henry with the rest, he baulked and fled. Henry took advantage of the fact that he had left the realm without permission to strip him of the earldom of Hampshire, which he had effectively held, and seize and demolish his many castles. He was left with his bishopric. But it was princely no longer.

With Bridgnorth and the fall of Bishop Henry, England was now Henry II's as unquestionably and unconditionally as it had been his grandfather's. But Henry was not content with England. Instead he aspired to the dominion, even the empire, of all Britain, which, under the vague title of *bretwalda*, had been claimed by the greatest of the Anglo-Saxon kings.

He began with Scotland, which under David I had taken advantage of the civil wars in England to push its borders south. Here Henry enjoyed his customary good luck. For David was succeeded by his grandson, Malcolm IV of Scots, who was aged only eleven at the time of his accession and was to be surnamed 'the Maiden'. Such a youth was no match for Henry, and when he was summoned to meet the king at Chester in July 1157, he agreed to surrender all his grandfather's gains in England. At the same time, he paid Henry homage and joined him in the major campaign which Henry now launched against the Welsh, who had also taken advantage of the anarchy of Stephen's reign to regain great swathes of territory from the Anglo-Norman marcher lords.

The meeting of Henry and Malcolm at Chester was, almost certainly, another piece of historicist playacting laid on by Henry as royal dramaturge. For it was at Chester that Henry's Anglo-Saxon predecessor, Edgar, following his 'imperial' coronation at Bath in 979, had been rowed in the Dee by six or eight Scottish, Welsh, and Irish kinglets in an act of ritual homage. Henry, I think, was ticking off this list. Following Malcolm's homage, only Ireland was left.

Henry determined to tick that too. And, as his luck would have it again, he had an important ally in the quest. For, a few days before his own coronation in December 1154, a new pope had been crowned: Nicholas Breakspear, who reigned as Adrian IV. Breakspear was the first (and last) Englishman to ascend the throne of St Peter. After a flattering embassy from Henry, the new pope had no hesitation in giving his blessing to Henry's conquest of Ireland.

It remained only to secure the agreement of the English political establishment. Once again, Henry's sense of the dramatic came into play: the deed would be done at Winchester. Bishop Henry's flight from his see had set the seal on Henry's political dominance in his original kingdom of England. Where better to inaugurate the conquest of his new?

The great council duly met at Winchester on 29 September 1155. But Henry encountered stiff opposition and the project had to be shelved. The king did not forget it, however. Nor, fired with the prospects of fresh conquests and fresh spoil, did his leading courtiers.

But England, even Britain, was only a part of the vast conglomeration of territories that Henry ruled. These now demanded his attention, and almost six out of the next seven years, from 1156 to 1162, were spent on the Continent – seeing off rivals, recovering old claims and pressing new ones.

His first challenge came from his younger brother, Geoffrey, who had been left their father's territories in Anjou and Maine. Anjou lay at the heart of Henry's French dominions. He wanted it. So first he contained Geoffrey by diplomacy, isolating him at a family conference and having their father's will set aside by the ever-obliging Adrian IV. Finally, in compensation, he reduced him to the single castle of Loudun. Then he installed Geoffrey in Nantes. And when Geoffrey died unexpectedly in 1158, Henry got his hands on Nantes as well.

He also wanted the territories of the Vexin, which lay between Normandy and the Ile de France. Henry had sacrificed the Vexin in 1151 to secure Louis VII's recognition of his claim to Normandy. Now he set himself to recover it. In a summit conference at Paris in 1158, Henry and Louis agreed on the marriage of Louis's daughter Marguerite to Henry's eldest surviving son Henry, with the Vexin as Marguerite's dower. Louis thought that the marriage was a promissory note rather than cash in hand since the groom was less than four and the bride was only a few months old.

But he reckoned without Henry. Adrian, Henry's tame English pope, died in 1159. A disputed election followed, which resulted in a pope, Alexander III, and an anti-pope, Victor IV. In 1160, Henry recognized Alexander. His reward was Alexander's sanction for the immediate marriage of Marguerite and Henry. The Vexin, to Louis's impotent fury, became *de jure* part of Henry's dominions forthwith. Its successful acquisition was crowned in 1162 when Henry met Alexander at Déols, on the banks of the River Indre. Henry greeted the pope with the extravagant abasement which the sovereign pontiff then required of mere earthly kings. But the real balance of power between the two was clear: the meeting took place on Henry's territory, while the pope himself was the man whom Henry had – in effect – chosen.

Finally, in 1159, Henry launched a great campaign to enforce his wife's claim to the county of Toulouse, which lay to the south of Aquitaine. Like the Welsh campaign of 1157, the expedition was carefully planned and lavishly resourced (largely at the expense of the English taxpayer). But, as with the Welsh campaign also, the results were disappointing.

Nevertheless, Henry had remade the monarchy. As William of Newburgh wrote: 'in all parts of his realm the king won the renown of a monarch who ruled over a wider empire than all who had previously reigned in England, for it extended from the far border of Scotland to the Pyrenees'. Henry was always on the move in his empire like, it was said, a human chariot pulling everyone behind him. It exasperated his friends and foes alike. 'At one moment the king of England is in Ireland, the next in England, the next in Normandy,' complained Louis VII, 'he must fly rather than travel by horse or ship.' Thanks to his restless energy, commanding personality and indomitable will Henry II had made himself the greatest king in Christendom.

II

'Lo! to fight and to judge: that is the task of a king.' While Henry was fighting in France (or, as he preferred, achieving the aims of war by the means of diplomacy), he was judging in England – either in person on his occasional visits or by proxy through his representatives.

Henry was as serious and hands-on in the business of justice as he was in most other aspects of kingship. He chose his judges with care and held them to account for their stewardship. What most kept them on their toes was the fact that Henry was at least as good a lawyer as they. He was, writes the great legal historian Frederic William Maitland, 'quite competent to criticize minutely the wording of a charter, to frame a new clause and to give his vice-chancellor a lesson in conveyancing'.

And he could impose his justice even when he wasn't there in person, thanks to his innovations in the law, which became a sort of mirror reflecting and multiplying royal authority. The main writing office was known as the Chancery, and it issued a multiplicity of 'writs' – that is, standardized royal orders. The writ itself was written out on a slip of parchment and then authenticated by attaching the great seal. The seal was deliberately large and impressive and it carried the king's image to the furthest corner of his dominions. It also makes an important point about the nature of kingship. On the front the king is seated, as a lawgiver and judge. On the reverse he is mounted and armed as the warrior-defender of his people.

In the course of Henry's reign, writs were developed to deal with all the most common legal problems of the king's subjects. They were mass-produced by Chancery clerks and they were available, for a fee, to every freeman. Previously, the king's justice had depended on the king's actual presence; now with the writ, the seal and the magic of writing, the king and his justice could be everywhere, for everybody.

For two decades England had been weak. But now the crown was worn by a man whose personality matched the pretensions of the position. Henry overawed and faced down opponents at every turn, high and low, at home and abroad. One contemporary observed: 'He is a great, indeed the greatest of monarchs for he has no superior of whom he stands in awe, nor subject who may resist him.'

In all of this activity, whether in fighting or in judging, Henry's principal agent and adviser in these early years was his chancellor, Thomas Becket. They had, contemporaries noted wonderingly, 'but one heart and one mind'. It went even beyond their personal relationship, close though it was. For Becket was the only one of Henry's ministers whose power was as extensive as the king's own. The responsibility of the treasurer, for example, was limited to England. But Becket's Chancery issued Henry's orders throughout all his dominions. And the chancellor himself, like the king his master (except that some unkind tongues said it was Becket who was the *real* master), seemed to be everywhere and to do everything.

In 1156, for example, Becket was an itinerant judge in three counties; in 1158, Becket, as we have seen, had gone to the Paris summit with Louis VII ahead of Henry, to prepare the ground and smooth the way. Later in the year, he was again justice itinerant in England. In 1159, he was the key figure, after Henry himself, in the Toulouse campaign: he organized the heavy taxation needed to finance it (which fell especially heavily on the Church); he commanded a troop of hand-picked knights and was the foremost in every fight. As the supreme mark of trust, he was given responsibility for the upbringing of the king's son and heir Henry, and in 1162 returned from Normandy to England with him, charged with the task of getting the magnates to agree to his nomination as heir.

He succeeded in this as in everything else.

When, therefore, Thomas's former patron, Archbishop Theobald, died in 1161, Becket was the obvious candidate to replace him. Theobald had 'hoped and prayed' that he would be his successor. More to the point, Henry had determined on it as well.

Becket was aghast and begged to be excused: he could not both fulfil his duties to the Church as archbishop and retain Henry's affection, he explained. Henry was insistent. Only the Empress Matilda, who had had personal experience of an earlier transformation, when the imperial chancellor had been made archbishop, counselled against the promotion. But her fears were ignored and Becket's were overcome. 'I acquiesced', he explained later, 'more for love [of Henry] than for the love of God.'

The elevation of the royal favourite was triumphant. He was elected unanimously on 23 May; the royal assent was signified by Becket's ward, the young Prince Henry; he was ordained priest on 2 June and the following day was consecrated archbishop by Bishop Henry of Winchester in a spectacular ceremony.

Who would be proved right: Henry or his mother Matilda?

It did not take Henry long to find out.

III

Henry had high hopes for his friend in his new office, though not, perhaps, quite as high as Becket had for himself. As archbishop and chancellor – for Henry took it for granted that Becket would continue in his old position as well – Becket would be supreme in both Church and state. His place in each would add lustre to the other and both would lend a reflected glory to Henry himself. For only the greatest of kings could confidently employ such an omnipotent and omnicompetent minister. Indeed, among contemporary rulers only one other had a chancellor-archbishop, the Emperor Frederick Barbarossa.

How better to reinforce Henry's own claims to quasi-imperial status?

But, above all, Becket's appointment was intended to play a central part in Henry's grand political strategy. This centred on his seven-year-old son and heir, Henry. Becket, as the king's best friend and alter ego, had already been heavily involved in the upbringing of his son. Now, as chancellor-archbishop, he would – Henry intended – finish what he had begun: he would crown the young Henry as king in his father's lifetime and head up a subordinate administration that would rule England in his name.

Finally, and almost as an afterthought against these high matters of dynastic policy, Archbishop Becket would be able to take the English Church in hand on Henry II's behalf as well. For Henry II's was not the only monarchy in England. There was another power in the land: the Church. The Church was a state within a state: it had its own language, Latin; its own system of law, known as 'canon' law; its own property, which extended to upwards of a fifth of the land in England; its own symbols of power in the churches, cathedrals and monasteries, which are still among our most impressive structures. Above all, it had its own personnel and its own organization, which paralleled the machinery of royal government.

Indeed, England would not have been England without the English Church and the king could not have ruled England without its cooperation either. The landed wealth of the bishops and abbots made their appointments important sources of royal patronage. The king also looked to the leading clergy as councillors, advisers and administrators. Nor was the king the only one: indeed, the services of the clergy were needed by all levels of secular society. For the Church had more or less a monopoly on learning and the teaching of Latin, which, following the post-Conquest abandonment of Anglo-Saxon as a written language, had become the language of both government and public and private administration.

So all jobs that we would still call 'clerical' were filled by clergymen. They were the lawyers, accountants, dons, secretaries, doctors and mere pen-pushers. And they were everywhere: one in six of the population were in some form or other of holy orders. This raised awkward questions of demarcation. What happened when a cleric committed a crime against the king's peace? Who should try a case between a clergyman and a layman? Who had jurisdiction over Church property? Where, in short, did the king's justice stop and the Church's begin?

These questions were further complicated by the fact that the Church was not only a state within a state. It was also, since it embraced all western Europe, above and beyond the state as well – just as the power of the pope was beyond and arguably above that of the king. And the more vigorously reform was pressed and the sharper the line that was drawn between the spiritual and the temporal, the more scope there was for a clash between the claims of pope and king.

In the Old Testament, kings were the chosen and anointed of God; in the New, Jesus enjoined his followers to 'render unto Caesar the things that are Caesar's, and to God the things that are God's'. This seemed clear enough. But, above and beyond the general rule, the papal monarchy had a special claim to divine sanction. For had not Christ himself given St Peter, who was believed to have been the first pope, 'the keys of the kingdom of heaven'?

In the Middle Ages almost no one doubted that this text gave the pope a universal spiritual authority. And it extended to kings and emperors as much as to the merest peasant. In particular, it meant that if a king sinned, the pope could chastise him like any other errant Christian. In extreme cases he could excommunicate him: that is, exclude him, more or less permanently, from the Christian community. He could also, as a further sanction, lay his territories under 'interdict', which had the effect of depriving, not only the miscreant king, but all his subjects of the ministrations of Holy Church.

The result in Continental Europe and the German Empire in particular was a clash on an epic scale. It culminated in 1077, when the Holy Roman Emperor Henry IV was compelled to make his way through the snows of an Alpine winter to Canossa, there to prostrate himself as a penitent at the feet of the indomitable Hildebrand, who reigned as Pope Gregory VII.

Neither Normandy nor England experienced anything like that. For William I, despite his ostentatious piety, was unwilling to yield an inch to the papacy. He used it when it was necessary or convenient to do so, most importantly to sanction his claim to England. But all this was achieved by about 1072. Thereafter William's concern was to insulate his dominions from Roman interference. He flatly refused the pope's demand for homage; no pope was to be recognized nor any papal letters received without his permission; no legislation was to be proposed in a council of the English Church without his agreement; and no baron excommunicated without his consent. And he imposed a ban on bishops going to Rome, even when they had been specifically summoned by the pope. The effect was to neutralize each and every weapon in the papal armoury.

But not even the Conqueror could insulate England entirely, and under his successors there were eddies and echoes of the great European conflict. During the civil war, in particular, the Church, like most other forces in society, moved to assert itself against a weakened crown. The attack was led by Bishop Henry of Winchester. At first sight he seems an unlikely champion. Opulent, magnificent, as at home in armour as in pontificals and with an adventurous artistic taste that extended to importing ancient Classical statues from Rome to decorate his palace at Winchester, Bishop Henry was nevertheless zealous in the defence of clerical rights and privileges.

The result was that the power of the Church reached its zenith in the years of the Anarchy. Stephen had been put on the throne by churchmen and had his title confirmed by the pope. In return he was prepared to grant whatever the Church asked – in effect complete autonomy against royal authority. Stephen was also quick to reconsider. His failure to observe the excessive clerical privileges provided Bishop Henry with his main justification for deserting his brother's cause. And it was at the council of Winchester, which followed Stephen's defeat, that Bishop Henry's claims for clerical supremacy became most extravagant, with his assertion that the Church not merely crowned the king but actually chose him.

Not even Becket himself could have claimed more.

After Bishop Henry's fall from grace at Rome, the leadership of the English Church passed to Theodore, archbishop of Canterbury. He was a man of very different character from Bishop Henry: the latter was lordly, the former austere and devout. But that did not stop Theodore from being a better politician and a much superior diplomat.

The result was that Theodore presided over the closest and most fruitful period of Anglo-Roman relations since the heroic, missionary days of Anglo-Saxon Christianity. Englishmen of promise went to Rome, chiefly to work in the administration of the papal curia. This encouraged the notion that contacts between England and Rome were not exceptional or alien but part of the natural course of things. Likewise, bishops and monasteries, nervous of faltering royal authority in England and the concomitant breakdown of public order, started to seek papal protection and confirmation of their possessions. Even more importantly, they (and lesser folk too) also started to appeal to the Roman court – not exceptionally but as a matter of routine.

This change coincided with a revolution in the scope and sophistication of canon – that is, Church – law. In 1137, Gratian, a monk of Bologna, set himself to systematize canon law on the model of the great Roman imperial jurists. The result was his *Decretum*. It was published in 1151 and it transformed both the teaching and the practice of canon law. The effects were felt even in remote England, as Theodore brought over Vacarius, a Lombard jurist, to teach Roman and canon law to the group of bright young men he had assembled in his household.

Theodore's entourage – the 'Canterbury men', as they were known – became a self-sustaining intellectual community. They formed a university, civil-service training college and debating society rolled into one. They included young men like Thomas Becket who were on the thresholds of careers that would take them to the summit of Church and state. But, above all, they were lawyers. They argued 'from prayers to meal time' on points of law, on knotty theological problems, and on current affairs. And they did so 'in the manner of pleaders in courts of law'.

It was in Archbishop Theodore's household, in other words, that Becket had learned to argue a case – passionately, effectively and with an unflagging enthusiasm. That never altered. All that would happen was that he changed client. He had already changed from Archbishop Theodore to King Henry. Now, although Henry did not yet realize it, he was about to change again, from his king to his Church and – he would have claimed – to his God.

IV

And the inadvertent agent of change, of course, was Henry himself. Henry must have discussed his plans with Becket before he made him archbishop. And they offered a glittering prospect indeed. As minister for everything, Becket had been in the king's shadow; as both viceroy to his son and heir and papal legate in England, he would have been a virtually independent potentate.

For the son of a rural knight turned failed urban property speculator, the temptation was well-nigh irresistible. Like the Devil with Christ, the king had offered him the rulership of the whole world (or at least of England). And, like Christ, Becket *was* tempted. Indeed, he admitted as much in a later letter. 'If we had been willing', he wrote, 'to have been agreeable to [Henry's] will in everything, there would have been no one, under his authority or in his kingdom, who would not have obeyed us absolutely.' But, like Christ also, Becket eventually resisted temptation and in effect said 'Get thee behind me, Satan' to an astonished, hurt and increasingly angry Henry.

Why? Had Becket undergone a religious conversion? Was he a consummate actor, throwing himself with relish into a new part? An advocate, pleading on behalf of a new client? Or was he trying to prove himself to his fellow clergy, who widely suspected him of being a royal stooge?

Bearing in mind the state of the evidence, any and all of these explanations are possible. For the months following his appointment as archbishop are among the worst documented of Becket's whole career. And contemporaries were as puzzled as posterity. Only direct divine intervention, they thought, could explain what had happened.

The change in Becket may have been complete and apparently miraculous but it was by no means instantaneous. '*After a time*', William of

Newburgh writes, 'considering piously and sagaciously the responsibility of so high an honour [as the archbishopric], he on a sudden exhibited … a change in his habit and manners.' *'After a time'*. There appears to be a studied ambiguity in the phrase. Did William not know when it had happened? Or was it not an event at all but a process? The latter seems the more likely. Becket, that is, did not *assume* his new role, he *grew* into it. One thing of course was clear from the beginning: he was determined to be a great archbishop just as he had been a great chancellor. He had made the latter office; he would remake the former. But how?

His first thoughts seem to have tended simply to a clerical grandeur. Theodore had had his household of clerks; Becket would have his dozens of clerks. He would be lavish in his hospitality and extravagant in his alms-giving. And he would carry out his duties meticulously: he spent time in his private devotions; he studied theology and he set himself to recover and augment the rights of his see.

But, despite the outward show, there seems at first to have been a certain reticence, even self-doubt. Perhaps it was a genuine diffidence about the propriety of his appointment. For certainly his promotion to Canterbury broke every rule in the new clericalist handbook. The proper position was that no bishop should be consecrated 'who had not been freely elected and without previous nomination by the secular power'. But, far from Becket being 'freely elected', each constituency that was invited to endorse his appointment was aware of overwhelming pressure from the king.

This presented him with an awkward dilemma. How could he pose as the champion of the Church when his election was uncanonical and he owed his appointment to his royal friend and master?

The first step towards his liberation came with his receipt of the pallium from Pope Alexander III. Normally the archbishop was required to go in person to Rome to receive the pallium – the narrow woollen stole that was the symbol of his office – directly from the hands of the pope. But Henry, solicitous as always for the welfare and convenience of his favourite and with many other things for him to do in England, arranged for Becket to receive it by proxy.

The pallium arrived in England in August 1162 and Becket received it barefoot and prostrate in Canterbury Cathedral. The extravagance of the gesture was characteristic of a man whose theatricality matched, if it did not outdo, Henry's own. It spoke, of course, of Becket's reverence for the papal office. But it also betokened something much more personal. For Becket treated the pallium, which, as was customary, had been blessed by the pope himself, as a calling, even as a laying on of hands. With its receipt, he felt, the stain of his appointment had started to be wiped away. Like Peter, he had been called to be a fisher of men; like the disciple, he would renounce wealth and family and friends. And he would start by renouncing his king.

Immediately after the ceremony at Canterbury, he resigned the chancellorship, proffering as his excuse that he was 'insufficient for one office let alone two'. Henry, who had just obtained a dispensation for him to continue to hold the chancellorship, was taken utterly by surprise and could hide neither his disappointment nor his pique. If he could not have an archbishop as chancellor, he resolved, he would not have a chancellor at all. Instead, so long as Becket lived, the office was left unfilled and its duties discharged by a vice-chancellor, Geoffrey Ridel, who had already acted as deputy to Becket. But Henry decided to make Becket suffer as well and insisted that he resign the archdeaconry of Canterbury, which was the most valuable non-episcopal appointment in the English Church, in Ridel's favour.

It was the beginning of a dangerous game of tit-for-tat.

But even more important for Becket and the English Church as a whole was the General Council of the Church which the exiled Pope Alexander III summoned to meet at Tours in the Loire valley in May 1163.

English kings had traditionally exercised a jealous control over the attendance of their bishops at General Councils. But Henry, despite his mounting disappointment with Becket, was in an expansive mood. Following his successful meeting with Alexander at Déols, he was confident of the political cooperation of the papacy and he waved through the attendance of his bishops at the council.

The council turned out to be a life-changing experience for Becket and his fellow bishops – and a political disaster for Henry. Its sessions took place 'with much pomp' and debated and passed a radically reforming set of canons: no cleric was to appoint a salaried deputy to perform his office; or to involve himself in usury or lending at interest; or to leave a monastery to study law or medicine.

Bearing in mind his own past, none of this should have made comfortable listening for Becket, the former lawyer and man of affairs. Even before he entered the royal service, he had been a great pluralist, with many more ecclesiastical offices than he could possibly perform himself. As a young man too he had been in the service of his kinsman, the great London merchant Osbert Huitdeniers. Osbert was a banker and, it is safe to assume, did not lend money free of charge. A different character might have drawn the lesson of humility from the contrast between his own earlier behaviour and the standards which he now joined in imposing on his fellow clergy.

But that was not Becket's style. Instead, Becket seems to have decided that the right way to atone for his previous failings was to espouse the new rulings with unbending rigour. This exposed him, then and now, to the charge of hypocrisy. But Becket brushed that off, as he did all criticism, and carried on regardless.

And it was not only Becket. For Henry had allowed more or less the whole bench of bishops to attend the Council of Tours. It is difficult, I think, to overestimate the consequences. Hitherto, the effective ban on bishops travelling abroad had kept the English Church significantly isolated from Continental turmoil in Church–state relations which had culminated in the Emperor Henry IV's submission to Pope Gregory VII. But now the attendance of the English bishops in a body at the Council of Tours exposed them directly to the full blast of the Continental movement for Church reform.

It proved a brisk and bracing air. They were able to see how far English custom departed from what was now ecclesiastical best practice. And they were strengthened in their determination to do something about it. But at least as important was the effect of Tours on their *esprit de corps*. Meeting with their fellow bishops and without the watchful eye of the king or his justiciar, they developed a novel sense of confidence and collegiality. This meant that Becket, to his surprise as much as Henry's, was able to face the king in the forthcoming storm with a united bench of bishops behind him.

Becket and his fellow bishops came back from Tours in the early summer. A few weeks later, Henry, who had recently returned to England after an absence of over four years, encountered Becket at a council held on 1 July 1163 at Woodstock. They immediately came to blows. The issue was a payment known as the sheriff's aid. Hitherto the payment had formed a perquisite of the sheriff; Henry was determined that it should be paid directly to the Exchequer instead. Becket set himself with equal determination to resist the change and the two exchanged high words.

Henry realized that he had been abandoned by the man whom he had made great and who had stood by his side. But he pulled back from the brink of all-out conflict. Was he trying to preserve a necessary working relationship? Or was he keeping his powder dry for the real issue?

This was not long in coming. Immediately after his return to England, Henry was bombarded with a series of disturbing reports from his justices. They, according to William of Newburgh, 'intimated ... to the king ... that many crimes against public order, such as thefts, rapes and murders, were repeatedly committed by the clergy'.

The justices spoke out of frustration, and perhaps dented professional pride, since the clergy's exemption from lay justice meant that they got off, in effect, scot free: instead of the mutilation or execution that would be visited on a layman, they faced penance or unfrocking at worst. Shock statistics were also produced to bring the matter home. 'During his reign', Henry was told to his face, 'more than a hundred murders had been committed by the clergy in England alone.'

The tactic worked. Outraged by the offence both to his sense of justice and his royal dignity committed by thugs in cassocks, Henry decided that something must be done. Becket, on the other hand, was equally determined that clerical exemption from lay justice must be preserved to the last jot and tittle.

He had found the perfect last ditch to die in.

The issue of 'criminous clerks' was a long-standing one. Such aberrant individuals have always existed and – to the delight of popular Sunday newspapers – still do. And the reaction of the Church was and is the same: to prefer silence to exposure and the dignity and standing of Church and clergy to the welfare of the victims or abstract notions of justice. Now the issue is child abuse; in the twelfth century it was violence. It was a more violent age; the relative number of clergy was much higher and many were in secular employment and lived essentially secular lives. They had wives and children; wore ordinary dress; and, like Chancellor Becket himself, were as handy with weapons as the next man.

What to do with such men when passions or violence spilled over into criminal acts had been in dispute since the Conquest, when William the Conqueror had introduced Church courts and canon law into England: the Church wished to protect its own; the king to do justice and vindicate his sovereignty. Where should the balance fall?

Becket pursued a double policy. In a series of high-profile cases, he stoutly defended the privileges of the Church. But he also tried to show that the Church was able to impose appropriate penalties: a priest from the diocese of Salisbury, who was unable to exonerate himself from a charge of murder, was committed to strict confinement in a monastery; a canon of Bedford, who was controversially acquitted by a Church court of murdering a knight, was banished; while a clerk of London, who stole a chalice, was branded. But, though well meant, Becket's actions only added fuel to the flames: not only were the sentences unknown at canon law; they also trespassed flagrantly on the royal monopoly on criminal justice.

A more systematic solution would have to be found. Henry chose his moment with care. In October, the body of his sainted predecessor, Edward the Confessor, was solemnly reinterred in Westminster Abbey by Becket. Henry used this ceremony in honour of a royal saint to convene an old-fashioned council of the Church, summoned and presided over by himself as a Christian king.

Henry began by repeating his complaints over 'criminous clerks'. Then, when the bishops failed to offer concessions, he went on the attack. Would they submit to the 'ancient customs' of the realm, he demanded. These ancient customs were studiously vague. But Henry, with his lawyer's mind, reduced them to two principal components. The first was the Conqueror's determination to insulate the English Church from the most aggressive papal claims. The second was his own insistence that criminous clerks should be subjected to his own, criminal justice.

The bishops, led by Becket, stalled by saying that they could only accept the ancient customs 'saving their order'. This sounds like conditional acceptance. In fact, since the ancient customs, as Henry understood them, were contrary to the new canon law, it was a flat refusal.

The result was stalemate and both sides appealed to Pope Alexander III: Henry to have the 'ancient customs' confirmed; Becket to have them annulled. But the pope counselled compromise. At the beginning of December, Becket, assured that Henry only required his assent by word of mouth, agreed. Scenting victory, Henry immediately raised the stakes. He summoned a council at Clarendon in January 1164 and browbeat Becket into repeating his oral assurance in front of the entire assembly. Then, characteristically, he ordered the ancient customs to be set down in writing. The following day, the obviously pre-prepared text of the Constitutions of Clarendon was produced.

The Constitutions are one of the great texts of English history. They express an overarching vision of a Church subordinate to the crown in all, save matters of belief, and they work out its implications in minute, lawyerly detail. As in Clause 3, which lays down the procedure for dealing with criminous clerks. After conviction in the Church courts, they should first be unfrocked and then handed over to the secular courts for punishment as ordinary criminals.

The Constitutions were the antithesis of everything that Becket believed in. For Becket espoused the contrary vision – based on an extreme clericalist reading of the biblical text 'touch not mine anointed' – which saw the Church as not only independent of the state but manifestly superior to it.

But, under Henry's intense pressure, Becket swore to the Constitutions. As did the rest of the bishops. Henry, it seemed, had won – as he usually did.

Becket, for his part, believed that he had sinned by swearing to the Constitutions. Soon he repudiated the submission on the grounds it had been extorted under duress. Henry now tightened the screw by accusing the archbishop of embezzlement during his time as chancellor. In fear for his life Becket fled abroad.

V

From his haven in France, Becket continued to defy Henry by making ever more grandiose claims for the independence and authority of the Church. He was also pursuing diplomatic negotiations as enthusiastically as he had when in power – only this time it was with Henry's enemies.

And there was an added danger. In order to shore up the succession to the crown, Henry wanted his son Henry crowned king of England immediately, during his own lifetime. But with the archbishop on the run and the clergy hostile this was no easy task. The right to anoint a king belonged to the archbishop of Canterbury. To get his way Henry made the archbishop of York perform the coronation. But was it legitimate? There was also the larger question of Becket's own position. Becket on the loose and abroad was more dangerous, Henry felt, than Becket at home. He was undoing Henry's foreign alliances. He was also a magnet for dissent in England, which was now coming from within Henry's own family. So a compromise was patched up and Becket returned to England.

And what a return! At Christmas 1170 word reached Henry that Becket, who had learned nothing and forgotten nothing, was up to his old tricks. The archbishop, his enemies insinuated to the king, was careering round the country armed with knights and he was excommunicating bishops who were loyal to Henry. Something snapped and there resulted one of those famous Plantagenet rages. 'Will no one rid me of this turbulent priest?' the king exclaimed, or words to that effect. Henry had said such things before and nothing much had happened. But this time four royal knights took the king at his word and they rode furiously to Canterbury to bring Becket to account – whatever that might mean.

On 29 December the four knights – Reginald fitzUrse, William de Traci, Hugh of Morville and Richard Brito – arrived at Canterbury Cathedral. The other clergy begged Becket to flee while there was time. But he refused, deciding to make a final stand. It was fitzUrse who struck the first blow, taking off the side of Becket's head. Still denouncing his assailants, the archbishop fell to the pavement of his cathedral and the others piled in. Moments later Becket lay dead.

When he heard the news Henry plunged into an agony of grief, hiding himself away for three whole days so that his friends feared for his life. Was it personal grief for the death of his one-time friend? Or horror at what had been done in his name? In either case the king's response fully matched the enormity of the deed. For Christendom was stunned by the murder of an archbishop in his own cathedral on the orders of his own king. And letters rained down upon the pope, even from Henry's own family, demanding that he proceed, with all the awful powers of the Church, against this sacrilegious king who was worse than a Nero or a Judas.

Meanwhile, Becket's ghost, growing more powerful year by year, served as the perfect cover for resistance or rebellion against the murderer king.

11

THE CURSE OF ANJOU

Richard I, John, Henry III

CANTERBURY CATHEDRAL LOOMS LARGE in the Kent countryside and also in English history. After the murder of Thomas Becket it took on almost mythic status. Since then, for Henry, everything had gone wrong. All the power he had built up threatened to unravel.

Only a grand gesture of self-abasement would exorcize the ghost that haunted the Angevin empire. In July 1174 Henry purged his soul with a fast, then walked barefoot wearing only a rough woollen shirt to Thomas's shrine in Canterbury Cathedral. There he prostrated himself before his erstwhile enemy. Next he, Henry, king of England, submitted to a public scourging by all the clergy present: bishops, abbots and each of the monks of Canterbury took it in turns to flog him. Finally he lay all night and all day on the cold stones in front of the shrine. It was an extraordinarily untypical gesture by that proud and passionate man.

The sight of a king humbled, especially so mighty a king, was shocking. But for the next century it would not be an uncommon sight as a line of English monarchs were forced, repeatedly, into humiliating concessions.

I

The penance that he performed at Canterbury, Henry calculated, was worth it if it contrived to separate Becket, the saint as he now was, from the coalition of enemies now arrayed against him. And so it proved almost immediately.

The king awoke the following morning to hear that an invasion of England had been thwarted. As if by miracle William I, king of Scots, was captured and a great armada poised to invade England from Flanders dispersed. Henry had indeed stooped to conquer. It brought to an end a crisis unleashed by the conflict with Becket, the lowest point in Henry's hitherto triumphant reign. For the rebels arrayed against him were his own family – Eleanor, his wife, and his three eldest sons, Henry (the Young King), Richard and Geoffrey.

For Henry had made a decision about the future of his kingdoms. He wanted to provide for the stability of his empire. He also wanted to try to keep the peace among his teenage sons, who had clearly inherited his own ferocious temper, by dividing up his empire among them. But in practice the division of his lands proved to be a disastrous miscalculation. The problem was that his eldest son in particular had been given glittering titles but no real power. Young Henry had been crowned king of England and in 1169 he had paid Louis VII of France (his father-in-law) homage – the ritual act of submission that English kings made for their holdings in France – for Anjou. But all this was his in name only. The young man had to watch as the mighty empire was further divided among his siblings. Richard was given Aquitaine and Geoffrey Brittany. This slight was compounded when Henry II gave the youngest son, John, three key fiefs in Anjou, *his* territory.

Seeing the divisions in the English royal family, Louis VII dripped poison into the ear of young Henry. Had he not been crowned king? Was he not sole ruler of Anjou? But what, in effect, was he lord of? Nothing. He was a gilded prisoner. And so too were his brothers, Richard and Geoffrey, whose power was equally illusory and dependent on their father. It was a matter of power and, above all, honour. The young Henry slipped away to join the French king and claim his just rewards. He had the full encouragement of his mother, Queen Eleanor, who had been plotting against her husband since the murder of Becket. Henry II had tried to divide and rule his family; instead he had united them against him. Richard and Geoffrey joined their mother and brother in revolt.

In the face of inter-familial strife, Henry's empire weathered the test and the king deployed his honed and doughty intelligence against his family. Eleanor was captured and imprisoned. After his grand act of abasement at Canterbury, Henry set off for Normandy full of confidence and backed by an army. The sons tasted military defeat at the hands of their all-conquering father and came to heel.

It was a pattern which was to repeat itself for over a decade.

Young Henry still thirsted for power, but was fobbed off by his father with an allowance and the chance to shine as a chivalric super-star. Richard, who had impressed his father during the rebellion, learned the real arts of warfare as duke of Aquitaine. There he gained a reputation as a fearsome, sometimes cruel, soldier. More than any of his brothers, he was his father's son: resourceful, ruthless and a highly capable ruler. Geoffrey was kept under close supervision, but was eventually given control of Brittany. And John was made lord of Ireland, the emptiest title of all. He was nicknamed 'John Lackland' by his father.

And it was Henry's effort to provide land for the boy which once again threatened to bring his empire crashing down. For to give to John meant taking land from one of his brothers.

Now it was the sons who fought among themselves in an intense sibling rivalry for land, honour and empire. Romantically known as the 'Angevin Curse', it was the price to pay for so large an empire and too many heirs. In 1183 Henry the Young King once more rose against his father and his brothers but in the midst of renewed civil war he died of dysentery aged just twenty-eight.

Henry changed tack: rather than name an heir (which had caused the problems in the first place), he would keep tight-lipped. It proved to be another blunder.

For the death of young Henry did not make things simpler. Far from it. It only made the surviving three brothers more desperate for land, more hostile to each other and more suspicious of their father. Richard was the eldest of the surviving sons, but on what terms would he succeed? If he inherited England, Normandy and Anjou, and added these to Aquitaine, Geoffrey and John would not stand for it. Henry offered Richard England and Normandy if he gave Aquitaine to John, but Richard refused. In response John joined the fray, unsuccessfully invading Richard's Aquitaine.

Then there were two. Geoffrey died in 1186, leaving Richard and John to compete for the spoils. And it was Richard, the bloodied warrior of thirty-two, who began to challenge and then overtake the great Henry II. By 1189 they were in open conflict and after one heavy defeat Henry fled from his son.

The old king had to surrender on Richard's terms. It was his last act. Mortally sick and already a broken man at the age of only fifty-six, Henry was carried back in a litter to his castle of Chinon, in his native Anjou, to die. One of the conditions imposed on him by Richard and the king of France was that he should pardon the conspirators against him. When the list was read out it included the name of his beloved youngest son, John. It was the final blow.

'Why should I reverence Christ,' the dying king cried out when he was asked to make his final confession, 'and why should I honour him who has taken all my honour from me?' Confess nevertheless he did, and immediately afterwards, on 6 July 1189, Henry died.

Henry's body was brought for burial to the nearby abbey of Fontevraud, the traditional burial place of the counts of Anjou. Like a wounded animal he had gone home to die. Yet he had been one of England's most successful kings – able in his prime to enforce his authority on barons, bishops and even other princes. He had turned his vision of kingship into a reality and embodied in it institutions that would far outlast his dynasty. He had made the monarchy great. Would his heirs be equal to that greatness?

II

Greatness was the one thing Richard I desired. As soon as Henry II lay dead he set about claiming his inheritance. And what a patrimony it was! It was not just the extent of the empire but the way it had been administered for the best part of four decades. Richard hastened to England to be crowned. The country was peaceful, well governed and prosperous. Richard received a treasury of some 100,000 marks. Then he held a sale – of local offices and the privileges that came with them. He returned estates that had been confiscated by his father. The money poured in. But it could never be enough for Richard's needs. He would have put London up for sale, he is supposed to have said, if he could find a buyer rich enough.

For Richard was fired with a holy mission. In 1187 catastrophe had hit Christendom when Saladin captured Jerusalem. Richard responded by taking the cross, or pledging himself to join the crusade to recover the Holy Lands. He was the first prince in northern Europe to do so. The money he raised in England in his fire sale funded a mighty fleet and army which he led east. England was left in the hands of a capable government under the justiciar, or chief minister, William de Longchamp.

Richard Coeur de Lion has gone down in history as the greatest of holy warriors. And he certainly cultivated an image as a romantic hero. Magnificent, brave and chivalric, he almost lived up to the myth he created. Another figure of legend, thanks to the tales of Robin Hood, was John. In the Angevin manner John was hungry for honour and power. Above all he wanted to be recognized as Richard's heir. And the king knew it. When Richard left for the crusade he made John swear to keep out of England for three years.

He should have known better than to trust one of his siblings.

Within a year John was back in England, alarmed at news that his nephew Arthur of Brittany, Geoffrey's son, had been accepted as heir by Richard and William de Longchamp. John took possession of royal castles at Nottingham and Tickhill. He then moved against Longchamp. First Longchamp was forced to accept John as heir. Then John moved to depose him as viceroy. He was poised to take over effective rule of England in Richard's absence, which he no doubt hoped would be long or end tragically. But he had reckoned without the loyalty and political sense of the council, the Church and the nobility. They closed ranks against the young usurper. For there was a contingency plan already in place against John's duplicity. Longchamp was replaced by Walter de Coutances – Richard's nominee as justiciar. Clearly Henry II's system of government was standing firm, even when the monarch was far away and the pretender close at hand.

John was still without the power he craved. To get it, he was prepared to do almost anything. In 1193, the king of France, Philip Augustus, lured John away from England with great promises. Together they plotted to seize Richard's lands in France. John returned to England to raise allies and men. But again he had overreached himself. He lost many of the castles and lands he had taken in England, and, what was worse, gained a reputation as a traitor.

Richard, by contrast, had earned a reputation as the greatest of Christian kings for his deeds on the crusade. Then, on his return, he was captured by the Holy Roman Emperor and held captive. John and Philip Augustus saw another chance. The emperor demanded 100,000 marks in ransom for Richard: John and Philip Augustus offered to pay to keep him a prisoner!

This flagrant disloyalty was John's undoing. The council of England launched an offensive against him, taking back the rest of the castles he had seized except his stronghold in Nottingham. When Richard returned he retook this as well, pacified England with remarkable speed, and immediately left for Normandy, which, thanks to John and Philip's treachery, was in a much worse state. John, for his part, begged on his knees for Richard's forgiveness. Foolishly, if generously, it was granted.

Richard was forced to spend the rest of his reign trying to recover his empire in France rather than return to crusading. England was hard pressed by tax to fund his wars. But it was given with good enough grace. For Richard's wars were seen as just, whether they were against Saladin or France. He was popular with his subjects and admired by contemporaries as the very model of a good king.

Richard died in 1199, shot by a crossbow when he was putting down a rebellion in the Limousin. His body was buried at Fontevraud with his parents; his heart was buried at Rouen. It was appropriate, for as king Richard had spent just six months in total in England. He had left it well governed, however, and its reputation enhanced and his father's empire in rude health. He would be a hard act to follow, especially as England had got used to its absentee king, and the more so because his heir was, incontestably, John. 'My brother John', Richard sneered, 'is not man enough to conquer a country if there is anyone to offer even the feeblest resistance.'

III

There is no more contrary breed than professional historians. For John's contemporaries and for most succeeding generations of historians, John was the opposite of his brother Richard and the very model of a bad king. But a new generation of historians has come along who argue that, on the contrary, John was 'a good thing', or at any rate a good administrator. He was unusually interested in the mechanics of government, which he pursued with an often obsessive interest. And his reign sees the start of the great parchment rolls which record the government's correspondence and which form the foundations for the scholarly history of the Middle Ages.

But to praise John for being a royal filing clerk shows historians looking after their own with a vengeance. For John's obsession for record-keeping was a sign not of strength, but of weakness. He was so keen on documentation because he was so mistrustful of his subjects, and his subjects in turn distrusted a king who was nit-picking and always eager to revive an old, outdated royal imposition or invent a new one.

The result was tax, tax and more tax. But money on its own was not enough. John was no mighty warrior like his father Henry II. Nor a charismatic leader of men like his brother Richard. Still worse, there was an unfortunate streak of mistrustfulness, even paranoia, in his character. He had been easily manipulated in his abortive rebellions. Now the manipulator had turned into his tormentor. Philip Augustus, his former fellow conspirator, was that rare thing at this time, a capable king of France. Defeated by Richard, he now saw his chance against John.

Thanks to his reputation for treachery and cruelty John found it impossible to keep together Richard's allies on the Continent. Added to that he was a poor commander and diplomat. He failed to halt Philip's advances and his high-handed manner stirred up rebellions in his own lands. Norman barons swapped sides and John could not persuade English magnates to follow him in a war of conquest. Once nicknamed 'Lackland', he was now known as 'John Swordsoft'.

By 1204 John had been shorn of a third of his territories, including his ancestral lands of Normandy, Brittany and Anjou. For the first time since the Norman Conquest the king of England was that and little more.

Deprived of empire, he turned his gaze on what was left – England. From 1206 he began sucking the country dry. Taxes reached unprecedented levels. The Jews were persecuted. The barons were squeezed hard and those who fell into debt to the crown were deprived of land and hounded into exile. The wealth of the nation, exacted by increasingly arbitrary means, was hoarded in royal castles. The sums were enormous (some 200,000 marks); so was the resentment.

Next John decided to follow in his father's footsteps by striking at the power of the Church. But, once again, he had the misfortune to encounter one of the greatest medieval popes: Pope Innocent III.

The struggle began as a dispute about the appointment of the archbishop of Canterbury. But it quickly escalated as both sides wheeled in their heaviest weapons. Innocent III laid England under an 'interdict'; this was a sort of clerical general strike, in which the clergy refused to say mass, marry couples or bury corpses. In retaliation, John resorted to one of Margaret Thatcher's favourite weapons against the unions and confiscated all the property of the Church. Who would win? The clerical strikers or the royal strike-breaker?

Pope Innocent was a formidable politician. And he turned real weapons as well as spiritual ones against the king of England. For he not only excommunicated John but also declared him deposed and invited Philip Augustus, John's other great enemy, to launch a crusade and seize the throne of England for himself.

Under simultaneous threat by his two most dangerous enemies, John had to buy one off. The price he was prepared to pay was astonishing – it was England itself. On 15 May 1213 King John received the pope's representative at Dover Castle. At the meeting John agreed to everything that the pope demanded: to do penance for his offences against the Church; to accept the pope's choice as archbishop of Canterbury; and to pay compensation for all that he had seized from the Church. But the king also went much further and, in a dramatic move, issued a charter in which he acknowledged the pope as his overlord and promised to pay a large annual cash tribute.

John had handed ultimate authority over the kingdom of England to the pope and had agreed to pay him a yearly fee to lease it back. John had saved his neck. But at what cost? He was humiliated at home and abroad, as a king and as a man.

There was now only one way for John to re-establish his authority: to reconquer his lost lands in France. It was an expedition long in the planning. All that cash which had been wrung from his people and coerced from his barons had been amassed for one purpose. John was playing a desperate game for the highest of stakes. If the dice rolled in his favour and he won a great victory in France all would be well. But once again his luck failed.

On 27 July 1214 the English and French armies met at Bouvines in Flanders. At first the English seemed victorious and Philip himself was thrown from his horse. But the French struck back and overwhelmed the English. Paris rejoiced, but in England John faced mutiny. He had blown his vast wealth – England's wealth. Without it he could not bully and bludgeon his subjects. Instead, he was at their mercy.

The barons sank their own differences and presented a united front against the king. Never again, they decided, would a king be able to behave as John had done. And they backed up their demands with the threat of overwhelming force. The part of honest broker between the king and the barons was played by Stephen Langton, the archbishop of Canterbury. He professed to be neutral but in fact he inclined to the barons and secretly helped them structure their demands. In January 1215 the king met his barons in London. They agreed to reconvene in Northampton in April, where John would reply to their demands. But, as ever, he thought he had a trick up his sleeve. He rushed over foreign mercenaries and persuaded the pope to condemn the rebels. So it was no surprise when he did not turn up in Northampton.

The response was astonishing. John's opponents renounced their loyalty to the king. London opened its gates to them. Civil war seemed inevitable. But in June the king capitulated. On the 15th the two sides met in a field near Windsor known as Runnymead. The barons, who had come fully armed, presented their demands and King John reluctantly, and already in bad faith, granted what they wished. The agreement became known as the 'Magna Carta', the Great Charter. But in fact it was only the most famous and ambitious of a succession of attempts – stretching back through the coronation oath of Henry I and the memories of Anglo-Saxon England – to define the rights and duties of king and people.

The original Magna Carta sealed by John himself has long since vanished. After all, the king had no desire to preserve the record of his own humiliation. But copies were distributed to each county, of which four survive today. Nowadays the fame of Magna Carta rests on clauses like this: 'no free man shall be seized or imprisoned or stripped of his goods or possessions save by lawful judgement of his peers or equals or by the law of the land'. Or this: 'to no one shall I sell or deny or delay justice'. Provisions like these are, or have become, what we call basic human rights and echoes of them survive in the statute book and in the universal declaration of human rights. But they come a very long way down the document. At the top are the provisions that really concern the authors of the charter – the bishops and barons. The first clause states: 'the Church in England shall be free'. That is, free from royal interference. While the second clause limits the king's rights to exact death duties or fines from barons when their lands were handed over to their heirs.

Magna Carta quickly became and remained a touchstone of liberties throughout the Middle Ages and beyond. It also had very sharp contemporary teeth because one clause permitted the barons to use force if necessary to bring John into line if he showed any backsliding from Magna Carta. It seemed a total defeat. But John had one last card up his sleeve. Immediately he appealed to his new overlord the pope to have the charter annulled on the grounds that he had been coerced into agreeing to it. Innocent agreed and Magna Carta was promptly declared null and void.

The barons were outraged at the king's faithlessness and open war broke out. For the barons it was no longer a question of restraining John but of dethroning him. They even turned to the national enemy and invited Louis, son of the French king, to take the English throne. Louis invaded and by the autumn of 1216 had seized much of the south-east of England, including London itself. Would England be divided, or would there be the first violent change of dynasty since 1066?

Suddenly, at this point King John died on the night of 18 October 1216, unmourned and unloved. 'Foul as it is,' one contemporary wrote, 'Hell itself is made fouler by the presence of John.'

His heir was his son Henry, only nine years old.

The child's cause looked hopeless. But with John safely out of the way the prospect of a French succession lost its attraction for an important group of the barons and bishops. They decided that the young Henry should be brought to Gloucester and crowned as quickly as possible. On the morning of 28 October 1216 the impromptu coronation took place.

The boy, who was a grave, handsome, golden-haired child, was brought to Gloucester Cathedral. He wore a specially made set of little royal robes. First he took the customary coronation oath; then he paid homage to the pope's representative, the legate; finally, and with all the traditional ceremonies, he was anointed and crowned, though the crown was in fact one of his mother's tiaras or hair ornaments. Bearing in mind the circumstances, it was inevitable that Henry's coronation was something of a makeshift affair. But it was a real one nonetheless. It had imbued him with the mystical, even magical, authority of kingship and he never forgot the fact. Now it was up to him – or rather his regents – to persuade the country to accept him as king.

Their first moves were not military but propagandistic. For already there was something called public opinion and the regents appealed to it by issuing a letter in the king's name. This letter neatly turned Henry's most obvious drawback – his age – into an advantage by arguing that his youth meant that he had no part in the sins of his father: 'we hear that a quarrel arose between our father and certain nobles of our kingdom, whether with justification or not we do not know. We wish to remove it forever since it has nothing to do with us.' Next, Henry's regents made a major political concession. They reissued Magna Carta, but removed the clauses authorizing the use of force against the king. At a stroke the charter was rescued from oblivion and the cause of civil war removed. The French abandoned their claim to England and Henry was universally recognized as king. For the remainder of his minority, the spirit of Magna Carta was adhered to. Demands for tax were accompanied by reconfirmations of the charter to reassure the barons that there would be no return to arbitrary government. This made it harder to raise cash, and it subjected the crown to the opinions of the great landowners. But it was a case of needs must.

Magna Carta had saved Henry's crown. It remained to be seen whether he would honour the charter when he grew to manhood.

IV

At Oxford in 1227 Henry declared himself of age. He was nineteen. But he was still king in name only. And, despite his declaration, he remained so for another five long years.

Real power instead belonged to Hubert de Burgh, who had acted as justiciar since 1219. De Burgh had been a key figure in restoring the monarchy; he had rallied support and preserved its powers. But now he was reluctant to give up his regency. Henry chafed at his control. More and more, he felt slighted and powerless, and in any case de Burgh was losing his grip. He fumbled an attempt to retake Normandy and Poitou, and it ended in a shaming debacle. And when Henry made it clear that he wanted to get married, Hubert saw this as another threat and spread rumours that the king was deformed and impotent. Things reached such a pitch that the angry young king was said to have vented his frustration by attacking his protector with a blunted sword.

By 1232 Henry III had summoned up the courage to overthrow the men and mentors who had restrained him for so long. But breaking with Hubert, virtually a father-figure, was evidently hard for the inexperienced, isolated king. Finally, after a fearful quarrel between the two, Henry stuck to his resolve. Hubert was stripped of his offices and castles and was presented with a hefty bill for all his expenditure as justiciar. Now Henry was determined to be king in deed as well as king in name, and he was determined above all to break the shackles of Magna Carta.

For Henry was not only looking back to the glorious monarchy of Henry II. He was also influenced by the revived monarchy of France. He favoured French courtiers, and his greatest building project was wholly French in style.

The Westminster Abbey we know today is essentially the work of Henry, though its interior is only a pale shadow of the masterpiece he created, which glowed with red and blue and gold. Work started in 1245; it cost a fortune, employed hundreds of craftsmen and lasted for twenty-five years, in the most ambitious project of church building that western Europe had yet seen. Indeed, it was so ambitious that it almost bankrupted the king and inflicted severe political damage on him. But for Henry it was worth it, for he was building a monument to the greater glory of God and to the monarchy.

Westminster Abbey, with the shrine of the royal saint, Edward the Confessor, at its heart, was intended to be the crowning glory of Henry's vision of kingship. But it was a vision that was intensely controversial to some of his barons. For it seemed as un-English as the architecture of the Abbey itself: the models of Henry's kingship were foreign too – the French monarchy and the papacy; even its agents were foreign born.

Here Henry's psychology came into play as, throughout his life, he had a tendency to fall under the influence of stronger, more powerful characters. This meant that he got rid of de Burgh only to submit himself to another man who had nurtured him as an infant king, Peter des Roches, the bishop of Winchester. It was an ominous choice since des Roches had been close to King John. In the last years of that reign the bishop had held the position of justiciar and exacerbated the tensions between king and people as an enthusiastic tax-collector and authoritarian. It was a case of out of the frying pan and into the fire: de Burgh had been unpopular with the nobility because he was a *novus homo* – a self-made man and a grasping outsider. Des Roches was even more unpopular because of his association with John and, most of all, because he was not English. Henry's own behaviour made things worse. He was generous to a fault, giving land and office not only to des Roches but also to his foreign-born family and friends. The Frenchman became virtual ruler of England.

But he lasted only two years. The barons loathed des Roches. He had displaced them at court. His French kinfolk had squeezed taxes out of the country. He had got the pope to cancel previous charters which limited the rights of the crown. And rumours were flying about that the Frenchified court was egging Henry on to take up arms against the barons, claw back the power that John had lost and emulate the claims to absolute sovereignty of the Holy Roman Emperor, Frederick II.

England was at the brink of civil war once again. And indeed fighting did break out for some months. In February 1234 the barons, under the leadership of the archbishop-elect of Canterbury, Edmund Rich, denounced Henry in public at Westminster. Before his elevation to Canterbury, Rich – an ascetic former Oxford don – had been an outspoken opponent of foreign office holders and a champion of Magna Carta.

Henry responded, like his grandfather and namesake Henry II, with an ostentatious show of piety. But he lacked the theatrical brilliance of his predecessor. He trekked from shrine to shrine in the East Anglian countryside, hoping something would turn up to save him. But it did not. Real power now lay with the archbishop and the council. Edmund took decisive action to head off civil war and provide leadership in a divided country. In April the division between Henry and the barons and bishops was revealed in dramatic style at Canterbury during Edmund Rich's consecration as archbishop. Henry sat with Peter des Roches alone on one side of the choir; the other bishops all sat on the other side, facing them as if in a trial. A month later the new archbishop threatened Henry with the ultimate sanction: unless des Roches was dismissed the king would be excommunicated.

Henry backed down. Des Roches was sent away and the council was reconstituted. The king had learned the hard way that his power was not unconditional. For a decade and a half peace of sorts was maintained. This was helped by the poverty of the crown. Henry might dream of autocracy, but he couldn't afford it. After the dark years of John and the settlement of Magna Carta it had become harder for the crown to raise large taxes. Attempts to bypass restraints and squeeze out more revenue were resisted by nobles and prominent subjects armed with a sheaf of charters guaranteeing their rights.

As a result Henry's greatest ambition was thwarted. He wanted to restore his family's honour by rebuilding the great empire of his grandfather Henry II, which had been squandered by his father. But the great reconquest never quite worked. The king's coffers were always empty. And he was a hopeless general. He wavered, refused to make firm or timely decisions and had a tendency to fall into his enemy's traps. Having failed in France, Henry dreamed of redeeming himself by going on crusade like his valorous uncle Richard. But that, too, never got off the ground.

Ironically, these were the best years of his reign, as, in spite of the king, peace was preserved at home and abroad. Good relations were maintained with the nobility and their rights were respected. Henry's personal rule was tolerated as long as it was light of touch and inexpensive. And for Henry's part, weak and sensitive as he was, the horrors of civil war which he remembered from his childhood and early years as king were to be avoided at all costs.

But these salutary memories dimmed with age. Henry grew more reckless and his folly led to the unravelling of his rule. From the late 1240s he increased the pressure on his subjects. Not on the landed nobility, of course, who were in a position to resist him, but on the lesser folk and clergy, who were hit hard by increased demands for tax. The money raised was wasted on Henry's erratic and futile foreign adventures. And the king slipped further into debt. He also slipped into the mire of his own delusions. In the 1250s he hatched several madcap schemes, the most notorious being a plan to set up his son, Edmund, as king of Sicily. Sicily was a papal fief and Pope Innocent IV had put it up for sale. Henry was required to pay almost £100,000 for its crown. And, on top of that, he would have to provide an army to remove the current ruler, who was squatting on the island.

Henry was in debt to the papacy; he owed great sums to other great families of Europe; and all he had to show were vain dreams. The nobility flatly refused to bail Henry out. And the Church had come to feel that the king was under the thrall of the pope, to the detriment of the liberties of the English Church. Political support was wearing dangerously thin for Henry.

It was not just Henry's costly and quixotic adventures. His family, too, was deeply mistrusted. In 1236, he had married Eleanor of Provence, and her Savoyard family were showered with lands, titles and provided with good marriages. Eleanor's uncle Boniface was also made archbishop of Canterbury, a conspicuously poor successor to Edmund Rich, the renowned academic, the doughty champion of the English Church and the upholder of Magna Carta. Boniface, the chronicler Matthew Paris commented acidly, was noted more for his birth than his brains: in 'learning, manners and years' he fell short of what was expected of a successor of Dunstan, Anselm, Becket and Edmund. He too spent a lot of his time advancing the interests of his relations. Other members of the family became leading councillors. And after the wave of Savoyards came Henry's half-siblings, the many children of Henry's mother's second marriage. They were known as the Lusignans, and they swarmed to England from 1247. Like their rivals the Savoyards they were treated with extreme generosity by Henry.

The English barons resented this influx of foreign dependants who assumed positions of political importance. Above all they saw the Lusignans egging Henry on in his lunatic schemes abroad and arbitrary rule at home. They were, to boot, harsh landlords and arrogant courtiers. The connection between foreign advisers and domestic tyranny was clear in the barons' minds. And the bid to gain Sicily was seen as a means of freeing Henry to become an autocrat like his father. It was as if the lessons of the fall of Peter des Roches in 1234 had been forgotten.

Gossip about the king's shaky hold on the crown spread around the country. One who relished the ins and outs of the court was the Benedictine monk Matthew Paris. Paris was supposed to concentrate on more exalted matters as he was the official historian of the abbey at St Albans. But, like many scholars cloistered away in academic pursuits, he hungered for something meatier than the humdrum of parochial research. Thus his history of St Albans grew into a history of everything. Soon he had outgrown his monastic life as well; he was being wined and dined by the great and the good, who fed his appetite for court gossip and political tales. It is from Paris that we get the juicy titbits of information about, for example, de Burgh's accusations that Henry was impotent and other insights into court life that only a privileged insider would know.

He even met Henry at one of the king's grand ceremonies at Westminster Abbey. The historian monk and the king got on well and over the years they would swap stories and bits and pieces of learning.

This introduction allowed Paris to extend his collection of elevated informants who sent him letters and official documents. Several times Henry came to St Albans to catch up on Paris's monumental history. And probably to see how he would fare in it. For the king was a very eager back-seat writer and, as Paris said, he stayed up most of the night 'and guided my pen'.

But Henry comes off very badly in Matthew Paris's history. Presumably he showed the king a favourable draft only when he came to St Albans. He liked Henry the man, but deplored his weaknesses as a ruler. Paris was a patriotic Englishman: he was sensitive about customary liberties, and he was nauseated by foreign influence on the crown. And monk though he was, he mistrusted the papacy. Indeed, he came to believe that there were two millstones between which poor old England was being ground: the pope and the king. His description of the mood in the country revealed his own opinion of Henry:

> ... he did not keep his promises, having little regard for the keys of the church and for the conditions of the Great Charter so many times paid for ... he exalted his uterine brothers [the Lusignans] in a most intolerable manner, contrary to the law of the kingdom as though they had been born in this country ...
>
> Moreover, the king was reproached with advancing and enriching the interests of all foreigners, and with despising and pillaging his own natural subjects, to the ruin of the whole kingdom ... he was so needy, whilst others possessed money in abundance, that he could not, for want of money, recover the rights of the kingdom, nay, that he could not even check the injurious incursions of the Welsh, who were the very scum of mankind.

Most disastrously Henry's ruinous debts cast him on the unpopular members of his family for financial support. In turn they became even more autocratic, confirming the barons' worst fears. By 1258 the competing groups in the royal family and the court had fatally undermined Henry. Government was on the point of breakdown.

V

The nobles found a leader in Simon de Montfort. De Montfort himself was a Frenchman. Like so many of his compatriots, he had been brought to England by Henry, showered with favour, and given the earldom of Leicester. He even dared to marry the king's sister without Henry's permission. Nonetheless, Simon was given positions of high authority and command, becoming Henry's lieutenant in Gascony (the last remaining portion of the monarchy's French empire), where he acted more or less as a free agent. Henry was clearly impressed and in awe of Simon. Simon for his part was often contemptuous of his king; he believed he was indispensable. Simon, in other words, was only the latest in the long line of powerful characters who had overshadowed Henry. But, from the beginning, the relationship had a novel edge of tension. Once, when the two men were out hunting together, they stopped to shelter from a thunderstorm. Henry is said to have told Simon that much as he feared the lightning, he feared Simon more.

The key to Simon's character was his past as a crusader. Crusaders see the world in simple black and white. Once Simon's enemy had been the Infidel; now it was those who supported Henry's autocratic style of monarchy. First in the sights of Simon and his followers were the Lusignans. In 1258 de Montfort and six other leading barons swore an oath of mutual loyalty. Together they were more than a match for the king and they in turn had their own distinct ideas of how England should be run.

Henry was confronted with a litany of complaints in Parliament. This was the name – given more and more consistently – to the specially convened assemblies of barons and bishops which had begun with Magna Carta. On this occasion, according to Matthew Paris, Henry tried to wheedle his way out of this crisis:

> The king, on reflection, acknowledged the truth of the accusations, although late, and humbled himself, declaring that he had been too often imposed upon by evil counsel, and he promised and made oath at the altar of the shrine of St Edward, that he would fully and properly amend his old errors, and show favour and kindness to his

natural subjects. But his frequent transgressions rendered him entirely unworthy of belief, and as the nobles had not yet learned what knot to bind their Proteus with (for it was an arduous and difficult matter) the parliament was prorogued ...

It met again at Oxford. As if to mirror the disorder in government, the weather had been foul all summer. Harvests failed and there was widespread death and disease. The barons, meanwhile, armed themselves against the Lusignans. The council at Oxford drew up a revolutionary new way of governing the country that was intended to turn England into a crowned republic. And Henry, despite his high view of kingship, had no choice but to agree. The 'Provisions of Oxford', as the new constitutional blueprint was known, looked back to Anglo-Saxon England with its tradition of a strong national community. They also looked abroad to Germany and Italy, where new self-governing communes or city-states like Florence or Venice were appearing.

The result was to leave Henry as king, but king in name only. Instead, his powers would be exercised by an elected council of fifteen which would in turn answer to parliaments meeting at three set intervals a year. No other European kingdom had tried such an audacious constitutional experiment and no other king had been subject to such humiliation. Henry had experienced the rule of the barons before. But then he was nine years old. Now, at the age of fifty-one, he was being treated like a minor once more and deemed incapable of ruling like an adult.

Henry was left isolated in the crisis when his Lusignan half-brothers fled the fury of the barons. Once again he affected to retreat into a life of simple piety. He embarked on a tour of holy places and abbeys, as he had done before when power was taken out of his hands in 1234.

But, behind this religious front, the king was determined to avenge himself. The only way was force. And in 1264 the two sides confronted each other outside Lewes in East Sussex. Inspired by de Montfort's leadership and wearing the crusader's cross, his army quickly reduced the king's forces to a broken rabble.

After the battle Henry took refuge at Lewes Priory. There he was joined by his son Edward, who had been victorious in his section of the battle but had been unable to save the day for his father. Would the royalists give in or would they try to resume the fight? To concentrate minds,

Simon's troops shot off a volley of burning arrows, which set fire to the roof of the priory church.

Intimidated and surrounded, Henry decided to surrender. But Simon's terms were harsh. Henry had to swear once again to submit to the baronial government agreed at the Provisions of Oxford. Still worse, to make sure that this time he kept his word, he was compelled to hand over his son Edward as hostage for his good behaviour. The king of England was now a puppet with only the trappings of kingship as Simon in the name of defending freedom ruled both king and kingdom. Not even John had sunk so low.

Simon was now free to impose his own vision of monarchy on Henry. The king was reduced to a mere figurehead while all power was exercised by Simon's baronial clique, who claimed to be acting in the name of the whole community of England.

But de Montfort's ideas also appealed far beyond the baronial class. And this led him to broaden dramatically the membership of Parliament. Hitherto it had consisted of nobles and bishops. But in 1265 Simon enfranchised new groups. He summoned representatives, of knightly rank, from each county and burgesses or local bigwigs from the more important towns. Such representatives had been summoned before to consult on taxation. But this was the first time they had been invited to discuss and to decide the great affairs of the realm. It was a blatant bid for support for Simon's revolution from the groups immediately below the magnates – the wider community of the realm. It was also a milestone in the history of Parliament.

But despite such bold moves, Simon's revolution was to be short lived. There was a strong royalist party and, for all Simon's own high ideals, his followers proved to be as selfish and grasping as the king's fallen favourites. Just as the tide was turning, the king's son and heir, Edward, escaped from captivity and raised an army. Edward met his fellow loyalists at Ludlow Castle. He made the symbolic promise to uphold Magna Carta and then marched to confront de Montfort's forces.

The armies met just north of the town of Evesham. Simon was hoping every minute to be joined by his son at the head of a second force. But the reinforcements never arrived and without them de Montfort's army was completely overwhelmed by the royalists. De Montfort himself was killed, only fifteen months after his great victory at Lewes.

A monument was erected to de Montfort in the grounds of Evesham Abbey in the 1960s. And, in 1992, De Montfort University at Leicester also honoured his name. They are signs that, 700 years after his defeat and death, he is not forgotten. Contemporaries remembered him too. Already at the time of his death he was a folk hero. Soon there were reports of miracles at his tomb and his was even compared to that other great scourge of kings – St Thomas Becket. But the royalists hated him and in a grisly revenge they dismembered his body as the corpse of a condemned traitor. It would be less easy, however, to uproot the political ideas that de Montfort had planted.

The civil war lingered on until 1267, when the last pockets of resistance were rooted out. For the moment the royalists had triumphed. Henry's humiliation was avenged and the authority of the monarchy was restored – though in practice it would be exercised by the Lord Edward. But there was one final moment of glory left to the old king. In 1269, the new Westminster Abbey, which had cost so much money and political goodwill, was finally consecrated. The king himself and his sons bore the relics of the royal saint, Edward the Confessor, to their magnificent new shrine. Encrusted with gold mosaic and inlaid with precious marbles, the shrine was the work of Italian craftsmen and it spoke of Roman imperial power and grandeur.

For, despite all the crises of his reign, Henry's view of his own position remained equally exalted and he still saw himself as combining the powers of pope and emperor in his own kingdom. Many of his nobility, of course (led by Simon de Montfort), had taken the opposite view and they had come very close to victory. It was anyone's guess which way the balance would swing in future.

In the space of a century, both Henry II's empire and the pre-eminent status of the monarch had been undone. Foreign entanglements, family feuds, bids for autocracy and conflicts with churchmen and barons had weakened but not quite broken the authority of the crown. Henry III died in 1272 after a reign of fifty-six years – the longest to date and the third longest of all English monarchs. His body lies in splendour in his beloved Westminster Abbey. His heart was taken to Fontevraud to lie with his Angevin forebears. But their empire and their greatness were now a distant memory.

12

WAR MONARCHY

Edward I, Edward II, Edward III

CAERNARFON CASTLE IN NORTH WALES is not only a great fortress; it is a grand statement. Its vast walls are built out of layers of different-coloured stone in imitation of the walls of the imperial city of Constantinople. And on top of the battlements of the great tower, now worn to stumps by the sea winds and the rain, perch stone sculptures of imperial eagles. For this castle was built by a man whose ambitions were truly imperial, King Edward I, conqueror of Wales and hammer of the Scots.

Edward was the founder of a line of kings – father, son and grandson – who all bore the Anglo-Saxon or Old English name Edward. And they carried England to new heights of power. They would conquer Wales, Scotland and even France.

Or at least the first and third Edwards would. But the second Edward, unconventional and self-indulgent, reopened the old debate about royal powers. His weaknesses brought the monarchy to the brink of disaster and may have inflicted a uniquely horrible death on the king.

Nor was it only gore and glory. For the Edwards were lawgivers as well as soldiers, parliamentarians as well as conquerors, with the result that by the end of the Edwardian century the shape of an England ruled by the parliamentary trinity of king, lords and commons was becoming clear.

I

In 1272, Edward I inherited the crown from his father Henry III. When he heard the news he was in southern Italy, returning from the crusades. He did not hurry home. Instead he took part in a particularly vicious tournament in France and made a detour to put down a rebellion in Gascony. It was an appropriate start for a warrior king.

He did not return to England to be crowned until 1274. His succession was unchallenged but his inheritance was flawed. Edward would never forget his father's humiliation at the hands of Simon de Montfort. It was Edward who led the royalist fight-back. And it was Edward who learned the painful lesson of what could happen to a weak king.

These had been Edward's first in a long line of battles. He had learned early that he would have to fight for the rights of the crown. When he was young he fought like the leopard with speed and cunning; when he got older he fought like the lion with awe-inspiring power. And his physique matched his warlike character: he was six foot two inches tall and blond. He looked like a king, fought like a king and spoke like one. There is a story told that at his coronation he removed the crown from his head and swore that he would never wear it again until he had regained what his father had lost.

And to do this, Edward's first task was to reunite his realm, divided by the barons' revolt. But instead of waging a vendetta against his surviving opponents, he forgave them. He even allowed them to buy back the property that his father had confiscated. The result made Edward appear magnanimous. But it also raised considerable sums for the crown.

Edward had learned from the rebel barons as well, and he understood that it was in the towns and villages of England that the roots of his power lay. So he decided to reinforce the bonds between king and people by ordering a huge nationwide investigation into official corruption. It would be king and people versus the 'fat cats'.

The results were recorded in what are known as the Hundred Rolls. There was a mass of detail, perhaps too much. For example, the Stamford Roll contains a bit of dirt on the bailiff of the town, Hugo Bunting. One of the things he is accused of is levying an illicit toll of five shillings on a certain William Gabbecrocky when he took his millstones through the middle of the town: *'ducit per medium villé'*.

Now this is just Stamford: multiply for all England and you get information overload. As a consequence few actual prosecutions took place. But it is the PR that was most important. Edward was showing that he cared; that the king's rights complemented the rights of his subjects and that he was able to guarantee equal justice for all his subjects no matter how humble. There followed a succession of important statutes intended to reform the law. It would be hard to think of a better beginning for a reign or a more effective answer to those, like the baronial revolutionaries of his father's reign, who claimed that strong royal government meant oppressive royal government.

Edward's next task was to restore the authority of the king over the whole of Britain. For in different ways the rulers of Wales and Scotland had taken advantage of Henry III's weakness to regain power and independence at the expense of their English overlord.

In 1276, from his wild fastness in Snowdonia, Llwelyn ap Gryffydd had extended his control over most of Wales. But Edward was loath to accept the rise of Wales as an independent power. So he insisted on the homage – or ritual submission – which the rulers of Wales traditionally paid to the kings of England. There resulted a struggle of wills. For Llwelyn, his homage was a bargaining counter in a relationship of semi-equals. For Edward, it was a non-negotiable acknowledgement of his superiority over a subject and inferior. Three more times Prince Llwelyn was summoned to perform homage and three times he refused. Finally, and with plenty of time to make his preparations, Edward declared war.

Edward mobilized the whole country. Merchants and craftsmen laboured to supply the army. Huge arsenals of weapons were stockpiled. And Llwelyn was no match for the resources of England. In the face of the campaign of 1277 Llwelyn capitulated. Wales was forced to accept English laws, which struck at the heart of Welsh identity and national pride. The settlement was never accepted and the Welsh rebelled in 1282. They were countered with another vast army. There was little hand-to-hand fighting. Instead, Edward laid siege to Llwelyn in Snowdonia and starved him out.

Edward was not the first king of England to fight the Welsh. But Edward carried the policy to new extremes. There would be no more native princes of Wales acknowledging the vague overlordship of the king of England. Instead, Wales was crushed under the heel of a brutal military occupation. Its symbol was the mighty castles which still dominate the landscape, such as Caernarfon. Designed as much for their dramatic impact as for their military strength, they proclaimed that the Welsh were a subject people ruled over by an English elite.

Finally, there was Edward's treatment of the rebel leaders. This was not only spectacularly brutal; it also shows that he was a new kind of king, with the new, harder attitude to kingship that he had learned during his father's reign. Ever since the Norman Conquest, barons and kings had fought it out with each other with few hard feelings on either side. No longer, because Edward now declared that to wage war against the king was treason. Treason was effectively a new crime for which a new, terrible punishment was devised. And the first to suffer it was Daffydd ap Gryffydd, Prince Llwelyn's brother.

Because he had betrayed the king, he was dragged to the place of execution by horses. Because he had killed noblemen he was hanged. And because he had committed murder at Easter he was cut down while still alive, castrated, disembowelled and his entrails burned. Finally, because he had committed crimes in different parts of the kingdom, his body was hacked into four and the quarters distributed throughout the realm.

The fate of Wales itself was scarcely less harsh. If the Hundred Rolls had shown that Edward was an astute politician, the conquest of Wales showed his savage lion-like strength. Not surprisingly the Welsh brooded under this alien rule. Edward faced repeated rebellions throughout the rest of his reign. None was enough to reverse the conquest.

Edward's empire now stretched secure from east to west across the British Isles. But in the south the king of France was threatening Edward's lands in Gascony while in the north Scotland at last seemed about to fall into his grasp. This struggle on two fronts – to subdue Scotland and preserve his lands in France – was to dominate the remainder of Edward's reign and, for better and for worse, to shape the reigns of his son and his grandson as well.

II

Scotland's identity is a vexed and troubled subject. With devolution, Edinburgh is once again the seat of a Scottish parliament and the focus of a revived and intensified sense of Scotland's separate nationhood. But, when Edward came to the throne, that sense of separate identity was not nearly so developed.

Scotland was an ancient monarchy. But its kings were much intermarried with the English royal house. They had vast landholdings in England; swore fealty to English kings; fought for them as well as against them; and had a say in English councils and parliaments. So were they separate monarchs? Or were they the greatest subjects of the kings of England? In either case, it was a highly ambiguous relationship. But Edward, with his sharp lawyer's mind and his acute awareness of his own rights, hated ambiguity. When he could he would make the relationship of the king of Scotland and the king of England clear on his own terms and in his own interests.

And his opportunity came in 1291. The sole heir to the Scottish throne was Margaret, the 'Maid of Norway', granddaughter of King Alexander III of Scotland, who had died in 1286. Edward determined that she should be brought to Scotland and married to his eldest son, Edward of Caernarfon. This came to naught when she died en route to Scotland. The Scottish throne was now vacant. Not to be thwarted, Edward, as feudal overlord of the country, now claimed the right to choose the next ruler. He would be kingmaker in Scotland and he would remake the relations between the two kingdoms.

Edward chose John Balliol over Robert Bruce and twelve other candidates. Balliol had a good claim. But he was also, as the founder of an Oxford college and a major landowner in England, the most anglicized of the candidates. And this was the real reason Edward chose him.

But Edward was not content with an anglicized Scottish king. Instead, he made it clear that – even with King John Balliol on the Scottish throne – *he* remained sovereign lord of Scotland. As such, he, Edward, was finally responsible for justice and good government in Scotland. And he would enforce those responsibilities, just as he enforced his laws in England, by using his own English courts.

Knowing Edward's attitude, Scotsmen appealed to him to have their own king's judgements overruled. Even Balliol's acquiescence was tested. But when Balliol complained, Edward informed him that he could summon even Balliol himself to appear before him at Westminster. And before long he did just this.

For Balliol it was a humiliation too far. The Scots were provoked into rebellion and Edward to invasion. Berwick was the first town to fall. It was said that Edward was so angry that the town had resisted him that he fell on them 'with the anger of a wild boar pursued by dogs'. From Berwick Edward pushed up the coast to Dunbar. The Scots taunted the English troops, calling them tailed dogs. But the castle fell after only a few days. Edward then took his army on a military parade through Scotland. The great fortress of Edinburgh fell after only five days' siege and Stirling before Edward even arrived. He boasted that Scotland was conquered in only twenty-one weeks.

Now Edward had achieved what he had probably always wanted: direct rule of Scotland. In an inversion of a coronation, the vestments, symbols and regalia of kingship were stripped off Balliol. Edward was literally un-kinging him. Even more radically, Edward decided to un-kingdom Scotland. First, he removed the Stone of Scone. For 400 years the kings of Scotland had been crowned on this rough sandstone block – rich with legend – known as the Stone of Destiny. Edward took the stone to England and placed it under the coronation throne in Westminster Abbey where it remained for the next 700 years. By this gesture Edward was declaring that Scotland had ceased altogether to be a kingdom and become a mere province of England.

Edward was now at the pinnacle of his power. He was an English Caesar, a new Arthur, a mightier Conqueror.

Finally, Edward took on the king of France, Philip IV. Philip, in the first example of what became known as the 'Auld Alliance', had allied with John Balliol and confiscated Edward's remaining French territories. With his burning sense of right, Edward was determined to recover every inch.

To fight his great wars, Edward needed taxation. And the only effective way of raising taxes was to summon a parliament – usually to Westminster. Parliament was necessary constitutionally because Magna Carta laid it down that nobody could be taxed without their consent. It was also necessary practically because it had proved impossible to raise taxes any other way without the taxpayers going on strike.

As usual, the most important group of taxpayers were the middle earners – the knights or country gentlemen and the leading townsfolk. So, in 1295, on the eve of the Scottish invasion, Edward summoned representatives of these groups to what became known as the Model Parliament. They would have to pay but they would have a stake in his vision for England.

The result was that Edward, the most naturally autocratic of kings, followed in the footsteps of the great rebel Simon de Montfort and, in spite of himself, became the father of Parliament.

It was a shrewd gesture. But fierce guerrilla resistance to the English conquest broke out in Scotland and Edward was forced into war on two fronts against both the Scots and the French. As the costs escalated, the king faced broad-based opposition led by an important group of nobles. To appease them he was forced to reissue Magna Carta and promise once more that there would be no taxation without consultation of the whole realm. These were new political realities and they compelled him to explain his policies, negotiate and compromise. It did not sit easily with his personality. Nevertheless, his obsession with conquering Scotland remained. The policy was increasingly unpopular. But, to pursue it, Edward was prepared to do anything: to raise money outside Parliament as well as through it; even to put at risk his whole carefully constructed relationship with the classes represented in Parliament.

Finally, in 1305, victory seemed within his grasp. William Wallace, the leader of the Scottish resistance, was betrayed and Edward decided to make an example of him. Wallace was brought on horseback to London and put on trial in Westminster Hall. As was usual in cases of treason, there was no counsel for the accused. Otherwise, both the facts of the case and the forms of law were carefully observed. The judges accused Wallace of having encouraged the Scots to ally with Edward's enemies, the French; of having invaded England and killed women, children and churchmen; and above all of having traitorously conspired for the king's death and marched in war with banners flying against him. Wallace indignantly denied that he had ever been a traitor – presumably meaning he had never recognized Edward as king. In the eyes of English lawyers, this only made his crime worse, and he was sentenced to the worst punishment the law could give.

At Smithfield, now London's meat market, Wallace was subject to the same horrific form of execution as the Welsh rebel Daffydd: he too was hanged, disembowelled, beheaded and quartered.

It was a graphic message of what happened to those who crossed the king. But it also made Wallace a martyr. No sooner had Edward dealt with Wallace than a dangerous new enemy took his place: Robert the Bruce. Despite the absence of the Scottish crown and the Stone of Destiny, Bruce had himself crowned king of Scots in 1306. He continued to harry the English; Edward retaliated with punitive campaigns and brutal reprisals. For, as with Wales earlier, he saw Scottish resistance not as war but as rebellion against his legitimate rule.

It was on his way north in 1307 to wage yet another war against Bruce that Edward died at the age of sixty-eight. There is a story that his last wish was that his body should be boiled until the bones were clean of flesh and his skeleton be carried at the head of every English army until the Scots were finally crushed. It didn't quite work out like that. Instead, his body was buried in his father's great church, Westminster Abbey. Inscribed on his tomb were the words '*Malleus Scoturum*', 'Hammer of the Scots'. What Edward had done was right and just by his standards. But he had the weakness of his strength. If he had been less rigid and less hammer-like the union of England and Scotland, so close in 1291, might have come about smoothly and naturally. And both countries would have been spared centuries of war, bloodshed and devastation.

But that is asking Edward to be other than he was. He was a supremely self-confident king, with a clear sense of the power and rights of the crown. He may be remembered for his wars but his legacy was much greater. At home, Edward reaffirmed, sometimes in spite of himself, the direct bonds between the crown and people. Abroad, his victories began to foster a sense of national pride.

But how would England cope with his successor, a man ruled by private obsessions rather than royal ambition?

III

Edward I would have been a difficult act to follow for any son. But Edward II was particularly ill equipped to step into his father's shoes. He may have looked like his father – tall, handsome and strong – but they had little else in common. Even his recreations were odd. He shunned the traditional pastimes of princes, preferring 'common pursuits' like rowing, swimming and boatbuilding.

At the beginning of Edward's reign the contrast of character with his father was not necessarily seen as a bad thing. Edward I had undoubtedly been a great king. But, especially in his later years, England had paid a terrible price for his driving ambition and men were looking forward to a quieter life under his apparently more accommodating son.

The symbol of the change was the new oath which Edward swore at his coronation. Out went Edward I's ringing promise to defend the rights of the crown; in came a new oath that the king would uphold and defend 'the laws and rightful customs which the community of the realm shall have chosen'. 'I so agree and promise,' Edward swore. In those few words he had abandoned any claim to absolute royal power and he undertook instead to rule by consent and in cooperation with the nobles. A brave new world, it seemed, had dawned.

But Edward lacked – for good and ill – not only his father's strength of will; he also had a worrying personality flaw. This was evident even at his coronation. He was crowned with his wife Isabella by his side. But it was his childhood friend, Piers Gaveston, who stole the show. Edward had eyes and ears only for Piers, and Piers in turn gave himself the airs and graces of a royal favourite. He even wore purple robes at the coronation rather than the traditional gold. To add injury to insult Edward then presented Piers with the best of his new wife's jewels and wedding presents.

Whether or not the relationship between Piers and Edward was homosexual in our sense of the word is unclear. No contemporary explicitly says that it was. But they probably came as near as they could. One describes Edward's feelings for his favourite as like 'the love, that surpasses the love of a woman'. Another wrote: 'I do not remember to have heard that one man so loved another. Jonathan cherished David. But we do not read that they were immoderate. Our king, however, was incapable of moderate favour and on account of Piers was said to forget himself ...'

In short, Edward and Piers were breaking the rules and they were offending those who saw themselves as the guardians of the rules: the English nobility. The nobility wanted reform, and their grievances focused on Piers. They also saw it as an opportunity to exert power over the new monarch. Only two months after the celebrations of the coronation, the nobility delivered an ultimatum to their new king: either exile Piers or face civil war. Their loyalty, they said, was to the monarchy, not to the king.

Not exactly in the spirit of the demands, Gaveston was sent to Ireland to rule it on behalf of the king. But Edward was not to be browbeaten. He had, it turned out after all, inherited his father's determination as well as his looks. But only in small things: Edward I had aimed to conquer Wales and Scotland; the summit of Edward II's ambition was to keep his adored Piers by his side. For this there were no depths to which he would not sink. He cajoled, bribed and threatened his nobles. He conceded further measures of reform. Finally, they relented and allowed Piers to return.

Overjoyed, the king rode to Chester to be reunited with his friend. But Piers and Edward had learned nothing. Together they resumed war against the Scots, thereby placing strain on the tax system and reviving the opposition which had faced Edward I. Edward also ignored his vague promises of reform, while Gaveston refused to conciliate the nobility. Instead he continued to treat the leading magnates of the country with contempt. He gave them nicknames: Burst Belly, Joseph the Jew, the Cuckold's Bird and the Black Dog of Arden. This amused Edward. But it made deadly enemies of his targets.

Piers's mockery of the nobility was the classic response of the outsider confronted by a clique of crusty old insiders. The English nobility saw government as being rather like a club. Membership, they felt, should be limited to people of the 'right' background: in other words to nobles like themselves. And everyone should obey the rules, including the king himself. And the first and most important rule was to respect the rights and privileges, together with the sensitivities and values, of the nobility themselves. This attitude was of course selfish and class-ridden. But it was the only way that the idea of royal government as responsible government could be given real meaning. Only the nobility were strong enough to hold the king to account, and in the circumstances of 1310 this meant forcing him, by violence if necessary, to get rid of Piers Gaveston.

In March Edward was forced to send Piers away as the nobility strengthened their forces. Edward remained and agreed to surrender. Twenty-one Lords Ordainer worked out a document containing forty-one clauses. It was almost a rerun of 1258 when Henry III's personal rule was picked apart. The king was not allowed to make any gifts without the approval of Parliament; the revenue was taken out of the king's hands; and he was not allowed to make war or even leave the kingdom without permission. This was a savage limitation of Edward's sovereignty. But even worse was the Ordainers' all-out attack on 'evil counsellors', who, they said, had set the kingdom on the course to ruin. Gaveston was named. He was the 'evident enemy' of the monarchy and the people. And he was to be exiled, not just from England but all Edward's domains.

Edward had to accept the Ordinances. But he could not give Piers up to the noble mob. He played for time. But the storm was gathering. The nobles and bishops met at St Paul's Cathedral in March 1313 and ordered the arrest of Piers.

Edward and Piers fled north, Edward abandoning his pregnant wife, Isabella, to his enemies. She would not forget the insult. But it was all for nothing. Piers was caught and taken prisoner by the earl of Warwick – the man whom he had mocked as 'the Black Dog'. There was no formal trial. Instead Warwick and four nobles decided his fate. The verdict was death and he was beheaded at Blacklow Hill near Warwick.

Edward was grief-stricken at Gaveston's murder. But it was more than a personal loss. He had also lost face as king. Gaveston was the thing in the world that had mattered most to him. But he had not been powerful enough, or feared enough, to protect his life or to avenge his death. What was the authority of such a king worth?

Edward, under attack at home, decided to try to recover his position abroad. Bruce's long guerrilla campaign in Scotland was at last bearing fruit: he drove the English from key castles; he even dared strike across the border with devastating raids.

Edward and his nobles sank their differences sufficiently to mount a vast punitive expedition against Scotland. Here in the field of battle, Edward might yet redeem himself. The English and Scottish armies met on 23 June 1314 just outside Stirling. Much to the English surprise, the Scots took the initiative. At daybreak it was they who advanced. But then Edward's surprise turned to amazement. Edward was reported as saying 'they kneel and ask for mercy'. One of his Scottish officials knew his countrymen better and replied: 'they ask for mercy but not from you. To God they pray, for them it's death or victory.'

The battle began and the English knights charged the Scots' front line. But the Scots held firm. Unable to break the front rank, the English withdrew. But their retreat turned into a rout. Encumbered by heavy armour, many men drowned in the boggy ground. The losses were huge and Bannockburn became infamous as England's most shameful defeat by the Scots.

Leaving his troops to be massacred, Edward fled from the field of battle and, with only a handful of followers, rode desperately for Dunbar. He took refuge overnight in the castle, which was in friendly hands. The following morning he set sail for England.

The war with Scotland had given Edward the opportunity to redeem his reputation. Instead the shattering defeat of Bannockburn sent it to new depths. He proved to be as bad a general as he was a politician and his flight made him seem like a coward as well. He now appeared unmanly as well as unkingly. The political consequences were inescapable. Immediately after Bannockburn Edward was forced to swallow the Ordinances and accept that he had sacrificed his sovereignty. There were also other, more insidious, developments. How, people began to ask, could such a creature as this be the son of the great Edward? And they answered their own question by saying that he wasn't, that he was a changeling and not royal at all. And thus began the rumours about the king's birth which his own fondness for such peasant activities as rowing, thatching, fishing and boatbuilding seemed only to confirm.

Nor was Edward any more successful as a husband. As a young bride Isabella had had to accept her husband's devotion to Piers. But by the 1320s she was older, wiser and, crucially, the mother of the heir to the throne. Edward had also acquired a new favourite, Hugh Despenser. Like Piers, Despenser was given gifts and power. And once again the nobility sensed danger. It led to civil war, from which Edward managed to emerge victorious. He slipped free of the restraints imposed by the Ordinances. The result was autocratic royal government, another pointless campaign against Scotland and more power for the favoured Despenser.

The young Hugh Despenser achieved extraordinary influence over Edward. Enraged by this renewed humiliation, Isabella had taken a lover, Roger Mortimer, earl of March. She said that the 'bond' of holy matrimony had been broken by an 'intruder'. She vowed to be avenged and fled to France with Mortimer. And there they planned their invasion of England. In September 1326 Isabella landed in England and met with little resistance. Marching through a tired and war-weary country, she seized the crown in the name of her and Edward's eldest son, a third Edward.

Isabella and Mortimer had no difficulty in seizing the throne. But it proved less easy to justify their actions as there was no constitutional machinery to depose a crowned and anointed king. This meant they had to resort to the astonishing legal innovation of the Articles of Accusation. The articles accused the king, the fount of justice, of a series of high crimes against his country. Instead of good government by good laws he had ruled by evil counsel. Instead of justice he had sent noblemen to shameful and illegal deaths. He had lost Scotland and Gascony and he had oppressed and impoverished England. In short, he had broken his coronation oath – here treated as a solemn contract with his people and his country – and he must pay the price. For the first time in English history a reigning monarch was formally deposed from the throne.

Edward's miserable state was described in a poem which he may have written himself.

> In winter woe befell me
> By cruel fortune threatened
> My life now lies a ruin.
> Once I was feared and dreaded
> But now all men despise me
> And call me a crownless king
> A laughing stock to all.

Edward was imprisoned in the Guard Room in the keep of Berkeley Castle. He soon escaped but was recaptured. Thereafter his imprisonment became stricter and heavy locks and bolts were bought for the doors. Finally he was murdered. It could not, of course, be seen as murder and pains were taken to leave as few marks as possible on the body. According to most contemporary accounts he was pressed down with a table with heavy weights and suffocated. But another account, written only thirty years after his death, suggests a more horrible end. The king was held head down; a hollow instrument, like the end of a trumpet, was forced into his fundament and a red-hot poker thrust up it into his bowels. The Articles of Accusation had been a kind of inversion of Edward's coronation oath: if this story is true then his death was a vile parody of the pleasures he was supposed to have enjoyed with Piers Gaveston.

IV

In April 1331, a three-day tournament was proclaimed in the name of the new king, Edward III. His father, Edward II, had banned the tournament, preferring more rustic pastimes. But Edward III excelled at the joust. Indeed, while Edward II had disappointed the traditional expectations of what a king should be, Edward III embodied the perfect contemporary image of kingship. Like Elizabeth I and Queen Victoria after him, Edward personified the values of his age. Edwardian England was an age of knights and fantasy castles, of honours and arms, of pageantry and jousts. It was a culture and a country rooted in war. And leading the country into battle was a hero king, Edward III.

Despite the revolution that placed him on the throne, Edward had to fight to rule as well as reign. His mother's lover Mortimer had taken effective control of the kingdom in 1327. Edward was then only fourteen. Nevertheless, Mortimer saw the boy king as a threat. Edward was kept under the strictest control, watched and followed. Mortimer hoarded power and land for himself, lording over king and nobility alike. It was a new tyranny for England. And Edward had to use guile and subterfuge to break these bonds. He reached out to the nobility, building up support. In 1330, Mortimer got wind of the conspiracy against him. He summoned the king to Nottingham to interrogate the young man before a great council – that is, a parliament without the representatives of the commons. Overnight, however, Edward and his band got into Nottingham Castle through an underground tunnel. They surprised Mortimer the dictator, overpowered him, and had him arrested. He was condemned and executed as a common criminal at Tyburn.

Edward had won control by shrewdness and personal bravery. It was a fine start to his personal rule.

After the disasters of his father's reign it was natural that Edward would model himself on his grandfather, the heroic warrior king Edward I. But it was a return with a difference. Edward had none of his grandfather's ruthless driving energy or his stiff-backed authoritarianism either. Instead he cultivated an easy, winning charm. He was a good family man with a pretty wife and a rapidly growing brood of fine sons. He was capable of striking populist gestures, such as when he entered a town in triumph, not on horseback, but on foot and leading his wife and eldest son by the hand. And he would meet the humblest knight in the tournament, man to man, and win. In short, Edward was the perfect gentleman, affable, sporting and brave, who would rule England as the first among equals of his nobility.

This was a quiet revolution. For Edward, there would be no divisive, upstart favourite like Piers Gaveston. Instead Edward, unlike Mortimer, unlike his father or even his grandfather, truly accepted that he had to work in harmony with the nobility. Indeed, to do so was a pleasure as well as a duty.

The result was that Edward encouraged an aristocratic culture, which bound the king and nobles together. Its most vivid expression was in heraldry and coats of arms.

Originally a man's coat of arms had the purely practical function of identifying him on the battlefield when he was encased in a suit of armour. But soon a whole world of meaning was added. A man's coat of arms showed who his ancestors were; whom he had married; whether he was an elder or younger son and what honours he had won. Edward III was an aficionado of all this and he established a new order of chivalry based on the legend, then of course believed to be true, of King Arthur and the Knights of the Round Table. It was called the Order of the Garter.

The story goes that at a court ball a lady let slip her garter, which fell to the floor. Amidst the laughter, the king himself bent down, retrieved it and silenced the titters by saying *Honi soi qui mal y pense*: 'shame be to him who thinks evil of it'. Be that as it may, the Garter with its blue-and-gold ribbon encircling a man's coat of arms became the supreme mark of noble honour. And St George, the saint of soldiers and nobles, to whom the Order of the Garter was dedicated, became the patron saint of England.

But all this glamour and glitz masked a darker, deadlier imperative. Edward and his nobles belonged to a killing culture in which a man gained honour and respect by slaughter. Sport, in particular, was all about the kill. A man killed animals in the hunt and came near to killing human beings in the joust and the tournament. And war, where a man killed for real, was the noblest sport of them all.

Recording this society, in which spectacle, slaughter and romance were intertwined like threads of black and gold and red, was the chronicler Jean Froissart. He was born at Valenciennes in Hainault and he wrote in French, which still clung on as the principal language of the English elite. His *Chroniques* covered the years 1327 to 1400; eventually totalled some three million words and dealt with a vast and crowded panorama of events in England, Scotland, France, Spain, the Low Countries and beyond. Froissart himself lived through over sixty of those years, and he was widely travelled in the countries he described. He began his career in the household of Edward III's queen, Philippa, who was also a native of Hainault, and he knew all the principal players in events. He interviewed the heralds and generals and listened to the tales of old soldiers. He consulted records and treaties; visited the harbours and battlefields and was a familiar figure in the houses and palaces of the great. Eventually, like almost all previous historians, he became a priest and may even have spent his last days in a monastery. But it is impossible to think of anyone less cloistered or more completely at home in the world of chivalry whose values he celebrated and whose decline he mourned.

His subject therefore was war – and the pleasure rather than the pity of war. No one described it better or better recognized its importance. Especially in England. 'The English', Froissart wrote, 'will never love and honour their king unless he be victorious and a lover of arms and war against their neighbours and especially against such as are great and richer than themselves.'

Edward first turned his war machine against Scotland. Scotland had eluded his grandfather, Edward I, and defeated and humiliated his father, Edward II. So for Edward, war with Scotland was a matter of honour. Edward took personal charge of his armies and managed to instil them with his own military enthusiasm, from the nobles at the top to the ordinary common soldier at the bottom. And it was the common soldier who largely won Edward's wars, thanks to a powerful new weapon: the longbow.

Edward understood the value of the longbow and later in his reign he passed an act which banned other village sports, such as football and bowls, to force a concentration on archery. The border town of Berwick, now back in Scottish hands, was Edward's first target. On Halidon Hill, just outside the town, the English and Scots met. It was the first victory for Edward and his longbow. As the Scots approached, the English archers fired their deadly wave of arrows with devastating impact. England's honour, lost at Bannockburn, was restored.

Edward's victory at Halidon Hill was the making of him as a man and as a king. He had smashed the Scots even more completely than his grandfather, the 'hammer of the Scots', had ever done. He had won Berwick, which was then Scotland's main port and trading city. And, for the first time in over thirty years, he had freed the north of England from the risk of invasion. But his personal gains were even greater. He had shown himself to be a natural general and leader of men and a master of the new tactics of the longbow. And he had done all this at the age of twenty-one. Already he was hailed as a new Arthur. Would he, like Arthur, reunify Britain? Or would he seek wider fields to conquer?

Edward chose the wider fields of foreign military adventure over domestic consolidation. His next target would be France, the country with which England had been intertwined since the Norman Conquest. War with France offered the chance of rich booty, vast ransoms and the prospect of controlling trade in the English Channel. The French had also taken advantage of England's recent divisions to chip away at its possessions on the Continent and aid Scotland.

Edward staked his claim in 1340 when he asserted that he was the true king of France as the only male descendant of Philip IV, his grandfather. Not even Edward, however, could have guessed that he was about to start a war that would last a hundred years.

But if Edward and his nobles fought the war, it was the grey men of Parliament who paid for it. Parliament was based, then as now, at the Palace of Westminster. Back in Edward's reign, Westminster was the king's principal royal palace. But it was also becoming the home of

Parliament too, with a special parliament chamber. What was turning Parliament into a regular institution was Edward's need for money to fight his wars with France. Edward was willing to do whatever was necessary to persuade members of Parliament to dig their hands deep into their constituents' pockets. It meant doing deals, greasing palms, slapping backs. Edward's victories were reported in detail; Parliament was consulted on war diplomacy and ratified the peace treaties with France. It was good politics. But it was more because it turned Edward's wars into a joint enterprise between the king and the English nation. It made the English monarchy into a national monarchy of which Englishmen could be proud and in which they had a stake and an investment.

The length of Edward's wars also normalized taxation. Direct taxation, on income and property, continued to be voted only for war. But indirect taxation on trade became permanent, enhancing royal power and extending the scope of royal government. But England was also lucky enough to be a producer and exporter of a valuable raw material: wool. This meant that, by levying heavy export duties, much of the cost of Edward's wars could be shifted from his English subjects to the foreign purchasers of English wool – who did not, of course, have a vote in Parliament.

Thus, Edward's war became England's war. Bishops and priests led patriotic services and prayed for success. Dispatches from the front were read out in every town. And triumphant peals of bells celebrated the news of victories.

It was in August 1346 that Edward's style of kingship was fully vindicated. The English and the French met at Crécy near Calais. The French were confident that victory was theirs. For they outnumbered the English eight to one.

But Edward had unleashed the full martial potential of his country. Trained in the longbow, fired by the promise of rich plunder and led by a brave and charismatic king, the English army had become a truly terrifying force. Edward knew this, even if his followers could be forgiven for nervousness at the moment of battle. Froissart described how Edward's powers as a leader overcame their doubts:

> Then the king leapt on a palfrey with a white rod in his hand … he
> rode from rank to rank, desiring every man to take heed that day to
> his right and honour. He spake it so sweetly and with so good coun-
> tenance and merry cheer that all such as were discomfited took cour-
> age in the seeing and hearing of him.

The French attacked first. But they met an English army fortified by
their king and well drilled in tactics. Edward, his teenage son the prince
of Wales and the earl of Northampton led the three divisions of
dismounted men-at-arms. The French cavalry met these formidable divisions and came under fire from the longbowmen who flanked them. They
also faced English cannon – the first use of artillery in a European battle.
By nightfall it was over and a witness described the scene:

> When … no more shouting … or rallying cries could be heard, the
> English concluded that the enemy were routed. So they lit great
> numbers of lanterns and torches because it was very dark … They
> hailed it as a glorious victory. And several times that night they gave
> thanks to God for showing them such great mercies …

The French had fled leaving four thousand knights dead. No one bothered to count the humbler men.

The most striking surviving monument of this battle is the great
window in Gloucester Cathedral known as the Crécy Window. It was
built to commemorate the victory and it contains the shields of King
Edward and his companions in arms. In the middle is the coat of arms of
King Edward himself, which quarter the lilies of France with the lions of
England. Here also are the arms of Lord Badestone, who probably paid
for the window out of the fortune he had made from the war in France.
For the war in France made England rich and it also remade England.

England had been culturally in the shadow of France ever since the
Norman Conquest. But now that France was shattered and defeated,
England had gained the confidence to strike out on its own. This, too, is
seen in the architecture of Gloucester Cathedral. The window is an early
masterpiece of the new English perpendicular style. Indeed, it is more
than a window: it is a kind of symphony in which architecture, heraldry
and religion all come together into a single hymn of praise to England's

God, to England's king and to England itself. And Edward was the most English of kings to sit on the throne since the Conquest. He spoke English. And, following his example, even among the nobility 'Middle English' was beginning to take over from French.

After Crécy Edward's popularity reached its zenith. According to the *Walsingham Chronicle*, the English thought that a new sun had risen, because of the abundance of peace in England, the plenitude of goods and the glory of the victories.

The prospect of a land of milk and honey, however, met the forces of nature. In the years following Crécy, Europe was ravaged by the Black Death. A third or more of the population died as bubonic plague returned year after year. Edward's government responded to the crisis. Legislation helped to relieve the terrible shortage of labourers caused by the plague. And its enforcement changed English law as well: justices of the peace were created to see the emergency laws were obeyed. Edward and his ministers had not only led England to victory abroad, they had created stable government during a period of potential turmoil.

But, as ever, Edward's eyes were focused across the Channel. English victories came thick and fast in the 1350s. Edward led armies which caught France in a pincer: they advanced from both Normandy and Gascony. He also led an army against the Scots. But it was his son who scored some of the greatest victories of the reign. Edward, the Black Prince, scourged southern France. At the battle of Poitiers in 1356 he once again used superior tactics to defeat a larger French army. It was a famous victory and it should have been decisive. For Jean II, king of France, was captured along with some of the great men of the realm. It was the climax of Edward's wars, the greatest victories England had achieved for over a century and a half.

Would Edward realize his dream and become king of France? It seemed a possibility. But he was unable to press home the advantage. At the Treaty of Brétigny (1360) he renounced his claims to the French throne but consolidated his considerable territorial gains. For the rest of the reign war continued, but a crushing victory on the scale of Crécy and Poitiers eluded the king and his sons.

The dream of ruling France would continue to haunt English kings and it would have important consequences for the future. But the century of Edwards had reshaped the English monarchy more fundamentally. The king was now more closely identified with the interests of his people and he would never again rule effectively without the consent and cooperation of Parliament. He was expected to fight wars. But they had to be in the national interest – or at least to seem as such. For the most memorable legacy of the Edwards was the forging of a nation that defined itself through war, symbolized in the flag of the soldier-saint, St George.

A superman, like Edward I, could manage it, as could the man's man, Edward III. But could their successors?

13

DEATH OF A DYNASTY

Richard II, Henry IV, Henry V, Henry VI

ON ST GEORGE'S DAY 1377 two young boys stood before the altar in Windsor Castle to be invested with the Order of the Garter – the highest order of chivalry in the land. The ten-year-old Richard was heir to the throne. The eleven-year-old Henry Bolingbroke was his cousin and heir to the most powerful aristocratic family in England. This ceremony marked their entrance on to the public stage.

The future of the English monarchy seemed assured as the two boys swore never to take up arms against each other.

It was a promise they could not keep. Instead cousin clashed with cousin as Henry usurped Richard and made himself king, as Henry IV. The usurpation was the worst crisis in the English monarchy since Magna Carta. Over the next 100 years there were seven kings, and only three of them died in their beds. Three were murdered, one was killed on the field of battle and three followed Henry IV's own example in violently usurping the throne.

Part of the problem was the size of the royal family. Edward III produced five sons who lived to manhood. Four of them – the Black Prince, Lionel, John of Gaunt and Edmund – would produce princely dynasties which would fight for the throne in a vicious extended family feud that lasted over a hundred years.

These bloody civil wars formed the background to Shakespeare's series of great history plays and their royal stars: the overweening Richard II, the heroic Henry V, the pathetic Henry VI. In these wars the whole basis of the English monarchy was questioned and upturned and the royal house tore itself apart in a slow and painful suicide.

I

In 1376, Edward III was a shadow of his mighty younger self. The war against France had stalled and the so-called Good Parliament stood up to the king, forcing the dismissal of his councillors, withholding tax and banishing his mistress, Alice Perrers. Worse still, Edward had slumped into feeble-mindedness, the result of a series of strokes. For the first time, the full force of Parliament was unleashed upon the monarchy. It was in no position to resist the storm. Edward was too ill to attend this fractious parliament. And most worryingly of all, nor was his eldest son, the Black Prince.

Edward the Black Prince was the great hope for the future. He was made very much in the image of Edward III – as great a warrior and already an experienced ruler. But, like his father the king, he found his glory days behind him. The victories had dried up. He had declined into chronic ill health. His eldest son, another prince named Edward, had died in France. Then, in the summer of 1376, he too succumbed and died aged forty-five in the middle of the session of the Good Parliament.

In his place his second son, Richard, became heir to the throne. Once again England faced the instability of a boy king. Once again gossip had it that one of the boy's uncles would seize the crown when the time came. The most likely uncle was John of Gaunt, duke of Lancaster, the father of Henry Bolingbroke. This prospect was headed off by a dazzling display of royal ritual. Honours and titles were showered on the boy: he was made earl of Chester, duke of Cornwall and prince of Wales. He sat above his royal uncles at a banquet and he even opened Parliament on the old king's behalf.

The investiture of his grandsons Richard and Henry Bolingbroke as knights of the Garter was one of the last acts of Edward III's life. Two months later the great king died.

One of Richard's toys was a set of dice loaded so that he always won, and life must have seemed just as rosy for the lad who grew up with a sense of an absolute and untrammelled right to power. At his coronation the crown of Edward the Confessor was placed on the head of the ten-year-old boy and the greatest bishops and earls knelt at his feet to pay him homage. The bishop of Rochester exhorted the nobility in prayer to honour and obey the boy.

And well he might. For there were no rules to dictate what should happen until Richard reached maturity.

Royal power relied on the support of England's nobility. Chief among them was John of Gaunt, the now oldest surviving son of Edward III. Gaunt had taken a leading role in ruling on behalf of his father in his last days and quietening the voices of dissent which had dared to be raised against the crown. He had a reputation as an authoritarian who was not prepared to tolerate resistance and who was happy to trample on liberties. Gaunt had not been given any official position during his nephew's minority. But that scarcely mattered. Gaunt was unpopular, but he was feared. For one thing he was of royal blood. But, even more importantly, he had immense power as a private landowner.

The House of Lancaster had thirty castles scattered across England. The jewel in their coronet was Kenilworth, which far outclassed most royal castles in scale and grandeur. The extent of their estates gave them a private army of some four thousand men. Gaunt was therefore the dominant noble in England and his opinions influenced the governance of the state even if he had no formal title to show for it.

Extravagances like Kenilworth were hugely resented by the common people of England. In the last fifty years the Black Death had swept through the country three times, wiping out perhaps half the population. Rents had collapsed and now landowners and the government were trying to recoup their position.

England was heavily burdened by taxation. The revenue had been lavished on what were now seen as worthless military forays. Taxpayers want at least something to show for their money. Instead the demands got heavier. Three poll taxes were brought in between 1377 and 1381 demanding a shilling of every adult in the land, whether duke, merchant or peasant. The collectors were ruthless in their hunt for cash. Not for the last time, a poll tax triggered a revolt. Riots in Essex and Kent spiralled into widespread rebellion and a march on London.

The rebels' target was not Richard, but the clique of noble families around him. The rebels even flew the banner of St George, and as they streamed to London they swore loyalty to their young king. It was as if they wanted to rescue their true monarch from the malign clutches of men like John of Gaunt.

As the rebels looted and burned in the City and suburbs, Richard, his mother, Henry Bolingbroke and a handful of councillors took refuge in the Tower. The revolt was of course a terrible threat. But it was also an opportunity for the young king. The lords who had hitherto ruled England in his name were suddenly powerless and directionless in the face of the triumphant mob. John of Gaunt's sumptuous palace, the Savoy, was burnt to rubble and his rural estates were in turmoil. The duke himself had only just escaped with his life, fleeing to Scotland.

On the other hand that same mob was crying enthusiastically for Richard as their true king. Richard took them at their word. Aged only fourteen and with a courage fully worthy of his father, the Black Prince, he left the protection of the Tower even when the knights supposed to be protecting him refused to venture out. He met the rebels three times with only a tiny entourage. And he faced them down. At the first meeting at Mile End he offered them a charter of liberties. When that did not quell the disturbances he met them again at Smithfield.

There he approached their leader, Wat Tyler. Greeting him as 'brother' he asked why the men of Essex and Kent had not gone home. It was a commanding performance. But it was undone when the Lord Mayor of London attacked and murdered Tyler. Quick in response to this nasty turn of events, which threatened to turn the situation into something much worse, Richard rode up to the seething ranks of rebels and shouted: 'I am your leader: follow me.'

Unbelievably, the mob did as they were commanded and followed their young king out of harm's way. Leaderless and their grip on the capital broken, they were easily dispersed by the London militia. The rebellion was crushed. And any romantic hope that the boy king was on the side of the common folk was soon smothered as well. Richard rescinded his promises of liberty. Indeed, he went to watch the execution of many of the rebels later in the summer. Any sympathy or fellow-feeling he had shown, or pretended to show, was gone. These men, he now believed, had committed the unforgivable sin of rebellion.

II

Having tasted real power, Richard was reluctant to give it up. He had taken personal steps to crush a serious rebellion. His masterstrokes of political calculation, subterfuge and charisma had succeeded where the nobles and officers of state had failed. He had, he believed, metamorphosed during those tumultuous days in London from an uncertain boy into a man. To signify this transition he found a bride and was married within a year. He was ready to rule in his own name.

The story of the next few years is the descent of Richard from the popularity and power he had gained after the Peasants' Revolt. He lavished gifts on a handful of favourites, the most prominent being Michael de la Pole and Robert de Vere. The latter had a title created just for him – marquis – which put him above all the nobility apart from the royal dukes. Then he was made duke of Ireland, which made him the equal of the royal family. Under Richard and his friends royal government became a high-tax, high-spend, cliquey affair. And once again taxpayers' money went nowhere: it was squandered on favourites and failed wars.

Richard had to be reminded to his face of the fate of Edward II. But the warnings did little good. Instead the demands for cash kept coming. Richard's failures in war meant that the country was facing invasion from France. The 'Wonderful' Parliament of 1386 agreed to help Richard, but only if he dismissed his favourites. Richard replied that he would not listen to Parliament even if it asked him to dismiss his kitchen scullion. It was a disastrous game of tit-for-tat. Parliament raised its demands. Richard then said he would invite in the French to help him against Parliament.

This was a shocking, silly thing to say. It was a burst of petulance from the lips of a twenty-year-old who had always had the dice loaded in his favour. And it had a devastating effect. Richard was threatened with deposition. That sobered him up. He surrendered to Parliament, which bound him to ordinances which set up a ruling council as in the days of Henry III and Edward II; impeached de la Pole and instituted an enquiry into royal finances. Richard stomped off in anger. It was called his 'gyration' – a tour of the country.

It was no meet-and-greet, however. Richard's intention was to gather armed support against the nobility and parliamentarians and gain legal judgements to rescue his prerogative. He formed his own private army, who wore his badge of the white hart as a sign of loyalty. Many of the men were drawn from his stronghold in Cheshire, giving him a handy force of archers. Richard was on a mission to assert his vision of monarchy.

An idealized version of this is depicted in the beautiful painting known as the Wilton Diptych. The Diptych is a work of private devotion and it takes us to the heart of Richard's intense, obsessive, solipsistic view of kingship, which raised him gloriously above his subjects and dangerously cut him off from them.

Richard was born on 6 January – the Feast of the Epiphany – when the three wise men, or kings, knelt in adoration before the Christ child and his Virgin Mother. In the centre of the picture is Richard, repeating that act of homage. January 6th is also the day on which the Church commemorates Christ's baptism by John the Baptist. He too appears in the Diptych beside the two English royal saints: Edward the Confessor, whose crown and ring had been placed on Richard at his coronation; and, next to him, the Anglo-Saxon martyr-monarch Edmund. Thus aided, Richard is ready to receive the banner of St George from the hands of the Christ child.

Even the angels surrounding the Virgin belong to Richard's dream world as, like his earthly trusties, the Cheshire archers, they wear his badge of the white hart. With the heavenly host in his pocket, Richard thought, who could stand against him?

The answer, in this new world, was the men who actually held power: the nobility. One of their natural leaders was Henry Bolingbroke, son of John of Gaunt.

Only ten years had passed since Richard and Henry had sworn never to take up arms against each other. But in the ten years the two boys had grown into very different men.

Henry had turned into a man of action, excelling at jousting and blood sports. And he had a soldier's harsh piety. Richard, on the other hand, had created a glamorous, luxurious court of which he was the glittering centre. 'He was of common stature,' wrote a chronicler, 'his hair yellow-ish, his face round and feminine, sometimes flushed; abrupt and stammering in his speech, capricious in his manners ... He was prodigal in his gifts, extravagantly splendid in his entertainments and dress.' Style was everything: he commissioned the first royal cookery book and invented the handkerchief.

But this was more than style wars: it was a clash of political values. Richard believed that a king was God on Earth; Henry that he was a first among equals.

The result was real war: Richard and his court favourites against the nobility.

On 19 December 1387 the two sides met at Radcot Bridge just outside Oxford. The royal army was led by Robert de Vere; the nobles by Henry.

Henry won. De Vere fled into exile, leaving Richard without troops and powerless. News of the catastrophe was brought to him at the Tower, where he was spending Christmas. Soon the rebel lords arrived as well and mercilessly browbeat the king, threatening him with force and even with deposition. There was nothing for it but complete and humiliating surrender. The 'Merciless' Parliament dismantled the king's power. Richard's friends were executed or driven into exile. The kingdom was to be ruled by a committee of the lords and even Richard's personal affairs were to be put into the hands of a board of guardians, as though he was a child or insane.

Richard was left only with the title of king. But it was enough. Slowly and painstakingly he rebuilt his position and power. The removal of the favourites satisfied many of his critics. After his twenty-first birthday he made a plausible case that he had matured. He reached out to John of Gaunt, who agreed to use his influence to pacify the country. He rebuilt his personal following. And above all he treated his former enemies with mercy.

But he had not forgotten his degradation. Adversity had taught Richard patience and cunning and, gourmet though he was, he had decided that revenge was a dish best eaten cold.

The depth of festering hatred was clearly illustrated when his beloved Robert de Vere died in exile.

In 1395 Richard arranged a funeral for him. All the sometime rebel lords were obliged to attend: the very men who had fought against de Vere at Radcot Bridge. Richard placed a ring on the dead man's finger and with this quiet gesture he signalled that vengeance would be his.

By 1397 Richard was strong enough to strike. One by one the lords who had rebelled against him were either executed or exiled on trumped-up charges of treason. No one was safe – among the victims was one of his own uncles, the duke of Gloucester. Parliament itself was surrounded by Richard's Cheshire archers in an unambiguous message that there was one sovereign in England. Richard had regained his prerogative, which had been taken from him over a decade before. And he had meted out the appropriate punishment.

But Richard II saved a special revenge for his cousin Henry. When Henry Bolingbroke was involved in a quarrel with another noble, Thomas Mowbray, Richard ordered that the two men fight to the death in judicial combat. God would be on the just man's side.

Richard's behaviour in the affair shows him at his most malign and vain. He deliberately played up the quarrel between Henry and Mowbray and he chose the means of settling it which showed off his own glory to the utmost. In an echo of the pageantry of the Colosseum, Richard would preside like a Roman emperor in the amphitheatre as the defeated man was stripped of his armour, dragged at a horse's tail from the field and strung up on the gallows that stood ready. But, in the event, Richard behaved more like a royal conjuror than a Roman emperor. For, just as the combatants were ready to charge, Richard, in a dramatic gesture, threw down his staff, stopping the fight and resuming judgement to himself. Henry, the king ruled, would go into exile for ten years and Mowbray for life. Thus King Richard, like a demigod, struck down his remaining foes.

III

In 1399, Henry Bolingbroke was an exile in Paris. Within the year he received a double blow. His father, John of Gaunt, died. And Richard seized all of Henry's vast Lancastrian inheritance for himself. Henry was left with nothing.

But Richard had overreached himself: all landowners in England now had cause to fear. The king was in his pomp as autocrat. He simply helped himself to other people's property. Twenty-two years had passed since Henry had been made a knight of the Garter with Richard but now any vestige of cousinly feeling had gone. Henry determined to reclaim what was rightly his by force.

Richard believed he had covered all eventualities. France was now on his side, and he had a private agreement with the duke of Burgundy that close watch should be kept on Henry. Richard even felt secure enough to go to Ireland. But fortune turned against the king. The duke of Burgundy was forced out of Paris by the plague. And Henry was free to do as he wished.

En route on this make-or-break journey back to England, Henry paused at the great royal abbey of St Denis. St Denis was where the kings of France were buried and it was also where they came to receive the sacred banner of the 'Oriflamme' (the standard of St Louis) on their way to battle. Henry was on his way to battle and he needed all the help, human and divine, that he could get. But he made sure that God at least was on his side by a single, revealing gesture. Before he left the abbey, he promised the abbot that he would restore to St Denis the revenues of the little priory of Deerhurst in Gloucestershire, given to the abbey long, long ago by Edward the Confessor and purloined, like so much else, by Richard. Already, therefore, before he even left France, Henry saw himself as the true king of England, fully able to redress Richard's wrongs.

With a fleet of only ten ships Henry sailed around England to the Yorkshire coast.

Yorkshire was the heartland of his stolen estate, and as Henry moved from castle to castle they surrendered easily to their rightful master. Henry marched south, his swollen army reinforced by the great northern earls.

Richard, back home, sought safety in Edward I's great Welsh castles. But Henry lured him out with the promise that he came only to claim his inheritance and had no intention of threatening the crown itself. It was a lie. But a successful one. As Richard emerged, an ambush of Henry's men lay in wait. The king of England was Henry Bolingbroke's prisoner. It was now clear that Henry wanted far more than the duchy of Lancaster: he would settle for nothing less than the crown of England itself.

But how to justify the dethroning of Richard and his replacement with Henry and the Lancastrian dynasty? The neatest solution would be to show that Richard had never been true king by hereditary right anyway. But that Henry was. Conveniently a story to this effect was an article of faith in the House of Lancaster. Henry and Richard were both descended from Henry III – Richard from the eldest son Edward, who had succeeded as King Edward I, and Henry from the second son, Edmund, earl of Lancaster, surnamed Crouchback. According to the story, however, Crouchback was really the eldest son but had been shunted aside in favour of Edward on account of his supposed deformity.

If this story were true, it was the perfect solution for Henry. So Henry referred the story to a specially convened panel of historians and constitutional experts. The panel was supposed to meet in secret. But then as now constitutional experts are a garrulous lot and one of the panel, Adam of Usk, recorded their deliberations in his *Chronicle*. Like all good historians, the panel went back to the sources, as Adam reports. Unfortunately for Henry these unanimously confirmed that Edward was indeed the eldest son: *Edwardus primogenitus regis Henrici*. The Crouchback story was indeed too good to be true. Henry would have to think again.

Richard, for his part, put up a brief struggle. But, faced with the threat of force, he abdicated his throne – to God.

For the first time since the Conquest the continuity of the succession had to be deliberately broken. Only one body could do that: Parliament.

Henry moved quickly and a parliament was summoned to meet at Westminster Hall. The hall had been splendidly rebuilt by Richard as a monument to his own glory. But now it was to witness his final humiliation. First, the terms of the king's abdication were read out. Then followed a long list of the charges against him. Finally, he was declared dethroned and deposed and his subjects absolved of their allegiance. All this had taken place in Richard's absence, and the royal throne under its great canopy of cloth of gold had remained empty.

But now Henry, in a theatrical gesture worthy of Richard himself, stepped forward to claim the vacant throne. He spoke simply and forcibly and in English. He descended, he said, of the true royal blood of the good King Henry III. Thanks to the help of God and his friends he had been able to reclaim that right and, in so doing, he had saved the realm from ruin by the bad government of his predecessor, Richard.

Put like that, Henry's claim sounds logical and convincing. But in fact it was a mere ragbag. For in reality he had only had a single compelling claim – he was the man of the hour.

In twelve weeks Henry Bolingbroke had transformed himself from landless exile into Henry IV, king of England. But to prove that he was more than a usurper, he needed God's blessing as well as Parliament's.

This was arranged, too. And at his coronation Henry was anointed with an opportunely discovered vial of oil reputedly given to Thomas Becket by the Virgin Mary. Divine oil would surely wash away the sins of the past. But Henry IV was about to commit the greatest sin of all.

Richard II may have been deposed by law before Parliament but he was still an anointed monarch. And so long as Richard lived Henry would have no security. So Henry decided to kill the former king – but secretly and without leaving marks on the body – by leaving Richard to starve slowly to death in Pontefract Castle.

Edward II, of course, had been murdered even more nastily. But none of the blame attached to his successor Edward III. In 1399, however, a king had indeed murdered a king. The taboo was broken. What was to stop others doing the same to Henry or his descendants? In 1400, only a year after his coronation, the Welsh rose up against English rule.

But the greatest threat to the Lancastrians came from within England and from the family who had been Henry's strongest supporters. The Percys, whose head was the earl of Northumberland, were the most powerful family in the north of England, with vast estates, strong castles and a multitude of armed followers. They had been the first to back Henry when he invaded England in 1399. And it was their support that had carried him to victory. But having made Henry king, why should the Percys stop there? Especially as Henry refused to behave as an obedient puppet. Perhaps they could do even better by backing another claimant? Perhaps a Percy could become king himself?

Henry recognized the threat and did his best to conciliate them. But in 1403 he learned that Hotspur – the son and heir to the earl of Northumberland – had joined the Welsh rebels and was invading England.

Hotspur rode south to join up with the Welsh. On 21 July 1403 the joint army arrived just outside Shrewsbury. From here Hotspur sent a defiant message to Henry challenging his right to the throne. Henry too was eager for a fight to the finish. The sides were evenly matched and the battle raged from midday to nightfall. The hardest fighting was around the king and Hotspur. In the end it was a personal battle between the two men.

Henry was victorious. About sixteen thousand men were killed in the battle; Hotspur's body was taken to Shrewsbury, where, as the corpse of a traitor, it was quartered. But the low-ranking slain on both sides were buried on the spot in a mass grave. In commemoration the site was renamed 'Battlefield' and a church, complete with an armed statue of Henry IV, was built as a monument to his victory. But this victory brought Henry no security. For no sooner had he cut down one enemy than another arose. Moreover, the king himself, doggedly though he fought, harboured private doubts. And if Henry doubted, why should anyone else believe in the Lancastrian title?

Henry IV's last years were a sad contrast to the promise of 1399. Gone was the vigorous youth who had won a country to his cause. Instead, he aged rapidly and developed a disfiguring skin disease: perhaps leprosy, perhaps a psychosomatic acute dermatitis. Whatever the diagnosis, to many contemporaries the disease seemed proof of God's displeasure with the usurper king.

In March 1413, Henry came to Westminster with the hand of death already on him. On the 20th, while praying at the Confessor's tomb, he had a seizure and was brought to the Jerusalem Chamber in the abbot's lodgings. The crown was placed beside his pillow; he seemed to cease breathing and his face was covered. Thinking like everybody else that his father was already dead, his son and heir, Prince Henry, took the crown. Suddenly the old king roused himself and demanded of Henry by what right he took the crown since he himself had none to it. Coolly Henry replied: 'As you have kept it by the sword, so I will keep it whilst I have life.' It is a good story and, as an insight into the prince's character, it is shrewd. For whatever doubts Henry IV may have harboured about his right to the throne, Henry V had none at all.

IV

Prince Henry might not have been born to be king. But no heir to the throne had served a more distinguished apprenticeship. He was created prince of Wales immediately after his father's accession, and, though he was only in his early teens, he quickly became his right-hand man and the pillar of the Lancastrian cause. He fought bravely against Hotspur at the battle of Shrewsbury and he led the English to victory in the ensuing hard-fought campaign against the Welsh. But mere military glory was not enough for Prince Henry. He wanted the reality of power as well. His father was disfigured, diseased and hopelessly tainted by his usurpation. Henry, in contrast, was the great white hope for his father's enemies as well as for his friends.

Henry V's first task was to unite the fractured realm his father had bequeathed him. He was firm in laying down the law and seeing it obeyed, and he stabilized the coinage. On several occasions he travelled through the country to foster loyalty to the crown. Above all he rooted out faction. As the son of a usurper, Henry knew from personal experience the importance of letting bygones be bygones. So Henry pardoned his father's enemies and Richard's supporters. He even restored the Percys.

By and large the policy paid off and Henry's former bitter enemies became his loyal lieutenants. Only one thing remained. Henry's smartest move was to make his peace with the unquiet ghost of Richard II. Henry IV had accorded Richard the dignity of a public funeral but he had refused to bury him in Westminster Abbey. The result was that Richard's memory continued to plague his successor. Miracles took place at his modest tomb; his name was constantly invoked to justify rebellion and many refused to believe he was dead at all. So when Henry V became king he moved to tackle the problem with his characteristic decisiveness. In December 1413, only eight months after his own coronation, Richard's body was brought to the Abbey in a magnificent procession and reburied among his fellow kings, in the tomb that Richard had commissioned for himself. The stain of 1399 was wiped out and Henry was able to benefit from the usurpation without incurring the stigma or the bad conscience of his father.

Having settled domestic politics, Henry was able to turn his attention to the project that would dominate his reign: the war of conquest with France.

The reign of the peace-loving Richard II had shown that the English war monarchy of the Edwards was ungovernable in peace. Better that the English nobles should fight the French than each other – or the king. But Henry's claim to France was also, for this intensely religious man, an article of faith.

For Henry, the war was essentially about justice for his ancestral claims. Through his ancestor, Henry II, he had a claim to the whole of the Angevin empire, to Normandy, Anjou and Aquitaine, while from his other ancestress, Isabella of France, queen of Edward II, he claimed the throne of France itself. Only let these claims be conceded, Henry announced, and there would be no war.

From the French point of view this was an outrageous demand and they refused. Denied his legitimate claim, Henry decided his conscience was clear: the French had refused peace with justice so the god of battles must decide. Henry also presented his case effectively in England; won support for his policies and brought the might of the nation behind the campaign. Most importantly, he was a systematic planner and his French expedition, like all his great projects, was carefully prepared in advance.

Henry set sail for France on 11 August 1415. His first campaign is the stuff of legend. 'For Harry, England and Saint George'. This was the battle-cry that Shakespeare gave the English soldiers on the field at Agincourt. Here Henry showed himself everything that an English king should be: resolute, heroic and a born leader of men. The English soldiers were in retreat, exhausted and far outnumbered by the French – by three to one – but fired up by loyalty to their king and country, they won an astounding victory.

It seemed proof positive that Henry V was God's chosen king. It was also proof that his war policy would work. Within two years he was back. This time his aim was conquest. The English army swept through Normandy, systematically besieging and capturing the greatest cities: Caen, Falaise and Rouen. But the key to France was Paris.

By 1420, Paris was in his grasp. But, rather than risk reuniting the French by attacking the capital, Henry, who was a subtle politician as well as a dashing general, decided to exploit the profound divisions within the French court. He made apparently enormous concessions: he would no longer claim western France as heir of Henry II. The present king of France could even keep his titles.

The ploy worked. By a treaty signed at Troyes on 21 May 1420, Henry seemed to have won the prize that had eluded even Edward III and the Black Prince. He was recognized as the legitimate heir to the then king of France, Charles VI, and, a few days later, in Troyes Cathedral, he married Charles's daughter Catherine. Henry, in other words, was seeking to apply in France the same model of traditional kingship which had served him so well in England. He would rule France not as a conqueror but as a legitimate king, and he would rule it in the French way according to French customs.

England had not known such victories. The status of the monarchy soared, as this piece of doggerel expresses:

> And he is king excellent
> And unto none other obedient
> That liveth here in earth – by right
> But only unto God almight[y]*
> Within his own, Emperor
> And also king and conqueror.

King, conqueror, emperor: these exalted titles were given living expression when Henry wore a closed arched crown. This style of crown signified imperial status. As an emperor Henry had no superior on earth, not even the pope.

On 1 December 1420 Henry entered Paris in triumph as heir and regent of France. He was warmly received and the French *parlement* ratified the Treaty of Troyes. It wasn't so simple, however. Many French nobles had understandable reservations about acknowledging an Englishman as king of France. Henry renewed hostilities to force the French resistance to accept the Treaty of Troyes. It was a hard slog of campaigning in northern France alleviated only by the knowledge that his wife Catherine had given birth to a son and heir.

But suddenly, at the age of thirty-five and in the middle of yet another campaign, Henry caught dysentery and died.

In only nine years Henry V had reunited England and taken France. And he had done it all as a consciously English king: speaking and writing English even for official documents. For the first time since the Conquest, England was a nation-state once more.

Henry was laid to rest in Westminster Abbey in a magnificent funerary chapel. The king's image was covered in silver gilt while among the rich sculptures were two coronation scenes representing Henry's two kingdoms of England and France. And in both he is shown with the imperial crown. But what really impresses is the sheer scale of the chapel and its magnificent location, directly at the east end of the Abbey. Here,

---

* The odd form 'almight' is to give a rhyme with 'right'.

everything seems to say, is the apogee of the medieval English monarchy and the monument to the perfect medieval king. The institution could scarcely go any higher. Could it even survive at its present high-water mark? Everything would depend on Henry's son, the nine-month-old infant, who in his cradle was heir of England and France.

V

With Henry's death on 31 August 1422 his son became king of England as Henry VI. If this were not enough, two months later his French grand-father also died and he was named king of France. Once again England had an infant king. But this time there was no serious rival nor any suggestion that an adult, perhaps an uncle, should be preferred in his place. This was a remarkable state of affairs, given that the dynasty had come to the throne through an act of usurpation less than a quarter of a century before. But the triumphs of Henry V blotted out the shame of his father, Henry IV, and extended a protecting hand over his son.

In these benign circumstances, the polished machinery of English government adapted easily. Acting in the name of the 'community of the realm', the nobility made arrangements for the rule of the cradle king. They divided the government of England and France between the king's two uncles, each of whom was assisted by a council.

Then, in 1429, the nine-year-old boy was crowned king of England at Westminster Abbey. The form of the coronation was unique and, reflect-ing his position as king of two realms, much of the French coronation ritual was incorporated into the English service. The boy surveyed the pomp and splendour 'saddely and wysely' as the crown was placed on his head. This brought a formal end to the regency. But it did not mean that others ceased to rule in Henry's name.

In France, meanwhile, important victories were won. And, despite the rallying of the French by Joan of Arc, the situation seemed sufficiently stable in 1430 for Henry's council to decide that the time had come for the ten-year-old Henry VI to take possession of his second kingdom. In April 1430, the young king, accompanied by the nobility, senior bishops and a large army, went to Rouen. There the court remained for a year. A month into the sojourn Joan of Arc was captured. But it was too risky and too expensive to escort Henry to Reims, the traditional place where

French kings were crowned. Instead, in December 1431, Henry was taken to Paris, where he was crowned Henri II in Notre-Dame. The event was not a success. The English and French clergy quarrelled and the Parisians rioted. Within a month Henry was bustled back to Calais and thence to England. It was to be his first and last visit to France.

Whether France remained English would depend on the kind of king Henry VI turned out to be. And no effort was spared to turn him into another edition of his great father. For the first four years of his life he was brought up, as Henry V had wished, with his mother. But in 1427–8 Queen Catherine had an affair with a dashing young nobleman, Edmund Beaufort, later duke of Somerset. And a year or two later she married an attractive Welsh squire of her household, Owen Tudor, by whom she had four children.

Thereafter, his mother saw little of Henry. Instead, responsibility for his upbringing was given to Richard Beauchamp, earl of Warwick, who was appointed Henry's governor, tutor and master. Warwick seemed ideally qualified for the role. He was one of Henry V's closest companions, and was brave, cultured and pious. And he tried hard to inculcate Henry with the same qualities. Two little suits of armour and a long-bladed sword were bought for the boy.

At first, all seemed to go well and Henry was described as a promising boy, unusually tall and advanced for his age. But there were worrying signs. He was indecisive. He was generous to a fault and he loved pardoning people. But of the sterner virtues that were indispensable to fifteenth-century kingship there was not a trace.

What had gone wrong? Maybe the veterans of Agincourt had tried too hard. The legacy of his French grandfather, the feeble Charles VI, who had died insane, cannot have helped. Not did his warring uncles, each with his diametrically opposed vision of how the war with France should be fought or whether it should be fought at all. Each sought to dominate the boy and capture him for his own point of view. In so doing, they appear to have stunted his mind and paralysed his will. As for Henry III and Richard II before him, a royal minority proved to be a personal, as well as a national, disaster.

In short, Henry never became his own man. Indeed, by fifteenth-century standards he never became a man at all since his passion was not war but religion.

How a king wishes to be remembered takes us to the heart of his kingship. And Henry's chosen monument was not a battlefield or a great castle; instead it was the chapel at Eton College. As he said to a group of scholars there: 'be you good boys, gentle and teachable, and servants of the Lord'. It was a good recommendation for earnest schoolboys; it was a poor model of kingship in the fifteenth century. Nowadays we think of Eton as the most famous school in the world. But the school as such was more or less incidental to Henry's purpose. Instead he was interested in the size and scale of the chapel. He wanted it to become one of the biggest, richest and holiest churches in England. As long as Lincoln Cathedral, as wide as York Minster, his very own Westminster Abbey. But, thanks to constant changes of plan, which led him to demolish parts already built and start again, only a fragment of the vast scheme was finished at the time of his fall from power. It is an apt symbol of a reign that began with high hopes and a magnificent inheritance and ended in failure and disaster.

But not merely was Henry unwarlike. Once he took government into his own hands, he pursued an active peace policy. He detested war. It was cruel. It was costly. And above all it destroyed Christian unity. Henry was the only king since the Conquest never to have commanded an army. He was even prepared to surrender parts of his father's conquests. This was to incur the wrath of the English nobles, who had done so well out of the war.

The most dramatic signal of Henry's intentions came in 1444, when, at the age of twenty-two, he married a French princess, Margaret of Anjou.

Margaret was the symbol of the controversial peace policy with France. Moreover, after she came to England and married her impressionable husband, she became its most effective partisan as well. This played into the hands of its opponents. The English always distrusted politically active queens, especially when they were foreign. And especially when, like Margaret, they looked suspiciously like a French secret agent at the heart of the English court.

Soon the worst fears of the English nobility came true. By the time Henry was thirty he had lost everything his father had won. Only Calais remained in English hands. Thanks to Henry, a hundred years of war with France had yielded nothing and the prestige of the English crown was destroyed at home and abroad.

But most lethal for the monarchy was the fact that the war, like most unsuccessful wars, was marked by vicious quarrels between the English generals. Most dangerous was the feud between Richard, duke of York, and Edmund, duke of Somerset. Both were members of the royal house, and York arguably had a better claim to the throne than Henry himself. Both his parents were descended from Edward III's sons – his paternal grandfather was Edmund, duke of York, and his maternal great-great-grandfather was Lionel, duke of Clarence. And he was by far the richest noble in the land with a string of estates and a large following. As such he resembled another great landowner of royal blood who fancied he held the balance of power in England: John of Gaunt.

York was an energetic soldier. He had commanded the armies in France and served as English viceroy in Ireland. In all this, he contrasted strongly with the timid Henry VI. York's bitter rival and the king's new favourite, the duke of Somerset, was a man of a similar stamp. He, too, was royal and Lancastrian after a fashion, as he descended from John of Gaunt – but via Gaunt's liaison with his long-term mistress and eventual third wife, Katherine Swynford. And he had been a much-decorated soldier as a young man. But, in 1449–50, having succeeded York as commander in France, Somerset surrendered first Rouen and then Caen and all Normandy to the French with scarcely a blow struck. Gascony, English for 300 years, followed. At best it was staggering incompetence. York thought it was treason and never forgave Somerset. Their quarrel now dominated English politics and led to civil war.

But it was the popular and parliamentary outrage at the catastrophe in France that brought the two dukes back to England. As news of the loss of Normandy reached London, the House of Commons turned on Henry's government. Ministers were accused of treason abroad and misgovernment at home. They had lost France, bankrupted the king and perverted justice. And what Parliament began popular violence completed as several leading councillors were done to death by mobs. Worse was to follow. In the summer Kent rose in revolt and the rebels, led by Jack Cade, entered London. Henry fled, leaving Queen Margaret to negotiate a settlement of sorts.

Both Somerset and York now took their chance. Cade had called on Henry 'to take about his noble person his true blood of the royal realm, that is to say, the high and mighty prince the Duke of York'. And, on cue,

York had returned from Ireland, proclaiming his loyalty to Henry on the one hand but, on the other, presenting himself as the great white hope of good government against the corrupt court clique – and Somerset in particular. Somerset, for his part, had already returned from France. His aim was to defend his reputation. He hardly needed to have bothered as Henry, with a confidence that is scarcely credible bearing in mind Somerset's performance in Normandy, immediately turned to him as the military strongman of his tottering regime.

The dukes' roles were now defined. Somerset became Henry's chief minister while York set himself up as the leader of an increasingly disloyal opposition. Their relationship was further poisoned by the problem of the succession. Henry's marriage was still childless. In these circumstances, York had an excellent claim to succeed Henry and Somerset a more doubtful one – though it was greatly strengthened by his 'Lancastrian' blood and Henry's favour.

The next few years were an extraordinary switchback. In the autumn of 1450, events seemed to be running strongly in York's favour. He was received enthusiastically by Parliament and Somerset was sent to the Tower. But York had 'gone too far without going far enough'. His professed loyalty to Henry meant that he could not force his services on the king – and Henry would not accept them any other way.

The tables were now turned. Somerset was released and resumed his old place in government. Two years later, York, despairing of making headway any other way, took up arms. He justified his rebellion by claiming, in time-honoured fashion, that it was not directed against Henry himself but against his evil councillors in the court, especially Somerset. But, receiving little popular or noble support, he was forced into a humiliating surrender and submission. Then, in 1453, Queen Margaret, still barren after eight years of marriage, 'miraculously' became pregnant. York seemed destined for oblivion.

But, once again, events somersaulted. The English suffered a final, shattering defeat in Gascony and Henry VI, probably in reaction to the news, had a mental breakdown. His stupor was so severe that for months he had to be spoon-fed.

Three months after the onset of Henry's illness Margaret gave birth to a son and the future of the Lancastrian dynasty seemed secure. But Henry acknowledged his son only with the flickering of his eyes and he could not even raise a finger in the government of his kingdom. Without a king as the final decision-maker, England was paralysed. Who would act in his name? Margaret – her position immeasurably strengthened as mother of the heir – put herself forward as queen regent. But Margaret commanded little support among the lords. Instead they nominated the duke of York as protector and defender of England.

York ruled England for close to a year. And he did so well and moderately – in everything, that is, apart from his treatment of Somerset. Somerset was promptly arrested and held in prison without trial for the duration of the protectorate. But at Christmas 1454 Henry's bout of insanity ended as suddenly as it had begun. Things now came full circle once more. York was dismissed from the protectorate and Somerset released and reinstated. But this time York was not prepared to accept the reversal. And this time he had allies – powerful ones.

One of the symptoms of the decline of royal government under Henry VI was the growth in the number and intensity of private feuds in the localities. Worst was the dispute between the two great northern families of Neville and Percy. The fatal development of 1455 was the alignment between the Percy–Neville feud in the north and the struggle between York and Somerset in the centre. The Nevilles, led by the earls of Salisbury and Warwick, allied with York, the Percy earl of Northumberland with Somerset. York and his allies marched on London and the two sides met in the marketplace at St Albans. York triumphed: Somerset was cut down in the street and Henry, deserted beneath the royal banner, was slightly wounded in the neck. Civil war had begun.

Once more York professed loyalty to Henry and once more he became protector. But he had overreached himself. The situation was quite different from 1454. The king was no longer mad; there was an heir to the throne; and the Lancastrian nobility had regrouped. York resigned as protector. But the country was still close to anarchy and the king had slumped into apathy. Instead Queen Margaret took the reins of power. She rallied the nobility to the crown and in 1459 she brought charges against York. He was left more or less isolated and fled to Ireland.

But the Yorkists remained a powerful force. Less than a year later York's son Edward and the earl of Warwick raised an army and defeated and captured Henry at Northampton. York himself returned from exile and entered London in royal state. In the ensuing parliament York formally laid claim to the throne. He was greeted with a shocked silence, because no one – not even York's followers – wanted a repetition of the usurpation of 1399. So York was forced to accept a compromise: Henry would remain king while he lived, and York would succeed only after his death. But they all reckoned without Margaret's ferocious mother love.

Margaret refused to see her son's inheritance forfeit and broke the truce when she led the Lancastrian forces against York. Margaret was victorious: York was killed in battle and his head, adorned with a paper crown, displayed on the walls of York.

But Henry VI was at this time, according to the pope, 'more timorous than a woman, utterly devoid of wit and spirit'. He was a broken man, ill, helpless and utterly incapable of ruling. Nor had the death of York ended the challenge to the throne. For York's son, Edward, and his allies were still at large. And Margaret's act of vengeance against York had raised the stakes. Promises counted for nothing. It was kill or be killed; rule or be crushed by the victors.

Edward and his close ally the earl of Warwick were defeated at the second battle of St Albans (during which Henry sat under a tree, singing to himself). But Margaret was deeply unpopular, especially in the south, where London shut its gates against her after the battle. Thereafter she was unable to repeat her successes. Owen Tudor and his son Jasper (Henry's half-brother) raised another Lancastrian army in Wales. But Edward defeated them at the battle of Mortimer's Cross in Herefordshire.

The tide had very definitely turned. Edward marched on London and the City opened its gates to the Yorkists. The earl of Warwick proclaimed Edward king of England at St George's Fields in Southwark and a hastily convened and one-sided council concurred. The next day he was crowned as Edward IV. A month later the Yorkists comprehensively defeated a much larger Lancastrian army at Towton in Yorkshire in a notoriously bloody battle. Henry was captured and imprisoned; Margaret and her son fled into exile. York's son was king of England. But he could not sit securely on the throne.

VI

The monarchy had reached its lowest point since the ninth and tenth centuries, when the unitary kingdom of England had first coalesced round the regional monarchy of Wessex. Wessex, I have argued, was a participatory society, which balanced an effective monarchy at the centre with institutions of local government that required and got the active involvement of most free men. It was this combination which enabled Wessex to survive and absorb the Viking invasions and finally to thrive. It is also why, after the destructive violence of the Norman Conquest and its immediate aftermath, the Norman kings decided that both the ethos and the methods of Anglo-Saxon government were too useful to be abandoned. Instead, the great lawgiver kings of the Middle Ages, such as Henry II and Edward I, embodied them in an elaborate framework of institutions: the common law, the Exchequer and Parliament.

But by the late fifteenth century much of this was played out. The sense of mutual responsibility between crown and people, which was the great legacy of the Anglo-Saxon nation-state, had eroded, and Parliament was flatly refusing to impose adequate taxation. And the nobility were more and more successfully interposing themselves between the king and his subjects. They were not dividing England into separate statelets, as happened in France and had threatened to happen in England in that earlier period of crisis under Stephen. Instead, and more insidiously, they were taking over the machinery of royal government itself.

Their instrument was the noble household. As the vast size of their surviving houses and castles shows, the nobility kept households of scores or even hundreds of servants. They came from every rank of society: from labourers and craftsmen, through clerks and lesser gentry, to fellow nobles, who were proud to serve in princely households like those of John of Gaunt or Richard of York. Their prime task was domestic, to keep their lords in the luxurious style to which they were accustomed. But they also ran their estates, extended their local influence and, above all, fought their wars – whether against the French abroad or their fellow nobles or even the king himself at home.

Historians call this phenomenon 'bastard feudalism'. And it coloured all aspects of late medieval English society: its art, literature, religion and, especially, its politics. It even had its own language. The servant in this special sense was known as a 'retainer'; he was bound to his lord by a contract known as an 'indenture', and he wore his lord's emblem known as a 'badge'.

And the badge is the key to it all. The Red Rose of Lancaster and the White Rose of York were the badges of the two rival branches of the royal house. The name 'Wars of the Roses' is a later, Romantic invention. But the wars, which include some of the biggest and bloodiest battles fought on English soil, were real enough. As was the takeover by badge-wearing retainers of the machinery of local government, justice, representation in Parliament and even the throne itself. Twice, in 1399 with Henry Bolingbroke and now again in 1461 with Edward of York, the biggest bastard-feudal lord had become king. Where would it stop?

Contemporaries too were aware that something had gone wrong. Indeed, with the chaos and violence of the Wars of the Roses, it was hard not to be. And the various competitors for the throne vied with each other in issuing manifestos for reform. In 1399, the House of Lancaster had promised to revive the monarchy. Sixty years later, the House of York was making similar, even more extravagant, promises. But would it be able to keep them? Or was it more than a matter of mere personalities? Would the institutions of English kingship fashioned under the Anglo-Saxons, and perfected under the Henrys and Edwards, have to change as well? Was England on the threshold not merely of a new dynasty but of a new monarchy?

PART III

THE IMPERIAL
CROWN

14

THE MAN WHO WOULD BE KING

Edward IV, Edward V, Richard III, Henry VII

IN LATE 1487, THE KING commissioned a new crown. And he would first wear it on the Feast of the Epiphany, 6 January 1488. This was the climax of the Twelve Days of Christmas, when in English court ritual the monarch re-enacted the part of the Three Kings who had presented their gifts of gold, frankincense and myrrh to the Christ child.

The new 'rich crown of gold set with full many precious stones' caused a sensation. As well it might. The circlet was thickly encrusted with rubies, sapphires and diamonds, highlighted with large and milky pearls. From the circlet there rose five tall crosses alternating with the same number of similarly proportioned fleurs-de-lis. These too were thickly set with stones and pearls, with each fleur-de-lis in addition having on its upper petal a cameo carved with an image of sacred kingship. The crown was surmounted by two jewelled arches, with, at their crossing, a plain gold orb and cross, and it weighed a crushing seven pounds.

It was the Imperial Crown of England. As such it sits on the table at the right hand of Charles I in his family portrait by van Dyck as the symbol of his kingly power.

The man who ordered the Crown Imperial to be made was the founder of the Tudor dynasty, Henry Tudor. But Henry was a man who should never have been king at all. He seized the throne against the odds, amid bloodshed and murderous family feuds. But behind the beheadings and the gore was the fundamental question of how England should be ruled. Henry thought he knew the answer. But his cure proved as bad as the disease.

I

The story begins in 1453, four years before Henry Tudor's birth, when a nine-year-old girl was summoned to court. Her name was Margaret Beaufort, and with her fortune of £1000 a year, she was the richest heiress in England. Even more importantly, as the direct descendant of John of Gaunt, duke of Lancaster, Margaret was of the blood royal. Her cousin, the Lancastrian King Henry VI, had decided that she should marry his own half-brother, Edmund Tudor – a man more than twice her age. It was a sordid mixture of money and power, with the technicalities fixed by a venal and accommodating Church.

But the key issue was the succession to the throne. As we have seen, Queen Margaret had just become pregnant after eight years of marriage. But the succession could hardly depend on a single life. The union of Margaret and Edmund would, Henry hoped, strengthen the depleted royal family. It might even, bearing in mind the uncertainties of the times, produce a plausible heir to the Lancastrian throne.

When Margaret was barely twelve, the earliest legally permissible age for sexual intercourse, Edmund brought her to Wales, where they lived together as man and wife. Shortly before her thirteenth birthday Margaret became pregnant. But six months later, weakened by imprisonment during a Welsh feud and finished off by the plague, Edmund died on 1 November 1456. His child bride, widowed and heavily pregnant, sought refuge with her brother-in-law, Jasper Tudor, at Pembroke Castle.

And it was in a tower chamber in the castle that Margaret gave birth to the future Henry VII on 28 January 1457. Actually, it was a miracle that both mother and child survived. It was the depths of winter and the plague still raged, while Margaret, short and slightly built even as an adult, was not yet fully grown. The birth probably did severe damage to her immature body because, despite two further marriages, Margaret was to have no more children. Yet out of this traumatic birth an extraordinary bond was forged between the teenage mother and her son.

Margaret would need to be the strong woman behind her son. For after the battle of Towton the Lancastrians were down and out. The boy was simply an irrelevance. Richard of York's son Edward IV sat on the throne; Henry VI was deposed, on the run and ground down by mental disability; and the heir to the Lancastrian dynasty, Prince Edward, was a miserable exile. Jasper Tudor also went into exile and the earldom of Pembroke was given to a loyal supporter of the House of York. Henry Tudor owed his birth to the efforts to keep the Lancastrian family well stocked. What did that matter now?

Edward IV was a young, charismatic king who had won the throne in battle. Like his namesake kings, Edward was a warrior and looked it – over six feet four inches tall. Although he was nineteen when he won the throne, he was a shrewd and capable soldier and leader. He promised much after years of disaster under a meek and incapable monarch. And he used his personal qualities to make good his military conquest of England. He won over former enemies with his charm and magnanimity. Those he could not bring to his side he overcame by force of arms. He sent feelers out to his brother monarchs on the Continent to bolster his position at home and abroad. He even began negotiating marriage with the royal houses of France – not a bad prospect for a young man who had so recently fought his way to the throne.

But the qualities which made Edward an attractive king were also his undoing. He was open and affable and this easy charm got him into trouble. In 1467 he made a startling admission to his council at Reading. Three years before, he told them, he had married in secret. And it was not even a good match in a political or diplomatic sense. Elizabeth Woodville was one of the most controversial women ever to have been queen of England, with a past that could provide plenty of ammunition for Edward's enemies. She was beautiful, ambitious, greedy and a widow of modest family background, on her father's side at least. Her first husband had died fighting on the Lancastrian side at the second battle of St Albans. Edward first met her when she petitioned him about a problem with her late husband's estate. Edward, young, handsome and sensual, immediately propositioned his pretty supplicant. But Elizabeth defended herself, it is said, with a knife. Edward, as seems then to have been his habit when women resisted his advances, offered her marriage. But this time it was not an empty promise to ensure a seedy seduction and the two were married secretly at her father's house.

Perhaps Edward had intended to repudiate this clandestine marriage to an attractive but nonetheless obviously unsuitable wife once he had got what he wanted. But he did not. Had the marriage turned out to be valid after all? Had Edward the playboy fallen in love? Whatever the case, Edward's supporters were amazed. Marry me, marry my family, Elizabeth might have said. Elizabeth's family queued up for reward and power. Her five brothers and five sisters were married into the nobility. And her male relatives were given positions of power and influence. Suddenly there was a ready-made royal family which could not believe its luck.

But there was already a royal family – Edward had two equally hard-nosed and ambitious brothers, George, duke of Clarence and Richard, duke of York. And there were those who considered they were as good as royal. Edward had come to the throne with the help of one of the most powerful landowners in the country, his first cousin the earl of Warwick. After he had made Edward king of England, Warwick had made himself governor of England. As a Frenchman joked in a letter about the English to Louis XI: 'They have but two rulers, M de Warwick and another whose name I have forgotten.' Such was the power of the earl that Edward had kept the news of his impulsive marriage from his mentor. Now, however, the kingmaker was being edged out, as he saw it, by the cuckoos in the nest – the greedy Woodville clan.

The Woodvilles stepped into the role of 'evil counsellors', well known from history and recent events. They were blamed for high taxes and all other disasters in the short reign. The duke of Clarence joined Warwick in opposing the king and the Woodvilles. Together they stirred up trouble, hoping to eliminate their rivals and have themselves restored to the inner royal circle. But the king did not give in to them. Together they reminded Edward of what had happened to Henry III, Edward II, Richard II and Henry VI, when those kings had 'estranged the great lords of their blood from their secret Council and [were] not advised by them'. Then they decided to repeat history in a more vivid way: they would dethrone Edward. But who would be king? Clarence perhaps? Or what about poor old Henry VI?

The rebellion awoke the Lancastrian cause. In 1470 Margaret the warrior queen, with her son Edward, began to plot their return and the ever-loyal Jasper Tudor invaded England with French backing and Warwick's support. This time it was Edward IV and loyal Yorkist nobles who had to flee into exile. Henry VI was back on the throne after just nine years, put there by Warwick the kingmaker. And Warwick sealed his dominance by marrying his daughter to the prince of Wales.

Edward was forced to fight to reclaim his throne. Once again he was roused to action by a crisis. From Burgundy he regrouped the Yorkists and secured foreign alliances. In March 1471 he landed on the Yorkshire coast. Clarence abandoned his new allies and joined his brother. In April they were in London and on Easter Day Edward IV defeated the earl of Warwick at the battle of Barnet, in the midst of which the earl was slain.

The final showdown came a month later at Tewkesbury in Gloucestershire. Margaret and Prince Edward had landed at Weymouth and were making for the Welsh marches to join up with Jasper Tudor's forces. En route, they were cut off by a united front of the Yorkist royal family and nobility at Tewkesbury. Clarence was back on the side of his elder brother Edward, and they were joined by their younger brother Richard. The battle soon turned into a massacre, leaving thousands dead on the field. It was a decisive victory for York; a disaster for Lancaster.

After the battle, many of the Lancastrians fled to Tewkesbury Abbey, where they took refuge in the church. The victorious Edward and his men then burst in. There are two different versions of what happened next.

According to the official account, Edward behaved with exemplary decorum, pardoning the fugitives and offering up solemn thanks at the high altar for his victory. But the unofficial accounts tell a different and much more shocking story. Edward and his men, rather than turning their thoughts to God and mercy, began to slaughter the Lancastrians. A lucky few were saved by the intervention of a priest, vested and holding the holy sacrament in his hands, in front of whom even the bloodthirsty Yorkists felt some shame. Edward then recovered control of the situation by issuing pardons to his defeated enemies. But already enough blood had been spilt to pollute the church and to require its reconsecration.

The Yorkists also claimed that the prince of Wales had died in the carnage of the battlefield. But darker rumours had it that he had been taken prisoner and brought before Edward, who accused him of treason, pushed the boy away and struck him with a gauntlet. He was then murdered by Clarence and Richard. A day or two later, despite his solemn pardon, Edward ordered the beheading of most of the remaining Lancastrian leaders. Now only the life of the feeble Lancastrian king, Henry VI, stood between Edward and an unchallenged grasp of the throne.

On 21 May Edward entered the City of London in triumph. That night, between the hours of eleven and midnight, Henry VI was murdered in the Tower of London, probably with a heavy blow to the back of the head. Only one man is named as being present in the Tower at the time: Edward's youngest brother, Richard, duke of Gloucester, who already, at the age of only eighteen, was emerging as the most effective hatchet man of the Yorkist regime. As he struck the fatal blow, he is supposed to have said, 'Now there is no heir male of King Edward the Third but we of the House of York!' Now, surely, the Wars of the Roses were over.

No one, a Yorkist chronicle also exulted, of 'the stock of Lancaster remained among the living' who could claim the throne. But one Lancastrian claimant, however remote, *did* remain: Henry Tudor. Fourteen years had passed since Margaret had had her son. Now the teenage Henry was in danger of his life. Not even the massive walls of Pembroke Castle could protect the boy against the vengeful power of Edward of York, and his mother urged him to flee. He took ship at Tenby, and crossed the Channel to Brittany. And there Henry had to endure a decade and a half of politically fraught exile before he would see either England or his mother again.

II

Having annihilated his Lancastrian enemies, Edward of York was now King Edward IV of England indeed. But the problem of nobles who were almost as rich and powerful as the king himself remained. And richest and most powerful of all was Edward's middle brother George, duke of Clarence, the man Shakespeare described as 'False, fleeting, perjur'd Clarence'.

The phrase is memorable. But it is misleading. It suggests that the key to Clarence's story lies in his character defects. It doesn't. It lies instead in his position. For Clarence was what Queen Elizabeth I, who would occupy the same unenviable place herself, called 'second person'. His title, duke of Clarence, was the one that was given in the Middle Ages to the king's second son. As such, he was endowed with vast estates and many grand castles such as Tutbury and Warwick. Here he kept what he called his 'court' with a state that was indeed royal. He had stepped into the role of Warwick the kingmaker, whose eldest daughter he had married and whose lands and immense following he now controlled. Only the life of Edward himself, and in time Edward's two sons, stood between Clarence and the throne itself. Some second persons were content to remain merely loyal lieutenants. Clarence was not one of them. He had a power over the king that was at once malicious and deeply harmful to the peace of England. Clarence's knowledge, should he choose to reveal it, concerned the future of the House of York itself and all that the brothers had fought for. It related to his sister-in-law, Elizabeth.

Edward's hasty marriage was the cause of much of his woe. The secrecy, the haste and the sexual hold that Elizabeth seemed to have over the king made it a juicy and seedy controversy. For Edward's enemies it was the gift that kept on giving. But, whatever could be said against it, the marriage had at least proved fruitful. By the mid-1470s, Elizabeth had presented Edward with five daughters and, crucially, two sons. Immortalized in stained glass at Canterbury Cathedral, they look like the perfect royal family. Edward had what every king desired: an heir and a spare and a collection of marriageable daughters.

The elder son was called Edward; the younger, Richard. History would know them as the Princes in the Tower. But if their parents' marriage proved to be invalid, the serene image of a happy royal family that would carry on the Yorkist line long into the future would be shattered. The boys would become bastards, and Clarence would be heir once more. So the ambitious second person revived an old rumour. It was said that the libidinous king had been married to another woman at the time he married Elizabeth, thus making the present union bigamous and therefore illegal.

The rumour of a previous marriage may well have been true; certainly, bearing in mind Edward's notorious way with women, it was plausible. That only made it the more dangerous, and by throwing his weight behind it Clarence had tested his brother's patience too far. Clarence was arrested and put on trial before a specially convened parliament in January 1478. Edward had packed the parliament with his own supporters. He was himself both judge and prosecutor, and no one dared to speak on behalf of the accused but Clarence himself.

The verdict of guilty was a foregone conclusion, and on 18 February 1476 Clarence was executed in the Tower, famously by drowning in a butt of malmsey. The middle brother of York was gone. But the problem he represented was not. The monarchy had been weakened by the Wars of the Roses. Much royal land had been given away to buy support from the nobles, some of whom, like Clarence, had threatened to become mightier than the king. Such overweening subjects were difficult to manage at the best of times. But when there were rival claims to the throne, they became a dangerous source of instability, as Clarence's own career had shown.

To guard against the possibility of future Clarences, Edward needed to strengthen his own position and that of the crown. To help him do it, he enlisted a surprising ally: a man who had spent thirty years working for the enemy. Sir John Fortescue had served as the Lancastrian Lord Chief Justice; had spent years in exile with the Lancastrian prince of Wales, and had been captured after the battle of Tewkesbury. But the king not only pardoned him; he placed him on his council.

At first sight, it's rather surprising that Edward decided to spare Fortescue. An enthusiastic hanging judge, Fortescue had planned the judicial murder of the young Edward and the whole Yorkist family. He had also written powerfully and learnedly against Edward's claim to the throne. But Edward set these personal grievances aside. He had work for the old man to do. Fortescue, the leading intellectual of Lancastrian England, would play an important part in the construction of the new, reformed Yorkist monarchy of England.

Fortescue could be called England's first constitutional analyst, his key ideas shaped by the years he had spent in exile in Scotland and France. For his experience of how other countries were governed led him to reflect on his own, and to ask a series of fundamental questions. What was unique and valuable about the English system of government? What had gone wrong with it to breed the dreadful malaise of the Wars of the Roses? And how could the disease be cured without killing the very benefits that made England what it was?

Fortescue set out his answers in a short but remarkable book. It is usually called *The Governance of England*, but its full title, as it appears in the early printed edition, is *The Difference between an Absolute and a Limited Monarchy*. Or in Fortescue's own lawyerly Latin terminology, between a *'dominium regale'* and *'dominium politicum et regale'*.

France, Fortescue says, is the supreme exemplar of absolute monarchy, *dominium regale*, and England of limited, or mixed, monarchy, *dominium politicum et regale*. And the key to the difference between the two lies in the rules governing taxation. In France, the king could tax the common people at will, a system Fortescue strongly disliked as it made the king rich, but kept the people poor. But in England the rule established since at least the thirteenth century was that the king could tax only with the agreement of Parliament. For the English had an inviolable right of private property, and in that lay their liberty.

This certainly made the English rich, with a standard of living that was the envy of foreign visitors and the boast of patriotic Englishmen like Fortescue. But did the rules limiting taxation make the English king poor, and because he was poor, weak and incapable of military conquest and enforcing the rule of law against a fractious and turbulent nobility? Fortescue thought that they did, and that this weakness was the explanation for the Wars of the Roses. For the administration of the laws which guaranteed the property rights and liberty of Englishmen worked only when the monarchy had the independence and authority to govern the powerful men of the kingdom. And that in turn depended on the relative balance of wealth and power between the king and his greatest subjects, the nobility. As it was, in the late fifteenth century the king was relatively poor, whereas a handful of the nobles were extremely rich, which made them in Fortescue's vivid phrase 'over-mighty' and potentially ungovernable.

One solution would have been for the king of England to follow the path of French absolutism and impose by force taxes that Parliament wouldn't vote by consent. But such a challenge to traditional English freedom, or more accurately to the rights of property owners, would be dangerously revolutionary. The question, therefore, was how to achieve the apparently impossible, and reconcile monarchical authority with the liberty of the subject. Fortescue's proposal was to strengthen the crown within the existing system of limited monarchy. The king, he said, should acquire land, and rule by virtue of being the richest man in the kingdom. For if the king had an independent source of income, Fortescue argued, the English people would enjoy their wealth and liberty without being imposed upon by the monarch, who would in turn uphold the law because he would 'exceed in all lordship all the lords of his realm, and none of them would grow to be like him, which thing is most to be feared of all the world'. The execution of his brother allowed Edward to do just that, by keeping Clarence's vast estates for himself.

The royal revenues from land increased rapidly, which meant that Edward didn't need to call a parliament again for the unusually long period of almost five years. But land, Fortescue also understood, was about power as well as cash. And Edward took advantage of his new-found freedom to redraw the political map. He carved England up into territories, each controlled by a trusted member of his own household or family. It was all very cosy, but it depended to a dangerous extent on the force of Edward's own personality. It also loosened ties of loyalty, since it meant that those outside the charmed circle didn't care very much one way or another about who the king happened to be.

But as long as Edward remained alive and well, none of that mattered. Indeed, for the next five years the king grew rich; his Yorkist regime grew strong and it seemed that Lancastrian Henry Tudor, still sheltering in Brittany, would live out the rest of his life in exile. But at Easter 1483, disaster struck the House of York. Edward was taken ill with a fever after going fishing on the Thames. Within ten days he was dead. Only Richard, youngest of the brothers, remained of the generation of Yorkists that had defeated the Lancastrians at Tewkesbury. He was no more his brother's heir than Clarence, but true to family form he too would make his own brutal bid for power.

III

After the unexpected death of King Edward IV, all eyes turned west, towards Ludlow in the Welsh marches, where Edward's son, heir and namesake Prince Edward was being brought up. But at twelve, was the boy old enough to rule in his own name? Much of the Yorkist clique, particularly the queen's family, who had become powerful after the secret marriage, staked their future on the premise that the child could reign in his own right. They had been responsible for his education and upbringing; they had much to gain in the new reign. But a faction emerged in favour of appointing the prince's uncle Richard as 'Protector' or regent until the boy was old enough to exercise power himself.

Queen Elizabeth, sensing danger, was determined to get her son crowned quickly, and the council agreed that the coronation should take place without delay. On 23 April, following the council's decision, Edward left Ludlow for London, his coronation and his reign. His escort, as his council insisted, was limited to two thousand men. It was enough to put on a fine show as the young king took possession of his kingdom. But the great lords of the kingdom were able to muster as many men or more. And unbeknown to the boy or his mother, Richard was summoning his own troops. He too was heading south.

Late on the night of 2 May, Queen Elizabeth Woodville, waiting in London for the arrival of her eldest son, received alarming news. Edward's cavalcade had been intercepted by his uncle, Richard, who had taken possession of his young nephew. The duke professed loyalty to the late king's son and heir, his own nephew after all. But Elizabeth, immediately suspicious of Richard's motives, fled that night with her younger son into the safe sanctuary of the Abbey at Westminster. Richard entered London with his nephew a few days later. The council quickly ratified Richard's role as 'Protector'. Young Edward's coronation was 'postponed' until late June, and he was placed in 'lodgings' in the Tower.

What was Richard doing and why? Hitherto, he had had a reputation, in contrast to the flighty Clarence, for rock-solid loyalty to his brother Edward, who had rewarded him with the government of the whole of the north of England. There he had won golden opinions as a fine soldier and a fair judge, and the model of a king's younger brother. Nevertheless, his portrait suggests a man not entirely at ease with himself or others. He is tight lipped, and he is fiddling nervously with the rings on his fingers; he also had the tic of biting hard on his lower lip and constantly pushing and pulling his dagger in and out of its sheath. Was he repressed, paranoid? A hypocrite with an iron grip on himself? Or did he genuinely believe, in view of Edward's tangled marital history, that he, Richard, was now rightful king of England?

On 10 June Richard, an over-mighty subject indeed, summoned his troops to London. His bid for the crown had begun in earnest. A week later, Queen Elizabeth was compelled to give up her younger son Richard into his uncle's charge. The young prince now joined his brother in the Tower.

Their uncle Richard now had both boys, first and second in line to the throne, under lock and key. On 22 June a compliant Parliament decreed that King Edward's marriage to Queen Elizabeth was invalid, and the princes bastards. Richard had succeeded where his brother Clarence had failed. He had robbed his nephews of their right to the crown and cleared his own path to the throne. He was crowned King Richard III at Westminster on 6 July, with the full blessing of Parliament.

During those frantic weeks, the two princes had been seen less and less around the Tower. Now they seemed to have disappeared altogether. By the late summer of 1483 everybody, including the princes' own mother, Elizabeth Woodville, took for granted that they were dead. They also took it as read that the responsibility for their deaths rested with Richard. For only Richard had the power, opportunity and above all the motive.

To this day, their exact fate remains a mystery. Writing thirty years later, Thomas More claimed that the constable of the Tower was ordered to do them to death, but refused. Others, however, proved willing, and the two boys, More says, were smothered to death in their sleep with pillows, on the orders of their uncle.

His elder brothers were dead, the princes gone. The crown was his. But apparently doing away with the rightful heirs to the throne was a step too far, and opposition to Richard was now growing. Richard had been popular and might in theory have been a suitable king. But his sudden and bloody means of gaining power were seen as bringing a curse on England and perverting the sacred rule of succession. Soon he would be fighting to the death for the crown he had taken by fraud and force.

Opposition came to centre on a plot hatched between two powerful and aggrieved mothers: Queen Elizabeth Woodville, whose sons were lost, and Margaret Beaufort, whose son Henry Tudor was in exile. Their machinations would prove Richard's undoing, and decide England's fate.

Some time in the late summer of 1483 Queen Elizabeth Woodville, still in sanctuary in the abbot's lodgings at Westminster, received a visit from a singular Welshman, Dr Lewis Caerleon. Dr Caerleon was a scientific jack-of-all-trades – mathematician, astronomer, astrologer and physician – and, unlike many polymaths, he was a master of all of them. The sanctuary, of course, was heavily guarded by the king's men, but Dr Caerleon was waved through because he was the queen's physician. He was also, not coincidentally, physician to Lady Margaret Beaufort, and in his doctor's bag he carried, on Lady Margaret's behalf, a remarkable proposal. The queen's eldest daughter, also called Elizabeth, should marry Margaret's son Henry. Thus the bloodlines would converge, and York, Woodville and Tudor would join together against the usurping Richard III. That Elizabeth accepted the proposal confirms that she was convinced her sons were dead.

That Margaret made it shows that she had realized Richard's murderous ambition had opened the way for her son to gain the throne of England. Margaret had been nursing her ambitions for her exiled son, Henry Tudor, for years. Now, thanks to Richard's murderous path to the throne, she could put them into practice.

His mother's plot under way, the thirty-year-old Henry set sail from Brittany, where he had lived in exile for the fifteen years of impregnable Yorkist rule, to make his bid for England's throne. On 7 August 1485, at Milford Haven, just a few miles from his birthplace at Pembroke, Henry Tudor's army made landfall in the evening. His years of exile were at an end.

As soon as he stepped ashore Henry knelt, overcome with emotion at his seemingly miraculous return, and began to recite the psalm 'Judge me Lord and fight my cause'. Then he kissed the sand and, making the sign of the cross, called on his troops in a loud voice to follow him in the name of God and St George. It was a magnificent beginning for a would-be king of England.

But only 400 of Henry's men were English. Most of the rest of his little army of two or three thousand were French, and they had come in French ships with the aid of French money and the blessing of the French king. Indeed, most of Henry's own ideas about kingship were probably French as well. So just what kind of king of England would he be? That question was not asked for the moment. First, he had to wrench the crown from Richard's powerful grasp.

The two sides came face to face at Bosworth in the Midlands, where the fate of England's monarchy would be decided. The battle began when the vanguard of Richard's army, thinking to overwhelm Henry's much smaller force, charged down the hill. But instead of breaking and running,

Henry's front line smartly re-formed themselves into a dense wedge-shaped formation. Against this, the attack crumbled.

Richard, high up on Ambian Hill, now caught sight of Henry with only a small detachment of troops at the rear of his army. With courage or desperation, Richard decided that the battle would be settled by single combat, Richard against Henry, York against Lancaster. Wearing his battle crown, with a light robe with royal symbols over his armour, Richard led a charge with his heavily armed household knights down the hill. With magnificent courage he cut down Henry's standard-bearer and came within an inch of Henry himself. But once again, Henry's foot soldiers proved capable of assuming an effective defensive position. And Richard, isolated and unhorsed, was run through by an unknown Welsh pikeman, mutilated and stripped naked, more like a dishonoured outlaw than a vanquished king of England.

The third and last of the brothers of the House of York was dead. By his reckless ambition Richard had split the Yorkist party and handed victory and the crown to Henry Tudor. The symbolic union of York and Lancaster was made flesh in January 1486, when Henry Tudor married Elizabeth of York, just as their respective mothers had planned. A new iconography of union was created, merging the two once warring roses, red and white, into one – the Tudor Rose. A new dynasty was born.

But two years after the wedding, Henry ordered the new, ostentatious crown to be made, one that hinted at political ambitions that went well beyond Fortescue's limited monarchy. The crown was soon known as the Crown Imperial. Its unusual size, weight and splendour symbolized the recovery of the monarchy from the degradation of the Wars of the Roses and the expurgation of the foul crimes of Richard, which had brought down a curse upon the kingdom. The French fleur-de-lis, alternating with the traditional English cross round the band of the crown, looked back nostalgically to England's lost conquests in France. But might there be more to it than that? Henry had witnessed at first hand the powers of the absolute monarchy in France and, some said, he had liked what he had seen. Might the Crown Imperial be the means by which these ideas could, as Fortescue had feared, be smuggled back into England?

IV

At Winchester Cathedral in 1486 it seemed that the new Tudor dynasty had set the seal on its triumphant beginnings. The queen had borne King Henry VII a son and heir. He was named Arthur, and his christening was designed to signal the start of a new Arthurian age. The baby's godmother was the Yorkist dowager queen Elizabeth Woodville, whose kinsmen also played a prominent part.

King Henry really had, it seemed, ushered in a new age of reconciliation. But it was to be short-lived. Just six months after the christening, Elizabeth Woodville was stripped of her lands and sent to a nunnery, effectively banishing her from court for ever.

What had happened? Events had been triggered, almost certainly, because there were too many queen mothers and would-be queen mothers around. For Elizabeth Woodville, in her moment of restored glory, had reckoned without her sometime fellow-conspirator, Lady Margaret Beaufort. Henry VII had already honoured Lady Margaret with the title of 'My Lady the King's Mother'. But, since she hadn't actually been crowned queen, she had to defer to Edward IV's widow Elizabeth Woodville, who had. Lady Margaret didn't like that one little bit. So Elizabeth Woodville, she decided, had to go. Indeed, Margaret gave precedence only reluctantly to her daughter-in-law the queen herself. She wore the same robes; she signed herself 'Margaret R'; and she walked only half a pace behind the queen. Lady Margaret, in short, was proving to be the mother-in-law from hell.

Margaret's behaviour was a political disaster. She was the heiress of the House of Lancaster; the humiliated Elizabeth was the matriarch of the House of York, and the Yorkist nobility felt spurned too. Henry's dream of reconciliation was fading in the face of family feuds and sidelined aristocrats. And within a year he faced a major uprising by rebellious Yorkist nobles, which he only narrowly beat off.

But in 1491 foreign affairs intervened. The French invaded Brittany, where Henry had spent his exile. Hoping to strengthen his position at home through victory abroad, Henry followed the traditional path of declaring war on France. The result was a curiously half-hearted affair for a man who had fought his way to the throne. A reluctant Parliament made part of its grant conditional on the duration of the war; while Henry himself delayed setting sail for France until almost the end of the campaigning season in October 1492. Three weeks later the French offered terms, and on 3 November Henry agreed to withdraw in return for an annual payment of £12,500. The English soothed their injured pride by calling the payment a tribute. But the world knew better. Once the English armies had aroused terror throughout France. Now they were a mere nuisance to be got rid of by the payment of a cheap bribe.

It was a sharp lesson for Henry. England's limited monarchy had let him down; it couldn't match the financial and military might of French absolutism. Now he had failed to achieve glory in war, just as he had failed to unite York and Lancaster. There was nothing left but to lower his sights and return to the financial methods previously advocated by Fortescue and implemented by Edward IV. He did so with a novel degree of personal involvement, as each surviving account book of the Treasurer of the Chamber shows.

Like a diligent accountant, Henry checked every single entry in it and, to confirm the fact, he put his initials, HR – known as the sign manual – alongside each one. It was not entirely regal behaviour. Rather than lead Englishmen in battle, Henry distinguished himself as an unusually scrupulous auditor. It was privatized government, medieval-style, with England run as the king's personal landed estate and the monarchy as a family business. It would make Henry rich, but would it make him secure?

Events showed not. In the autumn of 1496 he faced another rebellion. This one nearly cost him his throne. The uprising was led by a ghost from the past, a man claiming to be Richard, duke of York, the younger of the Princes in the Tower, who had apparently and miraculously survived his uncle's bloody purge and had at last returned from exile to claim his crown.

He was a fraud, a Fleming called Perkin Warbeck, but he had powerful backers, the Scots, who threatened to invade England. A reluctant Parliament ratified a substantial grant to the king of £120,000, and the royal army began to move north. But the tax sparked a rebellion in Cornwall. The rebels could see no reason why they should pay to fight the 400-mile-distant Scots. And with the south empty of troops, a rebel Cornish army marched unopposed across the breadth of England.

As the Cornish rebels approached dangerously near London, Queen Elizabeth of York collected her second and beloved son, Prince Henry, from Eltham and took refuge with the boy in the Tower. It was a close-run thing. If his father were defeated, Prince Henry would share the fate of his Yorkist uncles the Princes in the Tower and be done to death in the grim London fortress. Instead, on 17 June 1497, Henry VII defeated the Cornish rebels at Blackheath, and on 5 October Perkin Warbeck himself was captured. But Henry VII had learned his lesson. In the remaining dozen years of his reign he would summon only a single brief parliament, and he would impose no more direct parliamentary taxation.

Without parliaments, contact between king and people was weakened, and the narrowing of government was further intensified by a series of personal tragedies. In 1502, Arthur, Henry's son and heir, died, perhaps of tuberculosis, aged fifteen. Worse was to come. Two years later, Henry's much-loved wife Elizabeth died in childbirth. She was only thirty-seven, and her funeral saw an outpouring of public grief.

Most grief stricken of all was Henry VII himself, and the deaths in quick succession of his son and wife changed him greatly. His character became harder, his style of government more authoritarian. The sole purpose of Henry's kingship now became the soulless accumulation of riches. Racking up rents on royal lands was no longer enough; instead, in direct defiance of Magna Carta, he resorted to selling justice. The law was rigorously and indiscriminately enforced not according to strict principles of justice but as a means of drawing people into Henry's net of financial coercion. The usual punishments for crimes could be avoided by bribing the king, or, put more politely, paying a fine. The nobility bore the brunt, for they were fined large sums of money for feuding or retaining large private armies. The once powerful great men of the kingdom had finally been brought to heel, but as part of Henry's obsessive quest for revenue.

He had ceased to be a king and become, so his disgruntled subjects thought, a money-grubbing miser. He had crushed his over-mighty subjects, subduing the turbulent and lawless passions of the nobility, and avoided the trap of weak kingship; but along the way he had become a tyrant, an absolute monarch who manipulated the law at his pleasure. Was Sir John Fortescue turning in the grave, where he had rested for the last thirty years since his death in 1479? For Fortescue had believed passionately that a monarchy richly endowed with land and independent of faction would be a guarantor of English freedom and property rights. But it hadn't quite turned out like that. Henry had acquired the land and the money, getting his hands on more of both than any other king since the Norman Conquest. What he hadn't delivered on, however, were Fortescue's twin ideals of freedom and property. Instead, by the end of his reign they both seemed as dead and buried as the old Chief Justice himself.

Henry died on 21 April 1509, after a reign of almost twenty-four years. He was buried, next to his beloved wife, in the magnificent Lady Chapel which he had commissioned in Westminster Abbey. A few feet away would soon lie the other significant woman in his life, but for whom he might never have been king: his mother.

Henry died in his bed and he died rich. But if the last forty years had proved anything at all, it was that the traditional English limited monarchy had, in an age of Continental absolutism and increasingly professional armies, ceased to work. Henry's successor would give it one last try. And then, to his surprise and everyone else's, he would create a new and revolutionary imperial monarchy, different alike from that of his medieval predecessors and his authoritarian father. This successor was Henry's second son and namesake and, reigning as King Henry VIII, he would change the face of England for ever.

15

KING AND EMPEROR

Henry VIII

ON 24 JUNE 1509, HENRY VIII was crowned in front of the high altar at Westminster Abbey. The supreme symbol of the Tudor monarchy, the Crown Imperial, was now his.

But despite the myths and hopes embodied in the crown that sat on the seventeen-year-old boy's head, it was a debased inheritance. All Henry VII's dreams of an imperial English monarchy that ruled Scotland, Ireland and France and was a dominant power in Europe had ended in frustration. The old king, in his last inglorious years, was regarded as a miser and a tyrant hardly worthy of the crown he had designed. Instead, Henry VII ruled his 'empire' like a private landlord, strictly and with a beady eye on his rent. For those who knew anything of history, this was not how the ruler of a great nation was supposed to behave.

The son agreed, and his subjects knew it. His personality – sunny, gregarious and romantic – was the opposite of his father's, and it promised a fresh start, although no one could have guessed how radical, even revolutionary, it would prove to be. Naturally, the young king was greeted with an outburst of joy after so many years of repugnant rule. 'Heaven and earth rejoice,' wrote Lord Mountjoy; 'everything is full of milk and honey and nectar … Avarice has fled the country, our king is not after gold, or gems, or precious metals, but virtue, glory, immortality.'

He was right, and Henry's reign turned into a quest for fame as obsessive as that of any modern celebrity. It took many different forms. At first, Henry would try to breathe new life into the old monarchy. But it would essentially be a last gasp of traditional medieval kingship. Thereafter, the search for glory would eventually lead Henry into territory where no

English king had ever dared to venture before. But it came at a price. Above all, it threatened to upset the traditional balance between freedom and authority and to turn English kingship into an untrammelled despotism that claimed power over men's souls as well as their bodies.

I

At the time of Henry's birth in 1491, the Tudors were a new, not very secure dynasty. His father had failed to reconcile the defeated Yorkist nobility and was about to embark on an unsuccessful war in France. Threats of rebellion and civil war stalked in the background, and the once hopeful king retreated ever more into privacy; ever more into the role of a greedy landlord.

And, in any case, the future of the Tudor dynasty was not destined for Henry himself, but for his elder brother Arthur, prince of Wales. Henry, as the second son, wasn't expected to be king, and as a result he received a rather modern, unkingly kind of upbringing. Instead of having the rigorous demands of kingship knocked into him by male tutors and role models, he was brought up at Eltham Palace by his mother and with his sisters, who idolized the robust and self-confident boy.

This early experience of women's love made Henry a romantic, and paved the way to the great passions and crimes of his adult life. Yet he was no mere pampered prince. Instead, Henry would always combine his romantic passions with sincere, if second-rate, intellectual ambitions. Once again it went back to his mother. She made sure that his education was of the best and a succession of distinguished tutors gave him a thorough grounding in the latest Latin scholarship. Even the super-learned Erasmus was impressed, and when he met Henry, aged only eight, he was bowled over by the boy's confidence, precocious learning and star quality.

In 1502, when he was eleven, Henry's life was struck by family tragedy. His brother Arthur died suddenly, followed soon after by their beloved mother. Henry was now the sole heir to the Tudor dynasty.

For the boy, his new status was a double-edged sword. He might be the prince of Wales, but the carefree life that he had known as a boy was gone for ever. Quickly brought to court, he learned at first hand the uncertain and inglorious reality of Tudor monarchy. Nor was there much love lost between Prince Henry and the king. Henry was growing up fast and he was already taller and broader than his father. But the king, aware that the whole future of the Tudor dynasty depended on the life of his only surviving son, was fiercely protective.

A chief source of the conflict came over participation in extreme sports. Henry wanted to take part in the manly, aristocratic sport of jousting. But, because it was so dangerous, his father allowed him to ride only in unarmed training exercises: the inheritance of Bosworth was too precious to be risked in mere games. So, when the real thing took place, Henry had to sit it out, chafing on the sidelines while his friends slugged it out like men. The result was a clash, not of arms, but of the conflicting values between father and son about what it meant to be an English king.

But on 21 April 1509, after a twenty-four-year reign, Henry VII died, and Henry VIII was proclaimed king amid wild scenes of popular rejoicing. The most impressive tribute came from Thomas More, the great scholar and lawyer, whose life and death were to be inextricably linked with Henry's. 'This day', he wrote of the new king's coronation, 'is the end of our slavery, the fount of liberty; the end of sadness, the beginning of joy.'

Meanwhile others at the heart of power had already taken steps to turn More's vision into reality. As the old king lay dying at his favourite palace of Richmond, his council had split between the churchmen and nobles on the one hand, and the common lawyers, on the other. The latter had been the agents of Henry VII's fiscal tyranny; and the former, who had been among its principal victims, had not forgiven them for it. Now it was time for revenge – and to turn over a new leaf.

The coup – for such it was – was led by William Warham, Lord Chancellor and archbishop of Canterbury. Warham looked back to his great predecessors, such as Anselm, Becket and Langton, and he acted with equal boldness. First, he bought time by keeping the king's death secret. This enabled him to take the two principal lawyers on the council, Edmund Dudley and Sir Richard Empson, by surprise. They were attending to business in London. Before they knew it they were in the Tower, from which they only emerged for their trial and eventual execution. Finally, he led a set-piece debate in the council which decided to abandon Henry VII's strong-arm financial policies and return to the traditional method of raising taxation by consent. Parliament, which had been heading for extinction like representative assemblies throughout Europe, was saved. And it is Warham we should thank for it.

Fired with the idealism of youth, Henry also had strong ideas about kingship. He had been brought up on the myths of King Arthur and the exploits of his ancestor Henry V, and like them he believed that a great king should be a great warrior. When he was fourteen, Henry first saw what was then believed to be Arthur's Round Table at Winchester. The great visual and literary myths that surrounded the new Tudor dynasty may have been mere political contrivances for Henry VII; but for Henry VIII they were real. Now he was king, he was determined to take Arthur and Henry V as his models of kingship. Like them, he would be a great jouster, he would have a brilliant court, and above all he would follow in their footsteps and conquer France.

Funded by the large inheritance left to him by his father, and benefiting from the first peaceful transition of power since the Wars of the Roses, Henry's court took on the feel of a magnificently armed camp, with an endless round of tournaments and jousts. There was an insatiable appetite for martial entertainments and courtly splendour. All Europe was dazzled by the English court's new-found glamour and extraordinary pageantry. A Spaniard reported home that the courtiers had instituted a twice-weekly foot combat with javelin and spear 'in imitation of ... knights of olden time, of whom so much is written in books'. Many young nobles participated: 'But the most conspicuous ... the most assiduous and the most interested ... is the king himself.' It satisfied the longing for a splendid monarchy. It also signalled Henry's intention: the conquest of France.

To that end, one of Henry's first acts as king was to marry his brother's widow, the Spanish princess Catherine of Aragon, who was six years his senior. The marriage would sow the seeds of upheaval and revolutionary change in the English monarchy. At the time, however, it was much simpler. Henry loved Catherine, but the marriage also cemented England's alliance with Spain against France. In 1510, peace with France was renewed, but when the ambassador came to thank Henry, he angrily retorted with an unwisely phrased French sentence, 'I ask peace of the King of France, who dare not look me in the face let alone make war on me!' Henry was rearming England, and in 1511 he got both the council's agreement and a moral justification for war. The French king had committed the most mortal sin as far as Henry was concerned: he threatened to depose Pope Julius II and he had insulted the English ambassadors. On 28 June 1513, the English army crossed the Channel to France with Henry's banners intertwined with those of the pope. For the first time in almost a century, Parliament had proved willing to vote serious war taxation. The result was the largest and best-organized English army since Agincourt. This was a holy war, and Henry was the pope's greatest ally against schismatic France. The French king was stripped of the title 'Most Christian King', and it was given to Henry.

Henry, like his great hero Henry V, led the English army in person. He even came under fire occasionally. He defeated the French in the Battle of the Spurs, so called because the French knights ran away so quickly; captured important prisoners; and took two French cities after set-piece sieges. Henry hadn't conquered all France, of course, but he had restored the reputation of English arms. He had made England once more one of the big three European powers alongside France and the Habsburg Empire. Above all he had covered himself in glory.

At the same time, however, Henry, or rather Catherine, since it was always the woman who was blamed, had failed to produce an heir. She gave birth to a short-lived son in 1511, but then followed miscarriage after miscarriage. Henry was surprisingly understanding, but how long could he wait for a son?

II

King Henry VIII had triumphed in France, and had covered himself in glory, but he hadn't done it alone. The architect of his victories was Thomas Wolsey, a butcher's son from Ipswich. Wolsey had risen from nothing through his intelligence, drive and ambition. Though nominally only a royal chaplain, it was he who had organized the whole French campaign. Wolsey had an affinity with the king; they were both pleasure-seekers and men of broad vision. He flattered the young monarch, provided him with royal pleasures and relieved the king of the irksome, inglorious, pleasure-denying day-to-day business of ruling a country.

His rewards were commensurate with his usefulness: in quick succession he became bishop, archbishop and cardinal. Abroad his power and international standing added to the dignity of the English monarchy. At home, by virtue of his role as papal legate and a prince of the Church, he was de facto pope in England: so long as Wolsey held his personal supremacy there was no possibility of a foreigner interfering in the internal affairs of the kingdom or of the spiritual power of the Church challenging the temporal power of the crown. He was also a territorial magnate and dominated the ecclesiastical establishment. And as Lord Chancellor, he held executive and judicial power.

Thus, by 1515, Wolsey was supreme in Church and state. But as much as by his power, contemporaries were impressed by his overweeningly flamboyant character, by his taste, his magnificence and his sense of display. His supreme monument is his great palace at Hampton Court, where he kept a court every bit as lavish as Henry's own and demonstrated with his every move that the levers of power were in the hands of the cardinal legate. But we should not let this outward display deceive us about the reality of Wolsey's power. He had risen only because he was able to deliver what Henry yearned for – glory and war – and he would survive only if he were able to continue to deliver what Henry wanted, whatever it might be.

But it was becoming harder to see how Henry's lust for power could continue to be satisfied. For the gains of the war proved fleeting, and by 1516 Henry was no longer the teenage star of Europe. There was a new, young, warlike king of France, Francis I, and a new, even younger Habsburg emperor, Charles V, Queen Catherine's nephew, who ruled in his own right Spain, Germany, the Netherlands and most of Italy.

Since both commanded much larger resources than Henry, glory in war was no longer a possibility. But peace, he was told, could be as noble and religious; it was also realistic. Henry was still only twenty-seven, and the same ambitions to reclaim the throne of France burnt within him. How had he become the peace broker of Europe? Just as Wolsey fixed the king's wandering attention to mundane business with a rich gift or an appetizing dish, so he made peace attractive. It was not merely peace with honour: it was peace with glory. England's military and material weakness had been transmuted into nobler metal. She was now, it seemed, the leader of Europe and Henry truly the Most Christian of Kings.

The change was also underpinned by material considerations. For the moment, England seemed to hold the balance of power between Francis and Charles, and was courted by both sides. But could it last when the great rulers of Europe eyed each other with hostility? Wolsey, dextrous and inventive as usual, turned the situation to England's advantage by organizing a magnificent peace conference, the Field of Cloth of Gold, which took place on a dusty, windswept plain in the north-east of France on 6 June 1520. It centred on a personal meeting between Henry VIII and Francis I. And, in another first for Wolsey, it was one of the earliest modern summit conferences. But the jamboree was much more than that. Wolsey had pulled off the seemingly impossible: English and French aristocrats met in peace and friendship. Centuries-old conflict had been replaced by martial sports. Wolsey sought to overawe Henry, the aristocracy and the people with something so grand that it made up for what many believed to be a shameful peace. It had all the ritual of war, but none of the blood. It was an Olympic Games with international jousting and wrestling competitions; there were displays of lavish cloth-of-gold tents, fantastic pavilions and almost competitive feasting. The English were generally reckoned to have won.

But it proved to be a mirage. England's role as arbiter of Europe depended on the continuing balance of power between Francis and Charles. Sooner or later Francis and Charles would fight, and one of them would win. What would Henry and Wolsey do then? Still with Arthur and Henry V on his mind, Henry renewed his determination to defeat France. For all the posturing on the Field of Cloth of Gold and the rhetoric about the glories of peace, Henry was edging closer to Charles and the Holy Roman Empire. Together, they plotted to violate the sacred peace and vanquish Francis. Henry and Charles wanted to fight immediately, but Wolsey knew that England wasn't ready. With all his skills as a diplomatist, he continued to play both sides off against each other.

Henry had cast aside his humanist pretensions, and was animated by what the cardinal (with typical flourish) called the 'Great Enterprise' against France. By 1523, they seemed ready. But in reality the aims of Charles and Henry were very different. A tentative English invasion of France failed before it got further south than Agincourt. But where was Charles? The allies were far from accord. In the autumn of 1523, a revolt by the leading French nobleman, the duc de Bourbon, provided the perfect opportunity for an invasion. But Henry's army invaded and fought on its own; what was supposed to be a multi-pronged invasion by England and the empire ended in farce. The duke of Suffolk led the English army deep into France and it was poised to besiege Paris. But with winter coming on and no allies in the field, he was forced to abandon the campaign. The essential food supplies promised by Charles never arrived. England's best chance to defeat France came to nothing.

On 9 March 1525 Henry was woken by the arrival of a messenger come from Charles's army in Italy. He reported that the French had been crushed at Pavia, the capital of Lombardy; leading French nobles had been killed and Francis himself was a prisoner. Henry was elated. The Great Enterprise must surely enter its final phase, when England would reclaim her inheritance. He sent ambassadors to Spain to arrange the final destruction of France. Charles and Henry should launch an immediate invasion and take Paris, where Henry would be crowned king.

But the victory, which had promised so fair, was to be the final blow to Henry's great ambitions. For Charles had no intention of setting up Henry as the most powerful monarch in Europe. Instead he called Henry's bluff: if Henry wanted his share of France, he must conquer it himself. That required money. Parliament was unlikely to vote new taxes. In their place, Wolsey suggested an extra-parliamentary levy, to which, as spin doctor in chief, he gave the emollient name of 'Amicable Grant'.

It made no difference. All taxes are unpopular. This one caused riots, and the worst one took place at Lavenham in Suffolk, which was then a prosperous wool-weaving town. On 4 May, four thousand protesters poured through the streets, the church bells rang the alarms and the rioters swore that they would die for their cause. Other smaller protests took place throughout the south-east. In Lavenham, the rioters pleaded poverty. But in London, sophisticated constitutional objections were raised to a tax that hadn't been voted in Parliament.

In the face of the protest, the government abandoned the Amicable Grant and with it Henry's projected invasion of France. Both Wolsey and Henry put a brave face on the climbdown. But it was a terrible humiliation. To Henry, it seemed that he had failed in both peace and war, and his dreams of glory were dashed. After sixteen years of trying to emulate Arthur and Henry V, this Henry was no better, in his estimation, than his failure of a father. But there was a ray of sunshine; Henry had fallen in love again.

Henry had some years earlier fallen out of love with his wife, Catherine of Aragon. Like most kings before him, he'd had mistresses and even an acknowledged son by one of them. The real problem was not with his wandering eyes and hands, but instead came from Catherine's own situation.

She was the aunt of Henry's great betrayer, Charles V. She had urged the Anglo-Imperial alliance. Any advantage that should have come from their marriage in 1509 was, some sixteen years later, and after so many disappointments, hard to spot. Fatally for her, Catherine was identified with Henry's crushing international embarrassment. And there was scant compensation. The age difference between Henry and Catherine was now really beginning to tell, as the miniatures of the couple painted in 1525 show.

Henry himself, then aged thirty-four, had kept his youthful looks, but Catherine, already forty, was wearing badly. As the massive neck and shoulders in the portrait show, her once trim figure had run to fat, while her face, which used to be so pretty, had become round and blotched and bloated. The explanation, of course, was childbearing. Catherine had been more or less continuously pregnant in the first ten years of her marriage and it had played havoc with her figure. If the progeny had been sons, none of this would have mattered, but of all those pregnancies there was only a single child that survived – a daughter, Mary. And a woman who had lost her looks, was past childbearing age and hadn't produced an heir was vulnerable indeed.

Henry and Catherine's marriage wasn't the first royal union to get into difficulties. The man whose responsibility was to sort out such problems was the pope in Rome, head of the Catholic Church, to which England, like all the rest of western Europe, belonged.

But at just this moment, the pope's position was under greater threat than ever before. The attack was led by a young German academic, Martin Luther, who in 1517 had launched the furious assault on the corruption of the Roman Church which began the Protestant Reformation. Henry and his minister, Cardinal Wolsey, were united in their horror at Luther's heretical attack on the Church. In May 1521, Wolsey condemned Luther's works in a great book-burning at St Paul's Cathedral, while Henry, the would-be Most Christian King, after all, wrote a reply to Luther called the *Assertio Septem Sacramentorum* or 'Defence of the Seven Sacraments'. It was the first book to be written by an English king since Alfred the Great. Composed in Latin, it was set in the latest Roman type for circulation to a sophisticated, select European audience.

Above all, Henry's book was loud in its defence of the papal monarchy over the Church. So much so that Thomas More, then Henry's friend and intimate counsellor, warned the king that since his present good relations with Rome might change in the course of time, he should 'leave that point out or else touch it more slenderly'. But Henry was adamant in his championship of Rome and his reward was the title of 'Defender of the Faith' from a grateful pope.

Henry never wavered in his detestation of Luther and all his works. But his attitude to Rome, just as Thomas More predicted, underwent a revolution. The reasons were Henry's need for a son and heir and love.

The woman he'd fallen in love with was Anne Boleyn, sister of one of his former mistresses. Sexy rather than beautiful, Anne behaved as no mistress had dared to before, and with consequences that no one could have imagined.

III

By the mid-1520s, Henry's reign had hit the buffers. He'd failed in his quest for glory in both peace and war. He'd failed to father a son and heir. He'd even failed to persuade Anne to sleep with him.

For Anne, supremely confident in her hold over Henry, refused him sexual relations unless he agreed to marry her. The difficulty, of course, was that Henry was already married to Catherine, who would never agree to a divorce. So Henry and Anne tried to find legal grounds for dissolving Henry's marriage.

Their best hope lay in the Bible, where the Book of Leviticus forbade a man to marry his dead brother's widow, on pain of childlessness. It was for this reason that Henry had received a special dispensation from Pope Julius II to permit him to marry Catherine, the widow of his late brother, Arthur. But now Henry's lawyers argued that, since the marriage broke biblical law, Rome had exceeded its powers, and the marriage was invalid. The case was submitted for decision to the man who was both the pope's personal representative in England and Henry's own chief minister, Cardinal Wolsey.

In the subterranean bowels of the Ministry of Defence building in Whitehall in London, amid the ducting, the central heating pipes and the spooks, there is an extraordinary survivor of the Tudor world. It is the wine cellar of Cardinal Wolsey's town palace, known as York Place, which once stood on this site. On the first floor there was the principal reception room of the palace, known as the great chamber. It was, almost certainly, in this room on 17 May 1527 that the first trial of the marriage of Henry VIII opened.

It was known as the secret trial, since Catherine was kept in the dark to let Wolsey move as quickly as possible. For Henry was confident that the cardinal, armed with his formidable spiritual authority, would rule his marriage invalid. Instead, to enormous surprise, on 31 May Wolsey adjourned the court indefinitely, on grounds of the difficulty of the case.

Why did Wolsey, who owed everything to Henry, defy the king's wishes? Did he fear Anne Boleyn's power as queen? Were his legal doubts genuine? Or was it, above all, because he knew that without the pope's agreement, no one else could hope to adjudicate in so delicate a matter? Whatever his reasons, the delay was crucial.

For, at exactly the same moment, events were unfolding in Rome which would make it impossible for the pope to come down on Henry's side, even if he had so wished. Two days after Wolsey adjourned the court, news reached England that troops of the Emperor Charles V had taken Rome, sacked and pillaged the city, and driven Pope Clement VII to take refuge in the Castel Sant'Angelo. The pope was now in the power of Catherine's nephew and Henry's enemy, and he would remain so for the foreseeable future. Henry's hopes of a quick divorce were at an end.

Wolsey knew that his power and his life were at stake. Desperate to find his way back into Henry's favour, he wrote the king a long letter, setting out the case for his own approach to the divorce. He sat down at his desk at four in the morning, 'never', his valet noted, 'rising once to piss, nor yet to eat any meat, but continually wrote his letters with his own hand'. But not even Wolsey could change the reality of European power politics.

But he could and did disguise them from the king. Back in early 1527 Henry and Anne had thought to be married in months. Instead, the months stretched into years as the pope, with Wolsey's connivance, strung out Henry with legal manoeuvres and diplomatic subtleties. It was not a personal affair. Given Catherine's relationship to Charles, it was the empire and its vassal pope against England. But the crunch came with the second divorce trial in 1529, for Henry and for Wolsey most of all.

Getting the trial under way at all was something of a triumph for Wolsey. But it soon became clear that, faced with the brute fact of Charles V's power, Wolsey, for all his cleverness and confidence, and for all his claims of supremacy over the Church in England, had been unable to persuade the pope to disavow his predecessor's dispensation. Without that, all the formalities of the trial were empty and the court, once again, was adjourned without a verdict. Henry's patience was at an end. So, just as importantly, was Anne's.

As the second divorce trial neared its abortive end, the duke of Suffolk had expressed contempt at Wolsey's powerlessness to do the king's bidding. Wolsey replied that he was but a 'simple cardinal'. It was a humbling admission. Henry had no time for such creatures. Throughout his reign, Henry had been able to maintain his independence from Rome and even be seen as superior to it. Had he not taken the moral leadership of Christendom as the bringer of peace? If the pope was supposedly an equal partner and Henry supreme in his own kingdom, Wolsey's weakness had exposed it all as a sham. This failure cost him his job as the king's minister, and it would have cost him his head, if he had lived longer. Wolsey died cursing Anne for causing his downfall, and predicting the ruin of the Church.

Before he fell, Wolsey warned the pope that if the divorce was blocked, Henry would be forced 'to adopt those remedies which are injurious to the Pope, and are frequently instilled into the King's mind'. The refusal of Rome to deal with Henry honourably meant that 'the sparks of that opposition here, which have been extinguished with such care and vigilance, will blaze forth to the utmost danger of all'. This was an allusion to the Lutheran heresy, which was flourishing in Germany and the Low Countries and creeping into England, despite government repression of heretics and the public burning of heretical books. And there was no secret as to who had 'instilled' such radical ideas in Henry's mind. Blocked in Rome, Anne Boleyn, who was a Lutheran sympathizer, encouraged Henry to turn to Rome's English opponents.

Anne was an avid reader of heretical books that had been banned by the orthodox and loyal Catholic king. But these blasphemous books became increasingly appealing to Henry. When a radical clergyman was arrested for distributing Lutheran tracts and William Tyndale's English translation of the Bible, Anne stepped in to save him. It was a crucial moment. For not only did Anne protect heretics, she also brought their books to her lover's attention. One of them, Tyndale's *Obedience of the Christian Man*, had a particular relevance for him. As the books of Kings and Romans in the Bible made clear, it was kings whom God ordained with His power, not priests. Kings had rights as spiritual leaders. Such an argument flattered Henry's ambition. Kingship gave him a special place in Christendom, but that God-given authority had been usurped through the centuries by others. 'This is a book for me and all kings to read,' he declared, animated by this new vision of kingship. That might be true, but Henry needed more: he needed to find a way round the long-acknowledged authority of the pope, an authority that, a few years earlier, he had defended to the hilt.

It's not what you know but who you know, we're told. In the case of Thomas Cranmer it was both. When the divorce crisis began, Cranmer was an obscure theology don at Cambridge. But in the summer of 1529, a chance meeting with two Cambridge acquaintances brought Cranmer to the notice of Henry and Anne. The consequences transformed Cranmer, his world and ours.

For Henry, Cranmer insisted, had been going about the divorce in the wrong way. He had been treating it as a legal matter. But it wasn't: it was moral. And in morals the Bible supplied absolute answers as to what was right and what was wrong. And there were experts who knew which was which – they were university theologians, like Cranmer himself.

Let Henry only consult the universities, therefore, and he would have a clear, unambiguous verdict in favour of the divorce which even Rome and the pope would have to recognize.

'That man hath the sow by the right ear,' the king exclaimed. Henry was already coming to believe that the pope was not the sole judge in Christendom. Now Cranmer had confirmed it with all the weight of his theological scholarship. Immediately, the canvass of university opinion began, starting, like so many new ideas, in Cambridge itself. Cranmer had thought that it would be high-minded and straightforward. In fact both sides played dirty and used every device known to the academic politician: rigged committees, selected terms of reference and straightforward bullying and bribing. But after two days toing and froing, the university delivered the verdict that Henry wanted. Cambridge would be on the side of the winners in Tudor England.

With Cambridge and (more reluctantly) Oxford secured, Henry's envoys set out for the Continent to pit the arguments of the king of England against the authority of the pope. In universities across Europe they bribed, cajoled and threatened theologians to give a verdict in Henry's favour.

Over the next few years the whole power of the Tudor state was to be thrown against Rome and Catherine. But Catherine wasn't without her defenders. One of the boldest was her chaplain, Thomas Abell, who combined the very different roles of scholar and man of action.

In the winter of 1528, Henry sent Abell on a mission to Catherine's nephew, the Emperor Charles V, in Spain, where Abell played the desperately dangerous game of double agent. Outwardly he was working for Henry; secretly he was undermining the king's whole strategy on Catherine's behalf. Mission accomplished, Abell returned to England, where he quickly emerged as Catherine's most effective and outspoken scholarly propagandist.

Abell called his principal work, with magnificent defiance, *Invicta Veritas*, 'truth unconquered and unconquerable'. In it he attacked the verdict of the universities which provided the whole intellectual basis of Henry's case. The attack struck home, as the king's infuriated scribbles throughout the book show. At one point, Henry's irritation actually overcomes his scholarship and he scribbles in the margin in mere English: 'it is false'. But by the time he'd finished, Henry's composure had recovered sufficiently for him to deliver his damning verdict on the book in portentous Latin, on the title page. 'The whole basis of this book is false. Therefore the papal authority is empty save in its own seat.'

Not even that magisterial royal rebuke was enough to shut Abell up. Instead, it took the full weight of the law. He was twice imprisoned in the Tower, where he carved his name and bell symbol on the wall of his cell, and was eventually executed as a traitor in 1540. Even so, Abell's courage proved fruitless. As learned opinion in England swung in his direction, Henry became bolder. He now asserted that, by virtue of his God-given office, the king of England was an 'emperor'. As such, he was subject to no authority on Earth, not even that of the pope. When the papal nuncio came to Hampton Court to protest, the dukes of Norfolk and Suffolk and the earl of Wiltshire told him that 'They cared neither for Pope nor Popes in this kingdom, not even if St Peter should come to life again; that the king was absolute both as Emperor and Pope in his own kingdom.'

Once Henry had been the stoutest defender of papal authority. But that had changed with the divorce, which had blown open the ambiguities of the monarchy's relationship with Rome. Now the achievement of his most fervent hopes for Anne and for an heir depended on the idea that religious truth was to be found not in Rome but in the Bible. Rome instead was the obstacle that had delayed his divorce for five long years. It was the enemy that stood between him and Anne.

But what of the pope himself? Here again, the Bible spoke. For there were no popes in scripture, but there were kings. And it was kings, Cranmer and his radical colleagues argued, who were God's anointed, ordained by Him to rule His Church on Earth. The idea appealed to Henry's thirst for glory. It offered a means to cut the Gordian knot of the divorce, and it even promised to make Henry, not the pope, heir to the power and status of ancient Roman emperors.

It was intoxicating. Henry now stood on the threshold of a decision that would transform the monarchy and England utterly, and for ever.

IV

On 19 January 1531, Convocation, the parliament of the English Church, met in the chapter house of Westminster Abbey. It faced an unprecedented charge of exceeding its spiritual authority. Henry offered it pardon, in return for £100,000. Fatally, the clerics agreed to pay. Having forced them to admit their error, Henry increased his price: the clergy must acknowledge that the king was 'sole protector and also supreme head of the Church in England' with responsibility for the 'cure of souls' of his subjects. Over the next two weeks they fought that demand word by word and letter by letter.

Finally, subject to overwhelming royal pressure, the archbishop of Canterbury proposed that Henry should be accepted as Supreme Head on Earth of the Church of England 'as far as the law of Christ would allow'. His announcement was greeted with a stunned silence, which the archbishop ingeniously took to mean consent. The weasel words 'as far as the law of Christ allows' meant what anybody wanted them to mean, and the next year they were dropped. Until then, the pope had still been acknowledged as nominal head of the international Church. But Henry's new direction was radical. The pope was left as a sort of figurehead, but kings in their realms held a power directly from God. Also, in 1532, the House of Commons, having been given the green light by Henry's council, submitted a provocatively worded petition against the Church's remaining independent legislative power. This was a step too far and Convocation repudiated the arguments of the petition with outrage.

Their reply was brought before the king, who reacted by screwing up the pressure. On 10 May, he ordered the clergy to submit to royal authority: all new clerical legislation would in future be subject to royal assent and existing law would be examined and annulled by a royal commission. This was a direct order from the king. Nevertheless, the clergy persisted in their defiance, citing scripture in defence of their rights and privileges against secular interference. The king's response was a hammer-blow. He summoned a delegation from Parliament and uttered those famous and emotive words: 'well beloved subjects, we thought that the clergy of our realm had been our subjects wholly, but now we have well perceived that they be but half our subjects, yea, and scarce our subjects: for all the prelates at their consecration make an oath to the Pope clean contrary to the oath they make to us'.

In effect, Henry was accusing the clergy in its entirety of treason for giving oaths of loyalty to someone other than the king. In the face of this, Convocation had little choice but to surrender. On 15 May, it caved in, and gave up its independence. Parliamentary statute would dot the i's on Henry's new title of Supreme Head. But all the crucial steps had been taken. Henry had also broken Magna Carta and the first clause of his own coronation oath, by which he had sworn that the Church in England should be free.

And he had become a bigamist as well. In October 1532, Anne finally gave in and slept with Henry. By Christmas she was pregnant, and in January 1533, in strictest secrecy, Henry married her, despite the fact that Catherine was still legally his wife. A solution was now urgent. If Henry's second marriage was not declared valid, then the child (a boy if all was well) would be a bastard. The future of the Tudor dynasty would once again be in danger. The next month, Cranmer was made archbishop of Canterbury. He was placed in the uncomfortable position of having to swear loyalty to the pope, even though his purpose, as archbishop, was to implement the divorce and complete the break with Rome. 'I did not acknowledge [the pope's] authority', he swore in a secret disclaimer, 'any further than as it is agreed with the express word of God, and that it might be lawful for me at all times to speak against him, and so impugn his errors, when time and occasion should serve me.'

Time and occasion arrived very soon. Cranmer derived his authority from Henry, God's representative in England, not the pope, despite the oath he had made. It was Henry, in this capacity, who gave him permission to determine the validity of his marriage to Catherine, 'because ye be, under us, by God's calling and ours, the most principal minister of our spiritual jurisdiction within this our realm'.

A new trial was held at Dunstable Priory in Bedfordshire. Catherine was not represented, and crucial documents were missing. This did not matter. Using the verdict of the universities, Cranmer ruled the first marriage void and upheld Henry's marriage to Anne. There would be no appeal to Rome. After seven years, Henry had the woman and queen he wanted. The London crowds grumbled, Charles V was furious and the pope eventually excommunicated the king. But Henry and Anne defied them all.

Henry's second marriage and its intellectual foundation in the Act of Royal Supremacy, which finally passed into statute in November 1534, were profoundly divisive. Some opposed them viscerally because they hated Anne or loved the old Church. Others were more nuanced and, subtlest of all, as befits the man who warned Henry about exaggerating the pope's powers when the king wrote the *Assertio*, was Henry's old friend and counsellor, Sir Thomas More. Opponents of whatever sort were whipped into line by laws, which required them to swear oaths upholding the new settlement. They had to swear an oath of allegiance to the Royal Supremacy. They also had to swear to the Act of Succession, which declared that Henry and Anne's baby daughter Elizabeth was the true heir. The implications went deeper than merely ratifying the king's marital and dynastic decisions. By agreeing, the country was being made to acknowledge that the break with Rome was permanent, and to assent to it. To refuse the oath meant treason and death. Thomas More was still loyal to the papacy, and he knew that his conscience forbade him to take the oath.

Thomas More was imprisoned in steadily worsening conditions in a cell in the Tower for over a year. But when, on 1 July 1535, he was removed for his trial at Westminster Hall, it looked as though he might escape with his life. More now did what he had hitherto steadfastly refused to do and spoke his mind. He could not be guilty, he said, because the English Parliament could not make Henry VIII Supreme Head of the Church, for the common consent of Christendom, of which England was a tiny part, gave that title to the pope and had done for over a thousand years. The judges reacted with consternation to the force of More's argument. But the Lord Chief Justice recovered the situation with a characteristic piece of English legal positivism. English law was what the English Parliament said it was, he asserted. More was condemned and beheaded on 6 July.

Working *with* Parliament rather than against it, Henry had hugely outdone his father. He had invested the so-called Crown Imperial with a truly imperial authority over Church and state. He would even get his hands on more land and money than the ravenous Henry VII could have dreamt of, and he got it by plundering the wealth of the Church.

Henry's personal authority over the Church gave him access to incredible riches. There were about five hundred monasteries scattered over England, some desperately poor but many rich and well run, and maintaining a thousand-year-old tradition of prayer, work and learning. But a change of intellectual fashion away from monasticism made them vulnerable, and their collective wealth made them tempting. So in 1536, the process of dissolving the monasteries began. At first, the objective was presented as reform. The habits of the religious community were investigated and vices and irregularities were found, many petty and some serious. In the guise of enforcing the rules, all the smaller monasteries and abbeys were dissolved and ransacked. But it soon turned to outright abolition: the zeal of the investigators ensured that abuses were found in every aspect of monastic life. By 1540 the last abbey had gone and the crown had accrued a fortune. The monks were pensioned off and their lands, buildings and treasures confiscated. A few abbeys were retained as parish churches or cathedrals, but most were not. They were stripped of the lead on their roofs, the gold and jewels on their shrines, and left to rot. It was desecration and sacrilege on the grandest scale.

It provoked shock, outrage and, finally, open revolt. If the full implications of the Supremacy were not fully appreciated at the time, the spoliation of the monasteries made real the break with Rome and the change in the nation's religious life. And it was too much for many. The result was that, in the autumn of 1536, Henry faced the worst crisis of his reign, the rebellion known as the 'Pilgrimage of Grace'. The first uprising was in Lincolnshire, and spread quickly across the north of England. Under their banner of the Five Wounds of Christ, noblemen and peasants joined together, demanding the restoration of the monasteries and the return of the old religion. Monks and priests played a leading part in the revolt, preaching incendiary sermons and even wearing armour. Adam Sedbar, abbot at Jervaulx Abbey, wasn't one of them. Instead, when the rebel hordes turned up at the gates of his monastery, he fled to the surrounding moorland. But the threat to burn down his monastery forced him to return, however reluctantly, and join the revolt.

Secure in their control of the north, the formidable, well-disciplined rebel army marched south. By the time they reached Doncaster, only the king's much smaller forces stood between them and London and, perhaps, Henry's throne.

Scawsby Leys, now an unprepossessing track, was once the line of the Great North Road where it crosses the broad plain of the northern bank of the River Don. And it was here at dawn on the morning of 26 October that the rebels called a general muster of their troops. The flower of the north was there, and when the final count was taken they numbered 30,000 men with another 12,000 in reserve at Pontefract. It was the largest army that England had seen since the Wars of the Roses, and it wasn't the king's. But even though the rebels faced only eight thousand of Henry's forces, they chose to negotiate. They persuaded themselves that the attack on the Church was the work not of the king but of his wicked advisers such as Cranmer. They were also double-crossed by the king's representative. He promised them pardon and, believing him, the huge rebel army dispersed.

But a few months later, a new minor revolt in the north gave Henry the excuse he needed to break his promises and exact revenge. The leaders of the revolt were arrested and sent to London for trial. Henry was especially severe on clerics who had been involved, even when, like Abbot Sedbar of Jervaulx, they had been coerced into joining the revolt. Sedbar was arrested with the rest and sent to the Tower. Then he was tried, condemned and saw Jervaulx Abbey confiscated. The aristocratic leaders of the revolt were beheaded, but the rest, including Sedbar himself, suffered the full horrors of hanging, drawing and quartering. Henry's Supreme Headship of the Church, which had begun in the name of freeing England from the papal yoke, was turning into a new royal tyranny, to be enforced in blood.

No one was exempt. In May 1536, after only three years of marriage, Anne was executed on trumped-up charges of adultery, incest and sexual perversion. But her real crimes were less exotic. She had failed to adjust from the dominant role of mistress to the submissive role of wife and, above all, like Catherine before her, she had failed to give Henry a son.

Within twenty-four hours of Anne's execution Henry was betrothed again, and on 30 May he married his third wife, Jane Seymour. Demure and submissive, conservative in religion, Jane was everything that Anne was not. And in October 1537, she did what Anne and Catherine had both failed to do, and gave birth to a healthy son and heir, Edward. Jane died a few days later of puerperal fever, but the boy lived and became Henry's pride and joy.

All the problems that had led to the break with Rome – the king's first two disputed marriages, his lack of a male heir – were now solved. With the occasions of the dispute out of the way, why didn't the naturally conservative Henry return to the bosom of the Roman Church?

The answer lies in Hans Holbein's great dynastic mural of Henry VIII. The original, of which only a copy survives, was sited in the king's private apartments and as such takes us into his very mind. The date, 1537, is the year of Prince Edward's birth. In the foreground is the proud father, Henry VIII, together with the recently deceased mother, Jane Seymour. Behind are Henry's own parents, Henry VII and Elizabeth of York, while in the middle there are inscribed Latin verses which explain the meaning of the painting. 'Which is the Greater,' the verses ask, 'the father or the son?' 'Henry VII was great,' they reply, 'for he brought to an end the Wars of the Roses. But Henry VIII was greater, indeed the greatest for while he was King true religion was restored and the power of Popes trodden under foot.'

This, then, is why Henry refused to return to Rome. The Supremacy may have begun as a mere convenient device to facilitate his marriage to Anne Boleyn. But it had quickly taken on a life of its own as Henry had persuaded himself that it was his birthright, his *raison d'être* and above all his passport to fame, not only in relation to Henry VII and all the other kings of England, but in the eyes of posterity as well.

Henry had got what he wanted. But to do so he'd had to use ideas based on Lutheranism, which he detested. The symbol of these compromises was the new English translation of the Bible. The title page shows how literally Henry took his new grand title of 'Supreme Head in Earth of the Church of England'. At the top of the page, of course, appears Christ as God the Son, but he's very small. Instead, the composition is dominated by the huge fleshly presence of Henry VIII. As king *and* Supreme Head, he sits enthroned in the centre with, on the left, the bishops representing the clergy and Church and, on the right, the Privy Council representing the laity and the state. Below there are the people, who all join together in the grateful, obedient acclamation of '*Vivat, vivat Rex*': Long live the King, God save the King.

The title page of the Great Bible represents in microcosm the extraordinary achievement of Henry's reign. He had broken the power of the pope, dissolved the monasteries, defeated rebellion, beheaded traitors and made himself supreme over Church and state. All the powers and all the passions of a ferocious nationalism were contained in his person and at his command. No other monarch had ever been so powerful. Fortescue believed that the liberties of Englishmen consisted of the independence and power that nobles and yeomen had in relation to the crown. But that balance had been upset by the Royal Supremacy. The monarchy, rich in land, money and spiritual authority, had no competition in the kingdom, not from over-mighty subjects, not from freeborn yeomen. Henry had been seeking glory all his life. At last he had found it.

But the Royal Supremacy also contained the seeds of its own destruction. For in employing the new biblically based theology, Henry had allowed into England those very subversive religious ideas he had once tried so hard to suppress. The genie of Protestantism was out of the bottle.

And it was Protestantism which, only a hundred years later, would first challenge the powers of the monarchy, and finally dethrone and behead a king of England.

16

SHADOW OF
THE KING

Edward VI, Mary I,
Elizabeth I

IN 1544, KING HENRY VIII, now in the third decade of his reign, bestrode England like an ageing colossus. By making himself Supreme Head of the Church of England he had taken the monarchy to the peak of its power. But at a huge personal cost.

For the Supremacy had been born out of Henry's desperate search for an heir and love. The turmoil of six marriages, two divorces, two executions and a tragic bereavement had produced three children by these different and mutually hostile mothers. It was a fractured and unhappy royal family. Now the king felt it was time for reconciliation.

Henry's reunion with his family is commemorated in a famous painting, known as 'The Family of Henry VIII'. The painting shows Henry enthroned between his son and heir, the seven-year-old Edward, and, to emphasize the line of dynastic succession, Edward's long-dead mother Jane Seymour. Standing further off to the right is Henry's elder daughter Mary, whom he bastardized when he divorced her mother, and to the left his younger daughter Elizabeth, whom he also bastardized when he had her mother beheaded.

But this is more than a family portrait. It also symbolizes the political settlement by which Henry hoped to preserve and prolong his legacy.

To secure the Tudor succession, he decided that all three of his children would be named as his heirs. His son Edward would, of course, succeed him. But if Edward died childless, the throne would pass to his elder daughter, Mary. If she had no heir then her half-sister Elizabeth would become queen. The arrangement was embodied both in the king's own will and in an Act of Parliament.

Henry's provisions for the succession held, and, through the rule of a minor and two women, gave England a sort of stability. But they also ushered in profound political turmoil as well, since it turned out that each of Henry's three children was determined to use the Royal Supremacy to impose a radically different form of religion on England.

First, there would be the zealous Protestantism of Edward; then the passionate Catholicism of Mary. Finally, it would be left to Elizabeth to try to reconcile the opposing forces unleashed by her siblings.

The divisions within Henry's family reflected the religious confusion in the country as a whole. The Reformation of the Church had been radical at times, cautiously conservative at others. In some parts of the country, people had embraced Protestantism and stripped their local churches of icons and Catholic ceremonies. In others, the people cleaved to the old ways, afraid of the radical change that had been unleashed. Like the royal family, Henry's subjects were divided among themselves, unsure of the full implications of the Supremacy.

Containing this combustible situation was Henry VIII, with all his indomitable personality. On Christmas Eve 1545, Henry made his last speech to Parliament. It was an emotional appeal for reconciliation between conservatives who hankered after a return to Rome and radical Protestants who wished to press on to a complete reform of the Church. Henry sought a middle way which would both preserve the Royal Supremacy and prevent their quarrel from tearing England apart. It was also an expression of his personal views: he held on to the old ceremonies of the religion he had known from his youth; at the same time, he had repudiated the papacy that was their bedrock. And, as he was determined that his people should continue to tread the same narrow path, he made no secret of his contempt for the extremes in the religious disputes. Both were unyielding and zealous. Both were in some way flouting royal spiritual authority. Radicals and conservatives alike were under notice that unseemly disputes in the religious life of the country would not be tolerated.

I

Just over a year later, on 28 January 1547, Henry was dead, aged fifty-five, and with him died any prospect that the Royal Supremacy would be used to save England from religious conflict. Three weeks later, Henry's nine-year-old son was crowned King Edward VI at Westminster Abbey. The ceremony was conducted by Thomas Cranmer, England's first Protestant archbishop of Canterbury, who, sixteen years earlier, had helped Henry VIII to achieve supreme authority over Church and state. But the Supremacy had not taken the Church as far as he had wanted down the road of reform. Now Cranmer used Edward's coronation to spell out fully the Supremacy's awe-inspiring claims.

During the ceremony no fewer than three crowns were placed successively on the boy king's head. The second was the Imperial Crown itself, the symbol of the imperial monarchy to which Edward's grandfather Henry VII had aspired and which his father, Henry VIII, had achieved.

And it wasn't only the crown. Instead, Cranmer turned the whole ceremony into a parable of the limitless power of the new imperial monarchy. First, he administered the coronation oath to the king. But then, in a moment that was unique in the thousand-year history of the coronation, he turned directly to the king and congregation to explain, or rather to explain away, what he had done. He had just administered the oath to the king, he said, but, he continued, it was a mere ceremony. God had conferred the crown on Edward and no human could prescribe conditions or make him abide by an oath. Neither he nor any other earthly man had the right to hold Edward to account during his reign. Instead, the chosen of God, the king, was answerable only to God. 'Your Majesty is God's Vice-regent, and Christ's Vicar within your own dominions,' Cranmer told the little boy, 'and to see, with your predecessor Josiah, God truly worshipped, and idolatry destroyed, the tyranny of the Bishops of Rome banished from your subjects, and images removed.'

The full nakedness of the absolutism established by Henry VIII now stood revealed. And both those who ruled in Edward's name and in the fullness of time Edward himself were determined to use its powers to the uttermost.

For Edward was being tutored by thoroughgoing Protestants, and he learned his lessons well, writing in an essay at the age of twelve that the pope was 'the true son of the devil, a bad man, an Antichrist'. Edward and his councillors now determined to use the Supremacy to force religious reform, and make England a fully Protestant, godly nation. It was a resort to one of the extremes that Henry had warned against in his last speech.

And there was much to reform. For, as part of Henry's cautious middle way, most English churches and much ceremony had remained unchanged. But thanks to Edward's education in advanced Protestantism, *he* believed that his father's reign had been marred by undue caution in religious reform. So now Edward and his council ordered the culmination of the Reformation, or, in other words, a revolution in the spiritual life of the country. Stained-glass windows, the crosses over the choir screens and the crucifixes on the altars were torn down and burnt. The pictures of saints were whitewashed, and the Latin mass replaced by the English of the 1549 Book of Common Prayer, written by Cranmer himself. England had had a Reformation; now, many said as bonfires raged through the country and statues were vandalized, it was going through a 'Deformation'. Where once the crucifix hung high above the heads of the congregation for veneration, there was now just one image: the royal coat of arms.

A highly emotional religion of ritual and imagery gave way to an austere one of words, as Protestantism, for the first time, definitively replaced Catholicism. And it was not just a cosmetic reform. The old Easter processionals, saints' days and pilgrimages of the unreformed religion allowed lay people to participate in religious life. But Protestants saw them as blasphemous ceremonies that took the mind away from true devotion, and they were abolished. The new religion was one where the people should receive the word of God intellectually, not take an active, passionate part in the colourful rituals of Catholic worship.

And with the icons and processions also went charitable institutions such as hospitals, colleges and schools, town guilds and chantries, which had been part of the old religion. These institutions were paid for by people who believed that good works on Earth would speed their souls to Paradise when they died. But Protestants didn't believe in Purgatory; therefore there was no need for these charitable institutions designed to help the soul through the intermediary stage of the afterlife. They also believed that the soul would be saved by faith alone, not good works. And so a way of life was brought to an abrupt end. The effect was devastating. The fabric of religious life was torn to pieces, and many were left fearing that they would be condemned to hellfire. The popular reaction was riots and uprisings, especially in the south-west, protesting against the Act of Uniformity and the introduction of the Book of Common Prayer.

In 1549, in their camp outside Exeter, the rebels drew up their list of demands for concessions from Edward's government. It survives in the government's printed counter-propaganda, and it is remarkable both for the bluntness of its language – 'we will', the rebels state repeatedly – and for the picture that it presents of their religious beliefs.

For what the rebels wanted was the restoration of a whole series of religious ceremonies: 'We will', the seventh article reads, 'have holy bread and holy water made every Sunday, psalms and ashes at the times accustomed, images to be set up again in every church, and all other ancient, old ceremonies used heretofore by our Holy Mother Church.'

Religion, in other words, was a matter of belief made real by ritual. And it was the abolition of these time-honoured and well-loved rituals which had so outraged the common man and common woman and driven them to rebel. They believed that if the artefacts and practices of their religious life – the candles and rosaries, holy water and Easter processions, relics and icons, pilgrimages and prayers – were taken away, their souls would be damned. But Cranmer disregarded the sincerity of their rebellion and responded in the language of self-confident nationalism. It was not, he said, an issue of traditional forms of worship. The rebels' demands amounted to a treacherous call for the country to submit to the laws of the pope and 'to make our most undoubted and natural king his vile subject and slave!' The protesters were a fifth column; they had demanded the mass be said in Latin: 'And be you such enemies to your own country, that you will not suffer us to laud God, to thank Him, to use His sacraments in our own tongue?' Protestantism was England's national religion. Moreover, Edward was God's vice-regent. To oppose his reforms was heresy and treason combined.

In fact, the rebellion was easily defeated. But Edward soon found a more dangerous opponent in his own half-sister Mary. It was to divorce her mother, Catherine of Aragon, and marry Anne Boleyn, that Henry had broken with Rome, and so for Mary the Supremacy had always been a personal as well as a religious affront. Now, faced with the radical reforms of her brother and his council, she discovered her true vocation to be the beacon of the old, true religion in England. In defiance of the law, therefore, she openly continued to hear mass in the traditional Latin liturgy.

The clash between Mary and Edward, who was as stridently Protestant as Mary was Catholic, began at Christmas 1550. It was a family reunion, with Mary, Edward and Elizabeth all gathered together under one roof for the festivities. But, as so often, Christmas turned into a time for family quarrels, as the thirteen-year-old Edward upbraided his thirty-four-year-old sister for daring to break his laws and hear mass. Humiliated, Mary burst into tears. She replied: 'I have offended no law, unless it be a late law of your own making for the altering of matters in religion, which, in my conscience, is not worthy to have the name of law.' The law that she recognized was that which had been laid down by Henry VIII. He had retained at least the outward essentials of the old religion. She would not accept that Edward, a child, could have any kind of authority, especially not *spiritual* authority, to change the religion of the country. She believed instead that the country should be preserved as it was in 1547. But Edward was capable of holding his own opinion, and defend it he would. He truly believed what he had been told at his coronation. He was God's anointed, and he would purge Catholic blasphemy from his realm.

When she was next summoned to court a few weeks later, Mary came with a large retinue, all of them conspicuously carrying officially banned rosaries as a badge of their Catholicism.

Mary had arrived in force for what she knew would be a confrontation with the full weight of Edward's government. But when she was summoned before the king and council and taxed with disobedience, she played her trump card. Her cousin on her mother's side was the Holy Roman Emperor Charles V, the most powerful ruler in Europe. Mary now invoked his mighty protection, and the imperial ambassador hurried to court to threaten war if Mary were not given freedom of religion. Faced with the combination of foreign war and Catholic insurrection at home, the council backed off. It was Edward's turn to weep tears of frustration.

And there was worse to come. In the winter of 1552, Edward started to cough blood, and by the following spring it was obvious to everyone that the young king was dying.

In the same year the Reformation reached its high point. What little there remained of Henry's moderation was abandoned as Protestant reform reached its climax. The real presence of Christ in the sacrifice of Eucharist during mass was rejected by Cranmer's second Book of Common Prayer. Altars which symbolized the sacrifice of Christ during the Eucharistic rites were stripped from churches throughout the country and replaced with rough communion tables. It was a complete rejection of the old faith and the end of the compromise between Catholicism and Protestantism that Henry had advocated. Reform was hurtling in one direction. But Mary's intransigent Catholicism now became more than an obstacle to the progress of reform – it threatened the very survival of Protestantism itself. For Mary, her father had declared, was Edward's heir. She would succeed as queen and Supreme Head of the Church, and like her father and brother before her, she would be able to remake the religion of England according to her own lights. It was clear to everyone, even Edward, that this was only a matter of time.

The thought of Mary as his Catholic successor was intolerable to the hotly Protestant Edward. So, with a confidence that was breathtaking in a dying fifteen-year-old boy, he decided unilaterally to change the rules.

He set down his commands in an extraordinary document. It is headed in his bold schoolboy hand 'My Device for the Succession'. It was against statute law and drawn up without parliamentary consent. But the sickly king believed that his God-given authority would extend beyond the grave. First, he excluded Elizabeth as well as Mary from the succession on the grounds that both his half-sisters were bastards. Second, he trans-ferred the throne to the family of his cousins the Greys; and third, he decided that women were unfit to rule in their own right, though they could transmit their claim to their sons, or, in legal jargon, their 'heirs male'.

The problem was that all his Grey cousins were women, and though they had been married off at breakneck speed, none of them had yet had children. In the course of time, no doubt, the problem would have solved itself, but in view of Edward's rapidly declining health there wasn't time. Instead Edward swallowed his misogyny and called for his 'Device'. With two or three deft strokes of the pen he altered the rules one last time. Originally he had left the crown to the sons of the eldest Grey sister, the Lady Jane: 'the Lady Jane's heirs male'. One crossing out and two words inserted over a caret changed this to: 'the Lady Jane and her heirs male'. If Edward could make his choice stick, the impeccably Protestant and deeply learned Lady Jane Grey would be his successor as queen.

On 6 July 1553, Edward died. On the 10th the sixteen-year-old Lady Jane Grey was brought to the Tower to be proclaimed queen. The Tower was the traditional location for such a declaration. The difference in this case was that Jane Grey would never leave its precincts again.

II

By leaving the throne to Lady Jane Grey, Edward had flouted both his father King Henry VIII's will and the Act of Succession. This flagrant disregard for the law was unacceptable even to many Protestants. It would have given the crown even greater powers, putting it above Parliament and the law. Moreover, Lady Jane's supporters had made a fatal mistake – they had failed to arrest Edward's Catholic sister Mary, who was, according to Henry's will, the legitimate heir to the throne.

Instead, forewarned by friends at court, Mary fled out of reach to the depths of East Anglia, were she had vast estates and a loyal following. On 10 July, she proclaimed herself rightful queen of England, and two days later she took up residence at the great castle of Framlingham, which she made her headquarters for armed assault on the throne of England. Troops flooded in and Mary inspected her army in front of the castle in true royal style.

But no blow needed to be struck. Faced with Mary's overwhelming strength the Grey faction threw in the towel and Queen Jane was deposed after reigning for less than a fortnight. It was legality, legitimacy and the sense that she was Henry VIII's daughter which had won the day for Mary, but she herself didn't see it like that. 'In thee O Lord I trust, that I be not confounded forever,' Mary said; 'if God be for us; who can be against us?' She was convinced that her accession against all the odds was a miracle brought about by God for His own purposes; it was a sign, and she was now a woman with a mission to restore England to the Catholic faith.

In public, Mary promised to return to something like the consensus of her father's last years: there would be no forced conversions, her propa- ganda implied. In private she was more candid: 'she boasted herself a virgin sent of God to ride and tame the people of England'. The contrast was reflected in the hesitant start to reconversion: to begin with people were 'encouraged' to return to the old faith after nearly twenty years of Protestant reforms, and Edward's policies were assaulted only slowly. But it would not be long before Mary increased the pace of bringing England back to true religion.

First, however, to prevent the country ever returning to the heresy of Protestantism, Mary must marry and produce an heir. For otherwise her father's will left the throne to her Protestant half-sister, Elizabeth. Long ago in her youth, Mary had been briefly betrothed to the Emperor Charles V. Now Charles offered her his own son and heir, Philip, who had been brought up in Spain and was imbued with that country's passionate Catholicism. More importantly, his father had dedicated the empire's resources to stamping out Protestantism throughout Europe. Now England would be brought back to due obedience to the pope. But the idea of a Spanish king ruling in England was wildly unpopular. Even though a yearning for Catholicism remained widespread in England, decades of anti-papal, nationalistic propaganda had also done their work. The papacy was looked upon as foreign and un-English. Thus, when the Spanish embassy arrived, boys threw snowballs at them, and the rest of the crowd, 'nothing rejoicing, held down their heads sorrowfully'. More seriously, an uprising in Kent in 1554, led by Sir Thomas Wyatt, fought its way to London, and for a while Mary's throne was in jeopardy.

Mary rose to the occasion, won over Londoners with a magnificent speech in Guildhall and crushed the revolt. She then exacted a terrible revenge, executing all the leaders of the conspiracy, and Lady Jane Grey herself, whom she had hitherto spared. Elizabeth was implicated in the rebellion and sent to the Tower. With the rebellion defeated, and with Parliament's reluctant acquiescence, there was now no barrier to Mary's marriage to Philip.

Philip landed in Southampton on 20 July 1554. It was close to the first anniversary of Mary's accession. Five days later Philip and Mary were married at Winchester Cathedral. The couple processed through the west doors along an elevated walkway to a high platform in the centre of the nave, where the ceremony took place. It deliberately invoked an older and better world. Mary used an old-fashioned wedding ring made of a band of plain gold, and she swore the woman's old oath, to be 'Bonny and buxom in bed and at board'. If the couple were able to have children, that older, better Catholic world would live again.

Mary was thirty-seven and prematurely aged. But she sincerely believed that God would once again favour her and England with a miracle. A few months later, Mary, like her namesake the Blessed Virgin, declared that the 'babe had stirred in her womb'. The prospect of a Catholic heir greatly strengthened Mary's hand, and Parliament voted to return the Church of England to the obedience of the pope. The Royal Supremacy, which Henry VIII had forced on the English people, seemed to be over.

In early April 1555, Mary moved to Hampton Court for the birth of the child that would crown her life and reign, and guarantee the future of Catholic England. Her confinement, as customary, began with the ceremony of 'taking to her chamber', in which she bade farewell to the male-dominated world of the court and withdrew instead to the purely female realm of her birthing chamber. There, etiquette required she remain secluded and invisible until the birth. But Mary couldn't keep her joy to herself. Instead, on St George's Day, she appeared at a window to watch her husband Philip lead the Garter celebrations, and she turned side-on to show off her big belly to the crowd below.

Good Catholics rejoiced with the queen, as they did when the serious business of enforcing Catholicism began. Part of the return to Rome was the restoration of heresy laws that punished those who denied the Catholic faith with the terrible death of burning alive.

The burnings began in February 1555. Over the following three years more than three hundred men and women died in agony at the stake. Faced with such persecution, many other leading Protestants fled into exile. One of the exiles was the Protestant cleric John Foxe, who decided to write a history of the persecution. Using the trial records, eyewitness accounts and the writings of the martyrs themselves, he compiled his *Acts and Monuments*. Soon known as *Foxe's Book of Martyrs*, it became, after the Bible, the second-most widely read book in English, and it damned Mary's reputation for ever as Bloody Mary, especially the gruesome woodcuts.

But Foxe's propaganda would have amounted to very little if it hadn't quickly become obvious that Mary's condition was a phantom pregnancy. By early summer she was a public laughing stock, with stories circulating that she was pregnant with a lapdog or a monkey. By August even Mary herself had abandoned hope. Moreover, at thirty-nine, it seemed unlikely she would ever conceive again.

With her pregnancy exposed as a delusion, power started to ebb away from the queen. Philip, now with no long-term interest in England, abandoned his wife to return to his Continental possessions. Still worse, her failure to produce an heir, and with it the guarantee of a Catholic future, broke Mary's hold on Parliament.

Crucial to the government's plans for the final suppression of Protestantism was a Bill to confiscate the landed estates of the Protestant exiles. If the Bill passed, the economic foundations of their resistance would be destroyed. The government strained every nerve, but so too did the opposition, led by Sir Anthony Kingston. With the connivance of the sergeant-at-arms, the doors of the House were locked from the inside. Kingston thundered his protests and the Bill was defeated. Such scenes would not be seen again in Parliament until the seventeenth century.

Despite the loss of the political initiative, Mary grimly persisted with the persecution of Protestants. Her most illustrious victim was Archbishop Thomas Cranmer. But Cranmer was caught on the horns of a dilemma. In creating the Royal Supremacy, he had argued that monarchs were God's agents on Earth and were owed obedience as an absolute religious duty.

But what to do when the monarch was of the wrong religion? Obey the queen? Or Christ? Cranmer's prosecutors at his trial for heresy probed the dilemma ruthlessly, and Cranmer, old, worn out and terrified of the fire, recanted his Protestantism. It was a huge propaganda coup for Mary. But foolishly, she wasn't satisfied. She bore Cranmer a deep and personal grudge for divorcing her mother and, even though Church law said that a repentant heretic should be pardoned, she was determined that he would burn.

Cranmer's execution was to take place in Oxford, preceded by a public repetition of his recantation. After a good supper, Cranmer slept well, and early on a rainy morning he was brought to the University Church. It is still possible to see where sections of the pillars of the church were cut away to build a high platform to give maximum publicity to what the authorities were confident would be a repetition of his recantation and confession.

Instead, in an astonishing theatrical coup, Cranmer repudiated his recantation, and as the hubbub rose through the church he managed to shout out a final denunciation of the pope as Antichrist. He was pulled down from the scaffold and hurried to the stake.

But Cranmer hadn't finished. As the flames rose he stuck out his right hand, which had signed his recantation, and pushed it deep into the heart of the fire. It had sinned, he said, so it should be punished first. It was a magnificent gesture which vindicated Cranmer's personal integrity, and saved the good faith of Protestantism. Mary's vengefulness had turned the propaganda coup of Cranmer's recantation into a PR disaster, which fired her opponents with a new zeal to resist Bloody Mary.

Among them was John Ponet, a Protestant bishop who'd fled into exile in Strasbourg when the burnings began. He was an old friend of Cranmer's. But Ponet's experience of Mary's tyranny led him, unlike Cranmer, to question the intellectual foundations of the Supremacy, and reject outright the idea that the king was God's anointed, ordained by Him to rule His church on Earth.

In 1556 he published a revolutionary book, *A Shorte Treatise of Politike Power*. Its title page, with the motto taken from Psalm 118, says it all: 'it is better to trust in the Lord than to trust in princes'. This meant that kings, far from being the God-like figures of Cranmer's and Henry VIII's imaginations, were human at best and subhuman at their all-too-frequent worst. And this meant in turn that kings were human creations and had to be subject to human control.

If, therefore, Ponet went on to argue, a king or queen broke human or divine law they should be reproved or even deposed. And if, like Mary, they were cruel and persecuting idolaters then it was a virtuous act to assassinate them as a tyrant. Henry VIII had realized that the Royal Supremacy could survive only if the monarchy kept to a middle way in religion. But Edward and Mary had ignored his warnings, and now, in Ponet's groundbreaking work, had provoked a head-on challenge to the authority and legitimacy of kingship itself.

Mary was soon beyond the reach of Ponet's seditious theorizing. In 1558 she became seriously ill, although she fondly imagined she was pregnant again. She even wrote her will, leaving the throne to her unborn Catholic child.

But six months later, with her health rapidly fading, even Mary had to face reality, and she added a codicil to her will. In it, she finally acknowledged that it was likely that she would have 'no issue or heir of her body', and that she would be succeeded instead 'by her next heir and successor, by the laws and statutes of this realm'. That of course was her half-sister Elizabeth, though Mary couldn't even bring herself to write her name. Seeing visions of heavenly children to the last, she died on the night of 16 November 1558. She was forty-two.

Two of Henry's three children had succeeded to the throne and, by their contrasting religious extremism, had imperilled both the Supremacy and the crown. Would his last surviving heir, Elizabeth, do any better?

III

After years of danger and uncertainty, Henry VIII's last heir, his daughter Elizabeth, stood on the verge of becoming queen of England.

A portrait of Elizabeth aged fourteen, painted in the last weeks of her father's life, shows her as the very model of a religious, learned princess. But the reality of Elizabeth's life under the reigns of her brother and sister was to be very different from the studious calm suggested by this picture, especially under her sister Mary.

During Mary's reign, Elizabeth occupied the impossible position that she would later call 'second person'. By their father's will, she was Mary's heir presumptive; she was also, as a covert Protestant, guaranteed to undo everything that Mary held dear. This made her both the focus of every conspiracy against Mary, and the target of her sister's fear and rage.

Mary had sent her to the Tower after the Wyatt rebellion in 1554 on charges of treason, and would certainly have had her beheaded if she had been able to scrape enough evidence together. Such experiences left Elizabeth with a set of indelible memories, which meant she took a very different view of policy from either her brother or her sister.

News of Mary's death was brought to Elizabeth at Hatfield. The story has it that she fell on her knees, impulsively exclaiming with the psalmist: 'This is the Lord's doing; it is marvellous in our eyes.' Actually, Elizabeth had been preparing herself for this moment for weeks. Her right-hand man in her preparations for power had been Sir William Cecil. It was to be the beginning of a lifelong partnership.

Cecil, born the son of a Tudor courtier some thirteen years before Elizabeth, had shared many of her experiences and, as a Protestant, suffered the same fears under Mary when he too had saved his skin by conforming to Catholicism. But there was a difference. Cecil, unlike Elizabeth, responded to the fears he had experienced under Mary by hardening his opinions: never again must there be a Catholic monarch or heir, and if by mischance one appeared then people, council and Parliament together could and should remove them.

These were Ponet's arguments, though Cecil was a moderate in comparison. Nevertheless, it would make for an interesting relationship between Cecil and his imperious, headstrong young queen, with her high view of royal power and her moderate line in religion. And indeed, establishing a new religious settlement was Elizabeth's first task as queen. Mary's parliament had made Catholicism once more the religion of England and only another parliament could change it. But to what?

Elizabeth's first parliament met in January 1559. It was opened with a speech by the acting Lord Chancellor. He spoke in Elizabeth's name but his phraseology deliberately invoked her father's great speech on religion to the parliament of 1545. Since then, England had been to the extremes of religion. It had been, as Henry predicted, bloody and destructive. Most had tried to avoid being caught up in the conflict between Protestants and Catholics. The people, clergy, many of the council and Elizabeth herself had compromised with Mary and outwardly conformed to Catholicism. Elizabeth herself had heard mass in Latin and professed loyalty to her sister's faith. She, like the majority, had dissembled her true religious views. For she was never a Protestant in the mould of Edward. Like her father, she appreciated religious ceremony and deplored the name-calling of bigots from both sides of the divide. And so, like Henry, Elizabeth wanted the middle way in religion, partly because she believed in it, and partly because she too saw it as the best defence of the Royal Supremacy, which she was determined to revive as her God-given right. Only once the explosive passions of religion were contained would the throne and Elizabeth's life be secure.

But Elizabeth's plans for a moderate religious settlement came under fire from both extremes, from Catholics in the Lords and Protestants in the Commons and council. Which group offered the best chance of pacifying England with a workable religious settlement? Extreme Protestantism was a danger for Elizabeth. It had gained a new, radical way of thinking during the dark days of Mary's reign. It saw those who had hidden their beliefs as enemies of true religion. It had its martyrs, Cranmer foremost among them. And there were many who thought that even the Edwardian Reformation had not gone far enough and that Cranmer had been cut down before the Church had become fully reformed, leaving it stranded midway between mild, watered-down Protestantism and Catholicism. Moreover, these enthusiastic Protestants did not like female rule and had worked out a theory of justifiable resistance to monarchs during Mary's reign. They were politically and personally offensive to Elizabeth. But, just the same, they were a bulwark against the Catholics, who opposed the Supremacy.

Finally, to overcome her Catholic peers and bishops, Elizabeth had to join forces with her Protestant commons and councillors. She duly got the settlement and the Supremacy, though with the narrowest of majorities in the Lords of three votes. The price, however, was her acceptance of Cranmer's second, much more radically Protestant Book of Common Prayer of 1552. In the infighting between the religious extremes, it seemed that Elizabeth's hope for moderate settlement had been lost.

The outcome of the parliament of 1559 had been a triumph for Cecil. He had outmanoeuvred and strongarmed the Catholics to restore the Royal Supremacy, and he had, so it seemed, outmanoeuvred Elizabeth as well, to bring back the full-blooded Protestantism of her brother Edward. Elizabeth was equal to the challenge, however. She insisted, against fierce opposition, on inserting the so-called Ornaments Rubric into the legislation. This empowered her, on her sole authority, as Supreme Governor of the Church, to retain traditional ceremonies, such as making the sign of the cross in baptism, and to require the clergy to wear traditional vestments, like the surplice and the cope. These vestiges of Catholicism were offensive to radical Protestants. If they had had their own way, they would have sped the Church of England on the road to extreme Protestantism of the kind that existed in Europe and Scotland – a Church without bishops and ceremonies. It was only the queen's personal supremacy which prevented this. Far from hurtling along the road of reform in the way that Edward and his supporters had envisioned, the Church of England was frozen in time. The result was a Church that was Protestant in doctrine, Catholic in appearance and which would, Elizabeth hoped, satisfy all but a handful of extremists on both sides.

And Elizabeth's hopes would almost certainly have been fulfilled but for the issue of the succession. It was the succession which had driven the giddy switchback course from Protestantism to Catholicism and back again, and it had the potential to do it again. It was clear to Cecil that the best way to secure the succession was for the queen to marry and produce an heir. But Elizabeth was less sure. She had seen how her half-sister's choice of a husband had sparked dissent and rebellion. Elizabeth determined that England would 'have one mistress and no master'.

But if Elizabeth could not and would not marry, who should succeed her? Her father's will had an answer for that too, for, if Elizabeth died childless, a clause prescribed that she should be succeeded by the descendants of her Aunt Mary, Henry's younger sister, the Greys.

But Elizabeth hated the Grey family, because they had helped put Jane Grey on the throne. Then Elizabeth had been publicly branded a bastard and barred from the succession. In revenge, she would never allow the throne to pass to a Grey. But what to do about her father's will? Her brother and her sister, to whom its terms were equally unacceptable, had challenged it head-on and failed. Elizabeth was subtler. The will was given one last public outing in the second parliament of the reign and then it was returned to the safe deposit of the treasury and put in an iron chest. And the key to the chest in effect was thrown away. It was a case of out of sight, out of mind.

With the lightest of touches Elizabeth had nudged her father's will into oblivion. This left as her most obvious heir her cousin Mary, the granddaughter of Henry's eldest sister Margaret. Mary was queen consort of France and queen of Scots in her own right. She was also a Catholic.

In August 1561, after the death of her husband, the French king, Mary, having spent most of her young life on the other side of the Channel, returned to Scotland as queen. Brought up among the splendours of the French court, Mary was far more interested in her claim to the English throne than her paltry Scottish inheritance, and in September she sent her personal emissary, Sir William Maitland, to negotiate directly with Elizabeth. His mission was to secure formal recognition of Mary's status as Elizabeth's heir.

Elizabeth was all graciousness in her private, face-to-face interviews with Maitland. She acknowledged that Mary was of the blood royal of England, was her cousin and her nearest living kinswoman, and that she loved her dearly. And she also, under Maitland's subtle prodding, went further. She knew, she said, no one with a better claim to be her successor than Mary, nor any that she preferred to her. She even swore that she would do nothing to impede Mary's claim. But the final step declaring Mary her heir, Elizabeth told a crestfallen Maitland plainly, she would never, ever take. But Elizabeth had already gone far too far for Cecil. He had lived through the reign of one Mary and her attempt to re-Catholicize England, and he was determined never to suffer another one.

Matters came to a head in the parliament of 1566, which attempted to force Elizabeth to name a successor, and by implication to exclude the claim of Mary Queen of Scots. Furious, Elizabeth summoned thirty members of each House to her palace in Whitehall, where she delivered an extraordinary speech.

Elizabeth was at her fiery, brilliant best. She would never name an heir, she said, because he or she would become 'second person'. And Elizabeth, better than anyone else, knew the danger of that position, since, as Mary's legally appointed heir, she had been 'second person' herself. As such, her own life had been in constant danger and she had been the focus of plots and treason. At this point Elizabeth became sharply personal. Many of the MPs, she said, turning to the Commons delegation, had been among the plotters, and only her own honour prevented her from naming names. Similarly, turning now to the Lords, she proclaimed that many of the bishops, under Jane Grey, had preached treasonably that she, Elizabeth, was a bastard. 'Well, I wish not for the death of any man,' she said, not altogether convincingly. No head can have felt too secure on its shoulders by the time the queen had finished.

The issue of the succession would bedevil Elizabeth's entire reign. Parliament was terrified that they would be faced with an interregnum on the queen's death. As history made clear, a throne with no known heir guaranteed civil war and bloodshed when the monarch died. What would become of the monarchy? Would the absence of a known heir turn England into an elective monarchy? Would the religion of the country have to change once more depending on who emerged as the successor? But Elizabeth knew equally well that the 'second person', however convenient for Parliament and the country, would be her worst enemy. If Mary was named as successor, her accession was a knife blow away – a tempting prospect for a foreign power or a Catholic.

But however much it was ignored or passed over as too dangerous to discuss openly, the problem of the succession wouldn't go away, and it was brought into sharp focus when a rebellion brought about by disgust at her scandalous personal life forced Mary to flee Scotland in May 1568 and seek Elizabeth's protection in England. The presence of Mary Queen of Scots in England would force Elizabeth into the very actions that she had tried so hard to avoid.

IV

Mary Queen of Scots' flight to England was a disaster for Elizabeth. In Scotland, Mary, despite her Catholicism, had been lukewarm about religion. She had lived with a Protestant government, and she had even taken a Protestant as her third husband. But in England it was a different story. Here Mary played up her Catholicism, and Catholics in turn identified with her.

The issue for both Mary and the English Catholics was the succession. Mary was Elizabeth's obvious heir because she was her closest relation, but Elizabeth steadfastly refused to recognize her as such. The implications for the monarchy were vast. If not Mary, then who would inherit the crown? For if the succession was not determined by unalterable descent of blood, what gave the monarchy its legitimacy and divine right to rule? Mary played on this sensitive issue. By bidding for Catholic support, she was hoping to force Elizabeth's hand, and, in turn, the prospect of an heir of their own faith gave English Catholics, who had almost lost hope, stomach for the fight once more. The spectre, which Elizabeth had striven so hard to lay to rest, of a 'second person' who differed in religion from the monarch was about to rise once more. And its baleful effects were to be quickly felt.

For the next twenty years Elizabeth was to keep Mary prisoner, moving her from one secure castle to another. In all that time the two queens never met. And as Elizabeth had foreseen, the plots soon began. Catholics saw Mary as a means back to power, and used her as a focus for rebellion. Despite her precarious position, Mary was naive enough to allow herself to be implicated in several of these plots. But Elizabeth refused to take action against Mary. Her instinct was to try to defuse the conflict, and above all she did not want Mary to become a martyr.

But Elizabeth's hopes of avoiding conflict were dashed when her middle way came under attack from both extremes. First to move was Rome with a papal edict or Bull, issued by the pope in 1570. Known by its opening words as *Regnans in Excelsis*, 'reigning on high', it sets out the most extreme version of the papal claim to rule 'all people and all kingdoms'. Then, for her defiance of this claim, it condemns Elizabeth; deposes and excommunicates her, and absolves all her subjects from their oath of allegiance.

The Bull was the Catholic version of the arguments of the Protestant Ponet, and, as with Ponet, its logical outcome was tyrannicide, the assassination or murder of the errant ruler. The pope had, in effect, declared war on Elizabeth by calling for her death. But two could play at that game, and Elizabeth's council responded in kind.

Violent times breed violent measures and few have been more violent than the Bond of Association. Drawn up by the Privy Council in 1584, the bond is a kind of licensed lynch law. If Elizabeth were to be assassinated in favour of any possible claimant to the throne, then those who took the bond swore to band together to 'prosecute such person or persons to the death' and 'to take the uttermost revenge upon them by any possible means'. Furthermore, the bond would forbid anyone on whose behalf such an assassination took place from succeeding to the English throne. Finally, for any Catholic rebel or foreign power that thought Mary would automatically succeed if Elizabeth met an untimely end, the bond made clear that the right of nominating an heir belonged to 'Elizabeth, the Queen's Majesty that now is, with and by the authority of the Parliament of England'. The Protestant nobility and gentry flocked to subscribe to the bond in their hundreds, as the masses of signed and sealed copies that survive at the Public Record Office show.

Mary wasn't mentioned by name in the bond but everybody knew she was the target. The bond was subsequently legalized by an Act of Parliament, which also set up a tribunal to determine her guilt or innocence. But Cecil had wanted to go much, much further and establish a Great Council to rule England in the event of an assassination and the inevitable interregnum that would follow. The Great Council would exercise all the royal powers and together with a recalled Parliament would choose the next monarch. This was a radical constitutional innovation. If a council in alliance with Parliament had the authority to choose monarchs, it would also have the authority to set conditions on them and challenge their subsequent actions. This was Ponet translated into a parliamentary statute, and Elizabeth was having none of it.

For Elizabeth saw the bond as being as offensive as *Regnans in Excelsis*, since it too set religion above the crown, and permitted subjects to judge a sovereign and elect a new one. But not even Elizabeth could protect Mary from her own folly or Cecil's vendetta. In 1586, Mary was lured into giving her explicit endorsement to a plot to assassinate Elizabeth. Faced with incontrovertible evidence of her guilt, Elizabeth was forced to agree to her trial and condemnation. She even signed the death warrant. But she gave instructions that the execution wasn't to be carried out without her further command. For once, Cecil did not obey his queen.

Instead, a secret meeting of the council was convened in his private rooms at court and, acting on their own authority, and in defiance of the queen's express command, the councillors dispatched the death warrant to Mary's prison at Fotheringhay Castle. There, in the Great Hall, Mary was publicly beheaded. She died magnificently, clutching the crucifix and wearing a scarlet petticoat as a martyr to her Catholic faith.

But the removal of a threat to the monarchy and the Church of England had serious implications. Queen regnant anointed by God though she was, Mary had been publicly executed like any other common criminal. The 'divinity that doth hedge a King', which Elizabeth had fought so hard to preserve, had evaporated, never to return.

The execution of Mary was a watershed. Henry and his three children had sought to reshape the religion of England according to their own preferences. But as a fierce, nationalistic Protestantism took root in England, it was becoming clear that a monarch or an heir who fell too far out of step with the religious prejudices of the nation would do so at their peril. The dangerous liaison between monarchy and religion had claimed its first royal victim in Mary Queen of Scots. She would not be the last.

17

REBELLION

Elizabeth I, James VI & I,
Charles I

IN AUGUST 1588, Europe was convulsed by religious war, and Protestant England faced the world's foremost Catholic power. With the Spanish Armada in the Channel and a large and fearsomely professional Spanish army in the Low Countries, England was under dire threat.

On 18 August Queen Elizabeth came to review her troops at Tilbury. She wore a breastplate and carried a sword and addressed them in words that have echoed down the centuries: 'I know I have the body of a weak and feeble woman, but I have the heart and stomach of a King, and of a King of England too; and think foul scorn that Parma or Spain or any Prince of Europe should dare invade the border of my realm.'

But even as the queen spoke, the moment of danger had passed. The English fireships had broken up the Armada's 'invincible' formation off Calais, and coastal storms would do the rest. Nevertheless, despite the defeat of the Spanish Armada, England would not escape the horrors of religious war, and some of those who had heard Elizabeth at Tilbury might live long enough to see another English monarch raise his banner in defiance on English soil. But this time the king's enemies would not be foreign princes, but his own people.

I

Within a generation the monarchy was to move from a position of strength under the Tudors to abject weakness under the Stuart succession. With the defeat of the Spanish Armada, Elizabeth's reputation stood at a zenith at home and abroad. Even Pope Sixtus V, who had helped finance the Armada expedition, expressed his admiration of her and regretted only that they were unable to have children together! Inheriting their combined talents, he said, their offspring would rule the world.

Defending the realm was the most fundamental duty of an English monarch and Elizabeth had acquitted herself admirably. But, by virtue of the Crown Imperial, she had a further responsibility. She also had different opponents and they were at home. As time moved on from the dizzying religious convulsions that had engulfed England since Henry took the momentous step of assuming the Supremacy, it was becoming increasingly clear that the monarchy's power over religion was a double-edged sword. The problem was not now simply Protestant against Catholic but also Protestant against different kinds of Protestants. As queen, Elizabeth presided over a national Protestant Church and, as Supreme Governor, she made religion in her own image. It was a right that she affirmed came direct from God. Could Elizabeth, mere woman that she was, maintain this lofty claim? And how could she, as Supreme Head of the Church, avoid being drawn into the religious conflict, which threatened to turn quarrels about religion into disputes with the crown?

Elizabeth did her best in establishing a Church of England that was Protestant in its doctrines but Catholic in the appearance of its ceremonies and clerical dress. Elizabeth's policy was successful in heading off much Catholic opposition, but it had the opposite effect of opening up divisions on the Protestant side between those who wanted the rigorous, stripped-down Protestantism of the Continent and Scotland, and those who followed Elizabeth in her attachment to bishops and ceremonies.

This was not a struggle between government and opposition; rather it was a schism within the highest ranks of the Elizabethan establishment, with Elizabeth's chief minister and eldest confidant, William Cecil, on one side, and her archbishop of Canterbury, William Whitgift, on the other. The bad feeling between the two men burst into the open in the queen's own presence, and Elizabeth came down publicly and heavily on Whitgift's side.

Matters of religion, she insisted, were for her and her bishops alone. Neither the council nor Parliament had any say in the matter. Instead, since her Supremacy over the Church came to her from God alone, she was answerable only to God in how she chose to exercise it. This was Henry VIII's high view of the Royal Supremacy, and in sticking to it Elizabeth showed herself every inch her father's daughter.

But this version of the Church would, as everyone knew, last only as long as the queen's life. Would the next monarch continue the difficult but necessary balancing act of the middle way in religion after the ageing Elizabeth died? Or would he or she impose a new version of Protestantism on the Church? Her nearest blood relation was King James VI of Scotland. Son of a Catholic mother, but brought up in the rigorous and austere Protestant Kirk, the possibility of James's accession aroused wildly contrasting hopes. While he was still only a claimant, he could flatter them all. But when – *if* – he became a king of England, he would have to choose which way the Church of England would go.

Born in 1566, James was the only child of Mary Queen of Scots' disastrous marriage to Lord Darnley. His mother, widely suspected of murdering his father, had been forced to flee to England by a Protestant revolt. James would never see her again. Instead, the Scottish nobility and Kirk saw the baby as a king they could mould into a monarch of their own choosing. They intended that, king from the cradle, he would have none of the absolutist pretensions of other monarchs and none of his mother's Catholicism. The very first coins of James's reign showed him carrying an oversized sword; the motto read, in reference to the sword, *pro me si mereor in me*, 'for me, but against me if I deserve it'. James was crowned at the parish kirk at Stirling on 29 July 1567, when he was just thirteen months old. He was king of Scotland in his own right, despite the fact that his mother was still alive. He was also heir to Mary's claims to the English throne.

This boy, of great rank and greater prospects still, was largely brought up at Stirling Castle. It was a strange, insecure kind of childhood. A series of regents who ruled Scotland on his behalf were murdered in quick succession, and the boy's own life was more than once in danger. On his fourth birthday, a tutor arrived at Stirling Castle, charged with the responsibilities of creating a king in his own image. George Buchanan was a scholar known throughout Europe, and through him James would have one of the most rigorous and academic educations possible. Dour and self-opinionated, Buchanan was also a leading figure in the Scottish Presbyterian Kirk. He and his fellow Presbyterians believed that the supreme authority in the state was not the king, as it was in England, but the General Assembly of clergy.

Kings also, Buchanan believed, were mere servants of their people, who could and should be punished if they misbehaved. Indeed, his hatred of monarchy was not even disguised and, in his little pupil, he had a convenient target to hand. Like many sixteenth-century teachers, Buchanan thought that sparing the rod spoiled the child, especially if that child was a king, and he set about beating and birching his beliefs and learning into King James with gusto. It was a kind of pre-emptive punishment of a ruling monarch, intended to beat out any residual monarchical pretensions. Buchanan was charged with creating a Scottish monarch out of the small boy, one who would submit to the authority of the Kirk and the dominant Scottish lords and learn that kings were not absolute or possessed of divine powers, but weak-minded mortals. And, as James would in all probability be king of England one day, zealous Protestantism would be immeasurably strengthened there as well.

This treatment indeed succeeded in making James a considerable scholar. But in terms of religion and politics, it produced only an equal and opposite reaction to which James was able to give expression with unusual force and clarity when he grew up.

And the result was a work of scholarship that rejected every aspect of Buchanan's anti-monarchical lessons. It is called *The Trew Law of Free Monarchies*, which James wrote and published in 1598. In it, he says succinctly: 'Kings are called Gods; they are appointed by God and answerable only to God.' James grounded these assertions, just as Henry VIII had his claim to the Royal Supremacy, in the biblical story of the Old Testament kings. But James went beyond even Henry VIII by claiming that kings were accountable to no human law at all, above all in affairs of state. They were bound by God's laws, and were answerable to Him only. This was what he meant by a 'free monarchy'. Subjects, for their part, had the obligation to treat kings as if they were God's representatives and judges on Earth. To act against the king was to rebel against God.

But all this was fantasy in Scotland, where James had neither money nor following with which to challenge the dominance of the Kirk and the aristocracy. Here his grandiose claim of divine majesty was a reaction to a situation in which he was one of many competing powers in the kingdom. Only in England, where kings were indeed supreme, could he hope to realize his vision of monarchy. But his claim to the English throne was not secure. Just as Elizabeth had refused to name Mary Queen of Scots as her heir, so she refused to name James, terrified that if the succession were known an attempt would be made on her life. James was, for her, a 'false Scotch urchin', and he was left waiting.

But matters were taken out of her hands. In 1601, with the ageing queen's health beginning to fail, Elizabeth's leading ministers began to make moves to secure James's path to the throne. A successor had to be established before the queen's death, or else there would be an interregnum, perhaps a violent one. James was closest in blood to Elizabeth. He had to succeed to keep intact the claims of the monarchy to be a divine institution for which God provided a known line of successors. Worried Englishmen looked back wistfully to Henry VIII, who had left a will and an Act of Parliament ensuring that the crown would pass peacefully through the generations. But that certainty was at an end while Elizabeth retained the authority to nominate a successor but kept silent. Indubitable succession by the closest relative was historically the most peaceful method. The alternatives were horrifying. In the past kings had taken the crown by conquest, civil war or election when the succession was in dispute. The spectre of ambitious families jostling for supreme power brought to mind the Wars of the Roses.

The matter became pressing during the Christmas holidays of 1603, when both Elizabeth's health and her temper suddenly worsened. In mid-January she moved to Richmond for a change of air, but within a few weeks she was clearly dying. She lay on a pile of cushions on the floor of her privy chamber, refusing to eat and unable to sleep. Finally she was carried to her bed, became speechless and died in the small hours of the morning of 24 March after Archbishop Whitgift had lulled her into her last sleep with his impassioned prayers.

Elizabeth had restored Protestantism, preserved the Royal Supremacy, protected her country from invasion, and allowed nothing to challenge either her crown or her popularity. Above all, her studiously broad religious settlement had brought peace, though at the inevitable price of alienating extremes of all forms. With the Great Queen dead, all eyes now turned to Scotland and to James.

II

James VI of Scotland was proclaimed king of England within eight hours of Elizabeth's death. And his first parliament proclaimed that he was by 'inherent birth right and undoubted and lawful succession' the successor to the Imperial Crown of England and Scotland. It sounded good because it retained the monarchy's constitutional position. But it was a dangerous doctrine since it implied that James's title to the throne was above and beyond the law, as of course James himself, as the author of *The Trew Law of Free Monarchies*, firmly believed.

In April 1603, James arrived in London in triumph, the undoubted heir of his great-great-grandfather, Henry VII. Henry VII had commissioned the Imperial Crown as the symbol of the recovery of the monarchy from the degradation of the Wars of the Roses. Now James, the first ruler of all Britain, would endow it with a larger significance still. James's aim was to be *rex pacificus*, the peacemaker king. He had ensured the smooth passage of the crown without bloodshed. He would reconcile Catholic and Protestant, thus re-establishing Christian unity at home and abroad. He would end England's debilitating war with Spain, and above all he would terminate the ancient feud between England and Scotland, and fuse instead the two warring kingdoms into a new, greater united realm of Britain. It was an enormously ambitious programme, and to realize it James, in a strikingly modern gesture, summoned three major conferences on peace, religion and union with Scotland.

The peace conference and ensuing treaty at Somerset House were commemorated in a notable painting, which shows the English and Spanish delegates confronting each other across a richly carpeted table. Through its successful outcome James ended the twenty-year war with Catholic Spain. It was an auspicious start for James the international peacemaker. But the result, paradoxically, was trouble at home. On the one hand, the Somerset House treaty meant that the hotter Protestants were shocked to discover that England, now at peace with the leading Catholic power, would no longer be the champion of their fellow

Protestants in Europe. And, on the other hand, the more extreme Catholics were equally dismayed to find out that Spain had not exacted toleration for Catholics as a price of the peace. Abandoned by their allies abroad, such Catholics turned in desperation to direct action at home.

At the beginning of November 1605, James was shown a tip-off letter warning that the political establishment of England would receive a 'terrible blow' in the parliament he was due to open on 5 November. James immediately appreciated that the wording of the letter pointed to an explosion. But in order to catch the plotters red-handed it was decided not to search the vaults under the Parliament chamber until the night of the fourth.

At 11 p.m. the search party entered and found a man standing guard over a pile of firewood, thirty-five barrels of gunpowder and with a fuse in his pocket. His name was Guy Fawkes. If the gunpowder had exploded as planned it would have been the ultimate terrorist bombing, wiping out most of the British royal family and the entire English political establishment.

Nevertheless, the immediate political consequences were small. To James's credit there was no widespread persecution of Catholics in England and the peace with Spain held. But in the longer term the plot played an important part in the development of the anti-Catholic myth in England. At this early stage of the seventeenth century the reality was that English Catholicism was a beleaguered minority faith. But in the fevered imagination of the hotter sort of Protestants it became instead the fifth column of a vast international politico-religious conspiracy masterminded by the pope in Rome and aiming not only at the conversion of England but at the subversion of English Protestantism and English freedoms by the foulest possible means.

And so, at the second of James's great conferences, held at Hampton Court in January 1604 to determine the nature of religious settlement under James, those hot Protestants, known pejoratively as Puritans, demanded that the English Church be purged of what they regarded as its damnable popish elements, which had been retained by Elizabeth. But they reckoned without the seductive powers of the English monarchy and the English Royal Supremacy.

In Scotland, James VI had sat in the body of a church as the preacher 'bore down upon him, calling the king but God's silly vassal'. Another time the minister of St Andrews said that 'all kings are devils' children'. He was lectured that as far as the General Assembly of the Presbyterian Kirk went, he was not a king or master, but a member equal with all the rest. But in England it was the same man, now known as King James I, who sat on high in the Chapel Royal, enthroned in a magnificent royal pew while the preacher, under correction, went about his humbler task far below. It was the most graphic possible illustration of the power of the Royal Supremacy, which James was determined to keep in England and, if he could, extend to Scotland.

Instead of making the Church of England more like the Scottish Kirk, therefore, as the Puritans had hoped, James used the Hampton Court conference to proclaim that he was satisfied with the Elizabethan religious settlement, and was resolved to keep it, as it stood. Beaten by Buchanan and hectored by zealous Presbyterians, James associated Puritanism with disloyalty to monarchy. He would not, any more than Elizabeth, soften Whitgift's hard line in enforcing ceremonies and vestments, which the Puritans thought scandalously Catholic. And, above all, he would allow not an inch of movement by bishops away from the English government of the Church towards a role for assemblies of presbyteries or clergy as in Scotland. 'No Bishop, No King,' he summed up memorably.

He even managed to subvert the Puritans' demands for a new translation of the Bible. James eagerly agreed, since he detested the so-called Geneva version of the Bible, which was then used by Presbyterians in Scotland and Puritans in England, because of its marginal notes, which show typically hot Protestant disrespect for kings and queens. The King James version of the Bible, on the other hand, as the large and learned team of translators explained in the preface, was to tread soberly the middle way between 'popish persons' on one hand and 'self-conceited brethren' – that is, the Puritans – on the other. Thus this monument of the English language was born out of a long-dead politico-theological dispute, and it is the only classic to have been written by committee. Nevertheless, the King James Bible became the book which, more than any other, shaped the English language and formed the English mind.

James's other lasting legacy was to be the union of the crowns of England and Scotland, and he set out his case in a speech from the throne at the opening of his first English Parliament in March 1604. His succession had united the kingdoms of England and Scotland, ending the ancient divisions of the island of Britain. It was, said James, impossible to rule two countries, 'the one great, the other a less'. It would be easier 'for one head to govern two bodies, or one man to be husband of two wives'. Moreover, the king claimed, these divisions were largely in the mind. Were not England and Scotland already united by a common language, the Protestant religion and similar customs and manners? Was not the border practically indistinguishable on the ground? It was as though God had always intended the union to happen.

To resist union, therefore, James concluded, was not simply impolitic but impious: it was to put asunder kingdoms that God Himself had joined together. But the English Parliament, impolitically and impiously, decided to look the gift horse of union in the mouth. Partly their decision was governed by straightforward anti-Scottish xenophobia. But more fundamental causes were involved as well. These centred on James's apparently innocuous wish to rename the Anglo-Scottish kingdom 'Britain'.

A new name meant a new kingdom. It would, one MP said, be like a freshly conquered territory in the New World. There would be no laws and no customs and James, by his own rules in *The Trew Law of Free Monarchies*, would be free to set himself up as an absolute, supra-national emperor of Great Britain. The English Parliament, in contrast, would be left as a mere provincial assembly. It was not an enticing prospect for MPs, who saw themselves as the Great Council of the realm.

James's reaction to their opposition was to try to enact the union symbolically, using his own powers under the royal prerogative. By proclamation he assumed the title of king of Great Britain. He restyled the royal coat of arms, with the lion of England balanced by the unicorn of Scotland, and he insisted on a British flag, known as the Jack after the Latin form of the name James, again by proclamation. But not content with symbols, James also practised a kind of union by stealth. The English political elite had prevented him from establishing an evenly balanced Anglo-Scots council. But a king could do what he liked with his own court. So, in revenge, James filled his bedchamber, the inner ring of his court, almost exclusively with Scots. It was a pleasure, since James took a more than fatherly interest in braw Scots lads with well-turned legs and firm buttocks. But it also suited him politically since it compelled proud

Henry IV claiming the vacant throne after the deposition of Richard II in 1399. Henry, heir of John of Gaunt, duke of Lancaster, had played a leading part in the opposition to Richard II. In punishment, Richard had exiled him and, after his father's death, confiscated his vast estates. This proved a step too far and Henry overthrew Richard with ease. But he never lived down the stain of usurpation and Richard's subsequent murder.

Henry V, in a Tudor copy of a contemporary portrait. Driven, intensely religious, highly educated and a superb administrator, as well as a great general and leader of men, Henry was the ideal medieval king. He laid the ghosts of his father's usurpation and swept to victory in a divided France. But he died at the moment of triumph, leaving an infant son as heir to both England and France.

Henry VI at prayer before the Virgin, with the lords and commons. Henry, scarred by his long minority, showed himself indifferent, if not actually hostile, to his father's legacy and devoted himself instead to works of piety, as here in the charter recording his foundation of King's College, Cambridge.

Edward IV and Queen Elizabeth Woodville with their family of two sons and five daughters in a stained glass window at Canterbury Cathedral. Edward of York, tall, strapping, an insatiable womanizer and descended twice over from Edward III, was everything that Henry VI was not. Even so, it took ten years and the bloodletting of the battle of Tewkesbury in 1471 before his throne was secure.

Richard III in a near-contemporary portrait that hints at the complexities of his character. Youngest and apparently most loyal brother of Edward IV, Richard took advantage of the unpopularity of the Woodvilles to usurp the throne and dispose of Edward's two sons.

The family of Henry VII with St George and the dragon. A few months after his victory against Richard III at Bosworth, Henry married Elizabeth of York, the eldest daughter of Edward IV. But the promised reconciliation of York and Lancaster never materialized and Henry was always plagued with pretenders.

Catherine of Aragon in a miniature by Lucas Horenbout. Henry VIII married Catherine immediately after his accession in 1509. But she aged badly and, in 1527, Henry decided to divorce her – at any cost.

The title page of the first official English translation of the Bible, in which an enthroned Henry VIII distributes the Bible to both clergy and lay-folk, shows what the Royal Supremacy meant in practice.

The cost turned out to be a break with Rome and a thousand years of English history as Henry declared himself supreme head of the Church. It was the most fundamental reshaping of English kingship since the Norman Conquest, as shown in this copy of Holbein's dynastic mural of the first two Tudor kings and their wives, who are grouped round a monument inscribed with their rival claims to greatness: Henry VII for ending the Wars of the Roses; Henry VIII for establishing the Royal Supremacy.

The family of Henry VIII, with (LEFT TO RIGHT) Mary, Edward, his third wife, Jane Seymour, and Elizabeth. Henry's decision to leave the throne to each of his children in turn condemned England to wild religious swings.

Henry VIII on his deathbed, handing over power to the regime of the boy king Edward VI. Led at first by Edward's maternal uncle, Edward Seymour, duke of Somerset (standing at Edward's left), the government supported Archbishop Thomas Cranmer in introducing more and more radical Protestantism.

This *Allegory of the Tudor Succession* contrasts the reigns of Mary and Elizabeth. Mary and her husband Philip of Spain, accompanied by Mars, bring war abroad and persecution at home; Elizabeth, escorted by Minerva and Ceres, brings peace, plenty and Protestantism.

Mary, Queen of Scots, granddaughter of Henry VIII and heir presumptive to the English throne. Her behaviour in Scotland as spoiled seductress (LEFT) led to her flight to England. There she became a Catholic rallying point (RIGHT) and undid Elizabeth's attempt, hitherto successful, to return to Protestantism without violence or persecution.

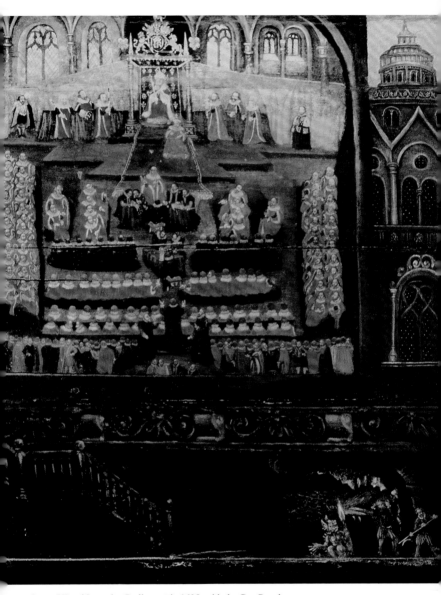

James VI and I opening Parliament in 1605, with the Gun Powder plotters below. James, son of Mary, Queen of Scots, succeeded Elizabeth I peacefully in 1603. He made peace with Spain, rode out the Catholic terrorist threat of the Gun Powder Plot without reverting to mass persecution and tried but failed to turn his dual kingship of England and Scotland into the unified state of Great Britain.

Charles I, Henrietta Maria and their two eldest children, Charles (later Charles II) and Mary (mother to the future William III). On the table is the massive, jewel-encrusted Imperial Crown of the Tudors and in the background a view of the royal palaces of Whitehall and Westminster. But Charles's mishandling of religious tensions both in England and between England and Scotland led to parliamentary revolt and civil war.

Oliver Cromwell as lord general. Cromwell's generalship led to the defeat and capture of Charles I and turned the army into a new force in English politics. It was the army which forced through the execution of Charles I on 30 January 1649 (BELOW), the abolition of kingship and the elevation of Cromwell to power as military dictator. But, in order to legitimate his rule, Cromwell more and more surrounded himself with the trappings of royalty and his funeral effigy was actually crowned.

Two years after Cromwell's death, the Stuart monarchy was restored and Charles II tried to efface the memory of the Interregnum by putting on a fine show: the Coronation Procession was magnificent and the regalia, which had been destroyed by the Parliamentarians, was remade as closely as possible after the old models.

William of Orange was determined to topple the power of autocratic Catholic France. His chance came in 1688 when, as the husband of James II's elder Protestant daughter Mary (BELOW), William launched a successful invasion of England, and with Britain's power added to that of the Netherlands, began a second Hundred Years War against France.

The Apotheosis of William and Mary. Sir James Thornhill's ceiling in the Painted Hall of the Royal Naval Hospital at Greenwich employs the visual language of Louis XIV's Catholic absolutism to celebrate his defeat at the hands of the limited Protestant monarchy which was established in England after the Glorious Revolution of 1688. William, with Mary at his side, is borne aloft in the centre, as he uses a barbaric-looking Louis as his footstool.

But succession was a problem once more: Anne, Mary's younger sister, succeeded the childless William and Mary but her only surviving child, shown with her, had already died.

In view of the childlessness of Anne, it was decided to pass over fifty Catholic claimants and give the throne to the Protestant George, Elector of Hanover, the grandson of James VI and I's daughter Elizabeth. George, who landed at Greenwich in 1714, enjoyed a trouble-free accession, while his son and grandson, who appear beside him, guaranteed the continuity of the new, thoroughly German dynasty.

The failure of the war against American Independence to which George III (ABOVE LEFT) had been deeply opposed, made the king very unpopular. Conversely, the war against revolutionary France highlighted his modestly straightforward virtues and made him, even in his long years of senility (ABOVE RIGHT), Father of the Nation.

The Coronation Banquet of King George IV in Westminster Hall was the most magnificent – and the last – in English history. George, who became king in 1820 after serving as Prince Regent for a decade, was indolent, wildly extravagant and quarrelled very publicly with his wife. But his building works – at Windsor, Buckingham Palace and the West End of London – created the setting of the modern monarchy and turned London into an imperial capital.

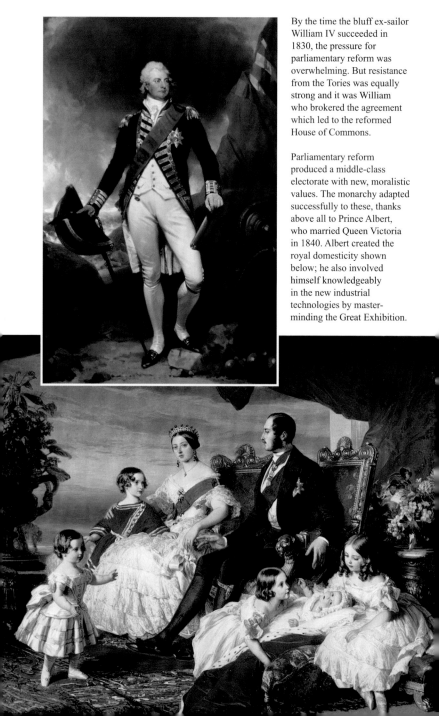

By the time the bluff ex-sailor William IV succeeded in 1830, the pressure for parliamentary reform was overwhelming. But resistance from the Tories was equally strong and it was William who brokered the agreement which led to the reformed House of Commons.

Parliamentary reform produced a middle-class electorate with new, moralistic values. The monarchy adapted successfully to these, thanks above all to Prince Albert, who married Queen Victoria in 1840. Albert created the royal domesticity shown below; he also involved himself knowledgeably in the new industrial technologies by master-minding the Great Exhibition.

George V, shown here preparing to give a radio broadcast from a room at Sandringham House, *c.* 1933, was happy to forge an alliance between the monarchy and the recently formed British Broadcasting Corporation.

George VI, with his close-knit family whom he called 'Us Four', exemplified the family values which his brother, Edward VIII, had so flagrantly defied. Here he relaxes with his wife, the queen consort Elizabeth, and his children, Princesses Elizabeth and Margaret at the Royal Lodge, Windsor.

The events of 1992 shook, or seemed to shake, the House of Windsor to its foundations. Queen Elizabeth II, seen here with firemen inspecting the damage after the fire at Windsor Castle, described it as an 'Annus Horribilis'.

Diana – alone – in front of the Taj Mahal, the symbol of marital love and fidelity. Following the breakdown of her marriage to Prince Charles, Diana's uncanny ability to play the tabloid press not only won her overwhelming public sympathy, it also destroyed the carefully crafted image of the Windsor Family Monarchy. The monarchy has not yet found another, equally powerful 'narrative'.

Englishmen to sue his Scots favourites for patronage and to bribe them as well.

But James's policy of union by stealth had a fatal flaw. He had inherited a substantial debt from Elizabeth. He had a large family to maintain, and he wanted to continue pouring money, and, to his eyes, his new-found wealth, on his favourites and his pleasures. For all this, the crown's so-called 'ordinary income' from land and custom duties was hopelessly inadequate. There was no choice but to ask Parliament to vote money. The English Parliament, however, saw no reason why taxpayers' money – their money – should end up in the pockets of Scots favourites, and they said so rather crudely. How, asked one MP, could the cistern of the treasury ever be filled up if money continued to 'flow thence by private Cocks'? 'Cocks' meant taps and, well, what it means now …

So James's project for British union remained an unfulfilled dream, while his relations with Parliament, which he thought he could master, turned into a disaster. The king was forced to fall back on his scriptural argument about the divine rights of kings. And, mundanely enough, the issue was tax. Blocked by Parliament in his pursuit of an adequate income, James used his prerogative to levy money from indirect taxation. Many saw this as unconstitutional, but, backed by the opinions of judges, James got his own way. But it meant a head-on collision with Parliament. If ever an English king managed to raise enough money by indirect means without consent, MPs reasoned, he would be able to dispense with parliaments altogether and reign as a tyrant.

Addressing Parliament in 1610, James went far beyond all his predecessors in arguing for his rights as king. Although he would respect Parliament, he said, MPs had no right to question his prerogative of taxing without consent. It may have been a constitutional or legal matter, but James went one step further. 'The state of monarchy is the supremest thing upon earth,' he told Parliament; 'for kings are not only God's lieutenants upon earth, and sit upon God's throne, but even by God Himself they are called gods.' James had after all been brought up a scholar, and this was the intellectual justification for what he was doing. He would not turn the monarchy into quite the absolutist institution which many were coming to fear would be the ultimate outcome of the Stuart succession. But that was because of his moderation and not because of any limitation on his quasi-divine majesty.

But James's words fell on deaf or deliberately uncomprehending ears. And, faced by widespread obstruction, by the time of his death, in 1625, he had retreated into a sort of internal exile, abandoning the task of government, and secluding himself with his favourites and horses at Newmarket. Nevertheless, he had managed, by a mixture of tact, duplicity and masterful inaction, to stick to the middle ground and hold together the warring extremes of the Church of England on the one hand and the differing religious policies of England and Scotland on the other. The result was a smooth succession on both sides of the border of James's son Charles to the glittering inheritance of the Imperial Crown of Great Britain. Within a decade and a half, Charles, by his intransigence and his ineptitude, had thrown it all away.

III

Charles was crowned king of England at Westminster Abbey on 2 February 1626. For James, divine right had been an intellectual position; for Charles it was an emotional and religious one. This was immediately made clear by his coronation service, which, meticulously organized by the up-and-coming cleric William Laud, lovingly reproduced all the splendour, solemnity and sacred mysteries of the medieval Catholic rite.

The ceremony is one of the best-documented as well as the best-organized of coronations thanks to the survival of two fascinating service books. One is Charles's own copy of the coronation service, which he used to follow the ceremony. The other is Laud's version of the same text, which he used as a kind of score to conduct the service. He also made notes in the margins in a different-coloured ink to record unusual features of the ceremony as it actually took place.

These notes take us into Charles's own mind. During the five-hour ceremony the king was invested with the carefully preserved robes and regalia of Edward the Confessor, the last sainted Anglo-Saxon king, and Charles's attitude to these ancient relics was unique. Laud notes that he insisted on placing his feet inside the sacred buskins or sandals which were normally only touched against the royal leg, and that he actually used, apparently for the only time in the 1500-year history of the corona-tion, the Anglo-Saxon ivory comb to tidy his hair after he had been anointed on the head with the holy oil.

This wasn't mere idle curiosity or historical re-enactment for its own sake. Instead Charles was treating each and every item of the regalia as a holy sacrament of monarchy. With each touch of the precious oils and the ancient fabrics, jewels and comb, God was washing away the merely human in him and leaving him purely, indefeasibly and absolutely a king. Or so Charles at least thought.

Charles, as his behaviour at his coronation would suggest, was an aesthete, a lover of beauty, elegance and order. His tutor had been chosen not for his scholarship but for his taste in fashion, and Charles himself grew up to be not only fastidious in dress and manners but also the greatest connoisseur ever to have sat on the throne of England. He built up a staggering collection of paintings and he commissioned portraits of himself and his family from the greatest contemporary artists, such as Sir Anthony van Dyck. And it is van Dyck above all who shows us Charles as he wanted to be, suggesting the grandeur of his kingship on the one hand and the Christ-like wisdom and self-sacrifice with which he hoped to rule on the other. It masked the reality. Charles was short of stature, weak and shy. Even when he was a teenager, his father nicknamed him 'Baby Charles'. The lustre of majesty with which Charles surrounded himself was intended to make up for his personal failings.

Like most royal heirs, Charles defined himself by espousing policies that were the opposite of his father's. Throughout his reign, James had been unfavourably compared with Elizabeth, the queen who had defeated the Armada. Throughout his reign, many had wanted a war to help the beleaguered and persecuted Protestants of France, Denmark, the Low Countries and Germany. Charles was pro-war, but Parliament, despite its vocal enthusiasm for a Protestant crusade in Europe, was never prepared to vote enough taxation to make war an affordable option. Frustrated by Parliament's unwillingness to put its money where its Protestant mouth was, Charles, instead of fighting the Catholic French, married the French, and of course Catholic, princess Henrietta Maria in 1626. On account of Henrietta Maria's religion the marriage was extremely unpopular with Parliament. It didn't even succeed in cementing an alliance with France.

The result was that Charles soon found himself in the worst of all possible worlds – without money, with a Catholic wife and fighting a hopeless war against both major Catholic powers, France and Spain. Charles, looking for a scapegoat for the debacle, found it in what he saw as Parliament's sullen obstructiveness. He decided that parliaments were more trouble than they were worth and that in future he would rule without them.

All over Europe, monarchs were dispensing with parliaments. So in attempting personal rule, Charles was simply following the European trend. But unlike his European counterparts, he lacked the legal ability to tax his subjects at will. Only Parliament could legislate new taxes. So, like his father before him, Charles's only recourse was to squeeze more revenue out of his customary rights and prerogatives. In order to launch a campaign to save the French Protestants persecuted by France, he asked for a 'Free Gift' from his subjects. In reality it was a forced loan, raised by threats. The subsequent campaign was a disaster, and much of the money, rather than being used to raise and support soldiers, was spent on the royal art collection.

Those who bravely refused the 'Free Gift' were sent to prison. As the 1630s continued, the unconstitutional methods of revenue-gathering, the threat to liberty and the flagrant waste of money on rash military adventures hardened parliamentary opinion against Charles. The king seemed to be augmenting his wealth at the expense of freedom. Parliament would not vote him money unless he gave guarantees that he would rule constitutionally. Parliament's attitude, in turn, hardened Charles. He resolved to rule regardless of its obstructiveness and belligerence. Fortunately, he had a crack team of lawyers to help him.

The most ingenious of Charles's lawyers was the Attorney General, William Noy. 'I moil in the law' was the anagram of his name, and he moiled – that is toiled or laboured – in the legal archives to great effect. His masterpiece was ship money.

Ship money was a traditional levy imposed on the port towns to raise vessels for the navy in times of war, as, for example, against the Spanish Armada in the heyday of Elizabethan England. This was uncontroversial, but Attorney General Noy said that the law allowed the king to extend ship money from the ports to the inland counties and to impose it in peacetime as well as in war. All this at the king's mere say-so. The extended ship money was first imposed in 1634, and within a year it was yielding over £200,000 annually and producing 90 per cent of what the king demanded. This was the Holy Grail of royal administration, which had eluded English kings ever since the Middle Ages: a large-scale permanent income which came in regularly, year by year, without the bother of consulting troublesome parliaments.

Those who refused to pay the tax on the grounds that it was unconstitutional soon found themselves confronted with the full force of royal government. The MP John Hampden was one of these people. His trial was a test case for Charles's new style of government by royal decree. Hampden was found guilty and the judge ruled that the king might levy money whenever he liked 'for the preservation of the safety of the commonwealth'. Without this power, one of the judges continued, 'I do not understand how the King's Majesty may be said to have the magisterial right and power of a free monarch'. But for a growing number of people, the king's actions marked the beginning of absolute royal government. It appeared that Charles had the right to confiscate private property and punish people at will. All legal and property rights were at his mercy. 'Grant him this,' wrote John Milton of extra-parliamentary levies, 'and the Parliament hath no more freedom than if it sat in his Noose, which when he pleased to draw together with one twitch of his Negative, shall throttle a whole Nation.'

The idea of taxing without any parliamentary consent was bound to cause grievances, as James I had found. But Charles exacerbated matters still further by attempting religious innovation at the same time.

Whatever the formal rules of the Church of England, many of the parish churches in the country had seen the development of a stripped-down fundamentalist Protestantism, very little different in practice from the Scottish Kirk. But a richer, more ceremonious vision had been preserved in a handful of places, in particular the Chapels Royal and the greater cathedrals. Here there were choirs, organs and music, candles and gold and silver plate on the communion tables, and rich vestments for the clergy. William Laud, now Charles's archbishop of Canterbury, determined to use the Royal Supremacy to impose this opulent religious tradition on the whole country. He did so because he thought religion should be about sacraments as well as sermons, and appeal to the senses as well as to the mind. Above all he wanted to stamp out the menace of Puritanism that was gaining a hold on the Church.

In England some welcomed the new policy, but many more saw it as an assault on the very essence of their beliefs and a covert attempt to re-Catholicize the Church. Had not Charles married a Catholic? And had he not failed to help European Protestants? It all began to seem like a sinister conspiracy. But, despite some foot-dragging and grumbling, there was little overt resistance. Emboldened, Charles and Laud decided the policy should be extended to Scotland as well. Here the Reformation had been far more thoroughgoing and radical and the risks of change were correspondingly greater. But Charles, confident as ever in his God-given rightness, was undeterred. He decided that a barely modified version of the English Book of Common Prayer should be used throughout Scotland. And he did so on his own personal authority without consulting either the Scottish Parliament or the General Assembly of the Kirk. Charles was behaving as though he were the Supreme Governor of the Scottish Kirk. But would the Scottish Presbyterians accept his authority?

The answer came on Sunday, 28 July 1637, when the new prayer book was used for the first time in St Giles Cathedral in Edinburgh in the presence of the assembled Privy Council of Scotland. As soon as the dean had begun the service a great shout erupted from the crowds at the back of the church. Heavy clasped Bibles and folding stools were hurled at the councillors and the clergy, and the rioters were ejected from the church by the guards only with difficulty. And even outside they continued pounding on the doors and pelting the windows, until the service was finished.

It was the same throughout Scotland wherever the prayer book was used. Then the protest turned political. And in Greyfriars Kirk in Edinburgh an influential group of citizens and noblemen drew up and signed an undertaking to resist Charles and 'the innovations and evils' he had introduced into the Kirk. Borrowing the name from God's solemn compact with the Jews in the Old Testament, the undertaking was known as the Covenant, and its adherents were called Covenanters.

The scene at Greyfriars was repeated in churches all over the Lowlands. It was now the Covenanters, not Charles, who controlled Scotland. Britain, which so far had escaped the wars of religion that had devastated much of the rest of Europe, now faced the horrors of sectarian conflict on its own soil. The Covenanters demanded that Charles withdraw what they saw as a Catholic prayer book and all the rituals and innovations. But Charles would not tolerate any challenge to his royal authority, in matters of money and especially in matters of religion. 'I will rather die', he bluntly stated, 'than yield to their impertinent and damnable demands.'

IV

By 1640, Charles's religious policies had brought about a crisis throughout Britain. Scotland was in the hands of the Covenanters, while in England Charles's opponents drew strength north of the border. But it was the recall of Parliament after eleven years which brought things to a head.

Charles had no choice, since only Parliament could vote the money needed to suppress the Covenanters, but equally Parliament provided an unrivalled public forum for the king's opponents. Most dangerous and effective of these was the hitherto obscure lawyer and MP for Tavistock, John Pym. Like other Puritans, Pym believed that Charles's policies in Church and state were the result of a Catholic conspiracy to subvert the religion and liberties of England. But instead of wasting his time in fruitless opposition, he had used the eleven years without a parliament to build up a compelling dossier for his case.

During the 1630s Pym read voraciously; followed every detail of politics at home and abroad, and noted down useful headings and extracts in his notebook. This meant that, when Charles was forced to recall Parliament in April 1640, Pym was the best-informed and the best-prepared man in the House, ready with both a rhetoric of opposition to Charles's government and a plan of action for curbing royal power. Charles had hoped to prey on English xenophobia to persuade Parliament to impose an immediate and vast tax to crush the traitorous Scots. Pym countered by dragging up his list of political and religious grievances against Charles's government of the 1630s. Parliament was willing to listen and to support Pym's demand as well as to avenge itself after over a decade of neglect and unlimited royal government. Charles countered with a move designed to break the deadlock. He hinted at the surrender of ship money, but the hint only emboldened Pym.

Finally Charles lost patience with a parliament that had, once again, refused to deliver, and whose demands proved troublesome. The Short Parliament was dissolved after less than a month. Rather than help their king fight the rebellious Scots, most parliamentarians admired, in secret at least, their stand against Laud's offensive religious policies. In the face of their resistance, Charles resolved to fight the Scots without a parliamentary grant. It was a catastrophic decision.

The disaster happened at Berwick-on-Tweed, which Henry VIII had fortified with mighty ramparts as a border fortress to protect England from the Scots. Expensively refortified by Charles, it stood as a seemingly impregnable barrier between the two countries. But in August 1640, the Scots army, large, well armed, well disciplined and well provisioned, took the daring decision to outflank Berwick; cross the River Tweed further upstream and head straight for Newcastle, which in contrast to Berwick was only lightly defended. Only the River Tyne now stood between the Scots and Newcastle. They forced a crossing at Newburn, and entered Newcastle in triumph on 30 August 1640. Never had so many run from so few, it was said, and never had Scotland won a greater victory on English soil or one with such momentous consequences.

With the Scottish army camped in England, Charles was forced to call Parliament again. Once again Charles faced Pym. And, once again, Pym cleverly focused on the financial, constitutional and religious grievances against Charles. Here Parliament was united in its opposition, and Charles was forced into a wholesale surrender of ship money and all the other objectionable aspects of his reign. His court was purged of the men Parliament regarded as 'evil counsellors', including Laud. Most humiliatingly, he was forbidden to dissolve Parliament without the consent of its members. It seemed as if opposition to the king would be permanent and that his powers would be stripped one by one in return for a dribble of cash. Charles believed that Parliament had 'taken the government all in pieces, and I may say it is almost off the hinges'.

But Charles would not accede to Pym's demand that he should abandon all his religious policies, to the extent of abolishing bishops. 'No Bishop, No King', as his father had famously said. The parliamentarians also wanted to remove Catholics from Henrietta Maria's court and to appoint a 'well-affected person' to teach the prince of Wales 'matters of religion and liberty' so that he would not repeat his father's mistakes when he came to the throne. Not only had Parliament taken away most of his powers, it now wanted to dictate the day-to-day running of the court and, worst of all, his family.

There was only one way out of this intolerable situation. Boxed in by his opponents in the English Parliament, Charles tried to break out by coming to terms with the Scots. In the summer of 1641 he journeyed to Edinburgh and in an astonishing change of front accepted the religious and political revolution of the last three years. He worshipped in the kirk; agreed to the abolition of bishops and filled the government of Scotland with the leading Covenanters and his own sworn enemies. The king also played several rounds of golf and, reasonably confident that he had solved one of his problems, returned in an excellent mood to England.

Events in England also seemed to be moving in Charles's direction. He was greeted with joy in London, as if nothing had happened over the last few years. And the parliamentary alliance that had exacted so many concessions was beginning to fracture. For, with Charles's surrender of ship money and other unconstitutional measures, the religious divisions in the Commons between Puritans like Pym and those who were sympathetic to Charles's ceremonious religion were opened up. Pym tried to whip his troops into line and put 'The Grand Remonstrance' to the vote. This was Pym's searing condemnation of Charles's conduct throughout his entire reign, and an explicit statement of dissatisfaction with his government, in particular in religious matters. These amounted, the Remonstrance claimed, to an all-embracing Catholic conspiracy to subvert the religion and liberties of England. The king himself, it was careful to point out, had been only the unwitting agent of the conspiracy. Nevertheless, Charles's gullibility meant that he could never be trusted to choose his own advisers or to command his own troops again. And, most importantly, after a hundred years the Royal Supremacy would be abolished in all but name. All Charles's and Laud's reforms would be reversed and Catholicism would be suppressed.

The Remonstrance was nominally addressed to the king. But in fact it was a manifesto, for a constitutional revolution at the least, perhaps even for an armed revolt. The Remonstrance was also bitterly divisive and, after days of acrimonious debate, it was passed on 1 December 1641 by 159 votes to 148 – a bare majority of eleven. The vote showed that the broad-based opposition to Charles had broken up. And the more Pym pushed the Puritan attack on Charles's Church reforms, the more his majority risked disappearing entirely. But then Charles overreached himself.

By dismissing Parliament's armed guard, he fuelled dark rumours that he intended to restore his power by force. Plenty of Irish Catholic veterans from the Scottish war were skulking in London. Henrietta Maria was suspected of negotiating with a Catholic country to help her husband. Suddenly, all those conspiracy theories regarding a Catholic coup were revived, and Parliament's united hostility to Charles was renewed. Pym said that he had picked up on 'whispering intimation' that there was 'some great design in hand' to ensure that 'the necks of both the parliaments should be broken'.

As if to confirm the fears, Charles made his greatest blunder. Convinced, probably correctly, that among MPs there were traitors who had colluded with the invading Scots in 1640, Charles determined to bring five Members of Parliament, including John Pym and John Hampden, to trial on charges of high treason. He ordered Parliament to give them up, but instead they voted him in breach of parliamentary privilege.

Charles was unsure how to deal with this latest rebuff. His mind was made up for him. 'Go you coward!' Henrietta Maria shouted at him, 'and pull those rogues out by the ears, or never see my face more.' On 4 January 1642, King Charles strode into the chamber of the House of Commons to arrest his principal opponents. His guards stood outside, fingering their weapons as, to uneasy silence, the king sat himself in the Speaker's chair. 'Where are the five members?' the king demanded, calling them by name. In response, the Speaker fell on his knees, protesting that he could answer only as the House directed him.

In fact, the five members, forewarned of the king's movements, had made good their escape by boat from the back of the Palace of Westminster as Charles and his guards had entered on the landward side at the front. Instead, it was Charles himself who had walked into a trap. By trying to seize the five members by force, he had shown himself to be a violent tyrant. By failing, he had revealed himself to be impotent. As Charles left the chamber empty-handed, he murmured disconsolately, 'All my birds have flown.' So too had most of his power.

Parliament exploited its advantage and took control of all aspects of government, including the militia. MPs claimed to be 'watchmen trusted for the good and welfare of the King, Church and State'. It was, they said, only temporary. They had been forced to act in this way because Charles had proved himself unfit to rule. The king could only complain that he was 'no idiot, nor infant, uncapable of understanding to command'.

Battle lines were now drawn up. Charles's violent, ill-thought-through gesture not only preserved Pym's parliamentary majority but also turned London decisively against the king. Throughout the rest of the country it was a different story as Pym's increasingly extreme Puritan attack on the Church won Charles a devoted following. But in fact Charles was no longer really king of Great Britain or even of England. Instead he was only the leader of a faction.

For history had come almost full circle. The attempt to expand the powers of the Imperial Crown so that it ruled both Church and state, and Scotland as well as England, had backfired. Instead England was about to return to the factional strife of the Wars of the Roses and Britain to the national struggles of the Anglo-Scottish wars. And it began at Nottingham in August 1642, when Charles raised his standard in a war against his Parliament and half his people. He had fewer than four thousand men under his command.

18

NEW MODEL KINGDOM

Cromwell

ON 23 NOVEMBER 1658, a solemn procession wended its way through the silent streets of London towards Westminster Abbey. It was the funeral cortège of the most powerful ruler the British Isles had known since the fall of Rome.

For this latter-day emperor had achieved what had eluded the greatest warrior kings of the Middle Ages. He had welded the countries of England, Scotland and Ireland into one United Kingdom. He had bent Parliament to his will; levied taxes as he pleased; stilled the fratricidal religious conflict of the Reformation and created the most feared navy and army in Europe. He lay in his robe of state, a sceptre in one hand, an orb in the other, with an Imperial Crown laid on a velvet cushion a little above his head. Yet this ruler was not a king. He was in fact a regicide – a king-killer.

His name was Oliver Cromwell, and his story is the tale of how England abolished its age-old monarchy only to find that it couldn't do without it after all.

I

Just fourteen years before, in 1644, England had been embroiled in a bloody civil war. On one side was King Charles I, insisting on his supremacy over Church and state. And on the other, parliamentary forces that believed the king's powers should be limited and that religion was a matter for individual conscience (providing it was Protestant), rather than royal decree.

Despite thousands of dead and an economy in tatters, neither side had been able to force a decisive victory. And Parliament's original war aims, which were, in essence, to limit Charles's authority in matters of state and religion, and to place his authority under the control of Parliament, were about to be replaced by the almost inconceivable notion of executing the king for treason. Playing with increasingly high stakes, Parliament fell to bickering.

Matters came to a head in November 1644 when Edward Montagu, earl of Manchester and major general of the parliamentary forces, questioned how the war should be prosecuted. Were they fighting the king to crush him, or merely to bring him to the negotiating table? The latter was Manchester's view. Aristocrat that he was, he couldn't conceive of a kingless world. He also had a thoroughly realistic fear of Charles's residual authority. 'If we fight the King 100 times, and beat him 99, he will be King still,' he said. 'But if he beat us once or the last time, we shall be hanged, we shall lose our estates and our posterities will be undone.'

This was the paradox of Parliament's war aims. Parliamentarians saw themselves as 'watchmen' over the constitution, who wanted to preserve the essentials of the ancient monarchy. Indeed, in 1645 only one MP voted for a republic while the vast majority still saw kingly government as the best of all the possible alternatives. But there was no sign that Charles would ever compromise with them. As the king bluntly stated, 'There are three things I will not part with – the Church, my crown, and my friends; and you will have much ado to get them from me.' He would fight to the end. Where did that leave Parliament?

Confronted with these realities, the original aims of Parliament were coming under attack. John Pym and John Hampden, its earliest leaders, had both died in 1643, while their manifesto, the Grand Remonstrance, with more than two hundred demands, offered no coherent, unifying war aim. But beneath the surface of the parliamentary armies were brewing new forces, and Manchester's moderate conservatism was met with fierce resistance from one of his officers, General Oliver Cromwell. For Cromwell, a Puritan, a radical and now a rising parliamentarian, rejected not only the king's authority in religious matters but also any accommodation with the crown. If he were so defeatist, he asked Manchester, why was he bothering to fight at all?

Cromwell, despite his rank, belonged to the wilder shores of religious belief. He and his fellows repudiated all human authority in religion and all fixed outward forms of belief. Instead they believed in their Christian liberty to seek after truth and to follow it wherever it led them personally and individually.

Born in 1599, Cromwell had Protestantism in his blood, and it was further drummed, indeed beaten, into him at school and university. Like many religious men, Cromwell experienced a crisis of faith in his thirties from which he emerged with a burning confidence in his own salvation. But there was nothing otherworldly about Cromwell's faith. He was a big, bony, practical, rather awkward man – hands-on, sporty, unscholarly despite his Cambridge days, but with the gift of the gab and a knack for popular leadership. Fearless, with no respect for persons however grand or institutions however venerable, Cromwell was a man waiting for God to reveal Himself to him in actions. But as the war ground into stalemate, there were few obvious signs of divine favour. Cromwell noticed early in the Civil War that the royalists fought with fervour and almost religious conviction. They truly believed in kingly government and the righteousness of their cause. Parliamentarian soldiers, on the other hand, bogged down in constitutional quibbles, lacked inspiration.

The New Model Army, filled with men who were seekers like himself, proved to be the answer to his prayers. Created in February 1645 by a Parliament that was increasingly despairing of victory, the New Model Army was England's first truly professional fighting force: a meritocracy founded on strict discipline, thorough training and ability rather than social rank. It was said that they fought with a pike in one hand and a Bible in the other. Cromwell, for these men, seemed to epitomize the Christian warrior. As a contemporary said after one of Cromwell's early victories, 'It was observed God was with him, and he began to be renowned.'

The first great test of the New Model Army came at Naseby on 14 June 1645. On one side were the royalist forces led by King Charles himself in gilt armour and mounted on his beautiful Flemish horse. On the other a company of 'poor prayerful men', many of whom were new to battle but who nevertheless outnumbered the more experienced royalist forces. During the course of the day, the solid ranks of Cromwell's New Model cavalry and Cromwell's own generalship proved decisive. By one o'clock in the afternoon, Charles had lost his infantry, his artillery and in effect the kingdom. 'God would', Cromwell wrote after the battle, 'by things which are not bring to nothing things that are.' It was a biblically inspired, messianic confidence which Cromwell shared with his troops.

The New Model Army proved to be the decisive weapon in Parliament's struggle with the king. But in forging this weapon, Parliament had called into being a new power in the land, one whose strength would grow with each victory that it won. Indeed, Cromwell's victory with the New Model Army at Naseby was not only the beginning of the end for the royalist forces; it was also the beginning of new ideas about the role of the monarchy – indeed, about its very existence.

After the battle, the army was visited by a clergyman, Richard Baxter. Baxter was a noted Presbyterian who had preached against the king's religious policies. Instead, like all Presbyterians, Baxter believed in an austere authoritarian national Church run not by king and bishops but by committees of zealous clergy and laymen known as presbyteries. Nevertheless, like most Englishmen, he anticipated that the king would eventually agree to a negotiated settlement and consent to a reformation of the national Church.

But Baxter now encountered in the New Model Army a body of men among whom radical ideas were eagerly embraced. They were fed on a diet of tracts and pamphlets that cast Charles as an evil tyrant and godly MPs and soldiers as God's true 'Vice-regents' on Earth. They believed that kingly government was ordained by God, for they read in Deuteronomy: 'one from among thy brethren shalt thou set king over thee'. But if kings were ordained by God, it did not mean that all kings were godly. Some monarchs did God's work, while others, like Pharaoh, were scourges that the pious were charged with fighting as a religious duty. Charles, it was clear to them, was akin to an Old Testament tyrant who set up false idols and oppressed the people of God. Such a man must be resisted, lest Englishmen commit blasphemy themselves by acquiescing in the sacrilege of a latter-day king of Babylon. It was not that Charles was just a secular despot: he was a tyrant over Christianity itself. One writer described the parliamentarian forces as a 'quiver so full of chosen and polished shafts for the Lord's work'. And another urged them: 'let us proceed to shed the blood of the ungodly.'

These tough, Bible-quoting, disputatious soldiers were agreed on two things – that the state had no right to interfere in their religion and that Charles was a tyrant and a traitor who must be defeated and brought to account for his crimes. For the Presbyterian Baxter, who believed in a God who ordained order and discipline, this was a nightmarish vision of un-Christian anarchy. But it was also a vision, Baxter realized, that the men of the New Model Army were determined to turn into reality.

To Baxter's horror these religious extremists were to have no qualms in calling for the trial, and eventually the execution, of their monarch.

II

After his defeat in the Civil War, King Charles had been prisoner first of the Scots, who handed him over to Parliament for money in January 1647; then he was seized by the New Model Army in April. For most parliamentarians, the thought that Charles should be put on trial, let alone executed, was abhorrent. Moreover, as Charles travelled through the country as Parliament's prisoner, he was met by cheering crowds everywhere, even in Puritan Cambridge, which was the constituency of Oliver Cromwell himself. The majority of the people, it was clear, were not ready for a revolution, and might even support the king if things were pushed too far. Sensibly, in view of this sentiment, Charles was offered a generous settlement to end the war.

But characteristically, Charles overplayed his hand, rejecting the astonishingly lenient political terms he was offered by Cromwell and the other army leaders in order to guarantee religious toleration. Instead, in a cynical *renversement d'alliance*, the king joined forces with his original enemies – the Scots Covenanters. In return for the king's promise to impose Presbyterianism throughout the British Isles, which he had no intention whatever of keeping, the Scots were to invade England to restore King Charles I and wipe out the New Model Army.

In 1648 the Scots army invaded England, initiating what became known as the Second Civil War, which was finally decided in a wet and bloody three-day-long battle at Preston in Lancashire. By a masterpiece of strategy, Cromwell and his New Model Army turned the Scots' defeat into an annihilating rout. The parliamentarians were indeed victorious. But it was the New Model Army which had won the war and was now determined to dictate the terms of peace.

They were decided at a three-day prayer meeting in Windsor in April 1648, when the army claimed to be fighting 'in the name of the Lord only'. The ultimate war aim now was 'to call Charles Stuart, that man of blood, to account for the blood he had shed, and mischief he had done to his utmost, against the Lord's cause and people in these poor nations'. But they were at odds with Parliament, which was terrified by the army's radical religious views. In November, MPs rejected the 'Remonstrance of the Army', a demand that Charles be brought to trial for treason because he had started the war and called in the Scots. Parliament was prepared to make yet another deal with the king.

But the army wasn't prepared to concede again. Its officers now moved with lightning speed. On 1 December it seized the king, who had escaped into light, protective custody on the Isle of Wight; on 6 December Colonel Thomas Pride entered the House of Commons and purged it of the Presbyterian majority. One hundred and eighty-six members were turned away, forty-one were arrested and eighty-six didn't turn up. Cromwell left the north for London, making known his support for the purge. And on 4 January what remained of Parliament, a group known as the Rump consisting of 150 MPs, proclaimed itself the Supreme Power in the nation. It was a military coup fronted by a pseudo-parliamentary dictatorship.

The Second Civil War and his great victory at Preston had produced a marked hardening in Cromwell's attitudes, especially towards the king. Until Pride's Purge he had kept his opinions secret. Henceforward, he, too, saw Charles – who had engineered war on his own initiative and for his own selfish ends – as a man of blood who must be punished for his crimes. Convinced as always that God revealed Himself in events, he quickly shifted ground to take a leading part in the decision to put King Charles on trial for his life.

The army and remaining parliamentarians knew full well that Charles, for all his blunders and obstinacy, retained significant support in his kingdoms. Even some radical elements in the army were objecting that the purge of MPs was an act of tyranny. The officers and remaining MPs had to act quickly. A High Court of Justice comprising 135 Commissioners was set up to try Charles. Opposition was bulldozed, as were constitutional niceties. When one Commissioner said that there was no known, legal way to try a monarch, Cromwell shouted him down: 'I tell you we will cut off his head with the crown upon it!'

On 20 January 1649, King Charles was brought to Westminster Hall to be tried for high treason. According to the indictment, Charles was 'a tyrant, traitor, murderer and a public and implacable enemy to the commonwealth of England'. The unthinkable act of killing the king was drawing even closer. Charles's strategy, which he stuck to with remarkable persistence, was to refuse to recognize either the authority or the legality of the court, and throughout the week-long trial both the king and his judges sat with their hats firmly on their heads in a stand-off of mutual disrespect.

Charles laughed openly at the charges and questioned the right of a minority of Parliament to try him. 'Is this the bringing of the King to his Parliament?' he asked. '… Let me see a Legal Authority warranted by the Word of God, the Scriptures, or warranted by the Constitution of the Kingdom.' He warned that a parliamentary or military tyranny would be a disaster for England. After him there would be anarchy or oppression when the known constitutional landmarks were torn away.

Charles was correct in saying that he was not being tried by the Parliament that had initiated opposition to his style of government. Under Cromwell's leadership, the radicals had grown from a fringe element to control not just the army but also the Parliament that now sat in judgement on the king, preparing for the almost inconceivable step of killing their anointed ruler. The death warrant of Charles I was signed and sealed by fifty-nine of his judges, ordering his execution by the severing of his head from his body on 30 January 1649, with the requirement that the execution should take place in the open street before Whitehall. It is a bold and brave document.

But it also highlights the titanic effort of will that was needed to bring even this panel of committed parliamentarians to take the terrible, irrevocable step of publicly executing the king. Both the date of the warrant itself and the date of the execution are inserted over erasures. The names of two of the men who were in charge of the execution have been changed following the refusal of the original nominees to act, and many of the signatures, we know, were obtained only after long, hard lobbying. Overseeing it all, driving it all and allegedly even guiding the pens of the reluctant signers was the third man to sign, Oliver Cromwell.

The day of the execution, 30 January, was bitterly cold. Charles put on two shirts: he did not want to be seen shivering lest onlookers mistake it as a sign of fear. At about noon the king drank a glass of claret and ate a little bread, and then he was escorted through the Banqueting House at Whitehall, the scene of the gaudy triumphs of the Stuart court, and stepped through one of the windows on to the high, black-draped scaffold in the street below. 'I go from a corruptible to an incorruptible crown,' the king said to his chaplain, Bishop Juxton, 'where no disturbance can be, no disturbance in the world.' And then the king removed the garter jewel of St George, made of a single onyx encircled with diamonds, from round his neck, and handed it to Juxton with the instruction that it was to be given to the prince of Wales with the single word, 'remember'.

Charles's most valuable legacy to his son was the manner of his death. Sixty years before, Charles's grandmother, Mary Queen of Scots, had died flamboyantly as a passionate martyr to the Catholic faith. Charles instead offered himself up with quiet dignity as a sacrifice to his vision of Christian kingship.

Barely two months later, on 17 March 1649, the House of Commons passed an Act stating 'That the Office of a King, in this nation ... is unnecessary, burthensome, and dangerous to the liberty, safety, and public interest of the people of this nation; and therefore ought to be abolished.' An attempt was made to eradicate the very word 'king' from the language, and all the images and icons of monarchy were removed. After almost two centuries, the supreme symbol of monarchy – the Imperial Crown itself – was smashed. The Commonwealth of England, ruled by the Rump Parliament, was established.

But getting rid of kings was easier said than done. There had been kings in England since before England itself had existed. Kings had made England and had forged the Imperial Crown with its claim to rule Church as well as state, and Scotland as well as England. Could this king-made, king-centred country successfully become a kingless republic? In eleven years of audacious political experiment, the parliamentarians tried every means possible and every bold constitutional experiment to transform England into the kingless society of their dreams.

The parliamentarians' first problem was that in killing one king they had created another. Charles II, the eldest son of Charles I, had spent part of the war fighting for the royalist cause, most notably at the battle of Edgehill. But defeat had forced him into exile in France. Monarchs and rulers throughout Europe all expressed their horror of the English regicide, but none was willing to supply a single soldier to help Charles regain his throne.

Only the Scots were ready for that, and then only on terms that Charles II found profoundly distasteful both personally and politically. For, the Scots demanded, Charles must not only accept the Presbyterian Kirk in Scotland itself, he must also promise to impose the Presbyterian system in England and Ireland as well. For eighteen months Charles wriggled until finally he was forced to accept the inevitable, swear the Covenant and give the undertakings the Scots demanded. The result was that in 1650 a Stuart once again rode at the head of an army on British soil. But it was a Scots army dedicated to the imposition of a Scottish Presbyterian empire by force throughout the British Isles.

Convinced of the holiness of his cause, and that he would find a large number of royalists who had been horrified by the murder of his father, Charles II took on the New Model Army once more. But as he travelled through Scotland and later England, he found a population eager to come out and cheer his ragged army, but reluctant to lay down their lives for the royalist cause. His plans of invasion and a glorious restoration of the Stuarts now ended in humiliation. Once again the Scots faced Cromwell's New Model Army. At Dunbar, despite mustering a force twice the size of Cromwell's, the Scots suffered a crushing defeat. And in 1651, Charles's invasion of England also ended in defeat at Worcester.

Charles, who had been crowned king of Scots on New Year's Day, became a fugitive, hunted throughout England for forty days. It was a remarkably long time, for Charles was unusually tall and had a dark complexion. The government had put out a description, but the young king was able to evade capture with the help of a few loyalists and his own playacting skills. He fled the Commonwealth's troops under the name of Will Jackson, a servant. Stopping to reshoe a horse, he made pleasant conversation with the blacksmith. 'What news?' he asked. The man told him of the defeat at Worcester, adding that the king was still at large. Charles replied amiably 'that if the rogue were taken he deserved to be hanged, more than all the rest, for bringing in the Scots'. Charles said that the blacksmith replied 'that I spoke like an honest man'. As he continued through England, the king saw bonfires and heard church bells pealing in celebration of his defeat. At last the king was able to slip across the Channel in a fishing boat.

Otherwise Cromwell's victory was complete. The English, as Charles II found, would not rebel against the Commonwealth in favour of the Stuart cause. Scotland, too, was conquered and occupied by the English army, and the General Assembly of the Kirk dissolved by force. It was Cromwell's last battle as an active commander. Now, leaving others to mop up in Scotland, he started the journey back to London.

Cromwell, like Julius Caesar before him, now bestrode the world like a colossus. He had outdone the greatest of the medieval kings and had succeeded where even King Edward I, the hammer of the Scots, had failed. He had conquered Ireland, Scotland and, in a series of coruscating victories, had forged a new united Britain. Except, curiously, in England. For the government of England remained in the limbo that had followed Charles's execution. The monarchy had gone, but it was unclear what would replace it.

Having won the war, the new republic now had little idea what to do with the ensuing peace. By 1653, Britain had been without a king for nearly five years and a decade of war had left the country economically drained. But the remaining Rump Parliament proved incapable of producing a new reformed constitution or providing effective leadership. There were calls that every adult male should be given the vote, that land should be redistributed and that the government should adopt a fully republican constitution. But radical proposals such as these were fiercely rejected as the English Republic became increasingly conservative. Indeed, by refusing to stand for re-election and meeting in continuous session the members of the Rump threatened to become a permanent and self-perpetuating oligarchy. Was it for this that the army had brought down Charles I? Parliament and the army were locked in mutual hatred, and only Cromwell was strong enough to hold power without the two coming to blows. But, after all, he owed his position to the army. As Parliament tried to take more power, his dominance was being challenged. The last straw came when the Rump began moves to deprive Cromwell of his position of Commander-in-Chief.

On 20 April 1653, Cromwell entered the Commons dressed as a mere citizen, in a plain black coat and grey worsted stockings. He rose to address the House, putting off his hat as was then customary and speaking moderately in praise of parliaments. But, as his passion and his confidence rose, he began to pace up and down, put his hat back on his head and thundered, 'You are no Parliament. I say, you are no Parliament. I will put an end to your sittings.' He looked down at the mace and said, 'What shall we do with this Bauble? here, take it away.' He then moved towards the Speaker's chair and told the assembled members that 'some of them were Whoremasters. That others of them were Drunkards, and some corrupt and unjust men, and scandalous to the possession of the Gospel, and that it was not fit they should sit as a Parliament any longer.'

'Call them in,' he cried, 'call them in.' Members of Cromwell's regiment burst into the Commons, the Speaker was removed from his chair, the mace from the table and the members of the Rump dispersed. England had already lost her king; now it had lost its parliament. Cromwell managed to do what Charles I had so humiliatingly failed to do when he came in 1642 to arrest just five MPs. Power flowed unmitigated and undisguised from the barrel of a musket.

III

Now Cromwell, with the backing of the army, ruled England without Parliament as Commander-in-Chief. A portrait of him, painted shortly after Charles I's execution, shows how far Cromwell – the erstwhile gentleman farmer – had transmuted into a princely figure, in armour, attended by his faithful page, wielding the field marshal's baton and able to exercise supreme power in civil as well as military affairs.

But Cromwell was a reluctant revolutionary and eager to cloak his military dictatorship in decent constitutional garb. Surveying the post-war situation, he mused on what form of government was suitable for England now the Stuarts were gone. He admitted that for 'the preservation of our Rights, both as Englishmen, and as Christians ... a settlement, with somewhat of Monarchical Power in it, would be very effective'. But he would not say as much, in public at least. Neither Parliament nor the army wanted another king, but they did recognize the need for a new kind of authority and so, under a new constitution, the office of king was renamed Lord Protector (the then usual English name for a regent) and offered to Cromwell, who accepted it.

Cromwell then summoned a parliament as provided for by the constitution. But the parliament of Cromwell immediately picked up where the parliaments of Charles I had left off, by arguing about the Lord Protector's control of the army, his income and his right to appoint advisers. And Cromwell responded by behaving like Charles I, first denouncing Parliament, then dissolving it.

As Lord Protector (and now untrammelled by Parliament), Cromwell was invested with all the authority of a dictator. And, having come into power as the nominee of the army, he set himself to carry out that which the army had set forth in its petitions and manifestos. Cromwell's most dramatic concession to the army came in 1655 with his agreement to the appointment of eleven major generals as military governors of the English regions. The major generals were doubly unpopular. First, because they were responsible for the enforcement of the Protectorate's programme of social reform. This showed that the Puritans really were puritanical since it not only involved an assault on swearing, drunkenness, gaudy female fashions and fornication, but also attempted abolition of such staples of English life as horse races, theatres, casinos and brothels. Not even pubs were exempt. Still worse, from the point of view of the constitutionally minded, was the fact that the major generals were to be paid for by a 10 per cent income tax on ex-royalists, known as the 'decimation' and levied purely on the authority of the Lord Protector.

But the decimation tax was seen as taxation levied without parliamentary consent, and it came under remorseless attack when a revised version of the Rump Parliament finally returned in September 1656. Concerned by what they saw as Cromwell's arbitrary use of power, and unable to recognize this new form of republican authority, Parliament now sought a return to the kind of constitutional government it had been used to in the past – working not with a Protector but a king.

They set out their claims in 'The Humble Petition and Advice', hoping that Cromwell would exchange the title of Protector for that of king. The title and office of a king, they argued, had been long received and approved by their ancestors. And had not Cromwell always wondered whether he might not be the Lord's anointed? What if a man, even a humble God-fearing man like himself, were king?

Cromwell was obviously fit to be king, but why should Parliament, which had just killed one king, now seek to create another? The reason was that the powers of the king, unlike those of the Lord Protector, were known and limited. A king had to respect ancient custom, and to seek the consent of Parliament to make laws and to raise taxes. King Oliver would have been an altogether more circumscribed figure than Lord Protector Cromwell.

But the army was aghast that its godly revolution might amount to no more than the replacement of the House of Stuart by the House of Cromwell. So they lobbied hard against the title of king, and Cromwell himself, after weeks of agonized indecision, decided that God had 'blasted the title and the name of King'. He would accept the powers and indeed more than the powers of a king, but not the title. Cromwell, asserting that he was 'not scrupulous about words or names or such things', brushed over the implications of his decision.

Cromwell's second inauguration as Protector took place on 26 June 1657 in Westminster Hall. The first had been modest; this was virtually regal. Edward I's Coronation Chair was brought from Westminster Abbey. Cromwell was invested with an imperial robe of purple velvet lined with ermine. He was presented with a gilt-bound and embossed Bible, a golden-hilted sword and a massive solid gold sceptre. He swore a version of the Coronation Oath and finally, seated in majesty in the Coronation Chair, he was acclaimed three times to the sound of trumpets and the cry 'God Save the Lord Protector'.

All that was missing was the crown itself, and that appeared on his coinage and Great Seal. Oliver was now indeed king in all but name. Cromwell had rid Britain of its king but as Lord Protector he now held more power than any king of England had ever held. His achievements rivalled those of any English monarch.

But just one year after his investiture, Cromwell fell ill, and on 3 September 1658 he died at the royal palace of Whitehall. In Cromwell's magnificent funeral ceremonies, which stretched out over fifteen weeks, any coyness about his royal status was finally abandoned. Cromwell had ruled like a king. He was buried as a king with solemn ceremony, a vast cortège, which included no fewer than three state-salaried poets, and at enormous expense. Presiding over it all, as was traditional in royal funerals, was a lifelike effigy of Cromwell himself, which wore in death the remade Imperial Crown that he had first destroyed and then refused in life. Few British rulers have left a grander legacy or one that seemed more stable.

But if Cromwell had taken on the forms of a king without the name, one very important thing was missing. Did the laws and constitution die with him? Was the Protectorship hereditary or elective? These matters were never cleared up, despite pleas that Cromwell should make the office hereditary to preserve the good order and stability of the Commonwealth after his death. But Cromwell, as usual, refused to antagonize the regicidal army by restoring a full hereditary monarchy. He acted at the very end, however, when he was beyond the jealousy of the generals. On his deathbed Cromwell nominated his eldest surviving son Richard as his heir, and within three hours of his father's death Richard was, to the sound of trumpets, proclaimed Lord Protector by the grace of God. Loyal addresses flooded in from the counties and towns, and messages of condolence and congratulations from foreign sovereigns. Few royal successions have been as smooth.

Richard was not without his personal qualities either. He had been brought up to be a simple country gentleman, spending part of his youth in Ely at his father's modest house. Perhaps fearing that if he were seen to be grooming an heir the army would object, Oliver had kept his son out of the way. Nonetheless, as Lord Protector Richard went on to display charm, dignity and even an unexpected eloquence. But he lacked the killer instinct for power on the one hand and a secure power base in the army on the other. Richard also inherited the unresolved political dispute between the army and Parliament. His father had been strong enough to control it, but it quickly threatened to overwhelm the son.

His first parliament met in January 1659, but by April the council of officers was calling on Richard to dissolve Parliament and entrust himself to the army. Their intention was to preserve the Protectorate under military rather than parliamentary control. Richard, unwilling that one drop of blood should be spilled to preserve his greatness, as he was supposed to have said, reluctantly agreed. He dissolved Parliament and threw himself on the mercy of the council of officers.

But dissension in the ranks quickly thwarted the council's plan, as junior officers and republicans joined together to call for the restoration of the Rump Parliament that Richard's father, Oliver Cromwell, had dismissed in 1653. The generals were forced to concede and the Rump, reassembled on 7 May 1659, immediately voted to abolish the Protectorate. Richard resigned from office just eight months after his investiture. The reign of Queen Dick, as Richard was derisively known, was over.

Once the army would have stepped decisively into the breach. But the army, for the first time, was divided. There was no unifying vision of how England should be governed and no recognized commander. In London its leadership was weak, self-interested and vacillating. In Scotland, however, General George Monck had power and influence enough to decide the situation. Monck was a canny politician who had fought on the royalist side in the Civil War until his capture and imprisonment by parliamentary forces. In exchange for his promise to command a parliamentary army, Monck was released. Now, as leader of the English army in Scotland, he took action.

But Monck was a restorer, not a revolutionary. He decided that Britain would never be at peace until the traditional forms of government were brought back. That certainly meant a new parliament; but might it also mean a king? On 26 December 1659, under pressure from Monck, the Rump Parliament was restored yet again and it appointed him commander-in-chief of the military forces. A week later, Monck and his army crossed the River Tweed and entered England.

For the first time events in England now offered Charles II, still in exile in the Low Countries, real hope. His advisers had been quick to spot the opportunity offered by the split in the army and the rise of Monck, and they put out secret feelers to him. But Monck had played a subtle game. So subtle indeed that his real motives still remain debatable. Was he resolved on the restoration of Charles II all along, or was he open minded about everything apart from the necessity for constitutional legitimacy? At any rate, Monck kept his contemporaries guessing and hoping long enough to head off the risk of renewed civil war and to let events acquire their own momentum. And it was a momentum, as irresistible as a force of nature, towards monarchy.

IV

By spring 1660, the English Parliament and its army were in disarray. England teetered on the brink of another civil war. It seemed to everyone, especially Monck, that the only authority that could rule England was a Stuart monarchy. Samuel Pepys recorded, 'Everybody now drinks the King's health without any fear, whereas before it was very private that a man may do it.'

On 4 April, Charles II wrote formally to the Speaker of the House of Commons from exile in the Netherlands. It was a tactful letter, offering his help and stating how the presence of the monarch might give the country the stability it had been lacking since the death of Lord Protector Cromwell. His approach was a masterpiece of clemency and statecraft.

The Declaration of Breda, as it became known, was intended to serve both as a manifesto for his restoration and as a blueprint for a comprehensive settlement after the turmoil of twenty years of civil war and unrest. And it shows that the lessons of those years had been well learnt. Its principal argument in favour of monarchy was that the proper rights and power of the king were the guarantor of the rights of everybody else, and without the king's rights nothing and no one was safe. As Cromwell had found, only monarchy could tame a fractious army and a power-hungry parliament. But as Charles now argued, only a Stuart monarchy had the legitimacy to guarantee known laws and a stable line of succession.

Most importantly, the Declaration stated that there would be no bloody reprisals or the restoration of the Stuart monarchy as it had existed under Charles I. Instead, the restoration would not be the victory of the royalist cause, but a continuation of strong government as it had existed under Cromwell. Finally, the Declaration of Breda promised to bind up the wounds of a bleeding nation. It offered pardon to all, save effectively those directly participating in the late king's execution. But most strikingly and unthinkably for the heir of Charles I, it also offered liberty of worship. 'We do Declare a Liberty to tender consciences; and that no Man shall be disquieted or called in question for Differences of Opinion in matter of Religion, which do not disturb the Peace of the Kingdom.' Was the genie of the Royal Supremacy, with its fatal harnessing of politics and religion, to be exorcized at last?

In April 1660, a new parliament, known as the Convention, was elected. Edward Montagu, earl of Manchester, who a decade and a half earlier had opposed the king's trial and execution, was appointed Speaker of the House of Lords. Overwhelmingly pro-royalist, the Convention first undertook to debate the question of the restoration of the monarchy. The parliament that only eleven years earlier had helped kill the king now debated the return of his son, Charles II.

On 30 April, the Convention MPs processed to hear a sermon in St Margaret's, Westminster. Preached by the Presbyterian Richard Baxter, who, a few years previously, had been so shocked by the religious anarchy of the New Model Army, it was entitled 'A Sermon of Repentance'. It argued that both the Episcopalians and the Presbyterians had sinned by fighting each other to establish their exclusive vision of the Church. Instead they should unite in as comprehensive a national Church settlement as possible. His call was heeded, and the next day both sides joined together to vote for the recall of the king.

On 1 May 1660, Parliament declared that the government should be by king, Lords and Commons. A week later, Charles was proclaimed by both Houses. The king and his court made haste to return to England. He was greeted with joy in London, where he processed through the streets. The diarist John Evelyn recorded: 'I stood in the Strand, and beheld it, and blessed God: And all this without one drop of blood, and by that very army, which rebelled against him.'

On 23 April 1661, Charles II, who had already been crowned king of Scotland a decade earlier, processed to Westminster Abbey for his second coronation, this time as king of England, almost a year after his return. It was St George's Day, and everything was done to restore the traditional forms. The king had even revived the eve-of-coronation procession from the Tower to Westminster that had been dispensed with by his father and grandfather. The procession took over five hours to pass and was of unparalleled magnificence, as was the coronation. All the ancient robes and regalia, which had been deliberately destroyed after the abolition of the kingship, were lovingly re-created as far as possible to the old dimensions and forms.

The service followed the text used for his father and grandfather, and at the ensuing coronation banquet held in Westminster Hall the King's Champion flung down his gauntlet in the traditional challenge to fight in single combat any who would deny the claim of Charles II to be the rightful heir to the Imperial Crown of England.

It was almost as though the Civil War, the Republic and the Protectorate had never been. But political clocks cannot be turned back so easily, as Charles II, his Church and people quickly discovered.

PART IV

EMPIRE

19

---◦❧❦◦---

RESTORATION

Charles II, James II

AT ROCHESTER ON 23 DECEMBER 1688, King James II of England, who had reigned less than four years, fled into exile. It was the second time in forty years that the English had dethroned a king.

There was to be none of the high tragedy of the trial and execution of Charles I, James's father, the last time the English rid themselves of a king. Instead, James's downfall was a pitiable farce. He had already tried and somehow failed to flee from his subjects a fortnight earlier on the 11th, when, after throwing the Great Seal into the Thames, he rode disguised as an ordinary country gentleman to the north Kent coast. There he embarked for France. But his boat was intercepted by suspicious and disrespectful fishermen and forced back to Faversham. And even his second attempt at flight succeeded only with the connivance of his son-in-law and usurper, William III, who sensibly wanted him out of the way.

But, despite these elements of black humour, James's dethronement brought about lasting change in a way which his father's hadn't. This, the fourth part of the book, tells the story of how this came about. It follows the resulting spread of the values of property, prosperity and freedom from these islands across the globe. And it shows that despite some conspicuous exceptions individual kings and queens tended to help rather than hinder the process.

But it begins at the monarchy's lowest point, by explaining how the House of Stuart lost the throne again only thirty years after James's elder brother, Charles II, had regained it in the Restoration of 1660. The old issues of religion and succession had arisen once more. But so too did a new question: which model of modernity should the British monarchy follow – the French or the Dutch? At stake were fundamental choices: between persecution and religious toleration, between absolutism and government by consent, and between success and failure.

I

Outside the Banqueting House in Westminster every Friday from June 1660 a huge crowd waited impatiently to be admitted into the presence of their newly restored sovereign, King Charles II. Many of them may well have remembered a very different scene at this same spot eleven years previously, when King Charles I had been publicly beheaded following his trial for treason.

But now England's experiment with republicanism was at an end, and once more a son of the House of Stuart sat beneath the canopy of state to receive his people. But they were here not merely to pay their respects. They had come instead to be cured by the magical caress of their sovereign, for it was firmly believed that the king's hands could banish scrofula, a disfiguring tuberculosis of the lymph nodes. Every Friday Charles would touch for the King's Evil, and over the course of his reign he would lay his hands on more than ninety thousand of his grateful subjects.

The ceremony of touching for the King's Evil was a sign of the divine nature of English kingship. But ever since the reign of Henry VIII, the connection between divinity and kingship had been more than mystical – it was political.

The assumption of religious authority was an enormous boost to royal power and prestige, but for Henry's successors the Supremacy had proved to be something of a poisoned chalice as, inevitably, the monarchy had become the focus of the violent religious conflicts provoked by the Protestant Reformation. Charles II had grown up as these disputes reached their culmination in political meltdown, civil war and regicide. Now he had been swept back with popular rejoicing to take the crown that had been abolished with his father's execution. He would soon find, however, that the quarrels that had led England into civil war were far from settled.

At first sight, King Charles was well suited to pick his way through the political quagmire that followed Cromwell's death. Charles I had lost the throne by his unbending adherence to principle: to the authority of the king in the state and of the bishops in the Church. In contrast, the only rigid thing about Charles II was his male member. He fathered at least fourteen children by nine different mothers and more or less single-handedly repopulated the depleted ranks of the English nobility. When he was egregiously hailed as 'Father of his people', Charles laughed, replying that he had certainly fathered a great number of them.

Otherwise there was nothing to which he would not stoop his six-foot frame; no corner, however tight, which he could not turn; and no loyalty, however deep, which, once it ceased to be convenient, he recognized as binding.

Like many such men, he had an easy charm. He was affable, good humoured and witty, though his intelligence was practical rather than scholarly. But he was as lazy as he was treacherous, and really applied himself only when his back was to the wall. In short, Charles could ride almost any tide. But steering a consistent course was beyond him.

The first test of both Charles's resolution and his honesty came over religion. As one MP said, the principles of the restored monarchy were that Charles should 'not be king of this or that party, but to be king of all'. Charles realized that it was good politics to live up to this. In the Declaration of Breda, the manifesto that had helped win him the throne, Charles had made an unequivocal promise of 'liberty to tender consciences', or religious toleration, for all the disparate groups that had rebelled against the Stuart monarchy. All the other undertakings of Breda about disputed title to land, war crimes and arrears of army pay were swiftly passed into legislation by the Convention Parliament, often using the precise, carefully chosen words of the Declaration itself.

But not religious toleration. Before the Civil War, Parliament had split over the intertwined issues of royal power and religion. The king's Anglican supporters took as their biblical text Paul's letter to the Romans, in which he states that 'the powers that be are ordained of God'. Anglicans interpreted this to mean that their highest religious duty was to obey the monarch, no matter what he did.

Opposing them were the Presbyterians, and other more extreme Protestant dissenting sects, who countered with Peter's saying in the Acts of the Apostles: 'It is better to obey God than man.' These opponents of absolute royal power had won the Civil War, but with the Restoration they had lost the peace.

In the elections to Charles's first parliament those who had fought alongside his father to defend the established Church of England and the king's role as its supreme governor were returned in large numbers, hence its nickname, the 'Cavalier Parliament'. In the political ascendant at last, the Cavaliers insisted on the enforcement of rigid Anglican conformity by oaths to be administered on all clergymen, dons, teachers and members of town and city corporations.

The result was known as the Clarendon Code, after Charles's chief minister and Lord Chancellor, Edward Hyde, earl of Clarendon. There is dispute as to whether Hyde had planned to subvert Charles's offer of toleration all along or whether he simply took advantage of circumstances. But there is no doubt that the Code reflected Clarendon's view that the Church of England was the only true Church and that only the Church of England taught the proper obedience of subjects to the king.

Charles had little sympathy with the Church's Protestant opponents, whom he blamed for the Civil War and his father's execution. But with Roman Catholics it was a very different story. The queen mother, Henrietta Maria, was a proselytizing Catholic, and there were persistent rumours that Charles himself had converted to Catholicism, or at least was dangerously partial to it. In fact he had few firm beliefs, and deplored the intolerant zeal of every group. As he said, he 'should be glad that those distinctions between his subjects might be removed; and that whilst they were all equally good subjects, they might equally enjoy his protection'. Charles sought to address these problems and to salve his conscience over the broken promise of toleration in the Declaration of Breda by issuing a second declaration in December 1662. It referred to the king's discretionary power to 'dispense' with the Clarendon Code for both Protestants and Catholics who 'modestly and without scandal performed their devotions in their own way', and called on Parliament to pass an Act to make such a suspension of the Code general and permanent.

But the ultra-royalist Cavalier House of Commons, with its hardline Anglican majority and absolute loyalty to the monarchy, refused their monarch point blank. They had not fought the Civil War and suffered under Cromwell to see the monarchy adopt their enemies' principles. And Charles, aware above all that Anglicans were the strongest supporters of the restored monarchy, had to acquiesce.

II

After these domestic frustrations, foreign policy seemed to offer an opportunity for decisive action and the glory of war.

The seventeenth century had been the Golden Age of the Dutch Republic. After surviving the Spanish attempt at reconquest in the late sixteenth century with English help that was neither consistently given nor very effective when it was, the Dutch had gone on to become an economic superpower that threatened to take over English trade. The English had already tried to cut them down to size in the first Anglo-Dutch War in the 1650s. Now Charles was persuaded that he should seek to outdo Cromwell by launching a second conflict.

The war began well with the great victory of Lowestoft in 1665, when the fleet, commanded in person by Charles's brother James, duke of York, as Lord Admiral, defeated the enemy and blew up the Dutch flagship, together with the Dutch commander, Admiral Opdam. But then the attempted seizure of the Dutch East Indies fleet in a neutral port misfired; the domestic disasters of the Great Plague in 1665 and the Great Fire of London the following year hampered the war effort and things hit rock bottom when the Dutch admiral De Ruyter sailed up the Medway, where the English fleet was anchored, captured the flagship the *Royal Charles*, on which the king had returned to England in 1660, burnt others and forced the rest to scatter and beach themselves. As was said in London, 'The bishops get all, the courtiers spend all, the citizens pay for all, the King neglects all, and the Dutch take all.'

It was a national disaster, which led to a profound bout of introspection. 'In all things,' reflected the diarist Samuel Pepys, who was in the thick of events as a naval administrator, 'in wisdom, courage, force, knowledge of our own streams, and success, the Dutch have the best of us, and do end the war with victory on their side.' Why was England apparently so feeble in defending even its own shores? A spate of books on the Dutch rushed to offer the explanation. The most interesting is Sir Josiah Child's *Brief Observations Concerning Trade and the Interest of Money*. Written even before the war was over, it argued that the Dutch Republic was so strong because it had developed secure financial institutions that gave it long-term security and the ability to wage war and expand its commerce, in spite of its geographical disadvantages. Most European monarchs had made a habit, when financially squeezed by the demands of war, of repudiating their creditors, which meant they could borrow only at a high rate of interest. But through the Bank of Amsterdam, with its enviable reputation for honouring its debts, the Dutch could borrow cheaply: a financial advantage that translated into military strength. And Child is to be taken seriously, since he was an expert on finance, having built up one of the greatest City fortunes of his day. Other authors pointed to Dutch religious toleration, which gave the republic domestic peace, as opposed to the civil wars produced by persecution in England. And others again to the superiority of Dutch hygiene, education, poor relief and technical expertise.

Why not, in short, imitate the Dutch instead of fighting them? Why not even ally with them? Especially since a new potent threat to England's security was arising in Louis XIV's aggressive, Catholicizing France.

III

France offered an alternative model for a modernizing monarchy. If the Dutch owed their success to innovative republican institutions and consensual government that had made a small and disunited country a world power, then France had become strong by following the opposite path.

France, like England, had been torn apart by civil war in the middle decades of the seventeenth century. But the wars, known as the *Fronde*, were very different. Instead of pitting the king against his subjects, they were a quarrel *within* the highest ranks of the nobility and the royal family itself. They came to an end at roughly the same time, however, when in 1661 the twenty-three-year-old Louis XIV, who had been king since the age of five, began his personal rule.

Louis was Charles's first cousin and the two were similar in appearance, with their powerful physique, swarthy complexion, full lips and hooked nose. They also shared the same insatiable sexual appetite. But there the resemblance ended.

For Louis, despite his lustfulness, was a man of rigid dignity, inflexible will and unbending self-discipline. His iron self-control meant, for instance, that he was able to give a public audience immediately after an operation, without anaesthetic of course, to treat an anal fistula. And what he expected of himself, he demanded of others.

Louis's motto, seen to this day on the ceiling of the Hall of Mirrors at the heart of his great palace of Versailles, was *Le Roy gouverne par lui-même*: 'the King rules by himself'. This meant that there would be no great minister or corrupt court faction or even parliament to come between the king and his people. Instead, he, Louis, would personally direct a close-knit group of departmental officials. They came from modest backgrounds and shared Louis's appetite for hard work and belief in discipline. Above all, they were at one with his commitment to the glory of France and her king.

Colbert, the minister of finance, directed an ambitious programme of state-sponsored industrial growth and overseas imperial expansion; Vauban, a military architect of genius, protected France's borders with vast fortifications; Louvois, the minister of war, reorganized the army and oversaw a series of aggressive campaigns that expanded French territory towards her 'natural frontier' on the Rhine and beyond; even the arts – painting, music, architecture, the theatre – and science were subjected to central direction and made to hymn the glories of *le Roy soleil*, 'the Sun King'.

And the medicine seemed to work as, in little more than a decade, France turned from the sick man of Europe into the European super-power. It also became the very model of a modern monarchy.

The rise of France posed for the English the same dilemma as the earlier rise of the Dutch. How would the English see the new France? As a threat? Or as a model?

For most of Charles's subjects, Louis's aggressive Catholicism meant that the issue was not in doubt: France not only threatened to become a universal monarchy but what was even worse a universal *Catholic* monarchy.

The result was that when, less than a year after the debacle of the battle of the Medway, England not only made peace with the Dutch but joined them in an alliance against France, the news was greeted with widespread rejoicing.

But not by Charles. The king harboured a grudge against the Dutch for the stain on his honour of defeat by a mere republic. He also took a very different view of both Louis and Catholicism from most of his subjects. Partly it was a matter of family connection. Charles himself was half French through his mother, Henrietta Maria. And the ties were strengthened when his youngest sister, also named Henrietta Maria, married Louis's brother, Philippe, duke of Orleans. Henrietta, who was as intelligent as she was pretty, promptly became a firm favourite of Louis (indeed, his interest was rumoured to be more than brotherly) and a powerful conduit between the two courts.

And there was a similar family inclination to Catholicism. So when in 1668 Charles's brother James informed him that he had converted to Rome, Charles, far from expressing horror, confided in him his intention to do the same. It remained only to work out the means.

A secret meeting was summoned on 25 January 1669 in James's private closet or study, at which only the king, his brother and three confidential advisers were present. Tearfully Charles explained his determination to adopt the true faith. But how? The fear of a Catholicized monarchy was, as everyone knew, enough to rouse Englishmen to arms. In the face of this threat the rest unanimously advised him to inform Louis and seek his powerful advice and assistance.

Charles and Louis had already opened secret negotiations, with Henrietta Maria, duchess of Orleans, as go-between, for a *renversement d'alliances* that would see England and France joining together to make war on the Dutch. Now Charles's professed resolution to convert to Catholicism raised the stakes still higher.

It took over a year to reach agreement. Finally, in May 1670, under cover of a flying visit by the duchess of Orleans to see her brother, the secret Treaty of Dover was signed. (It was called 'secret' because it was so closely guarded that most of Charles's ministers were not informed of its existence.) In it, Charles reaffirmed his 'plan to reconcile himself with the Roman Church', while Louis, for his part, promised Charles a subsidy of 2 million *livres* to help him suppress any armed resistance to his conversion, together, if need be, with six thousand French troops. The two monarchs were then to coordinate an attack on the Netherlands, with Louis bearing the brunt of the land war and Charles the naval.

Was Charles's undertaking to convert real? Or a diplomatic ploy that proved too clever by half? In any case, though the actual text of the Treaty of Dover remained a closely guarded secret, the rumours surrounding it led to a dangerous polarization in English politics. The worst fears of Charles's opponents were confirmed by the final steps that led to the outbreak of war. On 5 January 1672, Charles unilaterally suspended all payments from the Exchequer for a year; on 15 March he published the Declaration of Indulgence, which, on the model of the abortive declaration of a decade earlier, used the royal prerogative to suspend the Clarendon Code for Catholics as well as Protestant dissenters. Then, two days later, he joined Louis in declaring war on the Dutch.

The effect was to reconfirm the fatal association in the public mind of arbitrary government with Catholicism and an unpopular and, as it turned out, unsuccessful foreign policy. For the Dutch, despite the French occupying five out of their seven provinces, refused to roll over. Instead, they broke the dykes and used the flood waters to stop the French advance into the heartland of Holland. Still worse, from Charles's point of view, the man who led the heroic Dutch resistance was his own nephew, William, prince of Orange.

For the system of hereditary monarchy meant that the rivalries of the great European powers were also family quarrels. France was ruled by King Charles's cousin, Louis XIV, while France's Continental rival Holland was ruled by his nephew William, the son of Charles's eldest sister, Mary, princess royal of England, and William II, prince of Orange.

But William III was a very different ruler from Louis, the Sun King, the absolute monarch of all he surveyed. For the head of the House of Orange was not sovereign in the Dutch Republic, but first among equals. Sovereignty instead resided in the Estates of the seven provinces. But ever since William the Silent's leadership of the Dutch Revolt against Spain in the late sixteenth century, his descendants as princes of Orange had traditionally been made *stadholder* or governor of each of the provinces and captain-general and admiral of the armed forces of the republic.

It was an important position. But to exploit its potential required talent and tact on the part of the reigning prince. He also had to cope with strong republican elements among the Dutch urban elites, who were jealous of the quasi-regal pretensions of the House of Orange and were determined to cut it down to size. William would prove more than equal to the task.

His beginnings were inauspicious enough, however. In 1649, his English grandfather, Charles I, was executed, and the following year his own father died of smallpox at the age of only twenty-four. Eight days later, on 14 November 1650, William was born as a posthumous child in a black-hung bedchamber.

Quarrels between his widowed mother, Princess Mary, and his grandmother, Princess Dowager Amalia, for his guardianship played into the hands of the anti-Orange faction in the republic, led by the Grand Pensionary or chief administrator of Holland, De Witt, who not only managed to withhold the family's traditional offices from the young prince but even went so far as to abolish them.

None of this had much impact on the young prince, who was brought up in his birthplace, the Binnenhof Palace in The Hague, first in his mother's apartment and then in his own. At the age of six he was given his first tutor, a local clergyman, and at the age of nine a governor, who came from the cadet Nassau branch of the princely house.

From his tutor he absorbed a firm Calvinistic Protestantism and from his governor a sense of the historic destiny of the House of Orange and a passionate love of hunting. He also emerged as a man's man, with little time for women but a lot for attractive young men.

And all of these things – his religiosity, his family pride, even his homoeroticism – came together in the crisis of 1672, when he discovered his lifelong vocation as leader of the military resistance to French hegemony and the champion of Protestantism first in the Netherlands and then throughout Europe.

William was not the only Protestant in Charles's family. Only a few months after the Restoration, Charles's brother James, duke of York, had married Anne Hyde, daughter of Lord Chancellor Clarendon, the author of the notorious Code that defended the Church of England against Catholics and dissenters. Many, including the queen mother, Henrietta Maria, were scandalized at the *mésalliance* between a prince and a commoner. But Anne proved a dignified duchess and a loyal wife. She also brought up her two daughters, Mary and Anne, as committed Anglican Protestants despite their father's zealous devotion to the Roman Catholic Church.

And this Protestant grouping within the royal family became even stronger in 1677, when, as a result of the perpetual switchback of politics at Charles's court between Protestantism and Catholicism and France and the Netherlands, it was decided that William of Orange should marry his cousin, James and Anne's eldest daughter Mary. Charles's alliance with Louis and James's Catholicism had outraged the nation. It seemed as if the suspiciously Catholic royal court was subverting the national religion by joining Louis's campaigns against the Netherlands. The sudden U-turn to a marriage alliance with the Protestant Dutch Republic was intended to reassure the public and Parliament.

The wedding took place at Whitehall on 4 November 1677, the prince's birthday. Despite the auspicious anniversary, however, the marriage was hardly a meeting of minds or bodies. The fifteen-year-old Mary, beautiful and vivacious, towered over the dour bridegroom, who, despite his reputation as a warrior prince, was weak in body, hunched and asthmatic. She is said to have wept for a day and a half when she was told she was going to marry the Dutchman; while William, for his part, had made prudential enquiries via the wife of the English ambassador in The Hague as to Mary's suitability for a man like himself, who 'might not perhaps be very easy for a wife to live with'.

The answers seem to have satisfied him. And, after a shaky start, the forecast proved to be correct. Rumours of pregnancies soon dried up and Mary was jealous of William's quick and, as it turned out, lifelong attachment to her lady-in-waiting, Elizabeth Villiers. But this was an affair of the head rather than the heart, and William and Mary soon became mutually devoted. Indeed, Mary would put her loyalty to her husband above that to her own father. English history would have been very different otherwise.

IV

The marriage of William and Mary took on a further significance. Mary would inherit the English throne after her father James died, and would then, of course, bring her kingdom's might into alliance with William's Holland. For Mary and her younger sister Anne were the only legitimate children of the royal house of the younger generation. William himself was fourth in line, after his wife and sister-in-law.

For King Charles, so philoprogenitive with other women, had no children with his wife, Catherine of Braganza. When Charles had first seen the princess, with her hair dressed in long projecting ringlets in the Portuguese fashion, he is supposed to have exclaimed, 'they have brought me a bat!' But, despite her repeated miscarriages and at least one serious exploration of the possibility of divorce on grounds of her barrenness, Charles – perhaps out of guilt, perhaps out of affection – stuck with her.

The result was a replay of the twin crises of religion, in the form of the Royal Supremacy over the Church, and the succession, which had plagued English politics since the reign of Henry VIII. Known as the Exclusion Crisis, because it focused on the attempt to exclude Charles's brother James from the succession, it threatened to set the Stuarts on their travels once more. And his handling of it showed Charles at his best and worst.

James was made of very different stuff from his sinuous elder brother Charles. Every bit as highly sexed (indeed, he slept with a stream of common whores so ugly that wits claimed they had been prescribed as penance by his confessor!), James was otherwise formal, unimaginative and good at receiving orders and delegating them to subordinates. In short, there was something in him of the centurion in the Bible who told Jesus: 'I am a man under authority, having soldiers under me: and I say to this man, Go, and he goeth, and to another, Come and he cometh.'

So it was with James. Unlike Charles, who regarded his secret and half-hearted attachment to Catholicism as a matter of mere diplomatic and political expediency, James, after he had embraced the true faith as he saw it, never once deviated from it in word or deed: 'it was like a rod of steel running through thirty years'.

It was also to prove an absolute dividing line in English history.

The first test of James's resolve came quickly. In February 1673, the strongly Anglican Parliament was recalled and immediately set itself to force the king to overturn the Declaration of Indulgence. Lured by a generous promise of taxation, Charles agreed. Parliament then pressed home its advantage by passing the Test Act. This banned from all public office, civil or military, anyone who would not swear to the Acts of Uniformity and Supremacy; take communion according to the rite of the Church of England; and just to make sure sign a declaration against the key Catholic belief of transubstantiation, by which the bread and wine in the mass were held to become the actual body and blood of Christ.

James, as Lord Admiral, held such a public office; but, as a now convinced Catholic, he could take neither the required oaths nor the Anglican sacrament. The deadline for swearing the oaths was 14 June; that day James surrendered the Admiralty to the king. His resignation resolved the immediate issue; it raised, however, a much bigger one: if, as a Roman Catholic, James could not be Lord Admiral, how could he be entrusted with the infinitely greater responsibility of kingship? And, if not, could Parliament break the sacred line of succession and the integrity of its monarchy for the sake of its religion? It seemed like another version of resistance theory, this time in the name of the Church of England.

But down that route most respectable Englishmen, traumatized by the execution of Charles I, were not prepared to go unless something very extraordinary occurred.

In the late summer of 1678, the extraordinary duly happened in the shape of the Popish Plot. It is one of the strangest episodes of mass delusion and hysteria in English history; it starred one of the most remarkable hoaxers, Titus Oates, while its setting was the teeming metropolis of London, where Parliament, court and City all lived cheek by jowl with what was now the largest urban population in Europe. It was where men went to make their careers and to disappear.

One of those perhaps with more to escape from than most was Titus Oates. Lame, stunted, homosexual and extraordinarily ugly (his mouth was described as being in the middle of his face), he had failed at everything. He had been expelled from school; passed through two Cambridge colleges without getting a degree; been ordained on false pretences and driven out of his parish for making a false accusation of sodomy; been cashiered as a naval chaplain for committing buggery himself; and finally, after a probably false conversion to Catholicism, he had been frogmarched out of no less than three Jesuit seminaries.

By July 1678, the twenty-nine-year-old Oates was back in London and desperate for survival and for revenge on the world in general and on Catholics in particular. His scheme was to invent a gigantic Catholic conspiracy, masterminded by his erstwhile teachers, the Jesuits, to murder Charles and forcibly reconvert England. He found a willing listener in a fanatically anti-Catholic clergyman and, at his suggestion, wrote the whole thing up in the form of a deposition of forty-three articles.

On 13 August, a copy was handed to Charles while he was taking his usual brisk morning walk in St James's Park; on 6 September Oates also swore to the truth of his deposition before Sir Edmund Berry Godfrey, a fashionable, rather publicity-seeking magistrate; and on 28/29 September Oates appeared before the Privy Council itself.

Charles shredded his evidence from his own knowledge. But his advisers, from a mixture of motives, were inclined to take Oates more seriously and gave him a free hand to arrest the alleged plotters. And here Oates, for the first time in his life, struck lucky. Anne, duchess of York, had died in 1671, and two years later James had remarried the Catholic Mary of Modena. One of those Oates accused was Edward Coleman, Mary of Modena's secretary.

Coleman was almost as great a fantasist as Oates himself. Unfortunately, he had tried to put his schemes into action by soliciting money from Père la Chaise, Louis XIV's highly influential confessor. Copies of the correspondence were discovered when his papers were searched and they contained a damning paragraph: 'Success for his schemes', Coleman wrote, 'would give the greatest blow to the Protestant religion that it had received since its birth … They had a mighty work on their hands, no less than the conversion of three kingdoms, and by that perhaps the utter subduing of a pestilent heresy, which had so long domineered over great part of the northern world.' Here at last, it seemed, was proof positive of Oates's allegations, with a conspiracy extending to the heart of the royal family itself.

Oates's winning streak continued, even more sensationally, when Justice Godfrey, before whom he had sworn his deposition, disappeared in mysterious circumstances on 12 October. Already that evening rumours were sweeping through the City that he had been murdered by the papists. Five days later the rumours seemed to be confirmed when his body was found face down in a ditch on Primrose Hill. There was heavy bruising round his neck and his own sword had been driven through his heart so hard that the point protruded several inches from his back. Despite the violence, however, none of his valuables had been taken.

Even at the time, some suspected that the death was a suicide disguised as a murder. But such doubts were brushed aside and the coroner's jury returned the verdict of 'murder'. And there was no doubt in the popular mind that it was murder by Oates's papist conspirators. Godfrey was now reinvented as a Protestant martyr. His body was laid in state in his house and, on 31 October, given an impressive funeral at St Martin-in-the-Fields, at which the preacher preached a fiery sermon on the text 'As a man falleth before the wicked, so fallest thou'. Medals were struck in his honour and pamphlets written.

Fears of a massacre of Protestants now swept the capital; the preacher at Godfrey's funeral stood between two heavies dressed as clergymen and ladies carried daggers inscribed 'Remember Justice Godfrey' for their own protection from Catholic assassins.

In the midst of all this, on 21 October 1678, Parliament assembled. As the hysteria of the plot gathered force, no fewer than thirty-five people, mostly Catholic priests, were condemned to the hideous death of a traitor on the mere say-so of Oates and his steadily increasing band of associate informers.

But the parliamentary opposition, led by the earl of Shaftesbury, aimed at the biggest Catholic target of all: James, duke of York, the king's brother and the heir presumptive of the Imperial Crown of Britain.

V

Anthony Ashley Cooper, first earl of Shaftesbury, was one of the most complex and controversial figures of a complex and controversial age. He was very short, had strongly marked features and was known as 'Tapski', from the tube and tap which, in a dangerous and innovatory operation, had been inserted by his physician, John Locke, into his abdomen to drain an abscess on his liver.

His career was pretty fraught too, as he shifted, not always in the same direction, from being one of Cromwell's ministers to Charles's Lord Chancellor. From that exalted position he moved into opposition once again, to become one of the king's greatest and most dangerous opponents. For he was bold, unscrupulous, demagogic and a master of propaganda. As such, he chose the most modern and emotive icon as the symbol of his political strategy. The Monument, built to commemorate the Great Fire of London, and finished in 1677, just a year before the outbreak of the Popish Plot, was a modern marvel at 202 feet, the highest vantage point in the City and rivalled only by the spires of one or two of Wren's equally new, rebuilt churches, which had likewise risen phoenix-like from the ashes of the fire.

And the Monument was the sensational setting of the most effective piece of propaganda to emerge from Shaftesbury's circle. Entitled *An Appeal from the Country to the City*, it enjoined Londoners to climb the 311 steps to the top of 'your newest pyramid' and admire the rebuilt city.

Then they should imagine it on fire once more; the guns of the Tower turned on the City; the streets running with blood and the fires of Smithfield burning their Protestant victims at the stake again, as they had done in the reign of the last Roman Catholic monarch, Bloody Mary.

All this would happen, the *Appeal* insisted, if a Catholic king were allowed to succeed.

The *Appeal* didn't name James directly. Instead, keeping up the topicality, it alluded to the bas-relief on the base of the Monument, which shows James assisting his brother Charles to extinguish the Great Fire. All this was a sham, it announced. Instead 'one eminent Papist' – James – had connived at the disaster, 'pretend[ing] to secure many of the incendiaries' – thought to be Catholic, of course – 'but secretly suffer[ing] them all to escape ... for a Popish successor cannot but rejoice in the flames of such a too powerful city'.

Fired by such propaganda, between 1679 and 1681 the electorate returned three parliaments in which there was a clear Commons majority for James's exclusion. Each was quickly dissolved by Charles, who was prepared to concede limitations on James's powers as king but would not yield on his brother's indefeasible hereditary right to succeed.

Charles also had more cards than it at first seemed. The first was the division among his opponents about who should succeed if James were excluded. The more moderate Exclusionists favoured the Dutch line and wanted the succession to leapfrog a generation so that James's daughter Mary would become queen on Charles's death. Her marriage to the champion of Protestant Europe, William of Orange, satisfied everyone that the monarchy's association with French Catholicism would then be over for good. But Shaftesbury and the radicals backed instead Charles's eldest illegitimate son, James, duke of Monmouth.

Born in 1649 of Charles's affair with Lucy Walter, his first serious liaison, and made duke of Monmouth in 1662, James was handsome, charming, charismatic and amorous. He was also spoiled, badly educated, sensitive about his illegitimacy and, having been personally involved in both a mutilation and a murder, had an ugly streak of violence. The army was a natural career for such a man, and by 1678 he had succeeded to Oliver Cromwell's old office of captain-general or commander-in-chief and won what military glory was available under Charles. More importantly than all that, Monmouth was unequivocally, ostentatiously Protestant.

The Popish Plot and the ensuing Exclusion Crisis made Monmouth – popular, Protestant and princely – an obvious alternative to the dour and Catholic James and a natural ally for Shaftesbury.

The only problem was his illegitimacy. But was he illegitimate? Rumours, carefully fanned by Monmouth himself, circulated to the effect that his parents had been secretly married. There were supposed to be witnesses and a black box containing irrefutable written evidence.

But Charles, fond though he was of the strapping first fruit of his loins, was not prepared to allow Monmouth to shunt his legitimate brother James aside. Indefeasible hereditary right could not be undermined, however high the stakes. For this was the deepest principle of the Stuart dynasty. The result was one of the stranger scenes in English history when, in early January 1679, Charles, having summoned the Privy Council, solemnly declared 'in the presence of Almighty God that he had never given or made any contract of marriage, nor was ever married to any woman whatsoever but his wife Queen Catherine'. The declaration was then signed by the king, witnessed by those present and enrolled in the records in Chancery.

In a further, vain attempt to lower the temperature, both rivals for the throne, first James and then Monmouth, were packed off into honourable exile. James, unwisely, went to Catholic Brussels before being made governor of Scotland, while Monmouth went to Holland, where he was correctly but coolly received by Mary and William of Orange, his Protestant rivals for the succession.

The inability of the Exclusionists to agree on a single candidate was one thing strengthening the hand of Charles and James; the other was the perceived extremism of the Exclusionists of whatever stripe. For everything – their language, their demagogy, their violent anti-popery, their allies among the Protestant sects – revived uncomfortable memories of the Civil War.

The result was a pamphlet war and a clash of ideas out of which was born our modern two-party system. The Exclusionists were known as Whigs, or Scottish Covenanting rebels; the anti-Exclusionists as Tories, or Irish outlaws and cattle thieves.

The Whigs believed in religious toleration, limited government and a kingship that finally answered to the people; the Tories in divine-right monarchy, indefeasible hereditary succession, passive obedience and a monopolistic Church of England that was equally hostile to Catholics on the right and to Protestant dissenters on the left. The Whigs were pro-Dutch; the Tories generally pro-French. The Whigs had made the running in the Exclusion Crisis; now it was the Tories' turn.

For they made the forceful point that there was no precedent for preventing the next in line from taking his or her rightful inheritance. Mary Queen of Scots was an example of a Catholic heir. She had been executed before she could succeed Elizabeth, but that was because of her treason, not her religion. The Tories also pointed out that if James were excluded from the throne, the monarchy would be ruined for ever. In effect, England would become a republic. The nominal ruler would come to the throne only if he or she met the conditions laid down in advance by Parliament. However much Anglicans detested Catholicism, the alternative prospect of an elected, circumscribed monarchy was many times worse. In this Tory scenario, the Exclusionists were portrayed as modern Cromwellians, who were refighting the Civil War and attempting to destroy the monarchy and the Church of England. It was an emotional and effective appeal to English loyalties.

Charles met his fourth parliament in the Convocation Hall at Oxford. The Commons and Shaftesbury's group in the Lords were, as usual, hot for Exclusion. But Charles, sensing the turning of the political tide, stood firm. 'I have law and reason and all right-thinking men on my side; I have the Church' – and here the king pointed to the bishops – 'and nothing will ever separate us.'

After sitting for a bare week, the Parliament was dissolved. Nor, thanks to a new subsidy from Louis XIV and booming revenues from trade, did Charles ever have to summon another one. Instead, he could turn to the congenial task of taking his revenge on Shaftesbury and the Whigs for the Popish Plot and the Exclusion Crisis. Charles began by attacking the stronghold of the Whigs in the City and the other towns' corporations. Their charters were revoked and their governing bodies purged of dissenters and Whigs and packed with Tories.

In despair at the sudden turn of events, the Whig leaders now made the mistake of dabbling, very half-heartedly, in treason. A faction plotted to assassinate Charles and James, and put Monmouth on the throne. It was badly planned and attracted few followers. But the king struck them down ruthlessly. And, although the plot was the work of a small group, the Exclusionists as a whole were tainted by their treason. One Whig lord committed suicide in the Tower, two were publicly beheaded and most of the rest, including Shaftesbury and Monmouth, fled into exile in the Netherlands. There Shaftesbury died. But his secretary and intellectual factotum, John Locke, who had devised the operation for the insertion of the tube and tap into his master, continued writing and working in the congenial atmosphere of Dutch tolerance and freedom, completing his great work, *An Essay Concerning Human Understanding*.

Meanwhile, England witnessed a Tory triumph, which, like the French absolutism it so much resembled, expressed itself in soaring stone and brick. The statue of Charles I – the Tories' martyred hero – was re-erected in London; at Winchester, a huge new palace, destined to be the English Versailles, was being rushed to completion; and, above all, the huge bulk of St Paul's was rising over the City of London as the noblest, most eloquent and most crushing symbol of an Anglican absolutism.

If St Paul's was the symbol of the Tory triumph, its intellectual centre was Oxford. And it was there that, in Convocation on 21 July 1683, the University of Oxford issued a solemn declaration 'against certain pernicious books and their damnable doctrines'. It is an Anglican syllabus of errors, in which all the doctrines of Whiggism and their authors are condemned as 'false, seditious and impious, and most of them ... also heretical and blasphemous'. Instead, the university proclaimed that Toryism was an eternal verity and the duty of 'submission and obedience [to kings] to be absolute, and without exception'.

In other words, Anglicanism and royalism were one, as they had been from the beginning under Henry VIII and right through the Civil War.

But what would happen if the king ceased to be Anglican?

England would soon find out. For on 6 February 1685, Charles II died, having converted at last to Catholicism in his very final moments, and was succeeded without a struggle by the proudly Catholic James. The result would test the relationship of Church and state to destruction and send a Stuart on his travels once more.

20

ROYAL REPUBLIC

James II, William II, Mary II

WE ALL KNOW THAT ENGLAND WAS CONQUERED by William the Conqueror in 1066. But we have forgotten, or do not care to remember, that, 600 years later, England was also conquered by another William. William of Orange was Dutch, rather than Norman, and, while there's no doubt that the Norman Conquest changed England radically, the consequences of the Dutch conquest of 1688 were similarly profound, and not just for this country but, arguably, for the whole world.

It began to heal the breaches of the Civil War, which the Restoration of 1660 had tried but failed to do. It turned England from a feeble imitator of the French absolute monarchy into the most powerful and most aggressively modernizing state in Europe.

In short, it invented a modern England, a modern monarchy, perhaps even modernity itself.

I

All this would have seemed like the dream of a madman only a few years previously in 1685, when James II had succeeded to the throne. Then, England was a country still shaped by Henry VIII's religious settlement and the vast dynastic mural of Henry, which showed him as head both of his family and the Church, was still one of the wonders of Whitehall Palace for the new king to admire and to imitate. For successive monarchs had tried to exploit the vast powers of the Supremacy to build up power and wealth and rule unfettered by influence from Parliament.

And towards the end of his reign, it looked as if Charles II had finally succeeded. Bolstered by the support of the High Anglican Tories (as well as secret subsidies from his cousin Louis XIV) Charles managed to rule without Parliament for the last four years of his reign, although the cost was a passive foreign policy that gave France a free hand in Europe. And when Charles unexpectedly died in February 1685, aged fifty-five, the strength of the Stuart monarchy he had restored was underlined by the unchallenged accession of his brother James to the throne.

Just a few years earlier James's position as his brother's rightful heir had been in grave jeopardy following his open conversion to Catholicism. Yet together they had ridden out the storm, even if Charles, acutely aware of the power of anti-Catholic sentiment, had been heard to prophesy that James would be king for no more than three years.

But no one paid much attention, least of all James himself. Now, as he was proclaimed king on 6 February, crowds of Londoners toasted him in free wine and cheered. The fellows and undergraduates at Oxford 'promised to obey the King *without limitations or restrictions*'. There were similar oaths throughout the country and no sign of resistance to the first openly Catholic monarch since Bloody Mary. It seemed a miracle. And such James devoutly believed it to be.

That a convert to the Church of Rome could nonetheless become head of the Church of England was testimony to the power of the idea that underlay the Royal Supremacy: that the highest religious duty of an Anglican was to obey the king, who was God's anointed vice-regent on Earth.

The smoothness of James's accession was underscored by the magnificence of his coronation. It took place on St George's Day and it was the king's command to do 'All that Art, Ornament and Expense could do to the making of the Spectacle Dazzling and Stupendous'. Henry Purcell, Master of the King's Music, composed and directed the music, which culminated in his great anthem 'My heart is inditing'. Samuel Pepys, as one of the barons of the Cinque Ports, helped support the canopy over James in the initial procession from Westminster Hall to the Abbey. The final grand firework display centred on a blazing sun, the emblem of the absolute monarchy of Louis XIV of France, while the great crowned figure of *Monarchia* ('Monarchy') strongly suggested that England was going the same way.

Not everyone was happy, of course, in particular a group of Whig exiles in the Dutch Republic. They had been the architects of the parliamentary attempts to keep James from the throne, and they had been forced to flee when they had lost the political battle to Charles's Anglican Tory supporters. Now James's accession and the election of a complaisant Tory parliament that seemed ready to do James's bidding were the fulfilment of their worst fears. Only an armed invasion, they thought, could save England from Catholic absolutism. Its natural leader was Charles II's bastard son, James, duke of Monmouth, who, unsatisfactory as he was, had been the Whig candidate for the throne during the Exclusion Crisis.

Monmouth, who had come to enjoy the ease of a comfortable exile, took some persuading, however. But eventually he felt honour bound and, on 24 May, he set sail from Amsterdam with a pathetically small force of three ships and eighty-three men. They made for Lyme Regis in Dorset because this was an area where the Good Old Cause of English republicanism lived on. It was also a stronghold of dissenting Protestantism. And Monmouth's manifesto, which even seemed to leave the issue of the monarchy open, was designed to appeal to such men. He promised to free the English from the 'Absolute Tyranny' instituted by his uncle. He accused James of responsibility for the Popish Plot against Charles, the murder of Sir Edmund Godfrey and even of Charles II. Given the success that Titus Oates had enjoyed in working up the country to a pitch of anti-Catholic hysteria, and the popularity of the Exclusion parliaments, Monmouth believed that the country would be eager to rebel against the new Catholic king. But just three thousand at most joined his ranks. And they included no gentlemen.

Desperate to win over such leading figures in society – the so-called 'better-sort' – Monmouth had himself proclaimed king. It was intended to give his cause the veneer of legitimacy and demonstrate that a successful outcome of his rebellion would be nothing more radical than a restored Protestant monarchy. The result was to alienate his existing supporters without gaining any new ones. It also meant that, as a rival king, he could expect no reconciliation with his uncle. James II, for his part, worried about his hold on both Scotland and London, was able to spare only two or three thousand troops against Monmouth. They were badly led but at least they were professional soldiers. And that proved decisive.

The showdown came at Sedgmoor in Somerset on 6 July 1685. Boxed in by the royal army, Monmouth decided that his only chance was to launch a surprise night attack. The tactic made sense but his scratch forces were incapable of carrying it out and, once day broke, were routed by the king's troops: 500 were killed and 1500 taken prisoner.

By then Monmouth had already fled, disguised as a shepherd. But it was only two days before King James II of England, as he called himself, was found hiding in a ditch in his disguise, captured and taken to London. There was no need for a trial, since he had already been condemned as a traitor by an Act of Attainder rushed through by the Tory Parliament. Nevertheless, Monmouth humbled himself by begging for his life on his knees before James. At once his boastful claims to majesty disappeared as he pleaded that he had been forced against his will to declare himself king. His uncle, appalled at such cowardice, was implacable. Monmouth was brought to Tower Hill for execution on 15 July.

Monmouth's death, like his life, was a mixture of tragedy and farce. The two Anglican bishops who accompanied him to the scaffold tried to force a public acknowledgement of guilt out of him. He reluctantly said 'Amen' to a prayer for the king but refused absolutely to swear to the Anglican shibboleth of non-resistance to royal power.

Finally, the wrangling, widely felt to be indecent in the face of death, stopped, and Monmouth prepared himself for execution. He begged the executioner not to mangle him and bribed him heavily. Then he knelt down. But the first blow merely gashed him, and he turned his head as if to complain. Now thoroughly unnerved, the headsman took four further strokes but still failed to kill him. At last, he severed the duke's head with a knife. Many of Monmouth's supporters followed him to a bloody end at the hands of the public executioner.

The Whigs had another martyr and James, so he thought, another miracle. But the challenge to James's monarchy was to come not from the divided and dispirited Whigs but from the apparently all-powerful and all-loyal Tories. The Tories had given James rock-solid support throughout the Exclusion Crisis; now in return they naturally expected that he – Catholic though he was – would be equally unwavering in his support for the Church of England. And, at first, it looked as though he would be.

Things got off to a good start with James's speech to the first Privy Council meeting of his reign. He spoke off the cuff. But an official version was worked up and published with royal approval:

I have been reported a man for arbitrary power; but that is not the only story which has been made of me. I shall make it my endeavour to preserve this government, both in church and state, as it is by law established. I know the principles of the Church of England are for monarchy, and the members of it have shown themselves good and lawful subjects: therefore I shall always take care to defend and support it.

His audience applauded and James basked in their approval. Parliament voted him a vast income. Few kings had come to the throne with such wealth, loyalty and goodwill.

In fact, there was misunderstanding on both sides: the Tories thought that James had promised to rule as though he were an Anglican; James assumed that the Tories and the Church would continue to support him whatever he did. Both were quickly disillusioned.

For James was a man with a mission. The last Catholic monarch to rule in England was Mary Tudor. The piety, the sacrifices and the vicissitudes of his ancestor gave James hope. Like James, Mary had succeeded to the throne against overwhelming odds, which she took to mean that God had given her a mission to reconvert England to the true faith. The new king had overcome the full force of Parliament and the country's inbred hostility to Catholics. Divine purpose must lie behind these miracles. What clearer sign could God give that He supported the Catholic cause? The king also believed that he was on a personal journey of salvation. He had sinned by sleeping with innumerable women of easy virtue. He had to atone for those sins, and the one sure way of doing so was to fulfil his mission. James, we know from his own private devotional writings, was driven by this burning sense of divine purpose: "T'was the Divine Providence that drove me early out of my native country and 't'was the same Providence ordered it so that I passed most of [the time] in Catholic kingdoms, by which means I came to know what their religion was ...' 'The hand of God' was demonstrated in the failure of the attempt to exclude him from the throne: 'God Almighty be praised by whose blessing that rebellion [of Monmouth] was suppressed ...'

Such was James's mission. But what of the *method* of Catholic conversion? Was Britain to become Catholic within his lifetime, or was this the beginning of a long process of counter-reformation? Would it be by coercion? Or persuasion?

Here memories mattered. Bloody Mary had used the rack and the stake and, thanks to Foxe's *Book of Martyrs*, the memory was still fresh in England. So too were the stabbings, drownings and defenestrations of Protestants in the Massacre of St Bartholomew's Eve, the pogrom of Protestants which had occurred in Paris during the French Wars of Religion in 1572. Now these memories, which had scarcely faded, were reanimated in the most dramatic possible fashion by Louis XIV of France, the outstanding contemporary Catholic king and James's model and mentor.

For on 22 October 1685, Louis revoked the Edict of Nantes, which, by granting toleration to French Protestants, had brought the Wars of Religion to an end. News reached England quickly and the effect was dramatic. John Evelyn recorded in his diary:

> The French persecution of the Protestants raging with the utmost barbarity … The French tyrant abolishing the Edict of Nantes … and without any cause on the sudden, demolishing all their churches, banishing, imprisoning, sending to the galleys all the ministers, plundering the common people and exposing them to all sorts of barbarous usage by soldiers sent to ruin and prey upon them.

In fact James, who was no lover of persecution, protested, albeit discreetly, to Louis. But in vain. From now on, every move James made to ease the burdens on English Catholics and bring them back into political life would be read against the background of the events in France. Only six months after his accession, James's honeymoon was over.

II

Could something like the Revocation of the Edict of Nantes happen in England? A Catholic army harass English Protestants and compel them to convert or to emigrate? Circumstances in England made it infinitely improbable. But James, by his single-minded determination to allow Catholicism a level playing field in England with the established, Protestant Church, did his best to make the improbable seem a real possibility.

In response to Monmouth's Revolt, James had recruited a professional army 20,000 strong. And included in the officer corps were a hundred Roman Catholics. This was acceptable in an emergency; it was a red rag to a bull once the revolt was suppressed, since the employment of Catholics in the army, as in all public posts, was forbidden by the Test Act, which had been passed under Charles II in response to James's own conversion to Catholicism.

This was the background to the recall of Parliament, which James opened on 9 November 1685, just as the first wave of French Protestant refugees, numbering several thousand, reached London.

Like his father, Charles I, the king came to Parliament 'with marks of haughtiness and anger upon his face, which made his sentiments sufficiently known'. Then, with characteristic bluntness, James tackled the issue of Catholic officers head-on in his speech from the throne, when he vowed that nothing would ever make him give them up: 'to deal plainly with you, after having had the benefit of their services in the time of danger, I will neither expose them to disgrace, nor myself to the want of their assistance, should a second rebellion make it necessary'.

This was to fling down a challenge to both Houses of Parliament. In the Commons, a backbencher invoked the spirit of the Long Parliament in 1641, on the eve of the Civil War: 'I hope we are Englishmen and not to be frightened from our duty by a few high words.' He was arrested and sent to the Tower for his disrespectful language. There were other, more influential voices being heard. In the Lords, the bishop of London declared that the Test Act was the chief security of the Church of England.

Furious and frustrated, James dismissed Parliament. He would have to get round the Test Act some other way. The only other body whose authority remotely compared with that of Parliament was the judiciary. During the period of his personal rule, James's father, Charles I, had used the judges to authorize the collection of taxes that Parliament refused to grant; now James turned to the judges to get round the Test Act that Parliament refused to repeal.

First the bench of judges was purged of waverers; then a test case was brought on behalf of a Catholic army officer to whom James had granted a royal 'dispensation' or waiver from the requirements of the Test Act.

The Lord Chief Justice read the verdict on behalf of his almost unanimous colleagues. It could hardly have been clearer. Or more subversive:

We think we may very well declare the opinion of the court to be that the King may dispense in this case ... upon these grounds:

1. That the Kings of England are sovereign princes.
2. That the laws of England are the King's laws.
3. That therefore 'tis an inseparable prerogative of the Kings of England to dispense with penal laws in particular cases, and upon particular necessary reasons.
4. That of those reasons and those necessities the King himself is sole judge.
5. That this is not a trust invested in ... the King by the people, but the ancient remains of the sovereign power and prerogative of the Kings of England.

This ruling transformed Parliament into a mere sleeping partner in the constitution: it might pass what laws it liked; whether and on whom they were enforced was purely up to the king.

But, most of all, the judges' ruling was exquisitely uncomfortable for the Tories since it turned one of their fundamental beliefs, in the unconditional nature of royal power, against their other, in the sanctity of the Church of England. And James's subsequent exploitation of the judges' ruling only impaled them on the horns of the dilemma more cruelly.

James made the most of the intellectual quagmire in which the Tories found themselves. Their loyalty to the monarchy, they said, was unlimited, and they preached against any form of resistance. How far could this be pushed? James was convinced that Protestantism flourished in England only because it had banished religious truth by monopolizing education. If Catholic thinkers were only given equality with Protestants, the country, he believed, would learn that they had been lied to, and that the truth resided in Roman Catholicism. Then his mission of conversion would be possible. He therefore ordered the fellows of Magdalen College, Oxford, to elect a Catholic master. The fellows had vowed to obey their king in everything. Now they were being ordered to break the law of the land and their own college's statutes and acquiesce in the destruction of the Anglican monopoly on education. They refused James's order, arguing that it was illegal. The king, outraged that his loyal churchmen should defy him, went in person to Oxford. 'Is this your Church of England loyalty?' he demanded of them. '... Get you gone, know I am your King. I will be obeyed and I command you to be gone.'

James did not understand or affected not to understand the distinction that Anglicans were beginning to make between resistance and obedience. Although they had sworn oaths not to rebel against the king, many were coming to believe that this did not necessarily mean that they were obliged to aid James's policies. Moreover, this was especially true when they felt that he was breaking the law. They believed that this was not just a matter of letting a handful of Catholics serve as army officers or academics, but rather that it presaged a full-scale assault on the Church, the laws and the nation itself.

For James saw the *dispensing* power, which enabled him to exempt individual Catholics from the Test Act on a case-by-case basis, simply as a first step. Instead, his Holy Grail was to secure a recognition of the *suspending* power, which would enable him to abrogate the laws against Catholics (and Protestant dissenters too) in their entirety. This would have the effect of the king's repealing, unilaterally, legislation that had been agreed by all three elements of the Crown-in-Parliament – king, Lords and Commons.

French kings could do this, as Louis XIV had shown with the Revocation of the Edict of Nantes. English kings could not. They were supposed to seek the consent of their subjects and respect the permanence of the law. But if any English king had the potential to go down the path of French absolutism, it was James, with his ample tax revenues, his standing army, his iron will and his sense of divine mission. England was at a dividing of the ways.

James chose his ground with care. First he issued the Declaration of Indulgence, which tried to press all the right buttons. It invoked the 'more than ordinary providence' by which Almighty God had brought him to the throne; and it offered universal religious toleration as a guarantee of Dutch-style economic prosperity as opposed to Louis XIV-style religious persecution, which 'spoiled trade, depopulated countries and discouraged strangers'.

It was powerful bait. But would the Church of England be prepared to sell its monopoly position for a mess of potage?

On 27 April 1688, James ordered the clergy to read the Declaration of Indulgence from their pulpits. The archbishop of Canterbury, William

Sancroft, who, only three years before, had crowned James in the magnificent ceremony at Westminster Abbey, summoned his fellow bishops to a secret supper party at Lambeth, where seven of them signed a petition to the king against the Declaration.

In it, the bishops contrived both to have their Tory cake and to eat Whig principles. On the one hand, they invoked 'our Holy Mother the Church of England [which was] both in her principles and her practice unquestionably loyal [to the monarchy]', and, on the other, they argued like good Whigs that 'the Declaration was founded on a dispensing power as hath often been declared illegal in Parliament'.

It was a frontal – and, as the petition was soon circulated in print – public challenge to royal authority.

James determined to slap the bishops down by prosecuting them for seditious libel. But the bishops showed unexpected courage and a surprising flair for public relations. First, they stressed their loyalty. When James accused them of rebellion they recoiled in horror. 'We rebel! We are ready to die at your Majesty's feet,' said one bishop. 'We put down the last rebellion, we shall not raise another.' Then, by refusing to raise securities for bail, they got themselves imprisoned (rather briefly) in the Tower. It was a terrific coup: crowds of Londoners cheered them from the riverbanks as they were taken there by water; the soldiers of the garrison received them on their knees and the governor treated them as honoured guests.

Even more importantly, the bishops' trial, in the huge space of Westminster Hall, turned into a public argument about the legality of the dispensing power itself. Decorum broke down as the spectators cheered counsel for the bishops and booed and hissed the royal lawyers, and even the judicial worm turned against the king as one of the bench declared in his summing up that, if the dispensing power were allowed, 'there will need no Parliament; all the legislature will be in the king, which is a thing worth considering'.

'I leave the issue to God and your consciences,' he concluded to the jury. The jurors stayed out all night in continuous deliberation. Then, the following morning, they returned the verdict: 'Not guilty'.

Instead, it was James's government which had been condemned.

III

James II's zealous desire to legitimize Catholicism in England had brought him into open conflict with Parliament, the bishops and now the courts. But it was an unexpected event that took place at St James's Palace which finally brought matters to a head, an event that would under other circumstances have been an occasion for national rejoicing. Mary of Modena, James's second, Catholic wife, came from famously fertile stock. And she duly conceived frequently. But all the babies either miscarried or died in infancy, leaving James's Protestant daughters by his first marriage, Mary and Anne, as his heirs presumptive.

In the late summer of 1687, however, James went on pilgrimage to Holywell while Mary took the waters at Bath. Both medicine and magic seemed to work, and in December her pregnancy was officially confirmed. James was elated. The Jesuit monks who surrounded the pregnant queen promised that she would give birth to a boy. Now, with a Catholic heir on the way, the programme of converting the country could be continued long into the future.

The news was a disaster for English Protestants. There was sheer disbelief that the pregnancy could be genuine. Surely it must be another Catholic plot to subvert the laws and religion of the country? And the most important among these disbelievers were the members of James's own, Protestant first family: his daughters Mary and Anne and his son-in-law, William of Orange. William had expected that his wife Mary would eventually inherit the throne, thus bringing England on to his side in his struggle against Catholic France. They were now, by the pregnancy, to be dispossessed and disappointed.

Anne, who was still resident at her father's court despite her marriage to Prince George of Denmark, had also taken a hearty dislike to her stepmother's airs and graces when she became queen. Now she played a key role in endorsing and disseminating the malicious rumours about her pregnancy. It all looked suspiciously trouble free. Mary of Modena was too well. James, bearing in mind his wife's previous disastrous gynaecological history, was too confident. And he was too confident in particular that he would have a son.

Anne wrote to her sister Mary to tell her that the queen was only pretending to be pregnant. There was, she said, 'much reason to believe it a false belly'. Even so, the supposedly fake pregnancy ran its full course. The queen's pains began at St James's on the morning of 10 June 1688, and, after a short labour impeded only by the crowd of witnesses crammed into her bedchamber, she gave birth at about 10 a.m.

The baby, christened James Francis after his father and maternal uncle, was indeed the prophesied boy, and once his doctors had stopped feeding him with a spoon on a gruel made of water, flour and sugar, flavoured with a little sweet wine, and allowed him human milk from a wet-nurse, he was healthy and destined to live.

But was he the king and queen's child or a changeling?

Normally, the birth of a prince of Wales would have crowned James's attempt to reassert royal authority and re-Catholicize England. When, for instance, such an attempt had been made a century before, under Mary Tudor, it had been shipwrecked by the queen's failure to produce a child and so guarantee the permanence of her legacy. But the birth of James Francis had the opposite effect. Faced with the prospect of a Catholic succession, James's opponents decided that they could tolerate the course of his government no longer. Before the birth of a healthy prince, at least James's actions were reversible when his solidly Protestant daughter, with her husband William at her side, came to the throne. But now they must instead bring him to heel or even bring him down.

The first step was to develop the rumours about the queen's pregnancy into a full-scale assault on the legitimacy of James Francis. The pregnancy, the story went, had been suppositious all along, as Anne had said, and therefore the child must be a changeling, smuggled into the queen's bed in a warming-pan by the cunning Jesuits after a carefully stage-managed performance of childbirth. It was all nonsense, of course. But Princess Anne believed it. She persuaded her sister Mary in the Netherlands to believe it. And her brother-in-law, William of Orange, found it convenient to believe it too.

By 1688, William, now in his late thirties, was a hardened general and politician. But his goal to unite the Netherlands and England in a Protestant crusade against the overweening Catholic power of Louis XIV's France remained unchanged. Bearing in mind his position as both James's nephew and son-in-law, he had every reason to suppose that Mary would inherit England naturally. But James's Catholicizing policies and, still worse, the birth of a Catholic son and heir threatened to rob him of the prize. William would not let it go without a struggle.

He needed a decent justification for action, however. He took the birth of Prince James to be an act of aggression against him on James's part: 'there hath appeared, both during the Queen's pretended bigness, and in the manner in which the Birth was managed so many just and visible grounds of suspicion'. In view of these, William was compelled to take action because 'our dearest and most entirely beloved Consort the Princess, and likewise ourselves, have so great an interest in this matter, and such a right, as all the world knows, to the Succession of the Crown'. He was, in short, fighting not for his own selfish ends, but for his wife's rights and the rights of the English people.

William made his preparations on two fronts: in England and in the Netherlands. Learning from the mistake of Monmouth's puny expedition, he realized that he must invade in overwhelming force. During the course of the summer, he assembled a formidable armada on the Dutch coast, consisting of 60 warships, 700 transports, 15,000 troops, 4000 horses, 21 guns, a smithy, a portable bridge and, last but not least since it enabled the pen to assist the sword, a printing press.

William also benefited from Monmouth's experience in England. Monmouth had struck too soon, before the extent of James's intentions had become apparent. William, instead, reaped the fruits of the mounting disillusion with the king, which united Tories with Whigs in resistance to the crown and reached its high-water mark with the controversial birth of James Francis. The result was that, on 30 June, three weeks after the birth of James Francis, four Whig peers and gentlemen and three Tories signed an invitation to William to invade Britain, since 'nineteen part of twenty of the people ... are desirous of a change'. They exaggerated, of course. But their sense of the popular mood was right.

But none of this would have been possible but for a fateful decision taken by Louis XIV. There were two crisis points in Continental Europe in 1688: one in Cologne, where the pro-French prince archbishop had been replaced by one hostile to Louis, and the other much further south, where the Habsburg Emperor Leopold was engaged in a life-or-death struggle with the Ottoman Turks, who had laid siege to Vienna. If Louis decided to strike against Cologne, which lay near the Dutch border,

William could not risk denuding the republic of troops for his English expedition. Instead, in late summer, Louis resolved to pile the pressure on Leopold by invading southern Germany. The fate of James, Louis's English would-be pupil in absolutism, was sealed.

But at first the weather seemed to offer James the protection that Louis XIV had not. William had intended to sail on the first high tide in October. Instead he was first bottled up in port for several days by adverse winds and then driven back to shore by a storm. Meanwhile, James was still clinging to Divine Providence. 'I see God Almighty continues his Protection to me,' he had written on 20 October, after learning that the storm had driven William back to shore, 'by bringing the wind westerly again.'

But then the wind turned easterly and stayed that way. It blew hard due east, giving William a smooth voyage down the Channel and bottling James's fleet up in port. It was not lost on people that, a hundred years before, Protestantism had been saved by the destruction of the Spanish Armada. Now, for the hotter Protestants, England would be delivered from Catholicism by a very different sort of armada. But again, it was done by a wind. In 1588, the Armada medals were inscribed 'God's winds blew and they were scattered'; in 1688 the breeze that blew William towards England was called 'the Protestant wind'.

William landed at Torbay in Devon on 5 November – another auspicious date for Protestants – and marched through cheering crowds to Exeter, where he set up camp and his printing press to churn out carefully prepared propaganda. The 'Protestant wind' that blew William to England also blew away James's confidence and with it his authority as the signs, which for so long had been in his favour, turned against him. On 19 November, he arrived in Salisbury, intending to stiffen his army with the presence of their undoubted monarch. Instead, he underwent a psychosomatic crisis and succumbed to repeated heavy nosebleeds. Incapacitated and depressed, on 23 November he decided to retreat to London, his army and his subjects' loyalty untested.

That night, his up-and-coming general, John, Lord Churchill, fled to join William, whither he was followed twenty-four hours later by James's other son-in-law, Prince George of Denmark, husband of Princess Anne.

Behind every great man, it is said, is a strong woman. John Churchill's strong woman was his wife, Sarah. But Sarah was also, as Princess Anne's principal courtier and closest friend, a power behind the throne. When Churchill and Prince George deserted to the enemy, James immediately ordered the arrest of their wives, Sarah and Anne. But Sarah was ahead of him and she and Anne fled secretly from Whitehall late at night on 25 November. Their flight went undetected for seven hours, and when James re-entered his capital on the afternoon of the 26th he was greeted with the news that his youngest daughter too had joined the rebels. 'God help me,' he cried, 'my very children have forsaken me!'

Abandoned by his God as well as his children, James's only thought now was for flight. He believed wrongly that history was repeating itself and he was in the position of his father, Charles I. His enemies would execute him and murder his beloved baby son. It was clear that he was suffering a mental crisis and was incapable of judging the true nature of the situation. Outwardly, he conducted negotiations with William. But they were only to provide a cover for his real purpose. He contrived to bungle even this. The escape of the queen with the prince of Wales had to be postponed several days and took place only on 10 December, when she left Whitehall disguised as a laundry woman. James himself quit the capital next day, first flinging the matrix of the Great Seal into the Thames. After his embarrassing capture by the fishermen on the Kent coast, he was taken as a prisoner to Faversham, whence he was rescued by a loyal detachment of his guards and escorted back to London.

There he received a rapturous welcome and, for a moment, thought of making a stand. Many believed that if William ever tried to use force to snatch the throne, the army would rally behind James. This was never put to the test. James's resolution crumbled when William sent a powerful detachment of his army to occupy London, seize Whitehall and order James to withdraw from the capital. The ultimatum was delivered to James in bed at midnight. Twelve hours later he was sent under guard to Rochester, whence, on 23 December, he was allowed to escape to France. This time, with his son-in-law's connivance, he succeeded.

As James left London for the second time, William entered it. In six weeks, and without a shot being fired, England was his. But on what terms?

IV

A late-seventeenth-century engraving shows William the Conqueror swearing to the laws of his sainted Anglo-Saxon predecessor, Edward the Confessor, and thus preserving the traditional rights of the English.

Faced with their own William the Conqueror, the men of 1689 determined to tie him down even more firmly; others were resolved not to have him as king at all. As part of the propaganda for his invasion, William had committed himself, irretrievably, to be everything that James apparently was not: a friend of English law and liberties, of England's religion, and, above all, a supporter of Parliament. He could do nothing, therefore, without a free parliament. The assembly – in the event called a Convention since only a king could legally call a parliament – met on 22 January 1689, a month after William's entry into London.

The Tories retained a small, but weighty, majority in the Lords. But the Commons was made up of the men of the last parliaments of Charles II's reign, who had voted to exclude James from the throne in the first place and had subsequently been marginalized during the Tory ascendancy.

For the first fortnight of the Convention, the two Houses fought over the implications of the extraordinary last few months, which had left James still very much alive, if not in full possession of his mental faculties or indeed present in the country itself. Faced with these facts, the Commons made up of James's Whig enemies and under the chairmanship of Richard Hampden, son of Charles I's implacable enemy, made a bold resolution. It was also a daring constitutional innovation. James II, they declared, had broken the 'original contract' between king and subjects. He had also violated the 'fundamental laws' of the realm. And, most importantly, by removing himself from the country, he had abdicated the throne. The country had not been conquered by William; James had not been deposed. The king had deserted his people, not the other way round. It was a piece of fiction, but it was a very convenient one.

Nevertheless, the Tory-dominated Lords hesitated long and hard before they accepted it. But swallow it they did. James II having been disposed of, the key issue was now the succession. What was to become of the monarchy, now that there was no one on the throne? The Tory peers were determined to preserve the principle of Stuart hereditary right by denying William the title of king – a title to which they believed he, as fourth in line, had no right. He must wait his turn, and let the next in line take the throne. But the next in line was the baby Prince James Francis, the so-called 'pretended Brat'. The implication of sticking to indefeasible hereditary succession was yet another Catholic monarch.

The Whigs were not so wedded to such unyielding principles of monarchy. The Commons neatly sidestepped the problem of James Francis by declaring that it had been found 'by experience' that it was impossible for England to have a Catholic monarch. Whether the baby was legitimate or a changeling did not now matter. It was his Catholicism which rendered him ineligible to inherit the throne. The next Protestant in line for the succession was, of course, Mary. But it was clear that William would not accept being second string to his wife. The only real-istic solution was to have William the saviour of the country as king, whether it was constitutionally correct or not.

In the event, it took William himself to break the deadlock. The Tories hoped to string out the debates so that they could preserve the principle of monarchy. William threw cold water on their endless constitutional nit-picking. He would act neither as regent for his self-exiled father-in-law, James II, nor as consort for his wife Mary; instead, he would be king or he would return to the Netherlands and leave England to constitu-tional squabbles, anarchy and the possibility of a restored James II. Even Tories found that, even if they would rather do without King William, in practice England could not do without the Dutchman now that the coun-try had no legitimate ruler.

Faced with his ultimatum, Lords and Commons agreed to a face-saving compromise. William and Mary would rule as joint king and queen to give the impression that the Stuart line of descent was still valid. But in practice, the exercise of sovereignty would be vested solely in William.

But having given William the crown he wanted, Whigs and Tories united to limit the powers that he or any future monarch could exercise by drawing up the Bill or Declaration of Rights. The rights in question are not so much those of the individual against the government; rather they are 'the ancient rights and liberties' of the nation as represented in Parliament against the crown.

So, the Bill declared, the crown could not dispense with or suspend laws made in Parliament; it could not raise taxation except through Parliament and it could not have a standing army without the consent of Parliament. On the other hand, the crown should allow elections to Parliament to be free and parliaments frequent. Finally, and above all, the Bill declared it 'inconsistent with the safety and welfare of this Protestant kingdom' for the monarch to be Papist or to be married to a Papist.

The principle of the Royal Supremacy, that the English should have the religion of their king, had been stood on its head. It was a revolution indeed.

All was now ready for the formal offer of the crown to William and Mary in the Banqueting House at Whitehall. Mary, who had arrived in England only the day previously and, it was widely felt, had stepped into Mary of Modena's apartments, her possessions and her very habits with indecent glee, joined her husband under the Cloth of Estate. The Lords on the right and the Commons on the left, led by their Speakers, approached the steps of the throne; the clerk read out the Bill of Rights and a nobleman offered William and Mary the crown in the name of the Convention as the 'representative of the nation'.

William then accepted on their joint behalves, promising in turn to do all in his power 'to advance the welfare and glory of the nation', and they were proclaimed king and queen to the sound of trumpets. Two months later, William and Mary were crowned in Westminster Abbey, with the ceremony and the oath in particular having been transformed to reflect the new realities of power.

Each in turn swore to govern 'according to the statutes in parliament agreed on'; to maintain 'the Protestant reformed religion established by law' and to do 'justice in mercy' with no damn nonsense about 'discretion' as previously. Just as innovatory was the coronation sermon. Ever since the coronation of Henry VIII's young son, Edward VI, when Archbishop Cranmer had proclaimed that oaths could not bind the boy king nor holy oils add anything to his inherent, God-given sanctity, preachers at the coronation had vied with each other to elevate the monarch-cum-Supreme Head of the Church to an almost God-like plane.

In 1689, however, all this changed. 'Happy we,' the preacher proclaimed prosaically, 'who are delivered from both extremes: who neither live under the Terror of Despotick power [as in Louis XIV's France], nor are cast loose to the wildness of ungovern'd multitudes [as England had been during the Civil War and Commonwealth].'

As the preacher finished, the congregation broke into 'infinite applause'. They were responding as though the ancient mysteries of the coronation had transmuted into the inauguration ceremonies of a popular prince-president of a middle-of-the-road republic – as of course William was, in effect, in his native Holland. But not only was the monarchy brought down to a merely human level, so too was the Church, which, since the Royal Supremacy, had been its most stalwart supporter and mouthpiece.

William's propaganda had promised, and the Convention speedily enacted, freedom of conscience, of worship and security from persecution to all outside the Church of England – Roman Catholics as well as Protestant dissenters – who would live 'as good subjects', recognize William and Mary as king and queen and repudiate the temporal authority of the pope.

The effect, and on the part of the Whigs the intended effect, was also to diminish the Church of England. The Church remained uniquely privileged and only its members could hold public office, from the throne down. Nevertheless, it had ceased to be a monopoly and become one church among many.

The Church split over the changes between diehard Tories and Whigs, such as Gilbert Burnet, the preacher at the coronation, who not only accepted the new dispensation but also understood that the Church would have to argue for Christianity, not in the old voice of absolute authority, but by reason and persuasion. Chance and taste played their part too. William (among his many other ailments) was asthmatic and detested the urban, riverside position of Whitehall Palace with its fogs and mists. So too did Mary, who felt able to see nothing but 'water or wall'. Within a few months, therefore, the royal couple bought Nottingham House, with its extensive gardens and pleasant suburban situation on the edge of Hyde Park, and rebuilt it at breakneck speed as Kensington Palace. The result, described by a contemporary as 'very noble, though not great', was exactly the kind of residence that William was used to as *stadholder* and prince in the Netherlands.

Meanwhile, Whitehall, called 'the largest and ugliest palace in the world' by the duc de la Rochefoucauld, and seat of all English kings since the time of its builder, Henry VIII, was abandoned for all save ceremonial occasions. Neglected and forlorn, like so many underused buildings, it burnt down in 1698 and was never rebuilt.

Perishing in the flames and ruins was the great dynastic mural of Henry VIII and his family, which, more than any other single image, represented the awesome powers of the Royal Supremacy over Church and state. The painting had survived the destruction of the Supremacy and the royal absolutism it had entailed by less than a decade.

21

BRITANNIA RULES

William III, Mary II and Anne

TWO YEARS BEFORE HER DEATH IN 1714, a statue of Queen Anne was placed equidistant, as wags said, between her two favourite places, St Paul's Cathedral and a brandy shop. Whether the queen's preference was for the bottle or the building, certainly St Paul's was the setting for the high points of her reign.

The queen herself came to the cathedral in solemn procession in 1704 to lead the service of thanksgiving for Blenheim, the great victory won over Louis XIV of France by her general John Churchill, duke of Marlborough, husband of Anne's favourite, Sarah, who rode in the queen's coach and accompanied her every move.

The last monarch to come to St Paul's for a victory service had been Elizabeth I, and the parallels between the two queens were invoked in the celebrations:

> So France and Spain shall do to Anna now.
> As threatening Spain did to Eliza bow
> So France and Spain shall do to Anna now.

But whereas the dire state of Elizabeth's finances had never allowed the defeat of the Armada to be followed up with a crushing offensive campaign against England's enemies, each year of Anne's reign brought fresh victories and another state procession to St Paul's, until, by 1712, the year Anne's statue was erected, Britain could name her own terms for peace with France.

And by then it was no longer England, but Britain. She was the dominant power in Europe. Fifty years later, another victorious war was celebrated at St Paul's. The country's crushing defeat of France in Europe and the Americas marked Britain's emergence as the *world* power.

Few countries have risen to great-power status so quickly and so unexpectedly. Why had the England of Anne succeeded where the England of Elizabeth had failed? The answer can be found in the events that followed the revolution of 1688, which had settled most of the political and religious disputes that had torn England apart since the Reformation.

But much of the credit must also go to the man Anne abused in her private letters as 'Caliban' or 'the Dutch monster': her cousin, brother-in-law and predecessor, William III. It was William who created a new kind of English monarchy, with a new relationship between crown and Parliament, and in doing so transformed Britain from a divided, unstable, rebellious and marginal country into the state that would become the most powerful on the planet.

I

Soon after their inauguration as joint monarchs in February 1689, William of Orange and his queen, Mary Stuart, escaped from London to enjoy the country air at Hampton Court. It was love at first sight, and the palace and gardens we know today are essentially their creation.

But though William and Mary could flee the capital, they could not escape so easily from the quasi-religious rituals that hedged the divinity of the Tudor and Stuart kings. The dour Calvinist king was not impressed. He had mocked 'the comedy of the coronation', which was full of 'foolish old Popish ceremonies'. But his obligation to enact the spiritual dimension of English monarchy did not stop there. Many of these rituals centred on the Chapel Royal and followed the ancient rhythms of the Church's calendar. A particularly important group of dates clustered round the great feast of Easter, which in 1689 fell on 31 March.

On the day before Good Friday, the monarch, re-enacting the role of Christ, would wash the feet of as many poor persons as he was years old in the ceremony of Maundy Thursday. Three days later, on Easter Sunday, he would take his place in the Royal Pew, then, at the climax of the service, descend the stairs, process to the altar and receive communion alone to symbolize his unique relationship with God. There was also a clamour for William and Mary, acknowledged now by God and man, to follow in the footsteps of their predecessors and heal the sick by touching for the King's Evil.

William and Mary managed to go through the Easter Day ceremonies, though they thought the practice of receiving communion alone a 'foolish formality' and changed it as soon as possible. But William baulked at other, more outlandish ceremonies. On Maundy Thursday he refused to wash the feet of the poor, limiting himself instead to giving them the traditional alms. Even more extreme was his reaction to touching for scrofula. Since the Stuart Restoration in 1660, this ceremony had been the primary point of contact between monarch and subject and the symbol of the divine nature of kingship. Charles II had touched vast numbers of the people. James II had gone beyond Charles's enthusiasm for the practice and had reintroduced the old Latin Catholic ritual as well. For William, this was to add idolatrous superstition to old-fashioned absurdity and he suspended the practice entirely. 'God give you better health and more sense!' he mocked the hopeful afflicted.

Within days, William's refusal to continue the old royal rituals was hot news in Paris. It signalled to his French rival and everybody else that here was a different kind of king. For William's Tudor and Stuart predecessors, the monarchy and its powers, prerogatives and titles was a sacramental trust, committed by God to their ancestors, and, with God's will, to be transmitted to their descendants. But none of this, despite his own Stuart mother and wife, applied to William. He had come to the throne not through strict lineal succession, but because of the mess of purely human affairs. And since he was childless and with no prospect of offspring, he had no descendants to worry about. Finally, as a strict Calvinist, he didn't – as his attitude to the coronation, the Maundy and the Touching shows – believe in sacraments, royal or otherwise.

What William *did* believe in was predestination or divinely ordained destiny: in particular his own God-given mission to be the champion of Protestantism and the nemesis of Louis XIV's France. To become king of England, therefore, was only a step to this goal and not an end in itself. This meant that William's view of kingship was *instrumental*, in contrast to the jealous *sacramentalism* of his Tudor and Stuart predecessors. And this meant in turn that for William literally nothing was sacred (following the Dutch custom, he even kept his hat on during religious services). He was not sentimental about the trappings and symbols of monarchy. Nor was he in thrall to the sacred mystique of kingship. So William was willing, if not necessarily happy, to bargain away the powers of the monarchy for the hard cash that was needed to fight his great war against France.

This, it turned out, was a good thing, since the attitude of William's subjects to the monarchy had changed as well. The change was neatly summarized for the king by one of his ministers. During the last few decades, kings had known where they stood: the Tory half of the nation supported royal power while the Whig half opposed it. But the revolution that had brought William to power had muddied the waters. For the Whigs, though they were William's natural supporters, retained their habitual mistrust of monarchy. While the Tories, though remaining theoretically committed to royal power, did not, in their heart of hearts, think that William was the rightful king. They had made solemn and binding oaths to James II, which they were painfully conscious of having broken. And so the Tories mistrusted William at least as much as the Whigs did.

The result was that, divided in everything else, William's leading subjects were united in their determination to drive a hard bargain with their new king William. One MP spoke for all when he told the House: 'If you settle such a revenue as that the King should have no need of a Parliament, I think we do not do our duty to them that sent us hither.'

Parliament had made this error of rendering themselves useless by granting the king enough money to rule on his own in the Restoration Settlement of 1660 and, even more flagrantly, at the beginning of James II's reign in 1685. It was not to repeat the mistake again.

So in 1689 it refused to make any permanent settlement of the revenue at all, postponing it for another year. And even in 1690 it granted William only the Customs (or taxes on foreign trade) for life, while the Excise (or internal indirect taxes) was to be reviewed four years later. In personal conversations, William freely expressed his outrage at such ingratitude, as he saw it. 'The Commons used him like a dog,' he would say. 'Truly, a King of England … is the worst figure in Christendom,' he moaned at another time. And, in exasperation at the carpings and criticisms of the English, he snapped: 'The nation entertained such distrust and jealousies of him that he intended to go abroad.'

But, having vented his frustrations in private, in public (as he had learned to do by bitter experience in the Netherlands) he calmly settled down to bargain. The result was a financial and constitutional revolution far greater in effect than the revolution itself. In 1689 he offered the Commons scrutiny of public accounts. He surrendered his prerogative of calling and dissolving parliaments at his own pleasure in 1694 by agreeing to the Triennial Act, which provided instead for the automatic summoning of a new parliament every three years. And in 1697, by agreeing to a Civil List to cover the expenses of the royal household and peacetime domestic administration, he yielded to Parliament control over the expenditure, as well as the raising, of all revenue for the army and the navy.

Thanks to this subtle give-and-take diplomacy, Parliament, which in 1690 had been barely willing to finance William's expedition to reconquer Ireland from a French-financed invasion personally led by a reluctant James II, by the middle of the decade was raising an unheard-of £4 million a year in taxation. And every penny was needed. For the war that William declared against France within days of his coronation was the largest, longest, most expensive conflict England had engaged in since the Middle Ages. John Churchill, duke of Marlborough and after the king himself England's leading general, predicted that it would last 'forever'; in sober fact it was to be merely a new hundred years' war which was not finally settled till the Congress of Vienna in 1815.

The scale of the war and the taxation it entailed completed and made permanent the revolution of 1688/89. The result was literally built in stone. The Board Room of the Admiralty in Whitehall, which is still in use, was built to put the administration of England's hugely expanded navy on a proper footing. The Royal Hospital at Greenwich, founded by Queen Mary in 1692 after the great naval victory over the French of La Hogue, was built to care for invalided and aged sailors. Grander than any royal palace, it became a monument both to England's naval greatness and, with its lavishly painted interiors, to the Glorious Revolution and William's own triumphs over France.

If England was gaining secure and permanent civil and military institutions safely ensured by sturdy buildings, surely the most innovative and durable was the Bank of England, established in 1694 at Mercer's Hall in the City of London. Its origins had, like much else, less to do with root-and-branch reforms than with William's pressing need to manage the government debt incurred in fighting the war against France. Copied, once again, from the Dutch model of the Bank of Amsterdam, the bank's security was based, not on the king's credit (for kings, including Louis XIV, could and did go bankrupt), but on the guaranteed steady income stream of parliamentary taxation.

Security of payment meant that English interest rates plunged, while those in France, which stuck to the old system of royal credit and experienced the familiar crises of royal bankruptcy, soared. Thus, though pound for *livre* the English tax base was smaller than that of France (which is four times as big a country and then had three times as big a population), gearing meant that the English could match or even outspend the French.

In his own lifetime, William was able only to fight Louis to a standstill rather than inflict the crushing defeat for which he yearned. But he had created the financial, military and political machinery which, as events would show, swung the balance of power decisively in England's favour. It was an extraordinary achievement, which makes this Dutchman one of England's greatest monarchs.

II

William got little thanks from his subjects at the time, and posterity has been no kinder. For William, with so many great gifts, had few of the small ones that humanize greatness and make it popular, or at least bearable. He had no small talk. He suffered fools not at all. He hated company, preferring instead to unwind with a handful of intimates.

Secure in the privacy of the suburban or rural royal courts, William was free to carouse with his mainly Dutch male cronies in seclusion. English ministers who were used to a royal court where the king was accessible and business could be conducted face to face were annoyed by William's reclusive tendencies. Rather than sleep in the magnificence of the State Bedchamber, which was traditionally the buzzing hub of the royal court, William took his rest in a simple private chamber. And it was very private indeed. The king could not be troubled by overly attentive servants, demanding ministers or prying eyes. The locks were on the inside and only one other man had the key, Arnold Joost van Keppel, whose extensive apartment was next door. And Keppel's good looks and easy and exclusive access to the king fuelled ugly rumours of homosexuality.

Worst of all, perhaps, William and his favourites remained obstinately Dutch, and that the xenophobic English found intolerable. His wife and joint monarch, Queen Mary, however, deflected much of the bitterness over the fact that England had been conquered by a warmongering Dutch obsessive. Mary represented the unbroken Stuart descent and continuity with the past. Above all she was English. If William had delivered England from a Catholic king and waged war on France, Mary represented English virtue and piety. As far as William was concerned this was a good arrangement. For Mary believed that ruling was a man's business, and she was no threat to William's sole exercise of power. At the same time, she was indispensable to him as a figurehead to quell his new subjects' xenophobia. As William stated: 'He was to conquer Enemies, and she was to gain Friends.'

But when Mary died of smallpox in 1694, the Stuart fig leaf was torn from William's throne. Mary was loved by the people, and her death provoked an outpouring of grief from the country. But William had always been a very unpopular king, nicknamed the 'Rotten Orange', 'Hook Nose' or 'The Little Spark'. King Louis and the exiled James II celebrated when they heard of the death of Queen Mary. They did not believe that William could survive long on his own. He was hated by the English, and if he wasn't deposed or assassinated, then at least he would never risk leaving the country to go and fight France.

But William was able to face down his enemies. The king's evidently sincere grief at his bereavement won him some temporary popularity, and his supporters urged the population to respect the memory of the late lamented queen by remaining loyal, as she had done, to her husband. The PR campaign worked. Despite Louis's and James's predictions, William was secure enough to leave the country to continue the war against France as usual during the campaigning season. If the English did not love William as they had loved Mary, or even respect him that much, they were at least prepared to tolerate him for all his faults.

But by the turn of the eighteenth century Parliament had begun to resent William's aggressive foreign policy and to resent paying for it most of all. The Commons demanded that he disband most of the army and send home his Dutch guards. Once again, the stage appeared to be set for another round in the chronic conflict between king and Commons that had removed two monarchs within living memory. As he had done before, William petulantly threatened to return to Holland and wait until the English came to their senses and begged him to come back to save them from France and James II. He even drafted an abdication speech. For the sake of a few pounds, William said, the English were prepared to reduce the army and invite invasion. 'It is impossible to credit the serene indifference with which they consider events outside their own country,' William wrote of his truculent and insular subjects.

Things got worse as Parliament and king clashed over foreign policy and England's rights and responsibilities in Europe. But then the rule of the House of Orange came to an abrupt and unexpected end. On 21 February William was hunting in Hampton Court Park when his favourite horse, Sorrel, stumbled at a mole hill, throwing him and breaking his collarbone in the fall. The bone was set successfully but a chest infection set in and William died at his other favourite palace of Kensington on 8 March, aged fifty-one. Five weeks later, on 12 April, he was buried privately at midnight in Westminster Abbey. The Privy Council announced plans for a monument in the Abbey and another in a 'public place'. But no one could be bothered to build them – least of all his successor Anne.

Anne was thirty-seven. She had never been a beauty like her sister Mary. But she had a handsome, womanly figure, rather running to seed after repeated miscarriages and stillbirths. Her best feature, however, was her beautiful speaking voice, for which she had received professional coaching in her youth. Above all, she knew how to rise to a public occasion.

This meant that her first speech to Parliament, only three days after William's death, was a triumph. She wore a magnificent crimson robe, lined with ermine and bordered with gold. She blushed prettily. And she proclaimed in her thrilling voice that 'I know my heart to be entirely English'.

It was a deliberate distancing of herself from William, the foreigner who barely respected England and Englishmen. The English, pleased as they were to be rid of William, loved her for her bullish and patriotic sentiments, and from that moment she became, and remained, as popular as William had been disliked. Her accession seemed like the best of all possible worlds. She was a Stuart, but she was fiercely committed to the Protestant Anglican Church. She was a supporter of the modernized monarchy, but she had an instinctive and inbred regard for the ceremonies and mystique of the ancient monarchy. Touching for the King's Evil was back in fashion.

But despite these changes of personal style and belief, the substance of government altered very little. She would, Anne confirmed in her first speech to Parliament, continue her predecessor's policies at home and abroad. And that meant, above all, that she would continue with the war against France. She told the Dutch Republic that she would do everything that 'will be necessary [for] preserving the common liberty of Europe, and reducing the power of France to its just limits'. But this was an English queen speaking, and Anne was determined to cast herself in the mould of historic warrior queens; this would be an English war, and the country would fight it for its own interests and glory, and not on behalf of others.

For the stalemate peace that Louis and William had been forced to sign in 1697 quickly collapsed. The issue was the succession to the childless King Carlos II, who ruled Spain and her still vast empire in Europe and South America. Among the intermarried royal families of Europe, the choice lay between two remote cousins: the Austrian Habsburg Emperor was one candidate, the other was Philip, the younger grandson of Louis XIV of France. In the event, it was Philip whom Carlos left as his heir on his death in 1700.

For William the prospect of such a gigantic addition to French power was intolerable and, just before his death, he had reassembled the Grand Alliance against France, consisting of Britain, the Netherlands, the Empire and the German princes. But the declaration of war, on 5 May 1702, was left to Anne. Louis is supposed to have replied mockingly that he must be old indeed if women waged war on him. But oddly it was the fact that Anne was a woman which proved his downfall. For William, as was still commonplace among kings, had acted as his own commander. This was a mixed blessing: he was brave to the point of foolhardiness and indomitable; but he was no general.

But the man Anne chose to act in her stead as commander was. Indeed, ranking with Caesar and Napoleon, he is the only world-class general that England has ever produced. John Churchill had defected to William during the revolution, but, like many leading Englishmen, he had been pushed aside by the new king's Dutch intimates. In 1692 he was dismissed from court and deprived of his commands for spreading dissatisfaction in the army against the Dutch generals. Forgiven at last, he was appointed captain of the forces by William near the end of his reign, in 1701. He was retained in this leading post by the new queen, not just for his qualities, but because his wife was the queen's best friend.

Losing her mother at the age of only eight and quickly separated from her father because of his conversion to Catholicism, Anne became shy, reserved and lonely. She had found consolation in a series of close friendships with women. Much the most important and long lasting was that with Sarah Churchill, and testimony to it are the countless letters they wrote each other under the levelling pseudonyms of Mrs Freeman (Sarah) and Mrs Morley (Anne). Back in 1692, when the Churchills had been disgraced, William had demanded that Anne dismiss Sarah and John from her household. But Anne won the lasting hatred of her brother-in-law the king when she refused. Anne had pledged herself to Sarah as follows: 'never believe your Mrs Morley will ever submit, she can wait for a Sunshine Day, and if she does not live to see it, yet she hopes England will flourish again'. Now, with William's death, the Sunshine Day had arrived for England and, especially, for the Churchills.

Within a week of her accession, Anne had delivered her person and her kingdom to John and Sarah. Sarah was made Groom of the Stole and head of the royal bedchamber. The office was known, after its official symbol, as 'the key to the prince', and it controlled access to the queen's private apartments, her jewels and robes, and her personal cash. At the same time, John was appointed captain-general, master-general of the ordnance and ambassador extraordinary to the Dutch Republic, which in turn appointed him its own captain-general with the elegant Mauritshuis in The Hague as his residence.

His occupation of the Mauritshuis, which had belonged to the junior branch of the House of Orange, emphasized that John had now inherited William III's role as joint commander of the Anglo-Dutch alliance. Indeed, in military terms the Dutch were still the senior partner, as they had once been in trade and public finance. Their army was professionally drilled and equipped with the most modern weapons, such as flintlock muskets with fixed bayonets, while the Dutch logistics and commissariat were the most efficient in Europe.

But the English, as in other areas, copied them, and, thanks to their superior resources, soon outdid them. In all this Marlborough was the beneficiary of William III's pioneering efforts. But he achieved what William had only dreamed of doing. In 1702/3 he freed the Dutch Republic from the French stranglehold. That won him the dukedom of Marlborough. In 1704 he shattered the French threat to the emperor, the other key member of the Grand Alliance, with the victory of Blenheim on the Danube. The French commander was captured, along with 13,000 of his men, and 20,000 were killed. It was a crushing defeat for France, and England's greatest victory since Henry V's at Agincourt.

Marlborough scribbled the news to Anne on the back of a tavern bill and was rewarded with the royal estate of Woodstock in Oxfordshire. Here a vast palace grander by far than any of Anne's own was built for him and his wife at public expense. Called Blenheim, it is a temple to Marlborough's series of victories in the 1700s. Its every feature memorializes his triumphs: Blenheim itself; the victory at Ramillies in 1706 which drove France out of modern Belgium; and Oudenarde, the victory in 1708 which opened up the door to France itself.

But, despite Marlborough's triumphs, there remained profound tensions in Britain. For the issue of the succession had reopened. Back in 1689, the full implications of dethroning James II, whose general Marlborough had once been, had been masked because the House of Stuart would, it seemed, continue in the persons of his daughters and their issue.

Indeed, that very July Anne, despite her unfortunate tendency to miscarriages, had had a son who lived. He was christened William, created duke of Gloucester and became the apple of his uncle William III's eye. The succession would continue, and it would be through a male, a Protestant, a descendant of the direct Stuart line and an Englishman. The people could be reassured that the rule of a foreigner was only a temporary sacrifice. But in 1700 the boy died. Who should now replace him in the succession after Anne?

There was always the possibility of reverting to the male Stuart line, still temptingly near in their exile in France. The dethroned James II died in 1701 but was succeeded by the 'warming-pan baby', James Francis, whose birth in 1688 had started it all. Known to history as the Old Pretender, he was recognized by Louis XIV as King James VIII of Scotland and James III of England immediately on his father's death.

The Old Pretender was brave, moderately intelligent and charming – one to one at least. But he had his father's stiffness of public manner, his arrogance and his unyielding rigidity in his commitment to Catholicism. In short, the Old Pretender was the kind of man to arouse loyalty but, almost invariably, to disappoint it.

A few English and more Scots remained devoted to the cause of James III and were known, from the Latin form of his name, as 'Jacobites'. But, overwhelmingly, the English elite remained opposed to a Catholic king. Instead, Parliament – Tories as well as Whigs – passed the Act of Settlement in 1701. This reaffirmed the principle of the revolution that a Roman Catholic should never be king. The problem was that they had to look very far to find a Protestant in the line of descent from the Tudor and Stuart dynasties. Parliament passed over fifty other popish claimants who stood legitimately in the line of succession, including the Old Pretender. At last, it gave the succession, after Anne, to the impeccably Protestant Sophia, granddaughter of James I and electress dowager of the insignificant north German principality of Hanover. It was a link with the royal line, but a very distant one.

Two months after the passing of the Act of Settlement an English embassy arrived in Hanover to honour the future dynasty. They presented the widowed Electress Sophia with a copy of the Act of Settlement and her son, Georg Ludwig, with the Garter. (Georg was ruling prince of Hanover, because there, unlike in England, women were prevented from reigning in their own right.) Five years later, Sophia's grandson, the electoral prince, Georg August, was also made a Knight of the Garter and created duke of Cambridge as well.

But though Anne was happy to shower honours on her successors, she refused absolutely to allow any member of the electoral family to set foot in England. Successors were a magnet for opposition, as the queen knew, for she had been a difficult heir herself. Anne, wisely, was taking no risks. In England the choice of the House of Hanover was widely welcomed. But in Scotland, which shared a monarch with England but not a parliament, it precipitated an immediate rupture in relations with its southern neighbour. It was not automatic that the House of Hanover would succeed to the throne of Scotland. The spectre of renewed hostility between the two kingdoms raised its ugly head once again.

Would Marlborough have to break off the greater ambition of taking on Europe, in order, like that earlier captain-general Cromwell, to subdue the rebellious northern kingdom?

III

In March 1703 the Scottish Parliament was opened with the customary 'riding'. The mounted procession set out from Holyrood Palace, rode up the High Street, past St Giles Cathedral, and turned into the Scottish Parliament House. First came the nobles in their robes; then the barons representing the shires; and finally the town burgesses. The members were accompanied by their armed retainers and rode through a lane of citizens, also armed.

The carrying of arms was traditional. But, on this occasion, the atmosphere was feverish with barely suppressed real violence: 'our swords were in our hands or at least our hands were at our swords', one leading member recalled. And the object of this impassioned feeling was England.

Before the revolution, the Scottish Parliament was a poor thing, managed for the absentee monarch by a committee called the Lords of the Articles. But the revolution liberated Parliament in Scotland as well as in England. Freed from royal management, it could take an independent line against the crown – and a crown that was seen, above all, as the prisoner of its English ministers. Indeed, there was now talk of actual independence, or at least of selling freedom dearly.

The bargaining counter was the Hanoverian succession. The English Act of Settlement, which gave the crown to the House of Hanover, had been passed without consulting the Scots. Now the Scots would play the English at their own game and settle their succession independently too. The Scottish Parliament of 1703 did so in the Act of Security. This provided that, after Anne's death, the next monarch of Scotland should be a Protestant and of the royal line, but need not be the same person as the successor to the English crown. The English Parliament had actually named who the successor would be. This was to ensure that none of the fifty or so Catholics who stood in the line converted to Protestantism in order to fulfil the obligations of the Act of Succession and claim their right. As the Scots framed their Act of Security, there was nothing to stop the Old Pretender, the so-called James VIII of Scotland, from converting to Protestantism to claim the throne, and then switching back to Catholicism when circumstances suited. The British Isles would once again have two monarchs facing each other with mutual enmity.

Anne refused to give her consent to the Act of Security for almost a year, until overwhelming pressure forced her to yield. A few days later, news of Marlborough's great victory at Blenheim reached London. Freed from the immediate threat of a French-sponsored Jacobite invasion of Scotland, the English Parliament could now respond in kind to the Scottish.

The result was the Aliens Act, passed in spring 1705. All Scots, except those resident in England, were to be treated as aliens, and the major Scottish export trades to England banned unless, by Christmas 1705, significant progress had been made to agreeing a union of the two kingdoms.

The Aliens Act aroused predictable outrage in Scotland. But the deadline did concentrate minds. Two sets of commissioners, thirty or so on each side, were appointed to thrash out an agreement. The commissioners began work in April 1706 in government offices in what had been Henry VIII's cockpit at Whitehall. To soothe Scottish sensibilities, the two sets of commissioners met in separate rooms, communicated by written minutes only and strictly avoided socializing with each other.

On 22 April, the English room sent the following proposal to the Scottish:

> That the two kingdoms of England and Scotland be for ever United into one kingdom by the name of Great Britain. That the United Kingdom of Great Britain be represented by one and the same parliament, and that the succession to the monarchy of Great Britain [be vested in the House of Hanover].

On the 25th, the Scottish commissioners came back with a counter-proposal. They would accept union and the Hanoverian succession but on condition of freedom of trade, not only within the United Kingdom but also within 'the Plantations'. The English replied promptly that they regarded such mutual freedom of trade as a 'necessary consequence of an entire Union'.

It had taken only three days to work out the bones of an agreement. For both sides had got what they wanted. The English wanted Scotland unshakeably onside during their newly embarked-upon geopolitical struggle with France; while the Scots, having tried but failed catastrophically to establish a colonial empire of their own, wanted free access to the English 'Plantations' as a way out of their own desperate national poverty.

The 'Plantations', or colonies, largely in North America, were the great English success story of the previous hundred years, as, in spite of civil strife at home, the English had built an empire abroad. By Anne's reign, indeed, America seemed a separate realm and appears symbolically as such on the base of Anne's statue outside St Paul's, alongside figures representing her three other kingdoms of England, Ireland and Scotland. Henceforward, this American realm was to be as much Scottish as English. Or rather, like the empire itself, it was to be British.

And it was to St Paul's that Anne, wearing the combined orders of the English Garter and the Scottish Thistle and accompanied by 400 coaches, came to celebrate Union on 1 May 1707, the day that it came into effect. It was, she said, even among so many victories, the day that would prove the true happiness of her reign.

The Union was a nice mixture of the conservative and the radical. Most that was distinctively Scottish (or indeed English) was preserved, and along with 'the most ancient and most noble order of the Thistle', Scotland kept its own law and law courts (complete, at the outset, with the torture that was an intrinsic part of its criminal law), its universities and educational system and, above all, the intolerant, monopolistic Presbyterian Kirk that had been restored in the religious upheaval that was Scotland's peculiar contribution to the Glorious Revolution.

But equally, the institutions of the United Kingdom were new and were framed with the innovative, rational methods of Anglo-Dutch political economy. Most pressing, however, was the issue of Scottish representation in the Union Parliament at Westminster. It could be determined either by population or (since the principal business of Parliament was to vote taxation) by taxable wealth. Using the former basis would have given Scotland eighty-five MPs; using the latter (since Scotland's wealth was only a fortieth of England's) only thirteen. Eventually the commissioners compromised at forty-five, and honour was more or less satisfied.

Nevertheless, there were no celebrations for Union in Scotland. But, as the intellectual and economic transformation of eighteenth-century Scotland would show, the Scots probably got the better deal.

On 19 August 1708, Anne processed once more to the spiritual home of her reign, St Paul's, to give thanks for Marlborough's victory of Oudenarde. Accompanying her in her coach, as etiquette demanded, was Marlborough's duchess, Sarah. There had been much resentment at the duke and duchess of Marlborough's influence over the queen. Sarah was a committed Whig, contemptuous of princes and princesses, proudly atheist and opposed to the Anglican monopoly. She believed that it was her job to keep Anne from the Tories, whom the queen instinctively supported. Many detested Sarah as the malign power behind the throne.

All this came to a head on the way to St Paul's. En route, the two women had a terrible quarrel because Anne, who hated cumbrous clothing, had refused to wear the rich, heavy jewels that Sarah, as Groom of the Stole, had put out for her. As they stepped out of the coach, Sarah was heard to hiss 'Be quiet' to the queen, lest (she claimed) others overheard their quarrel. It seemed to confirm Sarah's unnatural power over the monarch. But more importantly, Anne never forgave the insult to majesty and the long and fraught friendship was over.

The quarrel was in fact only the straw that broke the camel's back. For Sarah had fought her own war at home against the Tory leaders whom she accused, not altogether wrongly as it turned out, of being secret Jacobites. Aware of James III's insidious charms, Sarah campaigned, with all her husband's relentlessness but none of his panache, for the Tories to be removed from government and for her Whig friends to retain power. But Anne, desperate to preserve her freedom of action between the competing political parties, refused. The result was that Sarah's company became increasingly disagreeable to the queen, who resented the political lectures and nagging. Lonely, unwell and in need of friendship, she transferred her affections to another courtier, Abigail Masham, who, unlike the domineering and high-handed Sarah, was demure and undemanding. Abigail was also close to the Tories, and her favour with the queen threatened to break the Whigs' monopoly on power. Sarah, outraged in turn, then accused the queen, in barely concealed terms, of lesbianism.

Sarah's loss of favour dangerously exposed Marlborough on the home front. For in any case, Anne, and much of the nation, were getting sick of the war, the deaths and the spiralling taxation. The turning point was Marlborough's last great set-piece battle of Malplaquet. It was an English victory of sorts. But the casualties were enormous and the French, faced with the invasion of their own soil, dug their heels in to fight a patriotic war. Marlborough's reaction was to demand the captain-generalship for life, like Oliver Cromwell. Anne's was to exclaim, 'when will this bloodshed ever cease?' and to decide that Marlborough must go.

Marlborough was dismissed in December 1711 and his Whig allies were replaced by a Tory ministry determined to make a unilateral peace with France. Secret negotiations were opened and agreement quickly reached. Louis XIV's grandson Philip would retain Spain and her American empire, but renounce any future right to France. England would be granted huge exclusive commercial concessions in the Spanish Empire, including a thirty-year monopoly on the slave trade. The Tories also had a secret plot. They had provoked outrage in Europe by abandoning their allies. One very important loser in this matter was Georg Ludwig, the elector of Hanover and heir to Sophia, who stood to inherit the English crown. Once on the throne, Georg would be unlikely to forget or forgive this gross betrayal. The outcome of the Act of Succession would be to place the Tories in danger. The leaders would therefore dump Hanover and offer the crown to the Old Pretender, provided he renounced Catholicism.

The separate peace was formally agreed at Utrecht in 1713 and celebrated with yet another grand thanksgiving service in St Paul's. And there was much to celebrate, since the peace, despite its consciously moderate terms, marked England's eclipse of the two powers that, only half a century before, had overshadowed her: England was now more powerful militarily than France and more commercially successful than the Netherlands.

And she had found her own unique way to modernity. At the root of this success was a new relationship between monarch and Parliament, in which the sovereign reigned, but for the most part the ministers ruled. Forged in the revolution of 1688, developed under William and consolidated under Anne, this new constitutional monarchy had proved more than a match for the absolutist political model represented by France. Over the coming centuries it would do so time and again.

But Anne, despite her passionate personal support for the peace, was too frail to attend the ceremonies. On Christmas Eve she fell suddenly and dangerously ill. She made a recovery of sorts. But it was soon clear that she had only months, if not weeks, to live. The Tory ministers now made a secret offer of the crown to the Old Pretender, subject only to his conversion. But James III had inherited his father's arrogance as well as his unyielding commitment to Catholicism. He now calculated that the Tories had so alienated Hanover that they would have to bring him back, conversion or no conversion, and refused point blank to change his religion.

That was the end of the Pretender's chances and, it turned out, of the Tories' as well.

IV

On 30 July Anne suffered two violent strokes, which left her able to say only yes or no. Two days later, at the age of only forty-nine, she was dead, and Marlborough and his duchess, who had gone into ostentatious voluntary exile in disgust at the peace, returned in triumph to London.

Anne's reign was a paradox, between public power and popularity and personal physical weakness. The latter was unsparingly described by one of the Scottish Union commissioners in his account of an audience with the queen:

> Her Majesty was labouring under a fit of the gout, and in extreme pain and agony ... Her face, which was red and spotted, was rendered something frightful by her negligent dress, and the foot affected was tied up with a poultice and some nasty bandages ... Nature seems to be inverted when a poor infirm woman becomes one of the rulers of the world.

This was possible, of course, only because of the machinery of England's new constitutional monarchy, in which the queen was a powerful figurehead, but the actual government was left to ministers.

Nevertheless, a woman who could resist and finally face down Marlborough and his formidable duchess was nobody's tool. Likewise the peace with France was hers, as much as the Tories'. But her most important contribution was to remain steadfastly loyal after her own fashion to the Hanoverian succession. And so, England and Scotland were likely to get another female ruler, Sophia of Hanover. But Sophia died before she could inherit, and the heir to the British crown was her son, Georg Ludwig.

When Anne died shortly after, the two principal claimants were both several hundred miles from London: Georg Ludwig in Hanover and the Old Pretender in Lorraine, where he had been forced to withdraw after the peace with France. If he had made a dash for it, the Old Pretender could have given the Hanoverian a run for his money. But James III did not do dashing.

Instead, correctly confident in the machinery of the Act of Settlement, George, as he now signed himself in English, took a leisurely six weeks to arrive in England. He landed at Greenwich on 18 September at 6 p.m. Accompanied by his son, Georg August, and a great crowd of nobles, gentry and common folk, he walked through the grand colonnades and courtyards of the Royal Naval Hospital to the Queen's House in the park, where he spent his first night in England.

The following morning, in the Queen's House, George held his first English court. He made plain his high regard for the leaders of the Whig Party and he administered a very public snub to the Tory leader: he allowed him to kiss his hands but said nothing to him in return. If George had anything to do with it, the sun, it was clear, would shine on the Whigs, while the Tories were destined for the wilderness.

And George did have a lot to do with it, despite the constitutional nature of the monarchy. And royal influence, combined with distaste at the Tories' slitheriness about the Hanoverian succession, helped win the Whigs a comfortable majority in the Commons. They now turned the Tory defeat into a rout by impeaching the former Tory ministers for their treachery in the peace negotiations at Utrecht. One was sent to the Tower; the other fled to the Old Pretender to encourage his bid for the throne.

But at this moment, Louis XIV of France, the inveterate enemy of the new English monarchy and the principal casualty of its success, died and was succeeded by a regency that was committed to good relations with England. Deprived of French active support, a Jacobite rising conducted by northern English Catholics was easily defeated at Preston. But in Scotland, though the rebels were held back from the Lowlands by the drawn battle of Sheriffmuir, they took the Highlands and occupied Perth.

After lengthy delays and disguised as a French bishop, the Old Pretender finally set sail for Scotland, where he landed just before Christmas 1715. At first, it was a triumphal progress: the magistrates of Aberdeen paid him homage; he made a state entry into Dundee; and proclaimed his forthcoming coronation as King James VIII and III at Scone. He then took up residence at Scone Palace and kept his court with the royal state of his ancestors.

But, after this good start, things began to crumble. With his shy, cold public manner, James couldn't even keep the loyalty of his existing follow-ers, let alone recruit new ones. 'If he found himself disappointed with us', one of his soldiers wrote, 'we were tenfold more so in him.' It was no basis on which to stand and fight the government forces that were marching on them through the snow of winter.

After retreating to Montrose the Old Pretender took ship secretly to France on 3 February 1716, abandoning his army to their fate. He never saw Britain again. The House of Hanover had seen off the Stuart dynasty.

The arrival of George I and ensuing triumph of the House of Hanover were also commemorated in the Painted Hall at Greenwich, a few paces from where George actually landed.

But that was the only realistic thing about the painting. Done in grisaille (or shades of grey) to imitate a Roman stone relief, it shows George arriving in a Roman triumphal chariot, while personifications of Tyrannic Power and Rebellious Despair quail before his harbinger, Liberty, with her cap.

The reality had been very different as the painter, James Thornhill, who had been an eyewitness and shows himself as such at the edge of the composition, well knew. It was night, he noted. George's clothes were unworthy of the event. And most of the receiving peers were Tories, which was the wrong political party. Hence, he explained, his decision to go for high-flown allegory.

But the sober reality had been right. George was a modest man and would preside over a modest monarchy. No British king would ever again inhabit a palace as large as Greenwich or hold court in a space as splendid as the Painted Hall. And if more and more of the globe would indeed be British, it was not the king but his ministers who made it so.

Nevertheless, Thornhill's vast swirling allegories were not wholly disproportionate to the events they represent. For the Revolution and its aftermath in the Hanoverian Succession were glorious. By good luck, as well as good management, Britain had freed herself from political and religious absolutism and in so doing freed herself for the rapid and most significant expansion of any European power since Rome. No wonder Thornhill, like most subsequent commentators on the British monarchy, was uncertain of what language he should use to describe the limitation of the Crown and the triumph of the Nation.

22

❖❖

EMPIRE

George I, George II, George III

IN 1782, FACED WITH A COMMONS MOTION to make peace with Britain's rebellious American colonies and recognize their independence, George III resolved to abdicate and return to his other kingdom of Hanover in Germany. He even got so far as drafting his abdication address:

> His Majesty … with much sorrow finds he can be of no further util-
> ity to his native country, which drives him to the painful step of
> quitting it forever.
>
> In consequence … his Majesty resigns the Crown of Great Brit-
> ain … to his … son and lawful successor George, Prince of Wales,
> whose endeavours for the prosperity of the British Empire he hopes
> may prove more successful.

Was the House of Hanover about to go the way of its unlucky predecessors the Stuarts? And the British to lose the empire they had only recently won? If it had been left to the Hanoverians themselves, who were the least able and attractive house to sit on the British throne, it is unlikely there would have been much to lose in the first place.

But in fact Britain in the eighteenth century witnessed an extraordinary and unprecedented political development: the rise of a second, parallel monarchy in Britain – the premiership. It was monarchs of this new kind who created the first British Empire, and the old monarchy which eventually destroyed it.

The seeds of the premiership lay in the Glorious Revolution of 1688/89. But it was the accession of the House of Hanover in 1714, and the awkward, unattractive personalities of the first two Hanoverian kings, which accelerated its development and made it irreversible.

I

For most of the eighteenth century, the monarchy veered between deep unpopularity and a national joke. When George I became king in 1714 the English had, for the second time in thirty years, a foreign monarch. Indeed, George of Hanover was much more foreign than William of Orange. For William had an English mother, spoke fluent English and was married to an English princess. George, on the other hand, was resolutely, unremittingly German: he arrived with German ministers, German-speaking Turkish body-servants, and German mistresses. (Indeed, the mistresses had been a necessary part of his life since he condemned his wife to life imprisonment in a German castle following the discovery of her sensational affair with a Swedish count.) Even subsequently, he never learned more than a few words of broken English and his interests remained essentially German too, centring on the welfare of his beloved north German principality, where he went whenever he could and stayed as long as possible.

It was all neatly symbolized by his heraldry, which showed the white horse of Hanover superimposed on the British royal coat of arms. Moreover, the German takeover of 1714 had consequences almost as momentous as those of the Dutch conquest of 1688. The conquest and the ensuing Glorious Revolution had been the work of Tories as well as Whigs and, for the following thirty years, the two parties had continued to alternate in power.

But George saw things very differently. Passionately interested in the military glory of Hanover, he blamed the Tories for the Peace of Utrecht, which halted the Grand Alliance's chances of a crushing victory over France and, more importantly for George, the aggrandizement of his beloved Hanover. He blamed them even more for their flirtation with his rival, the Old Pretender. The Tories, for their part, believed that the new monarch was really the puppet of the Whigs. Under the control of their opponents, they feared, the monarchy would become the powerless figurehead of a republic and the Church of England would lose its privileged status. For them, 1714 was the victory of the old parliamentary cause of the Civil Wars and the triumph of the Protestant dissenters.

Nor was George popular with the country. On the day of his coronation banners mocking the new king were displayed throughout the country. There were riots and talk of plots to restore the Stuarts. The general election of 1715 was violent, with more banners proclaiming 'No Hanover' and 'Down with the Roundheads'. And if the country seemed turbulent and dangerously polarized at the beginning of the reign, the king blamed it on the troublemaking Tories. Thus their prophecy that the new dynasty would exclude them in favour of the Whigs became self-fulfilling. After their crushing defeat in the election, Tories were deprived of office at every level, down to the gardener at Dublin Castle.

It was a century before the Tories would win a general election again, and sixty years before a Tory held high political office. The resulting long Whig domination has been hailed as the Restoration of Political Stability. It could equally be characterized as six decades of one-party rule, with all the problems of one-party rule that our own times have familiarized us with once more. For the Whig consensus was dogged by bitter internal division and competing factions. And this struggle became linked with another poisonous dispute within the new German royal family itself.

'The Hanoverians', it has been cruelly said, 'like pigs, trample their young.' The dictum was exemplified by the very public mutual loathing of fathers and eldest sons. There was good reason for this in 1714. At first sight, George's eldest son, George Augustus, prince of Wales, was a much more attractive character than his father. He was married to a vivacious, intelligent wife, Caroline. He was as fond of public pomp and circumstance as his reclusive father detested it. He had displayed conspicuous bravery at the battle of Oudenarde, where he fought on the English side under Marlborough and had his horse killed under him in the thick of the fighting. He spoke voluble, if heavily accented, English and had thoroughly acquainted himself with English affairs. Indeed, he played the English card shamelessly and proclaimed, rather unconvincingly, 'I have not one drop of blood in my veins dat is not English.'

Matters between father and son came to a head in 1716, when the king, who had been pining for Germany, returned to Hanover for a six-month visit. Custom dictated that the prince should have been left as regent; instead, an obscure precedent was dug out from the Middle Ages and he was created 'guardian and lieutenant of the realm' with severely restricted powers. All important decisions would be referred to the king in Hanover, as if his son were simply incapable of any kind of responsibility. The prince was left feeling humiliated and sidelined.

But still the prince was the figurehead of government and he and Caroline determined to exploit the fact for all it was worth. On 25 July the prince and princess and their daughters moved to Hampton Court, where, with a short interval, they remained for four months. Many people were angry that the new king had so little respect for his new people that he had left the kingdom as soon as he could. As was said, George 'is already become the Jest, the Contempt and Aversion of the Nation'. He had been cuckolded by his wife, whom he had been forced to lock up; he had two ugly mistresses nicknamed 'the elephant and the maypole' for their mismatched appearance; and he was stiff and humourless. All this was ripe for jokes and innuendo. But George's ill-disguised dislike for England was also offensive. His son and daughter-in-law, on the other hand, made great effort to show that they at least were pleased to be in England. And the young couple won popularity and loyalty for it.

Hampton Court Palace had lain unfinished and largely neglected since William III's death. But now it burst into life as George and Caroline moved into the state apartments, which had been specially refurbished for them, and kept the kind of splendid open court that had not been seen in England since the days of Charles II. It attracted the aristocracy and politicians, poets such as Alexander Pope, the writer Joseph Addison and scientists including Isaac Newton and Edward Halley. Once again, there was a flourishing court culture and a popular prince. The royal couple dined in public, held balls, fêtes and picnics; they also went on a successful tour of the south-east.

George I reacted to his son's public favour with jealous rage and, when he returned to England, entered against all his instincts and preferences into a public-relations war with the prince. So in the following summer of 1717, the king himself took up residence at Hampton Court, alongside the prince and princess. In uncomfortable proximity in the same building, the two adjacent but rival courts continued to maintain different styles: the king's studiously informal, the Waleses' preserving something of the traditional formality of the English court, with the consequent need for grand state apartments, such as the Guard Chamber and, beyond it, the

Presence Chamber, which were designed for them by Sir John Vanbrugh. It was a war of style and culture, and the prince and princess seemed to be winning it.

But King George had his own genius with whom to strike back: George Frederic Handel. On 17 July, just before his departure for Hampton Court, the king bade farewell to the capital in fine style with a grand water party to Chelsea and back. Accompanying the royal party was a barge with a large band of fifty musicians, who played the music that Handel had composed for the occasion. The king liked it so much that he had it 'played over three times in going and returning'. And no wonder, for it was Handel's *Water Music*. Let the prince of Wales try to beat that!

In November the royal family returned from Hampton Court to London for the winter season. Within a few weeks the quarrel between father and son became an open breach, and the king ordered the Waleses in writing to leave St James's Palace. In the new year they took up residence at Leicester House, in what is now Leicester Square. There were now two rival courts in London; Tories and dissident Whigs flocked to Leicester House in the expectation that when Prince George came to the throne they would be the favoured few. And the Jacobites rejoiced at the family feud, which, they hoped and prayed, presaged the fall of the House of Hanover.

II

One of the leading members of the Leicester House Set, as the followers of the prince of Wales were known, was the up-and-coming Whig politician Sir Robert Walpole. Walpole, the son of a middling Norfolk squire, was a mountain of a man, with a gigantic appetite: for food and drink, sex, money, power and work. He was shrewd, affable (when it suited him) and knew the price of everything and everyone. But, despite his coarseness and corpulence, he was attractive to women and understood them thoroughly.

What he understood most of all, however, was the House of Commons, of which he was the long-time undisputed master. For such a man, opposition, even when sanctioned by the prince of Wales, was of limited appeal. For one thing, George I showed no signs of dying any time soon and no man could gain power without access to the patronage that was the gift of the monarch, even if he had Parliament on his side. So in 1720 Walpole brokered a general reconciliation of sorts: between the king and the prince and within the fractured Whig Party. But what propelled him to undisputed power was his handling of the financial crisis known as the South Sea Bubble.

For the Glorious Revolution not only brought in modern public finance, with the Bank of England and the national debt, it also introduced other, less obviously desirable features of capitalist modernity such as the stock market, speculation and boom and bust. And the South Sea Bubble was the mother of all busts.

The centre of this feverish activity was the Royal Exchange, where shares in ventures like the South Sea Company were traded. The company had been established in 1711 as a Tory riposte to the Whig-dominated Bank of England. Its original purpose was to reduce the burden of the national debt by converting loans to the government into shares in the company. The company did have real assets, in particular the *assiento* or forty-year monopoly on the slave trade to Spanish America, which the Tories had won at the Peace of Utrecht. But its value was talked up beyond all reason. In March 1720 South Sea Company shares stood at 170, before peaking at 1050 on 24 June. Then they crashed, bottoming out at 290.

Everybody got their fingers burnt; still worse, everybody seemed to have their fingers in the pie: from the king, who had been made governor of the company, to his mistresses and his ministers, who had all received significant gifts of shares. Everybody, that is, apart from Walpole. With his usual good luck, he had been out of favour when the final scam was launched and so, for once in his life, appeared as whiter than white. He also used his financial skill to wind the crisis down, without provoking either a financial or a political meltdown.

On the other hand, his Whig rivals fell victim to the cry for vengeance: one died of a heart attack after angry scenes in Parliament; another committed suicide; and a third was sent to the Tower. With rivals eliminated and his own reputation riding high, Walpole emerged as unchallenged first or 'prime' minister.

And he made sure to advertise the fact to the world. Houghton Hall, which Walpole built on the site of his modest ancestral home in north

Norfolk, symbolized his immense power. He moved with his usual purposeful expedition. Designs were commissioned in 1721, the year his premiership began; the foundation stone was laid the next year and the building was finished in 1735. And for 'the Great Man', as he soon became known, nothing but the best would do. Walpole built with the best materials; he used the finest architects and designers, such as William Kent, who was responsible for the opulently gilded interiors and furniture; and he embellished the house with the biggest and best collection of pictures in England.

The result was perfection: according to one contemporary connoisseur, it was 'the greatest house in the world for its size' and 'a pattern for all great houses that may hereafter be built'. But at first it seemed as though Walpole might have counted his chickens before they were hatched. For in the summer of 1727 George I died, fittingly en route to Hanover. At first, his son refused to believe the news, thinking that it was another trick played by his father to entrap him into incautious expressions of joy. But once George II was persuaded of its truth, he made clear that the monarchy would be transformed from the dour, reclusive and Germanized version that Britain had suffered for thirteen years.

He indulged his love of splendour by having a magnificent coronation with music by Handel, whose great anthem, *Zadoc the Priest and Nathan the Prophet crownèd Solomon King*, has been played at every subsequent coronation. He vowed that unlike his father he would rule as a *British* king, not a reluctant German. Queen Caroline said that she would 'as soon live on a dunghill as return to Hanover'. There would be other radical changes with the new reign. Above all, George told Walpole, whom he had never forgiven for going over to his father, to take his marching orders.

But Walpole kept his head. He still had a large following in the House of Commons and showed his usefulness by getting it to vote George a bigger Civil List (or personal income) than his father. But for all his abilities and backing in Parliament, Walpole could remain in office only as long as he retained his favour with the king. He tried to make sure of this by appointing his followers to court positions so that no faction could be built against him. Such Walpole courtiers controlled access to the royal family, and they could exclude the prime minister's enemies from gaining the king's ear.

But most importantly, he had a powerful ally. Other politicians had paid court to George's insipid mistress. But Walpole knew better. Instead, he rebuilt his close friendship with Queen Caroline, whom he had betrayed in 1720: 'I have the right sow by the ear,' he boasted ungallantly. He was right, and Caroline played a vital role in managing her husband – who quickly turned out to be even more curmudgeonly and more in love with Hanover than his father and much less intelligent – on Walpole's behalf. Together they subtly governed the king, directing him towards Walpole's policies. The minister and the queen would meet in secret, so that she could discuss matters with the king before Walpole had his private interview. Thus primed when the prime minister met him, the king would already have been manipulated into agreement. Walpole had nothing but praise for the queen's arts in moulding the king's mind: she 'can make him propose the very thing as his own opinion which a week before he had rejected as mine'. And Walpole was skilful at keeping Caroline herself onside, flattering her with carefully chosen compliments. 'Your Majesty knows that this country is entirely in your hands,' he would lie, to the queen's delight.

In fact, the country was in Walpole's hands, as his premiership sailed on over the blip of George II's accession. But it trembled once more ten years later. George and Caroline had an odd marital relationship: he had numerous affairs and snubbed her all the time in public, but she always bounced back and was able to control him. Nevertheless, when Caroline fell fatally ill in 1737, George was heartbroken and tearfully refused her deathbed injunction to marry again by exclaiming: 'No! I'll have mistresses!' Walpole's premiership survived, even though he was terrified that the easily led George would fall under the spell of someone hostile to him now that Caroline was dead. He remained as prime minister, however, despite being deprived of his greatest ally. But now his enemies were gathering strength. Most important was the group known as 'Cobham's Cubs', who gathered round Richard Temple, Viscount Cobham. Cobham was a soldier, a statesman and a landscape gardener.

His greatest creation was the garden at Stowe, his Buckinghamshire estate. Vistas, trees and water were punctuated with artfully sited temples to create the sort of idyllic Classical landscape imagined by painters like Nicolas Poussin and Claude Lorrain. It was intended to delight the eye but also to exercise the mind. One of the Classical monuments was the

Temple of British Worthies. It is a Whig pantheon, with, on the left, the proponents of political liberty, such as the poet John Milton and the philosopher John Locke, and, on the right, the heroes of the struggle against Catholic Spain and France, such as Elizabeth I and William of Orange. But there was another, very different monument. It looked like a ruin containing a damaged, headless statue. Actually it was built like this. The ruin was satirically entitled the Temple of Modern Virtue, while the ugly, headless torso was 'the Great Man', Walpole himself.

For Walpole, Cobham and his Cubs believed, had comprehensively betrayed Whig principles by stealing the Tories' clothes. The Whigs had been the great anti-court party, determined to keep the powers of the king within bounds. But Walpole discovered that the way to keep office was to cultivate the king's favour and then use the royal patronage of titles, jobs and straightforward bribes to control Parliament. Whig heroes, or *Worthies*, should not be court toadies, as the oleaginous Walpole had become. The Whigs had also been the war party. But both the king and Walpole wanted peace with France: George to protect Hanover and Walpole to restore the public finances from the effects of the vast expense of Marlborough's wars.

Faced with mounting opposition, in 1742 Walpole won what amounted to a vote of confidence by only 253 votes to 250. The margin of victory was too small for effective government and three weeks later Walpole resigned. Within three years, deprived of the energizing effects of power, he was dead. And at first it seemed as though he might, like Samson, bring down the pillars of the Hanoverian temple with him.

For 1745 showed every sign of being a catastrophic year for Britain. In April, the French, against whom Walpole had reluctantly resumed hostilities, defeated the British under William, duke of Cumberland, the king's second and favourite son, at the great battle of Fontenoy in Belgium. Still worse, the French victory opened the way to another Stuart invasion of Britain. It was led by the Old Pretender's eldest son, Charles Edward. Aged only twenty-four, and tall, handsome and dashing, 'Bonny Prince Charlie' had all the Stuart charisma and charm that his father and grandfather had so conspicuously lacked.

He landed in the Outer Hebrides in June. At first the Highlands were slow to respond. But over the summer the rebellion gathered force. By September, Charles had taken Edinburgh, routed the tiny Hanoverian army in Scotland and announced the dissolution of the Union. In November, he invaded England and got as far as Derby before the failure of the English to rally to his cause forced him to retreat back to Scotland.

The final battle took place at Culloden in April 1746, when Charles's Highland army was confronted by a much larger, better-disciplined professional force under Cumberland. This personal struggle between two royal princes for the crown was like an episode of the Wars of the Roses, and both the battle and the repression of the Highlands after Charles's inevitable defeat were medieval in their savagery.

Charles, after many hardships and adventures, escaped, to die an early death of alcoholism and disillusionment; while Jacobitism itself died too, or rather, perhaps, was killed by Cumberland's scorched-earth policy after Culloden.

The Forty-Five was a turning point. Scotland threw itself more heartily into the Union, which was now yielding visible economic benefits; while in England the Tories, freed at last from the incubus of Jacobitism, were able to re-enter ordinary political life. But the greatest beneficiary of the year of crisis was Cobham's nephew by marriage, William Pitt the Elder, who was to emerge, despite George II's profound personal loathing, as the most remarkable politician of the age.

III

Of all the shades we can imagine wandering through the Elysian Fields of Stowe amid the follies and temples, William Pitt's is the greatest and the strangest. The favourite grandson of Thomas 'Diamond' Pitt, a tough, irascible East India merchant who had made a fortune and founded a gentry family, Pitt had first been introduced to Cobham in his thirties when his dazzling parliamentary oratory against Walpole had immediately made him one of the leading Cubs. The connection became much closer when, years later, Pitt married the childless Cobham's niece, Hester. The couple were middle-aged – he was forty-six and she was thirty-four – but it was a passionate courtship that led to a devoted marriage.

Hester often acted as her husband's secretary; even more importantly, she was his nurse. For Pitt was plagued with illness, physical and mental, and subject to swings of emotion, from elation to prostration, that were so extreme as to sometimes amount to madness. At their worst, his mood changes laid him low for months on end; at their best they drove him to heights of oratory that convinced his hearers that he was the voice of destiny: Britain's destiny.

And that national destiny too was prefigured in the Temple of British Worthies at Stowe with its roll-call of naval heroes: King Alfred, who was honoured as founder of the English navy; Sir Francis Drake, who became the first Englishman to sail round the globe in an expedition of magnificent, insolent plundering of the riches of the Spanish Empire; Queen Elizabeth I, who had knighted Drake and gave her name to the first great age of English sea power; and Sir Walter Raleigh, Drake's younger contemporary, who first projected an English colonial empire in America. Completing the pantheon of greats is the Elizabethan merchant-prince Sir Thomas Gresham, who stabilized the coinage and founded the Royal Exchange. Britain, in this version of history, was founded on the marriage of buccaneering sailors and solid mercantile wealth.

And Pitt, himself the grandson of a merchant-robber-baron-cum-empire-builder, took these ideas and made them his own. The result can be boiled down to three axioms. First, the proper field of British endeavour was overseas and worldwide, not Continental and European; second, the navy, not the army, was the right instrument to advance British power; and third, overseas trade was the means to the wealth, and hence the power, of the nation.

All this was guaranteed to set Pitt on a collision course with George II that was both personal and political. For the king, who had led his army to victory against the French at Dettingen in 1743 at the ripe age of sixty, regarded the army as his own peculiar pride and joy. He was also as devoted to Hanover as his father and, like him, regarded foreign policy as the flower of his prerogative.

As such, he was overjoyed at the victory at Dettingen. And he expected that his subjects would share the celebrations of their victorious king when he returned home with Handel's *Dettingen te deum* ringing in his ears. He was the last British monarch to personally lead an army in battle, and he had done so bravely. But there were those who would downplay his success, in particular William Pitt, who sneeringly disparaged it in Parliament: 'His Majesty was exposed to few or no dangers abroad, such as the overturning of a coach or the stumbling of his horse.' But there was more pointed criticism than the merely personal. A sizeable group in Parliament did not think that Britain should be fighting in Europe for the sake of Hanover at all. Indeed, victory or no victory, it was a betrayal of Britain. Pitt spoke for them too: 'It is now too apparent that this great, this powerful, this formidable kingdom is considered only a province to a despicable electorate,' he declared. 'We need only look at the instances of particularity that have been shown; the yearly visits that have been made to that delightful country.'

Such language was unforgivable. And George was a good hater with an excellent memory for slights. The result was that Pitt spent the next decade in a sort of political limbo. He was admitted to government and in office because he was both too useful and too dangerous in Parliament not to be. But he was not in power because the royal veto prevented it. This was frustrating for someone as aware of his own abilities as Pitt. But it did give him the opportunity to reconsider his instinctive opposition to Continental alliances; indeed, he became something of a convert – as he proclaimed with his accustomed breathtaking effrontery. 'I have,' he confided to the House of Commons, 'upon some former occasions, by the heat of youth and the warmth of a debate, been hurried into expressions, which upon cool reflexion, I have heartily regretted.' Being Pitt, he got away with it.

Being Pitt also, his moment came. War with France broke out again in 1756 and it began disastrously with the loss of Minorca and the control of the Mediterranean. Popular clamour arose for the punishment of the commanding officer, Admiral Byng, who was shot on his own quarter-deck to encourage, as Voltaire acidly observed, the rest. The cry also went up for Pitt: 'I know', he said, 'I can save this country and no one else can.' In the circumstances, George had to yield to his appointment as secretary of state with the direction of the war, albeit with a bad grace.

Almost immediately, the tide of war began to turn. For Pitt was a new sort of minister, who demanded and got a new sort of control over both policy and its detailed execution. There was a uniform, overarching strategy, which combined Continental and overseas war. Britain's principal Continental ally, Frederick the Great of Prussia, was given money but no men, while both money and men were flung to the far corners of the globe against the key points of France's colonial empire. For this too was to be a new sort of war in which no quarter was given: 'his administration [would] decide which alone should exist as a nation, Britain or France'.

The result caught France in a vice. On the Continent, the military genius of Frederick the Great kept up the pressure, against formidable odds. But what was decisive in the wider struggle was the quality of the British navy. For Britain had moved fast to equip itself with the infrastructure to meet the requirements of worldwide war. The great dockyard at Chatham was the jewel in the crown of the new policy. The naval dockyards were then by far the largest industrial establishments in Britain, and only a hundred years later, in the nineteenth century, did private enterprise begin to catch up in size, managerial efficiency and technical sophistication. Britain had four or five dry docks, such as the ones that still exist in Chatham, to France's one. And they were bigger and better too. The pulleys and tackle for manoeuvring sails were much superior. British naval stores of food and drink were also better, longer lasting and half the price.

This transformed the scope of British naval and combined operations. At the beginning of the eighteenth century a ship was lucky to be able to remain at sea for more than a fortnight; fifty years later cruises of three months and more were common. With voyages of this length, and the technical expertise to run them, all the world was now a stage for Pitt's great imperial drama.

It was fought in four principal theatres: Canada, the West Indies, Africa and India. In each, Pitt was victorious: General Wolfe defeated the French general Montcalm on the Heights of Abraham before Quebec in 1759 and all Canada fell the following year; at the same time, Martinique and Guadeloupe were captured in the West Indies and Dakar in Africa; Clive carried all before him in India, while both the northern and southern French fleets were smashed in European waters, giving Britain what she often asserted but rarely held: an absolute mastery of the sea. 'Our bells', wrote Horace Walpole, the witty, waspish son of the great Sir Robert, 'are quite worn threadbare with ringing for victories. Indeed, one is forced to ask every morning, "what victory is there?" for fear of missing one.'

It was a triumph too for Stowe and its new master, Pitt's brother-in-law, Earl Temple. The landscape was once more transformed with fresh shrines to British prowess and her new generation of heroes, more than equal to Alfred, Drake, Elizabeth, William III and all the other Worthies of history. An obelisk was erected in memory of General Wolfe, who had been killed at the moment of victory at Quebec. The Temple of Concord and Victory depicted an enthroned Britannia receiving tribute from the rest of the world. A selection of heraldic icons also mark a victory, one that was just as hard fought and won over a foe nearer home. They represent the august Order of the Garter, an honour on which Pitt's brother-in-law had set his heart.

But George loathed Temple even more than he did Pitt. Nevertheless, Pitt insisted and the king had to back down and confer the coveted honour. But he made his feelings plain at the investiture. Instead of decorously placing the ribbon over Temple's shoulder, as etiquette demanded, he threw it at him and immediately turned his back. Faced with the power of Pitt, the king of Great Britain was reduced to making an impotent protest, like a naughty child. Pitt was able thus to humiliate the king, not only because he was uniquely successful, but also because he had a new sort of power. He had been called to office, he asserted, 'by his sovereign' – which was conventional – and 'by the voice of the people' – which was a radical and bold claim.

Not even Walpole could boast that. Now, as George II moaned, 'Ministers are Kings in this Country.' Frustration built up over the years; when he was in Hanover in 1755 he almost did not go back to England: 'There are Kings enough in England. I am nothing there. I am old and want rest, and should only go to be plagued and teased there about the damned House of Commons.' In 1727, when he had come to the throne, a minister as formidable as Robert Walpole had to win and retain royal favour, as his assiduous and unctuous flattery of Queen Caroline showed. Since then, the king had been forced to accept men he hated as ministers, above all William Pitt, who never ceased to denigrate his beloved Hanover and oppose Continental wars. Power was no longer gained by a minister's standing at court and personal relationship with the king, but by his ability to break down the doors and impose himself on the sovereign. How had George found himself in this situation at the end of his long reign?

Partly, it was simply a matter of Pitt's translation of his war aims into bold and vivid language that had a resonance far beyond Parliament. But there were also more concrete alliances, such as the one commemorated in the Guildhall, the centre of the government of the City of London.

Pitt's own statue dominates the hall. But standing up on high to equal the great prime minister is the statue of Alderman William Beckford, millionaire, City politician and radical press lord, who marshalled City opinion behind Pitt with his weekly paper, *The Monitor*. Imperial might, parliamentary legitimacy and prime ministerial power stood four-square with City finance, mercantile wealth and the press.

Winston Churchill, who resembled Pitt in so many ways, called the Seven Years War 'the first world war'. But unlike the world wars of the twentieth century, it did not exhaust the country. When it began, Britain was one of two or three leading European powers. When it ended, she was all powerful and mistress of the first empire to stretch across four continents. But George was not there to see it and Pitt was not in office either.

IV

The morning of 25 October 1760 began like any other for George II. He rose early, drank his chocolate and retired to relieve himself on his close-stool. But there, without a day's illness or a moment's warning, he died, at about 7.30 a.m.

The gruff, choleric seventy-seven-year-old was succeeded by his grandson, the fresh-faced, twenty-two-year-old George III. George had been a late developer. Sulky, idle and apparently rather dim at first, he had been transformed in his late teens by a sympathetic mentor into a paragon of hard work and self-discipline. He was intensely musical, fluent in French and German, a competent draughtsman and an omnivorous bibliophile with a particular interest in history.

He had been a late developer sexually too. But following his marriage, eleven months after his accession, to Charlotte of Mecklenburg-Strelitz, he made up for lost time by fathering no fewer than fifteen children.

Above all, he was aware, unlike his two predecessors, that he was English through and through by birth and by inclination. He was also determined to fulfil his duties, as he saw them, as a patriotic British king. Perhaps, indeed, he was too determined, too demanding both of others and, critically, of himself.

The clash with the great war minister, William Pitt, who saw himself as having something of a monopoly on patriotism, came within hours. In his accession speech, given at 6 p.m. on the day of his grandfather's death, George referred to the 'bloody war' in which Britain was engaged. At Pitt's outraged insistence, this was toned down to 'expensive but just and necessary war' in the published version. Within the year, however, Pitt had resigned and in 1763 the Treaty of Paris was signed, bringing the war to a triumphant conclusion.

Triumphant or not, the war still had to be paid for. So, too, did the new British Empire. The war had doubled the national debt, from £70,000,000 to £140,000,000. This meant that interest payments alone totalled £4,000,000 a year, or half the tax revenue. Ongoing costs had multiplied as well. Before the war, the annual cost of the American establishment was £75,000. Now it had increased more than fourfold to £350,000. All this fell on a British population of only 8 million. Why shouldn't, ministers asked, British America bear a part? After all, the war, as Pitt had repeatedly stated, had been fought on their behalf, and they had been its principal beneficiaries with the removal of the threat from the French in Canada and the French allies among the Indian tribes. As Pitt had said in 1755, 'The present war was undertaken for the long-injured, long-neglected, long-forgotten people of America.' France had been expelled from much of North America while Britain and her allies tied up the French in Europe. 'America had been conquered in Germany,' Pitt bluntly asserted.

And there is no doubt that British America had deep pockets. Philadelphia, New York and Boston were large and rich; Charleston was catching up fast. And these were only the urban centres of an overwhelmingly rural economy in which about two million people were unevenly divided between thirteen colonies. The colonies were wildly different in size, religious complexion, economic interest and geographical focus, and were almost as suspicious of each other as of the British government. Nevertheless, there *was* a sense of British America and of the fact that it was already four or five times the size of Old England.

February 12 1765 was a quiet day in the House of Commons, with only a Bill to tap American wealth by imposing stamp duty on American property and legal transactions to be debated. As colonial business rarely aroused much interest (unless Pitt was displaying his pyrotechnics), the Bill was nodded through an almost empty chamber with minimal opposition.

But the Stamp Act set America alight. For the British Parliament was not the only one in the British Empire. Indeed, in America there were thirteen such assemblies – one for each colony – which, in their own worlds, thought themselves the equal of the Westminster Parliament.

The eighteenth-century Capitol, in Williamsburg, was the seat of the General Assembly of the Colony of Virginia. The Assembly was the oldest colonial legislature, first meeting on 20 July 1619. It was the closest in structure to Westminster, consisting of an elected Lower House, presided over by a Speaker, a nominated Upper House and the Royal Governor, who opened the sessions with a speech and wielded the veto on all Bills. Above all, perhaps, the personnel of the Virginian Assembly was nearest to that of the Westminster Parliament, since it was dominated by wealthy gentle-man-planters, such as the Lee family of Stratford Hall.

Stratford Hall, built in the 1730s, is a not-so-miniature version of an English country house. And the Lees, with their wealth derived from the surrounding tobacco plantation cultivated by dozens of black slaves, lived a provincial version of the life of the English country gentlemen who made up the great bulk of Westminster MPs, and they displayed a similar self-confidence and sense of their own importance. Thus it was that, on 30 May 1765, with Lees in the lead, the Virginian Assembly passed the first resolution against the Stamp Act. This solemnly declared that 'the taxation of the people by themselves, or by persons chosen to represent them ... is the distinguishing characteristic of British freedom, without which the ancient constitution cannot exist'.

This was Whig language turned against the British Parliament, which had first invented it. Less decorously, as the date for the coming into operation of the Stamp Act approached, Richard Henry Lee organized a protest procession, featuring his own slaves in costume and the mock-hanging of the collector of stamp duties. Similar resolutions and protests, many of them violent, spread like wildfire across the colonies, and British America became ungovernable. Wholly unprepared for the reaction, the Westminster Parliament repealed the Stamp Act. But it tried to preserve the principle of British parliamentary sovereignty by declaring that Westminster was competent to pass laws for the British colonies 'in all cases whatsoever'.

There remained only the little matter of translating the principle into practice. This every succeeding British government tried to do and failed. American resistance continued and the net yield of American taxation, at a few hundred pounds a year, was derisory. A final attempt was made in

1773. The usual British duty of 12 pence a pound on tea was lifted and a low American duty of 3 pence imposed. The effect was to make tea cheaper in America than in Britain, and the 'Sons of Liberty', as the American radical opposition called themselves, were afraid that Americans, who loved their tea, might sell their liberty for a nice, cheap cuppa.

To forestall them, in December 1773 they perpetrated 'the Boston Tea Party', in which forty or fifty 'patriots', disguised as Mohawk Indians, boarded three ships in the harbour and forcibly threw 343 chests of tea overboard. Goaded beyond endurance, the British government took a hard line at last. The port of Boston was closed, the Massachusetts Assembly remodelled and British troops exempted from trial by American juries.

But instead of being cowed, the Americans summoned a Continental Congress of representatives from all thirteen colonies to coordinate their response to the coercive British measures. Once again, the Virginian Assembly, meeting as usual in Williamsburg and steered by Richard Henry Lee, had taken the lead. But the most interesting Virginian initiative had its origins in the College of William and Mary, which lies at the other end of Duke of Gloucester Street from the Capitol.

The college was the Virginian University and the second oldest of the seven university colleges in colonial America. And it was here that Thomas Jefferson, who came from the same wealthy, slave-owning background as Lee, became a student and began to form the ideas expressed in the paper he wrote for the forthcoming Continental Congress. Entitled 'The Summary View of the Rights of British Americans', it takes the Whig idea that all government ultimately depends on a social contract, entered into by the people in a state of nature, and applies it brilliantly to America.

In Old England the state of nature was a mere abstraction – albeit a very useful one. But in America it was real in the endless, rolling acres of Jefferson's native Virginia. Here, Jefferson points out, his ancestors had come, voluntarily, to a New World, occupied and cultivated it by their own efforts, formed their own societies and chosen and established their own forms of government. Therefore, for the British Parliament, which represented only the British people, to presume to legislate for the people of America, who already had their own representatives in their own assemblies, was a gross usurpation. Instead, only George himself, as king and ultimate sovereign of America, had a right to intervene.

This idea of a monarch who, as sovereign of free and independent peoples, holds an empire together was both ingenious and far-sighted. Indeed, it became the foundation of Britain's twentieth-century imperial policy as the empire evolved into the commonwealth of self-governing dominions, united only by allegiance to a common crown. But in the circumstances of the eighteenth century it was impossible.

Parliament and premier had only just got some sort of control of the monarchy. To allow George to become king of America would be to give the crown a new and expanding power base that might once again allow the old monarchy to challenge the new. Nor did George want the power of an American monarch independent of Parliament, for he was far too loyal to the settlement that had brought the Hanoverians to the throne. Instead, he threw his weight behind the British Parliament's determination to impose its will on the rebellious colonies. 'I will never make my inclinations alone nor even my own opinions the sole rule of my conduct in public measures,' he said, confirming the power of the premiership. 'I will at all times consult my ministers and place in them as entire a confidence as the nature of this government can be supposed to require of me.' If the minister had been Pitt, there is little doubt he would have succeeded. But faced by a weak prime minister, the king himself increasingly emerged as the figurehead of the struggle. The result was indecision and disarray.

Troops, including German regiments personally raised by the king, were dispatched, and in April 1775 the first armed clash, in which the colonials acquitted themselves surprisingly well against seasoned professional troops, took place near Boston, at Lexington. The Americans took this as a declaration of war and a month later in May the Second Continental Congress convened in the State House in Philadelphia, the seat of the Pennsylvanian Assembly, to organize military resistance. On 15 June Congress appointed George Washington as commander-in-chief of the American army.

It could not have chosen better. For Washington, though not a great general, was a great man. He was another product of the planter gentry of Virginia, where his family were neighbours of the Lees of Stratford Hall. As a younger son, he became an officer in the Virginian militia; played an honourable part in the Seven Years War against the French; and tried but failed to get a commission in the British army. Marriage to a rich widow and deaths in his own family now enabled him to acquire his own plantation at Mount Vernon, where the mansion house, modest at first, was steadily enlarged and beautified over the years.

But despite his new-found wealth and status, Washington never lost his interest in military affairs, and he turned up to the congress in Philadelphia in uniform and using his rank of colonel in the militia. As commander-in-chief, Washington found himself in charge of a motley crew: badly armed, badly fed and clothed and badly paid when they were paid at all. To keep them in the field required tact, occasional firmness and infinite dogged patience. Washington had them all. He also had the natural leadership of a born-and-bred American gentleman.

The Continental Congress reconvened the following year at Philadelphia. The fighting had hardened positions, and in June Richard Henry Lee of Virginia moved the resolution for independence, while his fellow Virginian, Thomas Jefferson, drafted the Declaration itself, which was adopted on 4 July 1776 and became the Ark of the Covenant of the new republic.

Subsequent generations have focused on the grand principles of the preamble, with its ringing assertion (written by a slave-owner, of course) that all men, being born free and equal, have the right to determine how and by whom they are governed. Contemporaries were more interested in its violent and highly personal repudiation of allegiance to George III as a tyrant and 'unfit to be the ruler of a free people'. But the immediate importance of the Declaration lay elsewhere, in the claim that, as Free and Independent States, the United Colonies were entitled to contract what alliances they pleased.

And there was no doubt where their best hope of allies lay: the old enemy, France. For France was burning for revenge for its comprehensive humiliation by Britain in the Seven Years War. And how better to take vengeance than by separating Britain from the fruits of that victory – the better part of its newly acquired empire? Hence the bizarre marriage of convenience between the new republic and the oldest, proudest and most absolute monarchy in Europe. 'Do they read?' a French radical asked, as the French translation of the fiercely anti-monarchical Declaration of Independence was devoured at the Court of Versailles. He might well have asked, 'Do they think?', as the sweetly air-headed and super-fashionable queen, Marie Antoinette, demanded news of her 'dear republicans'.

And French help was desperately needed since, despite all Washington's efforts, the Americans barely hung on. New York and Charleston remained in British hands and the most likely outcome seemed a stalemate. The deadlock was broken at Yorktown, a few miles to the southeast of Williamsburg, where Lord Cornwallis, the British commander in America, set up his headquarters in 1781. Yorktown lies on the narrow peninsula between the estuaries of the York and James rivers as they debouch into the mighty Chesapeake Bay.

So long as the British navy controlled the sea, Cornwallis was impregnable. But the French threw money – all borrowed and at outrageous rates of interest – at their fleet while the British navy was overstretched and divided. The result was that Cornwallis found himself caught between a strong French fleet – which blockaded the York river – and Washington's army, which the French had also buoyed up with loans and gifts. Trapped and outnumbered by more than two to one, Cornwallis surrendered to Washington on 19 October with his whole army.

'Oh God, it is all over,' the British prime minister wailed when the news arrived. It was, though it took George III some time to realize it. In 1783 the Americans, in their first betrayal of their French allies, signed a separate preliminary peace with Britain that recognized American independence. George drafted and redrafted his abdication address. And the Holy Roman Emperor predicted that, with the loss of America, Britain would swiftly become a second-class power, like Sweden or Denmark. His words were echoed in Britain. 'America is lost,' said George. 'Must we fall beneath the blow?'

Thereafter, Britain and America went their separate ways. But only one remained loyal to its eighteenth-century roots.

These show clearly in Washington, the new American capital that was named after George Washington, who, after he had resigned his military command, became the first president of the new American Republic.

Laid out in the 1790s, its monuments, lawns and grand, sweeping vistas are the lineal descendants of the landscape gardens of Stowe. Similarly, it is America today which best embodies the ideas of freedom, power and empire which inspired that great denizen of Stowe, William Pitt, in the reign of George II.

And it does so for better or for worse.

23

THE KING IS DEAD, LONG LIVE THE BRITISH MONARCHY!

George IV, William IV, Victoria

KING LOUIS XVI OF FRANCE was executed on 21 January 1793 on the guillotine, the revolutionary killing machine which had just been introduced to humanize and industrialize the process of execution.

The night before, Louis read David Hume's account of the execution of Charles I. But the French king was prevented from re-creating any of the poignancy of the death of that English king. Instead, in his execution, everything was done to rob Louis of his dignity, both as a king and a human being. He was condemned as a mere errant citizen, Louis Capet; his hair was roughly cropped on the scaffold and he was ignominiously strapped to the movable plank before having his head and neck thrust into the guides for the twelve-inch, heavily weighted blade. Once severed, the bleeding head was held up to the mob before being thrown between the legs of the body, which was then buried ten feet deep in quicklime.

Not since the St Bartholomew Day Massacre had a foreign event provoked such horror in England. Audiences demanded that the curtain be brought down in theatres and performances abandoned; the whole House of Commons wore mourning dress; and crowds surrounded George III's coach, crying 'War with France!' In the event, the French Republic took the initiative by declaring war on Britain on 1 February.

Nothing would be the same again. The war, with only brief respites of short-lived peace, was to last eighteen years; it cost more in men and money than any before; and it rewrote the rules of politics. Henceforward, monarchies would be measured by their ability to respond to the new, post-revolutionary world. Those that could adapt survived; those that could not died, usually bloodily. Which the British would do was by no means a foregone conclusion.

I

Only four years earlier, in 1789, when the French Revolution broke out, nothing seemed less likely than this cataclysmic struggle. Much of the English elite welcomed the Revolution, which they saw in terms of France belatedly catching up with England's own benign and Glorious Revolution of exactly a century before in 1689. And, in any case, they took for granted that the revolutionary turmoil would cripple France as a great power for a generation.

Most confident of all was the prime minister, William Pitt. Son of the great mid-century prime minister of the same name, and known as Pitt the Younger, he had a meteoric career. Barely out of Cambridge, where he had excelled at mathematics, he became prime minister and Chancellor of the Exchequer at the age of only twenty-four in the aftermath of the American War of Independence, and quickly proved as great a peace minister as his father was a war leader.

This was because his qualities were almost the mirror-image of his manic-depressive father's. He was an optimist, a long and deep sleeper, and excelled as a financier, a fiscal reformer and a manager of his party and cabinet. He inherited few of the volatile passions of his father – he was somewhat rigid in demeanour and dry in speech but was a relentless workhorse. Thus, under his sober guidance, Britain shrugged off the effects of the American War of Independence and even enjoyed a trade boom with her former enemies, France and America.

Pitt's best qualities were on display in the Budget speech he made in the Commons in February 1792. 'Unquestionably', he told the House, 'there never was a time in the history of this country when from the situation of Europe we might more reasonably expect fifteen years of peace, than we may at the present moment.'

Not even he could predict that the outbreak of the greatest war in which England had ever been involved was a year away.

One man who did not join in the cheers was Edmund Burke, MP. Of a modest, half-Catholic Irish background, Burke had forged a remarkable career for himself in London as a writer, wit and politician. His maiden speech – a furious assault on the Stamp Act – brought him instant fame and he became a leader of the extreme Whigs, attacking, in classic Whig style, royal power and the king's influence in government. Indeed, his continued passionate defence of the American revolutionaries cost him his seat in populous Bristol, forcing him to seek re-election from a handful of compliant voters in the 'rotten borough' of Malton.

But despite the famous mock epitaph, which accused Burke of giving to party the talents that were intended for mankind, he never lost his original love for literature or the imaginative powers that went with it. These were now powerfully excited by the tremendous spectacle of revolutionary France.

Crucial was Burke's interest in the 'Sublime'. This he had defined as a young man, in a notable, pioneering essay, which is the turning point in the whole history of the taste of eighteenth-century Europe, as 'a sort of delightful horror, … a tranquillity tinged with terror', which we get from the contemplation of darkness, danger and death. It was this insight which enabled him to perceive, long before anyone else, the enormity of the passions unleashed by the French Revolution. In doing so, it turned him from a mere politician into a prophet whose words echo down the generations.

Burke published his *Reflections on the Revolution in France* in 1790. The Revolution, though he already called it 'the most astonishing [thing] that has … happened in the world', was then barely a year old. Absolutism and feudalism had been abolished; Church property confiscated; the Bastille had fallen; the new constitution and the Declaration of the Rights of Man had been promulgated; and the king and queen marched from Versailles to Paris.

But the Terror, the abolition of the monarchy and the execution of the king, the revolutionary wars that convulsed Europe for more than a decade and a half and led to the deaths of millions, still lay in the future. Burke, however, prophesied them all.

Burke did so because he correctly identified from the beginning that the operating principle of the Revolution was inhuman, abstract Reason, which thought that it could and should remodel politics, society and humanity itself from scratch. This levelling Reason saw history, habit and tradition as mere obstacles to progress that like any human opposition were to be destroyed in the joyous, all-consuming bonfire of the vanities: 'The Year One' of human history.

For Burke, on the other hand, history and tradition were the foundation of civilization and habit – the things that made us human. From time to time, they might need reform. But reform should preserve, not destroy, their essence. Monarchy, as the supreme embodiment of history and tradition, thus became a test case. Was it the key obstacle to the new world, as the French quickly came to see? Or was it the guarantor of stability and freedom, as the British had decided (on Burke's reading) in 1689, and would again, Burke predicted, once more?

Yet again, Burke was to be proved right. When he wrote the *Reflections* in 1790, his was a voice crying in the wilderness. But, over the next few years, public opinion swung, increasingly strongly, in his direction.

As in everything else, George, prince of Wales, the king's eldest son, was the barometer of fashion – handsome (before he ran to fat), intelligent, charming, sensual and a brilliant mimic. His relations with his father followed the normal Hanoverian pattern of mutual loathing and contempt. He thought his father mean and puritanical; his father thought his son a wanton and a wastrel. The prince of Wales also followed the traditions of his dynasty by putting himself at the head of the opposition party of radical Whigs, of which the pre-Revolutionary Burke had been the leading ideologue.

The prince's first reaction to the *Reflections* was thus, to Burke's immense hurt, to dismiss it as 'a farrago of nonsense' and the work of a turncoat. But, with the Terror, he changed his mind. The execution of Louis XVI, he wrote to his mother, Queen Charlotte, had filled him with 'a species of sentiment towards my father which surpasses all description'. He made his peace with the king (though it didn't last long); broke with the opposition and declared his enthusiastic support for Prime Minister Pitt. He even toyed with the idea of serving as a volunteer in the war against France.

And where the prince led, much of the Whig Party followed, joining Pitt in a coalition to wage war 'under the standard of an hereditary monarchy' against Republican France and all that she stood for. This increasingly ideological war irretrievably split the Whigs, and condemned them to the wilderness for a generation. The more conservative members, who believed that opposition to the war and calls for constitutional reform would culminate in the destruction of the constitution and the monarchy, as they had in France, soon followed the logic of their position and joined the government. This left only a rump of radicals in opposition, who were not only easily outvoted but were also tainted with republicanism and treason.

Once it was Jacobitism which had done for the Tories and left them in the cold; now it was Jacobinism (as the creed of the French ultra-Republicans was known) which dished the Whigs.

The great beneficiary was the monarchy. For much of his reign, as radicalism flourished in the cities and his American subjects rejected his authority, George III could do no right. Now he could do no wrong. Indeed, the less he did the better, as he turned (in the popular imagination at least) from a meddlesome would-be absolutist into the benign father of his people: uxorious, modest, moral, frugal and the very embodiment of a modern, eighteenth-century king. He liked to live simply, far removed from the formal ceremonies of monarchy, as an ordinary country squire. Those subjects who encountered him on his frequent walks found a man who conversed with them as equals. He enjoyed pleasant holidays in English seaside resorts, and when he was in Weymouth a year before Louis XVI was put to death, a lady of that town remarked on how wonderful it was to have George in their town, 'not so much because he was a King, but because they said he was such a worthy gentleman, and that the like of him was never known in this realm before'.

Thus, during the tumult of revolution and the recurring threats of French invasion, George III stood out as a reassuring symbol of stability who represented British virtues of simplicity, sincerity and good old-fashioned common sense. Indeed, he was the exact opposite of hot-headed Continental rulers or luxurious despots surrounded by the flummery of ceremony. He had the common touch without doubt. 'The English people were pleased to see in him a crowning specimen of themselves – a royal John Bull', in the words of the poet and journalist Leigh Hunt. The result was the astonishing popular success of his Golden Jubilee on 25 October 1809. There were illuminations, fireworks, dancing in the streets and celebratory verse:

> From Thames' to Ganges' common shores rejoice,
> A People, happy, great, and free;
> That People with one common voice,
> From Thames' to Ganges' common shores rejoice,
> In universal jubilee.

A year later to the day, George, who had already had two mysterious episodes of apparent mental illness, began his permanent and irreversible descent into a twilight world of madness, blindness and senility.

II

At the time of his father's collapse in 1810, the prince of Wales (disrespectfully known as 'Prinny' to his cronies) was already forty-eight and, under the combined influences of drink, drugs (like many of his contemporaries he took an opium compound known as laudanum) and a gargantuan appetite, his youthful good looks were fading fast and his skin had turned a deep coppery hue.

He spent gigantically too, and his own treasurer declared that his debts were 'beyond all kind of calculation whatever'. The contrast with his prudent and down-to-earth father could not have been greater and his profligacy and debauched antics had made him as deeply unpopular as the king was loved and respected. But worst of all was his disastrous marriage.

The marriage began hopefully as part of the closing of ranks within the royal family in the wake of the French Revolution. In return for the payment of his debts, the prince agreed to his father's urgent wish that he should marry and father an heir. German custom, however, dictated that his bride should be royal too. Best of a bad bunch of available Protestant princesses seemed to be his cousin, Caroline of Brunswick.

But when she arrived in England it was loathing at first sight. She was coarse, ill educated and none too clean. After his marriage in the Chapel Royal in St James's, George knocked himself out with brandy and spent his wedding night passed out on the bedroom floor with his head in the hearth. The following morning he recovered sufficiently to get Caroline pregnant, but only after he had steeled himself with more alcohol 'to conquer my person and overcome the disgust of her person'. A daughter, christened Charlotte, was born in January 1796. It was the first and last time the couple slept together, and they soon separated.

Such was the man who became prince regent of the United Kingdom. He got a bad press at the time, particularly from the great cartoonists like Gillray and Cruikshank, who had a field day with his shape and his private life. And posterity, on the whole, hasn't been much kinder.

But there's another side to the story. The prince regent wasn't much good at the business side of monarchy, which he found altogether too much like hard work. 'Playing at king', as he sighed shortly after becoming regent, 'is no sinecure.' On the other hand, few more imaginative men have sat on the British throne, and none has left more tangible results: in London, the royal palaces and the strange, hybrid concept of British identity itself.

Once again, it all goes back to the French Revolution. Burke's final prophecy and warning to the French had been that 'some popular general' would arise and become 'the master of your whole Republic'. This prediction too was fulfilled by the meteoric rise of Napoleon Bonaparte, the young, impoverished Corsican nobleman who became in quick succession France's most successful general, First Consul and finally, in 1804, self-proclaimed Emperor of the French.

Napoleon was self-crowned too in an extraordinary ceremony held in the hastily patched-up cathedral of Notre-Dame. Drawing on a range of royal and imperial symbolism, Napoleon and his stage designers came up with new rituals and regalia, a new imperial court, thickly populated with 'Grand'-this and 'Arch'-that, each in his own lavish new uniform, and a new imperial family, quarrelling as bitterly as any ancient dynasty.

Above all, the event, carefully recorded on canvas and in print, set new standards both for pomp and precision which the established monarchies rushed to copy. Not only, it seemed, could Napoleon beat kings and tsars on the battlefield, he could beat them at 'playing at king' as well.

The Republic had been bad enough for the prince of Wales. But this upstart emperor was worse, and doing him down and outdoing him became – insofar as his easy-going personality allowed – an obsession. The prince regent had over a decade to wait. But at last the day arrived, and on 18 June 1815, at Waterloo, to the south of Brussels, Napoleon engaged with a British army commanded by Arthur Wellesley, duke of Wellington. Each side played to their strengths: the French attacked with brio; the British doggedly resisted in defensive formations. 'Let's see who can pound longest,' said Wellington. In the event, the British did and held out until the arrival of the Prussian allied army gave them an overwhelming advantage.

The French retreat turned into a rout. On 3 July an armistice was agreed; on the 6th the allies entered Paris and on the 13th Napoleon wrote the most remarkable letter of his life. It was addressed to the prince regent. '*Altesse Royale* [Royal Highness],' it began, 'I have terminated my political career ... I put myself under the protection of British laws, which I entreat of Your Royal Highness as from the most powerful, the most constant, and the most generous of my foes.' In this contest of the imperial eagle against the royal popinjay, the popinjay, it seemed, had won.

But even in defeat and exiled to the British possession of St Helena – a tiny, remote Atlantic island – Napoleon continued to fascinate his enemies. And none more so than the prince regent. It began with the contest of capitals: London versus Paris.

Napoleon, like many despots, was a megalomaniac builder, who started to refashion the then largely medieval warren of Paris into the worthy capital of an empire which, at its height, stretched from the Bay of Biscay to the gates of Moscow. This was to throw down the gauntlet to Britain, since London, fattened by overseas empire and trade, already dwarfed Paris in size and wealth. But it was a rather dingy world capital, shrouded in fog and coal smoke and traversable only by rutted and narrow streets and lanes. St James's Palace, it was said by sophisticated European visitors, looked like a workhouse and Parliament like a coffee house.

Now, 'Prinny' decided, the City must look like the capital of a victorious empire. The man charged with realizing his dreams was John Nash. Nash's brief was simple: he must outdo Napoleonic Paris. And, thanks to his unusual combination of qualities as both visionary architect and shrewd property developer, he largely succeeded.

His scheme, which involved both landscaping and town planning on a heroic scale, created a grand processional route from the newly laid-out Regent's Park in the north, through Regent Street, to Pall Mall and the gates of the prince's then London residence in the south. Nash worked in sweeping curves and artful vistas; while his buildings, which were really terraces of middle-class brick houses, were covered in stucco plaster and painted to look like a succession of noble palaces. This was architecture as urban stage set: as theatrical as Napoleon's coronation and as successful.

Then, in 1820, there arrived a day for which the prince had waited almost as eagerly as he had Napoleon's downfall. For almost a decade after he became regent, his father, George III, had lived the life of a recluse in a little three-room apartment at Windsor. Dead to the world, he spent hours thumping an old harpsichord. But his condition suddenly deteriorated and he died on 29 June.

The regent was king at last. And he was determined that everybody should know it. But there was unfinished business with an enemy who stood equal in his eyes with Napoleon. One of his first decisions as king was to order his government to pass a Bill in Parliament dissolving his marriage to his hated wife, who now exulted in her position as Queen Caroline. She had been in voluntary exile in southern Europe, where she had enjoyed herself to the utmost with a succession of male admirers. It was the government's duty to present evidence of the queen's outrageous behaviour to the House of Lords, and secure a divorce for the new king. The ministry, on the other hand, saw that depriving a queen of her rights was politically impossible and attempted to make George see reason. But the king would not be deterred.

In the end, the cabinet was proved right. The country rallied behind Caroline, whom it saw as a wronged woman and the embodiment of female purity. (If she was, it was only in comparison with her estranged husband.) The monarchy slipped to the depths of unpopularity, and even the Lords found it hard to stomach George's hypocrisy. The government dropped the Bill.

George's coronation finally took place on 19 July 1821. He had delayed it for over a year in the hope that the longed-for divorce would mean that he would not have to share the greatest day of his life with Caroline. Thwarted by the half-hearted efforts of his government and the trucu-lence of his people, George got what he wanted by stationing prizefight-ers dressed as pages outside the doors of Westminster Abbey to exclude uninvited guests, with the queen top of the list.

Partly in compensation for the horrors of the past year it was, George resolved, to be the best-organized and most magnificent coronation in British history. It was certainly the most expensive, costing almost a quarter of a million pounds, while his father's had been staged for less than ten thousand.

For George IV was not measuring himself against a king but the Emperor Napoleon. Indeed, he was measuring himself literally, since his tailor was sent to Paris to copy Napoleon's coronation robe. The result imitates the form of Napoleon's robe and, being even more thickly embroidered and befurred, it took eight pages to carry it, and it was said that, had they let go, the king would have toppled on to his back.

George also copied Napoleon in demanding a precise and exhaustive record of the event in a series of coloured lithographs that preserved every detail of every costume for posterity. And, once again, the emulation was conscious and explicit. Sir George Nayler's *The Coronation of His Most Sacred Majesty King George the Fourth* was 'Undertaken by His Majesty's Especial Command', and Nayler received a £3000 royal subsidy. For it had to be the best – or at any rate, better than Napoleon's: 'This work will excel any of the kind in the known world; and the folio History of Bonaparte's Coronation, the most important and perfect yet published, will sink into nothing by contrast,' the Preface boasts.

Eventually, but only a decade after George's death, the ambition was fulfilled with the appearance of a set of splendid volumes, with their hand-coloured plates, lavishly heightened in gold, which captured more than a little of the magnificence of the day.

One of the spectators at the coronation was the Scottish historian, poet and novelist Sir Walter Scott, who was bowled over by the combination of 'gay, gorgeous and antique dress which floated before the eye'. If the coronation was supposed to bewitch, the magic certainly worked on Scott. And he tried to transmit the wonder of the day in a newspaper article, which asked his readers to imagine the Abbey lit by the

> sun, which brightened and saddened as if on purpose, now beaming in full lustre on the rich and varied assemblage, and now darting a solitary ray, which catched, as it passed, the glittering folds of a banner ... and then rested full on some fair form ... whose circlet of diamonds glistened under its influence.

Conjure up, he enjoined them, the 'sights of splendour and sounds of harmony'.

Scott, born in 1771, belonged to the generation that had grown up with the French Revolution and had reacted strongly against it. Profoundly influenced by Burke and by Burke's German disciples, he lived history and tradition and gave them life in his poetry and novels.

One of the most famous was *Kenilworth*, which focused on the great revels presented at Kenilworth Castle for Good Queen Bess by her favourite, the earl of Leicester. Published in 1821, the novel plugged into the same fashion for all things Elizabethan and Shakespearean that was tapped by the costumes George devised for his coronation. Now Scott, who had first met George in 1815, was given the opportunity to devise his own grand historical pageant when he was put in charge of organizing the king's visit to Edinburgh in 1822.

The visit – the first to Scotland by a reigning monarch since Charles II's coronation in 1651 – began on 14 August with the king's ceremonial landing at Leith and continued for a fortnight with balls, receptions and a grand procession from Holyrood Palace to Edinburgh Castle. There the king inspected the Scottish royal regalia, which had recently been unearthed by Scott himself.

Throughout, at Scott's insistence, all the gentlemen wore Highland dress, including the king, whose ample figure was compressed into something like the necessary shape by corsets and flesh-coloured tights. The climax came in the great banquet held in the Parliament House, where, a century earlier, Scotland's separate political existence had been extinguished by the passage of the Act of Union. The king called for a toast to the 'Clans and Chieftains of Scotland', to which the chief of the Clan Macgregor replied with one to 'The Chief of Chiefs – the King!'

It was all, as the hard-headed have not ceased to point out from then till now, nonsense. But, as befits Scott's genius as impresario, it was inspired, romantic nonsense. Above all, it was successful nonsense. It gave Scotland a proud cultural identity that, for over a hundred years, dwelt in a sort of parallel universe alongside the political subordination required by the Union. And, as the ardently Tory Scott intended, it firmly anchored this renewed Scots national identity to the Hanoverian monarchy.

For nationalism had played a part in the downfall of Napoleon's empire second only to British arms. The British monarchy instead, thanks in the first place to George IV's taste for theatrical pageantry, was able to harness the wild horses of nationalism, geld and domesticate them and turn them into the gaily decked palfreys pulling the royal state coach. Or, in the case of the Highland regiments, its foot soldiers, marching alongside and winning the empire's battles under the Union Flag.

For that, parading through the streets of Edinburgh in corsets and kilts was a small price to pay.

III

But George IV was unable to keep up the flurry of activity that marked the beginning of his reign. His health and mobility declined and his self-indulgence grew, as he washed down vast amounts of food with even larger quantities of alcohol and dulled what little sense remained with ever more frequent doses of laudanum. He died, unlamented, at Windsor on 26 June 1830 and, having been predeceased by his daughter and only child, was succeeded by his eldest surviving brother, William, duke of Clarence.

At first sight, William IV, who was already aged sixty-four, was not a promising prospect as king. He had been sent to sea at the age of thirteen as a midshipman in the Royal Navy, where he had spent a few happy years drinking and womanizing around the world; on his return he shocked his staid parents and polished brothers with his compulsive swearing. Deprived of the chance to further his career, he had then spent most of his life as a relatively impecunious younger son. It was an empty existence with no meaningful role, and he filled his time fathering a numerous progeny of grasping bastards. And he had been cashiered from the only senior post he had (briefly) held – that of Lord High Admiral – for refusing to submit to the prime minister's orders. He was also personally ridiculous, with a strange, pineapple-shaped head and a tendency to talk at length and at some distance from the point.

On the other hand, he was a moderate Whig in politics, in contrast to the rabid Toryism of other members of the royal family, while his naval service had given him both a common touch and robust common sense. He was described as 'A little old, red-nosed, weather-beaten, jolly looking person with an ungraceful air and carriage', rather like a retired sea captain. He was also – in striking contrast to his predecessor – completely indifferent to ceremony and pomp and circumstance.

Testimony to this is Clarence House, the elegant but comparatively modest London residence built for William while he was still heir to the throne. The king continued to live there after his accession and showed no wish at all to move into the neighbouring Buckingham Palace, George IV's last, grandest, most expensive and still embarrassingly incomplete building project. Instead, he asked whether the palace could be converted into barracks.

William was equally unexcited about his coronation. Indeed, he suggested doing away with it entirely as a mere occasion 'for useless and ill-timed expense'. Could he not simply take the oaths to the constitution and the Protestant religion prescribed by the Bill of Rights and have done with it? When he was in the robing room of the House of Lords preparing to dissolve Parliament, he snatched the crown from a startled courtier and, placing it askew on his head, said to Lord Grey, the prime minister, 'Now, my Lord, the Coronation is over.'

Horrified Tory protests forced him to go through with the real ceremony. But it was done on the cheap (costing less than a fifth of George IV's, it was nicknamed the 'Half-Crownation'), while the ancient ritual was ignorantly butchered and abbreviated. And ever the boisterous and laid-back sailor, William conspicuously mocked the gravity of the occasion during the service.

All this was of a piece with his usual behaviour. Early in his reign he would walk up St James's Street unattended, but had to give up when he was mobbed. On another occasion, society was shocked when William took the king of Württemberg for a drive round London and 'set down the King ("dropped him", as he calls it) at Grillon's Hotel. The King of England dropping another King at a tavern!' And again, impatient at the delays in getting the state coach ready for the dissolution of Parliament, he threatened to go in a hackney coach (the ancestor of the modern taxi) instead. Never, in short, has Britain come nearer to a bicycling or at least a taxiing monarchy than under William IV. But would these decent, unpretentious qualities be enough?

Barely a month after William's accession there was a brutal reminder of the fate of unsuccessful sovereigns. Paris once again rose in anger: the 'Days of July', when the king of France, whose monarchy had been restored after the fall of Napoleon, was ignominiously driven from the throne. Now, news came, he was on his way to seek refuge in Britain.

He was packed off to Edinburgh, where he spent a miserable winter in unheated and unfurnished rooms at Holyrood, protected from a hostile mob only by Sir Walter Scott.

Just how secure was the throne of his reluctant and ungracious English host? For, despite forty-odd years of almost uninterrupted Tory rule, from the 1780s to the 1820s, the ideas of the French Revolution *had* taken root in Britain. But was it to be full-blown revolution? Or reform?

In the hard days after victory in 1815, when the economy had taken a serious downward turn and aberrant climatic conditions caused the harvests to fail, radical agitation had reached a peak. In 1819, for instance, a great demonstration took place in St Peter's Fields, Manchester, as 60,000 men, women and children marched on the town. The town magistrates panicked and ordered the local yeomanry cavalry to disperse the peaceful throng. The charge killed eleven and wounded about four hundred in what, in a savage parody of Waterloo, became known within days as the Peterloo Massacre.

But the demonstrators had not threatened violence. The huge crowd was carefully marshalled, with the brass bands accompanying each division playing patriotic tunes, such as 'God Save the King' and 'Rule, Britannia!'. And when it was the turn of the national anthem most members of the crowd respectfully took their hats off. In 1820 the pro-Caroline demonstrators focused their anger on political corruption, not anti-monarchism. And the radical leaders paid court to the scorned queen, like any ardent royalist basking in the light of majesty.

Back in the heady days of the early 1790s, a minority *had* hoped for revolution red in tooth and claw. But this revolutionary group was quickly eclipsed by another, who wanted reform, not revolution. They thought change could be brought about *within* England's existing institutions, and by peaceful means, not revolutionary violence. They also differed from the ardently pro-French revolutionaries and their undercover, quasi-treasonable followers in that they paraded their John Bull British patriotism, as the Manchester and Caroline demonstrators had done. Finally, the striking thing is that the target of the reform agitation was not the monarchy, as it was in contemporary France and had been in seventeenth-century England, but Parliament.

In the early nineteenth century Parliament met, as it had done for centuries, in the medieval royal palace of Westminster, which had been long abandoned by the monarchy and handed over instead to Parliament and the Law Courts. Over the centuries, the ancient structure had been repeatedly hacked around and refurbished, the Commons most recently by Sir Christopher Wren in the eighteenth century and the Lords by James Wyatt at the beginning of the nineteenth.

The result was a kind of physical embodiment of Burke's ancient constitution, in which the antique buildings had been slowly and almost imperceptibly altered and adapted over the ages. They were also ramshackle, jerry-built and prone to fire.

Much the same could be said, by its critics, of the House of Commons itself. Many important and fast-growing towns had no MP at all, while tiny, half-abandoned villages with a handful of inhabitants returned two MPs each at the command of the owner of the rotten borough, as such constituencies were known. A handful of rich and powerful noblemen owned a dozen or more rotten boroughs each and could make or break governments.

It was William's misfortune that the pressure for parliamentary reform suddenly intensified at the beginning of his reign. For, five months after his accession, the Tory government fell and a Whig administration took office for the first time in almost fifty years.

The new government also looked to a different geographical constituency. For the capital was not the only town to undergo radical change in the first decades of the nineteenth century. The noble townscape of Newcastle-upon-Tyne, for instance, is the equal of anything created by the prince regent in London. But its grand terraced main street and monumental column are a memorial not to a king or prince, or a general or admiral, but to Charles, Earl Grey, the prime minister of the Whig government of 1830 and a local Northumbrian grandee.

Grey's father was a successful general who was raised to an earldom. He first became an MP at the age of only twenty-two and quickly established a reputation as a brilliant, if reckless, speaker and an accomplished adulterer, who numbered Georgiana, duchess of Devonshire, among his conquests.

In the Whig split during the French revolutionary wars Grey remained with the rump in opposition. But he disagreed with the leadership over their pro-French defeatism. Instead, he argued, the Whig Party must renew itself by discovering its earlier radicalism and joining – or rather leading – the movement for parliamentary reform.

For Grey was, and remained, a natural aristocrat, who saw himself acting on behalf of the people, and not at their command. Now, as prime minister, with nine out of thirteen cabinet ministers drawn from the Lords, he had the opportunity to put his ideas into practice. Over the next three years, three Reform Bills were submitted to Parliament – each to much the same effect: fifty-six rotten boroughs to be abolished; forty-four seats to be given to large towns, and then the most modest property holders to be enfranchised. The first was defeated in the Commons and provoked a general election that, even on the unreformed franchise, produced a Whig landslide. The second was defeated in the Lords. And it looked as though the intransigent Tory majority in the Lords would do the same to the third.

The only way, it seemed, to break the deadlock was for William to create enough peers to give the Whigs a majority in the Lords as well.

So far, William had given Grey unstinting support. He had done so on practical grounds, since he recognized that reform was the only alternative to revolution. He also acted on principle, since he saw it as his duty, whatever his personal wishes, 'to support the Prime Minister until Parliament by its vote determines that the Prime Minister no longer possesses the confidence of the nation'. But a creation of up to fifty peers, which would radically dilute the composition of the Lords, was a step too far. William refused; Grey resigned and, on 9 May 1832, the king invited the Tories to form a government.

England now had its 'Days of May', when it looked as though London, Newcastle and the rest would follow in the steps of revolutionary Paris. There were mass demonstrations and strikes; newspapers whipped up the frenzy with provocative headlines like 'The Eve of the Barricades', while in Birmingham a speaker at a rally of 100,000 people proclaimed Tory 'incompetency to govern' and invoked the people's 'Right to Arm' in the face of oppression from the Bill of Rights.

When the American rebels had used that language, George III had dug his heels in; William IV instead sought compromise.

The Tories, he suggested privately, should simply cut their losses, bury their pride and abstain. Reform was inevitable, and that way at least they would retain their inbuilt majority in the Lords. It was a bitter pill to swallow and they resisted as long as possible. But finally they had to admit that they couldn't form a government. William now had no choice but to recall Grey and to agree in writing to his demand for the mass creation of peers.

It was the most humiliating document a king had signed since the Civil War. But William turned it to his advantage by informing the Tory leaders of what he had done. Certain now that they would be swamped even in the Lords, they abandoned their resistance and the Reform Bill went through.

The key figure in these behind-the-scenes negotiations was the king's private secretary and long-serving courtier, Sir Herbert Taylor. Taylor wrote all William's letters (up to thirty or forty a day) and the suspicion must be that he helped shape much of their content as well. If so, it was a job well done. For, by their joint actions in the 'Days of May', William and Taylor had invented, more or less at a stroke, both the modern constitutional monarchy and the role of the private secretary as the principal cog in the royal machine.

On 7 June the Reform Act received the royal assent by commission. Grey had wanted William to give it in person. But, because he disapproved of the popular clamour, the king refused. It was perhaps his only false step in the whole affair. The new House of Commons, elected under the new franchise, was unencumbered by such fear of public opinion.

Two years later, on the night of 16 October 1834, the chambers of both Houses of Parliament and all the rest of the Palace of Westminster – apart from the Great Hall – were consumed by a raging fire. Reconstructing Parliament from scratch now ceased to be a disputed metaphor and became a practical necessity instead.

IV

William himself, now in his late sixties and beyond hope of legitimate children of his own, would not long survive the Reform Act. His health was declining and his tetchiness increasing. But he was determined to live long enough for his heir presumptive, Princess Victoria, to inherit the crown in her own right. For if he died before she reached her eighteenth birthday, a regent would have to rule in her name. And that person would be William's detested sister-in-law and Victoria's mother, Marie Louise Victoria, duchess of Kent. Contemplating the prospect of power, the duchess had become overbearing and nakedly ambitious. Outraged, nine months before the young princess's birthday, William made an extraordinary speech to the court. He did not mince his words, saying that he was determined to prolong his life for a few months longer, for 'I should then have the satisfaction of leaving the royal authority to the personal exercise of that young lady … and not in the hands of the person now near me, who is surrounded by evil designs and who is herself incompetent to act with propriety in the station in which she would be placed'.

William made it with days to spare. Victoria celebrated her eighteenth birthday (her royal coming of age) on 24 May 1837 and William, his goal achieved, died on 20 June.

Victoria was at Kensington Palace when her uncle died. And it was here that she had been brought up and educated. Her education was strong in foreign languages and traditional female accomplishments like drawing and music. But it had neglected the male curriculum of classics and mathematics.

On the other hand, her governess, Baroness Lehzen, whose ideal monarch was Queen Elizabeth I, had made sure that, despite the bias of her education, Victoria would be no meekly submissive woman. Lehzen brought her up to rule, and Victoria had the appetite and will to do so. She was also prepared for the necessary hard work. During the king's illness, her lessons had been cancelled. 'I regret rather my singing lesson,' she said, 'though it is only for a short period, but duty and *proper feeling go before all pleasures.*' Just eighteen, she was showing the qualities that would define her reign.

The news that she was queen was brought at six o'clock in the morning by the Lord Chamberlain and the archbishop of Canterbury, who were received by Victoria in her dressing gown. And the contrast between the glowing young queen and the sombrely dressed, elderly male political establishment was only underscored by her Accession Council, which was held later in the day. The next day she presided over another council meeting 'as if she had been doing it all her life'. All who saw her were bowled over by her confidence.

Particularly susceptible was the prime minister, Lord Melbourne. And the attraction was mutual. Charming, worldly wise and with the faint whiff of the danger of an ex-roué, Melbourne was the perfect mentor for the inexperienced young queen. He was also of the right political colour, since Victoria had been brought up as an ardent Whig.

The result was that the Tories soon called foul. But worse was to come when, only two years after her accession, Victoria displayed blatant partisanship during a ministerial crisis and wrecked a Tory attempt to form a government. Melbourne had won a crucial vote in the House of

Commons by just five votes and resigned the premiership. Victoria, still under the sway of the paternal old politician, grudgingly offered the premiership to first the duke of Wellington and then Sir Robert Peel. Peel, not feeling it the right moment to take power, would accept only on the condition that the queen replaced the ladies of her household, who were all aristocratic Whigs. Victoria took great pleasure in refusing this disrespectful order, and Melbourne, against *his* better judgement, was reinstated as the queen's pet prime minister. Even Whigs now had to acknowledge that a young, unmarried girl on the throne was a loose cannon.

But who was to be the husband? The front-runner was Prince Albert, a younger son of the duke of the little German principality of Saxe-Coburg. The connection between the houses of Hanover and Saxe-Coburg was already strong, as both Victoria's mother and her cousin by marriage were Coburgs. Moreover, when Victoria (who was highly susceptible to male beauty) had first met Albert some years previously she had been very taken by his excellent figure and rather ethereal good looks. But she noted his tendency to tire easily, in contrast to her own boundless energy.

Albert was exactly of an age with Victoria. But otherwise their early experiences had been very different. Albert's father was an inveterate womanizer and, in revenge, his wife had taken a lover of her own. The result was divorce and Albert's loss of his mother at the age of only five. His own upright morality was a reaction to this loss and to the loneliness of a motherless child.

The gap left by his mother had eventually been filled by Albert's tutor, who discharged his duties with a rare zeal and thoroughness. He had also benefited from formal instruction, both in Coburg and later at the university in Bonn, which was then at the height of its academic fame. All this added mineralogy and science, anthropology, philosophy, literary criticism and music to the basic curriculum he had learned at home. And, despite his rather weak constitution, he was no milksop either: he was a competent fencer and an excellent shot. In short, he was the very model of an accomplished, modern prince for the nineteenth century. All that he lacked, as a penniless younger son, was a wife.

Victoria was in no hurry to oblige: she was enjoying the delicious freedom of being a young queen regnant far too much for that. Nevertheless, despite her conspicuous lack of encouragement, Albert was sent over to England to be inspected a second time. He arrived at Windsor on 10 October 1839. Victoria was watching from the top of the stairs and confided her feelings to her diary: 'It was with some emotion that I beheld Albert, who is *beautiful*,' she wrote with a characteristically heavy underlining. It was love at second sight, but none the less profound for that. And it lasted for both their lives.

In view of the disparity in their status it was Victoria who had to propose. They were married at the Chapel Royal at St James's on 10 February 1840 and departed for a two-day honeymoon at Windsor. 'We did not sleep much,' Victoria noted of their wedding night. They revelled in each other's sensuality. Albert helped Victoria pull on her stockings; she watched him shave. Unsurprisingly, then, Victoria conceived within days and gave birth to a daughter in November. A son, Edward, prince of Wales, came just eleven months later, followed by seven more children, with never more than two years between them.

And it was this uxorious bliss which began to alter the relationship between them. From the beginning, they had had adjacent desks. But Victoria had made it clear that, as was constitutionally proper, the business of queening was hers alone. Albert was allowed to blot her dispatches, but only as a concession.

But her repeated pregnancies, regularly followed by intense post-natal depression, began to swing the balance of power. And the change was completed by Albert's increasing psychological dominance. She was tempestuous; he coldly rational. And he soon turned her temperament against her by making her ashamed of her uninhibited behaviour. The result was that Victoria not only became a submissive wife in private; she even surrendered public business to her husband, who acted as her private secretary with more power than any private secretary ever had. Once he had meekly blotted dispatches; now he dictated them.

This gave Albert a free hand to shape his own vision of monarchy. He had arrived in an England transformed by the Reform Act, which had created a new, predominantly middle-class electorate. And he had quickly attached himself to the most intelligent politician of the mid-century: the Tory leader, Sir Robert Peel. Peel, himself the son of a cotton manufacturer, saw it as his mission to adapt the Tory Party to the new world of industry and railways, powerful manufacturing cities and bourgeois morality which we call the Industrial Revolution.

In pulling it into the modern world, Peel split the Tory Party, sending it into the political wilderness for two decades. But Albert succeeded in adapting the monarchy to the same forces beyond anyone's wildest dreams. He began at home.

The young royal family would spend their summers at Osborne House, which Albert built on the Isle of Wight. Victoria's uncle, George IV, true to his decadent nature and the flamboyance of the time in which he ruled, had summered in his holiday home, the Brighton Pavilion. With its exotic minarets and domes, it appeared to be the home of a fairy-tale oriental despot. At Osborne the contrast could not have been greater. In place of the fantastic architecture and fantastic expense all was sobriety and efficiency. The site was bought at a bargain price and building works completed to time and to budget.

But most innovatory was the layout. For Osborne is really two buildings in one. There was the Family Pavilion and the Household Wing. Servants and the business of state were shunted off into the latter, while the former provided the setting for 'The Home Life of Our Own Dear Queen' – which was really Albert's creation and was a model of modern, almost bourgeois, privacy and respectability.

'That damned morality would undo us all,' snorted Victoria's first, old-school prime minister. Albert, on the contrary, saw the 'moral monarchy' as the one means by which royalty could appeal to the middle classes, perhaps even lead them.

And central to this was the mid-nineteenth-century faith in progress and entrepreneurial zeal. In the previous century, the monarchy had been at the forefront of innovation, patronizing nascent industry and sponsoring scientific experiments. But many of the great advances of the Industrial Revolution in the nineteenth century had been spurred by private effort. The Royal Society for the Encouragement of Arts, Manufactures and Commerce had been established by George III, but had slumped into dozy inactivity before Albert took over as president. Under his active patronage, it was revived with a successful programme of annual exhibitions of British manufactures.

Then it was suggested that the exhibition should become *inter*national to reflect the fact that one quarter of the world's population was now ruled by Britain. Albert took up the idea enthusiastically. But it required all his drive and determination to overcome the obstacles and objections.

The projected event was riddled with impracticalities and dangers. For it to work, suitable space in central London would have to be found and all the international exhibitors would have to be carefully managed. The pessimistic predicted that it would be a Great British farce. The unruly lower orders would riot; the fine elm trees on the Hyde Park site would be damaged; none of the 245 submitted designs for the exhibition building would work.

The day was saved by Joseph Paxton's scheme for a prefabricated 'Crystal Palace' of iron and glass, like a gigantic conservatory. Albert took only nine days to get 'the most advanced building of the nineteenth century' accepted; seven weeks later the concrete foundations were laid and four months later it was finished. The statistics are staggering. The palace was 1848 feet long, 108 feet high (easily accommodating the threatened elms) and covered by 300,000 panes of glass. Inside, 1¾ miles of exhibition space displayed 100,000 exhibits from 14,000 exhibitors drawn from Europe and the world. Machines hummed and whirred; telegraphs and cameras showed what the future might be like; both finely crafted and mass-produced artefacts were proudly on display; and the produce of the world – the fruits of empire and free trade – were brought together under the glass. All this was seen by 6 million people, or a third of Britain's entire population.

And it was all Albert's work. In a speech at the Lord Mayor's Banquet, Albert said that the Exhibition pointed to the future of mankind – unity through communication and mutual understanding. 'The Exhibition of 1851', he said, 'is to give us a true test and a living picture of the point of development at which the whole of mankind has arrived in this great task, and a new starting point from which all nations will be able to direct their further exertions.'

On 1 May 1851, Victoria, wearing silver and pink and with Albert at her side, opened the Great Exhibition. 'It was the greatest day in our history', she wrote, 'and the triumph of my beloved Albert.' The crowds came, but they were not disorderly; they were decent and respectable. The Exhibition, true to its commercial origin, turned a handy profit, which was put towards founding the Victoria and Albert, the Science and the Natural History museums.

Eight months later, on 3 February 1852, Victoria and Albert opened another, very different, building. Indeed, at first sight it looks as reactionary as the Crystal Palace was progressive. For when the rules were announced for a competition to rebuild the Palace of Westminster after the fire of 1834, it was specified that the design must be in 'the Gothic or Elizabethan style'. The winner, Charles Barry, and his assistant, Augustine Pugin, responded enthusiastically, combining the native English Gothic with the resonantly patriotic Elizabethan; every inch of the building, inside and out, is a riot of medieval and Tudor-inspired ornament.

It is especially rich and colourful in the sequence of magnificent spaces which lead to the House of Lords. These were designed as a stage set for the state opening of Parliament and used for the first time by Victoria and Albert in 1852. Albert was heavily involved here also, as chairman of the committee that chose the artists and the subjects for the wall-paintings, which were likewise exclusively historical and allegorical. The enormous Norman Porch has a stained-glass window showing Edward the Confessor. King Arthur and the Knights of the Round Table are painted on the walls of the Robing Room, where the monarch assumes the royal parliamentary robes and Imperial State Crown prior to the state opening. Paintings of the victorious death of Nelson at Trafalgar and the triumph of Wellington at Waterloo line the Royal Gallery. From here the sovereign processes to the Lords' Chamber, which was intended not only as a debating chamber, but as the magnificent climax of the state opening of Parliament. Stained-glass windows depicting the kings and queens of England and frescos with allegorical representations of Chivalry, Religion and Justice overlook the gold canopy and throne, upon which the monarch sits to open Parliament. Everything is crimson and gold and solemn splendour.

The result has been described and denounced as backward looking and Tory. Albert would have been astonished. He considered himself to be liberal, progressive and constitutionalist. He saw no contradiction between history and progress, or between the Crystal Palace and the Palace of Westminster. And he regarded the state opening of Parliament as the perfect reconciliation of medieval and modern, in which the institutions of English government showed themselves at once durable and flexible.

And the monarchy, as guided by his hand, was all of these things.

PART V

MODERNITY

24

THE MODERN MONARCHY

Victoria, Edward VII, George V,
Edward VIII, George VI

QUEEN VICTORIA DIED IN HER BEDROOM at Osborne, the seaside residence she and Albert had built together in the early days of their marriage, at half past six in the evening of 22 January 1901, with her pillow supported on one side by her doctor and on the other by her eldest grandson, Kaiser Wilhelm II of Germany.

At almost eighty-two, she was the longest lived of any English sovereign and, with over sixty-three years on the throne, the longest reigning also. In her funeral procession through London, her coffin was followed by two emperors and the heir to a third, three kings, two crown princes and leading members of every royal family in Europe. Never had the world seemed so safe for kings. Less than twenty years later, however, this royal Europe tore itself apart in the holocaust of the First World War. It began with the murder of the Habsburg heir and it ended with the fall of all three Continental empires: the Russian, the German and the Austro-Hungarian.

Now only one Western king-emperor survived: Victoria's grandson, George V of Great Britain. At the height of the conflict, in 1917, he had changed his family name to Windsor.

Windsor. The name, selected after careful consideration, is redolent of all things English. Shakespeare. Pageantry. Sweet, old-fashioned smells.

And the magic worked. Or something did. For, eighty years later, the House of Windsor still soldiers on, and George V's granddaughter, Elizabeth II, still sits on the British throne.

This part shows how and why this extraordinary survival against the odds took place. It asks what the nation has gained as well as lost from the continuance of monarchy. And it looks to the future, if indeed there is one. Will green become the new royal purple? Or will the glory of monarchy finally fade away having bored us and itself to death?

I

In 1859 Queen Victoria was painted as she appeared at the state opening of Parliament: robed, diademed and glittering in diamonds, with her Speech from the Throne and the Imperial State Crown, made for her coronation in 1838 and set with the finest and most famous jewels of the Royal Collection, on the table beside her. Rising romantically in the background are the towers and spires of the Palace of Westminster, which she and Albert had opened in 1852 and which was at last nearing completion. No doubt the painter flattered. But the spirit is right. With Albert to guide and steer her, she was enjoying the giddy whirl of being queen.

Two years later, it was all over. Though she had four decades more to live and reign, she would never wear the Imperial Crown again.

On 25 November 1861 Albert, who had been secretly warned that his eldest son, Albert-Edward, prince of Wales, was keeping a woman in his student rooms at Cambridge, travelled by train from Windsor to confront him. He spent the night at Madingley Hall just outside Cambridge, before returning to Windsor the following morning.

Already unwell before his journey, which had taken place in soaking-wet weather, his condition rapidly worsened. But Victoria was oblivious and his doctors powerless, doing little more than drugging him with ever more frequent slugs of brandy. Soon he was delirious, and on the night of 14 December his breathing began to change. Victoria was summoned and, confronting the truth at last, exclaimed, 'This is death' and fell on his body.

Once she emerged from the immediate paralysis of grief, Victoria's first thought was to preserve Albert's private memory for herself and her children. The Blue Room at Windsor, where he had died, was turned into a shrine, where she came to meditate each year on the anniversary of his death. Similarly, his rooms at Osborne were kept unchanged, with his pictures, knick-knacks and his omnipresent bust. Even his shaving-water continued to be put out as usual.

But would Albert's public achievements, in identifying the monarchy with the forces of progress in the arts, industry and politics, survive as well? Here, on the contrary, Victoria's behaviour seemed to risk throwing everything away. Locked in her own misery, she refused point-blank either to come to London or make public appearances. Buckingham Palace, the now all-too-visible symbol of monarchy, stood empty and shuttered, and in 1864 some joker tied a mock advertisement to the gates: 'These commanding premises to be let or sold, in consequence of the late occupant's declining business'.

Two years later, in 1866, under immense pressure from the government, she agreed to open Parliament for the first time since Albert's death. But she could not have made her real feelings plainer. She refused to walk along the Royal Gallery – *his* gallery. Or wear the crown. Or even read the speech. Instead, she sat, frozen and impassive, on the throne, with a black cap, a black dress and a long black veil, while the Lord Chancellor delivered the speech on her behalf.

The following year, Britain took 'a step in the dark' with the passage of the Second, much more radical, Reform Act. This gave the vote to the skilled urban working class and added more than a million voters to the roll.

The age of mass politics had begun.

Victoria reacted calmly, asserting, with her characteristically vigorous underlinings, that 'the country was never so loyal or so devoted to their Sovereign as now'. Her confidence was soon put to the test by the dramatic events in France. On 2 September 1870 at Sedan, the Prussians crushed the French armies and took the Emperor Napoleon III prisoner. France declared a republic and, early the following year, a left-wing rising – the Commune – left the centre of Paris and its great public buildings a blackened, smouldering ruin.

As a century before, the republican infection quickly spread to Britain. *The Republican* newspaper was founded and more than fifty republican clubs established from Aberdeen to Plymouth.

Faced with this direct challenge to her throne, Victoria bestirred herself at last and in 1871 performed more public engagements than in the decade since Albert's death. In February, she opened Parliament, wearing a new, small diamond crown. Weighing only a few ounces (in contrast to the two and a half pounds of the Imperial State Crown), it was designed to fit neatly over her widow's cap and veil and, perched on top of her head, quickly became her acknowledged symbol.

In March, she presided, wearing rubies as well as diamonds, over the wedding of her daughter, Princess Louise, to the marquess of Lorne at Windsor Castle, and followed it by joining the couple on a drive through London. At the end of the month, she opened the Royal Albert Hall, which was packed to capacity with eight thousand people. Finally, in June, she drove to the newly completed St Thomas's Hospital, where her statue commemorates her visit. She paid tribute to Florence Nightingale; toured the building, naming one ward 'Victoria' and another 'Albert'; and declared the hospital open. Albert's improving, philanthropic legacy was, after all, safe in her hands.

Despite all this activity, public opinion hung in the balance, and on 6 November 1871, Sir Charles Wentworth Dilke, a Liberal MP and a baronet, openly called for a republic: 'I say, for my part – and I believe the middle classes in general will say – let it come!'

The salvation of the 'monarchy business' came from an unexpected quarter. The behaviour of the prince of Wales – known to his family as 'Bertie' – had not improved since Albert's death, and only the previous year he had been summoned as a witness in the sensational Mordaunt divorce case. But in late November 1871 he fell dangerously ill of typhoid fever. It was just ten years since his father had supposedly died of the same disease, and it seemed more than likely that there would be the same outcome.

As the royal family, headed by Victoria herself, gathered round the prince's sickbed at Sandringham, a remarkable change took place in the popular mood. Hitherto the press had pilloried Albert-Edward as a good-for-nothing wastrel. Now it kept vigil with the afflicted family. The crisis came on 14 December, the anniversary of Albert's death. But instead of succumbing, the prince survived and began a slow but sure recovery.

The opportunity was too good to miss for the Liberal prime minister, William Ewart Gladstone. Throughout his sixty-year-long political career, which took him from High Toryism in youth to the wilder shores of Liberalism in old age, Gladstone remained constant to the belief that religion was central to politics and that monarchy was the best embodiment of that relationship.

How better to reaffirm this belief and dish Dilke and the republicans than by holding a Day of National Thanksgiving for the prince's recovery, with the queen and the prince of Wales processing through London to a service at St Paul's? The only obstacle, ironically enough, was Victoria herself. She preferred her religion plain and private. And she detested cathedral services with what she saw as their hypocritical combination of religion and pomp.

But Gladstone, for all his religiosity, was an astute politician: the moment was too good to miss and he browbeat Victoria into acceptance. Their personal relations, awkward from the start, never recovered. But, having given way, the queen played her part to perfection.

Temple Bar, which has now been moved to a site by St Paul's Cathedral, then still stood at the entrance to the City in Fleet Street. As the royal carriage passed through it, it halted to be greeted by the Lord Mayor. During the pause, Victoria seized her son's hand, held it up in front of the vast crowd and kissed it extravagantly. It was a gesture worthy of her great predecessor, Queen Elizabeth I herself. The republican movement collapsed and Dilke himself forswore the faith, only to be later forced out of public life by charges of adultery.

In 1874 Gladstone fell and was replaced as prime minister by the other great figure in Victorian politics, the Tory leader, Benjamin Disraeli. Disraeli, feline and slippery as opposed to the craggy Gladstone, was a bundle of contradictions: dandy, novelist and supremely professional politician; baptized Jew and hardline Tory; elitist and populist; cynic and courtier. The moment he became prime minister, Disraeli set himself to charm Victoria, ageing though she was, as his 'Faery Queen'. Victoria, used to Gladstone's lecturings, responded with coquettish glee.

But she also took advantage of the change. Intensely conscious of her royalty, she had been reluctant to yield precedence to the Continental monarchs who bore the title 'emperor' or 'empress'. But the declaration of the German Empire, which followed the defeat of France, raised a particular problem since in time her own eldest daughter, who had married the German crown prince, would be empress herself.

But wasn't she the doyenne of European sovereigns? The ruler of the world's greatest empire, with a fifth of the globe's inhabitants as her subjects? And in India, as heir of the Mughals, wasn't she even regularly called 'empress'? So from 1873 she began to badger about a formal assumption of the title.

The Bill to create her officially 'Empress of India' was introduced in 1876. Gladstone spoke vehemently against it. And even Disraeli harboured doubts, though he kept them to himself. But, once the Act had passed, he moved with characteristic dexterity to exploit it as the centre-piece of a new Tory 'imperial policy of England'.

In 1875, he guaranteed communications to India by buying a control-ling interest in the Suez Canal; in 1877 he engaged in a stand-off with Russia, Britain's chief imperial rival, in the Balkans and the Bosporus; then in 1878 the old prestidigitator pulled off a final coup at the Congress of Berlin by acting as arbiter of Europe and bringing home 'peace with honour'. As he returned to Downing Street in an open carriage, a huge bunch of flowers was thrust into his hands: 'From the queen,' the messen-ger bellowed above the cheers.

At the height of the crisis, the mob had chanted their new song:

> We don't want to fight but by Jingo if we do,
> We've got the ships, we've got the men, we've got the money too.

Then they let off steam by breaking the windows of Gladstone's fine house in Carlton House Terrace. 'Dizzy', Gladstone wrote, 'is looking for the weak side of the English people.' In 'imperialism', as it was soon called, he had found it.

But, deadly political rivals though they were (the mere thought of having to deliver Disraeli's eulogy after his death in 1881 gave Gladstone a fit of diarrhoea), the triumphant late Victorian monarchy is their joint creation. The increasingly grandiose acts of national dedication were Gladstone's progeny (though he intensely disliked the grandiosity); the mounting imperial stridency, enthusiastically abetted by the queen-empress herself, was Dizzy's contribution. And the two came together in the celebrations for Victoria's Diamond Jubilee in 1897.

European royalties were deliberately omitted: instead, pride of place was given to the prime ministers of the newly self-governing white colo-nies of the empire, together with troops representing all its diverse and many-coloured peoples. The celebrations culminated in a carefully rehearsed open-air service, held in brilliant July weather, in front of St Paul's. Looking down on the ceremonies was the statue of Queen Anne, who had reigned almost two centuries before. Anne had come frequently to St Paul's in great, popular processions to celebrate England's victories over the French.

But, despite her shyness and idiosyncrasy, Victoria's popularity was wider and deeper than that of any previous monarch. Her statue stands across the globe; she gave her name to hospitals and universities, cities and waterfalls, entire provinces, and to the greatest and most creative age in our history. She was Britannia, representing in her dumpy little person Britain and her empire, at once embattled and triumphant.

As the queen's carriage pulled off at the end of the service, the choir-boys broke rank to scoop up the gravel that had been crushed by its wheels as a sort of sacred relic.

II

But, for all Victoria's achievements, something was missing. On 23 March 1887, on one of her new-style royal progresses, Victoria visited Birmingham. She travelled by train and then drove from the station in a carriage procession to the magnificent town hall, for a civic reception which ended with a performance of Handel's 'Hallelujah Chorus'.

As she got back into her train, Victoria told the mayor she was delighted at the warmth of her welcome. But the Brummies felt cheated. 'Why had there been so few carriages?' Joseph Chamberlain, the Birmingham City boss, asked after dinner at Windsor a few days later. 'Where was the Household Cavalry?' The courtiers explained that Victoria preferred simplicity. 'Simplicity', replied Chamberlain, 'was suit-able to a Republic. But a Sovereign should make such visits with all possible state.' There would be no 'republican simplicity' in the new reign.

Three years after her triumphant Diamond Jubilee, Victoria, now aged eighty-one, died. Her last word was 'Bertie'.

Twenty-four hours later, Albert-Edward was making his accession speech at St James's Palace, London. And it contained a bombshell. He would reign, he announced, as King Edward VII, not Albert I, as his mother had wished. For 'I desire', the new king declared, 'that Albert's name should stand alone.' The Albertine monarchy, and its long Victorian aftermath, was over.

And this was only the start. Edward got rid of Osborne, which he detested, by giving it to the nation as a monument to his parents. He purged Windsor and Buckingham Palace, those 'Scottish funeral parlours', as he called them, of sixty years' accumulation of clutter and mementos. He redecorated Buckingham Palace in the smart new white, gold and crimson style of the grand hotels and theatres where he had spent so much of his time as prince. Even the national memorial to Victoria was used to redesign the Mall and Buckingham Palace as the setting for the grand state ceremonies that Victoria, alive, had so much disliked. Edward's sisters, devoted to Victoria's memory, were horrified; everyone else rather approved.

Edward was in his sixtieth year. Browbeaten by his father and side-lined by his mother, he had gone his own way. He shot, he sailed, and he was by far the most successful royal breeder of racehorses ever. He loved the theatre, opera and bridge. He ate enormously and smoked heroically. And he remained an inveterate, if reasonably discreet, adulterer. In short, like George IV, that earlier prince of Wales who had had to wait too long for the throne, Edward had made pleasure a profession.

But whereas George's dissipation had cost him his youthful good looks, Edward, unimpressive as a young man with bulbous eyes and a weak mouth and chin, gained girth and gravitas with age. He now looked every inch a king; he even looked a bit like Henry VIII. Above all, like both Henry VIII and George IV, he loved the pomp and circumstance of being king. Out went Victoria's republican simplicity; in came stately sovereign splendour.

Edward decided to revive the state opening of Parliament, which Victoria had first truncated and then abandoned, in its full, colourful ritual. So, on 14 February, only three weeks after Victoria's death, he processed to the gilded House of Lords. In place of his mother's widow's weeds, he wore the scarlet tunic of a field marshal under his crimson, gold and ermine robes; he read the speech himself; he even proposed changes to its contents until he was slapped down by the prime minister.

Not that Edward was hidebound by tradition, being, for instance, a pioneer motor-car enthusiast. Given his first spin by Lord Montagu at Beaulieu, Edward soon acquired a fleet of cars of his own, with their characteristic claret-painted bodywork; he converted part of the royal stables into garages; he added 'Royal' to the title of the Automobile Club and, looking every inch a Toad of Toad Hall in his loudly checked tweeds, he adored being driven at sixty miles an hour (three times the legal speed limit) on the straight stretches of the London–Brighton road. He even considered introducing a motor coach into the coronation procession.

Indeed, Edward's first thought had been that he would have a thoroughly modern coronation, magnificent of course, but free from all old-fashioned 'tomfoolery'. His advisers, too, split into traditionalists and modernizers. Eventually, the traditionalists won.

It was even decided to reuse St Edward's Crown as the actual coronation crown. Made for the Restoration of 1660 in imitation of the Tudor Imperial Crown, which the Puritans had smashed, it had last been used for the coronation of William and Mary in 1689. Now, lightened a little by paring away 12 of its 83 ounces of solid gold and restored to its original bulbous shape, it was refurbished to symbolize the historical continuity of the six other Edwards who had ruled before the king.

But, as once before in Edward's life, his state of health intervened to dramatic effect. The coronation was due to take place on 26 June 1902. But, three days previously, the rehearsal at the Abbey was interrupted to announce that the coronation had been postponed indefinitely because of the king's illness. He underwent an emergency operation the following day for a burst appendix. His recovery was rapid and the ceremony took place on 9 August. It was impressive enough but it was a shadow of what had been planned. Edward was not strong enough to wear the St Edward's Crown; the service was curtailed and he had to rest for half an hour before emerging from the Abbey.

But at least, on Saturday, 21 June 1902, Dame Clara Butt had premiered a new work by Edward Elgar at the Royal Albert Hall:

> Land of Hope and Glory, Mother of the Free,
> How shall we extol thee, who are born of thee?
> Wider still and wider shall thy bounds be set;
> God who made thee mighty, make thee mightier yet.

Make thee mightier yet! 'Land of Hope and Glory' caught the mood not only of celebration at the coronation but also of relief at the Treaty of Vereeniging, signed in May 1902, by which the Boer War was brought to a triumphant conclusion with the incorporation of the rebellious Afrikaner provinces into the self-governing Dominion of South Africa.

A year or two later, the huge Cullinan Diamond was found and the South African government decided to make a peace offering of it to Edward. The cheese-paring British government was reluctant to accept it because of its concerns about the cost of cutting and setting the stone. But Edward, with his characteristic love of splendour, insisted and the diamond, cut into two major stones, has become the brightest ornament of both the sceptre and the Imperial Crown. Edward, however, never used them.

But the war, with the near-universal sympathy for the Afrikaners in other countries, had also highlighted Britain's isolation – now perceived to be dangerous rather than glorious – in Europe. It also gave Edward his opportunity in foreign policy. Edward, with visits as prince of Wales to India, Canada and the Middle East, had been the first monarch to know the empire at first hand. But, unlike his mother, his real interest lay in Europe. He had been brought up to speak French and German as fluently as English, and he spent two months of each year on an early summer holiday in France, followed by a month in autumn taking the waters at a German spa.

Now he capitalized on his familiarity with France to undertake, on his own initiative, a state visit to Paris in May 1903. At first, with widespread pro-Boer sentiment, his reception was cool, even hostile. But during the interval at the Théâtre Français he gallantly saluted – in French – a French actress he'd known in London as representing 'all the grace and all the spirit of France'.

The remark spread like wildfire and the visit turned into a triumph. The following year, the French president paid a return visit to London and the *Entente Cordiale* was signed. For better or for worse, Britain was involved in the alliances of Continental Europe once more.

On 6 May 1910, Edward's bull-like constitution finally broke. After smoking his last cigar and taking a light luncheon, he collapsed and was helped to a chair. At five o'clock, he was told that his horse had won at

Kempton Park. 'I am very glad,' he replied. They were his last coherent words and he died at about quarter to midnight.

Edward's last words were characteristic, for he had enjoyed being king. He and his advisers understood, of course, that royal ceremony had needed to be polished and made more appealing to the men (though not yet the women) who formed the new, mass electorate and increasingly wielded political power. But Edward preened and paraded because he wanted to and not just to make the monarchy more 'democratic'. Historians who present his reign as a turning point in the history of the monarchy also forget that he reigned scarcely nine years and left most of his projects unfinished.

If he had been succeeded by his eldest son, the doe-eyed but dim, unstable and apparently perverted Eddie, it is more than likely that the usual Hanoverian pattern would have reasserted itself. The son would have rejected his father's legacy and Edward's ceremonious revolution would have died with him. But his eldest son had predeceased him in 1892 and he was succeeded instead by his second son, George.

Soon after his father's death, the new king, George V, wrote in his diary: 'I have lost my best friend and the best of fathers. I never had a word with him in his life. I am heartbroken and overwhelmed with grief.' For the first time in the two centuries of the House of Hanover a father had been succeeded by a son who loved and respected him.

But, despite his fondness for his father, George, who had spent his early career as a well-regarded naval officer, was his opposite in almost everything. He was slim, abstemious and rather shy. He wore the same elegant clothes to the same events and detested changes of fashion. He mistrusted the telephone, except for family gossip; was never driven at more than thirty miles an hour and loathed aeroplanes, submarines and all modern weaponry. He was a crack shot and a notable stamp collector. He was devoted to his wife, his weather gauge and the unchanging daily routines of his life as a country gentleman. Above all, he was driven by a strong sense of duty. The result was that, though George set himself to preserve and complete his father's programme, he also took it in a very different direction.

His first steps were devoted to his parents. His widowed mother, the beautiful, deaf and rather daffy Queen Alexandra, he decided, was to be known by a new title: 'queen mother', rather than the traditional, coldly formal 'queen dowager'.

Back in 1898, the great Victorian prime minister William Ewart Gladstone had lain in state in Westminster Hall. Now George, who had acted as one of Gladstone's pall-bearers, decided that his father should follow in the steps of the Great Commoner and lie in Westminster Hall before his burial in the royal vault at Windsor. The result was the grandest and most moving ceremony of a ceremonious reign, in which half a million people filed past Edward's coffin in what the *Illustrated London News* called 'The People's Lying-in-State'.

George, however, who had nothing of the celebrity in his temperament and loathed the very concept, was far less relaxed about the ceremonies in which, of necessity, he was the star. And, since he had never acquired his father's ease at public speaking, he was particularly anxious if they involved a talking role. 'The most terrible ordeal I have ever gone through,' George confided to his diary of his first state opening of Parliament. But his sense of duty meant that he persevered nonetheless. It even made him go beyond his father, with his natural appetite for ceremony. Edward, because of his illness, had not been crowned with the massive St Edward's Crown; his son was. Edward had no separate inauguration as emperor of India; George travelled to the subcontinent in 1911 to wear yet another specially made crown and receive the homage of his Indian subjects in the huge, spectacular Delhi Durbar. Finally, Edward had worn only a field marshal's cocked hat at the annual state opening of Parliament. But, from 1913, George decided that 'people wanted him' to wear the Imperial State Crown, now augmented with the massive South African Cullinan II diamond.

The crown, as the jewellers' labels inside it show, was subject to repeated alterations. But it was never successfully fitted to George's narrow skull, and, as he got older, it gave him dreadful headaches. All the same, he continued with his self-imposed burden of wearing it at the annual state opening.

This is the measure of the difference between George V and Edward VII. Edward revived ceremonies because he enjoyed pomp and circumstance and was a natural at it. His son kept them going and even augmented them, not because he liked them, but because he thought it was the right thing to do. This is ceremony as a monarch's hair-shirt,

undertaken, not through inclination, but as a solemn duty. It is this devotion to duty which would transform the monarchy once again as it faced
the challenge of ever more rapid and more radical social change.

III

George V had come to the throne in the midst of the worst political crisis
in generations. In 1906 the Liberals won a crushing general election
victory on a platform of social reform and state welfare benefits. The
proposals and the consequent need for heavy taxation were more bitterly
divisive than anything since the First Reform Act of 1832, and, like the
Reform Act, they pitted the Liberal House of Commons against the Tory
House of Lords. Also, as in 1832, the monarchy risked finding itself
pig-in-the-middle.

The death of the old king and the inauguration of the new reign had
imposed a truce on political strife. But not for long. In November 1910
the Liberal government decided to go to the country on a proposal known
as the Parliament Act to curb permanently the power of the Lords. But
first, they would get George's prior agreement to a mass creation of peers
if the Lords continued to resist.

The confrontation took place at Buckingham Palace. The Liberal
prime minister, Herbert Asquith, browbeat the inexperienced king mercilessly. He was also double-crossed by his private secretary, who concealed
from him the Tories' willingness to form an alternative government.
George never forgave those who'd taken advantage of him. But, probably,
it was for the best. The powers of the Lords were indefensible; the important thing from the king's point of view was to stop the monarchy going
down with the peerage.

Six weeks after the coronation, the Parliament Act passed the Lords
by a whisker, because the bishops decided to vote with the government
to save the monarchy from embarrassment and the Lords from
themselves.

Soon the crown confronted a far more dangerous threat, when the
system of Continental alliances, which Britain had rejoined under Edward
VII, sucked Britain and the empire into the slaughter of the First World
War. The royal family did its bit. The king visited the troops in the field;
Queen Mary cheered up the wounded in hospital and the prince of Wales

joined up though fear of his capture meant that, to his intense frustration, he was never allowed near the front.

But, by 1917, the strain was beginning to tell. Abroad, the February Revolution overthrew the Russian autocracy and Tsar Nicholas II, George's first cousin and spitting image. At home, there were strikes, mutinies and political radicalization. Confronting this double threat, George and his advisers embarked on a series of bold measures to shed old baggage and make new friends.

Most dramatically, he dumped centuries of German dynastic history, culture and family connection by renaming the royal family the 'House of Windsor'. His German relatives were stripped of their British honours and titles. And those who remained in Britain were given new, British-sounding names as well, so that, for instance, the Battenbergs became the Mountbattens.

Here the very deficiencies of George's education helped. Speaking only English (probably the first king to do so since before the Conquest), he identified himself solely with England and the empire. In other circumstances, his insularity and Little Englandism would have been a disadvantage; now they became an asset. The novelist and radical H. G. Wells might denounce 'an alien and uninspiring court'; George was able to reply, truthfully, 'I may be uninspiring but I'll be damned if I'm an alien!' Neither his polyglot father and grandmother, both of whom spoke English with a slight though unmistakable German accent, could have got away with that.

Next George used a wholesale remodelling of the honours system to accommodate the renewed Windsor monarchy to the new social forces that had emerged in the war years and just before, such as women, socialism and the vast growth of both the civil and the armed services. The key step was the establishment of the Order of the British Empire. The ancient orders of chivalry, such as the Garter and the Thistle, were deliberately exclusive, in both size and rank. And they were wholly male. The Order of the British Empire, on the other hand, was designed to be as large and inclusive as possible and to honour women as well as men.

The first investiture was equally revolutionary. It took place not in the plush and gilt interiors of Buckingham Palace, but in the open air, at Glasgow Rangers' football stadium at Ibrox Park in September 1917.

Here the star of the show was Miss Lizzie Robertson, who wowed the 70,000-strong crowd by turning up in her natty khaki overalls to receive the Medal of the British Empire, 'For devotion to duty in a national projectile factory'.

The original insignia of the order featured a figure of Britannia in the centre. But, after their deaths, it was replaced by the twin profiles of the founders of the order, King George V and Queen Mary. It would be hard to think of a more fitting memorial to the 'People's King', as contemporaries already called him.

Also founded at the same time was another consciously 'democratic' order, the Companions of Honour. This conferred no title of rank or special precedence and was aimed at those new powers in the land such as the trade union bosses and Labour mayors who professed a wholesome socialist contempt for such outmoded trappings of class and wealth. Prominent among the original seventeen Companions were the leaders of the Metal Workers, the Railwaymen and the Transport Unions.

But it soon became clear that the Palace had been wrong to take the socialists' levelling pretensions seriously. For it turned out that the new aristocracy of labour was every bit as keen on badges and baubles, knighthoods and peerages, as the old aristocracy of birth and wealth. The result was a remarkable trade-off. 'We are all socialists now,' declared the *Darlington Northern Star* after the sweeping changes of 1917. But it should also have added: 'We are all royalists now' – even trade unionists, socialists and suffragettes.

Most 'socialist' of all, perhaps, was George's treatment of his Russian cousin, the dethroned Nicholas II. The Russians had been Britain's allies against Germany. Nevertheless, tsarism was profoundly unpopular with Liberal and Labour politicians, who rejoiced at its fall. And George let this fact, rather than family ties or sentiment, govern his behaviour. He vetoed any offer of refuge to the imperial family, leaving them instead to their grisly fate at the hands of the Bolsheviks, after they seized power in the second, more extreme revolution of October 1917. Subsequently the king wept crocodile tears. Or perhaps he had simply suffered a convenient amnesia.

But there was more to the reinvention of the British monarchy in 1917 than a remarkable, and remarkably successful, heading off of the threat of Red Revolution. The monarchy had long been a welfare monarchy, honouring, and thereby encouraging, the charitable donations which in the days before the welfare state had financed healthcare, education and poor relief. Now, as the state, under the impulse of socialism, was starting to take over these areas, it shifted to become a service monarchy, rewarding those who did that bit more in their jobs and communities. It was committed to the ethos of public service, of which it saw itself as the apex and exemplar. It was not socialist, far from it. But it did believe that 'there was such a thing as society'. Which is why, from that day to this, it has tended to be more comfortable with Labour and wet Tory governments, rather than high and dry Thatcherite ones.

The monarchy had become a moral one. And it was morality, in its vulgar sense of sexual behaviour, which was to carry it both to its peak and its depths.

IV

The 'family monarchy' was also a product of the year of transformation of 1917. For the last 200 years the Hanoverians had continued the German practice of marrying only into fellow-German princely families. Now George altered the rules to decree that his children could marry Englishmen and women. 'This was an historic day,' he wrote in his diary. It was. A German dynasty had become an English family – even, perhaps, the representative Great British Family.

Here again George's deeply conventional character meant that the role fitted like a glove – and much more comfortably than his crown. At his father's coronation, Edward's collection of mistresses, past and present, had been given special accommodation, known irreverently as the 'Loose Box'. George, in contrast, had the most blameless personal life of any king since George III in the eighteenth century.

But for the family monarchy to establish itself also depended on the next generation. Here the prospects were mixed. George V had two older sons: David Edward, prince of Wales, born in 1894, and Albert George, duke of York, who followed a year later. Despite the closeness of their ages, they turned out to be very different in character.

David Edward took after his grandparents: he inherited Queen Alexandra's blond-haired and blue-eyed good looks and King Edward's temperament. He was intelligent, curious, a good linguist and a natural charmer. But he was also contrary, found it difficult to concentrate and reverted to the Hanoverian norm by getting on badly with his father.

Albert George, on the other hand, was a slower, dimmer version of his father. He passed sixty-eighth out of sixty-nine in his final school exams, was knock-kneed and cursed with a dreadful stammer. But he had application, stamina and at the age of seventeen became a convinced Christian. The two brothers, in short, were the hare and the tortoise.

Especially with women. David Edward acquired a *maîtresse en titre* even before the end of the First World War. But there was no sign of a wife. Two years later, in 1920, Albert George encountered Lady Elizabeth Bowes-Lyon. But Elizabeth was in no hurry and Albert George, inexperienced and justifiably afraid of rejection, hesitated. Not till 1922 and at what was rumoured to be the third attempt was his proposal accepted.

Elizabeth, daughter of an earl and cousin of a duke, was exactly the kind of spouse that George had envisaged for his children when he changed the royal marriage rules in 1917. The king was delighted, and his letter of congratulation to his son ended: 'I feel that we have always got on very well together (very different to dear David)'. The marriage thus neatly squared the circle. It was socially acceptable, as the king required; it was also rooted in romantic love, as the post-war popular mood demanded.

The popular mood also demanded that the wedding be turned into a public spectacle. It took place at Westminster Abbey on 26 April 1923, the first of a royal prince to be held there since the Middle Ages, and the sermon was preached by Cosmo Gordon Lang, archbishop of York. The great Victorian archbishops had been outstanding intellectuals. Lang instead was a courtier and committee man, with a view of Christianity in which the monarchy, rather than the cross, stood centre-stage as the symbol of the nation's faith.

George had already turned the monarchy into a monarchy of duty. Now Lang and his ilk added a new responsibility to the already overburdened royal shoulders: to have, or at least to appear to have, a perfect marriage: 'You cannot resolve that [your marriage] shall be happy,' his sermon warned the couple in a solemn admonition, 'you can and will resolve that it shall be noble.' Or, in less elevated language: you will stick together come what may and never, ever divorce.

Pressure had been mounting since the turn of the nineteenth century to liberalize England's highly restrictive divorce laws. But the opposition to reform was also strong. It had been led by Lang despite his own (probably non-practising) homosexuality in the name of the defence of Christian marriage; now, with his marriage sermon, he enlisted the family monarchy as a powerful ally in his campaign.

As it happened, the Yorks were happy. At least, George was: his marriage 'transformed him, and was the turning point of his life'. A daughter, Elizabeth, was born in 1926, and another, Margaret Rose, four years later. The result was an idyllic family life which, despite the trappings of wealth and royalty, the press contrived to present as 'normal'.

But Albert George was the second son. Meanwhile, the elder, David Edward, carried out a series of spectacularly successful tours of the empire – Canada, Australia and India – and the United States. He glad-handed, defied protocol and flaunted his sex appeal. The crowds went wild and he became the first royal star of the new mass media of the cinema, radio and the illustrated press. He was a celebrity and a royal rebel. But did he have a cause? Or was it mere self-indulgence?

In 1935 George V celebrated his Silver Jubilee. The king-emperor, now almost seventy, was worried about the effort and expense. But the coalition national government, formed to cope with the depression, was keen for a demonstration of national unity in the face of threats at home and especially abroad from the rising dictatorships of Germany and Italy.

On 6 May the king, queen and their children processed to St Paul's for a service of thanksgiving. The painting of the event shows a scene of almost Byzantine rigidity. Only two figures break rank: David Edward, who transfixes the spectator with an imperious stare, and Elizabeth, duchess of York, who simpers, Madonna-like, over her two little daughters. 'We all went away', the British prime minister remembered, 'feeling that we had taken part in something very much like a Holy Communion.'

Monarchy was no longer simply in alliance with religion; it had become a religion. It had also become a substitute at once calmer, saner and more decent for the virulent nationalisms of Continental Europe.

But on 20 January 1936, only six months after his jubilee, George V died at Sandringham. Once heralds had proclaimed the death of kings. Now it was the BBC.

The British Broadcasting Corporation was less than ten years old. It had been established by royal charter in 1927 and given a monopoly of the new medium of radio. Its first director general was John Reith. Like his friend Lang, Reith was an ambitious, driven, sexually ambiguous Scot who was determined to use the BBC to inculcate a morally cohesive society. Also like Lang, Reith saw the monarchy as central to his campaign. The result was an alliance between the monarchy and the corporation almost as close and important as that between the crown and the Church of England.

George made the first Christmas broadcast from Sandringham on 25 December 1932; he broadcast again for the jubilee three years later – 'I am speaking to the children above all. Remember, children, the king is speaking to you.' Now radio would announce his death to Britain and the empire. At just gone midnight on the 20th, Reith himself read the final bulletin: 'Death came peacefully to the king at 11.55 p.m.' The next day Reith altered the text of Prime Minister Stanley Baldwin's broadcast to the nation, 'bringing in the moral authority, honour and dignity of the throne'.

But as one tradition was invented, another was undone. At midnight on the 20th also, King Edward VIII, as he now was, ordered the clocks at Sandringham, kept half an hour fast since Edward VII's time, to be put back to the right time. Lang, who by this time had succeeded as archbishop of Canterbury, reacted as though the new king had committed sacrilege. 'I wonder what other customs will be put back also?' he demanded.

The answer was legion, for Edward delighted in treading on establishment toes and ruffling retainers' feathers. He wanted substantial cuts in the coronation service; he was most reluctant to move into Buckingham Palace; he made slashing reductions in the staff and running costs at Sandringham and Balmoral; he walked in the street; broke convention by insisting that his left profile appear on postage stamps; and said 'something must be done' about the unemployed. But all this was more an attitude than a serious programme of modernization.

Edward was serious about one thing, however: Wallis Simpson.

V

Wallis Simpson, born in 1896, and the impoverished descendant of two distinguished Southern families, was a classic woman on the make: hard-edged, firm-jawed, acquisitive and with a certain brittle style. 'You can never be too rich or too thin,' she is supposed to have said. She was also the most disruptive force in the twentieth-century British monarchy before the advent of Princess Diana.

David Edward had first met Wallis in 1931 and had quickly decided that, since 'to him she was the perfect woman', she was his natural sexual and intellectual partner in life. But there were obstacles. She was American, divorced and presently remarried to an American businessman resident in London. It would have been difficult to think of anyone further from his family's or the establishment's idea of a queen.

Edward was used to getting his own way. But, as prince of Wales, he had done so by breaking the rules. Now, as king, he would have to change them. This would have been difficult, though perhaps not impossible. He was popular and there was an embryonic 'King's Party' with Winston Churchill himself as its leader. But, instead of exploiting these advantages, Edward, Micawber-like, merely waited for something to turn up. And, whether out of embarrassment or calculation, the establishment, led by the prime minister, Stanley Baldwin, played a similar waiting game. As did the British press, which threw a veil of silence over the affair.

All this was brought to an end by the hostile reaction to the Simpsons' collusive divorce on the flagrantly absurd grounds of his adultery. On 16 November, Edward saw Prime Minister Baldwin and the royal family and told them of his determination to marry Wallis and, if need be, to abdicate in order to do so. Then there was a diversion while the idea of a morganatic marriage was floated in which Wallis would become Edward's wife but not his queen. This was submitted to and rejected by the cabinet, the opposition and the dominion governments. Edward made a final plea to be allowed to put his case directly to the people in a broadcast. This too was rejected and, cornered, on 11 December he signed the Act of Abdication. Only then, and with some trepidation, was Edward allowed to broadcast to the nation: 'You must believe me', he said, 'when I tell you that I have found it impossible to carry the heavy burden of responsibility and to discharge my duties as king as I would wish to without the help and support of the woman I love.'

The broadcast – improved if not substantially written by Churchill – showed Edward at his brilliant, media-savvy best, with all the qualities that, in different circumstances, might have made him the perfect modernizing king. But, by then, it was too late: the tortoise had beaten the hare; the conscientious, second-rate Albert George was king and the clocks, put forward at the beginning of Edward VIII's brief reign, were turned back with a vengeance.

Albert George chose the same royal name as his father and his signature was practically indistinguishable from his; he reverted to the same old-fashioned circle of friends and courtiers, such as Archbishop Lang, and he shared the same obsession with uniforms, with his only recorded innovation being the invention of pinched-in dress trousers to allow for the wearing of the Garter. They did not catch on. Above all, George VI, with his close-knit family whom he called 'Us Four', exemplified the family values that Edward VIII had so flagrantly defied.

In one area, however, there was less break with the immediate past. George VI was not as ostentatiously pro-German as Edward VIII had been. But he was a passionate supporter of appeasement, and when Neville Chamberlain returned from Munich with 'Peace in Our Time', he was paraded with the king and queen on the balcony of Buckingham Palace in front of huge cheering crowds. It was an act of gross political partisanship worthy of Victoria at her most unconstrained.

War came anyway, and Chamberlain was replaced by Winston Churchill as prime minister. As Churchill had also been Edward VIII's leading supporter, early relations with the king and queen were strained. But they soon developed an effective division of labour.

The royal family represented the sufferings of the British family on the home front. They remained in London, though spending most nights in the comparative safety of Windsor. Their food and clothes were rationed and George, who was frugal at the best of times, personally marked the five-inch maximum line on the baths in Buckingham Palace. And they took a direct hit when a daring daytime raid dropped a cluster of bombs on the palace, narrowly missing the king. 'Now we can look the East End in the face,' said Queen Elizabeth, who had been indefatigable in visiting bomb sites and comforting the survivors.

But the role of war leader, symbolic as well as real, fell on Churchill. George was temperamentally unsuited to the task. But, understandably, he came to view Churchill's prominence as a national icon with something like jealousy. Things came to a head when Churchill, with characteristic bravado, announced his determination to go in after the first wave of troops in the D-Day landings. Determined not to be outdone, the king scotched the scheme by threatening to accompany him! In the event, once secure beachheads had been established, they visited Normandy – but separately. All was forgiven, however, in victory, and on VE Day, 8 May 1945, Churchill joined the king on the balcony of Buckingham Palace to celebrate the end of the war in Europe.

Two months later, Churchill was crushingly defeated in a general election and a Labour government came to power committed to a full-blooded socialist programme of nationalization, redistributive taxation and welfare reform and with the huge majority needed to drive it through.

The king also had to deal with a very different prime minister, Clement Attlee. Described by Churchill as 'a modest man with plenty to be modest about', Attlee's trademark lengthy silences at first defeated the king, who had little small talk himself. In fact, they turned out to have much in common. Both were unassuming, hard working, ascetic and wedded to an unbending view of duty and public service which George had inherited from his family tradition and Attlee had imbibed in his public school days at Haileybury. United by this shared ethic of public service, socialism and the House of Windsor turned out, once again, not to be such uneasy bedfellows after all.

The result was that when George, having outlived Attlee's government by only a few months, died prematurely at the age of fifty-seven, he left an inheritance that was surprisingly unscathed. He also left it to a daughter who was determined to keep it that way.

25

NEW KINGDOM

Elizabeth II

'MY HEART IS TOO FULL', Queen Elizabeth II told her Accession Council in February 1952, 'for me to say more to you today than that I shall always work as my father did.' Ten months later, her grandfather, George V, had joined her father, George VI, as a model. 'My father, and my grandfather before him,' she said, in her first Christmas broadcast to Britain and the Commonwealth, 'worked all their lives to unite our peoples ever more closely ... I shall strive to carry on their work.' For all the brave talk of a 'New Elizabethan Age', this was to be a monarchy that looked firmly back to the past – but not perhaps all that far.

I

Elizabeth had always been a character: self-possessed, authoritative and aware of her position from an extraordinarily young age. She gave the Windsor wave in her perambulator; was curtseying to her grandparents by the age of two; and wore Norman Hartnell to her first state function at nine. In contrast, her education, at the hands of devoted governesses, was modest and undemanding. Outside experts were brought in only in history, French and, most successfully, riding, the latter of which, along with dogs, became a lifelong passion. Books, on the other hand, remained alien: reading was for state papers. Surrounded by doting parents and servants, she had a happy, secure upbringing. Indeed, for a preternaturally orderly, conformist child, it was perhaps a bit too secure.

It would be hard to think of a greater contrast with the childhood of Elizabeth's distant cousin, Prince Philip of Greece. Born on a kitchen table, exiled as a baby and homeless at nine when his parents split up, he'd lived the life of adventurer and poor relation with only his wits, his good looks and his royal connections to depend on. And it was these last which led to his meeting Elizabeth in 1939 on a royal visit to Dartmouth Naval College, where he was then a cadet. He was eighteen; she thirteen. He showed off; she fell, and remained, deeply in love. There was opposition, especially from the stuffier courtiers. But Elizabeth, as usual, got her way, and they were married in 1947. It was, and perhaps remains, a marriage of opposites.

Just over four years later, on 6 February 1952, George VI was dead and Elizabeth became queen. At the time, she was up a giant fig tree watching big game in East Africa, on the first leg of an imperial tour.

On the flight back her private secretary went over the rituals that surrounded the 'demise of the Crown'. The new queen got up once or twice to relieve her feelings in private. But there was none of her father's nervous anxiety about an unlooked-for and unwelcome burden; still less of her uncle's chippy resentment. Instead there was a calm acceptance – part religious and part robust common sense – of the job she had been born to do. She was aware of its history, though not especially curious about it. Above all, she was utterly unseduced by its romance. Others might enthuse about the New Elizabethan Age, but not the second Elizabeth herself. 'Frankly,' she said in her second Christmas broadcast, 'I do not myself feel at all like my great Tudor forebear, who was blessed with neither husband nor children, who ruled as a despot and was never able to leave her native shores.' Elizabeth II, in contrast, was wife, mother, constitutional sovereign of a democracy and head of the empire – or Commonwealth, as people were learning to call it. But she was still queen – a Windsor queen. And it was the rituals and values of the House of Windsor established by her grandfather, George V, which were unrolled once more.

Her father, George VI, lay in state in Westminster Hall, in the cere-mony invented by George V for his father, Edward VII. Her mother, Queen Elizabeth, was given the title of queen mother, first conferred by George V on his widowed mother, Queen Alexandra. Above all, and against the furious protests of her husband, she announced that the name of the royal house would remain the House of Windsor, as George V had decreed in 1917. To soothe Philip's feelings, she made him chairman of the committee to plan the coronation. He was eager for 'some features relevant to the world today [to] be introduced'. But his was a lone voice on a committee whose collective memory stretched back more than fifty years. The result was that the coronation of 1953 was a polished replay of the historicist pageantry of the earlier Windsor coronations of 1937 and 1910.

Elizabeth underwent the same earnest religious preparations at the hands of the archbishop of Canterbury as her parents in 1937. She rehearsed as meticulously as they had done, and sharply called Philip into line when he failed to take the esoteric rituals seriously. She was crowned with the massive St Edward's Crown, first used, after an interval of more than two centuries, for her grandfather in 1910. And, despite the Labour government of 1945–51 having eroded still further the political power of the Lords by the new Parliament Act of 1949, and having reduced many of them to virtual penury by its punitive taxation, the peerage continued to dominate the coronation. They also supplied its only moment of humour. This took place towards the end, when the backwoods peer Lord Mowbray, Seagrave and Stourton hurled himself down from the dais, where, as premier baron, he had performed homage on behalf of the baronage, with his robe bunched up, mothballs and bits of ermine flying, and with conspicuously filthy fingernails.

But there was one hugely important innovation nonetheless. For a new mass medium had appeared alongside radio and cinema: television. Microphones and cine-cameras had been allowed in the Abbey for the coronation of 1937; should TV be permitted to broadcast the crowning of Elizabeth II? The queen herself, with her conservative instincts, was firmly opposed. But a press campaign quickly forced a retreat. The result was that, on 2 June 1953, I, then a boy of eight in my Sunday best, gathered along with countless millions more to watch the coronation on a neighbour's television set, which had been bought specially for the occasion. It was the first time that I had seen television or a monarch. And I have never forgotten it.

Elizabeth's fear had been that television would trivialize or vulgarize the ceremony. She need not have worried. Instead, the mellifluous, silken-tongued Richard Dimbleby delivered a commentary whose stately language complemented and occasionally outdid the text of the service itself.

DIMBLEBY: Her Majesty returns the orb and the archbishop
now places on the fourth finger of her right hand the ring,
the ring whereupon is set a sapphire and on it a ruby cross.
This is often called the Ring of England.

ARCHBISHOP: Receive the ring of kingly dignity and the seal
of catholic faith and as thou art this day consecrated head
and prince so may you continue steadfastly as the defender
of Christ's religion ...

And so on, as the two voices and one language interwove like the verses
and responses in the Book of Common Prayer.

The coronation of 1953 was the apotheosis of the Windsor monarchy.
The ceremony was perfect. The empire, despite Indian independence in
1947, seemed more or less intact. The queen, with her youth and sincerity, was the most attractive embodiment yet of the Windsor values of
family, service and duty. And television, far from being a threat, had
proved itself to be the most effective means for their dissemination.
Elizabeth, it seemed, had been right to stick with the tried and tested
formula of Georges V and VI. And Philip's instinct to modernize had
been wrong. Or had it?

Philip had now been married to Elizabeth getting on for ten years. By
the same stage in his marriage, Prince Albert, Philip's predecessor as
royal consort, had established an absolute supremacy over Queen
Victoria's mind in both the public and the private spheres. This made him,
in effect, permanent prime minister and king-in-all-but-name. No one –
not the politicians, the royal household and least of all Elizabeth, who
jealously kept her red boxes to herself – was going to concede any such
position to Philip. Nor is there any sign that he wanted it, given his own
maverick tendencies. Instead, he acted as a sort of licensed dissident-cum-
court-jester, prone to break protocol, tread on toes and generally ruffle
feathers. But, for one who was so frequently rude himself, he had a singu-
larly thin skin. It was a combination that guaranteed bad relations with
the press.

More positively, Philip, like Albert before him, showed an informed
interest in industry and technology. He was passionate about sport and
worked tirelessly to ensure that the sprawling suburban housing

developments of the 1950s and 1960s had adequate recreation grounds. Above all, Elizabeth, who had created a minor sensation when she promised to 'obey' in her marriage vows, ceded him headship of their family. It was the same domestic role that Victoria had given Albert, and Philip exercised it in the same way by trying to make his sons new editions of his younger self. Albert's educational experiment with his children was intellectual; Philip's physical. But the results were just as disastrous.

Philip had completed his secondary education at Gordonstoun in Morayshire. Founded by Kurt Hahn, a refugee from Nazi Germany, the school was run on spartan principles and aimed to instil confidence and leadership through physical hardship and strenuous exercise. Philip, extrovert and naturally athletic, thrived, becoming captain of cricket and hockey and Head of School. But what suited Philip was a torment to his eldest son. Charles was shy, physically awkward and intense. His grandmother, the queen mother, fought hard for him to be sent to Eton, with its high culture, civilized tradition of individual rooms and reassuring proximity to Windsor. But Philip, humiliated over the issue of his children's surname, was in no mood to give way. So to Gordonstoun Charles went, despite his misery and his tears. As he has admitted, it scarred him for life. It also reopened the traditional Hanoverian tension, in abeyance for three generations, between father and son.

II

Meanwhile, Elizabeth – in contrast to her husband with his restless, relentless, frenetic activity – sailed serenely on. Each year was much like the last, with a round of engagements as regular as clockwork. It was more of a liturgy than a diary. Like the Church's liturgical year, which it so much resembled, the cycle of the royal year followed the changing seasons. Within it, each individual event was invested with a broader symbolic meaning; performed in a special, esoteric costume and choreographed to within an inch of its life. And it culminated in the annual secular sermon of the Christmas broadcast.

In 1996, the queen used her Christmas broadcast to list some of the highlights of the previous year and reflect on their deeper significance. In the spring, she had attended the Maundy Service at Norwich Cathedral. In the Middle Ages, the monarch, following Christ's example, had washed the feet of as many poor people as they were years old; now they were merely given specially minted coins. But the message was the same: 'The lovely service', the queen said, 'is always a reminder of Christ's words to his disciples: "Love one another; as I have loved you". It sounds so simple yet it proves so hard to obey.'

'In June', she continued, 'came the Trooping the Colour, a vivid reminder of this country's proud military tradition, and of the discipline and dedication which our servicemen and women show in their taxing tasks of peacekeeping in many distant parts of the world.'

'Then, in October,' she concluded, 'I opened Parliament. This is not just a state occasion, but also a symbol of the process of parliamentary democracy which we enjoy here in Britain, and in so many countries of the Commonwealth. It is a process which seeks to express the ideal of the equality of all citizens under the law.'

These ceremonies, as the queen again reminded us, 'have their roots in history'. True. But, in their current form, and centring on the monarch's personal participation, their roots are shallow indeed. The oldest, the Trooping the Colour and the state opening of Parliament, go back only to the reign of Edward VII, Elizabeth's great-grandfather; the Maundy was revived only in 1932 by her grandfather, George V; while the June Official Birthday, when Trooping the Colour is celebrated, is an innovation of her father, George VI's reign, which she retained out of both filial piety and convenience.

The Official Birthday is also one occasion for the publication of the twice-yearly Honours List, the other being New Year's Day. In each, the queen is pleased, in the official phrase, to confer honours on about a thousand individuals. They range from the rich, the famous and the powerful, for whom their gongs are only another glittering prize to be added to their quiverful, to ordinary people who have done extraordinary things. And it is the latter whom the queen really cares about, taking immense pains to memorize their details for the investiture ceremonies in which she personally gives them their honours. These mass investitures, for which the vast ballroom of Buckingham Palace is scarcely large enough, are the most important and characteristic ceremonies of Elizabeth's monarchy. And they are without any historical roots whatever further back than those of the Windsor monarchy.

III

On 29 July 1981 Prince Charles and Lady Diana Spencer were married at St Paul's Cathedral, almost five hundred years since a prince of Wales had been married here. Both weddings were overhyped and overblown. And both led to disaster: the former to the Reformation; the latter to the Diana affair, which shook, or seemed to shake, the House of Windsor to its foundations.

It was, said the archbishop of Canterbury in his sermon, 'a fairy-tale wedding'. Such indeed seems to have been Diana's feeling as she looked forward with adolescent glee to becoming a real-life princess. Charles's emotions were far more ambivalent and he had blown hot and cold on the engagement. Finally, Philip had put his foot down. Charles had gone too far and was honour bound to marry, he said. It was of a piece with Philip's other interventions in his son's life.

The result was that the fairy tale ended quickly and, before long, turned into a nightmare for both parties. There had been difficulties from the start, as Diana, young, highly strung and chaotically brought up, found it hard to fit into the rigid customs of the royal family. She had her suspicions, almost certainly unfounded at this stage, that Charles was continuing his affair with his old flame, Camilla Parker Bowles. And her eating disorders became worse and their symptoms more extravagant and embarrassing. The result was rapid estrangement. There were hopes that the births of two boys, Princes William, born in 1982, and Harry, who appeared two years later, would bring the couple together. Instead, their dynastic duty done, their estrangement became complete and, from about 1987, they led separate lives. Charles returned to Camilla in good and earnest; while Diana began a serious of short, tempestuous affairs with all and sundry.

All this was common knowledge in select circles in London. But the press – still besotted, like much of the public, with the fairy tale of Cinderella who'd found her Prince and Lived Happily Ever After – showed no inclination to probe. Instead, it was the couple themselves who went public with their rival versions of the failure of the marriage. Diana struck first with Andrew Morton's *Diana: Her True Story*, which she had effectively ghosted; Charles riposted with Jonathan Dimbleby's authorized biography. The latter was accompanied by a television interview in which Charles memorably confessed to adultery. Diana then had her 'revenge' (in her own words) with her television interview with Martin Bashir, in which she too admitted to being unfaithful but in the much more artfully crafted language of romance.

Indeed, throughout the War of the Waleses, as this game of tit-for-tat became known, Diana proved much the more adept media performer. She had the advantage of being a pretty woman and a fine ham actress; she also benefited from the fact that public opinion normally sides with the 'wronged' woman. As it did with her in spades. She was also imaginative, reckless of the consequences and developed posing for a photograph that would get the right headline in the *Sun* into a fine art.

Appalled at the damage the affair was doing, not only to the couple but to the monarchy itself, the queen, in one of her rare interventions in family affairs, effectively required them to divorce. But by then it was too late. Not only was the Waleses' marriage dead, so too was the family monarchy.

The Diana story – which reached its climax, at once tragic and tawdry, with her death in a car crashed by a drunken driver in 1997 – is also a testament to the revolution in British values that had taken place during the Windsor years. In 1936, Edward VIII had been widely reviled, not least by Archbishop Lang, for putting personal happiness above royal duty. In the 1990s, however, Diana – who, like Edward, was photogenic, a celebrity, a clothes-horse and profoundly self-indulgent – was praised to the skies for doing just that. Duty was fuddy-duddy; happiness a right whatever the cost.

In the face of this tide of sentiment, Elizabeth, with her determination to stick to the monarchy of her father and grandfather, with its values of duty and service, looked more and more out of touch.

IV

The year 2002 was the turning point of Elizabeth's reign. In February, her wayward but deeply loved sister, Margaret Rose, died, followed only six weeks later by Queen Elizabeth the Queen Mother. The queen was now the undisputed matriarch of her clan. In the summer, she celebrated her seventy-sixth birthday and the fiftieth anniversary of her accession.

But the Golden Jubilee also marked a turning away, towards the future and Prince Charles.

The first clear signal that something new was afoot came three years later, on 9 April 2005, with Charles's marriage to his long-term mistress and the real love of his life, Camilla Parker Bowles. The queen was detached, if not actually disapproving. For the marriage broke every rule in the Windsor book. In 1936, the taint of the divorces of his wife-to-be had forced the abdication of a king-emperor; in 2005, both parties were divorced and both had been openly adulterous. But they got away with it. Was it a betrayal of the fundamental principles of the family monarchy? Or a long-overdue recognition of changing times and values?

The ceremony, at Windsor rather than Westminster Abbey or St Paul's, also marked a return to the semi-private nuptials of the pre-family monarchy and even perhaps to something of their typical chaos. For, again depending on your point of view, the arrangements were a shaming muddle or a splendid piece of improvised, make-do-and-mend ceremonial.

The problem was that, if the monarchy – or at least the prince – had changed its spots on the remarriage of divorcées, the Church of England hadn't. This meant that the wedding had to be a civil ceremony before a registrar. Whether the legislation setting up such ceremonies was properly available to members of the royal family is a not-entirely-answered question. Moreover, it had been overlooked that the venue for civil ceremonies had to be licensed. And if it is licensed for one couple it is licensed for all. The thought of turning the state apartments of Windsor Castle into a public wedding parlour led to a hasty relocation of the ceremony to Windsor Guildhall – the humblest location for a royal wedding since the clandestine marriage of Edward IV and Elizabeth Woodville in 1464, which led to the fall of the House of York.

Ducks-and-drakes was also played with tradition in the matter of Camilla's titles. In an obvious attempt to appease Diana's diehard supporters, it was announced that she would be known, not as princess of Wales, but as HRH The Duchess of Cornwall. Nor, official spokesmen claimed (with an eye on the same constituency), would she be styled queen when Charles became king; instead she would be known as HRH The Princess Consort.

All this is legal and historical nonsense. If the wife of a king does not automatically, both by law and immemorial custom, become queen, then why did George IV have to try to divorce Caroline to deprive her of her title of queen? Or why did Edward VIII have to abdicate to marry Mrs Simpson? But, nonsense though it might be, this bold, unilateral innovation is characteristic of a royal house that had thrown over its name, its nationality and its closest relations in 1917 – all in the name of survival.

Prince Charles has given clear indications that his coronation will be very different too. He wishes, he says, to be known, not as Defender of the Faith, as every monarch has been since 1521, but as Defender of Faith. This is to challenge, head-on, the unique and exclusive alliance between the sovereign and the Church of England which has existed since the Reformation and has been a key to the survival of both. Is James I's famous dictum, 'No bishop, no king', really played out? And can Church and crown successfully go their separate ways?

The prince, I suppose, would point out that the Church's hostility to his remarriage had already broken their side of the bargain. It is not even clear, in view of his marital status, whether a future archbishop of Canterbury would be prepared to crown and consecrate him, much less Camilla. More positively, the prince's position also represents his well-known engagement with other faiths, in particular with Islam. As it happens, the first proposal for a multi-faith coronation came from that other would-be princely innovator, Edward VIII, who had his own quarrel with the Church of England. But Edward also pointed out, quite reasonably, that as emperor of India he was sovereign of subjects of a multitude of faiths, among whom Anglicans were a small minority. In 1953, there was even a small nod in the direction of Christian ecumenism when the moderator of the Church of Scotland was given the task of presenting the Bible to the queen. But a genuinely multi-faith service would involve a much more radical rewriting and rethinking of the ancient ritual.

And what of the peers? In 1953, as at every coronation since the High Middle Ages, the peers in their crimson robes and the peeresses in their white provided both chorus and backdrop to the ceremony. But in 1999 all but a rump of the hereditary peers were removed from the House of Lords, and the remainder are certain to go soon. This is the logical outcome of the progressive curtailment of the Lords' powers over a century or more, from the Reform Act of 1832 to the Parliament Acts of

1911 and 1949. But if the peers no longer sit in the Lords, why should they dominate the coronation? And who will replace them?

Indeed, with Church and peerage both in eclipse, will it be possible for Charles to have a coronation at all? Is it even desirable? Might it not be better instead to have a civil inauguration? Westminster Hall, the Coronation Chair and the regalia of crown, orb and sceptre could be used to provide historical continuity. But a new cast of characters and a different form of words would take account of the tumultuous social, political and religious changes of the several decades that will have elapsed since the last coronation.

And there is a precedent, too, with the inauguration in Westminster Hall of Oliver Cromwell as Lord Protector in 1657. That was the homage of the Republic to the monarchy it had abolished but could not replace. Charles's civil inauguration, on the other hand, would be a recognition that the United Kingdom has become – as it has indeed – the Royal Republic of Britain. The ceremony would thus represent a new and welcome accommodation between the two great strands in British political life: the royal and the republican. It could also redefine the royal role itself.

The last time the royal role was formally redefined was in the even greater upheaval of 1917. Then the crown, finally shorn of executive power, was left with two strings to its bow: as the family monarchy, it was 'the Head of Our Morality', the focus of national sentiment and the guardian of the British way of life; as the fount of the modernized honours system, it was the patron and prime mover of public service and the voluntary sector. The former was dominant for most of the twentieth century; the latter, I am sure, will come into its own in the twenty-first. The time is ripe; and it is also this which Charles with triumphant success has made his own.

And here too he is building on precedent rather than rejecting it. It was his great-great-grandfather, Edward VII, during his fifty-year stint as prince of Wales, who began to change the traditional royal role of patron of good causes. He and his wife Alexandra were assiduous in travelling the length and breadth of the country to open People's Parks and People's Palaces. But these were the fruit of local self-help and municipal enterprise. In medical charities, however, Edward was proactive, using his friends among the new plutocracy of the City to endow a fund later known as the King's Fund, which was central to the financing of the London Hospital in the half-century before the establishment of the National Health Service.

Beatrice Webb, the Fabian socialist and co-founder of the London School of Economics, was scathing about the King's Fund, which she saw (eccentrically) as unworthy and something that might have been dreamt up by a 'committee of village grocers'. Instead she had a vision of what 'a sovereign of real distinction' would do. He would, she confided to her diary, 'take over as his peculiar province the direction of the voluntary side of social life [and] cultivate in a rich and leisured society a desire to increase the sum of real intellectual effort and eminence'. 'What might he not do', she concluded, 'to further our civilization by creating a real aristocracy of character and intellect?'

None of Edward's successors had the character or the ambition to undertake such a programme. Nor were the times right, since they found 'the voluntary side of social life', as Webb put it, marginalized by the burgeoning welfare state. This was funded out of compulsory taxation rather than voluntary contributions, and, at its apogee in the 1940s and 1950s, aspired to replace voluntary effort more or less completely.

Typical was the experience of Victoria's granddaughter, Princess Marie Louise. Following her return to England and her peremptory divorce by her German princely husband, she devoted herself to art, good works and spiritualism. One of the plethora of charities she founded, the Princess Club, provided desperately needed practical antenatal education for poor women in the East End. But, come the NHS, Marie Louise was told it was 'of no more use, as the State and the County Council would do all I had tried to do'. If only!

And it was not only health. Schools, the universities, theatres, opera houses, museums, libraries and art galleries were all given state funding and subjected to increasingly direct state control. As was broadcasting and even that rarest, strangest and most personal of the arts, the writing of poetry. Moreover, alternative funding was cut off at its root as the punitive rates of taxation needed to sustain this elephantine structure all but destroyed the noble tradition of charitable giving on which so much of the creative achievement of Victorian Britain had rested.

But now at last the tide is turning. The arts and universities are slowly and often painfully being weaned off state funding. Alternative forms of finance are being sought for schools. Even the sacred cow of the National Health Service is being subject to covert privatization. And it is not simply a matter of resources. Most important of all, perhaps, the state has lost confidence in itself. State welfare is seen as part of the problem rather than the solution. The capacity of the state to deliver anything at all is challenged and its characteristic instruments of bureaucratic control despised. It is no longer even confident of its distinctive ethos. Instead, business values and the cash nexus rule all. New Labour vies with the Tories as the party of business and has continued the Tory policy of eroding the 'not-for-profit' ethos of the public service through market reforms, PFI, targets and managerialism in all its forms.

Nevertheless, it remains as true as it always was that human beings are not motivated only by money. They may even, as with increasing numbers of our new rich, want to give it away in prodigious quantities. But if the state and civil service won't recognize this, who will? And who will encourage and honour those who do? And shape, inspire and coordinate their efforts? The answer, surely, is the monarchy.

And with Charles we have, for the first time since Prince Albert in the nineteenth century or the young George III in the eighteenth, a royal patron who does aspire to 'direct the voluntary side of social life'; who dares to talk of 'real intellectual effort and eminence', and, above all, who puts his money where his mouth is.

A recent example is the rescue of Dumfries House. The house is that rarest of things: a noble Georgian mansion still furnished with the fixtures and fittings that were designed and made for it by the most eminent cabinetmakers of the day, including the great Thomas Chippendale himself. The state-funded heritage bodies laboured for years but were unable to come up with a solution that would save the house for the nation. Then, at the eleventh hour, and only weeks before a sale that would have dispersed the collection for ever, Charles cut the Gordian knot. And he did so by borrowing £20 million. The security was the assets of one of his charities; and the sum will be paid off by the development of a Scottish Poundbury – a model village, built in the Lowland vernacular style, on a site adjacent to the estate.

So not only have quangocrat heads been banged together, circles have also been squared and conservation and high culture will be combined with the economic regeneration of a depressed area. Only the prince could have done it. For only he has the necessary combination of social and economic power and imagination to pull it off.

A leading member of the prince's staff describes this as 'charitable entrepreneurship'. And its heart is the core group of charities known as the Prince's Charities. The prince raises their funding – £110 million each year – and sets their main areas of activity. These include 'opportunity and enterprise, education, health, the built environment, responsible business, the natural environment and the arts'. Most are leaders in their field; they venture into areas where others dare not and blaze trails that others – in particular, state organizations – follow. The outstanding example is the Prince's Trust. This helps disadvantaged young people into employment to become worthwhile members of society. Most of its clients have done badly at school, are poor and come from broken homes. But, above all, they are poor in aspiration. The Prince's Trust uses a wide variety of techniques including individual mentoring to give them confidence to help themselves. Its rate of success is striking and politicians – New Labour and Newer Tories alike – strive to learn from it and emulate it.

Here, then, is a new kingdom of the mind, spirit, culture and values which is not unworthy of a thousand-year-old throne.

LIST OF ILLUSTRATIONS

First plate section

Mosaic at Fishbourne Palace. *The Ancient Art and Architecture Collection Ltd*
The Venerable Bede. *The Bridgeman Art Library*

Helmet from the Sutton Hoo burial. *Photo copyright Michael Holford / British Museum*
Staffordshire Hoard cheek piece, fittings and zoomorphic mount. *Birmingham Museums & Art Gallery*

Æthelbert's Law Code. *The Dean and Chapter of Rochester and the Director of Education and Leisure, Medway Council*
Offa's coins. *British Museum*
Dragon-headed ship. Anglo-Saxon, tenth century, vellum manuscript. *British Museum / The Bridgeman Art Library*

Ring of Æthelwulf. *British Museum / The Bridgeman Art Library*
The Alfred Jewel. *Ashmolean Museum, Oxford*
Edgar. *British Library*

Cnut and Emma. *British Library*
Coin portrait of Edward the Confessor. *AKG-images*

Battle of Hastings. *The Bridgeman Art Library / Musée de la Tapisserie de Bayeux, France*
The Domesday Book. *Public Record Office Image Library*

The coronation of William II. *Chetham's Library, Manchester / The Bridgeman Art Library*
Westminster Hall. *Photo copyright A. F. Kersting / Houses of Parliament*

William I on horseback. *The Bridgeman Art Library / Musée de la Tapisserie de Bayeux, France*
John of Winchester's *Chronicle. The visions dreamt by King Henry I. Corpus Christi College, Oxford / The Bridgeman Art Library*

LIST OF ILLUSTRATIONS

Court of King's Bench, Westminster Hall, *c.* 1401–5 (vellum). *The Masters of the Bench of the Inner Temple/The Bridgeman Art Library*

Eleanor of Aquitaine. *Abbaye de Fontevrault, France*
Tomb effigy of Henry II at Fontevrault. *Photograph by Henri Gaud*

Becket's reliquary. *By permission of the Society of Antiquaries of London*
Chertsey titles. *British Museum*

King John's tomb at Worcester Cathedral. *Photograph by Mr Christopher Guy, Worcester Cathedral Archaeologist. Reproduced by permission of the Chapter of Worcester Cathedral (UK)*
The Magna Carta of Liberties, Third Version (1225). *Department of the Environment, London/The Bridgeman Art Library*

Tomb effigy of Henry III at Westminster Abbey. *Dean and Chapter of Westminster*
Self-portrait kneeling at the feet of the Virgin and Child (colour litho), by Matthew Paris, *c.* 1200–59. *Private Collection/Ken Welsh/The Bridgeman Art Library*

Battle of Evesham. *The British Library Board, Cotton MS Nero D II, f.177r*
Caernarfon Castle.

King Edward II, cast by Domenico Brucciani, *c.*1330s. *The National Portrait Gallery, London*
The execution of Hugh Despenser, 1324. *Mary Evans Picture Library*

Edward III in the Garter Book, 1435. *The British Library Board, Stowe MS 594, f.7v–8*
Richard II presented to the Virgin and Child by his Patron Saint John the Baptist and Saints Edward and Edmund ('The Wilton Diptych'). *The National Gallery, London*

Second plate section

Henry IV claiming the throne. *The British Library Board, Harley MS1319, f.57*
Henry V. *The National Portrait Gallery, London*

Charter upon Act of Parliament for the Foundation of King's College, Cambridge, London, 1446. Artist: William Abell (doc. 1450–d. 1474). Scribe: John Broke. *King's College, Cambridge. Photograph by Dr Julia Craig-McFeely*
(LEFT TO RIGHT) Richard Duke of York, uncrowned Edward V, then prince of Wales, Edward IV, the royal window, in the north-west transept of Canterbury Cathedral, fifteenth century. *Sonia Halliday Photographs*

King Richard III, by unknown artist, late sixteenth century (oil on panel). *The National Portrait Gallery, London*

While every effort has been made to trace the owners of copyright material reproduced herein, the publishers would like to apologize for any omissions and would be pleased to incorporate missing acknowledgements in future editions.

INDEX

Common Law 21, 132, 256; eradicate
Romanized Britain 4, 20–1, 28; feudalism
114–15, 119, 442; *Fürstengräber* ('princely
graves') 24–5; language 5, 19, 21, 59; law
32, 70, 73, 92, 232, 393; pagan 27–32, 33,
35, 36; political system 21, 50–1, 63, 66,
69–70, 71, 73–4, 75–6, 84–5, 97; Saxon
Conquest *see* Saxon Conquest; society 21,
22–4; wealth increases extremes of rich
and poor 24–5; *witan* (council) 47, 50, 56,
58, 66, 71, 73, 75, 76, 77, 82, 85, 87, 104,
117, 130
Anjou 102, 103, 117, 135, 151, 152, 157, 177,
194, 195, 196, 199, 246
Anjou, House of xii–xiii, 151–2, 157, 165–6,
170, 171, 172, 173–274
Anne, Queen 388, 389, 391–2, 398, 399,
405–10, 411, 412, 413–15, 416, 471
Anselm, Archbishop of Canterbury 127–8,
131, 133, 146, 281
Antoinette, Marie 438
Appeal from the Country to the City, An
373–4
Apollinaris, Sidonius 14
Aquitaine 178, 194, 195, 246
Arthur I of Brittany, Duke 197
Arthur, King 227, 229, 282, 285, 286, 462
Arthur, Prince of Wales (son of Henry VII)
275, 277, 280
Articles of Accusation (1327) 225, 226
Ashingdon Minster 72
Asquith, Herbert 477
Asser 46, 56–7
Assertio Septem Sacramentorum ('Defence of the
Seven Sacraments') (Henry VIII) 287, 295
Athaulf, Visigothic King 20
Athelney 48–50, 51, 53
Attainder, Act of 381
Attlee, Clement 486
Augustine (Italian monk) 30, 31, 32, 34, 37
Augustus, Emperor 7
Aurelianus, Ambrosius 19

Badestone, Lord 231
Baldwin V of Flanders, Count 46, 77, 102
Baldwin, Stanley 483, 484
Balliol, John 217, 218
Balmoral Castle, Scotland 483
Bank of Amsterdam 364, 403
Bank of England 402–3, 424
Bannockburn, battle of (1314) 224, 229
Barbarica conspiratio ('The Conspiracy of the
Barbarians') 10, 15
Barnet, battle of (1471) 265
barons: Edward I and 214, 215, 216; of the
Exchequer 143, 144; Henry II and 175,

196; Henry III and 204, 205, 207, 208,
209, 210, 211, 212; John and 199, 200–1,
202, 203; Magna Carta and 201–2, 209;
Norman 121, 132, 156, 157, 199; birth of
Parliament and 209–12; required to
demolish unlicensed castles, 'Treaty of
Winchester' 175; Stephen and 156, 157,
166
Barry, Charles 462
Bashir, Martin 494
Basset, Ralph 146
'bastard feudalism' 256–7
Bath 19, 62–4, 65, 160, 176–7
Bath peace conference (1140) 160
Bayeux Tapestry 79, 86, 91, 106
BBC 482–3
Beauchamp, Richard, Earl of Warwick 250
Beaufort, Edmund 250
Beaufort, Margaret 262, 272, 273, 275
Becket, Thomas 174–5, 180–1, 184, 185–92,
193, 194, 212, 244
Beckford, William 433
Bede 4, 12–13, 17–18, 22, 24, 26, 28, 29, 30,
31, 33, 34, 35, 56, 58, 60, 104, 134
Bellême, Robert of, Earl of Shrewsbury
137–8, 141, 176
Benedict, Saint 62, 63
Beorhtric, King of Wessex 42
Beorn, Earl 81
Beornwulf, King of Mercia 42
Beowulf 25–6
Bertha, Queen of Kent 29, 30, 31, 33
Berwick-on-Tweed, battle of (1640) 336
Bigod, Hugh, Earl of Norfolk 169
Bill of Rights (1689) 394, 395, 452
Biscop, Bishop Benedict 13
Black Death 232, 236, 242
Blenheim, battle of (1704) 398, 408, 411
Bluetooth, Harold 66, 69
Boer War (1880–1) 474
Boethius 58
Boleyn, Anne 288, 289, 290–1, 293, 294,
298, 304
Bonaparte, Napoleon 446, 447–9, 452
Bond of Association (1584) 318
Boniface of Savoy, Archbishop of Canterbury
207
Boniface, Saint 36
boroughs, establishment of English 54–5
Boston Tea Party (1773) 436
Bosworth, battle of (1485) 273–4, 281
Boudicca, Queen 8
Bouvines, battle of (1214) 200
Brémule, battle of (1119) 138–9, 140, 147
Brétigny, Treaty of (1360) 232
Bride's Ale Revolt (1075) 113, 114

INDEX

INDEX